# Comparative Economic Systems
## Models and Cases
*Models and Cases*

# THE IRWIN SERIES IN ECONOMICS

Appleyard and Field
**International Economics**

Baily and Friedman
**Macroeconomics, Financial Markets, and the International Sector**

Barron and Lynch
**Economics**
*Third Edition*

Baye/Beil
**Managerial Economics and Business Strategy**

Blair
**Urban and Regional Economics**

Bornstein
**Comparative Economic Systems: Models and Cases**
*Seventh Edition*

Brown and Moore
**Readings, Issues, and Problems in Public Finance**
*Third Edition*

Colander
**Economics**

Colander
**Macroeconomics**

Colander
**Microeconomics**

Denzau
**Microeconomic Analysis: Markets & Dynamics**

Hyman
**Economics**
*Third Edition*

Hyman
**Macroeconomics**
*Third Edition*

Hyman
**Microeconomics**
*Third Edition*

Hyman
**Modern Microeconomics: Analysis and Applications**
*Third Edition*

Katz and Rosen
**Microeconomics**
*Second Edition*

Lehmann
**Real World Economic Applications: The Wall Street Journal Workbook**
*Third Edition*

Lindert
**International Economics**
*Ninth Edition*

Maurice and Phillips
**Economic Analysis: Theory and Application**
*Sixth Edition*

Maurice, Thomas, and Smithson
**Managerial Economics: Applied Microeconomics for Decision Making**
*Fourth Edition*

Nadler and Hansen
**Microcomputer Macroeconomics with IBM Disk**

O'Sullivan
**Essentials of Urban Economics**

O'Sullivan
**Urban Economics**
*Second Edition*

Peterson
**Principles of Economics: Micro**
*Eighth Edition*

Peterson
**Principles of Economics: Macro**
*Eighth Edition*

Prager
**Applied Microeconomics: An Intermediate Approach**

ii

Rima
**Development of Economic Analysis**
*Fifth Edition*

Roger and Daniel
**Principles of Economics Software Simulation**

Rosen
**Public Finance**
*Third Edition*

Schwarz and Van Dyken
**Manager: Managerial Economics (Software)**

Seo
**Managerial Economics: Text, Short Cases**
*Seventh Edition*

Sharp, Register, and Leftwich
**Economics of Social Issues**
*Eleventh Edition*

Shepherd
**Public Policies Toward Business**
*Eighth Edition*

Shugart
**The Organization of Industry**

Slavin
**Economics**
*Third Edition*

Slavin
**Microeconomics**
*Third Edition*

Slavin
**Macroeconomics**
*Third Edition*

Streifford
**Economic Perspective**

Walton and Wykoff
**Understanding Economics Today**
*Fourth Edition*

# Comparative Economic Systems
## *Models and Cases*

**Seventh Edition**

Edited by

**Morris Bornstein**
*Professor of Economics*
*The University of Michigan*

**IRWIN**
Burr Ridge, Illinois
Boston, Massachusetts
Sydney, Australia

© RICHARD D. IRWIN, INC., 1965, 1969, 1974, 1979, 1985, 1989, and 1994

Senior sponsoring editor: *Gary Nelson*
Editorial assistant: *Tia Schultz*
Marketing manager: *Ron Bloecher*
Project editor: *Waivah Clement*
Production manager: *Laurie Kersch*
Designer: *Mercedes Santos*
Art coordinator: *Mark Malloy*
Art studio: *Benoit Design*
Compositor: *Bi-Comp, Inc.*
Typeface: *10/12 Times Roman*
Printer: *R. R. Donnelley & Sons Company*

**Library of Congress Cataloging-in-Publication Data**

Comparative economic systems: models and cases/edited by Morris
    Bornstein.—7th ed.
        p.    cm.—(Irwin series in economics)
    Includes bibliographical references and index.
    ISBN 0-256-09593-0
        1. Comparative economics—Case studies.  I. Bornstein, Morris,
1927–    .  II. Series.
HB90.C654   1994
330.1—dc20                                                          93–2552

*Printed in the United States of America*
*1  2  3  4  5  6  7  8  9  0  DOC  0  9  8  7  6  5  4  3*

# Preface

This book, like the six previous editions, is about the organization, operation, and performance of economic systems, both in theory and in practice. It deals with alternative methods of determining the bill of goods to be produced, the allocation of resources to produce it, and the distribution of the resulting income. These are some of the most vital questions of our time—urgent issues for all economies, both capitalist and socialist, both more and less developed. The book explores various alternative answers by analyzing different economic systems and comparing them with each other.

This collection of readings is primarily intended for use in college courses in comparative economic systems. It is somewhat unusual because it is specifically designed to serve either as collateral reading in conjunction with one of the textbooks in the field, or as the core around which a comparative economic systems course can be organized. With the latter purpose in mind, I have prepared editorial notes for each part and chapter of the book which integrate them and place them in an overall conceptual framework. With few exceptions, the selections are articles or essays reprinted in their entirety, rather than isolated excerpts. As a result, they present the author's full argument and at the same time are of an appropriate length for student reading assignments. At the end of each of the five parts of the book, suggestions for further reading are given.

The chapters in this volume are the fruit of an extensive search of the literature over a number of years in connection with my courses in comparative economic systems at The University of Michigan. They include "classic" articles by the most distinguished figures in the field, as well as lesser known, often overlooked articles by other authors. In many cases, the articles are from out-of-print volumes or less accessible journals. All of them can be read with understanding and profit by students in courses in comparative economic systems which require only principles of economics as a prerequisite. In a few instances, very technical passages, references to foreign language sources, or supplementary statistical tables have been omitted.

As befits a comparative economic systems book, the authors of the chapters in this volume include economists not only from the United States but also from Belgium, France, Germany, Great Britain, Hungary, Italy, Japan, the Netherlands, Poland, Singapore, and Switzerland.

This book covers the principal topics included in most college courses in comparative economic systems, although it is impossible in a volume of reasonable size to include all of the topics treated by different instructors in a field so broadly defined. This book excludes certain topics which are covered by relatively few instructors—for example, primitive economies—as well as other topics on which a considerable variety of material is readily available in inexpensive paperback form, such as the U.S. economy, Marxism, and problems of less developed countries.

Part I of the book provides a conceptual framework by explaining the scope and method of comparative economic systems. Part II presents theoretical analyses of the market economy and of regulated capitalism, followed by case studies of Great Britain, Sweden, France, the European Economic Community, and Japan which give a broader view of capitalist regulated market economies to readers familiar primarily with the U.S. economy. Part III includes chapters on different theoretical models of a socialist market economy, as well as a case study of Yugoslavia. Part IV covers socialist centrally planned economies and their reform. It contains theoretical articles on the nature and operation of these economies, and on the process and problems of economic reform. It presents case studies on the USSR and its successor states, Eastern Europe, and China. Part V compares economic systems in regard to unemployment and illegal economic activity.

Although the material is presented in this sequence, the selections are chosen and the book is constructed so that the chapters can logically and conveniently be assigned in several different orders and combinations to fit the individual instructor's approach to the subject.

More than half of the material in this edition did not appear in the sixth edition. This reflects the rapid development of the literature in comparative economic systems. I wish to thank the many persons who made suggestions for the new edition. The cooperation of authors and publishers who granted permission to reprint material included in the book is appreciated. Finally, I am grateful to my wife, Reva, for her encouragement and forbearance during the preparation of the book.

**Morris Bornstein**

# Contents

# Comparative Economic Systems
## *Models and Cases*

# Part I

# Comparing Economic Systems

An analytical framework for comparing economic systems is essential in the study of economic systems—both economic models and case studies of actual economies. The most common bases of comparison are (1) the ownership of the means of production and (2) the methods of resource allocation. The means of production may be owned privately, as in capitalism, or publicly, as in socialism. In turn, resources may be allocated by markets through prices, as in a decentralized market economy, or by administrative commands expressed in real (physical) terms, as in a centrally planned economy. Various combinations of these two dimensions are possible, and Parts II, III, and IV of this book are concerned, respectively, with capitalist market economies, socialist market economies, and centrally planned economies.

The chapters in Part I discuss the methodology of comparing economic systems. Chapter 1 explains the concept of an economic system, why systems differ, and how they may be compared. Chapter 2 discusses important methodological issues in the comparison of economic systems, or components of them. Chapter 3 shows how economic systems can be compared in terms of their aims and objectives, political choices among conflicting objectives, and the instruments used to achieve the chosen combination of objectives.

## Chapter One

# The Comparison of Economic Systems*

### Morris Bornstein

*This chapter explains the scope and methodology of comparative economic systems as a branch of economics.*

*The economic system is a particular kind of social system. Economic systems differ and change because of social and cultural forces, the level of economic development, and various "environmental" factors.*

*Economic systems are often analyzed in three dimensions: the social preference function, the institutions and instruments used by the government, and the resulting patterns of resource allocation and income distribution.*

*The performance of economic systems can be compared in many respects, including output, growth, efficiency, stability, security, inequality, and freedom. Because there are so many possible "performance criteria," to reach an overall evaluation one must use a preference function specifying the relative importance of the different criteria.*

*A thorough understanding and comparison of economic systems require the study of both theoretical models and actual cases, using concepts and techniques not only from economics but also from other disciplines such as political science and sociology.*

This chapter integrates various approaches to the comparison of economic systems. The first section briefly considers the concept of an economic system. The second examines various ways of comparing economic systems. The third explains key dimensions of comparative economic studies. The final section presents some conclusions. Throughout, the discussion focuses on an examination of the scope and method of the field, rather than a review of the principal literature on the many subjects composing it. Thus, although specific works are

* Revised 1993 from Morris Bornstein, "An Integration," in *Comparison of Economic Systems: Theoretical and Methodological Approaches,* ed. Alexander Eckstein (Berkeley and Los Angeles: University of California Press, 1971), pp. 339–55. Copyright © 1971 by the Regents of the University of California; reprinted by permission of the University of California Press. Additional material copyright © 1993 by Morris Bornstein; reprinted by permission.

cited for illustrative purposes at various points, the chapter is a methodological, rather than a bibliographic, essay.

## CONCEPT OF AN ECONOMIC SYSTEM

One may begin with the concept of a *system*, of which an economic system is a
type. A general definition is that a system refers to a collection of "objects,
ideas, or activities united by some regular form of interaction or interdependence." Thus, two dimensions are involved: what is being organized, and how
the components are related to each other.

A more sophisticated and complex definition is as follows: The *participants* in a system may be individuals or different groupings of individuals.
Through the *interactions* of participants, the actions of one participant simultaneously or sequentially affect other participants. Orders and rules govern these
interactions. *Orders* are dated messages calling for a specific response from the
participant(s) to whom they are addressed. *Rules* are messages stipulating (or
constraining) for an indefinite period the actions of (a set of) participants under
specified conditions. *Organizations* consist of a set of participants who regularly interact, according to rules and orders, to accomplish a set of activities
constituting the purpose of the organization. The *motivation* of a participant is
a function which associates with each course of action the utility of its outcome
to him. Such motivations govern responses to orders and rules within organizations. Thus, the study of a system involves the analysis of the interaction of
organizations, including the composition of the organizations, the orders and
rules signaling action, and the motivations affecting the participants' responses
to these signals.[1]

An *economic system*, in turn, involves the interaction of organizations of
participants engaged, according to rules and orders, in the production, distribution, and use of goods and services. It may be viewed as the set of arrangements by which the society determines (1) what shall be produced ("the bill of
goods"); (2) how it shall be produced, including (*a*) the institutions and instruments to be used and (*b*) the pattern of resource allocation; and (3) how the
resulting personal income and claims to goods and services shall be distributed
(and redistributed) among households.

## BASES OF COMPARISON OF SYSTEMS

Economic systems may be compared in regard to three main aspects: (1) What
forces influence the system, determining its character? (2) What is the nature of
the system? How does it operate? What are the nature and extent of state

---

[1] On general system theory, see, for example, Anatol Rapoport, *General System Theory: Essential Concepts and Applications* (Tunbridge Wells, England, and Cambridge, Mass.: Abacus Press,
1986).

intervention in economic life? (3) How well does the system perform, in regard to its own goals and in regard to additional goals which are esteemed by others if not, no more than, by the system itself? Thus, we wish to know (1) what makes systems similar or different, (2) what the similarities or differences in systems are, and (3) what differences in performance are associated with differences in systems. These three aspects will be discussed in turn in some detail.

## Forces Influencing the Economic System

These forces are so numerous and their relationship so complex that a comprehensive discussion is beyond the scope of this chapter. Instead, it is convenient to group them into three main categories, each of which subsumes a number of elements: (1) the level of economic development, (2) social and cultural factors, and (3) the "environment." Although these categories are not necessarily exhaustive, they illustrate how different kinds of forces shape the nature and performance of economic systems.

**Level of Economic Development.** The level of economic development can be measured and compared by various indicators, including the level of per capita income; the share of primary, secondary, and tertiary activities in total employment or GNP; birth and death rates; literacy rates; and so forth. Whichever measures are used, it is clear that economic growth alters the size and structure of the economy, and that these changes in turn modify the economic system.

Thus, economic growth and development in the United States in the last 50 or 100 years have been responsible for many changes in the economic system. They include changes in the nature and extent of government intervention to deal with problems of market power arising from the emergence of large firms and trade unions; problems of external diseconomies, such as water and air pollution; and problems of scientific discovery, such as the utilization of nuclear energy.

Another example is economic reforms in socialist planned economies which seek to adapt the economic system to changes in the nature of the economy. This process has frequently been described as a shift from a more centralized system in the "extensive" phase of economic development, to a less centralized system in the "intensive" phase. In the earlier period, the tasks of "economic construction" were socialization of the means of production, a sharp increase in the rate of investment, rapid structural change, and revision of the income distribution. In this period, resource allocation was dominated by physical planning and administrative rationing. In contrast, the intensive phase was characterized by emphasis on greater efficiency in the use of given resources, greater responsiveness to household demand for consumer goods and services, and greater emphasis on competitiveness in international trade. This phase was seen to require a more decentralized economic system, involving greater reliance on market forces rather than administrative allocation, more need for scarcity prices, greater enterprise autonomy, and more emphasis on incentives instead of commands.

Although these examples illustrate how changes in the level of development affect the nature of the economic system, it is clear that a given level or pattern of economic development is not uniquely associated with a specific economic system. Rather, different countries at approximately the same stage of economic development exhibit a great variety of economic systems. Thus, it was not very satisfactory to classify countries into such groups as "West," "East," and "South," because some of the Communist countries in "East" were no more developed than some of the non-Communist countries in "South."

Instead, an "exclusion principle" seems useful. Although a given level of development can accommodate more than one economic system, certain levels of development may be incompatible with particular economic systems. One reason may be that the level of development alters the system. Another is that the system eschews a level or pattern of development which is incompatible with (i.e., threatens) the system. Thus, tribal or oligarchic societies may resist economic changes which will disrupt the traditional social structure.

The level of economic development is also related to the economic system in several other ways. First, it is part of the environment in which the system operates and which affects the system's performance. Second, it influences the culture, which also shapes the economic system. Finally, one of the aims of the system may be to alter the level of development. These propositions are developed further below.

**Social and Cultural Forces.**   Many aspects of society and culture influence the economic system. One is social stratification, based on race, occupation, income, wealth, religion, or other factors. Another is the customs, traditions, values, and beliefs of society. By way of illustration, I shall examine the influence of ideology, which has received considerable attention in the literature of comparative economic systems.

An ideology is a set of ideas and values guiding individuals (and organizations composed of them) in interpreting their environment, choosing goals in regard to maintaining or changing the environment, and selecting the means to achieve these goals. An economic ideology is a set of ideas related to economic action. Ideology may affect the economic system in various ways. It influences both the ends and the means of the system: what its goals are, including the priorities among them; the institutions and instruments of the system and the patterns of their use; and attitudes about changes in goals and institutions and instruments. Thus, ideologies may maintain or alter systems.

However, there are a number of difficulties in identifying the influence of ideology on the economic system. First, a single consistent ideology is sometimes ascribed to a pure model of an economic system (e.g., "rapid industralization through comprehensive central planning based on public ownership"). But, in actual real-world economies, there are various interest groups with different ideologies about the ends or means of the system. Second, ideologies may be misleading. The ideology may seek to rationalize what is being done rather than constitute its true motivation. Or the aim may be to deceive—to conceal what is being done by describing it in completely different terms. Thus, the explicit ideology may not be the normative guide to action. Rather, the effective ideology may be implicit in the nature and operation of the economic system, from which it must be deduced. Third, there is a time gap between an ideology and the economic system to which it relates. An ideology can lag behind changes in the economy which it is supposed to guide, or it may lead the system it aims to change. The gap is narrowed in the former case when outdated ideas are finally abandoned, and in the latter case when ideology succeeds in changing the system.

In conclusion, ideology does not determine the economic system in the sense that a single consistent ideology unambiguously and effectively shapes the economic system. Rather, different ideologies—some explicit, some concealed—influence economic institutions, policies, actions, and results. For this reason, one may prefer to account for the effect of ideology in terms of more specific concepts such as perception, attitudes, norms (preference functions), institutions, and patterns of behavior, through which ideologies are expressed and operate.

**Environment.**   The natural environment of an economic system includes such elements as the size (in area and population), location (topography, climate, access to the sea), and natural-resource endowment of the economy. These features affect the nature of the economic system indirectly in various ways. For example, they help determine the level and character of economic development. They also affect ideologies and other aspects of culture—for instance, attitudes toward the need to emphasize national unity of geographically diverse and distant regions, the desirability or feasibility of a high degree of self-sufficiency, and the like.

Another aspect of environment is contact with other economic systems, which is a source of transmission of ideology and information about alternative arrangements and their results. An economic system may change as a result of its contact with another system. For example, a country may modify some facets of its economic system, such as its foreign trade arrangements, in order to accommodate international economic relations with a country having a different system. Or it may change important aspects of the economic system—indeed, even the system itself—because a powerful neighboring state insists upon it.

Thus, while an economic system operates in an environment which affects its performance, the system itself may be influenced directly or indirectly by its environment.

To analyze how these various forces—the level of development, social and cultural factors, and the environment—influence economic systems, is to study how economic systems change. It is an investigation of the dynamic process, as distinct from either interspatial (transnational) comparisons at a given time or intertemporal comparisons of the economic system of the same country at different times (e.g., the United States in 1938 versus 1993). For some purposes, it is convenient to classify these forces of change into exogenous factors, such as new technology and developments in world politics, and endogenous factors, such as the effect of increasing affluence in creating new interest groups or ideologies capable of modifying the economic system.

## Nature and Operation of Economic Systems

The nature and operation of an economic system may be analyzed in terms of its social preference function, its institutions and instruments, and its patterns of resource allocation and income distribution. These three aspects are, of course, related. The social preference function determines which institutions and instruments are used in which patterns of resource allocation and income distribution to pursue which social aims. And the most useful focus of analysis for all three aspects is the nature and degree of state intervention in economic life.

**Social Preference Function.** The social preference (or utility or welfare) function expresses the community's effective aggregate preferences regarding the ends and means of economic activity. In analyzing and comparing systems, we wish to consider both how the community's decisions are reached and what these decisions are.

In regard to the first aspect, three mechanisms may be distinguished: (1) individual preferences expressed through individual choice in markets (consumer sovereignty); (2) individual preferences expressed through the political process, either by direct voting on certain issues or by indirect voting through the selection of legislators and government officials; and (3) the preferences of a ruling group not selected through the electoral process. Several questions must then be investigated. What is the relative importance of each of these mechanisms in determining the community's preference on such matters as the composition of output, the distribution of income, and so forth? How does each of these mechanisms formulate its respective preference function? What is the resulting preference function generated by each mechanism? Finally, how are the several preference functions integrated into a single (consistent?) community preference function?[2]

In addition, we wish to compare the resulting community preferences in regard to the objectives of economic policy, the choice of institutions and instruments to achieve these aims, and the combination of these institutions

---

[2] On social preference functions, see, for instance, Dennis C. Mueller, *Public Choice* (Cambridge, England: Cambridge University Press, 1979), and *Public Choice II* (Cambridge, England: Cambridge University Press, 1989).

and instruments in particular patterns of resource allocation and income distribution. The society's objectives will include goals in regard to the level of employment, price stability, per capita consumption, the rate of growth of national income, the distribution of income and wealth, and so forth. These objectives may be expressed more precisely in specific economic policies and in quantitative terms as "targets."

**Institutions and Instruments.** *Institutions* may be defined as relatively fundamental organizational arrangements for conducting production and distribution. They are often prescribed by law and not altered as easily as instruments. Examples of institutions include firms, households, markets in which firms exchange with other firms and with households, banks, trade unions, and government economic agencies. Each of these institutions in turn has various types and subtypes. For instance, government economic agencies may be concerned with planning, regulation, redistribution (e.g., social security), or the provision of public goods. An important aspect of any institution is the motivation of its participants, because different participants may have different motivations, with their relative strength and interaction determining the motivation of the institution as such.

The institutional distinction most often made in the study of economic systems concerns the ownership of the means of production. The variants of *private* ownership include individual, partnership, cooperative, and corporate enterprises. When the means of production are *socially* owned, they may be operated by departments of government at different levels (e.g., federal, state, local), by autonomous public boards, or by the personnel of the enterprise ("workers' management"). In all of these cases, private and social, the actions of the enterprise may be restricted by other institutions, using some of the instruments noted below. However, the trend in the study of economic systems is to downgrade the significance of ownership as a critical element in the nature and operation of economic systems, on the ground that it is less important than the arrangements for decision making about investment, production, and consumption. Thus, it is now commonly held that "capitalism" and "socialism" are not useful classifications of economic systems, and that such distinctions are more of ideological or political significance. Nevertheless, although ownership is not decisive in determining the character of the economic system, it is significant both as a factor in income distribution (an important feature of any system) and as a source of power in the formulation of the community's preference function.

*Instruments* refer to the tools used by the state when it intervenes to (attempts to) achieve social goals in the economic sphere. In comparison with institutions, instruments are more often subject to quantitative expression, are more easily and more frequently altered, and are used by only one kind of institution (government agencies). At least five types of instruments may be distinguished: (1) *Fiscal* instruments include taxes, subsidies, transfer payments, and government purchases. (2) *Monetary* instruments involve changes in interest rates, reserve ratios, and credit rationing; government lending and borrowing; management of existing debt; and control of consumer credit. (3) Altering *exchange rates* is another instrument. (4) Among *direct controls* are production assignments, allocation orders, fixing of prices and wages, and allocation of foreign exchange. Finally, (5) *changes in the institutional framework*—e.g., in property rights or rules for the operation of markets—may be considered another type of instrument.[3]

Thus, the comparison of systems involves the study of the prevalence and operation of various institutions, as well as the purposes for which, and manner in which, the state uses the possible instruments of economic policy to direct the economic activity of these institutions toward social goals.

**Patterns of Resource Allocation and Income Distribution.**   The interaction of institutions and instruments generates the pattern of resource allocation and income distribution in the system. Three complementary approaches to the analysis of these patterns appear in the literature, each stressing somewhat different elements of the same economic processes.

*Centralization versus decentralization* involves the delineation of different hierarchies and the relationships among and within them.[4] This approach is concerned with the locus at which different decisions are made on investment, current production, the decision rules applicable to a given unit, and changes in the hierarchical structure. It also considers the flow of information, involving the form, content, purpose, and routing of "messages." Although the choices along the centralization–decentralization continuum in the two cases are related, they need not be identical. For example, the flow of information could be more centralized than the decision-making process. This occurs when the central authorities collect a great deal of information only in order to make it available to autonomous units which use it for decentralized decisions.

*Command versus exchange* contrasts resource allocation in physical terms via administrative orders with resource allocation in response to money flows and prices in markets. Money and prices may be used in a command economy. But they perform only "secondary allocation," helping to implement plans

---

[3] A comprehensive analysis of these instruments is presented in E. S. Kirschen and others, *Economic Policy in Our Time* (Amsterdam: North-Holland Publishing Company, and Chicago: Rand McNally, 1964), Vol. 1, and in E. S. Kirschen and others, *Economic Policies Compared* (Amsterdam: North-Holland Publishing Company, 1974). For a recent application to macroeconomic policies, see *Macroeconomic Adjustment: Policy Instruments and Issues,* ed. Jeffrey M. Davis (Washington, D.C.: International Monetary Fund, 1992).

[4] See, for example, Leif Johansen, *Lectures on Macroeconomic Planning, Part 2: Centralization, Decentralization, Planning under Uncertainty* (Amsterdam: North-Holland Publishing Company, 1978); Manfred Kochen and Karl W. Deutsch, *Decentralization* (Cambridge, Mass.: Oelgeschlager, Gunn & Hain, 1980); and Robert G. Lynch, "Centralization and Decentralization Redefined," *Journal of Comparative Economics* 13, no. 1 (March 1989), pp. 1–14.

drawn up through physical planning techniques. Although it is intended that money flows should supplement administrative orders, in practice they often conflict with them, inducing "violations" of the plan.

*Planning versus the market* focuses on the manner and extent of state intervention in the economy through "planning." This approach is concerned with such questions as the following: What is the coverage, in scope and detail, of the plan? How is the plan prepared—by what techniques and with what participation by lower units? How seriously is the plan implemented, and what instruments and adjustment mechanisms are used? In addition, one must be aware that some areas of government intervention may be outside the scope of what is customarily included in the "plan," and such extra-plan activities may reinforce or conflict with the plan.

In all three approaches, it is essential to investigate both the formal and the informal mechanisms and their relationship in actual operation, not merely official descriptions or theoretical models of the processes.

To summarize this section briefly: An economic system consists of a particular set of arrangements in regard to a social welfare function, institutions and instruments, and patterns of resource allocation and income distribution. Any specific economic system—whether a model or an actual case—represents a unique combination of these three related aspects. To compare the nature and operation of different systems, we must compare them in detail in all three respects, as systems are likely to be more similar or different in one respect than another. Next we want to associate differences in the nature of the system with differences in performance.

## Performance of Economic Systems

One may argue that the ultimate purpose of comparing economic systems is to find ways of improving the performance of a given system (in the light of its social preference function). For this purpose, we want to compare the results of different systems, operating in similar or different environments, in regard to various performance criteria which are deemed important.

The criteria commonly considered include the following:

1. The level of output. The objective ordinarily is a "high" or "full-employment" level, although the quantitative expression of this target depends upon assumptions or goals regarding labor force participation rates, the length of the workweek, and frictional unemployment.

2. The rate of growth of output; for instance, the annual percentage growth rate of GNP.

3. The composition of output: the shares of consumption, investment, and military programs; collective versus individual consumption; and so forth.

4. Single period ("static") efficiency. It is achieved when no reallocation of existing resources could increase total output.

5. Intertemporal ("dynamic") efficiency. This concerns the increase in potential output attainable from additional resources of labor, capital, and land. The increase in output depends on how the incremental resources are allocated, technological progress, economies of scale, and external economies.

6. Stability of output, employment, and prices.

7. Economic security of the individual, including security of income and/or of employment.

8. Equity—involving equality of opportunity and an "appropriate" degree of inequality of income and wealth.

9. Economic freedoms of occupational choice, consumption, and property.

Other criteria may be derived from these. For example, the level of per capita consumption, sometimes suggested as an index of welfare, is a combination of 1, 3, and the size of the population. Similarly "economic justice" usually refers to goals in regard to 7, 8, and sometimes 9.

Some of these objectives are complementary, that is, mutually reinforcing; for example, the higher the rate of growth, the greater the level of output (in the next period). Others may be competitive, that is, mutually conflicting; for example, price stability may conflict with a high level of output and a high rate of growth.

Thus, for an aggregate evaluation of an economic system's performance it is necessary to have a utility or welfare function according to which the different criteria can be assigned appropriate weights. Different preference functions will assign different weights to the various performance criteria. The prevailing community preference function may differ in this respect from the function of some part of the community (which may be a majority or a minority of the population) which is given little weight in, or is overruled by, the prevailing function. The function prevailing in one community (i.e., country) may differ from that in another community, or in the same community at another time. It may also differ from that of the analyst of systems, who must recognize when he or she is using a personal preference function to evaluate the system(s) studied.

Thus, the comparative evaluation or ranking of different economic systems will depend on (1) the performance of the systems in regard to the various criteria considered, and (2) the preference function(s) assigning weights to the several criteria. The latter is essentially a value judgment, somehow formulated for the community as a whole. The former is more nearly subject to objective scientific measurement.

Two steps are required for empirical comparisons of performance. First, each of the various criteria must be defined as precisely as possible to permit quantitative measurement. This is easier for some criteria than for others. For example, Lorenz curves can show the degree of inequality in the distribution of income and wealth. National accounts depict the level and composition of output. Statistics on employment (unemployment) and personal income provide a measure of economic security. Variations in output, employment, and prices indicate the degree of (in)stability of the economy. Efficiency is more difficult to quantify, but the extent of idle resources may furnish some measure of single-period efficiency, and calculations of aggregate factor productivity offer an indication of intertemporal efficiency. It is even possible to quantify some of the differences in economic freedoms. For example, one can use the respective shares of output produced by private and public enterprises as some index of freedom of enterprise.

Once the criteria have been defined carefully, the next step is to measure the performance of the economies to be compared, in as uniform a way as possible. This involves many well-known problems of international comparisons, such as differences among countries in the availability, reliability, coverage, and methodology of data.[5] Although such calculations are usually difficult and complex, they yield the final product toward which the comparison of economic systems is directed. They show the differences in performance—the merit of which is to be assessed in the light of one or more preference functions, and the causes of which are to be explained by the analysis of the nature and operation of the system.

## DIMENSIONS OF COMPARATIVE ECONOMIC STUDIES

The potential scope of comparative economic studies is broad. One can distinguish five dimensions which help delineate this field of economics: (1) the relationship between comparative economic systems and economic development; (2) system studies; (3) comparative topical studies; (4) work on the transformation of one economic system into another; and (5) interdisciplinary approaches.

### Comparative Economic Systems and Economic Development

The issue here is the extent to which the comparative study of economic systems should include the less developed countries and primitive economies. For this purpose, *less developed countries* are defined as those with low per capita income levels, which are associated with differences—from the more developed countries—in various aspects of economic structure. These aspects include the distribution of national income by sector of origin, the type of enterprise, the structure of the labor force, factor shares and the size distribution of income, patterns of income use, and foreign-trade proportions. One striking characteristic of many less developed countries is the coexistence of an

---

[5] See, for instance, Paul Marer and others, *Historically Planned Economies: A Guide to the Data* (Washington, D.C.: World Bank, 1992).

important "traditional" sector in agriculture alongside a "modern" industrial sector. *Primitive economies,* on the other hand, refers to isolated, non-monetized tribal societies in which economic activity is guided chiefly by tradition and custom, rather than by exchange or command. This definition may suggest some overlap with the traditional sector in the "dual" economy. The difference is that in the dual economy the traditional sector is in contact with and is being changed by the modern sector, whereas the primitive economy lacks such strong links to a parallel modern sector. With these distinctions in mind, I believe that the study of comparative economic systems may fruitfully include the less developed countries but not primitive economies.

The major reason for including the less developed economies is that the level or stage of economic development is one of the forces affecting the nature of the economic system, as well as the conditions (environment) in which it performs. Moreover, there are large and interesting intragroup differences among the less developed countries, for example, among Egypt, Algeria, Mexico, India, and Taiwan. It is desirable to investigate how differences in the level of development are associated with the nature and performance of economic systems. Finally, there are interesting questions about the interaction of the modern and traditional sectors in the less developed countries which do not arise in the study of more developed economies.

On the other hand, the study of primitive economies may reasonably be excluded. It is not very useful to compare cases where great differences exist in material technology and the stock of useful knowledge. The resulting differences in the economic activities of society cannot be attributed in significant measure to differences in the economic system. That is, "intra-epochal" comparisons are desirable, but "inter-epochal" comparisons are not very relevant. Of course, this position does not mean that the study of primitive societies is pointless or without interest. Rather, it suggests that the subject be considered part of economic anthropology, instead of comparative economic systems.[6]

## System Studies

Much work has been devoted to the description, analysis, and evaluation of the components of a particular economic system and their interaction. Other studies consider more narrowly a specific part of an economic system. In turn, each kind of research may concern theoretical models or case studies. Hence, one can distinguish four types of system studies: (1) a theoretical model of an economic system,[7] (2) a theoretical approach to an aspect of an economic

---

[6] On the scope and methodology of economic anthropology, see, for example, *Economic Anthropology,* ed. Stuart Plattner (Stanford, Calif.: Stanford University, Press, 1989), and *Beyond the New Economic Anthropology,* ed. John Clammer (New York: St. Martin's Press, 1987).

[7] For example, James A. Yunker, *Socialism Revised and Modernized: The Case for Pragmatic Market Socialism* (New York: Praeger Publishers, 1992).

system,[8] (3) an empirical treatment of an economic system,[9] and (4) an empirical investigation of an aspect of an economic system.[10]

*Models* of economic systems are simplified abstractions presenting the main institutional features and operating characteristics of different types of economic systems. They are often inspired by one or more important real-world economies, although they purport to represent general types rather than specific economies. A *case study* deals with an actual economy, which typically incorporates features from various pure models, as a result of such influences as the level of economic development, social-cultural forces, and environmental circumstances. Thus, each specific case has its own unique combination of social preference function, institutions and instruments, and patterns of resource allocation and income distribution.

The model approach to the study of systems has been criticized on the ground that it is concerned with oversimplified abstractions from reality. For example, it is asserted that it is not useful to consider a pure centrally administered economy, simply because none has ever existed or is likely to exist. A second objection is that it is not possible to measure and compare the performance of models, while this can be done in regard to case studies. As a result, it is argued, the comparison of models is especially vulnerable to ideological biases in interpretation and assessment.

In turn, the case approach has been challenged on the ground that the reality of an actual economy is so complex that any case must be considered selectively, in the light of some conception of the critical variables—that is, a model. Furthermore, it is a common pitfall to identify a case, explicitly or implicitly, as—in some sense and to some degree—representative of a group of countries with common characteristics. For example, often the United States was chosen as an example of capitalism and the Soviet Union as an illustration of socialism. The unsophisticated reader—student, citizen, or politician—may then erroneously assume that the features and results of the prototype country generally characterize the entire group, and that a comparison of the relative merits of the prototypes, according to one or more performance criteria, reveals the relative merits of the "families" the prototypes are supposed to represent. This may lead to incorrect conclusions because other countries in the group may differ from the prototype in important respects. The relative performance (merit) of the two groups will therefore depend on which member

---

[8] For instance, Paul G. Hare, *Central Planning* (Chur, Switzerland: Harwood Academic Publishers, 1991), and Thomas W. Wolf, *Foreign Trade in the Centrally Planned Economy* (Chur, Switzerland: Harwood Academic Publishers, 1988).

[9] For example, Alec Nove, *The Soviet Economic System,* 3rd ed. (London: Allen & Unwin, 1986), and Harold Lydall, *Yugoslav Socialism: Theory and Practice* (Oxford: Clarendon Press, 1984).

[10] For instance, Silvana Malle, *Employment Planning in the Soviet Union* (New York: St. Martin's Press, 1990).

is selected as the prototype, as well as which performance criteria are chosen for comparison. In short, intragroup differences are frequently so great that prototypes are not or cannot be representative. Intragroup differences may even exceed intergroup differences in regard to certain characteristics or performance criteria.

The model and case approaches should, however, be viewed as complementary rather than competitive. Models provide a framework for selecting and comparing cases. In turn, the comparison of cases with the models they are supposed to illustrate should lead to the revision and improvement of the models, for example the elaboration of various models of centrally planned socialism, or of market socialism, with different ownership arrangements and different combinations of command and exchange. In this respect, the West and East European economies have offered especially promising case studies which can suggest various intermediate models between the traditional model of regulated capitalism inspired by the United States and the classic model of centrally planned socialism suggested by the Soviet Union. These intermediate models can generate a number of testable hypotheses about the operation and performance of economic systems to guide subsequent case studies.

## Comparative Topical Studies

System studies deal with a particular economic system, or a specific part of it, usually leaving to other analysts subsequent comparisons with other systems. In contrast, comparative topical studies explicitly compare economic systems in regard to certain aspects. These aspects include, for example, employment,[11] productivity,[12] income distribution,[13] research and development,[14] exchange rates,[15] foreign trade,[16] and energy use.[17]

System studies and comparative topical studies should be considered complementary rather than alternative approaches. On the one hand, the topical approach needs a view of the entire system, because the characteristics of a

---

[11] Andrew J. Stollar and G. Rodney Thompson, "Sectoral Employment Shares: A Comparative Systems Context," *Journal of Comparative Economics* 11, no. 1 (March 1987), pp. 62–80.

[12] Abram Bergson, "Comparative Productivity: The USSR, Eastern Europe, and the West," *American Economic Review* 77, no. 3 (June 1987), pp. 342–57.

[13] Anthony B. Atkinson and John Micklewright, *Economic Transformation in Eastern Europe and the Distribution of Income* (Cambridge, England: Cambridge University Press, 1992).

[14] Philip Hanson, "The Economics of Research and Development: Some East–West Comparisons," *European Economic Review* 32, no. 2–3 (March 1988), pp. 604–10.

[15] Michael Melvin and Su Zhou, "Do Centrally Planned Exchange Rates Behave Differently from Capitalist Rates?" *Journal of Comparative Economics* 13, no. 2 (June 1989), pp. 325–34.

[16] Peter Murrell, *The Nature of Socialist Economies: Lessons from East European Foreign Trade* (Princeton, N.J.: Princeton University Press, 1990).

[17] John R. Moroney, "Energy Consumption, Capital, and Real Output: A Comparison of Market and Planned Economies," *Journal of Comparative Economics* 14, no. 2 (June 1990), pp. 199–220.

given activity in a particular country are determined by the system of which it is a part. On the other hand, comparisons enhance our understanding of the respective systems as a whole. Thus both approaches—and a synthesis of the results—are necessary.

## Economics of Transition

Another dimension of comparative economic studies includes theoretical and empirical work on the transformation of one economic system into another.

Almost 150 years ago, Karl Marx and Friedrich Engels sketched a scenario for a transition from capitalism to socialism and then to communism.[18] The actual transformation from capitalism to socialism began in the Soviet Union in the late 1920s[19] and in Eastern Europe[20] and China in the late 1940s.[21]

Now attention is focused on the opposite transformation, from a socialist centrally planned economy toward a capitalist regulated market economy, in Eastern Europe, China, and the successor states of the Soviet Union. In these countries, political and economic reforms are changing many facets of the economic system, including social preference systems, institutions and instruments, and patterns of resource allocation and income distribution.

Work on the transformation of an economic system requires analysis of (1) the old system's nature, characteristics, and problems; (2) possible alternative system arrangements compatible with relevant social and cultural forces; and (3) feasible transition paths from the old to a new system. The many aspects to be investigated include privatization of economic activity; markets for goods, labor, capital, and land; monetary, fiscal, and foreign trade institutions and policies; and social welfare institutions and programs. Moreover, alternative scenarios for "sequencing" various reform measures must be elaborated and evaluated. Finally, proposals and results for individual countries are compared in an effort to distill more general theories and models of the transition.[22]

---

[18] *The Communist Manifesto* (1848). See also Karl Marx, *Critique of the Gotha Program* (1875).

[19] See, for example, Maurice Dobb, *Soviet Economic Development Since 1917,* 5th ed. (London: Routledge & Kegan Paul, 1960); and Alexander Baykov, *The Development of the Soviet Economic System* (Cambridge, England: Cambridge University Press, 1946).

[20] See, for instance, Nicolas Spulber, *The Economics of Communist Eastern Europe* (Cambridge, Mass.: Technology Press of the Massachusetts Institute of Technology, 1957).

[21] See, for example, Carl Riskin, *China's Political Economy: The Quest for Development since 1949* (Oxford: Oxford University Press, 1987).

[22] See, for instance, *On the Theory and Policy of Systemic Change,* ed. Hans-Jürgen Wagener (Heidelberg, Germany: Physica-Verlag, 1993); *The Transformation of Socialist Economies,* ed. Horst Siebert (Tübingen, Germany: J. C. B. Mohr, Paul Siebeck, 1992); *The Transition to a Market Economy,* ed. Paul Marer and Salvatore Zecchini, 2 vols. (Paris: Organization for Economic Cooperation and Development, 1991); Jozef M. van Brabant, *Privatizing Eastern Europe: The Role of Markets and Ownership in the Transition* (Dordrecht, the Netherlands: Kluwer Academic Publishers, 1992); and *Fiscal Policies in Transition,* ed. Vito Tanzi (Washington, D.C.: International Monetary Fund, 1992).

### Interdisciplinary Approach

To what extent can the comparative analysis of economic systems, along the lines suggested above, be performed exclusively with the tools ordinarily found in the economist's tool box? Or should considerable use be made of the concepts and techniques of other disciplines, including history, anthropology, political science, sociology, and psychology?

Perhaps more than other branches of economics, the comparison of economic systems requires a multidisciplinary or—better still—interdisciplinary approach. Some aspects of the subject may need this approach to a greater extent than others. For example, the comparison of ideologies involves other disciplines much more than does the comparison of growth rates.

In this field, as in others, it is incumbent upon the investigator to use all of the relevant tools. In some cases, the economist may acquire and use them. In others, the most satisfactory solution will be to secure the collaboration of appropriate scholars in other fields who possess the additional disciplinary skills. Illustrations include joint work by economists and political scientists on government resource-allocation decisions, by economists and psychologists on enterprise management, and by economists and sociologists (or anthropologists) on social-cultural forces shaping the economic system. Fortunately, current trends in other social science disciplines are favorable to such collaboration. The comparative method has long been used in anthropology. Systematic comparative studies have received increasing attention in both political science and sociology. Comparative politics is concerned with transnational analysis of the social configuration, the interest group universe, political parties, ideological attitudes as they shape and condition political behavior, and elite structure. Comparative sociology is devoted to cross-societal studies of kinship, family, and marriage; polity and bureaucracy; social stratification and mobility; ecology, urban sociology, and demography; and cultural value orientation. The potential for mutual assistance and cross-fertilization between these fields and comparative economic studies is clear and exciting.

## CONCLUSION

The scope of comparative economic studies is broad, encompassing several main aspects. First, the field deals with the factors influencing economic systems, including the level of economic development, social and cultural forces, and the "environment." A second aspect is the nature and operation of systems, involving social preference functions, institutions and instruments, and patterns of resource allocation and income distribution. Third, the subject is concerned with the performance of systems, both empirical measurement of results for various performance criteria and aggregate evaluations in the light of the weights assigned to the various criteria by one or more social preference functions.

The broad scope of the field in turn accommodates—indeed requires—a variety of research methods and analytical approaches, disciplinary and inter-disciplinary. They include theoretical and empirical analyses of particular economic systems, or specific parts of them; comparative topical studies; and investigations of the transition from one economic system to another.

Finally, comparative economic studies make a unique contribution to economics as a whole, by providing the perspective to overcome the parochialism inherent in economic thinking—on both theoretical and policy questions—based on the experience of a single economic system. The comparison of systems enriches the analyst's understanding of his or her own system, sharpening appreciation of its merits and demerits and suggesting organizational and operational changes to improve its performance.

*Chapter Two*

# Comparing Economic Systems*

*Egon Neuberger[1]*

*In this chapter, Neuberger presents key methodological principles for comparing economic systems, or components of them.*

*First, he explains how the performance of an actual economy is the result of the interaction of the economic system, policies adopted by the government, and factors such as resource endowment, available technology, and actions of other countries.*

*Second, he examines alternative ways to analyze and compare economic systems. One approach considers the decision-making, information, and motivation structures. Another focuses on the roles of tradition, the market, and planning as mechanisms to coordinate decisions about production, investment, and consumption.*

*Next, Neuberger discusses issues in comparisons of the economic performance of nations with different economic systems. He notes a number of problems in the measurement of economic variables for a country, and, especially, in comparisons across countries. He stresses the need to distinguish the role of the economic system itself versus other reasons for differences in economic performance. He emphasizes that alternative preference systems provide possible sets of "weights" for the evaluation of economic performance.*

*Finally, Neuberger shows how his analytical framework can be applied to compare not only economic systems but also firms of different types—proprietary, employee-owned, user-oriented, and government-owned.*

* "Comparing Economic Systems." Copyright © 1993 by Egon Neuberger; used by permission. This essay includes some material from Egon Neuberger, "Comparative Economic Systems," in *Perspectives in Economics: Economists Look at Their Fields of Study,* ed. Alan A. Brown, Egon Neuberger, and Malcolm Palmatier (New York: McGraw-Hill Book Company, 1971), pp. 252–66, copyright © 1971 by McGraw-Hill, Inc.; used with permission of McGraw-Hill Book Company. Egon Neuberger is Leading Professor of Economics at the State University of New York at Stony Brook.

[1] I am very grateful to Morris Bornstein for his constructive criticisms and invaluable suggestions. His contribution to this study goes way beyond the usual editorial comments. However, he should not be blamed for any remaining weaknesses.

The comparison of economic systems is a complex task requiring a number of steps: (1) placement of the economic system into a general conceptual framework; (2) definition of the economic system itself, and identification of the features that should be stressed; (3) determination of what aspects of the economic system are being compared—its features or its performance; (4) selection of the appropriate criteria by which the comparison is to be conducted; and (5) solution of difficult measurement problems.

## GENERAL CONCEPTUAL FRAMEWORK

In order to deal with the first issue, the construction of a general conceptual framework within which to place the economic system for purposes of comparison, we adopt the Koopmans-Montias framework.[2]

We specify: $n(o) = n[f(e, s, p_s)]$, in which performance of the economy is measured by quantitative and qualitative outcomes ($o$), weighted by the norm ($n$), and the outcomes are a function of the environment ($e$), economic system ($s$), and government policies conducted within the system ($p_s$).

*Outcomes* comprise both final and intermediate goals. Final goals include per capita consumption, income and wealth distribution, stability of employment, incomes, and prices, protection of the physical environment, and national economic and military power. Among the intermediate, instrumental goals are static and dynamic efficiency, the rate of growth of GNP, and the ability of the economic system to permit orderly change. For some of these goals—such as per capita consumption, distribution of income and wealth, stability, efficiency, and rate of growth of GNP—many countries have statistical series that serve as appropriate measures of these goals. For other goals—such as national power, protection of the physical environment, and system adaptability to change—it is much less obvious what statistical data are appropriate, but this does not make these goals any less important.

In comparative economic systems terminology, *norms* are functions which determine the weights to be attached to each of the outcomes, including zero weights to all the outcomes that are not considered important. There are two basic approaches to determining the appropriate *norms* to use: the *comparer's norm* and the *prevailing norm*. In the former case, the person doing the comparison decides on the outcome variables to which to attach positive or negative weights, and the actual weights for each of the chosen outcome variables (e.g., per capita consumption, the extent of inequality in income distribution, growth of GNP, efficiency, and so forth). In the case of prevailing norms, we try to determine the outcome variables chosen, and the weights attached to them, in the "objective" or "preference" function of those who have the basic

---

[2] Tjalling C. Koopmans and John Michael Montias, "On the Description and Comparison of Economic Systems," in *Comparisons of Economic Systems: Theoretical and Methodological Approaches,* ed. Alexander Eckstein (Berkeley: University of California Press, 1971), pp. 35–38.

decision-making authority in the system. This authority may be held by one dictator, an oligarchy, or, in democratic societies, all the participants in the system or their elected representatives. If the decision-making group consists of more than one person, it is necessary to deal with the various problems one runs into when attempting to aggregate the preferences of several decision makers into one norm. This topic is central to the social choice literature.[3] We shall return to the choice of outcomes and norms when we consider the issue of what criteria to use in comparing economic systems.

In this framework, the *environment* is a general category including the known stock of human and material resources and technology; the size and location of the country in question; the tastes and preferences of the population; the prevailing social, political, and legal, but not economic systems; and the impact of weather, natural disasters, and actions of other countries. Thus, it is the most comprehensive category within this framework.

*Government policies* are conducted within the framework set by the economic system (discussed below in greater depth). For example, the existence of a central banking system, such as the Federal Reserve System, is part of the economic system. On the other hand, the decision by the central bank whether to make money tighter or less tight is a policy decision. Government policies include (1) macroeconomic stabilization policies (fiscal and monetary policies); (2) international trade and finance policies (tariffs and exchange rate policies, particularly export-propulsion or import-substitution policies); (3) regulatory policies (antitrust, consumer protection, health and safety); (4) industrial policies (policies encouraging certain industries to grow in order to establish a new dynamic comparative advantage); and (5) agricultural policies (subsidies and price floors).

At this point, we should distinguish carefully between the *economy* and the *economic system*.

When we speak of comparing the economy of the United States with that of Japan, for example, we are asking a much broader question than when we wish to compare just their economic systems. The economy includes, in addition to (1) the economic system, also (2) all the human, natural resource, and technological aspects of what we have defined above as the environment; (3) government policies; and (4) the outcomes.

## THE ECONOMIC SYSTEM

### Alternative Views of an Economic System

Because the *economic system* is one key determinant of performance and the focus of attention in this chapter, we shall treat it in much greater depth than the other components of the overall framework.

---

[3] For example, Dennis C. Mueller, *Public Choice II* (Cambridge, England: Cambridge University Press, 1989), and Donald E. Campbell, *Equity, Efficiency, and Social Choice* (Oxford: Clarendon Press, 1992).

There is no general agreement among economists about how to define the economic system. There are two key questions:

First, how broad and inclusive should the definition be? Should participants' preferences, the sociopolitical system, information technology, and so forth, be considered endogenous to (i.e., part of) the economic system or exogenous (i.e., outside the system and part of the environment)? For example, the "isms" approach (capitalism, socialism, communism, fascism) defined economic systems very broadly by including all of these factors (other than information technology) in the concept of the economic system. Most of the recent approaches have tended to favor narrower conceptions, discussed in detail below. In these approaches, the exogenous factors are not ignored. Rather, their interactions with the endogenous factors form an important area of systemic analysis.

Second, which aspects of the economic system should be taken as the most important ones? There are at least four approaches: (1) In the DIM approach the system consists of the Decision-making (D), Information (I), and Motivation (M) structures which determine how decisions are made, coordinated, and implemented.[4] (2) The ownership approach (e.g., Marx and his followers; adherents to the "isms" approach;[5] and the adherents of the "Chicago School"[6]) takes property relations as the key to understanding economic systems. (3) The RCP (Rules, Customs, and Procedures) approach focuses on the institutional structure of the system.[7] (4) In the RDT approach the economic system is described by Rules, Decision makers, and Transactions.[8]

The concept of rules, customs, and procedures is basically the same as that of "institutions." For example, North states: "Institutions are the humanly devised constraints that structure political, economic, and social interaction. They consist of both informal constraints (sanctions, taboos, customs, and codes of conduct), and formal rules (constitutions, laws, property rights). Throughout history, institutions have been devised by human beings to create order and reduce uncertainty in exchange. Together with the standard constraints of economics they define the choice set and therefore determine transaction and production costs and hence the profitability and feasibility of engag-

---

[4] This approach is fully developed in Egon Neuberger and William J. Duffy, *Comparative Economic Systems: A Decision-Making Approach* (Boston: Allyn & Bacon, 1976).

[5] For example, Andrew Zimbalist, Howard J. Sherman, and Stuart Brown, *Comparing Economic Systems: A Political–Economic Approach*, 2nd ed. (San Diego, Calif.: Harcourt Brace Jovanovich, 1989).

[6] For example, *The Economics of Property Rights*, ed. Eirik G. Furubotn and Svetozar Pejovich (Cambridge, Mass.: Ballinger Publishing Company, 1974).

[7] John Michael Montias, Avner Ben-Ner, and Egon Neuberger, *Comparative Economics* (Fundamentals of Pure and Applied Economics; Chur, Switzerland: Harwood Academic Publishers, forthcoming).

[8] Montias, Ben-Ner, and Neuberger, *Comparative Economics*. In this approach, the economic system is described in terms of the dominant types of *decision makers,* and of *transactions* among them that are permitted, tolerated, or forbidden, as determined by system *rules.*

ing in economic transactions.''[9] Although North limits his notion of institutions to exchange transactions, there is no logical reason for doing so.

## Working Approaches to the Concept of the Economic System

**The RCP–DIM Approach.**   In order to arrive at a working definition of the economic system for our purposes, we combine two different approaches. We take the Montias–Ben-Ner–Neuberger view of economic systems as consisting of formal and informal rules, customs, and procedures constraining the actions of system participants in their production and consumption decisions (RCP). We also utilize the conceptual division of economic systems into the three structures D, I, and M, and the resultant dominant coordination mechanism.

Thus, we shall define the economic system as a mechanism for coordinating decisions on the allocation of scarce resources among competing ends, and the distribution of the results among the system participants. It consists of the decision making (D), information (I), and motivation (M) structures—all three of them being determined by formal and informal system rules and customs. The interplay of these three structures determines the nature of the coordination mechanism: market, plan, tradition, or some combination of them. We shall discuss this approach at some length below.

This approach to economic systems includes the ownership approach as one important aspect. Ownership consists of a bundle of decision-making rights: right of control over the use of the owned object, right to determine allocation of the income attributed to the use of the object, and right to dispose of the owned object. Thus, ownership is one of the basic sources of decision-making power, and a key part of the D structure.

In the RCP–DIM approach the rules, customs, and procedures are of two basic types: (1) *A priori* restrictions are established by constitution or tradition, and are very important and very difficult to change (e.g., ownership patterns, right to one's job, tradition of individualism or collectivism). (2) Rules, customs, or procedures are considered less important, and therefore more easily changed (e.g., rules governing the method by which firms can incorporate, the size of the customary bribes that must be paid to get an import permit, procedures by which firms select members for the board of directors).

**The RDT Approach.**   An alternative but complementary way of looking at the function of systemic rules is that they establish the *decision maker–transaction nexus*. This is the nexus between (1) the types of decision makers (including organizations, such as proprietary firms owned by providers of capital, employee-owned firms, and government-owned firms) that are authorized to participate in economic transactions, and (2) the types of transactions which are

---

[9] Douglass C. North, "Institutions," *Journal of Economic Perspectives* 5, no. 1 (Winter 1991), p. 97.

encouraged, tolerated, or forbidden (e.g., which transactions are legal, and which are forced into the "second" or "underground" economy).

A useful way to think about transactions is in terms of *grants economics*. In this view, there are four types of transactions: (1) In *pure exchange,* a clear quid pro quo is given, each party gains utility, and neither party suffers a loss in net worth. (2) *Implicit exchange* is similar to pure exchange, but there is no explicit contract, e.g., in the case of reciprocal Christmas gifts. (3) *Explicit grants* include pure personal gifts or direct government subsidies. (4) *Implicit grants* involve a combination of exchange and grant (e.g., subsidized loans).[10]

In this context, the RCP–DIM approach determines (1) what transactions are permitted within the system (pure and implicit exchange, implicit and explicit grants); (2) who the decision makers are in each of these transactions, and on what their authority is based (the D structure); (3) the nature of the information channels, the languages, and the content of messages used in the transactions (the I structure); and (4) the mechanisms that can be used by the decision maker to influence others to implement his decisions and engage in transactions (the M structure).

## THE DIM APPROACH TO ECONOMIC SYSTEMS[11]

This approach views the economic system as a combination of three structures—decision making (D), information (I), and motivation (M)—which jointly define the dominant mechanism for coordinating and implementing decisions in the economy, such as the market, a central plan, or tradition. The D structure determines the locus of decision making (i.e., who is authorized to make what decisions) and the source of this authority (ownership, custom, coercion, access to information, and so forth). The I structure determines the manner in which the decision maker obtains the information needed to make rational decisions (the channels of information, the language used, how detailed the messages must be in order for all parties to agree on the meaning of the message, the content of the messages, and so forth). The M structure determines how the decision maker gets others to implement his or her decisions (material and nonmaterial incentives, coercion, custom, and so forth).

### The Decision-Making Structure

In dealing with the locus of decision-making power, one must consider the level of the economy at which decisions are made, the types of decisions made there (for example, the decision on how many houses are to be built in a tract is more

---

[10] Alan A. Brown, Janos Horvath, and Egon Neuberger, "Grants and Exchange: An Overview" (University of Windsor Working Paper no. 92-16, November 1992).

[11] This discussion includes material from Egon Neuberger, "Classifying Economic Systems," in *Perspectives in Economics: Economists Look at Their Fields of Study,* ed. Alan A. Brown, Egon Neuberger, and Malcolm Palmatier (New York: McGraw-Hill Book Company, 1971), pp. 252–66. It also draws on Neuberger and Duffy, *Comparative Economic Systems.*

important than the decision on the colors to be used for interior decoration), and the legal or extralegal sanctions (property rights, tradition, or bureaucratic position) provided to protect the right of a decision maker, or a group of decision makers, to make decisions.

What is our reason for placing ownership in a secondary position, making it merely one of several sanctions provided to protect the right of a decision maker to make a decision? The answer is that ownership rights, in themselves, may signify very little. They may mean anything from complete control over the owned object to virtually no control at all. For example, they may range from the almost absolute control you have in the decision to save or spend the dollar in your wallet to the almost zero control a child of three has over the same dollar deposited in his or her name in a savings bank by parents. In addition, ownership is by no means the sole sanction behind a decision maker's right to dispose freely of some object. The native chieftain who rules a tribe by virtue of tradition may have both the decision-making power and the ability to reap many benefits from the tribe's property without having actual ownership over anything. The same can be said of a high functionary in a socialist state, or of a top executive in many U.S. corporations.

The most important question concerning the D structure is the degree of its centralization or decentralization. While much has been written about this question, no fully satisfactory treatment exists. Of the many important issues, we shall attempt to clarify only three: (1) Instead of the simple dichotomy between centralization and decentralization, we shall deal with four basic types of decision-making structures—complete centralization, administrative decentralization, manipulative decentralization, and complete decentralization. (2) Next, we shall discuss shifts in decision making in cases where there are more than two levels in a hierarchy—the most common case. (3) Finally, we propose the substitution of concentration for centralization as a superior method of comparing different D structures.

**Centralization and Decentralization.**   It is easy to define *complete centralization* in the abstract. This exists when a unique, central, monolithic authority in an economic system makes all the decisions. No national economic system based on such complete centralization has ever existed. The cost and difficulty of obtaining the necessary information and the problem of assuring that everyone in the economic system does what he or she is told provide effective barriers against such centralization. The only conceivable way such a system could be made to operate is by means of a cybernetic revolution, where the information and control problems are solved by information technology and automation.

*Administrative decentralization* provides for the formulation of basic decisions by the central authority, but for the delegation of the responsibility to implement the decisions and the right to make the necessary subordinate decisions to lower-level authorities. The control over the actions of lower-level authorities is achieved by placing limitations on their freedom of action—for example, by commanding them to do something, forbidding them to do something else, or setting rules by which they must guide their decisions. A textbook case of administrative decentralization is the army. The army clearly represents the ultimate in a hierarchical, command organization, with all the important decisions being reached at the top of the pyramid, and so may appear to represent complete centralization. However, no commander worth his salt spells out for his subordinates the precise manner in which his commands are to be implemented—for example, a division commander is not likely to tell the company commander which squad to send out on patrol.

For the third type of decision-making structure we have coined the name *manipulative decentralization*. This is similar to administrative decentralization, but in this case the central authorities do not place explicit limitations on the freedom of action of lower-level authorities. Instead, they control their actions by affecting the environment within which these actions take place. For example, they may manipulate prices, bonuses, taxes or subsidies, or access to credit.

The fourth type of decision-making structure is *complete decentralization*. This provides for the dispersal of basic decision-making power among a number of independent decision-making centers. In the extreme case—again virtually nonexistent—each of these centers would have complete freedom of decision. The textbook case of complete decentralization is pure competition, where each entrepreneur has complete freedom to make his or her decisions and there is no higher organ to control those actions in any way. Paradoxically, in the case of pure competition it is obvious that all this freedom actually amounts to very little real power. This is because the invisible hand of the market serves as a demanding taskmaster. Thus, situations of oligopoly—where a few sellers divide the market—or of "countervailing power"—where strong buyers face strong sellers across a market—offer better examples of complete decentralization in the economic sphere.

The fundamental difference between administrative and manipulative decentralization, on the one hand, and complete decentralization, on the other, is between the delegation of authority to lower echelons merely to make decisions that implement the basic decisions reached by higher echelons, in the former, and the dispersal of decision-making power among independent decision-making organs, in the latter. In the one case, circumscribed rights are granted to subordinates and can be taken away at the discretion of the superior. In the other case, by rights of ownership, custom, or law many independent organs possess power that they cannot be deprived of, except by major changes in these sanctions. In view of this, we would argue that the most significant watershed lies between complete decentralization and administrative or manipulative decentralization, rather than between centralization and decentralization.

**Three-Level Hierarchy.**  The second important problem in dealing with centralization–decentralization arises when we consider shifts in decision-making power in a system that has more than two levels of authority. In a three-level hierarchy, the definition of decentralization, whether administrative or manipulative, is no longer clear. In this case, there are 12 possible shifts in decision-making power:

| | 1 | 2 | 3 | 4 | 5 | 6 | 7 | 8 | 9 | 10 | 11 | 12 |
|---|---|---|---|---|---|---|---|---|---|---|---|---|
| Central units . . . . . . . | − | − | − | + | + | + | | − | | + | − | + |
| Intermediate units . . . . | − | | + | − | | + | − | + | + | − | + | − |
| Primary units (enterprises) . . . . . . | + | + | + | − | − | − | + | | − | | − | + |

Let us define *decentralization* as a shift of decision-making power from the top toward the bottom of the hierarchy (that is, where the power of the highest unit decreases (−) and the power of the lowest unit increases (+)). It should be clear that there are three kinds of decentralization (columns *1*, *2*, and *3*), the most thorough being seen in column *1* and the least thorough in column *3*. *Centralization* is, of course, defined by the reverse process, as in columns *4*, *5*, and *6*. The most thorough centralization appears in column *4*, the least thorough in column *6*.

*Semidecentralization* occurs when there is a downward shift in decision-making power between any two adjoining levels. The two cases of semidecentralization are seen in columns *7* and *8*. *Semicentralization* is the reverse phenomenon and is pictured in columns *9* and *10*.

*Positive intermediation* occurs when the intermediate decision-making units gain power at the expense of the highest and lowest units, as in column *11*. *Negative intermediation* occurs when the intermediate units lose power at the expense of the highest and lowest units, as in column *12*.

Since almost all hierarchies consist of three or more levels, the above discussion is not merely a theoretical exercise. As just one example, in many of the centrally planned economies in the 1960s and 1970s, decision-making authority was shifted both downward from central planning organs, and upward from firms, to intermediate units (kombinats or associations)—a clear example of positive intermediation.

**Concentration Instead of Centralization.**   For systemic comparisons of D structures, centralization and decentralization are not the most felicitous concepts. How would we compare the D structures in a hierarchical centrally planned system, such as the former Soviet Union, and a nonhierarchical system in which the government and the *keiretsu* (large associations of enterprises and banks) share much of the power among themselves, such as in Japan?[12]

[12] Editor's note: See Chapter 13 on Japan's *keiretsu*.

Since centralization is meaningful only in a hierarchical D structure, it cannot be used for such comparisons. Therefore, we must shift our focus from centralization to concentration of decision-making authority.

In order to measure concentration, we adopt two concepts used in the measurement of concentration of income and wealth—the *Lorenz curve* and the *Gini ratio*. They will yield a better idea of the power distribution in an economic system than we can achieve by approaching it through the concept of centralization.

The Lorenz curve requires us to try to determine the set of decision makers holding authority over each economic decision that the society makes, and to determine the importance of each decision. Although this is a very difficult task, measuring the extent of centralization requires the same information. Once we have estimated the extent of decision-making power of each decision maker, we can construct the Lorenz curve by placing all the participants in the economy (whether they have any decision-making authority or not) on the horizontal axis. On the vertical axis we measure (cumulatively) the percentage of total decision-making authority.

Using the Lorenz curves in Figure 2-1, we may adopt the following definitions:

1. *Complete concentration:* one participant monopolizes authority over all decisions. In this case the Lorenz curve is $A$, following the horizontal axis to point $X$, and then the vertical axis up to point $Y$.

2. *Complete dispersion:* all participants share decision-making authority equally. In this case the Lorenz curve follows $B$, the diagonal.

In order to measure concentration between these two extremes, we use the Gini ratio. It equals the area between the Lorenz curve and the diagonal $B$, divided by the area of the triangle $OXY$. Thus, for Lorenz Curve $A$ the Gini ratio is one, and for Lorenz curve $B$ it is zero. The lesson is clear—the larger the Gini ratio, the more concentrated is the D structure.

Even after we obtain the information needed to fit the Lorenz curve, and therefore to calculate the Gini ratio, further criteria would be needed to rank all structures intermediate to $A$ and $B$. Consider structures $C$ and $D$, which have roughly the same Gini ratio. In $C$, all individuals have some decision-making authority, but 50 percent of the authority is concentrated in the hands of 10 percent of the system's participants, with the remaining 90 percent of the participants sharing the other 50 percent of the authority. In $D$, 50 percent of the system's members have no authority at all, although the 50 percent who do have authority share it relatively equally. Structure $C$ is more typical of modern market economies, as in Japan where a great deal of authority is concentrated in the small number of *keiretsu*. Structure D is more typical of ancient Athens, where all citizens shared authority more or less equally, but slaves had no decision-making power at all. This shows that the Gini ratio alone is not sufficient to describe a D structure, but the combination of the Gini ratio and the Lorenz curve enables us to get a very good idea of the nature of the D structure and its concentration.

**FIGURE 2–1**   Lorenz Curve of Distribution of Decision-Making Authority

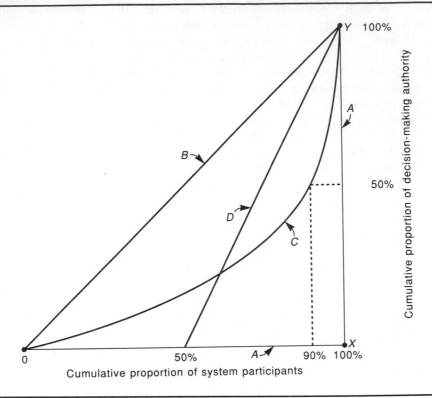

## The Information Structure

In order to make rational decisions, the decision maker requires information of various types, such as forecasts of future demand for a product, prices of competitive products and of the inputs needed to produce the product, potential expansion of capacity by competitors, government policy, and so forth. Information has been gaining importance recently because of changes both in economic systems and in information technology. We will define information very broadly to include the collection, transmission, processing, storage and retrieval, and analysis of economic data; the communication of orders or other signals; and the feedback necessary for evaluating decisions taken as a result of the signals. As we move from a subsistence economy to a traditional economy, from that to a market economy or centrally planned economy, or even to the extreme of a cybernetic economy, the importance of information in the economic system rises very greatly. The larger the number of participants in the economic process, the greater the division of labor, the more complex the technological processes, and the wider the assortment of goods and services an economic system produces, the more information-intensive the economic process becomes. Information becomes more essential not only for the system as a whole but for every participant in the economic process.

The amount of information entering into the decision-making process varies greatly among decision makers in the same economic system, with those nearer the center of economic power requiring and obtaining more information than those at the periphery. It also varies greatly among decision makers with similar positions but operating under different economic systems.

The three major types of informational signals are prices; data on physical units of inputs, outputs, capacities, and the like; and commands. Data on physical units and commands are hallmarks of Soviet-type central planning, while prices are hallmarks of the market system. However, each type of informational signal can be found in both centrally planned and market systems.

Information may be generated within a given organization or received from outside the organization. It may be obtained by horizontal channels—for example, from customers or rival businesses—or by vertical channels—for example, as commands from higher echelons or as data on levels of output and unused capacities transmitted from a firm to its ministry. Information may consist merely of scattered bits of data used to support an action based on intuition, or it may be generated by a well-established system of information collection and analysis, using the latest instruments of information technology.

Three indirect indicators of the degree of informational centralization may be found in an economic system: (1) horizontal channels of information; (2) reliance on price changes, manipulation of incentives, and generalized monetary and fiscal policy; and (3) limitations on the types of messages that can be demanded by the center and sent from the center to the enterprises. All three correspond to informationally decentralized systems.

The way an economic system is organized with respect to the demand it places on informational inputs to decision making, the channels of information that are established, and the ability of decision makers to obtain high-quality information in a reasonable time and at a reasonable cost—these are important factors in determining the efficiency of the system.

## The Motivation Structure

Once the decision maker reaches a decision, he or she must find ways of motivating others, let us call them *agents,* to implement the decision. There are four basic ways to accomplish this: (1) limit the set of options available to agents, (2) structure the consequences of the agents' actions so that the best consequences result when they implement the decision, (3) try to influence the agents' preferences to correspond to the decision maker's preferences (e.g., by indoctrination), and (4) manipulate information available to agents on their feasible options or the likely consequences of their actions.

The first approach (we have called it administrative decentralization) characterizes all hierarchical systems. The superior gives commands to subordinates or sets rules that they must follow. The second approach (manipulative decentralization) uses positive or negative material and nonmaterial incentives (e.g., bonuses, taxes and subsidies, commendations, publicizing of negative acts) to influence the decisions of agents.

Both approaches can be effective, although exercising influence over consequences (unless carried to the extreme) provides control to the decision maker without depriving the agents of all decision-making power. For this reason, economists strongly prefer manipulative to administrative decentralization. Approaches (3) and (4) are less direct and less certain of success. However, if successfully implemented, they are very powerful since the agent will voluntarily act as the principal wishes him or her to act. Therefore, these approaches will not require any further action by the decision maker to influence the agents.

A similar, complementary, and somewhat more general approach to the motivation question is to ask what motivates people. We might say that there are four basic motivators: reliance on tradition, appeal to egocentrism (material or nonmaterial incentives), appeal to solidarity (willing subordination of the individual to group objectives), and coercion.

## COORDINATION MECHANISMS

For an economic system to function effectively, it is essential that decisions made by all the various decision makers are coordinated in some manner. There are three basic mechanisms that accomplish this coordination: tradition, market, and plan.

### Tradition

This coordinating mechanism may be best explained by the following description of the Trobriand Island economic system:

> Every man knows what is expected from him, in virtue of his position, and he does it, whether it means the obtaining of a privilege, the performance of a task, or the acquiescence in a *status quo*. He knows that it has always been thus, and thus it is all around him, and thus it always must remain. The chief's authority, his privileges, the customary give and take which exist between him and the community, all that is merely, so to speak, the mechanism through which the force of tradition acts. For there is no organized physical means by which those in authority could enforce their will in a case like this. Order is kept by direct force of everybody's adhesion to custom, rules and laws, by the same psychological influences which in

our society prevent a man of the world doing something which is not "the right thing." The expression "might is right" would certainly not apply to Trobriand society. "Tradition is right, and what is right *has* might"—this rather is the rule governing the social forces in Boyowa, and I dare say in almost all native communities at this state of culture.[13]

## Market

The "invisible hand," as the coordinating mechanism in the market, consists of three major elements: every individual is motivated by self-interest; he or she obtains the commodities and services required through exchange with others; and by people's pursuit of self-interest, in competition with others, the welfare of society is maximized. Some quotations from Adam Smith illustrate these points:

> It is not from the benevolence of the butcher, the brewer, or the baker that we expect our dinner, but from their regard to their own interest. We address ourselves, not to their humanity but to their self-love, and never talk to them of our own necessities but of their advantages.[14]

While humans obtain most of what they need by means of exchange— "Give me that which I want, and you shall have this which you want"—this does not happen with other species: "Nobody ever saw a dog make a fair and deliberate exchange of one bone for another with another dog."[15] The most important, but by no means most obvious, aspect of the market is that, according to Smith, a man pursuing his own self-interest is

> . . . led by an invisible hand to promote an end which was not part of his intention. Nor is it always the worse for the society that it was no part of it. By pursuing his own interest he frequently promotes that of the society more effectually than when he really intends to promote it.[16]

Or again,

> Every individual is continually exerting himself to find out the most advantageous employment for whatever capital he can command. It is his own advantage, indeed, and not that of the society, which he has in view. But the study of his own advantage naturally, or rather necessarily, leads him to prefer that employment which is most advantageous to the society.[17]

---

[13] Bronislaw Malinowski, *Argonauts of the Western Pacific* (New York: E. P. Dutton & Co., 1922), pp. 158–59.

[14] Adam Smith, *The Wealth of Nations* (London: J. M. Dent & Sons, Ltd., 1910), p. 13. [First published 1776–78.]

[15] Smith, *The Wealth of Nations*, pp. 12–13.

[16] Smith, *The Wealth of Nations*, p. 400.

[17] Smith, *The Wealth of Nations*, p. 398.

## Plan

The third major coordinating mechanism is a plan. One of the earliest examples of planning is told in the Biblical story of Joseph, who prepared Egypt for seven lean years by gathering grain and storing it in the warehouses of the Pharaoh during seven fat years. A more recent example is the centrally planned economic system introduced by another Joseph, Joseph Djugashvili, better known as Stalin.

According to its adherents, the major advantages of a plan as the coordinating mechanism are (1) the possibility of *ex ante* coordination, which enables a given objective to be attained more smoothly and more speedily, and (2) the reduction of uncertainty as to the actions of competitors, suppliers, and buyers, which makes for more rational investment decisions and may help in internalizing external economies. As we have learned, these theoretical advantages of central planning are generally not fulfilled in reality.

In addition to requiring a coordination mechanism, an economic system must provide mechanisms for assuring that decisions are implemented. Implementation in a traditional society is based on voluntary adherence to custom, or, if need be, on the enforcement of custom by such means as ostracism. In a market system, implementation takes place through the operation of the price system. In a planned system there are many possible mechanisms for enforcing the decisions of the planners. The usual one is by informational messages in the form of commands from superiors to inferiors. But this role could theoretically be performed by a cybernetic system transferring information from one machine to another, by the setting of prices by planners, by the use of coercion, or possibly even by the willing cooperation of all the participants. All of these implementing mechanisms, of course, contain motivational or informational components, and could be dealt with as aspects of the motivational and informational structures.

## COMPARISON OF SYSTEMS

There are two quite different types of *systemic comparisons:* (1) comparisons of *systemic features* (DIM, RCP, RDT, etc.) and (2) comparisons of *performance,* that is, comparison of the outcomes as weighted by norms, namely $n(o)$.

### Comparison of Systemic Features

In this type of comparison, we must first agree on the definition of the economic system in order to decide on which aspects of the economic system we should concentrate. Should we stress DIM, RCP, RDT, ownership, or some other aspect?

**Choice of Systemic Approach.**   Since we have selected the RCP–DIM approach as the relevant one, we begin by examining the rules, customs, and procedures that determine the role of the market, the plan, and tradition in each of the economic systems subject to comparison. For instance, do the RCP favor central plans or markets? Are the capital, labor, and product markets relatively free of government intervention or controlled by the government? In this connection, we would be examining the sources of decision-making authority, the degree of concentration in the D structure, the dominant type of information channels in the system (vertical versus horizontal), the content of the informational messages (prices and quantities versus commands and information on capacities), as well as the major motivational mechanisms used in the system.

If we had chosen the RDT approach, we would have concentrated on the nature of the organizations engaged in transactions (proprietary, employee-owned, government-owned, nonprofit, and so forth) and the dominant types of transactions in the system (various types of exchange and grant transactions). Thus, we would ask what are the relative roles of the private and government sectors, and what proportion of the transactions are pure or implicit exchange versus implicit or explicit grants.

We should note again that the RCP–DIM and RDT approaches are complementary rather than mutually exclusive. In fact, in comparisons at the micro level in the next section, we rely heavily on the RDT approach.

If we had adopted the ownership approach, we would have asked what proportion of total assets, or of all organizations, are "owned" by stockholders, employees, government agencies, or others (e.g., donors and/or directors of nonprofit organizations).

**Weighted or Unweighted Approach.**   Even after we have decided to rely on the comparison of systemic features, and chosen the features to examine, we must still decide the difficult question whether to attach different weights to different features or use an unweighted approach.

Most system analysts adopt the former approach and select those features for comparison that they consider the most important. For example, in our approach we place great emphasis on the relative roles of the market, plan, and tradition; the degree of concentration in the D structure; and the nature of the I and M structures.

While this approach of selecting the most important features for systemic comparisons represents an obvious and reasonable way to approach this problem, it is not the only possible one. In the biological sciences, where taxonomy and comparison of species play a major role, a technique of numerical taxonomy has been developed. In this technique *all* the features of the organism (in our case, economic system) are compared without any weights being attached to them. The disadvantage of this approach is that relatively minor features, such as the existence or nonexistence of commercial arbitration boards, receive the same weight as some very important features, such as the existence or nonexistence of a system of commercial banks. Therefore, no analysts of economic systems have adopted the numerical taxonomy approach. Instead, the weights attached to each feature represent our evaluation of each feature's potential impact on the system's performance.

**Systemic Features and Their Effectiveness.**   There is one further important choice that the comparer must make. Should we concentrate on the existence of specific systemic features, or go one step further and examine the effectiveness of each of these features? For example, in comparing a highly centralized planned system with a system of manipulative decentralization, do we merely describe the components of the D, I, and M structures in each of these systems, or do we go further and ask how effective these mechanisms are in fulfilling the objectives of the central planners? For example, the creation of semiautonomous firms in centrally planned economies appears, at first sight, as an abandonment of control by the central planners. However, it can be explained as a rational move based on the desire to internalize within these firms some transactions (or externalize them from the point of view of the planning apparatus) that would otherwise have to be carried out, at a higher cost, through the planning hierarchy.[18]

## Comparison of Performance

In the comparison of performance, we face a number of very difficult and closely related problems: (1) how to isolate the impact of the economic system from that of the environment and government policies, (2) the choice of appropriate norms, (3) the "index number" issue, and (4) the measurement problem.

**The System and the Environment.**   As we indicated earlier, the performance of an economy is a function of the economic system, the environment, and government policies. Thus, a definitive comparison of the relative performance of different economic systems (i.e., how well they perform in achieving the goals valued highly in the norm used for the comparison) requires us to eliminate from the analysis the effects on relative performance of the environment and government policies. This is obviously not easy to achieve in practice.

There are two possible ways to deal with this problem. The *first* is to compare a number of countries with different economic systems, eliminate any environmental factors that are measurable (e.g., capital stock and quality of labor), and hope that there is no systematic bias introduced by other environmental factors. In addition, in such comparisons we would assume that the government policies pursued in each of the set of economies are closely tied to

---

[18] This argument is made in Avner Ben-Ner and Egon Neuberger, "Towards an Economic Theory of the Firm in the Centrally Planned Economy: Transactions Costs, Internalization, and Externalization," *Journal of Institutional and Theoretical Economics* 144, no. 5 (December 1988), pp. 839–48. It is parallel to the famous explanation for the existence of firms in market economies by Ronald Coase in "The Nature of the Firm," *Economica* 4, no. 16 (November 1937), pp. 386–405.

the economic system and do not introduce any separate bias into the comparison. For example, if we compare a number of developed centrally planned economies with a number of developed market economies, we can hope that the unmeasured environmental factors in the two groups do not differ sufficiently to negate our conclusion that the differences in performance are based on the impact of different economic systems.

This was the approach used by Abram Bergson[19] in comparing labor productivity in 1975 in a number of centrally planned and market economies. Bergson obviously chose to use the comparer's norm in selecting labor productivity as the performance criterion. He found that the market economies had a much higher labor productivity.

Similarly, John R. Moroney[20] analyzed the efficiency with which developed market economies and planned economies utilized their energy resources. He found that the planned economies used about twice as much energy per unit of capital and per unit of output. This is explained, in part, by greater emphasis on energy-intensive industries in planned economies, which is a result of planners' preferences. In addition, systemic factors—such as emphasis on gross output rather than efficiency, and a price system that subsidizes energy—played a major role in fostering relatively inefficient use of energy.

The *second* way is to attempt to select two economies that are as similar as possible in their environmental aspects but have different economic systems. This approach also faces great difficulties. For example, we might argue that East and West Germany, or Czechoslovakia and Austria, are appropriate for this type of comparison. However, in addition to the major differences in economic systems between the countries in each of these pairs of economies, the countries also differ in some very important environmental aspects (e.g., social, political, and legal system; level of technology; and in the case of the two Germanies, also size).

This type of comparison was done by Peter Sturm when he compared total factor productivity (the productivity of labor, capital, and land) in East and West Germany.[21] In order to measure differences in the productivity of labor, capital, and land (including natural resources), he took into account the level of technology, and adjusted for labor quality. In addition, he explicitly considered an important systemic variable (foreign trade intensity), and a variable that has both systemic and environmental aspects (allocation of factors of production among different sectors of the economy). Sturm found that the two critical variables explaining productivity differentials are (1) systemic differences and (2) the impact of economies of scale in the much larger West German economy.

[19] Abram Bergson, "Comparative Productivity: The USSR, Eastern Europe, and the West," *American Economic Review* 77, no. 3 (June 1987), pp. 342–57.

[20] John R. Moroney, "Energy Consumption, Capital, and Real Output: A Comparison of Market and Planned Economies," *Journal of Comparative Economics* 14, no. 2 (June 1990), pp. 199–230.

[21] Peter H. Sturm, "The System Component in Differences in Per Capita Output between East and West Germany," *Journal of Comparative Economics* 1, no. 1 (March 1977), pp. 5–24.

**Norms.**   We have already discussed the issue of the various norms, or ways of attaching weights to the systemic outcomes. It is clear that the evaluation of performance will hinge heavily on which norm (i.e., which set of weights) is adopted for the comparison.

If the comparer decides to use his or her norm for the comparison, the outcome of the comparison will be influenced by the proximity of this norm to one or the other economy's norm. The economy whose norm approximates more closely the comparer's norm is likely to appear more successful, other things being equal. This is true because both the country's economic system and its government policies will have been adjusted to try to achieve the outcomes weighted heavily in the norm. We should note that the three comparisons cited above (Bergson, Moroney, and Sturm) each used the comparer's norm. Moreover, each emphasized the efficiency with which each economy used its resources.

Part of the reason, although by no means the whole reason, that the market economies were superior in these three comparisons is that efficiency or productivity is not as highly valued in centrally planned economies as it is in market economies. In the planned economies, the total quantity of output, however achieved, is given more weight than the efficiency with which the output is produced.

An interesting example of the role of norms in comparing economic systems was pointed out by Peter Murrell[22] when he discussed the issue of the lack of product differentiation in centrally planned economies. He argued that one thing that struck all Western visitors was the sheer monotony of life in these economies due to the lack of variety in their products. However, there exists an important trade-off between product differentiation and economies of scale. Thus, if our norm gives heavy weight to per capita consumption, our judgment has to rest on the evaluation of the benefits to consumers of having a greater variety of products versus a larger amount of the goods.

**Index Number Problem.**   If the comparer decides to use the prevailing norm, rather than the comparer's norm, should the norm of economy A or economy B be chosen when comparing the performance of the two economies? This raises the "index number problem."[23] Using the norm of country A will generally lead to favoring country A in the systemic comparison since its system and policies will have been adjusted to try to achieve the outcomes valued highly in country A's prevailing norm.

---

[22] Peter Murrell, "Can Neoclassical Economics Underpin the Reform of Centrally Planned Economies?" *Journal of Economic Perspectives* 5, no. 4 (Fall 1991), p. 63.

[23] The usual form of the index number problem arises when statisticians calculate the consumer price index, and must decide whether to use the market basket of the base year or the current year. When calculating the price change between 1980 and 1993, we will get different results if we use consumer purchases in 1980 (the Laspeyres Index) or the different set of purchases in 1993 (the Paasche Index).

For example, in a comparison of the U.S. and Japanese economies during the 1960s to 1980s, the results will be very different if we use the level of per capita consumption or the rate of growth in GNP as the outcome given the heaviest weight. The United States will dominate Japan in terms of per capita consumption, and Japan will dominate the United States in terms of growth rates.[24]

Unfortunately, there is no single "correct" solution to the index number problem. So it is necessary to make the comparison using both economy A's and economy B's norms. This gives us the two extremes, both of which are "correct," and we know that a "true" comparison is somewhere between the two, although not exactly at which point. Any average of the two extremes serves as a convenience, but has no theoretical validity.

**Measurement Problems.**   Whatever norm we use, we may still face severe measurement problems. Whether the norm weights heavily per capita consumption, growth in GNP, income distribution, or stability, we need first to determine what available statistical data are most appropriate as measures of the desired outcomes. Even in what appears to be a simple case, growth in total output, we must decide whether the appropriate data set is Gross National Product, Gross Domestic Product, Net National Product, or National Income. If the outcome of greatest interest is stability, then are data on price stability, employment stability, or output stability the most appropriate? And, if we wish to measure price stability, should we use the consumer price index, the producer price index, or the GNP deflator?

Once we have decided what data are appropriate for our comparison, three key problems remain: (1) the reliability of the data, (2) the availability of a sufficiently large data set, and (3) the choice of an appropriate common denominator.

In any statistical analysis, it is essential to try to determine whether the data to be used are reasonably reliable. Again, it is a question of degree, since data vary from relatively reliable, such as the U.S. consumer price index, to basically fictitious, such as Soviet official data on their military expenditures.

The question of availability, as opposed to reliability, of data is generally less serious in cross-section comparisons of different economies at one time (e.g., of GNP of different countries in 1993). However, most norms involve time-series comparisons, that is, evaluation over time of the functioning of economies (e.g., growth in GNP, price stability, changes in efficiency). Such

---

[24] The only exception to this type of bias is the so-called "Gerschenkron effect," which occurs when the outcomes in which country B is especially strong are those that have higher valuations in country A. For example, if output of goods relatively expensive in country A happened to grow particularly rapidly in country B, use of the price weights of country A would favor country B. However, the "Gerschenkron effect" is clearly an exception to the general rule. In addition, it is much less likely in comparisons of income distributions, stability, and other more general outcomes, than in comparisons solely of rates of growth of output.

evaluation requires consistent data over a long period in order to provide results with statistical significance (i.e., a reasonable assurance that the results could not have occurred randomly). Such long series covering a large number of periods in each of the countries we may wish to compare are often not available. And, even when they are available, they may be misleading if significant changes in the system or the environment occurred in one or more of the economies in the comparison. For example, comparisons of the performance of the U.S. and German economies during the 1980s and 1990s will be misleading if the unification of East and West Germany in 1990 is ignored.

The choice of common denominator in comparing levels of per capita consumption, GNP, or other economic aggregates is closely related to the index number problem. We must compare the values of goods and services in one country with those in another country. The obvious, although not necessarily correct, procedure is to use the official exchange rate between the currencies of the two countries. However, since official exchange rates often overvalue or undervalue a currency, this method can give quite misleading results. Therefore, considerable effort has been made to develop a set of exchange rates that reflect more faithfully the purchasing power of each country's currency.[25]

## SYSTEM COMPARISONS AT MICRO LEVEL

Generally, system comparisons have been conducted at the level of national economies. However, more recently considerably more attention has been given to system comparisons of basic economic organizations (i.e., firms, households, and other economic organizations).[26] In order to keep our discussion relatively simple and brief, we limit ourselves to firms, and cover only a few basic points.

Just as we placed the economic system of a country into a broader framework, the same has to be done for the economic system of a firm. We must remember that the firm is one of many organizations within an economy, and the firm's economic system depends on the nature of that economy. We can approach this question by asking what factors are likely to influence the economic system of the firm. The major interconnected factors are (1) the eco-

---

[25] See Irving B. Kravis, Alan Heston, and Robert Summers, *International Comparisons of Real Product and Purchasing Power* (Baltimore, Md.: Johns Hopkins University Press, 1978), and Robert Summers and Alan Heston, "The Penn World Table (Mark 5): An Expanded Set of International Comparisons, 1950–1988," *Quarterly Journal of Economics* 106, no. 2 (May 1991), pp. 327–68.

[26] We draw extensively on a paper by Avner Ben-Ner, John Michael Montias, and Egon Neuberger, "Basic Issues in Organizations: A Comparative Perspective," *Journal of Comparative Economics* 17, no. 2 (June 1993), pp. 207–42. Various aspects of comparisons at the micro level are explored in this special issue of the journal on "Structure and Behavior of Economic Organizations: Theoretical Perspectives," ed. Avner Ben-Ner, Josef C. Brada, and Egon Neuberger.

nomic, political, and legal system of the country; (2) the identity of the firm's controllers, their goals, and their theory of organization; (3) the nature of the product produced by the firm, its technology, and its markets for outputs and inputs; and (4) the country's social norms, culture, and level of economic development. While all four sets of factors influence the firm's economic system, the first two are closely connected and have the greatest influence.

## Economic System of a Firm

Most of the problems involved in defining the economic system of a country reappear in the case of the economic system of a firm. We define the economic system of a firm the same way we defined the system of a national economy (i.e., by its RCP and DIM structures). In order to classify firms, we rely on the D structure as the primary criterion, and focus on the nature of the ultimate controllers or "owners"—those who have the dominant ownership rights over the assets of the firm (control, distribution of income generated, and disposal). A critical component of the control rights is the right to hire and fire the managers. We single out this right of "ownership," since frequently managers are the de facto controllers of the firm. Hence, power over them is a key defining element of *ultimate control.*

There are four basic categories of firms (each with its own variants), depending on who wields ultimate control: (1) In *proprietary* firms, suppliers of capital and/or entrepreneurship have ultimate control. (2) In *employee-owned* firms, control rests with suppliers of labor services. (3) In *user-oriented* firms— such as consumer cooperatives or nonprofit hospitals or theaters—donors or customers, who are primarily interested in the nature and quality of the product, are in control. (4) *Government-owned* firms are controlled by local, regional, or national government organs.

We begin by concentrating on two basic human traits that affect the economic system of all firms: bounded rationality and self-interest.

*Bounded rationality* means that individuals act under constraints imposed by their intellectual capacities. We include all aspects of human fallibility in making decisions, as well as in acquiring, digesting, analyzing, and transmitting information. One important aspect of bounded rationality is the limited computational capacity of the human brain, which leads to the adoption of simplified decision rules.

*Self-interest* means that individuals pursue their objectives (including personal material gain, satisfaction from a job well done, enjoyment of leisure, challenge, and respect of peers) even when this worsens the performance of the firm.

These two traits vary with education, native intelligence, and personal values, as well as social norms established by the society and those established by the firm. Varying degrees of these two traits create, respectively, technical-administrative (T-A) problems and agency-managerial (A-M) problems.

Due to bounded rationality, T-A problems arise in the D and I structures, including incomplete information available to decision makers and imperfect decision making. It is important to note that T-A problems exist even when all members of the firm share mutual goals and, therefore, operate as a "team." For example, in a producer cooperative where all members share the goal of maximizing the net income per member, they may not succeed in accomplishing this goal, due to T-A problems. Bounded rationality makes the transmission of information costly, and makes it impossible to engage in perfect decision making. Hence, they are forced to substitute imperfect but simpler rules based on partial information.

Self-interest, combined with *asymmetric information,* leads to A-M problems in all three (D,I,M) structures. The *principal–agent framework* has been developed as a useful way to deal with the analysis of A-M problems. In this framework, the principal determines the contract and the agent either accepts it or not. If only those individuals who will benefit most from a contract accept it—e.g., only those in desperate need will buy insurance, or only those workers who have no alternative job opportunities, due to lack of necessary skills, apply—the principals face *adverse selection.* If, after accepting a contract, the agent operates in a way to benefit himself at the expense of the principal (e.g., those with insurance use health care more than necessary or a worker uses sick leave in order to prolong a vacation), there is a case of *moral hazard.* In contrast to T-A problems, A-M problems do not arise when the firm operates as a team. For example, a member of a small producer cooperative will not shirk his or her duty by taking unnecessary sick leave, just as a member of a baseball team will not fake sickness when the team is playing in the World Series.

The ultimate controllers will exert great efforts to establish the D, I, and M structures of the firm's economic system in a way to counter both the T-A and A-M problems.

In order to deal with T-A problems, they will provide in-house education and training for managers and workers (or send them to special courses at universities), and they will invest in computers and communications equipment to improve informational exchange.

The attempt to minimize A-M problems requires more difficult and more complex solutions than measures to counter the T-A problems. There are two important types of moral hazard problems. One is "free riding": each individual tries to minimize his or her own effort in the hope of riding free on the efforts of others. The second is the provision of biased and incomplete information to the principal. For example, the manager of a division reports a smaller production capacity in order to get a task the division can fulfill very easily.

In order to address these moral hazard problems, the ultimate controllers try to use elements of the D, I, and M structures: (1) They can establish strict rules to be followed by all members. (2) They can appoint supervisors to monitor the behavior of the workers or employ sales managers to oversee the activity of sales representatives. (3) They can structure incentives so as to make it in each manager's or worker's self-interest to act in the firm's interest, and make free-riding or provision of biased information counterproductive (e.g., by stock options or profit sharing).[27] (4) They can try to develop an organizational culture that stresses solidarity (e.g., formation of quality circles).

Firms operating as teams tend to use associational structures. In an *association* members engage in joint decision making with essentially equal control rights. On the other hand, firms that face moral hazard problems tend to set up hierarchical structures. In a *hierarchy* superiors are empowered to issue orders to subordinates and to set rules to control the behavior of subordinates. Thus, hierarchies are established to counter A-M problems by limiting the ability of firm members to act against the firm's interests.

## Four Types of Firms

There are four basic types of firms, depending on who controls them: proprietary, employee-owned, user-oriented, and government-owned. We shall point out very briefly some systemic variations among the four types due to the differences in the goals of the controllers, and the T-A and A-M problems they face.

In proprietary firms the goal of the owners is generally profit maximization. In employee-owned firms it is maximization of net income (revenue minus nonlabor costs) per member. In user-oriented firms controllers seek the production and delivery of high-quality products. A government-owned firm tends to be assigned a multiplicity of goals by the government organ that creates it. These goals may include provision of high-quality products and services (as in user-oriented firms), profit maximization (as in proprietary firms), maximization of employment, providing patronage, and so forth.

These differences in goals and in the type of A-M problems that arise lead to different mechanisms in the economic systems of firms in these four categories. In addition, as we shall see later, the differences in goals raise again the problem of what norms to use and the index number problem.

**Proprietary Firms.**   In large proprietary firms there are four types of A-M problems: (1) the relations between shareholders (the ultimate controllers) and managers, (2) between managers and employees, (3) among shareholders, and (4) among employees. The first two have been given major attention in the literature, which discusses various mechanisms by means of which the share-

---

[27] A solution to this problem is the establishment of so-called "Groves-type" incentive schemes. In these schemes, the payoff to each member depends, in part, on the information the member provides, as well as that provided by all other members. This feature encourages each member to provide truthful information and limit his or her free riding. See Theodore Groves, "Incentives in Teams," *Econometrica* 41, no. 4 (July 1973), pp. 617–31.

holders (the principals) can reduce A-M problems with managers (agents), and managers (principals) can do the same with workers (agents).[28]

1. Unless there is a small group of shareholders who can exercise direct control, the principals must exert indirect control through a board of directors or an external market for control (mergers and takeovers). The former method of control is more common in Germany and Japan, where banks and allied firms play a major role on the board of directors, while the latter is more common in the United States and United Kingdom. In addition, principals can use improvements in I structure to provide more complete information to themselves and to those who are potential shareholders. Also, various incentive schemes (e.g., stock options) can eliminate the moral hazard problem by making it in the managers' interest to maximize the objectives of the shareholders.

2. The principal–agent problems between managers and workers have been dealt with primarily in the industrial relations literature.[29] The economic system of the firm has been structured to attempt to minimize A-M problems. The major mechanisms are hierarchy in the D structure and monitoring of the activities of workers in the I structure.

3. A-M problems among the principals concern reaching agreed decisions among many principals, and the advantage to each principal of trying to free-ride on other principals in controlling the managers. Such problems have been faced explicitly in some of the privatization schemes in Eastern Europe, where special institutions (investment funds) have been created to provide a "core" of shareholders capable of, and interested in, controlling the managers.

4. A-M problems among workers in proprietary firms may arise during negotiations over a wage and benefit package. Workers, as principals, may disagree on various components of the contract the union (their agent) is negotiating with management. For example, they may differ on the appropriate wage differentials for various skill levels, or on the relative weight to be given to wages compared to health benefits or job security.

**Employee-Owned Firms.**   Two parallel D structures exist in these firms. One structure has the workers as principals for purposes of policymaking and managers (whether members or hired) as their agents. The other structure has the

---

[28] For example, Andrei Shleifer and Robert W. Vishny, "Value Maximization and the Acquisition Process," *Journal of Economic Perspectives* 2, no. 1 (Winter 1988), pp. 7–20; and Bengt Holmstrom and Jean Tirole, "The Theory of the Firm," in *Handbook of Industrial Organization,* ed. Richard Schmalensee and Robert Willig (Amsterdam: North-Holland Publishing Company, 1989), vol. 1, pp. 61–134.

[29] For example, Paul Willman, *Technological Change, Collective Bargaining, and Industrial Efficiency* (Oxford: Clarendon Press, 1986).

managers as principals in the production process with workers as their agents. The former structure is generally an association, while the latter a hierarchy.

A-M problems tend to be somewhat less serious in employee-owned firms since the members share in the results of their activities, and there is a lesser need for managerial monitoring of workers since workers tend to monitor each other. However, A-M problems do occur even in employee-owned firms. Members are likely to differ in their attitudes toward wage differentials among workers with different skills levels or in the degree of their risk aversion. The problem of free-riding may also arise because most workers would prefer to have others expend the effort involved in monitoring the managers, and many also prefer leisure to participating in meetings where policy decisions are reached.[30]

These firms also face serious problems in obtaining capital. The contributions of equity capital by members are limited by their personal wealth and their willingness to invest in the firm. Members face much greater risks in investing in their own firm than do shareholders in proprietary firms. If members invest in their own firm rather than in other firms, then their income from both their labor and their capital investment would depend on the success of this single firm. This lack of portfolio diversification is the cause of the greater risk.[31] In addition, employee-owned firms generally have a more difficult time than proprietary firms in obtaining loans and selling bonds on the capital markets.

**User-Oriented Firms.**   Firms such as nonprofit hospitals or theaters are not oriented toward maximizing profits. If any profits are earned, they must be reinvested in the firm, and cannot be distributed to any member of the firm. The D structure in these firms is generally less clear-cut than in any of the other types of firms. There are no ultimate controllers with all three types of the ownership rights (control, distribution of income, and disposal). These firms are controlled by a board of directors (we shall call the members of the board the firm's controllers), with membership generally given to major donors, customers, top managers, or government representatives—none of whom have legal rights of ownership. The board of directors determines how income is to be distributed, with the proviso that no profits can be distributed. They have only a limited right to dispose of the assets of the firm.

---

[30] Using the DIM approach, Ben-Ner provides a comparison of systemic features in proprietary firms and employee-owned firms. See Avner Ben-Ner, "The Life Cycle of Worker-Owned Firms," *Journal of Economic Behavior and Organization* 10, no. 3 (October 1988), pp. 287–313.

[31] The finding that the investment by co-op members in their firm is limited by their wealth and the greater risk they face, compared to shareholders in proprietary firms, is supported by a major empirical study of employee-owned and proprietary plywood cooperatives in the Pacific Northwest. The study compared firms in the same industry, in the same region, and during the same time period. It showed that the value of the shares in the plywood cooperatives was lower than that of shares in comparable proprietary plywood mills. See Ben Craig and John Pencavel, "The Behavior of Worker Cooperatives: The Plywood Companies of the Pacific Northwest," *American Economic Review* 82, no. 5 (December 1992), pp. 1083–1105.

However, in one type of user-oriented firm, the consumer cooperative, the D structure is very clear. The customer–members of the co-op are the ultimate controllers who wield all three rights of ownership.

User-oriented firms face the same four A-M problems as proprietary firms, although their goals are very different. In fact, in those user-oriented firms which have adopted the nonprofit form of organization, the goals include production and distribution of large quantities of high-quality products, growth of the firm, and quality of life for managers and workers in the firm. This multiplicity of goals makes it more difficult to measure performance.

The lack of legal owners limits the options available to principals to control managers. While an external market for control is an important control mechanism in proprietary firms, it is not available in nonprofits. Therefore, it is critical for these firms to avoid the *adverse selection* problem in recruiting their managers and workers. They must exercise great care in hiring, especially for management positions, in order to employ only those who share the controllers' objectives of providing high-quality goods and services to the users. Otherwise, there is a danger that managers will neglect these goals in favor of making life pleasant for managers and employees—for example, by high wages, generous expense accounts, and luxurious offices. Moreover, hiring the right persons also helps to alleviate any possible *moral hazard* problems, since they will operate as a team, that is, work toward fulfilling the controllers' goals.

**Government-Owned Firms.**   In state-owned enterprises, the principals are theoretically the population as a whole. However, in fact, the actual principals tend to be government officials overseeing the firm. If the firm is to serve the people of the country or region—who are its ultimate principals—the selection of managers and employees is again critical. The D structure in a government-owned firm tends to be hierarchical, just as is the case for the government organ that controls the firm.

The nature of the economic system at the national level has more impact on government-owned firms than on other types of firms—both in terms of the proportion of all firms that are government owned, and in the objectives they pursue. In market economies, government-owned firms play a much smaller role than in centrally planned economies, and these firms may be forced to compete with proprietary firms within the country or in international trade. Thus, Renault in France, INA (a government oil company) in Italy, and other government-owned firms tend to operate much more like proprietary firms than do government-owned firms in centrally planned economies.

## Performance Comparisons

The problems faced in comparisons of firms with different economic systems are very similar to the problems encountered in comparisons of economic systems in different economies.

The issues include comparison of features versus comparison of performance; selection of appropriate criteria (the choice of norms and the consequent index number problem); and the measurement problems. When we compare firms within a given country, we avoid having to find an appropriate common denominator, since we can use the prices of the country in question.

For instance, a study by Vickers and Yarrow comparing the performance of proprietary and government-owned firms in the United Kingdom concluded that there is strong evidence that proprietary firms are superior in efficiency under competitive conditions. However, they found no hard evidence that proprietary firms perform better than government-owned firms when both have monopoly power or when both function under a similar regime of government regulation of industry.[32] Note that Vickers and Yarrow adopted the comparer's norm, using efficiency as the criterion, and thereby favored the proprietary firm, which does not have a multiplicity of goals.

## CONCLUSION

We began this chapter by asserting that the comparison of economic systems is a very important but complex and difficult task. By this time, the reader will very likely agree.

(1) we placed the economic system into a general conceptual framework: $n(o) = n[f(e, s, p_s)]$. (2) We defined the economic system in terms of the rules, customs, and procedures (RCP) as they affect the decision-making, information, and motivation structures (DIM). (3) We argued that comparisons of both systemic features and systemic performance are relevant. (4) We pointed out problems in choosing the appropriate criteria for comparing systemic features (weighted or unweighted approach), and for comparing performance (isolation of system from environment, the choice of comparer's versus prevailing norms, and the "index number" problem). (5) We considered problems of measuring relative performance: choice of appropriate data, reliability of data, availability of data, and selection of appropriate common denominator.

We have not stopped with macro comparisons of total economies—a common perspective in Comparative Economic Systems. Instead, we have also moved down to the micro level, comparing different types of firms—the viewpoint of Comparative Organizations. We have contended that in both kinds of comparisons it is appropriate to use the same general conceptual framework (within which the economic system is but one important variable) and the RCP–DIM approach to defining the economic system. We have shown that most of the problems that arise in macro comparisons have their analogues in comparisons of firms with different economic systems.

---

[32] John Vickers and George Yarrow, *Privatization: An Economic Analysis* (Cambridge, Mass.: MIT Press, 1988).

Despite all the difficulties, systemic comparisons at both the macro and micro levels are necessary to evaluate the basic differences among economic systems, and their relative performance. Choice of economic systems is not a frequent event. However, when it happens it is critical to judge the relative effectiveness of different systems. This has occurred in the case of the former Soviet Union and Eastern Europe, where the consensus emerged that the centrally planned economic system did not work well. This judgment made major systemic changes inevitable, both at the macro level and at the micro level. Similarly, the conclusion that the U.S. health system is both too costly and too inequitable is leading to a major restructuring. In both cases, the relevant decision makers based their decisions on comparative studies of the effectiveness of various systemic features, and of the performance of different systems.

Both our theoretical treatment of system comparisons and the case studies we have cited demonstrate that system comparison at the macro and micro levels is a very difficult but essential task. Therefore, the reader should welcome systemic comparisons but take them with a large grain of salt. One should not accept statements about relative performance without analyzing carefully each step in the comparison to see whether the comparer has satisfied all the requirements for systemic comparisons that we have discussed.

*Chapter Three*

# The Objectives and Instruments of Economic Policy*

*Etienne S. Kirschen*
*Lucien Morissens*[1]

*This chapter shows how a country's economic system can be analyzed in terms of the objectives of economic policy and the instruments used to pursue them. The principal objectives include full employment, price stability, economic growth, improvement in the balance of payments, satisfaction of collective needs, and modification of the distribution of income and wealth. To accomplish these goals, governments use instruments of public finance, monetary and credit measures, direct controls, alteration of the exchange rate, and even changes in the basic institutional framework. The authors explain which instruments are commonly used for which objectives, and they identify the conflicts which occur and the choices which must be made by government policymakers.*

*The framework proposed by Kirschen and Morissens can be applied in various ways. In Table 3–1, one can evaluate the importance of different aims—for exam-*

* Excerpted by permission from *Quantitative Planning of Economic Policy*, ed. Bert G. Hickman (Washington, D.C.: Brookings Institution, 1965), pp. 111–33. Material originally published in E. S. Kirschen and others, *Economic Policy in Our Time* (Amsterdam: North-Holland Publishing Company, 1964), is reprinted by permission of the North-Holland Publishing Company. Etienne S. Kirschen was Professor and Director, and Lucien Morissens was Professor, at the Department of Applied Economics of the Free University of Brussels.

[1] Much of the substance of the present paper is drawn from *Economic Policy in Our Time* (Amsterdam: North-Holland Publishing Company, 1964), by E. S. Kirschen (Belgium), J. Bénard (France), H. Besters (Germany), F. Blackaby (United Kingdom), O. Eckstein (United States), J. Faaland (Norway), F. Hartog (Netherlands), E. Tosco (Italy), and L. Morissens (Belgium). The study is in three volumes: I. *General Theory;* II. *Country Studies: Economic Policy in the United States, United Kingdom, and Norway;* III. *Country Studies: Economic Policy in Belgium, The Netherlands, France, Italy, and Western Germany.* This material is in general paraphrased, and on occasion blended in with additions made for the present paper. In any case, the authors are grateful to the North-Holland Publishing Company for permission for use of the excerpts and tabular material. An extension of this analysis appears in E. S. Kirschen and others, *Economic Policies Compared—West and East* (Amsterdam: North-Holland Publishing Company, 1974).

*ple, material welfare versus equity—and analyze how each objective fulfills a particular aim, for instance, the contribution of price stability to material welfare, equity, and the reduction of social tensions.*

*In Table 3–2, one can identify examples of each of the instruments, such as different types of taxes or transfer payments, and consider how they can help achieve different objectives, such as full employment, price stability, and modification of the distribution of income and wealth.*

*In Table 3–3, one can analyze the reasons for conflicts among objectives, for instance between full employment and price stability, or between competition and protection.*

*The "dominant-to-negligible" scale in Table 3–4 can be used to map the preferences, among various economic policy objectives, of rival candidates or political parties.*

## OVERALL TERMINOLOGY

By "policy," we mean action taken by the government in pursuit of certain aims, examples of which are:

Raising the population's standard of living.

Preserving law and order.

Guarding the freedom of expression and choice.

Reducing social tensions.

Defending the country from outside attack.

Making adequate provision for health and education.

It must also be recognized that governments in the eight countries chosen for special study were elected, and that one of their aims was to keep the electorates' support. All these aims have, to a greater or lesser extent, an economic aspect. The standard of living is obviously an economic matter, but the other aims, too, usually require some kind of government intervention in economic affairs. Preparations for defense or expenditure on health, for instance, require that resources are diverted from productive uses.

*Economic policy,* therefore, is the economic aspect of government policy in general: it is *the deliberate intervention of the government in economic affairs to further its aims.* In pursuit of these aims, governments have tended to set for themselves certain specific *objectives* which can be stated in economic terms, and which (at least in principle) are capable of measurement (either ordinal or cardinal).

To put its economic policies into effect, a government either alters certain economic quantities (such as bank rates or tax rates), or makes changes in the economic structure (such as nationalization). The economic quantities which the government can change, or the types of intervention in the economic structure, we call *instruments.* The government selects, from a wide range of instruments, those that will in its opinion most nearly achieve its objectives. The use of an instrument does not normally bring about changes in objectives directly: It operates on other economic quantities. For instance, a government may have expansion of production as its objective. It may choose to increase private consumption, investment, or exports, and to effect these increases it can select from a large number of possible instruments—such as a guaranteed minimum wage or export subsidies.

Finally, the use of a particular instrument on a particular occasion we call a *measure*. A measure is taken to promote one or more objectives. This means that there is no measure without an objective.

## THE OBJECTIVES OF ECONOMIC POLICY

For economic analysis as well as for political decision making, a classification of the objectives is necessary. There are many ways of classifying objectives, but none of them is perfect. The reasons for this deficiency are the following:

1. Economic policy was not devised in one day by a brain trust. Objectives appeared in the course of history, one by one, as new problems arose and as policymakers became more fully conscious of old problems. This process resulted in overlappings and contradictions. Some objectives are complementary—when the achievement of one helps in the achievement of another. Other objectives conflict—when the achievement of one is detrimental to the achievement of another.[2]

2. Problems are not considered in the same way by the politician (who makes decisions) and by the economist (who sometimes inspires decisions). The politician may be led to classify objectives according to the preferences expressed by the various policymakers who influence economic policy. From this point of view, he will distinguish objectives which serve the general welfare of the nation from those which serve particular interests, and, among the latter, he will consider separately the objectives aiming at the promotion of various particular interests. The economist, on the other hand, will tend to rationalize economic policy on the basis of his views about the workings of economic mechanisms. In his classifications, he might thus use such criteria as demand, production, or incomes, which will obviously lead to something very different from the list of objectives stated by politicians.

In *Economic Policy in Our Time* objectives were classified according to the following statement of principles:

> In producing our classification of objectives, we tried to find the one which was most useful in showing up the important differences in the policies of our nine countries.[3] The classification has been derived partly from the analysis of actual economic policy in these countries, and it takes into account the objectives which the various governments themselves have stated from time to time. It also uses the various systematizations which have been prepared by other economists.

---

[2] This point of conflict is discussed in the later section, "Conflicts and Choices,"
[3] Editor's note: The eight countries listed in footnote 1 plus Luxembourg.

The criteria applied in our classification are the following:

1. The number of objectives was kept small enough to render the classification easy to handle, but large enough to keep international comparisons meaningful.

2. The objectives were divided into two groups: mainly short-term and mainly long-term. This is because it is of interest to examine separately the various methods used in the different countries to counteract short-term cyclical fluctuations, and the methods used to pursue longer term economic policies. However, all the short-term objectives have long-term aspects as well. For instance, the objective of maintaining full employment was most commonly a short-term cyclical problem, but governments have also had long-term full employment objectives, such as that of reducing structural unemployment.

3. The longer term objectives were divided into major and minor ones. If, in the years we were surveying, most countries had an objective and most countries considered it important, then we classed it as a major objective—otherwise as minor.

4. When an objective appeared to be the result of a regrouping which is meaningful for the economist but not for the policymaker, we subdivided the objective. This is the case for the improvement in the allocation of factors of production. But when an objective had a composite nature that was not the result of economists' arrangements, the objective was not subdivided. Thus, we kept together the protections given to various industries, the satisfaction of the various collective needs, or the improvement in the pattern (i.e., relative importance of the various items) of private consumption.

5. When an objective could be given two opposite meanings, we did not subdivide it into two objectives. For example, the improvement in the distribution of income can mean a move toward greater or lesser equality. Similarly, according to its state, a balance of payments can be improved either by reducing its deficit or by reducing its surplus. Thus, when we use the word "improvement" this implies nothing more than that, in the judgment of the government which took the measures, any change was an improvement.

6. We have not included all the various objectives which may have been in the mind of some particular minister in one or another of the nine countries at some time. At various times, for instance, some people have elevated to the rank of objectives such things as the balanced budget, the reduction of the national debt, or the preservation of a particular exchange rate. We regard these matters as constraints on the use of instruments.

The classification of objectives (as formulated in *Economic Policy in Our Time*) is shown in the left-hand column of Table 3–1. At the head of the columns are listed the main aims that seem to have been expressed by the various objectives. There are, of course, many overlappings between the aims, mostly because aims incline to be philosophical notions. (The x's in the columns mean that the aim was expressed by the objective.)

In this section the first four objectives in Table 3–1 will be considered. For each objective we give a definition and the methods of quantification.

## Full Employment

**1. Definition: Prevention or Reduction of Unemployment.**  Governments have been mainly concerned with the objective of preventing and reducing short-term cyclical unemployment, caused, for example, by a decline in exports or by the ending of an investment boom. But some have also had long-term policies that were specifically directed to reduce noncyclical unemployment: for instance, *frictional unemployment*—unemployment due to the delay in matching vacancies with the unemployed who are capable of filling them; or *structural unemployment*—for instance, unemployment due to the decline of a particular industry, or to the fact that industry is moving away from a particular region.

**2. Methods of Quantification.**  *Full employment* may be expressed as a given or a maximum ratio between the number of unemployed and the working population; or it may be expressed as an equality between the number of unemployed and the number of unfilled vacancies.

\* \* \* \* \*

## Price Stability

**1. Definition: Maintaining General Stability of Prices.**  Throughout most of our period, most governments tended to regard price stability as a short-term problem: The tendency to rising prices was something to be corrected by "conjunctural" policies. More recently, an increasing number of governments began to regard this tendency as a long-term problem that might require structural changes in the economy.

**2. Methods of Quantification.**  The objective may be expressed as a maximum annual increase in the retail price index.

\* \* \* \* \*

## Improvement in the Balance of Payments

**1. Definition: Maintaining a "Satisfactory" Balance of Payments and a "Satisfactory" Stock of Gold and Foreign Exchange.**  Usually, the objective was the short-term one of maintaining or increasing exchange reserves. Sometimes

**TABLE 3–1**  Classification of the Objectives of Economic Policy and Aims Expressed by These Objectives

| Objectives | Internal Aims | | | | | |
|---|---|---|---|---|---|---|
| | Material Welfare | Equity | Reduction of Social Tensions | Promotion of Human Values | Ethics and Religion | Protection of Persons and Properties |
| Mainly Short-Term | | | | | | |
| 1. Full employment . . . . . . | x | x | x | x | | |
| 2. Price stability . . . . . . . | x | x | x | | | |
| 3. Improvement in the balance of payments . . . . | x | | | | | |
| Mainly Long-Term (Major) | | | | | | |
| 4. Expansion of production. . . | x | | | | | |
| 5. Improvement in the allocation of factors of production | | | | | | |
|    *a.* Promotion of internal competition . . . . . . . | x | x | x | | | |
|    *b.* Promotion of coordination . . . . . . . . . | x | | | | | |
|    *c.* Increase in the mobility of labor, within countries . . . . . | x | | | x | | |
|    *d.* Increase in the mobility of capital, within countries . . . . . | x | | | | | |
|    *e.* Promotion of the international division of labor . . | x | | | | | |
| 6. Satisfaction of collective needs: | | | | | | |
|    *a.* General administration . . . . . . . . | x | x | x | | x | x |
|    *b.* Defense . . . . . . . . | | | | | | |
|    *c.* International affairs. . . . | x | | | | | |
|    *d.* Education . . . . . . . . | x | x | | x | x | |
|    *e.* Public health. . . . . . . | x | x | | x | | |
| 7. Improvement in the distribution of income and wealth . . . . . . | x | x | x | x | | |
| 8. Protection and priorities of particular regions or industries . . . . . . . . | x | x | x | x | x | |
| Mainly Long-Term (Minor) | | | | | | |
| 9. Improvement in the pattern of private consumption . . . . . . . . | | | | x | x | |
| 10. Security of supply . . . . . | x | | | | | |
| 11. Improvement in the size or structure of the population . . . . . . . | x | | x | | x | x |
| 12. Reduction in working hours . . . . . . . . . . . | x | | | x | | |

Note: The x's in the columns mean that the aim was expressed by the objective.

| External Aims | | | |
|---|---|---|---|
| External Security | Political Power | International Solidarity | Personal Aims |
|  |  | X |  |
|  |  | X |  |
|  | X | X |  |
|  | X | X |  |
|  |  |  |  |
| X | X | X |  |
|  |  |  |  |
| X | X |  |  |
| X | X | X |  |
|  | X |  |  |
|  |  |  | X |
|  |  |  | X |
|  |  |  |  |
| X | X |  |  |
| X | X |  | X |

there was concern about the balance of payments on current and/or capital accounts (when a rise in the reserves results only from the inflow of short-term money). Some countries, in addition to the short-term difficulties with their exchange reserves occasioned by the trade cycle, also had a long-run need to improve the proportion of their output which is exported, notably to meet import developments. A balance of payments surplus was thus needed. Some countries aimed to reduce the rate at which their reserves were rising—partly because they considered that their export surplus was becoming inflationary, and partly because other countries were protesting that their own reserves were being run down too fast. There were other long-term balance-of-payments problems as well—such as the problem of changing the regional pattern of exports: for instance, by increasing the proportion going to dollar markets.

**2. Methods of Quantification.**   The objective could be expressed in one of the following ways: minimum level of exchange reserves; minimum ratio between the reserves and the value of imports; difference between exports and imports (in current and/or capital accounts).

* * * * *

## Expansion of Production

**1. Definition: "Satisfactory" Rate of Growth in the Real National Product.** Generally, the objective is to increase the rate of growth per head of the population, since this is a measure of the increase in the standard of living. In some cases, however, the overall rate of growth also mattered, when expansion was linked to the political power of the nation.

**2. Methods of Quantification.**   This objective could be expressed as a minimum rate of increase of the GNP (total or per head).

* * * * *

## THE INSTRUMENTS OF ECONOMIC POLICY

The instruments are commonly listed in five categories: public finance, money and credit, the exchange rate, direct controls, and changes in the institutional framework. Instruments included in each category are shown in Table 3–2.

   1. The instruments of *public finance* cover most income and expenditure items of central governments and local governments, as well as balances between income and expenditure.

   2. The instruments of *money and credit* include those which serve to make it either more difficult or easier for persons, companies, or governments to borrow money; they include, for instance, measures designed to change the rate of interest or to increase or reduce bank advances.

3. The *exchange rate* is the ratio between the national currency and one or more foreign currencies. Changes in the exchange rate include both general revaluations and devaluations, changes for particular transactions, or changes against particular currencies. They also include any change in the type of exchange-rate system.

4. The instruments of *direct control* include the powers to fix prices, quantities, or values, generally by fixing maxima or minima.

5. The general categories of *changes in the institutional framework* are identified in Table 3–2: (1) changes that alter the basic system within which other instruments are used—for instance, a substantial change in the credit system; (2) changes that do not affect the other families of instruments, but have a direct bearing themselves on the process of production—for instance, anticartel legislation; (3) changes that create new international institutions, and which, therefore, limit the freedom of national governments.

The uses of instruments may take various forms. Usually, they are imperative, backed by the force of the law. This is the case for government revenue instruments and, generally, for direct controls.

The government may at times use persuasion (mainly in the fields of money and credit and of direct control) with the threat—expressed or implied—of statutory measures if its wishes are not complied with. In some cases, however, persuasion amounts to little more than mild suggestion, or the government refrains from showing the instruments which it will use if need be. For example, it may be arbitrary to say that a general campaign against price rises is a use of price control, when in fact the government may have recourse to an increase in direct taxes. Such a campaign has nevertheless been considered as a use of price control, for there is no dividing line between the strong and the mild varieties of persuasion.

The dividing line between the various categories of instruments is not always clear, and the classification given in Table 3–2 can thus be criticized. Among the borderline cases of classification are the following:

1. Restrictions exercised in the field of credit were included among the money and credit instruments. This seemed more appropriate than leaving them with price and quantity controls.

2. All government debt operations—both new borrowing or lending and operations in existing debt—have also been considered as money and credit instruments, though there are strong grounds for listing them in public finance.

3. The dividing line between changes sufficiently large to be considered changes in the institutional framework and changes within the existing framework is also necessarily an arbitrary one. For instance, the decision to impose indirect taxes on a new range of goods would not be considered an institutional change big enough to be included here. On the

**TABLE 3–2**   Instruments Used for Each Objective: Synthesis for Nine Countries

| Families of Instruments → Objectives | A. Current Balance | A. Overall Balance | B. Government Investment | B. Subsidies and Capital Transfers to Enterprises | B. Transfers to Households | B. Government Stock Changes | B. Current Purchases of Goods and Services | B. Wages and Salaries | B. Transfers to the Rest of the World |
|---|---|---|---|---|---|---|---|---|---|
| | *Balances* | | *Government Expenditure* | | | | | | |
| 1. Full employment | x | x | I | x | x | x | x | x | |
| 2. Price stability | I | I | I | x | x | | x | x | |
| 3. Improvement in the balance of payments | x | x | x | x | | | x | x | x |
| 4. Expansion of production | x | | I | I | | | | x | |
| 5a. Promotion of internal competition | | | | | | | | | |
| b. Promotion of coordination | | | | | | | | | |
| c. Increase in the mobility of labor | | | | x | x | | | x | |
| d. Increase in the mobility of capital | | | | | | | | | |
| e. International division of labor | | | | x | | | | | x |
| 6. Satisfaction of collective needs | | | I | | x | x | I | I | x |
| 7. Improvement in the distribution of income and wealth | | | x | x | I | | | x | |
| 8. Protection and priorities to regions or industries | | | x | I | | x | x | | |
| 9. Improvement in the pattern of private consumption | | | | x | | | | | |
| 10. Security of supply | | | | x | | x | | | |
| 11. Improvement in the size or structure of population | | | | | x | | | | |
| 12. Reduction in working hours | | | | | | | | | |
| Number of objectives (x's, I's) served | 4 | 3 | 7 | 10 | 6 | 4 | 5 | 7 | 3 |
| Number for which the instrument was important (I) | 1 | 1 | 4 | 2 | 1 | 0 | 1 | 1 | 0 |

SOURCE: E. S. Kirschen and others, *Economic Policy in Our Time* (Amsterdam: North-Holland Publishing Company, 1964), vol. 1, Table VII-1, facing p. 148.

**Instruments of Public Finance** — C. Government Revenue

**Instruments of Money and Credit**
- A. Government New Borrowing and Lending
- B. Government Operations in Existing Debt
- C. Interest Rate Instruments
- D. Instruments Acting on Credit Creation by Banks
- E. Instruments Acting on Lending or Borrowing by Other Agents

Column key (instrument number. name):

Public Finance — C (Government Revenue):
10. Direct Taxes on Households' Incomes
11. Direct Taxes on Enterprises' Incomes
12. Indirect Taxes on Internal Transactions
13. Customs Duties
14. Social Security Contributions
15. Taxes on Property
16. Succession Duties
17. Transfers from the Rest of the World

Money and Credit — A (Government New Borrowing and Lending):
1. Lending Abroad
2. Lending to Households and Enterprises
3. Borrowing from Abroad
4. Borrowing from Households and Enterprises

Money and Credit — B (Government Operations in Existing Debt):
5. Open-Market Operations in Short-term Securities
6. Other Open-Market Operations in Existing Debt

Money and Credit — C (Interest Rate Instruments):
7. Bank Rate
8. Legal Imposition of Maximum Rates
9. Government Guarantees of Loans

Money and Credit — D (Instruments Acting on Credit Creation by Banks):
10. Reserve Ratios, etc.
11. Quantitative Stops on Advances
12. Approval of Individual Loans
13. Other Directives, Recommendations, and Persuasion

Money and Credit — E (Instruments Acting on Lending or Borrowing by Other Agents):
14. Control of Local Authorities' and Nationalized Enterprises' Borrowing
15. Control of Private Companies' Borrowing by New Issues
16. Control of Hire-Purchase Transactions
17. Control of Other Financial Institutions

| PF‑C 10 | 11 | 12 | 13 | 14 | 15 | 16 | 17 | A 1 | 2 | 3 | 4 | B 5 | 6 | C 7 | 8 | 9 | D 10 | 11 | 12 | 13 | E 14 | 15 | 16 | 17 |
|---|---|---|---|---|---|---|---|---|---|---|---|---|---|---|---|---|---|---|---|---|---|---|---|---|
| x | x | x | x | x | x |  |  |  | x |  |  | x |  | I |  | x | x | x | x | x | x | x | x | x |
| x | I | I | x | x | x |  |  |  | x |  | x | x | x | I |  | x | x | x | x | x | x | x | x | x |
| x | x | x | I | x | x | x | x | x | x | x | x | x | x | I | x | x | x |  |  |  | x |  | x |  |
| x | I |  |  | x | x |  |  | x | I | x |  |  |  |  |  | x | x |  |  |  |  | x |  |  |
|  |  |  |  |  | x |  |  |  |  |  |  |  |  |  |  |  |  |  |  |  |  |  |  |  |
|  |  |  | I |  |  |  |  |  |  |  |  |  |  |  |  |  |  |  |  |  |  |  |  |  |
| I |  |  |  | x | x | x |  |  | x |  |  |  |  |  |  | x |  |  | x | x |  | x | x |  |
| x | x | x | I | x | x |  |  |  | x |  |  |  |  |  |  |  |  |  | x | x |  | x | x |  |
|  |  | x |  | x | x |  |  |  | x |  |  |  |  |  |  | x |  |  |  | x |  |  |  |  |
| x | x |  |  | x | x |  |  |  |  |  |  |  |  |  |  |  |  |  |  |  |  |  |  |  |
| x |  |  |  |  |  |  |  |  |  |  |  |  |  |  |  |  |  |  |  |  |  |  |  |  |
| **7** | **6** | **7** | **7** | **6** | **6** | **2** | **2** | **3** | **9** | **3** | **2** | **3** | **3** | **4** | **1** | **7** | **4** | **3** | **4** | **5** | **3** | **5** | **4** | **3** |
| **1** | **2** | **1** | **3** | **0** | **0** | **0** | **0** | **0** | **1** | **0** | **0** | **0** | **0** | **3** | **0** | **0** | **0** | **0** | **0** | **0** | **0** | **0** | **0** | **0** |

**TABLE 3–2** *(concluded)*

| | | Exchange Rate | | Instruments of Direct Control | | | | | | | | |
| | | | | A — Control of Foreign Trade, Foreign Exchange, and Immigration | | | | | B — Control of Prices | | | |
| Categories of Instruments | | | | | | | | | | | | |
| Instruments | | 1. Devaluation | 2. Revaluation | 1. Control of Private Imports | 2. State Import Trading | 3. Control of Private Exports | 4. Exchange Control | 5. Control of Immigration | 6. Price Control of Goods and Services | 7. Rent Control | 8. Dividend Control | 9. Control of Wages |
| *Objectives* | | | | | | | | | | | | |
| 1. Full employment | | | | x | | x | | x | x | x | | I |
| 2. Price stability | | | I | x | x | x | | | I | x | x | I |
| 3. Improvement in the balance of payments | | I | | I | x | x | I | | x | | x | x |
| 4. Expansion of production | | x | | x | | x | | x | x | | x | x |
| 5a. Promotion of internal competition | | | | | | | | | x | x | x | x |
| b. Promotion of coordination | | | | | | | | | | | | |
| c. Increase in the mobility of labor | | | | | | | | | | | | |
| d. Increase in the mobility of capital | | | | | | | | | | | | |
| e. International division of labor | | x | x | I | x | x | x | x | | | | |
| 6. Satisfaction of collective needs | | | | | | | | | | | | |
| 7. Improvement in the distribution of income and wealth | | | | | | | | | x | x | x | I |
| 8. Protection and priorities to regions or industries | | | | I | x | x | | x | | | | |
| 9. Improvement in the pattern of private consumption | | | | | | | | | x | x | | |
| 10. Security of supply | | | | x | x | x | | | | | | |
| 11. Improvement in the size or structure of population | | | | | | | | x | | | | |
| 12. Reduction in working hours | | | | | | | | | | | | |
| Number of objectives (x's, I's) served | | 3 | 2 | 7 | 5 | 7 | 2 | 6 | 7 | 5 | 5 | 6 |
| Number for which the instrument was important (I) | | 1 | 1 | 3 | 0 | 0 | 1 | 0 | 1 | 0 | 0 | 3 |

| | Instruments of Direct Control | | | | | | | Changes in the Institutional Framework | | | | | | | | | | | | |
| --- | --- | --- | --- | --- | --- | --- | --- | --- | --- | --- | --- | --- | --- | --- | --- | --- | --- | --- | --- | --- |
| | C: Other Controls on the Internal Economy | | | | | | | A: Institutional Changes Involving Other Instruments | | | | | B: Affecting Directly the Conditions of Production | | | | C | | Number of Instruments Used | |
| | 10. Control of Investment | 11. Raw Material Allocations | 12. Control of Operations | 13. Regulation of Conditions of Work | 14. Control of Exploitation of Natural Resources | 15. Rationing of Consumer Goods | 16. Quality Controls and Standards | 1. Changes in the System of Transfers to Households | 2. Changes in the System of Subsidies to Enterprises | 3. Changes in the Tax System | 4. Changes in the Credit System | 5. Changes in the System of Direct Control | 6. Agricultural Land Reforms | 7. Changes in the Conditions of Competition | 8. Changes Increasing Labor's Influence in Management | 9. Changes in the Extent of Public Ownership in Industry | 10. Creation of National Institutions | 11. Creation of International Institutions | Total | Total Important Instruments (1) |
| | X | X | | | | | | | | X | X | | | | | | X | X | 38 | 3 |
| | X | X | X | | | X | X | | | X | X | X | | | | X | X | X | 44 | 9 |
| | X | X | X | | | X | X | | | X | X | | | | | | X | I | 48 | 6 |
| | X | | | | | | X | | | I | X | | X | X | X | X | I | I | 35 | 7 |
| | X | X | X | | | X | | | | X | | X | | I | | X | | X | 13 | 1 |
| | X | X | | | | | | | | | | | | | | X | X | X | 6 | 0 |
| | | | | | | | | X | | | | | | | | | | X | 5 | 0 |
| | | | | | | | | | X | | | | X | | | | | | 3 | 0 |
| | | X | X | X | | | | | | | | | | X | | | | I | 17 | 3 |
| | X | X | | | | | | X | | | | X | | | | | | I | 12 | 4 |
| | X | | | | | X | | I | | X | | | X | X | | X | | X | 25 | 4 |
| | X | X | X | | X | | X | | X | | | | | | | | X | X | 28 | 3 |
| | | | | | X | X | | | | | | X | | | | | | | 9 | 0 |
| | | X | X | | X | X | | | | | | X | | | | X | | X | 16 | 0 |
| | | | | | | | | | | | | | | | | | | | 3 | 0 |
| | | | | X | | | | | | | | | | | | | | | 1 | 0 |
| **Total** | 9 | 8 | 6 | 2 | 3 | 6 | 4 | 3 | 2 | 6 | 4 | 5 | 3 | 4 | 1 | 6 | 6 | 12 | 303 | |
| **Total Important Instruments (1)** | 0 | 0 | 0 | 0 | 0 | 0 | 0 | 1 | 0 | 1 | 0 | 0 | 0 | 1 | 0 | 0 | 1 | 4 | | 40 |

other hand, the creation of a tax on the value added counts as a change in the institutional framework. Similarly, the setting up of any major new machinery or institution for exercising direct control is included among changes in the institutional framework. The operation of the machinery or institution after it is set up is included among direct controls.

Table 3–2 shows which instruments were used for each objective and which objectives were served by each instrument in the eight countries (synthesized) during the period of our consideration. When the letter *I* replaces a cross in the table, this indicates that the policymakers considered an instrument to be particularly important for an objective.

Since such tables indicate the relations between instruments and objectives which the governments used in their economic policies, they provide a basis for beginning the construction of economic policy models. The information must, however, be supplemented by:

1. Relations between instruments and noncontrollable variables (such as private investment and foreign trade) and between such variables and objectives, as the instruments often act on the objectives through such variables.

2. Other possible relations between instruments and objectives which were not used by the governments but could have been used if the governments had so desired.

3. Relations indicating unintended effects of instruments on objectives.

4. Relations between objectives (some information on this subject is given in the section that follows).

## CONFLICTS AND CHOICES

So far, objectives have been dealt with independently of each other, and we have only endeavored to find out which instruments were used consciously in order to reach them. In actual fact, of course, matters are much more complicated, since in present-day economies interrelationships are numerous and important. Some of the instruments used for one objective may have effects on other objectives; some instruments interfere with each other; and the total number of available instruments is sometimes smaller than the total number of objectives. The objectives will be found to be independent, or complementary, or conflicting. These various interactions may reinforce the efficiency of instruments, but may also weaken their effects and lead to conflicts that can only be solved by choices.

One could conceivably construct a table that shows, for a given country and at a given time, all the relationships between objectives, but because of the changing effects of instruments on objectives, we have not attempted to do this. Some material, however, can be drawn from the national studies of economic policy. . . . As illustrations of practical cases of interrelations, we

**TABLE 3–3**   Main Cases of Conflicts between Objectives in Nine Countries

|  | Price Sta- bility | Balance of Pay- ments (Re- duction of Sur- plus) | Expan- sion of Pro- duction | Coordi- nation | Interna- tional Divi- sion of Labor | Collec- tive Needs (All) | Redis- tribution of In- comes | Protec- tion |
|---|---|---|---|---|---|---|---|---|
| Full employment . . . . | x | x |  |  |  |  |  |  |
| Price stability  . . . . . |  |  | x |  |  | x | x |  |
| Balance of payments (reduction of deficit)  . . . . . . . |  |  | x |  | x | x | x |  |
| Expansion of pro- duction . . . . . . . |  |  |  |  |  |  | x | x |
| Internal competition  . . |  |  |  | x |  |  |  | x |
| International division of labor . . . . . . . |  |  |  |  |  |  |  | x |

Note: The x's indicate the most important conflicts experienced in one or more of the nine countries studied.

present the main conflicts between objectives, . . . and the main cases of complementary. . . .

Table 3–3 indicates the main conflicts between objectives, with the x's in the columns indicating the most important conflicts experienced in one or more of the nine countries studied. In most cases the conflict is between an objective served by increased government expenditures and/or reduced taxes (full employment, expansion of production, satisfaction of collective needs, improvement in income distribution) and an objective served by reduced expenditure and/or increased taxes (price stability, reduction of the deficit in the balance of payments). Sometimes, however, the conflict is between an objective which requires trade liberalization (international division of labor, internal competition, price stability) and an objective which requires restrictions (reduction of deficit in the balance of payments, protection).

\* \* \* \* \*

The most common cases of intended complementarities found in the . . . countries studied were the following:

Full employment and expansion.

Full employment and protection.

Price stability and balance of payments.

Price stability and redistribution of incomes.

Expansion and collective needs.

Expansion and protection.

Redistribution of incomes and protection.

Redistribution of income and patterns of private consumption.

The order of priority of the objectives that are, in fact, selected depends on: the economic structure of the country; the disequilibriums (economic fluctuations as well as social or political events); the preferences of the various policymakers; and the influence of the various policymakers. Only the last two elements (which comprise the role of policymakers) are dealt with here.

In a democracy the powers of the state are exercised by parliament and the administrative government. The latter is, in its turn, the result of coalitions of political parties. However, the party (or parties) in power must come to terms not only with the opposition, but also with other categories of policymakers, notably the administration and interest groups. . . .

## Preferences of Political Parties

Table 3–4 indicates the a priori preferences of three political groupings found in eight of the countries. Three objectives not included in the table, since they were considered negligible by almost all of the political groupings in these countries, are: improvement in the pattern of private consumption, security of supply, and improvement in the size or structure of the population.

## Preferences of Administrations

Government administrations play a decisive role in the choice of instruments, for this requires the assistance of experts. And although the administration role is less important for the choice of objectives, it is still not negligible. Administrations are obviously preoccupied with objectives within their own fields of reference. Thus, a ministry of finance will be particularly concerned with short-term economic objectives (notably, price stability and improvement in the balance of payments), as also will the central bank. A planning commission or bureau, the industrial ministries, or the general directorate for industrialization will be preoccupied with the objective of expansion, while ministries for special sectors (agriculture, industry, commerce, transport) will frequently support the claims of corresponding interest groups for protection, priorities, and distribution of income.

The preferences of an administration are a function, on the one hand, of its recruitment system and of its standing and, on the other hand, of studies that it may undertake concerning the social and economic needs of the community. Thus, an administration which goes in and out of office with the political party in power (as in the United States) has few preferences clearly distinct from those of the party, at least for some time after an election. The most important exceptions are those parts of administrations with the most permanent structures, in particular (as in the United States) the armed forces, the public works department, the Federal Reserve System. Similarly, in Norway, where the Socialist party has been in power for 25 years, a slow penetration of the administration by the party—or at least its views and preferences—appears to have occurred, and the definitions of the main objectives of economic policy seem to

**TABLE 3–4**   Preference of Political Groupings with Regard to Objectives of Economic Policy: Synthesis for Eight Countries (excluding Luxembourg)

| Objectives | Socialists | Center | Conservative |
|---|---|---|---|
| Dominant . . . . . . . . | Full employment. Improvement in income distribution. | — | Price stability. |
| Dominant or significant . . . | Collective needs (other than defense). Expansion of production | Price stability. Expansion of production. | Collective needs (defense.) |
| Significant . . . . . . . . | Reduction in working hours. Allocation (coordination). | Full employment. Collective needs (all). Allocation (international division of labor). Improvement in income distribution. | Improvement in the balance of payments. Allocation (international division of labor). Protection-priorities. |
| Significant or minor. . . . . | Protection-priorities. Price stability. Allocation (international division of labor). Allocation (internal competition). | Protection-priorities. Allocation (internal competition). Improvement in the balance of payments. | Expansion of production. Full employment. |
| Minor . . . . . . . . . . | Improvement in the balance of payments. Collective needs (defense). | Allocation (coordination). Allocation (mobility of factors of production). Reduction in working hours. | Allocation (internal competition) Collective needs (other than defense). Allocation (mobility of factors of production). |
| Negligible . . . . . . . . | Allocation (mobility of factors of production). | — | Improvement in income distribution. |
| Negligible or hostile to the objective. . . . . . . . | — | — | Reduction in working hours. Allocation (coordination). |

SOURCE: E. S. Kirschen and others, *Economic Policy in Our Time* (Amsterdam: North-Holland Publishing Company, 1964), vol. 1, Table IX 2, p. 227.

be made in common, notably in the preparation of the four-year program before each electoral campaign for a new parliament.

But in the countries endowed with very stable administration (United Kingdom, Netherlands) and very centralized ones (France), the administration plays an active role in the choice of objectives, and divergence of views as between administrations and the politicians in power may very well occur when their standpoints diverge, owing, for instance, to different social backgrounds. Thus to define valid coherent objectives may become more difficult.

Perhaps as important as an administration's recruitment methods are its rejuvenation and the modernization of its intellectual training. A relatively young administration will be more receptive to objectives for expanding production than to those for price stability or the maintenance, at any cost, of the exchange reserves. Above all, it will be more acutely conscious of interdependence between objectives and instruments, of the essential unity of economic policy, and consequently of the need to test (as far as possible) its internal consistency *ex ante*. On the other hand, there is danger that a young administration will overlook the preoccupations of the people, and steep itself in technocracy.

Finally, it is the job of an administration to undertake studies, as objectively as possible, of existing or potential public needs. . . . Not only has the apparatus of official statistics been generally extended, but a number of objectives in political economy are no longer decided on without detailed study in advance, conducted by trained administrators. This is the case with housing, town planning, education, and public health.

Apart from these "public needs," the intellectual activity of administrations has developed differently according to country and subject. In countries politically attached to economic liberalism (Germany, Belgium, and the United states) or principally preoccupied with financial equilibrium (England), the role of the administration is especially important for definition and the measurement of objectives concerned with the trade cycle. In other countries, the role extends more and more to objectives concerned with structure—notably economic expansion, improvement in the allocation of factors of production, and the priorities and forms of protection for industries or regions.

This extension of the field of administration into matters of economic policy is not, however, caused only by the pressure of indisputable necessity. In part it is the effect of "Parkinson's Law," whereby all established administrations tend to develop and perpetuate themselves, whatever their utility at any given moment.

## Preferences of Interest Groups

The preferences of interest groups are concerned with partial objectives inspired by the particular interests which they defend. The efforts of these groups are therefore directed fundamentally toward the following objectives: protection and priorities to particular regions or industries; improvement in income distribution; improvement in the allocation of factors of production through internal competition. The criteria for their choices are simple: the defense of acquired positions and the conquest of new positions favorable for the economic or social group which they represent.

\* \* \* \* \*

# Suggestions for Further Reading
# for Part I

Barzel, Yoram. *Economic Analysis of Property Rights.* Cambridge, England: Cambridge University Press, 1989.

Eckstein, Alexander, ed. *Comparison of Economic Systems.* Berkeley and Los Angeles: University of California Press, 1971.

Lane, Jan-Erik, and Svante Ersson. *Comparative Political Economy.* London and New York: Pinter Publishers, 1990.

Montias, John Michael. *The Structure of Economic Systems.* New Haven, Conn.: Yale University Press, 1976.

Pryor, Frederic L. *A Guidebook to the Comparative Study of Economic Systems.* Englewood Cliffs, N.J.: Prentice Hall, 1985.

Symposium on "What Is Comparative Economics?" *Comparative Economic Studies* 31, no. 3 (Fall 1989), pp. 1–32.

Wiles, P. J. D. *Economic Institutions Compared.* New York: Halstead Press, 1977.

# Part II

# Capitalist Market Economies

The basic characteristics of a capitalist economic system are (1) private owner-ship of, and private enterprise with, the means of production; (2) the predomi-nance of economic gain as a guiding force in decisions about investment, pro-duction, and sales; and (3) reliance on markets and prices to allocate resources and distribute income.

Chapter 4 considers "human" aspects of a capitalist market economy, including the link to personal freedoms, the connection of incomes with contri-butions to production, and the relationship between differential incomes and efficiency.

Chapter 5 assesses benefits and costs of government intervention to alter the market's answers for the composition of output, the allocation of resources, and the distribution of income.

Chapter 6 examines the strengths and weaknesses of the price system. Then it analyzes and evaluates government action in the spheres of competition and regulation, consumer protection, and structural policy. It contrasts "mar-ket failure" with "government failure."

Chapter 7 explains the drive for privatization of public sector activities in Great Britain. It discusses British privatization's goals, methods, effects, and benefits—and possible lessons for other countries.

The Swedish economy is a distinctive case of a capitalist regulated market economy in three respects: generous social welfare benefits, an "active" labor market policy for "full employment," and centralized collective bargaining between employers and workers. Chapter 8 explains and assesses the labor market and centralized bargaining features of the "Swedish model," and their potential relevance for other European countries.

In France the government has attempted to steer the economy through a special kind of "indicative" planning very different from the comprehensive and detailed control of economic activity pursued in the centrally planned economies to be discussed in Part IV of this book. Chapter 9 explains the nature of French indicative planning, its key functions, and commitments to achieve plan goals.

The major economic and potential issue for Germany is the post-unifica-tion integration of eastern Germany, which had a socialist centrally planned economic system, with western Germany, a leading capitalist regulated market economy. Chapter 10 discusses the economic legacy of socialist central planning in eastern Germany, and the resulting macroeconomic and microeconomic problems of unification. It assesses the effort to create jobs and infrastructure in eastern Germany to narrow the economic and social gap between it and western Germany.

The progress of economic integration in Western Europe has curtailed national sovereignty over many aspects of economic policy, including measures affecting foreign trade, competition, and economic development programs. Chapter 11 explains and evaluates the latest step in West European economic integration—the Single Market Program which created a unified economic area for free circulation of people, capital, and goods and services.

Japan's economic success has been impressive. Chapter 12 appraises the extent to which the explanation is government industrial policy—an approach to government intervention in a capitalist regulated market economy advocated by prominent politicians, labor leaders, and business executives in the United States. Chapter 13 discusses the role in the Japanese economy of powerful industrial groups called *keiretsu*. Chapter 14 analyzes the contribution of Japan's unique labor relations system to its strong industrial growth and export performance.

## Chapter Four

# Rewards in a Market Economy*

## Arthur M. Okun

*This chapter considers three important "human" aspects of a capitalist market economy: the link to personal freedoms, the extent to which rewards are related to contributions to production, and the way differential incomes can enhance efficiency.*

    *Okun explains the types of contributions earning differential rewards. Then he evaluates the fairness of the resulting unequal distribution of income—the trade-off between equality and efficiency.*

Some conservatives would argue that, if a market economy is functioning properly, people simply get out of it what they put into it. And the resulting differences in income are acceptable and fair—perhaps even ideal. Fair games have losers as well as winners. Rights in the marketplace do not guarantee anyone an income, but then freedom of speech does not guarantee anyone an audience. By this reasoning, fair and equal treatment is provided by the opportunity to induce people to pay for services—just as it is by the opportunity to induce people to listen.

## REWARD FOR CONTRIBUTION

With a sprinkling of appropriate assumptions, it can be demonstrated that a competitive market will pay workers and investors the value of their contributions to output. This so-called marginal productivity theory of distribution is the economist's formal way of saying that you take out what you put in. The fruits of labor and capital are converted into dollars and given back to the suppliers. At the turn of this century, that theory of distribution was greeted by

---

* Reprinted by permission from his *Equality and Efficiency: The Big Tradeoff* (Washington, D.C.: Brookings Institution, 1975), pp. 40–50. Copyright © 1975 by the Brookings Institution. Arthur M. Okun was a Senior Fellow at the Brookings Institution.

some social thinkers as divine revelation of the justice of a competitive economy.[1] Today, however, economists do not invoke the name of the Lord in
support of the market. In fact, most of the ardent supporters of the the market
explicitly reject the claim that distribution in accordance with marginal productivity is necessarily just distribution.[2]

Nonetheless, the ethical appeal of reward for contribution remains very
much alive and shows up in subtle ways. When authors distinguish between the
deserving and undeserving poor, or the deserving and undeserving rich; when
Marxists challenge marginal productivity with a theory that attributes all value
to labor input, directly or indirectly; or when egalitarian economists rest their
case for altering the verdict of the market on allegedly scientific comparisons of
the "utility" of income to different people, they are all paying homage—as
supporters or detractors—to the initial presumption that income *ought* to be
based on contribution to output.

Therefore, it is worth exploring the ways contributions are rewarded in the
marketplace and evaluating the system of rewards in terms of ethical standards.
To begin with, the actual pricing of productive services differs from the textbook results of a competitive model in a dozen ways. I will mention only a few.
When there is "monopsony"—monopoly power on the buyer's side—in the
labor market, the employer may be able to pay workers less than they contribute. Even without monopsony, most markets for labor and capital lack the
auction system needed to ensure an equilibrium wage or price that avoids
shortages and excess supplies. Moreover, the contributions of two factors that
must operate together—like two men on a two-handled saw—cannot always be
assessed separately. Finally, as John Kenneth Galbraith has emphasized, the
contribution of workers is often judged and their pay set by managers who have
interests and objectives of their own, quite distinct from the profitability of their
firm.[3]

## SOURCES OF PRODUCTIVE CONTRIBUTION

The deviations from the competitive model are serious and significant; yet, I
believe, still more fundamental issues about income rewards arise even in the
unreal and ideal world of that model. What determines the competitive market
value of the services of any citizen? Are the resulting rewards really fair?

---

[1] For a discussion of this view as set forth by John Bates Clark, see Mark Blaug, *Economic
Theory in Retrospect* (Homewood, Ill.: Richard D. Irwin, Inc., 1962), pp. 403–8; also John Rawls,
*A Theory of Justice* (Cambridge, Mass.: Harvard University Press, 1971), pp. 308–9.

[2] See, for example, Frank H. Knight, *The Ethics of Competition and Other Essays* (New York:
Harper & Bros., 1935), pp. 54–58; and Friedrich A. Hayek, *The Constitution of Liberty* (Chicago:
University of Chicago Press, 1960), pp. 93–100. Friedman is the exception: he does not reject (nor
does he embrace) the ethics of reward for contribution; see Milton Friedman, *Capitalism and
Freedom* (Chicago: University of Chicago Press, 1962), pp. 161–65. For a contrasting position, see
Lester Thurow, "Toward a Definition of Economic Justice," *Public Interest,* no. 31 (Spring 1973),
p. 72.

[3] *The New Industrial State* (Boston: Houghton Mifflin, 1967), pp. 124–35.

The productive contribution of the services I could sell in a hypothetical competitive market depends on four sets of elements: (1) the skills and assets that I have acquired through my lifetime; (2) the abilities and talents with which I was born; (3) the effort I am willing to expend; and (4) the supply and demand situations for other services related to the ones I can offer.

## Acquired Assets

What I have to sell today reflects my entire life-history, including the nutrition and health care I have received, my education, my previous job experience, and any physical property I have acquired by previous saving or inheritance. To the extent that my current supply of marketable services is augmented by effort (or thrift) that I have exercised previously, I am reaping the harvest from the seeds I planted in the past. But to the extent that my present position reflects heavily the advantages of family background, or privilege, or status, I am reaping what others have sown.

To switch metaphors, some of the contestants get a head start while others have handicaps. Social and economic disparities among families make the race unfair. The importance of the uneven positions at the starting line and the possibilities of making the race fairer are complex and controversial issues. But it seems undeniable in principle that the prizes for the performance would be more defensible ethically if everyone had an even start.

## Natural Abilities

Those who shrug their shoulders at the social and economic differences in starting positions emphasize the differences in natural abilities. They argue that these biological differences are even more important. It isn't capitalism's fault that infants differ in endowments at the starting line of birth and even of conception. Such differential talents are, by definition, hereditary rather than environmental; they are given to the individual by his parents rather than developed or earned by him. Thus they preclude truly fair starts.[4] Should everyone therefore stop running races? Obviously not. In real track meets, no official has ever disqualified a runner for having "fast genes."

The non-shoulder-shrugger retorts that society should aim to ameliorate, and certainly not to compound, the flaws of the universe. It cannot stop rain, but it does manufacture umbrellas. Similarly, it can decide to restrict prizes that bestow vastly higher standards of living on people with greater acquired assets or greater innate abilities. With tongue in cheek, Henry Simons of the University of Chicago once developed a tantalizing case for reversing the income distribution: The talented are unavoidably favored by being more talented; giving them higher incomes compounds their accidental and unmerited advan-

---

[4] Frank H. Knight, *Risk, Uncertainty and Profit* (Boston: Houghton Mifflin, 1921), pp. 374–75; see also Friedman, *Capitalism and Freedom*, p. 164.

tages.[5] John Rawls's tongue was not in his cheek when he stated his "principle of redress": "to provide genuine equality of opportunity, society must give more attention to those with fewer native assets and to those born into the less favorable social positions."[6] Indeed, the principle of redress is a common feature of family life, where extraordinary efforts are often devoted to the education and happiness of handicapped children. Fairness is clearly not interpreted as reward for contribution in such cases.

## Effort

Differences in incomes that are associated with differences in effort are generally regarded as fair. If everyone were offered the same hourly wage rate and the opportunity to work as many hours as he or she chose, the resulting discrepancies on payday would be understandable. In fact, it would seem unfair for the person who takes more leisure to get just as much income. Leisure is a form of income and an element in one's standard of living; thus, a sacrifice of leisure must be compensated in other ways if fairness is to be achieved.[7]

Extra income for extra effort is unquestionably useful in providing incentives as well as fair compensation for parting with leisure. The two roles are hard to disentangle. When the fairness issue is viewed in a broad and searching context, some difficult questions arise. Shouldn't society be capable of tolerating diverse individual attitudes toward work and leisure? Would society really want to starve those who might conceivably have lazy genes? Suppose for a moment that incentives are not relevant. If the total input of effort were completely unaffected, would society want the beachcomber to eat less well than his fellow citizens, including others who do not work, such as children, the elderly, and students on fellowships?

Nor is it obvious, in that broader perspective, that incentives for effort to produce marketable output should take the form principally of purchasing power over marketable output. In a Robinson Crusoe economy, the individual putting forth the effort must get the resulting output. But other societies can provide different kinds of incentives. Many primitive societies allowed those who shirked work to eat just as well as workers,[8] but some insisted that the nonworker eat apart from the rest of the community and others had ceremonies in which the well-fed slacker was publicly scorned by his brother-in-law. When the advanced capitalist economy provides its incentives for productive effort primarily in dollars, that revives the Robinson Crusoe arrangement with the innovation of a monetary system. Should that be viewed as progress or retrogression?

---

[5] Henry C. Simons, *Personal Income Taxation* (Chicago: University of Chicago Press, 1938), pp. 12–13.

[6] Rawls, *Theory of Justice,* p. 100.

[7] The same is true about risky, unpleasant, or exhausting work.

[8] Karl Polanyi, "Our Obsolete Market Mentality," in *Primitive, Archaic, and Modern Economies,* ed. George Dalton (Boston: Beacon Press, 1971), pp. 65–67.

## Related Supplies and Demands

The value of my marginal product does not depend solely on my skills and effort. It can be altered greatly by changes in the behavior of other people, even though I keep doing the same old thing no better and no worse than ever. If more economists emerge who are willing to make speeches, or if audiences lose interest in talks given by economists, that would be bad news for my income. But would I then really be less productive? Would I *deserve* a drop in income? Is it ethically (as distinct from pragmatically) desirable for incomes to rest on the shifting sands of technology and tastes?

In view of those dependencies on other people, the concept of *my* contribution to output becomes hazy. Production comes out of a complex, interdependent system and may not be neatly attributable to individual contributors. Henry Ford's mass-produced automobile was a great success in a country with a high average income, 3,000 miles for unimpeded driving, an alert and ambitious work force, and a government that could protect travelers and enforce rules of the road. It would have been a loser in Libya. In that sense, most production processes involve "joint inputs," like the two-handled saw.[9] That aspect is recognized in a few private arrangements, which reward teams rather than individuals. The same World Series shares are given to Johnny Bench and the bench-warming third-string catcher, even though their salaries during the regular season are vastly different. Would it be a desirable innovation for some portion of the social output to be shared equally by all the players, like a World Series kitty?

In fact, if everyone received the full measure of his or her marginal product and no joint inputs existed, the economic benefits generated by great entrepreneurs and inventors would accrue entirely to them. There would then be no "trickle-down" of progress to the masses.[10] Benefits do actually trickle down precisely because the big winners do not obtain—or at least do not maintain—the full rewards for their contribution to improved technology, increased knowledge, and accumulated capital. The trickle-down of benefits is a merit of capitalism in the real world, and it works insofar as the distribution of income departs from the strict standard of reward for personal contribution to production.

## VARYING VERDICTS

I have dozens of good questions about the fairness of market-determined incomes. But I don't claim to have any good answers. The appraisal is obviously

---

[9] In viewing the whole social and political system as an "input," I am using an unconventional—but nonetheless relevant—concept of joint inputs.

[10] The formal analysis of trickle-down may be viewed along the following lines: Consider capital-deepening without technical change. The profit rate is driven down over time, and rent on previously invested capital is lowered to match the marginal product of new capital. Then benefits trickle down from the "old" capitalists. The marginal product of labor is raised by capital-deepening, so workers get the benefits of the trickle.

a matter of personal judgment. In mine, incomes that match productivity have no ethical appeal. Equality in the distribution of incomes (allowing for voluntary leisure as a form of income) as well as in the distribution of rights would be my *ethical* preference. Abstracting from the costs and the consequences, I would prefer more equality of income to less and would like complete equality best of all. This preference is a simple extension of the humanistic basis for equal rights. To extend the domain of rights and give every citizen an equal share of the national income would give added recognition to the moral worth of every citizen, to the mutual respect of citizens for one another, and to the equivalent value of membership in the society for all.[11]

Nonetheless, my preference for one person, one income, is not nearly so strong as that for one person, one vote. Equality in material welfare has much lower benefits and far higher costs than equality of political and civil entitlements. Perhaps because material objects do not seem all-important, it is far less invidious to deprive some citizens of automobiles than to deprive them of the right to vote or freedom of religion. Second, while the provision of equal political and civil rights often imposes costs on society, the attempt to enforce equality of income would entail a much larger sacrifice. In pursuing such a goal, society would forgo any opportunity to use material rewards as incentives to production. And that would lead to inefficiencies that would be harmful to the welfare of the majority. Any insistence on carving the pie into equal slices would shrink the size of the pie. That fact poses the trade-off between economic equality and economic efficiency. Insofar as inequality does serve to promote efficiency, I can accept some measure of it as a practicality. I can live with rules of the game that make it fair not to share—just as that lady from Boston insisted. But that is a feature of the universe that I regret rather than enjoy.

Many in our society, including some losers as well as most winners, seem to enjoy the rules of the game and the contest. They cheer loudly for success in the marketplace, and reinforce income incentives by vesting those who succeed with social status. The marketplace becomes a great American game; the winners are made proud and the losers embarrassed. The widespread mental depression that accompanied economic depression among the chronically unemployed of the 30s, the satisfaction derived by those who "make it" into the economic mainstream, and the bourgeois aspirations of the poor all reveal the deeply ingrained market ethic of American society.[12] In a sense, these attitudes

---

[11] I regard this Rawlsian basis for egalitarianism as far sounder than a foundation based on interdependent utilities or interpersonal comparisons of utility. R. H. Tawney had the same idea: ". . . because men are men, social institutions . . . should . . . emphasize and strengthen . . . the common humanity which unites them. . . ." See *Equality*, 5th ed. (London: Allen & Unwin, 1964), p. 49.

[12] For a discussion of the mental attitude of the unemployed during the 30s, see E. Wight Bakke, *Citizens Without Work* (New Haven, Conn.: Yale University Press, 1940), especially pp. 201–2. For a current treatment of the aspirations of the poor, see Leonard Goodwin, *Do the Poor Want to Work?* (Washington, D.C.: Brookings Institution, 1972), p. 112.

preserve some of the features of the primitive societies that invoke ceremonies to penalize the lazy and reward the energetic.

Those who enjoy the game seem particularly fascinated by jackpot prizes. The possibility of "making it big" seems to motivate many Americans, including some who have not made it at all. They dream of rags-to-riches and project that dream from generation to generation. There are enough examples of winners to keep it alive and to encourage education, saving, and bourgeois values. In 1972, a storm of protest from blue-collar workers greeted Senator McGovern's proposal for confiscatory estate taxes. They apparently wanted some big prizes maintained in the game. The silent majority did not want the yacht clubs closed forever to their children and grandchildren while those who had already become members kept sailing along.

On the other hand, those who reject the rules of the game on ethical grounds seem most offended by the reliance on "greed" as a key motivating force in economic life. Greed is deplored because it is an expression purely of self-interest, and because it aims at the acquisition of material things.

With proper awe for the fundamental philosophical issues concerning the virtues and practicalities of altruism as opposed to self-interest, I will still venture a few personal views. I do not find a reliance on self-interest offensive as an organizing principle for the economy. First, selfishness is a safeguard against the much greater danger of blind allegiance to a leader or to the state. Second, self-interest is consistent with an enlightened selfishness that creates loyalties to family, community, and country, as institutions that benefit the individual and extend his range of interests. Third, I read the lesson of history as teaching that efforts to suppress the tendencies toward self-interest by the individual—in societies as noble as monasteries or as base as Fascist dictatorships—have also severely restricted the rights of the individual.

Nor am I offended by a competition that seeks prizes in the form of material possessions. Surely, some kinds of alternative rewards would be far more oppressive and more invidious—like feudal privileges and membership in the elite party. Indeed, if the losers can still lead a decent life, prizes for the winners in the form of swimming pools and bigger houses seem especially innocuous in terms of their social impact. In short, while I do not find reward for contribution ethically appealing, neither do I find it ethically intolerable—within pragmatic limits.

## Chapter Five

# Economists' Changing Perceptions of Government*

## *Anne O. Krueger[1]*

*Governments intervene in capitalist market economies to alter the answers the market would yield for the goods and services to be provided, the allocation of resources to produce them, and the associated distribution of personal income across households.*

*However, the opinions of economists, other social scientists, and philosophers have changed regarding the case for government intervention, as they have become more skeptical and cautious about the justification for government intervention and its probable benefits and costs.*

*In this chapter, Krueger explains the earlier conception of the government as a "benevolent, costless social guardian." Then she examines recent challenges to this view, arising from the economics of information, analyses of collective action, the theory of rent-seeking, and the recognition of "bureaucratic capture." Thus, to decide what government intervention is appropriate, it is necessary to assess the magnitude of "market failure" and its costs and weigh them against "government failure" and its costs.*

## INTRODUCTION

A central question for economists has always been what the roles of governments and markets in the economy are, and what they should be. Until Adam Smith analyzed the functioning of markets, and the role of the invisible hand in guiding the economy, there was no separate discipline of economics. It was Smith's profound insight that when individuals respond in their own self-inter-

* Reprinted by permission from *Weltwirtschaftliches Archiv* 126, no. 3, 1990, pp. 417–31. Anne O. Krueger is Professor of Economics at Duke University.

[1] This essay is the text of my acceptance speech on the occasion of the award of the Bernhard Harms Prize at the Kiel Institute, Germany, on June 23, 1990.

est to the incentives with which they are confronted, the outcome may well enhance the social good. With that central proposition in place, there was scope for a separate study of markets and their functioning, and for the separate discipline of economics. To be sure, Smith recognized the need for a strong government, providing law and order, a framework for contracts, and the necessary infrastructure of transport, communications, and education.

As economic thought evolved, economists' and political philosophers' thinking about governments and markets altered subtly but importantly. Whereas Smith focused on the invisible hand and its benefits, a rising strain of thought sought to identify circumstances in which the market would not function perfectly. In these instances, it was thought, there was a case for government intervention.

In a sense, the case was automatic if it could be shown that markets were not perfect. Underlying this approach was a set of assumptions, usually implicit, about the nature of government. Implicitly, it was assumed that there could be no such thing as government failure. The view of a government was that it would and could function as a "benevolent social guardian" in the Benthamite[2] tradition. Such a government, it was believed, could costlessly and unerringly enter the market and function, just as could a private entrepreneur.

Given the premise that a government could perfectly and costlessly execute its objectives, it naturally followed that economists as technocrats could provide sensible welfare-maximizing rules, such as that public utilities should price according to marginal cost, or that in the presence of an externality, government intervention with taxes and subsidies can improve welfare, contrasted with laissez faire, and that these rules would be readily implemented in ways superior to market outcomes.

By the late 1940s, two additional lines of thought also led to the view that governments could and should play a major role in economic activity. The first was the Keynesian revolution, which arose out of the Great Depression, and suggested a strong role for government in the macroeconomic management of the economy. The second was the concern of all for income distribution: there was and is nothing in the theory of competitive markets that suggests that markets will generate a socially desirable income distribution.

Over the past several decades, economic thought has evolved further, and a new view of government, and its role in the economy, is emerging. In that view, behavior within the public sector can be analyzed in ways similar to, but not identical with, that in the private sector. The self-interest of bureaucrats and the incentives with which they are confronted affect behavior just as the self-interest of managers and workers affects firm behavior. Moreover, just as organizational factors within the firm affect its performance, so organizational

---

[2] Editor's note: Jeremy Bentham (1748–1832) was a British philosopher, economist, and sociologist.

features of government affect its performance. Additionally, however, collective action may lead to circumstances where behavior may differ profoundly from that encountered when analysis focuses upon individual optimizing agents.

The emerging view of governments and their interaction with markets is much more complex than earlier views. In particular, government behavior is now seen to resemble more closely the outcome of a complicated interaction of a number of groups and interests, rather than the result of purposive behavior of a maximizing benevolent guardian. While it is still widely recognized that there are "market failures" in a variety of circumstances, the change is that government failures must also be taken into account before policy recommendations are made.

I plan to set forth the considerations that have led to this emerging new, more complex, view of government as an economic actor and ask how that affects the policy prescriptions that were based on the implicit assumption that governments behave as benevolent guardians. As a starting point, it is useful to describe the attitudes of economists—perhaps caricature would be a better word–as they were expressed in the late 1940s and early 1950s. Thereafter, I will focus on those strands of thought and realizations that have altered the understanding of economic policy formulation and execution. Finally, the special characteristics of decision making within the public sector are considered, and the implications for economists' roles as policy analysts are considered.

There are three broad areas of governmental economic policy: those pertaining to macroeconomic issues, such as monetary and fiscal policy; those affecting microeconomic allocation of resources, such as public utility regulation, labor legislation, tariff and trade policy, and industry-specific policies; and those designed to influence income distribution. Changes in thinking have been significant in all three areas. However, in order to focus the discussion, I shall consider only government policies pertaining to microeconomic matters. It is in this domain that many of the issues prompting reconsideration of earlier thought have first arisen. Although I shall refer to the theory of economic policy and experience in a number of microeconomic areas, I shall illustrate extensively with the "infant industry rationale" for protection, both in theory and in practice.

## GOVERNMENT AS A BENEVOLENT SOCIAL GUARDIAN

Once Adam Smith recognized that the invisible hand could allocate resources in socially desirable ways, economists' attention quickly turned to analyzing the conditions under which "market failures" might occur. Smith himself had pointed out several such circumstances. He noted the businessmen's tendency to collude, and the desirability of prevention of monopoly and collusion.

As the discipline of economics developed, a number of contributions led to increased emphasis on government's role. In circumstances where there are industries in which the costs of providing service decrease as the number of units of service provided increase for each firm, the market may not be large enough to permit perfect competition. This was thought to be particularly a problem in public utilities, including electricity, telephones, railroads, and waterworks. When this decreasing cost continued over a sufficiently wide range of output, it was recognized that there would emerge a conflict: on one hand, if there were a sufficiently large number of firms so that there could be competition within the industry, then costs would be high. If, on the other hand, a monopoly were permitted, it would charge too high a price, and provide too little of its output for social welfare maximization, or it would either have to be run by government or be regulated by government. Likewise, in the presence of negative or positive externalities—instances where the presence of one productive activity raises or lowers the costs of other activities or otherwise harms or benefits persons other than those directly engaged in it—private competition would clearly result in a level of production in the activities generating it that was either too low (in circumstances where others benefited from the productive process without taking part in it) or too high (when others are harmed by the process, such as in the case of environmental pollution).

Yet another line of thought focused upon uncertainties, and the ways in which they might affect unfettered private decision making. Indeed, in the literature on economic development for developing countries in the 1950s, it was widely thought that uncertainties would, for a number of reasons, discourage private individuals from undertaking investments and thus result in underinvestment. The recommended outcome was for governments themselves to establish new firms and industries.

These considerations, and others, led to an analysis of what the differences, if any, might be between government ownership of the means of production and private ownership. By the early 1940s, it had been shown that if one gave decision makers in the public sector the right rules, it could make no difference whether economic activities were undertaken in the private or the public sector.[3]

The "infant industry" argument was applied in this spirit. Alexander Hamilton and Friedrich List[4] had been the first to note that there might be "infant" industries in countries whose overall economic development lagged behind that of the frontrunners. They believed that, in these circumstances, temporary protection might be warranted to permit an "infant industry," or set of industries, a period in which to catch up. This conjecture withstood close scrutiny. The theoretical proposition is straightforward: if there are externalities that

---

[3] This was the central thesis of a very influential book, Oskar Lange and Fred M. Taylor, *On the Economic Theory of Socialism,* ed. Benjamin E. Lippincott (Minneapolis: University of Minnesota Press, 1938).

[4] Editor's note: Friedrich List (1789–1846) was a German economist.

cannot be captured by the original investor in the industry, and if there are dynamic factors that will lead to reduced costs over time, and the later competitiveness of the industry will be sufficient so that profits are adequate to cover the initial losses entailed in starting the industry, temporary protection of that infant may be warranted.

The proposition is theoretically valid. For present purposes, it should be noted that the criterion is quantitative: future gains must be estimated and must compensate for initial losses. It is also a criterion which requires knowledge of the future. I defer, however, to later insights as to the role of government which have emerged, as country after country provided protection on infant industry grounds and found the outcome to be rather different than theory indicated.

By the 1950s, then, economists were accustomed to thinking about markets in the following way. One first established the conditions under which a perfectly competitive market would yield an outcome that could not be improved upon for everyone. These conditions included the absence of externalities and increasing returns to scale, the absence of dynamic effects, and the existence of markets in which uncertainty could be eliminated for individual decision makers. The presence of any of these "market failures" was regarded as constituting a case for government intervention. Even in the absence of a market failure, it was thought that production within the public sector was little different than that in the private sector, and that it was largely a matter of indifference—even when conditions for well-functioning competitive markets were present—whether production took place in the public or in the private sector.[5]

In developed countries, this thinking provided the underlying intellectual rationale for public sector enterprises, for anti-monopoly laws, for regulation of transportation and utilities or their inclusion within the public sector, for taxes and subsidies to individual industries, and for a variety of other interventions. In the developing countries, where many governments' stated objectives included rapid economic growth, the domain of intervention went further still. Not only were large segments of economic activity reserved for the government, but in addition, foreign exchange and trade restrictions, requirements that investments be licensed, credit rationing, and a variety of other measures circumscribed private economic activity—rationalized largely by the infant industry argument and the argument that there was "market failure."

It has been experience with these measures in both developed and developing countries that has called into question the entire view of government

---

[5] For example, Tinbergen recently concluded that: "As an outcome of many discussions . . . many European economists and politicians have concluded that the type of ownership of the means of production is much less important for an enterprise's efficiency than the quality of its management . . . Efficiency considerations need not be a stumbling block if public enterprise is chosen as a means for furthering a country's development." See Jan Tinbergen, "Development Cooperation as a Learning Process," in *Pioneers in Development,* ed. Gerald M. Meier and Dudley Seers (New York: Oxford University Press, 1984), pp. 113–31 (the quotation is from p. 326).

underlying the interventionist case. It is to that set of issues that attention now turns.

## CHALLENGES TO THE BENEVOLENT, COSTLESS SOCIAL GUARDIAN VIEW

It remains recognized that markets may fail. The change is that it is now recognized that there may also be government failure. Both theoretical developments and experience have led many to question whether government activities are undertaken costlessly and selflessly by public servants who can omnisciently determine exactly what constitutes a socially optimal set of techniques and volumes of production of various goods and services. Interestingly, these challenges have arisen apparently fairly independently in a number of fields of economic inquiry, such as industrial organization and international trade. They have come from two directions: from theoretical developments in the theory of markets and from experience.

It is useful first to review the theoretical developments. An early challenge, which has received a great deal of attention in recent years, has been from the economics of information. Another major set of considerations was raised from the analysis of the economics of regulation in developed countries. In yet another branch of economics, questions were raised by many who were concerned with the collective action aspects of government activity. Yet another set of considerations concerned the likelihood of rent-seeking, and special interest groups, that would affect decision making. Related to all these was the recognition that there might be "bureaucratic capture" of activities, and that there might be coalitions of various public groups that governed decision-making processes. Finally, experience—especially in developing countries—with efforts by governments to operate or control individual economic activities has led to an increased appreciation of the importance of markets as mechanisms for competitive pressures, entry, and exit in ways which are far more difficult in the public sector.

### Economics of Information

Smith's original insight into the invisible hand was based in large part upon the premise that "every individual can, . . . in his local situation, judge much better than any statesman or lawgiver. . . ."[6] Others, including, most notably, Hayek,[7] took up the argument and insisted that the wealth of particular, detailed information regarding technologies, products, and markets, was perhaps

---

[6] Adam Smith, *The Wealth of Nations* (Toronto: Modern Library, 1937), p. 423. (Originally published 1776–78.)

[7] Editor's note: See, for example, Friedrich A. Hayek, "The Use of Knowledge in Society," *American Economic Review* 35, no. 4 (September 1945), pp. 519–30.

the most important rationale for permitting private markets, rather than government agencies, to decide on the technique of production and the allocation of resources.

As economic growth has proceeded, it has in large part been a process of more and more specialization, that has been characterized by some as a process in which individuals are "knowing more and more about less and less." Although Smith anticipated this, with his discussion of increasing specialization of activities within the pin factory, division of labor has in fact probably proceeded further in terms of skill acquisition than it has in terms of different physical tasks.[8] As that has happened, and the importance of specialized knowledge of particular activities has increasingly been recognized, doubt has been cast upon the ability of economic planners to decide upon how resources should be allocated within and between activities. Indeed, it is the specificity of knowlege required for understanding various lines of production that lies at the basis of some of the phenomena discussed below.

The information requirements of modern economic activity themselves constitute an argument in favor of finding mechanisms that are "incentive-compatible." If incentives are not consistent with societally acceptable goals, the likelihood grows with the complexity of economic activity that there will be high costs for central direction of efforts.[9] As I shall argue below, in application of the infant industry argument, one difficulty was that protection was to be based on forecasts of future performance of individual firms and industries. Since government officials could not know what performance would be, and since the individuals seeking protection paid little or no penalty if their forecasts were optimistic, it should not be surprising that all industries rapidly acquired "infant" status!

## Economics of Regulation

Independently of the analysis of information, a group of economists concerned with industrial organization came to question some aspects of regulation. Earlier economists had tended to assume that when a natural monopoly, such as water or electricity, existed, regulation by governmental bodies could prevent

---

[8] Sherwin Rosen, "The Economics of Superstars," *American Economic Review* 71, no. 5 (December 1981), pp. 845–58.

[9] A major literature has sprung up in economics analyzing circumstances in which various decision-making mechanisms are influenced by "asymmetric information." Such informational asymmetries can flaw the functioning of private markets as well as of governments. Asymmetric information exists whenever one party to a transaction has information not possessed by the other and has an incentive not to reveal it. In insurance, for example, it is likely that high-risk individuals will seek insurance more than low-risk individuals, thereby raising insurance premiums and driving away low-risk persons. For a survey of these issues, see Joseph E. Stiglitz, "Information and Economic Analysis—A Perspective," *Economic Journal* 95, Supplement (1985), pp. 21–41.

any tendency for the monopoly to capture monopoly profits and to restrict output. In that spirit, there had existed a large number of regulatory commissions in America from at least the turn of the century.

By the early 1970s, however, important questions were raised about the theory of the regulatory process. This started when George Stigler[10] articulated the view that perhaps the regulators were "captured" by the process of regulation. According to this analysis, people who understand a particular line of economic activity have two choices of employer: they can work in the industry itself, or they can work in the regulatory agency. For a wide variety of reasons, including both the sociological proposition that these people are likely to know each other, and the self-interest argument that those currently regulating may later need jobs and be employable only in the firms they are now regulating, "capture" may take place. An agency that starts out to govern a particular economic activity may, thus, eventually end up serving the interests of the industry.[11]

The truth of the capture theory is frequently revealed when deregulation is proposed: it is, more often than not, those in the regulated industry themselves who are the loudest in their protests against deregulation! In the case of industries accorded infant industry protection in developing countries, proposals (often 20 and 30 years later) to reduce the level of protection have led to strong protests.

## Collective Action

At about the same time that George Stigler was questioning the extent to which regulation served the interests of the public, as contrasted with those of the regulated, Mancur Olson[12] was analyzing the logic of public policy decisions, and especially the role of special and general interests in the decision-making process.

Olson pointed out that, when large numbers of persons each have a small amount to gain by a particular action, while a few persons have a lot to lose, the losers will be likely to find it in their self-interest to organize in opposition to the measure, while the potential gainers may not find it in their interest. There are a number of reasons for this proposition, but the basic one is that when there are large groups of gainers or losers, any one individual is in the position of a "free rider"; whether he joins the group or not will not significantly affect the group's

---

[10] George Stigler, "The Theory of Economic Regulation," *Bell Journal of Economics and Management Science* 2, no. 1 (Spring 1971), pp. 3–21.

[11] For a recent survey, see David Baron, "Design of Regulatory Mechanisms and Institutions," in *Handbook of Industrial Organization*, ed. Richard Schmalensee and Robert Willig (Amsterdam: North-Holland Publishing Company, 1989), vol. 2, pp. 1349–1447.

[12] Mancur Olson, *The Logic of Collective Action: Public Goods and the Theory of Groups* (Cambridge, Mass.: Harvard University Press, 1965).

strength, and thus not significantly affect the outcome. Since most people in the large group are in a similar situation, the likelihood that they will organize effectively is smaller.

Taking the Olson logic to its conclusion, lobbies representing small particular interests are likely to have disproportionately large representation and effects on decision making in governments, while organizations representing the interests of large groups (consumers, the elderly) are likely to be underrepresented. For economic policy, an important implication is that producers' associations are likely to be especially powerful. If one then combines that proposition with the benevolent guardian theory of government, a contradiction is apparent. Insofar as decisions are influenced, and they surely are, by pressure groups, it is manifestly unrealistic to assume that decisions regarding regulation, taxation, protection, and so on will be made in a cool-headed technocratic environment where the social welfare is the paramount and only consideration. Instead, arguments made for regulation based on infant industries, externalities, and monopolies may in fact obscure the true motives and potential beneficiaries of the measures proposed.

## Rent-Seeking[13]

Olson's logic of collective action originated from consideration of the roles of special interests and lobbies in economic decision making in industrial countries, primarily the United States. In the context of developing countries, however, the economic role of the state had been vastly expanded by the late 1960s. With it, disillusionment arose on grounds additional to those discussed above.[14]

One of the most important of these was the proposition that many forms of regulation create opportunities—sometimes legal, sometimes illegal—for large private profit. When they do so, substantial resources can be wasted in seeking those profits.

An example may illustrate. In India, it was stated policy that licenses to import scarce intermediate goods and raw materials—which were highly valuable because of the overall shortage of foreign exchange—would be allocated to individual firms in infant industries in proportion to the individual firms' share of capacity in their particular industries. Not surprisingly, many firms

---

[13] Editor's note: Rent-seeking involves the use of real resources in an attempt to appropriate a surplus in the form of a rent.

[14] See Jagdish Bhagwati and T. N. Srinivasan, *India* (Foreign Trade Regimes and Economic Development Series; New York: National Bureau of Economic Research, 1975), for an articulation of the proposition that Indian economic intervention had often had consequences opposite to those intended. That influential work had followed upon the earlier volume by Jagdish Bhagwati and Padma Desai, *India: Planning for Industrialization: Industrialization and Trade Policies since 1951* (London: Oxford University Press, 1970), in making the case that there was a wide gap between theory—on which Indian intervention had been based—and practice.

were discovered to be investing even when they, and their competitors, already had substantial excess capacity. This was because any firm that failed to do so would lose market share if it did not follow the others. Obviously, such investment was socially wasteful as long as there was considerable excess capacity already existing, but it was privately profitable, and thus took place whenever the authorities could not find other policy instruments with which to attempt to control it.

Rent-seeking can take a wide variety of forms. It can consist of outright bribery, or smuggling, or of queueing in lines for commodities which are in short supply. When payoffs to civil servants are large, it can take the form of waiting for a long period of time for a job to open up, and of excess educational qualifications. It can also consist of a variety of merchants, each operating with substantial excess capacity, as the profits they do make per unit on their very small volume of imported goods compensate for the very small volume of their business. Workers may leave the countryside to seek higher-paying employment in the cities, only to be idle for months while attempting to obtain a job in an industry subject to minimum-wage legislation.

The phenomenon of rent-seeking is not confined to developing countries, although the pervasiveness of intervention to encourage industrialization has perhaps made it more visible there. To cite but one example in the context of developed countries, Averch and Johnson[15] showed that public utility firms which are regulated as to the rate of return they may realize on capital will have an incentive to overinvest in physical capital in order to earn higher returns, and in fact do so.

Estimates of the magnitudes of economic costs of rent-seeking have suggested that they may be 10 or more percent of GNP in some developing countries.[16] The magnitudes are large enough so that the likelihood and probable magnitude of rent-seeking behavior are a major consideration that must be weighed before a decision for intervention is made. The literature raises some interesting questions, as yet unanswered, as to forms of intervention less and more likely to encourage rent-seeking behavior. Until there are more satisfactory answers, however, an important question that must be addressed in the design of microeconomic policy interventions is the likely magnitude of rent-seeking that will be induced. From whatever probable social benefits are expected to result from intervention must be subtracted the likely costs of rent-seeking that may be entailed.

---

[15] Harvey Averch and Leland L. Johnson, "Behavior of the Firm under Regulatory Constraint," *American Economic Review* 52, no. 5 (December 1962), pp. 1052–69.

[16] Wafik Grais, Jaime de Melo, and Shujiro Urata, "A General Equilibrium Estimation of the Effects of Reductions in Tariffs and Quantitative Restrictions in Turkey in 1978," in *General Equilibrium Trade Policy Modeling,* ed T. N. Srinivasan and John Whalley (Cambridge, Mass.: MIT Press, 1986), pp. 61–88.

## Bureaucratic Capture

Another phenomenon has been observed that relates to intervention: that is, once an agency or institution for regulating economic activity has been established, the self-interest of those public servants employed by it becomes a political force. Officials whose job is to allocate import licenses (to protect infant industries or for other reasons), or to decide which industries will be protected, will constitute a major source of opposition to proposed liberalizations of the system. Indeed, when things seem to go wrong, the usual bureaucratic cry is for more controls, and more authority, rather than less.

In part it is only human nature for individuals to believe that whatever they are doing is important and valuable. In part, however, the jobs that might be lost, were an agency's functions to be reduced or eliminated, are a relevant political consideration.

One may combine considerations of bureaucratic self-interest with the notions of capture discussed earlier. This might suggest that bureaucrats and the regulated industries may go hand in hand for reasons other than commonality of technical knowledge posited: bureaucrats may preserve their employment by regulating in ways which engender political support from the regulated industry.

This logic has been carried one step further in the political science literature. Known as the "iron triangle," it is based on American politics, but it may have relevance elsewhere. The iron triangle is said to consist of politicians, bureaucrats, and voters. Voters vote for politicians whom they perceive to be doing them "special favors." Politicians want to be reelected to office, so they need to have special favors that can be done for their citizens. Meanwhile, bureaucrats obtain their power by virtue of the command they have over the implementation of various functions. They do favors for constituents of incumbent politicians, and in so doing increase the likelihood of incumbent politicians' reelection. Incumbent politicians are therefore not interested in reducing the scope of special favors done by bureaucrats, and support their administration of controls. Meanwhile, once the controls are in place, voters support politicians who can influence the bureaucratic apparatus favorably from their (the voters') viewpoint.

## Competition, Entry, and Exit in Markets and in Government

It seems to be inherent in the nature of governmental controls that, once established, an agency is very likely to continue: the likelihood that it will be subdivided into two agencies, and expand, is considerable, while the likelihood that it will be disbanded is very small. This is largely for reasons already cited: bureaucrats who administer the controls will support their continuation, and those benefiting from the controls will easily identify themselves and organize to perpetuate and, if possible, enhance the benefits they believe they derive from the agency.

By contrast, markets provide feedback which can result in the pressures to reorganize, or possibly even in the exit of unprofitable firms. In some circumstances, of course, unprofitable firms are able to appeal to governments for support; in so doing, they are shifting from the economic to the political marketplace in perpetuating themselves. When they do so, the productivity and growth of the economy are, in most instances, impaired. In many developing countries, infant industries have continued for 20 and 30 years protected by high tariffs or very restrictive import licensing procedures. Worse yet, in some countries, firms which were unprofitable—even with high levels of protection—have been taken over by governments rather than be permitted to go out of business. The result has been an ever-increasing size of public sector enterprises and their deficits, with negative consequences for both growth and efficiency.

## THE MICROECONOMIC ROLE OF GOVERNMENT

The view of a governmental process as the outcome of an "iron triangle" operating in an environment in which lobbyists are particularly influential and in which rent-seeking is the order of the day is far distant from the conception of civil servants and governmental decision-making bodies as disinterested Benthamite social guardians.

It raises questions far different from those considered by early theorists of economic policy whose view was that market failure implied an automatic case for direct government intervention. A more reasonable approach, if one is guided by these considerations, is to attempt to assess the magnitude of "market failure" and its costs, and to weigh it against the magnitude of "government failure" and its costs. When "market failure" is found to be sufficiently severe to warrant governmental interference, there remains the question of how intervention may most effectively be achieved to reduce the likelihood of bureaucratic capture and of rent-seeking, and to maximize the expected benefits of correcting market failure.

In theory, the answer is fairly straightforward: on one hand, quantification of the failure to intervene at all is an estimate of what will happen under unfettered market conditions, and is no different under the new view of government than it was under the earlier, selfless-benevolent guardian view. On the cost side, alternative mechanisms need to be identified through which the market failure might be partially or entirely corrected. These usually have included the traditional solutions of straightforward government operation of the activity and contracting for private performance of the activity.

The emerging view of governmental behavior, however, suggests that search should also be extended to inquiring why markets are believed likely to fail, and to seeking incentive-compatible policy instruments that might be used to correct these failures.

The infant industry case provides a case in point. Many developing countries adopted high walls of protection, and now find themselves saddled with

"senescent infants" who grew old before they grew up! These high-cost industries constitute major political lobbying groups opposing change toward more
efficient economic policies, and they simultaneously appear to be impervious to
government controls seeking to influence their efficiency.

A few countries, however, sought to industrialize through alternative policy instruments. Instead of seeking to decide which industries were reasonable
candidates for infant industry protection, they established incentives for exporters without regard to industry of origin. These incentives were sufficiently
large that those who could profitably develop and expand for exporting identified themselves. Those who could export were encouraged through a variety of
means, but those means were based on actual performance, and not upon the
exporters' promises of future behavior.

As described, this general model of "infant industry" protection is applicable to the Korean, Taiwanese, and Hong Kong experience. To a degree, it
also describes the successful export performance of Turkey and Chile in the
1980s. The failures of infant industry policy, as practiced through efforts at
futuristic identification of particular industries, are exemplified in the low rates
of economic growth (and negative productivity growth) of India and many
Latin American countries.

The lesson, however, is far more general. Although those deciding to
undertake particular economic activities have more knowledge of the markets
and their circumstances than do government officials, even they are confronted
with considerable uncertainty. Decision making that will be socially and privately profitable is difficult at best in that environment.

When governments intervene through mechanisms that do not penalize
those making less-than-optimal decisions, the mix of industries that will arise is
very likely to include some whose forecasts of their future were unduly optimistic. When, however, there are strong rewards for those correctly assessing
their prospects, and penalties for those who are overly optimistic (or merely
seeking governmental protection), the mix of activities that will be undertaken
will differ. Indeed, even the productivity and cost-effectiveness of the activities
that would be undertaken under either regime are likely to be greater under a
policy regime that rewards desirable behavior and penalizes undesirable behavior fairly automatically than they would be under a regime of indiscriminate
important substitution.

Seen in this light, the role of an economist as policy adviser is not to
identify specific industries, or to administer particular controls. Instead, it is to
seek mechanisms which can be put in place under which those who will behave
in the desired ways will find it in their self-interest to do so. In some instances—asymmetric information, for example—there will be no ideal mechanism, and policymakers may be forced to conclude that an imperfect market
outcome may be preferable to an imperfect governmental outcome. In other
cases, however, incentive-compatible mechanisms may be found, either
through experimentation or through reliance upon an understanding of individual behavior in response to incentives. Almost surely, incentive-compatible

mechanisms will be those which offer rewards to those carrying out the desired tasks, offering greater rewards the lower the costs incurred in so doing, while simultaneously penalizing those who fail to perform the desired activity, or do so at higher cost.

The rapid growth of infant industries in Korea and Taiwan into successful, low-cost exporters testifies to the existence of infant industries and the ability of producers to react rapidly when confronted with strong incentives. The failure to achieve rapid growth of infant industries through direct controls, governmental ownership, and protection from imports, in countries such as India and Argentina, testifies equally strongly as to the inefficiencies of those policy instruments as means of achieving the same objectives.

Although many other aspects of government activity have not been as visibly inefficient as some efforts for infant industries, the sheer size of government in most developed countries in the world today increases the urgency of finding ways of achieving societal goals that are consistent with incentives for economic efficiency and low-cost performance. While theoretical developments and experience over the past 30 years have been fruitful in challenging the older visions of government, a challenge for future research is to improve understanding of public organizations and processes. With this understanding, it should be possible to articulate more clearly the comparative advantage of governments and markets in various types of economic activity, and to identify incentive mechanisms and structures for lowering costs of public sector activities.

## Chapter Six

# Decision Making via the Price System*

*Bruno S. Frey*

*In a pure market economy, the composition of output, the allocation of resources, and the distribution of income are determined by supply and demand forces affecting prices in a set of related markets for goods, services, and assets.*

*The market system has long been admired as an efficient mechanism for resource allocation through decentralized decision making on the basis of prices reflecting relative scarcities. But markets and prices have their weaknesses. For example, competition among buyers and/or sellers may be weak for many reasons. Prices do not capture various positive or negative effects of economic activity that are "external" to the market. The income distribution generated by the market may not be considered "fair." Finally, full employment and price stability are not assured by the market system.*

*Thus, the government, in pursuit of its various objectives, intervenes with many instruments of economic policy to alter the outcomes that market forces would generate.*

*In this chapter, Frey analyzes in detail how the government in a capitalist regulated market economy seeks to improve the operation and results of the market system in three spheres. First, the government attempts to increase competition, or regulates firms where sufficient competition cannot be achieved. Second, the government strives to strengthen the position of consumers, relative to producers, in the market. Third, structural policy tries to make the relative rates of development of particular sectors, branches, and regions different from the market solutions.*

*However, Frey stresses, in all three spheres government intervention may not be completely successful, because of deficiencies in the democratic policy-making process and/or in the administrative implementation of policies. Hence, "market failure" of the price system has its counterparts in "government failure" and "administrative failure." Thus, one must evaluate to what extent imperfect government intervention improves the imperfect results of the market.*

* Reprinted by permission from Bruno S. Frey, *Democratic Economic Policy: A Theoretical Introduction* (Oxford: Martin Robertson, 1983), pp. 58–84. Bruno S. Frey is Professor of Economics at the University of Zurich, Switzerland.

## INTRODUCTION

Individuals and groups can choose among different methods of making social decisions by social consensus. The economic adviser can provide information as to which procedure is best suited to which decisions. The functioning of the social decision-making mechanisms and their corresponding institutions must be known. The decision makers seeking a social consensus can thus be informed of the advantages and disadvantages of each mechanism, allowing them to decide upon the most productive rule. Moreover, the economic decision makers must be informed about ways of improving the functioning of the social decision-making mechanisms.

The decision makers will not rely on one decision-making procedure alone. Rather, they will choose a combination of the mechanisms at their disposal. The "best" combination cannot be determined a priori. It will result from an evaluation of the properties of the various procedures by the individuals and groups at the level of the social consensus.

Social decision-making procedures can be classified in various ways. This chapter deals with the price mechanism, discussing its strengths and weaknesses and the main approaches designed to improve its functioning:

- *Antitrust policy,* which should serve to restrict monopolistic tendencies and to stimulate competition. *Government regulations* imposed on particular firms and economic sectors are also directed toward this goal.

- *Consumer policy,* which aims at strengthening the consumer's position against that of the producers.

- *Structural policy,* the goal of which is to promote adjustments in the structure of production. The most extreme form is the direct control of capital formation (known as "investment steering").

## PROPERTIES OF THE PRICE SYSTEM

In present times the price system seems to lose more and more ground in the decision-making process to administrative and bureaucratic factors. Even in countries whose economies are based on the market mechanism, there is an increasing tendency to plan and to regulate the economy. On the other hand, there have been some fundamental decisions to introduce the market and therewith the price system (as for example in the Federal Republic of Germany in 1948). The increased use of elements of the market in socialist planned economies, in particular in Hungary, is also noteworthy. Finally, in the United States there is presently quite a strong movement for freeing the economy from direct government intervention (for *deregulation*).

Within economic theory, the central role of the price system as a social decision-making mechanism was cast into doubt by the "Keynesian revolution," at least with respect to macroeconomics. In recent years the champions of the price system, under the leadership of the "monetarists" and the "supply-side economists," have once more gained in importance.

In order to be able to make a well-reasoned assessment of the role of the price system and the policies to improve upon it, it is necessary to compare the actual functioning of the price system with the actual functioning of economic policy interventions. There is little use in comparing a non-optimally functioning price system ("market failure") with idealized institutions of economic policymaking, or in comparing badly functioning economic policy institutions ("government failure") with an idealized market. Individuals and groups need to be informed by economic advisers about how the decision-making mechanisms actually function in a real-life politico-economic process. They have to compare *imperfect* decision-making mechanisms and *imperfect* institutions. With this knowledge they will be able to determine the weight they want to give to the price system and the supporting economic policies.

The most important *strengths* of using the price system are as follows.

- Economic resources are allocated efficiently.
- The selfish and competitive behavior of individuals leads (under specific circumstances) to the best outcome for all. There is no need to set any incentives for the "right" behavior by any outside authority.
- The decentralized system of decision making by consumers and producers reduces information and transactions costs.
- Everyone is free to choose according to his or her own preferences; behavior is not directly regulated.
- Changes in relative prices induce people to introduce technical progress, to change the structure of production, and to undertake organizational reforms.

There are two kinds of *weaknesses* of the price system: either it does not function well, or it cannot be applied. The major shortcomings of the market mechanism are more numerous.

- Markets may be incomplete, there being only few demanders and/or suppliers. In the case of increasing returns to scale, the competitive principles destroy themselves. The supplier with the largest output can offer goods at the lowest price, and will drive out the other competitors, thereby creating a monopoly.
- In the presence of external effects or the characteristics of a public good, the identity of those benefiting and those carrying the cost no longer holds. This leads to a misallocation of resources in that too much or too little is supplied. This is often referred to as the problem of "free riding" and the "tragedy of the commons."
- The allocation of resources can be biased if there is "moral hazard." This arises if a supplier of insurance against a risk is unable to distinguish adequately between true risk (of, say, a house burning down after being struck by lightning) and negligence (when, for example, a house burns because the owner does not take the precaution of extinguishing his fire properly, secure in the knowledge that he is insured). There can also be a

misallocation of resources owing to "adverse selection." This occurs if the supplier of insurance is unable to ask for a premium that is higher for bad than for good risks. This may result in there being no market for some types of risk, so that the corresponding (socially worthwhile) activities will not be undertaken.

- The price system is sometimes slow in bringing about the necessary supply reactions when they are needed—for example, when a war breaks out.

- Some markets do not exist or are considered to be immoral. Some transactions are forbidden in most societies because they conflict with basic human values (selling parts of one's body or even one's blood, for example—and, of course, engaging in slave trading), or because they are incompatible with democracy (for example, buying parliamentary seats or bribing public officials). It should, however, be pointed out that human history shows examples of almost everything having been marketed at one time or another; in England and France, at one time, parliamentary seats could be openly bought.

- The distribution of income resulting from the price system is usually not considered to be just. This aspect is of central importance for the practical application of the price system.

- Full employment of resources, especially labor, and stable prices are not guaranteed. The state must intervene with fiscal and monetary policy in order to stabilize the price system. This "Keynesian" view has recently been challenged by the "monetarists," who argue that the private market economy is stable, and that instability is produced knowingly or otherwise by the government or the central bank. Even if this is true, it may take a very long time for full employment and price stability to be reached after an exogenous disruption. The costs to individuals arising in this transition period may be intolerably high.

## ANTITRUST POLICY AND REGULATIONS

Institutional arrangements that serve to intensify competition can overcome some of the shortcomings of the price mechanism and reinforce some of its advantages. Such arrangements, of course, can only improve those shortcomings that result from hindrances to the price system's allocative qualities. On the other hand, it is not to be expected that an improved functioning of the price system will remove the problems created with respect to income distribution and stabilization. If anything, it is likely that they will be intensified.

The objective of strengthening competition is to break up monopolistic positions—in the widest sense—and to offer consumers an effective choice between various suppliers, which in turn forces producers to supply efficiently. *Antitrust policy* (which will be discussed next) seeks to achieve this goal by creating the conditions of a competitive market as far as possible. *Regulation* (which will be discussed subsequently) accepts the monopolistic positions as given and attempts to achieve by way of (generalized) instructions a better fulfillment of the consumers' wishes and more efficient production.

## Arguments For and Against Antitrust Policy

In the economic literature, various reasons are given for why competition ought to be strengthened:

- Allocative efficiency can be improved.
- Technical efficiency, or *X-efficiency* as it is often called, is higher, and therefore prices are lower, than in the case of a monopolistic market.
- More technical progress is made and introduced than under less competitive market conditions.

The following arguments are advanced against antitrust policy:

- If increasing returns do in fact exist, large firms can produce more cheaply than small ones.
- Only large enterprises can successfully compete on international markets.

Laymen and politicians, however, usually have quite different quarrels with large and monopolistic firms:

- Monopoly prices are unjust from the distributional point of view.
- Monopolies are responsible for inflation and unemployment.
- Monopolies restrain technical progress by suppressing new goods and processes protected by patents.
- Monopolies manipulate consumers through advertising.
- Large firms are the main culprits of environmental destruction.
- Monopolies push small firms out of business and lead to an alienation of the workers.
- Monopolies use their power for political goals and thus threaten a free society.

In order to find a social consensus on whether, and on how far, to restrict monopolistic firms, it is necessary to determine whether these charges are well founded. In this book, only some of them can be discussed. The next section deals with the allocative inefficiencies created by monopolies. The following sections are concerned with X-efficiency, technical progress, returns to scale, and the possibilities and actual working of antitrust policy.

## Monopolistic Supply and Allocative Efficiency

The model of perfect competition cannot be used directly for the purpose of economic policy because it depends on very specific conditions that are rarely, if ever, fulfilled or attainable. The conditions not being fully met, one has to turn to the *theory of the second-best*. This approach, however, does not allow any generally valid assertions as to whether more intensive competition improves allocative efficiency. Only if the sector considered is strongly isolated from the rest of the economy does an antitrust policy that brings about marginal cost pricing improve economic efficiency. The behavioral rules for the firms deduced for specific cases are extremely complex and hold only for narrowly determined parameter constellations.

Applying the theory of the second-best bears the danger that more and more biases are introduced into the economy, in particular when restrictions assumed to be immutable do in fact change. This may lead to a complete mix-up in economic policy. For these reasons the economic policy adviser will find little help in the theory of the second-best when he or she makes suggestions for an institutionalization of antitrust policy at the level of the social consensus.

The concept of *workable competition* opens up another, and more practically oriented, avenue to antitrust policy. Deviations from the conditions of perfect competition are taken as the rule rather than the exception. Whether competition is effective is judged by the results. Competition fulfills its role if it meets the preferences of the consumers as well as possible. There are various criteria for judging whether competition works—the level of factor productivity, the speed with which new products and new processes are introduced, the spectrum and quality of goods and services, and so on. Workable competition can exist within an oligopolistic or even monopolistic market structure. It may even happen that consumers are less well off where there is a structure of atomistic suppliers.

The concept of workable competition gives a better basis for the institutionalization of an antitrust policy than does the abstract model of perfect competition. In particular, the dynamic aspects of competition can be better assessed.

Whether to undertake an antitrust policy, and to what extent, depends crucially on how large the allocative inefficiencies brought about by monopolization actually are. There have been various attempts to measure empirically the welfare losses due to monopolies. These losses can be captured only at the level of the firm. Their macroeconomic importance is calculated by aggregating the results over all firms.

The welfare loss due to monopolization can be measured by the decrease of consumer surplus arising when the quantities and prices of a monopoly are compared with the Pareto-optimal supply of a firm under perfect competition. Figure 6–1 shows the corresponding equilibrium quantities and prices, and the loss in consumer surplus.

With perfect competition, profit-maximizing firms offer the quantity $X_c$, so that the given competitive price $p_c$ is equal to marginal cost $MC$. In the figure, the marginal costs are taken to be constant for simplicity; they are thus equal to average cost (they include normal interest payments for the capital invested). Profits are zero. Profit-maximizing monopolists, on the other hand, set the quantity they supply at $X_m$ and the price they charge at $p_m$ so that marginal revenue $MR$ equals marginal cost $MC$. The consumers have to pay a higher

**FIGURE 6–1**   Welfare Loss Owing to Monopolization

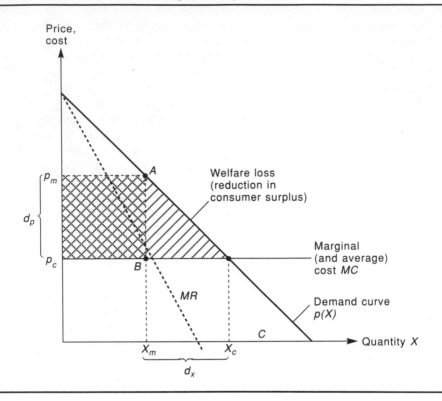

price and choose to buy a smaller quantity than under perfect competition. The welfare cost amounts to the reduced quantity of output $d_x$, evaluated at the corresponding price $p(X)$—this is shown by the trapezoid $X_mACX_c$—minus the value of the reduced resource input. They are evaluated at opportunity cost, that is, the competitive price. The value of saved resources thus is $d_x \cdot p_c$, which corresponds to the rectangle $X_mBCX_c$. The net loss for the consumers— the reduction of the consumer surplus—equals the hatched triangle $ABC$. This welfare loss is often named "dead-weight loss."

## Empirical Estimations

The first attempt to measure the welfare loss empirically was undertaken by Harberger. He assumes that the price elasticity of demand equals minus one, and concludes that the welfare loss amounted to 0.07 percent of gross national product in the United States in 1929. This loss is extremely small. Other authors, such as Schwartzman and Kamerschen, reach similar but slightly higher estimates, using somewhat different assumptions.

Newer estimates include additional negative effects of monopoly on welfare. All those expenditures can be considered socially wasteful that are used to keep up the monopoly position and the corresponding profits, for example by maintaining excess capacity, by differentiating products unnecessarily, by forcing protection from foreign competition, by giving funds to political parties and by bribing politicians and public officials. The maximum size of these expenditures is given by the size of the monopoly profits. It can therefore be argued that the social loss due to monopolization includes the whole area between the monopoly and competitive prices ($d_p$) from zero up to the quantity sold. This area, additional to the loss of consumer surplus, is indicated by the double-hatched quadrangle $p_m ABp_c$ in Figure 6–1. According to Posner, this results in a welfare loss of between 1.8 and 3.4 percent of gross national product (GNP) for the United States.

Some authors, such as Cowling and Mueller, also consider all advertising outlays as social loss. If these are added to the two types of cost already mentioned, there is a welfare loss of 13 percent for the United States in the years 1963 to 1966. The corresponding figure for the United Kingdom is 7.2 percent of GNP for 1968 to 1969.

The results of various empirical estimates of the welfare losses due to allocative inefficiency are given in Table 6–1. This table shows that the empirical estimates of the welfare losses due to monopoly yield increasingly higher values. Cowling and Mueller's estimates are roughly one hundred times larger than those of Harberger or Schwartzman (around 10 percent compared with 0.1 percent of GNP). This increasing size is due mainly to the broader definition of what constitutes the welfare losses attributable to monopoly.

**TABLE 6–1**   Welfare Loss Due to Monopolization

| Study (author) | Country | Year | Size (percent of GNP) |
| --- | --- | --- | --- |
| Harberger | U.S. | 1929 | 0.07 |
| Schwartzman | U.S. | 1954 | 0.1 |
| Kamerschen | U.S. | 1956–61 | 1.8 |
| Posner | U.S. | 1929, 1954 | 3.4, 1.8 |
| Cowling and Mueller | U.S. | 1963–66 | 13 |
|  | U.K. | 1968–69 | 7.2 |

SOURCES: Author's compilation from original studies:

Arnold C. Harberger, "Monopoly and Resource Allocation," *American Economic Review* 44, no. 2 (May 1954), pp. 77–92.

David Schwartzman, "The Burden of Monopoly," *Journal of Political Economy* 68, no. 6 (December 1960), pp. 627–30.

David Kamerschen, "Estimation of the Welfare Loss from Monopoly in the American Economy," *Western Economic Journal* 4, no. 3 (Summer 1966), pp. 221–36.

Richard A. Posner, "The Social Cost of Monopoly and Regulation," *Journal of Political Economy* 83, no. 4 (August 1975), pp. 807–27.

Keith Cowling and Dennis C. Mueller, "The Social Costs of Monopoly Power," *Economic Journal* 88, no. 352 (December 1978), pp. 727–48.

The empirical results presented here do not on the whole indicate that the social welfare costs of static allocative inefficiency are very high. It seems rather that society experiences only a small loss as a result of suppliers failing to follow the rules of perfect competition (not setting price equal to marginal cost). Moreover, when interpreting Table 6–1, three points should be kept in mind:

1. Antitrust policy can at best reduce the welfare losses *once;* the United Kingdom, for example, could increase its consumer surplus by 7 percent of GNP. This is not much compared to a steady growth rate of GNP which cumulatively raises output and welfare.

2. Expenditure on advertising is not necessarily wasteful, because part of it serves the useful function of informing consumers. Advertisement also often has an entertainment value. The estimates of loss by Cowling and Mueller given in Table 6–1 are therefore overstated. The same applies to the costs of defending a monopoly position: The size of monopoly profits indicates only a (probably quite irrelevant) upper boundary.

3. The estimates show what a *perfect* antitrust policy could at best attain if it were completely *costless*. The costs of undertaking the antitrust policy itself (administration, costs of errors, and so on) are disregarded.

## X-efficiency

The maximum output that can be produced with a given set of inputs is called *technical efficiency* or *X-efficiency*. In traditional economic theory, it is assumed that firms produce on their production possibility curve, and that the cost functions show the minimal attainable cost of producing a given output. Organization and the incentive structure within the firm are influences that the theory omits.

X-inefficiency can arise for three reasons:

1. The contracts between employers and employees are incomplete and at times vague; the input factor labor cannot, therefore, be used to the optimal extent by the firm.

2. It is either not possible or too costly to monitor the performance of employees precisely; the employees therefore have a chance to behave inefficiently, or even to shirk.

3. The firm's management is not fully informed about the production possibilities; in some areas the most efficient way of producing is unknown.

A monopoly that produces above-average profits is not directly confronted with the need to survive. Therefore it can be assumed that this market structure allows X-inefficiency to arise. When competition is stiff, however, firms not producing at minimum cost will be pushed out of the market by efficient firms. The likely existence of X-inefficiency in a monopolized market is one of the more important arguments in support of antitrust policy.

So far no compelling empirical evidence on the importance of X-inefficiency for the whole economy has been found. In the literature, one finds more or less anecdotal stories about cases of inefficiency with monopolies and large firms. These examples suggest that X-inefficiency is of considerable importance. The connection with the degree of competition in a market is, however, an open question. The possibility may not be excluded that lively competition between a few oligopolistic suppliers is more effective in preventing X-inefficiency than the "night-cap competition" between a large number of small competitors.

## Technical Progress

Monopolistic firms are the main innovators; this is argued by well-known economists such as Schumpeter and Galbraith. This proposition directs our attention to an additional and important aspect going beyond the static allocative efficiency of the model of perfect competition.

The connection between innovation and the extent of competition has been analyzed empirically in a great number of studies. Three relationships in particular have been examined.

1. Expenditure on research and development per unit of output has been shown to increase up to a threshold size of firm and then to decrease. This threshold differs as between sectors of the economy.

2. There is as yet no evidence for the view of Schumpeter and Galbraith that higher concentration leads to more research and development. The empirical studies suggest rather that a "medium" degree of concentration somewhere between perfect competition and pure monopoly brings about the highest degree of innovative activity.

3. If there is little rivalry between suppliers, small and medium inventions are introduced quickest. Large and important innovations, on the other hand, are more quickly brought in when there is a well-developed rivalry between suppliers.

## Economies of Scale

Should an antitrust policy be undertaken if production is subject to decreasing returns to scale resulting in small firms producing at lower cost? Or are large firms more efficient owing to increasing returns to scale? Empirical analyses have reached the following conclusions.

- In cross-section studies it is not possible generally to find any marked scale effects in one direction or the other. The "utilities" (transport, power plants, gas works) may be an exception. In the public sector, say, the postal service or police, increasing returns to scale have also been found. However, average costs fall only down to a threshold and rise thereafter. The size of the threshold (measured, for example, by the number of employees) differs between economic sectors.

• The time-series analysis of economies of scale is subject to great measurement problems because it is difficult, or even impossible, to differentiate between the effects of scale and the effects of technical progress occurring over time. The existing empirical studies suggest that there are approximately constant returns to scale.

On the whole, the research undertaken indicates that the supposed existence of increasing returns to scale is no convincing argument for tolerating large firms and monopolistic market structures. To justify a large firm on this ground it would be necessary positively to demonstrate that there are increasing returns to scale in this particular sector.

## Approaches to Antitrust Policy

Antitrust policy can be differentiated according to the point of application and its intensity.

Measures for intensifying competition can be applied by considering the market structure, conduct, or performance of firms.

In the first case it is assumed that the number of firms (as measured by the degree of concentration) is a sufficient indicator of the extent of competition. Concentration may take various forms. It can be horizontal or vertical, or it can extend over conglomerates (where completely different products are supplied within one firm). Capturing competition by the degree of concentration has the advantage that it may be measured in a relatively easy and objective way. Moreover, it approaches the problem at its base: the possibility of building up market power is prevented. It is, however, dubious to infer directly from the development of, and sectoral differences in, the degree of concentration how well the price system functions. This measure considers only one aspect among many. It is not at all clear whether consumers' preferences will be better fulfilled when the degree of concentration is reduced by antitrust policy.

Antitrust policy can also be applied by considering the behavior of firms. This implies that within a given market share the firms have considerable leeway to vary their behavior. The problem is to determine, and to measure empirically, whether a particular firm is behaving in such a way as to restrict competition. This approach also underlies regulation, because the antitrust institution usually tries to coerce firms to behave in a specific way by subjecting them to instructions (see the next section).

The third way that antitrust policy can be applied is to direct attention to performance. No intervention is deemed necessary if the firms produce at low cost and if they introduce new goods and processes rapidly. This approach, based on the idea of workable competition, is difficult to operationalize because performance entails many different aspects and because there is no definite point of reference. However, some hints may be gained by comparing the performance of firms across economic sectors, regions, and countries.

There are four different intensities of antitrust policy.

1. Competition can be strengthened or established if the entry of new suppliers into the market is encouraged by reducing legal and financial barriers and giving positive incentives through tax reductions and subsidies. Moreover, the government can establish public enterprises that compete in the market.

2. The behavior of those firms that restrict competition may be prevented. It is difficult to monitor restrictive practices, because there may be tacit collusion and "parallel behavior" between the suppliers. It is easier to control those restrictions that are directed toward a specific supplier (for example, by boycotting him) or to discriminate in the form of differentiated prices and terms of delivery. Antitrust policy can endeavor to prevent competing firms from being thrown out of the market or being subjugated to a dominating firm or a suppliers' interest group.

3. Antitrust policy is more severe if all explicit or implicit supply restrictions among the market participants are prohibited. Such agreements may, for example, refer to future prices, to the geographic region awarded to a supplier, or to the division of the supply quantity among the suppliers.

4. The most severe antitrust policy consists of prohibiting all forms of mergers between firms that may lead to a domination of a market by one firm. (In the case of merger, formerly independent firms form a new unit that often reduces competition among suppliers.)

## Regulation

If the conditions of competition are impossible or very difficult to attain, or if competition is inefficient, a government institution may be established to force firms to behave in a socially useful way. Regulation is particularly applied to natural monopolies, which produce under increasing returns to scale. Under these technical conditions average costs fall with increasing output. The Pareto-optimal equalization of prices with marginal cost then leads to a deficit. These relationships are illustrated in Figure 6–2. At the intersection of the falling marginal cost curve $MC$ with the demand curve $p(X)$, price is lower than average cost $AC$, resulting in losses. It would, on the other hand, be socially wasteful if a large number of small firms produced the quantity $X_{SF}$ each at a profit, because the advantages of mass production would not be exploited. It would be preferable if one firm produced, for example, quantity $X_T$ where average cost equals price $p_T$. No monopoly profits would exist and at least part

**FIGURE 6–2**   Regulating a Natural Monopoly

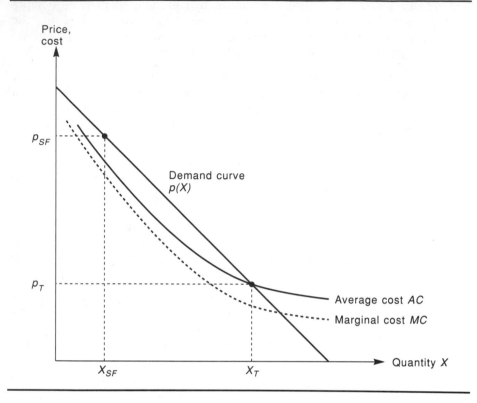

of the benefits of mass production would be exploited. The main objective of regulation is to bring about the quantity of supply $X_T$.

Regulation can proceed either by fixing a "fair rate of return" or by directly setting prices. Fixing a fair rate of return on capital is intended to protect the consumers against exploitation by the single (or few) supplier(s), but still to take advantage of the increasing returns to scale. This procedure is confronted by three major difficulties.

1. The prices that may be charged by a firm are based on cost and on the profit rate set by the regulatory agency (*cost-plus pricing*). This kind of price setting leads to distortions and inefficient production:

• The regulated firms have an incentive to overstate their cost in order for the regulatory agency to grant a higher price. The firms will attempt to label some part of profit (perhaps the perquisites of management) as cost.

- Regulated firms have no incentive to reduce cost. Lower costs could not increase (the regulated) profit but would have to be used to reduce the price.

In order to prevent such behavior, the regulatory agency must control the firms. It must monitor costs precisely and must be able to recognize and indicate possibilities for reducing costs by technical innovations and organizational reforms.

2. A regulated firm has an incentive to produce more capital-intensively than a nonregulated firm. In the case of a firm subject to a maximum rate of return on capital, increasing the stock of capital not only entails costs but also increases the admissible profit. However, empirical studies have been unable to locate this overcapitalization effect. This may be due to the fact that such firms do not intend to maximize profits, but rather pursue other goals.

3. A fair rate of return may lead to difficulties in the case of firms with low profits or losses. If the regulated firm is confronted with a price-elastic demand curve, raising the price will not help because revenue falls. Such a firm will attempt to get rid of those products not bringing profit or to reduce the quality of the goods and services supplied. The regulatory agency will make an effort to prevent both reactions. If it succeeds, the unprofitable firm must be supported by the government or be nationalized.

This discussion shows that effective regulation is very difficult. It is not sufficient to fix a fair rate of return. The regulatory agency is forced to establish a whole net of controls. It must monitor costs, see that technical progress is introduced, and survey the range and quality of goods and services supplied.

Instead of fixing a rate of return, the regulatory agency can also directly set prices. In order to promote certain products, low prices can be fixed which do not cover average cost and therefore lead to losses. In exchange, prices above average cost will be granted in other areas of production. The profits produced there will compensate for the losses in the areas with low prices. There are many examples of such *cross-subsidization,* for example in profitable/unprofitable air routes or in telecommunications.

The regulated firms react by supplying large amounts of the products with high prices and little of the products with low prices. The regulatory agency is therefore forced to control quantities as well as prices. Nonregulated firms coming from the outside will also attempt to supply in the area with high prices—to engage in "cream-skimming." In order to salvage its plan, the regulatory agency must keep out these competing firms by erecting entry barriers. Moreover, it must control the investment policies of the regulated firms to prevent the prices falling too much as a result of the enlarged supply. This means that there is another far-reaching intervention into the firms' behavior and into the market.

## The Behavior of Antitrust and Regulatory Agencies

The decision makers seeking a social consensus have to know how the institutions undertaking the antitrust and regulation policies function in practice, not how they should function ideally. The economic advisers can make it clear that these agencies are not able, nor do they intend, to maximize "social welfare." The persons involved in antitrust policy and regulation are best assumed to pursue their own selfish interests. The actual antitrust and regulatory policy observed depends on the behavior of three decision makers.

1. The *members of an antitrust and regulatory agency* have an interest in minimizing the conflicts with decision makers in order not to be burdened with unnecessary trouble. They will moreover be interested in establishing a good reputation, as well as in extending their agency to give them greater influence and possibly even higher income. These goals can be reached if the agency takes into account the interests of other decision makers, in particular those directly affected by their policy. As a rule, the latter are well organized and can create difficulties for the agency by passively obstructing the orders, by withholding information the agency needs, and by appealing to the courts. The population, on the other hand, will scarcely react to the policies. An individual citizen is rarely confronted directly by the issues and has little incentive to supply a public "good" in the form of an effective antitrust or regulatory policy. The agency therefore has little interest in paying special attention to the wishes of the general public. It is much more important for it to get along well with the economic sectors with which it directly deals. It will take into account their wishes, and possibly even will promote them actively. As one of the wishes of these sectors always is to prevent competition, the antitrust and regulatory agencies cannot be expected to undertake a vigorous policy to foster competition.

2. The *government* must evaluate whether it is advantageous to pursue an active competition policy against the well-defined interests of particular economic sectors. The interests of "capital" and "labor" in such sectors are in line with each other and therefore particularly effective in politics. As a rule, the government will conclude that it does not pay to antagonize the special interests of particular economic sectors.

3. The *economic sectors affected by an antitrust or regulatory policy* will attempt to make the policy fit their own interests. Barriers to entry and investment controls that reduce the competitive pressure are particularly advantageous. The sectors affected will try to persuade the agency to prohibit substitute products and to support complementary products. In order to reach these goals, the sectors will promise to support the agency and the government financially and politically, provided they adopt an "appropriate" policy.

The interaction of the decision makers leads us to expect the following type of antitrust and regulatory policy:

- Monopoly power in certain areas will be strengthened and the agency will be closely connected with the sectors to be regulated. The agencies even identify with the interests of "their" sector. In most countries, for example, it is a matter of course that the ministry of agriculture represents the interests of the farmers.

- In order to protect suppliers, competition will be restricted. Entry barriers will be erected, and some forms of competition, such as comparative advertising and discounts, will be prohibited.

Serious empirical research on the benefits and costs of antitrust and regulatory policy seems thus far to be available only for the United States.

## Empirical Evidence

A study by Breyer and MacAvoy of the U.S. Federal Power Commission, which regulates the area of gas pipelines and the production of gas and electricity, concludes that the consumers have gained no, or at best very little, net utility from regulation. The commission is an ineffective institution for the purposes for which it was established.[1]

An analysis by Posner of the social costs of regulation finds that the regulatory costs make up between 10 percent (for milk) and 30 percent and more (for medical services, road transport, and oil) of the revenue of the sectors affected. The overall regulatory costs are estimated to be around 1.7 percent of GNP.[2]

Weidenbaum differentiates between the direct administrative cost of the regulatory agencies and the indirect burden imposed on the private sector due to regulation. The total costs are calculated by taking the lowest cost estimates of a number of detailed studies of particular economic sectors. He estimates that in the United States in 1976 the direct administrative cost amounted to $3.2 billion, and the private sector had to carry indirect costs of $62.9 billion. The total cost of federal regulation of over $66 billion amounts to about 3.6 percent of GNP.[3]

One must hasten to add that these studies look only at the *costs* imposed by government regulation. If the benefit side is also considered the overall effect may well be positive.

---

[1] Stephen G. Breyer and Paul W. MacAvoy, *Energy Regulation by the Federal Power Commission* (Washington, D.C.: Brookings Institution, 1974), Table 5.1

[2] Posner, "The Social Cost of Monopoly," p. 818, Table 2.

[3] Murray L. Weidenbaum, "The High Cost of Government Regulation," *Challenge* 22, no. 5 (November/December 1979), p. 37, Table 4.

## Conclusions for Economic Advising

Whether or not individuals and groups reach a social consensus to institutionalize an antitrust and/or a regulatory policy depends on the evaluation of the relevant elements. In addition, the other aspects mentioned at the beginning of this chapter should be considered, though there is so far no sound theoretical and empirical evidence available (for example, on the influence of monopolistic firms on individual preferences through advertising).

The economic adviser can make the following suggestions, which may become part of a social consensus.

- Only unequivocal evidence of the effects of an increase or decrease of the existing state of competition is useful. The adviser has to identify those economic sectors and firms in which, for example, increasing returns to scale do exist, and in which technical progress is overwhelmingly promoted by large firms.

- Antitrust and regulatory policy should be directed toward decreasing the restrictions on competition. In particular, the barriers to entry should be removed. The resulting potential competition is likely to improve allocative and X-efficiency, and to increase technical and organizational change.

- Competition can be actively strengthened by establishing public enterprises to compete with private monopolists, and private firms with public monopolies.

- The institutional design of the antitrust and regulatory agencies must be paid great attention. If the institutions are badly constructed, competition will be hampered rather than strengthened. To reduce the tendency of the agency to identify too closely with "its" economic sector, it is useful to establish agencies that are monitored by both producers and consumers of particular goods and services. The opposition of those injured by a particular agency policy will then make itself felt within the agency. To improve the weight of consumers and taxpayers within the agencies, institutions of direct participation may be devised.

## CONSUMER POLICY

The price system is often criticized because it is taken to disregard the preferences of consumers. Three kinds of criticisms may be distinguished:

1. Consumption *per se* is criticized by the New Left and some environmentalists because it is believed to make people unhappy.

2. Consumers are manipulated by producers. According to Galbraith, this results in a disequlibrium between private and public consumption owing to firms' advertising.

3. Particular goods are of insufficient quality. The consumers cannot take advantage of the choice possibilities because they are badly informed and not adequately protected against deception. This view is advanced, for example, by the American "consumerism" movement.

The underlying theme of these criticisms is that the consumers have a much weaker position in the price system than do the producers. The market that is designed to meet the wishes of the demanders does not function properly.

Economic advisers can inform the individuals and groups of ways of enabling consumer preferences to be better fulfilled within the price system. They can suggest rules and institutions of consumer policy that may find a consensus. The antitrust and regulatory policies (discussed in the previous section), which may be considered to be a form of indirect consumer policy, are here supplemented by a *direct* consumer policy.

The consumers' role in the price system can be improved by strengthening the individual consumer's position, by collective action of consumers, and by weakening the relative position of producers.

1. An individual consumer is better able to fulfill his or her wishes in the market if better informed about the properties of the goods supplied. In many cases the producers have an incentive to offer product-specific information, because this improves the utility gained through the product, resulting in a greater demand for it. The consumers are also informed by commercial enterprises, which offer their specialized knowledge in the market at a price and thus operate as the consumers' agents. They will be able to sell their knowledge in the long run only if they are able to offer a useful service to consumers. This will be the case if they make an effort to inform as objectively as possible. Examples are the consumer guide journals or the French *Guide Michelin,* which is bought because consumers believe that it can judge competently the quality of hotels and restaurants.

Information will not be provided on all goods and services by the price system itself. As soon as there is a public good element involved (that is, when the information cannot be transmitted only to those consumers who pay for it)—and this is quite often the case—the consumers will be informed insufficiently. Also, there is in general very little information supplied on how best to use the goods and services supplied by government.

The individual's position in the market will also be strengthened by a good consumer education. Such education is not devoted to particular goods but is designed to make consumers more critical and more aware of properties of goods generally, thus allowing them to improve their buying decisions.

2. Activities designed to strengthen the consumers' position in relation to producers have, to a considerable extent, the properties of a public good. A particular consumer has little incentive to participate in the cost of

such activities but will tend to behave as a "free rider." There is little chance therefore that consumers will be able to form themselves into an effective interest group.

Self-organized collective action will take place only under the following conditions.

- When the shortcomings in the goods and services supplied are grave and very obvious, a spontaneous reaction in the form of consumers' strikes and boycotts is possible. These will, however, as a rule be effective only in the short run.
- In well-defined goods markets, consumer organizations may exist in the long run, provided they offer the individual consumers a specific incentive to join, in the form of a private good. Individuals may then find it advantageous to pay the membership fee because otherwise they would not receive the private good supplied jointly (or would have to buy it at higher cost). Automobile associations function on the basis of this principle. They are able to fight in the political sphere only because they offer their members a great many private services.
- The interests of consumers may be taken up by "political entrepreneurs," who hope to win votes and influence by supporting their case.

As self-organized collective action by consumers takes place under restricted conditions only, the decision makers may seek a social consensus about strengthening the consumers' position by establishing public institutions designed to support consumers. In many countries (in particular in the Federal Republic of Germany) such consumer organizations are financially supported by the state. Another possibility which has recently received considerable attention is the appointment of a (publicly financed) ombudsman for the consumers. He surveys advertising and marketing methods, accepts complaints about deficient goods and services, and seeks to remove the nuisances by voluntary bargains with the firm or sectors concerned.

Whenever consumer interests are collectively organized and promoted, there arises the problem of providing incentives to the executives of such organizations to fight for the real interests of consumers. It must be expected that these organizations will become concerned with their own affairs and pursue their own goals. Such a development is the more likely the larger the share of public subsidies received, the latter being independent of how successfully the cause of consumers is advanced.

3. The producers' position in relation to consumers can be weakened by consumer legislation. This may involve regulations concerning price, quality, marketing, and the introduction of goods. The producers can also be made liable for the goods supplied. These regulations are of use only if they can be made effective by the consumers at a low cost. Such costs may

be lowered by admitting "class actions," in which anyone can sue in the name of the many persons involved.

Laymen often think that, the better the protection of consumers by way of regulations, the better off consumers will be. In particular, they often assume that, the stricter the liability rules are, the better will be the position of consumers. It may, however, be shown that this is not necessarily so, and that there may also be disadvantages for the consumers.

*Liability rules* affect the behavior of both producers and consumers. When liability rules are introduced by social consensus, it is important to know the advantages and disadvantages connected with any such rule. The consequences of introducing four types of liability rules will be discussed here.

1.  The buyer carries all the risk associated with a product. The consumer will make an effort to be aware of the product quality (*caveat emptor*) and will have an incentive to choose and use products carefully. Buyers have a comparative advantage in this respect, because they know best the purpose for which they want to use the goods. The transaction costs are thus high for consumers only if they use the product rarely and at infrequent intervals.

2.  The producers are liable for deficiencies in the product. The consumers then carry only part of the risk; this induces them to choose the product less carefully. Compared to the rule of *caveat emptor,* the producers will supply fewer potentially deficient goods, because they must take into account the possibility that they might be held liable. They will also ask higher prices, because they will be induced to supply more goods at high quality and low risk of deficiency. The area of choice for consumers will thus be restricted. The supply of risky, but cheap, products will be smaller.

3.  The producers are liable when the consumer is dissatisfied with the product. There need not even be a deficiency in the material or construction of the good. This liability rule will induce consumers to be very negligent in their handling of the product. They know they will not carry the cost if they use it for the wrong purposes and thereby damage or destroy it. Because there will also be more accidents in product use, the social costs of consumption will rise. The producer will supply even fewer products that are susceptible to negligent and mistaken use. They will supply only very carefully checked and foolproof products, which will push up prices. The consumers' choice will be even more limited.

4.  The government compensates consumers for all damages that arise in the use of products, irrespective of who is responsible. The social costs of such a liability rule will be very high because neither the producers nor the consumers will have to carry any of the cost of negligence; they do not have to account for the consequences of their actions. The producers may

supply badly designed and deficient products, while the consumers have no incentive to be careful when choosing and using the goods.

Economic advisers can inform individuals and groups about the weak position of consumers in the economic process and can make suggestions on how it may be strengthened by information, education, collective action, and liability rules. By pointing out the advantages and disadvantages of the various institutional arrangements, advisers can help to bring about a consensus on the fundamental properties of consumer policy.

## STRUCTURAL POLICY

The price system results in a given structure of production with respect to economic sectors and regions. Individuals deciding at the level of the social consensus need not necessarily agree with this production structure but may consider rules and institutions that bring about a different pattern of goods. In the course of economic development, inefficient branches will disappear and others become important. It is difficult or even impossible to reach a consensus on the desirable structure of production in the current politico-economic process because the interests of individuals and groups are strongly influenced by the sector with which they are connected. Few would be ready, for example, to support a structural policy abolishing the sector to which they are attached. The basic institutions and rules about structural policy have therefore to be agreed upon by social consensus behind the veil of ignorance. That is, individuals will not know with which sector they and their heirs will be connected.

Structural policy has a very important impact on future economic growth. This policy can promote economic development in two ways:

1. It can help to bring about the structural changes necessary for growth by offering help with adjustment. Opposition to structural change on the part of the declining sectors can thereby be overcome. This effort can be directed at enterprises as well as at workers. Improved education and special courses for adapting new skills help to decrease unemployment resulting from structural changes.

2. Structural change can be actively promoted by supporting those sectors in the economy that are assumed to have good prospects. Alternatively, the government may withdraw all support from those sectors that are not considered viable in the future, particularly if they are inefficient.

The instruments of structural policy can affect supply or demand. On the supply side, the input of labor and capital, as well as of technical progress, can be influenced. Demand can be affected by varying the public budget. Often, direct subsidies and (less visible) tax relief measures are used. Protection may be offered by means of direct government regulation in the form of fixed or minimum prices, government guarantees to buy certain goods, barriers to entry and restrictions of capacity, closing markets against potential competitors, quantitative import restrictions, manipulated price increases of foreign goods (through import duties), and technical regulations which make it difficult or impossible for foreigners to compete.

The agrarian market of the European Economic Community provides many examples of a structural policy using the instrument of protecting suppliers. Prices are fixed politically and sales are guaranteed. As the prices are fixed above the world level, there is chronic oversupply of such goods as butter, corn, beef, and milk powder. Production is not directed to meet the consumers' wishes, but to maintain a certain structure of production, in particular to keep the agricultural sector alive.

Another instrument of structural policy is *investment guidance,* an approach extensively discussed in Germany. The government directs the sectoral distribution of private investment to take into account "social preferences," which are taken to be disregarded by private investors. According to the proponents of this approach, what constitutes these social preferences may be determined by the democratic mechanism of voting or by the views of an "enlightened elite" (among which the proponents of investment guidance count themselves). A hierarchy of wants is established, ranging from basic individual needs, to basic social needs, to superior individual needs, to superior social needs, and finally to private luxuries. The government has to see to it that private investments are undertaken in such a way that these needs are fulfilled in sequence.

Structural policy can be formulated by a council of scientific experts on structural questions; a political assembly in which the main social groupings are represented; or an executive agency for the practical implementation of the policy. The following major problems will arise when a structural policy is to be undertaken.

1. The technical problem consists in finding reliable data on structural changes in the past and in forecasting likely future developments. To undertake a reasonable policy, it is important to have an idea about which sectors have good economic prospects and which ones must be expected to shrink. Such forecasts are extremely difficult to make. The forecaster ideally should have available a model of economic and political developments in the whole world, which of course is impossible. Therefore more or less arbitrary assumptions will be made about future conditions within and outside the country. On this basis the likely structural change will be forecast, presupposing (among other things) knowledge about future technologies. The forecaster will have to know which new production processes will be introduced and which new goods will appeal to consumers.

2. It must be decided which groups should be represented in the councils and assemblies for structural policy, and what their proportions should be. There is a strong danger that well-organized groups will be overrepresented or that they will at least bring forward their interests too forcefully. We have to expect that in such institutions coalitions will form with the goal of maintaining existing economic structures, especially when labor

and capital in a particular sector act jointly. As structural change mainly benefits future generations by promoting economic growth, it should be considered which group (if any) represents the interests of future generations.

3. The agency given the power to undertake the structural policy does not necessarily contribute to more rapid structural change and thereby to an increase in future welfare. (As mentioned earlier, the formal goals of an institution should not be confused with its actual behavior.) As prestige and a quiet life may be assumed to be important arguments in the utility function of the top executives of such an agency, the intensive and well-organized interests will be privileged, whereas the less visible, broad, and badly organized interests will be neglected. The economic sectors whose size and existence are threatened by structural change will be given more weight than the anonymous taxpayers and consumers. Therefore it is likely that the agency will undertake a policy designed to maintain the existing economic structure, with the general public having to pay the cost. Economic advisers can make suggestions about the institutional form of the agency so that incentives are created to promote, and not to hinder, structural change.

## CONCLUSION

The price system has advantages and disadvantages (the latter are usually called "market failures"). Its functioning can be improved by various policies. This chapter has discussed antitrust and regulatory, consumer, and structural policies. It has been shown that all these attempts at improvement also entail social costs. Often, there is a wide gap between the officially declared goal of improving the functioning of the price system and the policy actually undertaken. Often economic policy measures lead to results that are in gross contrast to the official goals. A structural policy, for instance, as a rule does not promote structural change but rather helps outdated economic sectors to survive.

The large gap between official goals and actual policy can be attributed to two causes:

1. *Government failure,* entailing a distorted functioning of the democratic decision-making mechanisms.
2. *Administrative failure,* entailing an inadequate working of the public administration.

In accordance with this discussion, it should always be kept in mind that the advantages and disadvantages of the price system should be compared with the advantages and disadvantages of those decision-making mechanisms designed to improve upon the price system. The individuals and groups setting the basic rules in society have to choose between alternative ways of ordering the current politico-economic process. What they need, therefore, is a *comparative analysis of institutions.*

*Chapter Seven*

---

# Privatization: British Style*

*Colin Harbury*

*A distinctive feature of the British economy since 1980 has been the drive to privatize activities in the state sector: for example, in air transport, motor freight transport, telecommunications, and oil production. The Conservative Party has sought privatization for reasons of ideology and efficiency.*

*In this chapter, Harbury analyzes and evaluates key aspects of the British privatization program. First he considers its goals, such as greater productive and allocative efficiency, "popular capitalism" resulting from wider ownership of stock shares, and budget revenue from asset sales. Next he explains alternative methods of privatization, including ownership transfers, deregulation, and subcontracting. Then he examines the comparative performance of public and private enterprises, and the effects and benefits of privatization. In this connection, he stresses the need for proper regulation of privately owned "natural" monopolies; for instance, in telecommunications and delivery of gas.*

*Harbury concludes with some lessons from British privatization experience that are applicable in other countries. They include, for example, the desirability of breaking up large state-owned entities in connection with privatization, and the gains from greater competition resulting from subcontracting and deregulation.*

## THE MEANING OF PRIVATIZATION

Let it be stressed that there is no single sense in which the word *privatization* is used in Britain (let alone, internationally). Thiemeyer reported that the term was to mean no less than 17 different things.[1] A few are essentially political and need not concern us. But it is well recognized that privatization policies in the

* Reprinted by permission from *The Journal of Behavioral Economics* 18, no. 4 (Winter 1989), pp. 265–88, with the omission of a table, some notes, and references to unpublished studies and limited-circulation reports. Colin Harbury was Professor of Economics at City University, London.

[1] Theo Thiemeyer, "Privatization: On the Many Senses in Which This Word Is Used in an International Discussion on Economic Theory," *Annals of Public and Cooperative Economy* 57, no. 2 (April–June 1986), pp. 147–52.

United Kingdom[2] are designed to serve multiple objectives[3] and to describe almost any attempt to improve public sector performance.[4]

This study deals first with goals and instruments, and then traces the course of privatization since 1979, reviewing recent critical literature on the effects of asset sales, subcontracting, and deregulation. The following sections discuss the new regulatory machinery devised for the control of privately owned public utilities and conclude by considering the benefits and costs of the program.

## GOALS

It is convenient to collect the goals under three heads—efficiency, equity, and a miscellaneous category, though these are not, of course, watertight compartments.

### Efficiency

The first group of objectives is associated with allocative and productive efficiency. Broadly speaking, they involve policies that seek to replace decision taking by bureaucrats with those resulting from market forces—all aimed at improving economic performance where it has been held back by public sector activities.

One can perceive two strands to these policy goals. The first tries to create greater competition in sectors characterized by, at least, contestable markets. The second strand is concerned with markets where profit-maximizing behavior is suboptimal, because of the presence of (natural) monopolistic elements and/or concern with standards of quality or externalities. In these spheres, increased competition may still be an aim. But such competition is limited to that in the capital market, with the threat of hostile takeover bids playing a key role. Also relevant may be the popular notion that employees, especially managers, perform better in market environments than in bureaucratic ones.

In the second set of markets, some state intervention is still, *prima facie,*

---

[2] To save space, initial letters, common in the United Kingdom, are used in the text on second and subsequent occasions. A full list is as follows:

| | | | |
|---|---|---|---|
| AI | Amersham International | BT | British Telecom |
| BA | British Airways | CAA | Civil Aviation Authority |
| BAA | British Airports Authority | EFL | External Funding Limit |
| BG | British Gas | MMC | Monopolies and Mergers Commission |
| BR | British Rail | OFTEL | Office of Telecommunications |
| BSC | British Steel Corporation | PSBR | Public Sector Borrowing Requirement |

[3] J. A. Kay and D. J. Thompson, "Privatization: A Policy in Search of a Rationale," *Economic Journal* 96, no. 381 (March 1986), pp. 18–32.

[4] Simon Domberger and John Piggott, "Privatization Policies and Public Enterprises: A Survey," *Economic Record* 62, no. 177 (June 1986), pp. 145–62.

called for, and the actual operation of regulatory agencies is crucial for allocative efficiency. The United Kingdom has developed distinctive rules for such agencies, which are examined below.

The feeling that market forces should be given greater prominence in the search for improved efficiency in the British economy has two origins, one general and one specific. The *general* stems simply from the view that human motivation causes private sector units to perform better than public sector units. Valid or not, this argument holds that the best private firms outperform the best public corporations.

The *specific* argument related to particular conditions of the U.K. public sector at the time at which the privatization program was introduced. Three particulars may be itemized: (1) The nationalized industries had been underperforming in the 1970s compared with the previous decade (see below). (2) Some unprofitable private companies had been rescued and taken into the public sector for reasons such as the prevention of local unemployment, and such "lame ducks" were new to the scene. (3) Worry had been growing that day-to-day interference by ministers in the affairs of private and public corporations was a major source of inefficiency.

## Equity

We shall later consider the equitable consequences of privatization policies in general, but it should be recognized that some policies have distinct equitable objectives of their own. Prime among them is the notion of "popular capitalism"—especially of raising the proportion of the population owning ordinary shares, from the low of 5 percent in 1979.

A related objective, aimed also at improving labor force motivation, has been to extend share ownership by employees in the company in which they work. A third goal, on the theme of property-owning democracy, is offering for sale rented public (so-called) housing to tenants at attractive discounts.

## Other Goals

There are goals other than those discussed under the previous heads that do not directly concern us, but the existence of which can have important implications for our analysis.

The most important of these objectives relates simply to revenue raising, or "selling off the family silver," as a former (Conservative) Prime Minister, Lord Stockton (formerly Harold MacMillan) put it. Governments do not normally try to raise revenue without reason. The two main underlying motives in the United Kingdom in the 1980s have been to secure a reduction of the Public Sector Borrowing Requirement (PSBR) in pursuit of a strong counterinflationary policy, and to provide financial resources to fund reductions in taxation, especially the income tax.

Associated partly with macromanagement goals (though also, one suspects, with political motives) one discerns a desire to diminish the bargaining power of trade unions in certain state-owned sectors, especially power and communication. The strategic nature of these nationalized industries gave their unions power to hamper governments in the vigorous pursuit of anti-inflationary policies. Public-sector pay bargaining between management of nationalized industries and strong unions, whose threats of national strike action could not lightly be ignored, made the transfer of such industries to the private sector an attractive proposition.[5] A somewhat similar attraction may have influenced those responsible for the level of investment in public-sector corporations. Constrained by the External Funding Limit (EFL) component of anti-inflationary policy, desirable investment gets put aside. But if the industry is transferred to the private sector, no such constraint need operate. This may be a relatively minor motive for most privatizations but is believed to have been a consideration of magnitude when the communications corporation British Telecom (BT) was sold off, allowing for the raising of a large capital sum for modernization outside the confines of EFLs and PSBR.[6]

## INSTRUMENTS

Four main sets of instruments are available. Chief reliance has been placed on two of them—transfer of ownership from the public to private sectors, and deregulation/liberalization of activities hindered by previous state intervention. A third instrument, subcontracting government provision, has also been used, but the fourth set, substituting charging (whether in cash or vouchers) for free, or subsidized, provision has so far been of limited importance.

### Ownership Transfers

The transfer of publicly owned assets to the private sector can be done in several ways, some more likely to achieve certain privatization goals than others. Aside from the possibility (argued persuasively by Brittan and Riley)[7] that shares in state-owned corporations be given, free of charge, to every citizen, the main mechanisms are offers for sale at a fixed price, tender, placing, and "tapstock" sales (i.e., when market conditions are favorable). The two first-named have been used for the largest sales. These have been of mammoth proportions, even creating a very real danger of disrupting the capital market in Britain. For instance, the sale of BT was to yield £1.6 billion in 1984 (with further installments of £2.3 billion to come)—compared to an estimated

---

[5] Transfers could also make manpower cuts less difficult.

[6] C. G. Veljanovski, *Selling the State: Privatization in Britain* (London: Weidenfeld and Nicolson, 1987).

[7] Samuel Brittan and Barry Riley, "A People's Stake in North Sea Oil," *Lloyds Bank Review* 128 (April 1978), pp. 1–18.

£1.4 billion for all private-sector new issues of equities the same year.[8] British Gas (BG), sold off two years later, yielded £4 billion, and the planned sale of the national electricity industry is expected to yield at least £15 billion.

Matching sale methods to goals is a matter of great importance. For instance, encouraging wider share ownership, rather than increasing efficiency or maximizing revenue from transfer, would suggest low (fixed) price offers for sale. Sales can be enhanced, too, when a public corporation is "dressed up" (e.g., by writing off accumulated debt beforehand) or by sale as a single entity with retained monopoly power. Such enhancements may also help convert otherwise hostile top managers and other employees to support the transfer.[9] There is plenty of evidence of these happenings in the British experience. We discuss the conflicts so caused in later sections when we also consider the new regulatory regimes established to deal with newly privatized national utilities.

## Deregulation

The second privatization instrument is deregulation. It is not, of course, simply an alternative to transfer of ownership. Industries in both private and public sectors have been regulated in the past, and there is no reason why both should not be deregulated.

Private-sector deregulation has included a wide variety of measures, such as the ending of monopolies of solicitors in conveyancing real estate,[10] and of qualified opticians in the sale of eyeglasses, and the repeal of legislation going back to the 1930s which restricted competition in the provision of road passenger transport. Opening public-sector corporations to competitive forces can occur before, in the course of, or even without, transfer of asset ownership— one example being the Telecommunications Act of 1981, which curtailed the statutory monopoly powers of the (then, state-owned) BT.

## Subcontracting

The third set of privatization instruments to be considered is opening up state-provided goods and services to competition by subcontracting, or franchising. The device has been used, to a limited extent, in the privatization program (e.g., in refuse collection by local government authorities, and in hospital do-

---

[8] Colin Mayer and Shirley A. Meadowcroft, "Selling Public Assets: Techniques and Financial Implications," *Fiscal Studies* 6, no. 4 (November 1985), pp. 42–56.

[9] General trade union opposition to privatization has been effectively quashed by guaranteeing employees attractively priced share options. Mention should, in this connection, be made of an alternative technique, sale by management/employee buyout, usable only with smaller corporations, but successfully applied to National Freight, assisted by Barclays Merchant Bank, in 1982. Six years later, the company was ready for a public issue realizing large capital gains.

[10] Editor's note: In the United Kingdom, only solicitors (lawyers) could handle the transfer of title to real estate.

mestic services within the National Health Service). It has, however, long been used by some public corporations, for example, duty-free shops in airports operated by the British Airports Authority (BAA).

There are two principal methods of subcontracting. Both call for tenders from outside suppliers. One awards contracts to the highest bidder, effectively allowing for the sharing of any monopoly profits between the parties. The second awards contracts to suppliers who offer to sell on the most favorable terms to ultimate consumers—the so-called Chadwick-Demsetz principle.[11] The advantage of the latter type of contract for the attainment of allocative as well as productive efficiency is obvious. However, it requires monitoring to ensure, not only that the contract is honored as to price, but also that there are no quality deteriorations of output. Both types have been used in Britain and will be commented on later.

## THE PROGRAM

The origins of the privatization program are usually traced to a private document written by a research group in the Conservative party under the chairmanship of Nicholas Ridley before Mrs. Thatcher's first electoral victory in 1979.[12] It is a matter for comment that there was no detailed program before then. Previous post-war Conservative administrations had done little beyond marginally shifting the boundaries between the public and private sectors, and the only major state industry to be denationalized had been steel, as far back as 1953.

The reason for hesitation before embarking publicly on a large-scale privatization program is surely to be found in doubts within the party as to whether it would be electorally popular. The following years were to reveal that the apprehension had been unnecessary. To the contrary, some of the policies proved themselves election winners. Popular capitalism, in particular, became a roaring success, as witnessed by growing support for buying shares in state industries, as they were sold off on attractive terms. The substantial revenues raised by sales also aided counter-inflationary policy and helped the Chancellor of the Exchequer to reduce income tax. There was plenty of emotive support, too, among the "floating electorate" for taming some of the more powerful unions and for, somehow or other, stirring things up for the nationalized industries.

The political matters described above are mentioned not so much because it would be misleading to suppress them, but because of the role they played in the historical development of the privatization program itself. As it became apparent what was especially popular, so the policies took shape. Sell-offs of national assets on attractive terms and buoyant state coffers are inclined, one

---

[11] See Harold Demsetz, "Why Regulate Utilities?" *Journal of Law and Economics* 11, no. 1 (April 1968), pp. 55–65.

[12] It was leaked to *The Economist* weekly magazine in May 1978.

**TABLE 7–1**   Public Sector Asset Sales, 1981–1987

| Date | Company | Business | Proceeds (£ millions) |
|------|---------|----------|-----------------------|
| 1981 | British Aerospace | aerospace | 40 |
| 1981 | Cable & Wireless | telecommunications | 180 |
| 1982 | Amersham International | radio-chemicals | 65 |
| 1982 | National Freight | road haulage | 5 |
| 1982 | Britoil | oil | 630 |
| 1983 | Associated British Ports | seaports | 50 |
| 1983 | International Aeradio | aviation communication | 60 |
| 1983 | British Rail Hotels | hotels | 50 |
| 1984 | British Gas Onshore Oil | oil | 80 |
| 1984 | Enterprise Oil | oil | 380 |
| 1984 | Sealink Ferries | cross-channel ferries | 65 |
| 1984 | Jaguar Cars | cars | 300 |
| 1984 | British Telecom | telecommunications | 3,920 |
| 1984 | British Technology Group | miscellaneous | 715 |
| 1986 | British Gas | gas | 4,525 |
| 1987 | British Airways | airline | 900 |
| 1987 | Rolls Royce | aero engines | 1,360 |
| 1987 | British Airports Authority | airports | 1,230 |

imagines, to bring greater, and quicker, political rewards than driving toward improved economic efficiency through greater competition.

A quick way of summarizing the extent of privatization during 1979–87 is to note that 18 corporations were transferred from the public sector to the private sector (see Table 7–1). This transfer reduced the size of the public sector by about a third and employment in the nationalized industries by about 40 percent. However, these measures ignore the growth of deregulation and subcontracting. A better perspective on the way in which the program developed is obtained by considering the period as falling into three phases corresponding, more or less, to the periods of office of the three Thatcher administrations.

Phase I covered the rather cautious period up to 1983, when deregulation and subcontracting proceeded apace, with such measures as the Road Transport Act (1980), which freed express coaching,[13] and the British Telecommuni-

---

[13] Editor's note: "Coach" is a British term for bus.

cations Act (1981), which ended the Post Office's monopoly over express mail. Many of the state enterprises sold to private enterprise, such as Amersham International (AI) and British Rail Hotels, were already in competition with private firms, and they were mainly small compared to the massive denationalizations to come later. The largest sales in Phase I were of council houses to sitting tenants.[14] They were at an average discount of about 50 percent, and over one million (about a third of the total) were sold between 1979 and 1986.

Phase II covered the period of the second Thatcher administration and the run-up to the third. The early years saw continuance of the policy of selling competitive state businesses, such as Jaguar cars and Sealink car ferries, but a new dimension was introduced with the offer for sale of the giant state telecommunications enterprise (BT) in 1984. The sale's popularity was unquestioned. It was heavily oversubscribed, and share allottees enjoyed an immediate capital gain on the first day of trading of over 80 percent on the fixed issue price. It emboldened the government to embark on more large-scale asset transfers in Phase III.

Phase III covers Mrs. Thatcher's third term, during which an even more gigantic monopoly, British Gas (BG) was sold, also producing a healthy profit on the issue price, albeit of more modest dimensions. There followed two more large sales, of British Airways (BA), which had by then become sufficiently profitable, and of British Airports Authority (BAA), which owns and operates London's major airports. Plans for the remainder of the present administration are for the sale of national water utilities, worth approximately as much as gas, and the national electricity corporation, of such gargantuan proportions that it is expected to yield four or five times as much as BG.[15] Also due to be sold is the state-owned steel industry, British Steel Corporation (BSC), and there is talk for the more distant future of the sale of part or all of public assets in coal and the Post Office. Meanwhile the National Health Service has been undergoing a different form of privatization, as patient charges have been raised, and private self-provision encouraged.

## THE EFFECTS OF PRIVATIZATION

In this section some of the recent literature on the effects of privatization is reviewed. No attempt is made to give an overall assessment. Such is a virtually impossible task, given the multiple objectives of the set of policies described by the term *privatization* in Britain. Also, comparable before-and-after data are

---

[14] Editor's note: Housing owned by local governments (councils) was sold to tenants renting it.

[15] The swingalong nature of the assets transfer program may be illustrated by the announcement in 1988 that the government was disposing of the unprofitable parts of the British Leyland (motor vehicle) "lame duck" known as the Rover Group. Although the price turned out in this case to be negative, when account is taken of the prior write-off of accumulated losses, the government was no doubt glad to be rid of a long-endured embarrassment. It is interesting, too, that the purchaser (on attractive terms) is an earlier public corporation, British Aerospace (BAe).

lacking. For example, the data are distorted by actions taken to increase profit-ability, such as writing off accumulated debt and guaranteeing continuity of monopoly status. Another problem is that of choosing appropriate performance measures for enterprises with elements of natural monopoly about them. Profits in such cases are poor measures of allocative efficiency. Productive efficiency is, in principle, easier to monitor where total productivity data are available, though output per unit of labor input is often the only statistic con-sistently available.

Eventually, an adequate number of in-depth case studies of individual privatization projects may become available for an attempt at an assessment. All we offer here is report and comment on such evidence as is available on the effectiveness of some privatization policies, including the new regulatory ma-chinery. All should be read in conjunction with a public health warning that the interpretations and views are those of this single author. We look first at evi-dence of comparative performance in the public and private sectors in a British context, then at public utility regulation, followed by an examination of the record on equitable/distributive effects.

## Comparative Performance of Public and Private Enterprise

It is not the intention in this study to resurvey the international literature on this subject, which remains substantially inconclusive.[16] One of the principal contributors in this area is Pryke, whose two books, a decade apart, tell a story of interesting contrasts.[17] In the first, Pryke surveyed the performance of the major nationalized industries in the period to 1968, ending with the conclusion that, after the teething troubles of the early post-nationalization years, perfor-mance was, on average, at least as good as that in the private sector of the economy—with a rate of growth of labor productivity of over 5 percent per year, compared with the average for manufacturing industry of 3.5 percent. In his second book, Pryke reversed his conclusions, and made the much quoted observation that, with certain clear exceptions, the performance of the nation-alized industries should be classed as "third rate."

It may be noted in passing that such deterioration was particularly distress-ing in view of the fact that Pryke's second period coincides with one when the government had taken steps to emphasize the commercial, as distinct from the social, obligations of the nationalized industries. It called for the adoption of pricing policies based on long-run marginal costs and advocated investment appraisal using modern discounted cash flow techniques, requiring such deci-sions to be compared with the yardstick of a new Test Discount Rate set by the

---

[16] For some recent surveys, see Peter J. Curwen, *Public Enterprise: A Modern Approach* (Brigh-ton, England: Wheatsheaf Books, 1986), and Domberger and Piggott, "Privatization Policies."

[17] Richard Pryke, *Public Enterprise in Practice* (London: MacGibbon and Kee, 1971), and *The Nationalized Industries: Policies and Performance Since 1968* (Oxford: Martin Robertson, 1981).

government. Pryke's studies were recently extended by Molyneux and Thompson to the post-1978 period.[18] Productivity was shown to have recovered quite sharply, and to be rising considerably, again faster than in the manufacturing sector as a whole.

The industries examined by Molyneux and Thompson included some privatized, some due for privatization, and yet others with no firm plans for sale to private enterprise. Little light is therefore shown on whether change of ownership (with any accompanying changes in regulatory machinery) led to changes in performance. It is, in any event, too early to expect reliable evidence on that question. But one might, perhaps, be tempted by the observed trends in the data to conclude that factors other than ownership were dominant. The conclusion that change of ownership, per se, has less effect than changes in the degree of competition on performance is widely held among economists. It is a view probably shared, one suspects, by more industrialists than publicize it. The ex-chairman of the nationalized coal industry wrote recently on the subject of motivation, which, he said, many people seem to expect to be bound to be weak in a nationalized industry:

> I did not find this to be so—at any rate in the coal industry. In management the motivation of the mining engineer and the other professional personnel was very high. Equally, the principal motivation that I discerned among the miners was loyalty to the pit. . . . It was strongly felt and . . . it seemed to me that these two elements of motivation were as important as anything in the private sector.[19]

Another relevant recent study by Pryke attempts like-with-like comparisons where private and public enterprises competed alongside each other.[20] They were airlines (BA against private British Caledonian); cross-channel ferries (Sealink and BR Hovercraft against European Ferries and Hoverlloyd); and retail sales of gas and electrical appliances (BG and state-owned Electricity Boards against Curry's and Comet). Pryke's results showed private enterprise significantly outperforming public. The poor rating of BA is confirmed in another recent study by Forsyth and others, who compare the corporation with other major international airlines.[21]

These results should be treated with a certain caution and not regarded as necessarily representative, in that special circumstances may provide, at least partial, explanations for them. For example, BA's performance is quite heavily dependent on route allocations made by a government body (the Civil Aviation

---

[18] Richard Molyneux and David Thompson, "Nationalized Industry Performance: Still Third Rate?" *Fiscal Studies* 8, no. 1 (February 1987), pp. 48–82.

[19] D. Lord Ezra, "Privatization: A Middle Course," in *Privatization,* ed. Jonathan Neuberger (London: Macmillan, 1987), p. 86.

[20] Richard Pryke, "The Comparative Performance of Public and Private Enterprises," *Fiscal Studies* 3, no. 2 (May 1982), pp. 69–81.

[21] Peter J. Forsyth, Rob Hill, and Chris D. Trengrove, "Measuring Airline Efficiency," *Fiscal Studies* 7, no. 1 (February 1986), pp. 61–81.

Authority (CAA)), and the observed relative inefficiency of the state-owned gas and electricity appliance showrooms might be attributable to their being seen as part of the whole operation of fuel supply. It is true that the showrooms offered a great deal more by way of maintenance and after-sales service than did the outlets with which they were compared pricewise. Moreover, the private suppliers selected for this comparison were among the cheapest available, and not typical of the average to be found in the private sector.

## Subcontracting

We turn to consider evidence on the effects of the subcontracting instrument of privatization policy, where performance measurement is rather less difficult, and where firmer conclusions may be drawn. The studies of greatest interest are those which monitor changes in efficiency of operating services undertaken exclusively by public sector units until opened up to outside competitive tendering. Two areas in which this occurred are refuse collection and hospital domestic services, including cleaning and housekeeping. We illustrate with a description of the former, which in this instance probably is fairly typical.[22]

Studies of subcontracting in refuse collection have been made by Cubbin and others.[23] Their results have particular interest since subcontracting was introduced early in the privatization program, and had been adopted by about 10 percent of all local authorities responsible for this work. The efficiency of three groups was compared: (1) refuse collection by public authorities *not* put out to tender; (2) that performed "in-house" after tendering; and (3) that awarded to outside private contractors.

The studies were carefully conducted. There are no significant scale economies, and the work is broadly comparable wherever done, or differences fairly reasonably allowed for. The results, which the authors claim to be robust on the issue of cost reductions from tendering, show efficiency improvements in *both* groups (2) and (3) where tendering was instituted. Private outside firms *and* in-house public authorities which continued to provide the services *after* the introduction of tendering both had costs about 20 percent lower than those local authorities that did not put the work out to tender.

A subsequent study . . . estimated the technical efficiency of the three groups of workers. The procedure provided an indication of the sources of the observed productivity differences. The results suggested that the productivity differences of private contractors were broadly equal to the cost differences between them and the local authorities which did not have refuse collection put

---

[22] For a comparable study of the effects of competitive tendering in hospital services, see Simon Domberger, Shirley A. Meadowcroft, and David Thompson, "The Impact of Competitive Tendering on the Costs of Hospital Domestic Services," *Fiscal Studies* 7, no. 4 (November 1987), pp. 39–54.

[23] John S. Cubbin, Simon Domberger, and Shirley Meadowcroft, "Competitive Tendering and Refuse Collection," *Fiscal Studies*, no. 3 (August 1987), pp. 49–58.

out to tender. However, the same was not the case when local authorities which did employ tendering but retained the work in-house, were compared to private contractors. In this case, technical differences accounted for only some 50 percent of the cost differences. The important conclusion suggested is therefore that about half of the cost improvement achieved by local authorities which operated the refuse service themselves after tendering, was secured through personnel cuts and/or reductions in the level of remuneration of workers.

Opening up the provision of services to competitive tendering seems therefore on the evidence to have much to commend it from the viewpoint of increasing efficiency. However, it must be recalled that franchising is not necessarily an unmitigated blessing. Aside from distributive consequences, such as those referred to in the previous paragraph, it must be recalled that only 10 percent of local authorities surveyed had introduced tendering. Moreover, a study by Hartley and Huby,[24] which reported on a survey of local authority policy in this area, showed that in about a quarter of over 200 cases observed, contracts were not even awarded to the lowest bidder. It is also important to ensure that franchises are awarded on the Chadwick-Demsetz (C-D) principal rather than to the bidder offering most to the contract awarder.[25] BAA (the monopoly operator of London's major airports) has used the latter principle and was required by the Director General of Fair Trading to switch to C-D for chauffeur-driven car hire in 1984. There can be few economists passing through Heathrow or Gatwick airports who have not bemoaned the presence of a single duty-free operator, rather than a number of competing operators. Their worries must rise now that BAA has announced that the possibility of the ending of duty-free concessions in Europe in 1992 was leading it to consider the purchase of concessions at 15 airports in North America and the Far East—to avoid the loss of 10 percent of its total receipts and a significant slice of its profits, and a need to increase landing charges by 15 to 20 percent to make up the loss.

## Deregulation

A wide range of measures and sectors have been involved in the application of deregulatory instruments in the privatization program. State-owned corporations have suffered removal of statutory monopoly powers (e.g., BT was forced, before sell-off, to open its network to a new licensed competitor, Mercury; the Post Office lost its monopoly on express mail services). Private-sector businesses lost protections afforded by government actions (e.g., the ending of the restrictions on entry in road passenger transport which can be traced back

---

[24] Keith Hartley and Meg Huby, "Contracting-Out in Health and Local Authorities: Prospects, Progress, and Pitfalls," *Public Money* 5, no. 2 (April 1985), pp. 23–26.

[25] Editor's note: As explained above, under the C-D principle, contracts are awarded to suppliers who offer to sell on the most favorable terms to the ultimate consumer.

to the Road Passenger Transport Act of 1930). And there have been miscellaneous measures, such as those ending the legal profession's monopoly over the conveyancing of real estate.

The breadth of issues raised in deregulation is so wide that, unlike subcontracting, it is impossible to identify sufficiently typical cases worth describing in a paper of this nature. One generalization that should probably be made relates to standards of quality. The reason, often the excuse, for many restrictions originally placed on conditions of market supply is related to quality standards more often than to any other matters. Hence, one should be careful about drawing conclusions on price changes alone that might follow deregulation. There are many papers on individual liberalization acts, but the only one general enough to cite is by Thompson,[26] who surveys the experience in four areas—express coaching, telecommunications, airlines, and energy (fuel supply). One important, albeit unsurprising, conclusion was that

> the introduction of competition is worthwhile, but that it requires more than simply the removal of statutes prohibiting it.

Less obvious is the observation that deregulation does not necessarily result in the ousting of a dominant supplier, even when there appear to be no significant economies of scale. The express coaching sector remained dominated by the state-owned National Express after deregulation, but all the same the level of prices had been brought (and held) down substantially as a result of competition.

## Regulating the Natural Monopolies

Perhaps the most crucial test that needs to be applied in an assessment of the results of privatization in Britain, concerns the performance of the now privately owned telecommunications and gas industries, run by the giant corporations BT and BG (and in time to come, electricity and water utilities). That is not to say that these enterprises are clear natural monopolies, though there are unquestionably important sections of their business which are technically unsuitable for competition if costs are to be minimized. It was, however, recognized by the authorities that this was the case, and though exposure to capital market discipline was hoped to bring productive efficiency gains, additional measures were needed to try to ensure that allocative efficiency was not overlooked. It was therefore accepted that, where elements of natural monopoly were present, regulation was necessary in the public (i.e., consumer) interest.

The need for some kind of control is rendered more evident when it is appreciated that the form of transfer of both these utilities was such as to retain

---

[26] David Thompson, "Privatization in the U.K.: Deregulation and the Advantage of Incumbency," *European Economic Review* 31, no. 1/2 (February/March 1987), pp. 368–74 (the quotation is from p. 373).

much larger monopoly units than necessitated by the natural monopoly components. Both BT and BG were sold as single units with their monopoly powers largely intact. The decision to denationalize in such forms can be traced to a number of factors, the most important of which are probably (1) to maximize the revenue from sales, (2) to encourage wider share ownership (see below), and (3) to effect the transfer with the support, rather than the opposition, of the chairmen and boards of the public corporations.[27] Indeed, in some cases monopoly powers were deliberately maintained, even strengthened, to increase the attractiveness of the asset! Advice was not lacking on the key importance of increasing competition above other goals if efficiency gains were wanted,[28] but alternative options, such as regional break-up,[29] were rejected.

New style specialized regulatory agencies have been set up to monitor and control performance of the large privately owned utilities. We examine them shortly. However, we should also note other ways in which the freedom of these corporations is constrained. In the first place, there is the work of existing bodies concerned with competition (i.e., antitrust) policy—the Office of the Director General of Fair Trading and the Monopolies and Mergers Commission. Secondly, there are certain cases where government departments or agencies happen to have special powers (e.g., the CAA exercises very considerable power through its route-authorizing role in respect of airlines). Thirdly, there are cases where the government might be in a position to use its influence as a major customer of the corporation. The Ministry of Defense has such a position vis-à-vis British Aerospace (BAe), for example, and the government is BT's largest customer.[30]

There is one other control mechanism which might be thought relevant to the issue of control over the giant public corporations. This is the existence of shares with special rights, commonly known as "golden shares," which the central government retained in some three-quarters of the privatized corpora-

---

[27] A fourth reason given sometimes, but lacking quite the same plausibility, was that it would be difficult for the stock market to put values on parts of a company when the shares of the parent had not been previously traded.

[28] See, inter alia, Michael Beesley and Stephen Littlechild, "Privatization: Principles, Problems, and Priorities," *Lloyds Bank Review* 149 (July 1983), pp. 1–20; Elizabeth M. Hammond, Dieter R. Helm, and David J. Thompson, "British Gas: Options for Privatization," *Fiscal Studies* 6, no. 4 (November 1985), pp. 1–20; and David Starkie and David Thompson, "London's Airports: The Privatization Options," in *Privatization and Regulation: The U.K. Experience,* ed. John Kay, Colin Mayer, and David Thompson (Oxford: Clarendon Press, 1986), pp. 210–20.

[29] Regional breakups may be advantageous in three ways: exposing enterprises to competition in the market for capital, reducing the scope for cross-subsidization, and allowing for a modicum of product competition around regional boundaries.

[30] Not that there is any presumption that such power would be more likely to be exercised in the consumers', rather than in the government's, interest—if the connivance of the central government in Rank Xerox's discriminatory pricing policy, which benefited taxpayers rather than consumers, is anything to go by.

tions, including BT and BG (but not, surprisingly, BA). The purpose of the golden share provisions is, however, less related to efficiency objectives than to the popular capitalism goal, since they are designed to help small shareholders by limiting the size of individual holdings, often to a maximum of 15 percent. We mention them here, however, because they can have effects on efficiency, though probably the reverse of what is needed to promote competition. This is because they tend to reduce the threat of hostile takeovers, which can be a major, occasionally the only, way in which market forces can be felt. Note, too, that in some cases the government has the right to appoint directors of the denationalized corporations, but it is clear that such a person's responsibilities are intended to be to the company, not to the public. The significance of these matters has been neglected by most commentators, but see Wiltshire[31] and Veljanovski.[32]

## THE NEW STYLE REGULATORY AGENCIES

The model for regulating large national utilities was developed in the first instance for the telecommunications industry, as BT was due for sale in 1984. It has since been applied to BG and BAA, and may be the basis for control of the electricity and water corporations in due course. It followed the appointment by the government of Professor Stephen Littlechild to investigate and make recommendations on the most appropriate control system. Littlechild's report was naturally influenced by U.S. experience using rate-of-return controls, with their concommitant disadvantages of depressing profit incentives and of promoting productive inefficiency through overcapitalization—the well-known A-J effect.[33]

The essential argument for regulating prices rather than profits, put by Littlechild and accepted by the government, is that price control provides incentives for businesses to use such techniques as will maximize productive efficiency as well as profits. Moreover, if the regulator has full knowledge of cost and demand conditions, price controls can induce profit-maximizing monopolists to produce optimum outputs, thereby achieving allocative as well as productive efficiency.[34]

The basis of the control system adopted in Britain has, therefore, been price rather than profits. It has come to be known as (RPI-X) control because it is designed to encourage cost minimization, after allowing for inflation—RPI being the Retail Price Index—and because it sets no limits to profits. The (RPI-

[31] Kenneth W. Wiltshire, *Privatization: The British Experience: An Australian Perspective* (Melbourne: Longman Cheshire, 1987).

[32] Veljanovski, *Selling the State.*

[33] Harvey Averch and Leland L. Johnson, "Behavior of the Firm under Regulatory Constraint," *American Economic Review* 52, no. 5 (December 1962), pp. 1052–69.

[34] In the case of a natural monopoly, a lump-sum subsidy would, of course, also be necessary.

X) system is simple enough conceptually, and would be easy to operate in a simple economy. In the case of regulation of large-scale multiproduct corporations in a world riddled with incomplete data of doubtful reliability, and of uncertainty with regard to the future, the system is proving less than simple to operate, let alone to assess. The main problems with this form of price setting may be explained in the context of control of BT by the Office of Telecommunications (OFTEL), the agency set up in 1984 at the time of transfer.

OFTEL has been required to operate a version of (RPI-X) with X set for five years in the first instance by the Minister responsible,[35] the basis for control being a weighted average of a basket of major internal telephone charges. At the time of writing, OFTEL is reviewing the experience. In 1989, the (RPI-X) rule is due for renewal or modification. The problems involved in operating the system may be summarized by asking the following questions.

1. What is the proper value for X which, in principle, stands for all *unavoidable* increases (e.g., in the prices of inputs)? This involves estimating future changes in total factor productivity. OFTEL describes as "remarkable" the extent to which different and quite independent researchers have produced estimates for the behavior of *past* productivity changes.[36]

2. What is the optimum period for which to set a given price formula? The shorter the period, the closer the rule resembles rate-of-return control, as the regulated firm may not expect to be allowed to enjoy the fruits of increased efficiency. The longer the period, the greater the degree of uncertainty and the greater the chance that the value given to X will prove inappropriate, in the light of changing demand and cost conditions.

3. What prices should be covered by the formula? On the one hand, a weighted average of the prices of only some products leaves room for cross-subsidization within the basket as well as between the basket and services outside. On the other hand, individual price caps smack of over-bureaucratic intervention.

4. How great is the danger that quality will be sacrificed to profitability when a monopolistic firm is subjected to price controls? OFTEL has the task of monitoring quality. It is noteworthy that economists working in this field are on record as saying they believe that monitoring of service quality may, perhaps, be the regulator's main function. In the case of BT, complaints of deterioration of quality of service since privatization have been numerous and well-founded, though there has been evidence of some recent improvements.

---

[35] X was set at 3 percent for BT for the five-year period. It may be compared with 2 percent for BG and 1 percent for BAA. [Editor's note: For example, if X is set at 3 percent and the RPI rises 10 percent, a weighted average increase of 7 percent is permitted for the "basket" of charges.]

[36] A subsidiary question as to whether there is a better *available* deflator than the RPI must surely be answered in the negative.

It has to be said that OFTEL's functions are not confined to administering (RPI-X) but are extremely wide and varied,[37] including the task of monitoring BT's license, which has no fewer than 50 conditions attached to it.[38] One cannot help wondering whether an agency with limited resources can cope with so many problems. Worry may be greater because it is the single person of the Director General of OFTEL who carries the responsibilities. One is led to ask whether he is liable to "capture," to which question there is no easy answer. The first Director General, Bryan Carsberg, is a Professor of Accounting at the London School of Economics, and has developed a reputation for being on the tough side. But he relies heavily on BT for his data. It has to be recognized that BT's profit rate has risen steadily, since denationalization, from 17.5 percent in 1984 to 21.4 percent in 1987 (compared with 19.3 percent in the last year under state ownership). At the same time, BT has not taken full advantage every year of the maximum price rises available to it under the formula—suggesting that the difference between (RPI-X) and rate-of-return control may not be as great as was hoped?

A further relevant feature of the experience of the first four years of operation is that the price structure of the charging scheme used by BT changed very substantially.

The unit price of peak rate long-distance calls, used mainly by business, fell by as much as a third, while that of local calls rose by approximately the same extent. There is more than a suggestion that this followed BT's desire to meet competition in the trunk-call market from a new licensee, Mercury. It is, however, also the case that BT's prices were out of line with costs at the start of the period. Little more can be said at this point of time other than that the government seems to be hoping that a limited duopolistic private sector industry, under the eyes of a novel regulatory agency rule, may produce a more efficient industry than the public sector monopoly. It will probably take as long for a consensus to be reached on whether the result is an improvement, as it will to decide whether the breakup of AT&T in the United States was a success.

## NET BENEFITS OF PRIVATIZATION

We have confined our analysis so far to the question of efficiency and privatization. In order to be able to comment on whether there are net benefits from the program as a whole, we must incorporate some assessment of success with other objectives, and set the total against the costs involved, taking account of

---

[37] Tony Prosser, *Nationalized Industries and Public Control: Legal, Constitutional, and Political Issues* (Oxford: Basil Blackwell, 1986), pp. 90–96.

[38] It is for the Monopolies and Mergers Commission, however, to investigate alleged breaches of license.

distributive side effects. Our coverage will necessarily be incomplete. We shall avoid discussion of any benefits that relate to "freedom," trade union strength, and other essentially political matters. We shall also largely ignore the issue of macromanagement, the PSBR, and use made of the proceeds of asset sales, without in any way suggesting they are unimportant. We concentrate on the goal of popular capitalism, the costs of asset sales, and distributive consequences.

## Popular Capitalism

Earlier in this study we drew attention to the objective of widening share ownership in the population as a whole, and of trying to stimulate shareholding by employees in the companies in which they work. We mentioned, also, the intention to extend privatization to the housing market and, in the wider context of a "property-owning democracy," to encourage owner-occupation among those living in subsidized housing.

We deal first of all with the last of these, since it is the simplest to quantify. In the period up to 1987 approximately a fifth of council house tenants had bought their houses, at discounts related to the length of time they had lived in them, but averaging approximately 50 percent. We refrain from comment on the wisdom of the transfer from a wider perspective, and turn to the major objective of wider share ownership.

If one wishes to promote direct ownership in stock market securities among people who have never held them previously during a period coinciding with massive disposals of publicly owned assets, there are several things one can do. They basically require that the advantages of share ownership should become widely appreciated. This is not easy to achieve overnight. But if you can engineer guaranteed capital gains, and spend enough on advertising them, you are on the right road. If you add inducements of simple appeal—such as offering BT original shareholders discounts off their telephone bills, and loyalty bonuses to those who hold on to their stock for minimum periods—you have the essence of the policy adopted by the government for many of the substantial asset sales, though there were other devices, such as giving preference to small shareholders in allotting issues which were oversubscribed. The importance of the advertising should not be overlooked. The major issues of BT and BG stock were accompanied by unprecedented advertising campaigns, including the legendary "Tell Sid" slogan, which successfully created the impression that it was folly not to apply for shares in BT.

In the bull market when most of the share issues were made, it was not difficult almost to guarantee immediate capital gains, given control of the offer price of shares. The realized premia on the first day's trading on the Stock Exchange reached over 80 percent in the case of BT (1984), 68 percent for BA (1987), and percentages varying between 20 and 70 for other sales before October 1987. All major issues in the years up to that date were, more or less, heavily oversubscribed, as increasing numbers of people applied for each public issue of stock.[39]

Seen from the viewpoint of increase in the numbers of persons holding shares in joint-stock companies, there is little doubt that the privatization program of asset sales achieved its target. The proportion of the adult population who were shareholders rose from 7 percent in the 1979 to over 20 percent in 1988, most of the increase taking place in 1984 and 1987. Also successful must be judged movement toward the target of increased employee ownership in their companies. Over 90 percent of employees participated in buying shares in the privatization offers in BT, BG, and BA, though it must be added that employee participation was being aided generally by tax relief.

Viewed somewhat differently, the success with popular capitalism is muted. Four points can be made. First, the share of the stock of total equities held by persons, as distinct from institutions such as pension funds, continued to fall. It had dropped from 54 percent to 28 percent over the decades of the 60s and 70s. The fall continued because, although many more people held shares by 1980, the vast majority held very few, while the value of shares owned by the institutions rose rapidly.[40] In the second place, well over half of personal shareholders, mainly those starting share ownership with one of the privatization issues, owned shares in only a single company. Thirdly, the number of shareholders in several, especially of the early, privatization cases, dropped dramatically, presumably with profit-taking. For example, of the 158,000 initial shareholders in BAe in 1981, only 27,000 remained by the following year. Likewise, the 63,000 shareholders in AI had dropped to 6,500 by 1986. At the same time, other shareholdings were holding up (e.g., there were still 1.5 million holders of BT stock in 1986 compared to just over 2 million at flotation date in 1984). The fourth comment that may be made about success with popular capitalism is that wider share ownership might inhibit benefits for efficiency arising from exposure to capital markets, since greater dispersion increases the power of directors vis-à-vis shareholders.

## Transaction Costs of Asset Sales

Asset sales of the kind described in the previous section are not made without costs, direct and indirect, the estimation of which is extremely difficult. Direct

---

[39] Some idea of the extent of popularity of issues in the middle period (up to "Black Monday" [when a stock market crash occurred in October 1987]) may be gauged by the extent of (illegal) multiple applications for shares. One Member of Parliament was convicted of the offense, and one self-employed accountant made the headlines with 700 applications for shares in British Gas, 477 in British Airways, 533 in Rolls Royce, and 710 in British Airports.

[40] Paul A. Grout, "The Wider Share Ownership Program," *Fiscal Studies* 8, no. 3 (August 1987), pp. 59–74.

costs comprise underwriting and other fees to City[41] institutions and advertising—a very heavy item with some of the largest issues such as BT. Indirect costs, less easily estimated, are accumulated debts written off prior to flotations; discounts at which shares are offered for sale; and any special treatments which increase prospective profitability (e.g., the award of a defense contract in the long-delayed run up to the sale of BA).

Some of these cost components are, in part, trade-offs for wider share ownership. Many of them are unquantifiable with any serious claim to reliability, and attention has been focused in the City and the press on the size of discounts which fixed-price offers for sale implied. The Public Accounts Committee of the House of Commons also described asset sales as being at "unduly cautious levels." Independent estimates have been made of the costs of such sales. A recent one concluded that while the direct costs of the privatization exercise have not been substantially out of line with those in the private sector, "discounts on offers for sale of public assets (thus) seem well in excess of the average for private issues."

It must be pointed out that all assets have not been sold at fixed prices. There have been a few, relatively small, employee/management buyouts and placements, though these are naturally unsuitable for sales of very large corporations such as BT and BG. Some sales have been by tender, though virtually all have been undersubscribed, producing negative discounts. This might suggest that some of the discounts on fixed-price offers were smaller than they would otherwise seem. Support for this view comes from the argument that setting a market-clearing price is more than ordinarily difficult for the issue of shares in a business owned and run by the state, and whose future profitability may depend heavily on the functioning of a new-style regulatory agency.

Against this view it must be allowed that particular market circumstances at the time of sale may well have depressed some tenders (e.g., the volatile oil market). Another explanation of the poor tender performance is the practice of allowing City institutions both to tender and to act as underwriters, giving them a positive inducement to refrain from bidding—effectively turning the tender into a placement among underwriters.[42] The same authors also ask why the government should not consider itself able (with the Bank of England's help) to act as its own underwriter.[43] They advocate an alternative method of asset sales—the issue of an equity tapstock, which could be released as and when market conditions seemed favorable.

---

[41] Editor's note: "The City" is London's financial district, analogous to New York's "Wall Street."

[42] Roger Buckland and Edward W. Davis, "Privatization Techniques and the PSBR," *Fiscal Studies* 5, no. 3 (August 1984), pp. 44–53.

[43] The government was under pressure to be this when the sale of an asset (the state's holding in British Petroleum) came to market just after the stock market crash of October 1987, and when the underwriters were, partly, left off the hook.

## Distributive Consequences

Privatization, as we now know, has multiple, and partly competing, objectives. Our final task in this study is to consider the distributive consequences of the program. Some such are deliberate; others, by-products. We include both, without distinction. Without, also, making the slightest claim to be comprehensive, the following observations about possible gainers and losers may be made.

Among the gainers, the following groups stand out as clear winners— council house tenants who bought their houses at substantial discounts,[44] and persons allotted shares in denationalized companies sold at discounts.

Other gainers are employees in those same companies who were given priority share applications; and financial and other institutions allotted shares and/or not ungenerously rewarded for their services as underwriters, etc. (including overseas allotees in some cases).

A different set of gainers are consumers in industries favored by the operation of liberalization (e.g., long-distance bus passengers) and of the regulatory system (e.g., business telephone users). A similar group are employees, probably mainly professional and skilled workers, whose pay was pushed up by forces of competition or by the way in which the regulatory system worked. Perhaps it is not too cynical to count the government itself as a gainer, because the privatization program seems to have turned out to be an election winner.

Among the losers, parallel groups may be distinguished. First, the general body of taxpayers whose loss may be measured by the extent of asset sale discounts (compensated though they may be in other ways).[45] Secondly, we find losers among consumers of products of industries where efficiency declined and/or of others not favored by the regulatory process (e.g., domestic telephone users). A third set of losers are employees in state-owned industries which lost the protection of a degree of monopoly power (e.g., in refuse collection). Finally, and for consistency, a cynical view would count opposition political parties who lost two elections after privatization in the losing group.

---

[44] Interestingly, the increase in the proportion of the population owning their own houses should make the distribution of personal wealth look more equal. In a celebrated early study, the notably smaller proportion that did so in the United Kingdom compared to the United States turned out to be an important explanation of the greater degree of observed wealth inequality in the former country. See Harold F. Lydall and John B. Lansing, "A Comparison of the Distribution of Personal Income and Wealth in the United States and Great Britain," *American Economic Review* 49, no. 1 (March 1959), pp. 43–67.

[45] The sale of BT alone has been estimated to have cost just under £65 for each British citizen (which implies a figure of well over £100 per taxpayer). See Mayer and Meadowcroft, "Selling Public Assets."

## PRIVATIZATION: THE LESSONS

The privatization program in Britain began less than 10 years ago and is not yet complete. Serious estimates of its complex impact are only now being attempted. Nevertheless, it is possible even at this early stage to suggest a few, limited lessons to be learned from the experience.

1. The most likely source of gains probably comes from increasing competition arising from subcontracting and deregulation.
2. The least likely source of gains (or possibly of losses) comes from the transfer of large state-owned public utilities as single going concerns.
3. The main reason for (2) above is to be found in the government's attempt to use privatization to achieve several conflicting objectives—popular capitalism, maximizing revenue from sales, and efficiency.
4. Greater attention has, on the whole, been paid to improving productive than allocative efficiency—understandably, as easier to monitor.
5. The verdict on regulation, British style, lies open. There is almost certainly some benefit from having an independent agency to monitor output quality of natural monopolies, but the apparent attractiveness of price (RPI-X) over rate-of-return control remains unproven, either way.
6. The privatization program has had complex distributive consequences, both intentional and accidental. Inter alia, redistribution has occurred from general taxpayers to newly allotted shareholders of issues floated at discounts, and to purchasers of council houses. (This ignores what is done with the proceeds of asset sales.) Sundry consumers and employees must have gained, or lost, depending on relative movements of product and factor prices following asset sales, liberalizations, and the functioning of the regulatory system.
7. The *prima facie* view that ownership *per se* is a secondary matter is neither denied nor confirmed; but less interference in day-to-day running of a business by the state is probably still a major key to the door of higher efficiency.

To end on an optimistic note, present plans for the sale of the national electricity assets suggest that the government may have learned lesson 2.

## Chapter Eight

# The Swedish Model: Relevant for Other European Countries?*

*Lei Delsen*

*and*

*Tom van Veen*[1]

*The Swedish economy has long been regarded as a distinctive case of a capitalist regulated market economy in three respects.*

*Sweden has an ambitious "welfare state" which provides generous social insurance and pension benefits, essentially free health care, and education at no charge at all levels (with stipends for post-secondary students). In Sweden, total public expenditures (comprising government purchases of goods and services as well as transfer payments) are equal to about two thirds of the gross national product. In turn, tax rates are high. For example, payroll taxes are equal to more than one third of the payroll, and the marginal personal income tax rate is 40 percent for the average industrial worker.*

*Also, the Swedish government seeks to keep unemployment low through a combination of fiscal and monetary policy measures sustaining aggregate demand, on the one hand, and labor market measures such as placement services and retraining, on the other. Thus, frictional umemployment of 1 to 2 percent of the labor force has been considered acceptable, but the overall rate of unemployment has not exceeded 4 percent even in recessions.*

*Another feature of the "Swedish model" has been highly centralized collective bargaining by representatives of workers and employers. The aim has been to reach reasonable wage settlements with a minimum of labor disputes. To preserve the international competitiveness of Swedish industry, the general principle was established that—in terms of average annual percentage increments—wage in-*

* Reprinted by permission from the *British Journal of Industrial Relations* 30, no. 1 (March 1992), pp. 83–105, with the omission of tables and references to unpublished papers and limited-circulation publications. Lei Delsen is Associate Professor of Applied Economics at Nijmegen University, the Netherlands. Tom van Veen is Associate Professor of Economics at the University of Limburg, the Netherlands.

[1] The authors would like to thank R. Meidner and H. Gospel and two anonymous referees for their comments on an earlier version of the paper.

*creases should not exceed the sum of labor productivity growth and the rise in export prices.*

*In this chapter, the authors consider the second and third elements of the "Swedish model"—government labor policy and centralized collective bargaining.*

*Swedish labor market policy is characterized by the principle of "the right to work" rather than "the right to income." Thus, Sweden pursues "active" labor market measures such as job placement services, training and retraining, relocation grants, and subsidies to private firms to create jobs. Although Sweden has a generous unemployment compensation program, benefits may be stopped immediately if a person refuses to take a job or a training assignment.*

*For decades, strong national employers' and workers' organizations undertook centralized negotiations to keep wage increases within the limits of "macroeconomic balance" determined by the inflation rate and the trade balance. Employers favored central bargaining in the expectation that it would retard wage growth and avoid strikes. Unions believed centralized bargaining would help achieve a policy of "equal pay for equal work," regardless of the specific financial position of a firm, and thus reduce wage differentials across enterprises, industries, regions, sexes, and age groups. This centralized wage bargaining supported an incomes policy that restrained wage growth despite the low rate of unemployment resulting from the government's labor market measures. However, since the mid-1980s, wage bargaining has become more decentralized, as employers, especially producers of exports, seek smaller wage increases and workers pursue larger wage increases for particular industries and enterprises.*

*The authors compare the performance of Sweden versus other European countries with respect to unemployment, economic growth, inflation, and inequality in pay. The authors conclude that other nations could reduce (especially, long-term) unemployment by adopting some of Sweden's active labor market measures. But the authors question whether centralized collective bargaining can be achieved and can succeed in curbing wage increases.*

## INTRODUCTION

By the 1970s, supply-side theory had become something of a new economic orthodoxy. From the supply-side perspective, labor market inflexibility explains mass unemployment. In this context the presumably greater flexibility of the labor market in the United States was seen as an explanation of its superior employment record relative to European economies. Many European employers' organizations and public authorities came to believe, in fact, that flexibility and deregulation are a useful weapon in the fight against unemployment. Although many have adopted policies in this direction, unemployment rates in Europe seem to have stabilized at a high level. Unlike most European countries, Sweden, which is highly regulated, does reasonably well in employment terms. The country seems to be in an enviable position. In addition to the low unemployment rate, another remarkable aspect of employment in Sweden is the high labor force participation rate. Recently, however, the Swedish model has been the subject of debate both inside and outside Sweden. Inflation has risen, and economic growth and the balance of payments have deteriorated.

This has led to discussion about the stability of the system. The study goes into this debate. The central question addressed is: What can be learned from the Swedish experience by other European countries suffering from high (long-term) unemployment?

This study is organized as follows. First, the main characteristics of the Swedish model are outlined. Next, some major outcomes that have been achieved are presented and compared with those in other European countries. In the final section, the relevance of (parts of) the Swedish model for other European countries is examined.

## THE MAIN CHARACTERISTICS OF THE SWEDISH MODEL

The term *Swedish model* has some very different connotations. It sometimes refers to the fact that the Swedish economy is a cross between a market economy and a state-regulated economy—a combination of private ownership in the production sphere and collectivization of consumption, and a highly centralized wage policy with powerful confederations of unions and employers' organizations as the main agents, based on the principle of solidarity. Another way to define the Swedish model is to take as a starting point its two dominant goals: full employment and equality. The highly developed labor market policy and the exceptionally large public sector in Sweden resulted from the commitment to these goals. In a narrow sense, the Swedish model can be seen as a model for combining full employment and price stability by a restrictive general economic policy complemented by selective measures for maintaining high employment and investments. Others refer to the Swedish model as a negotiation/consensus model in the labor market. Following Ahlén,[2] we define the Swedish model as a combination of an unusual labor relations system with a sophisticated bargaining approach founded on macroeconomic concerns.

Sweden has a high rate of unionization and employer organization. It probably has the highest (overall) unionization rate in the world (80–85 percent). During the first two postwar decades, the main players in the Swedish model (apart from the government) were the Swedish Trade Union Confederation (LO),[3] the largest employees' organization (primarily blue-collar), and the Swedish Employers' Confederation (SAF), the main employers' organization in the private sector. The LO represents some 90 percent of the blue-collar workers, and the SAF represents about 42,000 firms in private industry, including all of the largest firms. In the 1970s, with the expansion of (public-sector) services, came the rise in prominence of public-sector and white-collar unions, and the dominance of the LO-SAF axis came to an end. By 1978 the

---

[2] Kristina Ahlén, "Swedish Collective Bargaining under Pressure: Inter-Union Rivalry and Income Policies," *British Journal of Industrial Relations* 27, no. 3 (November 1989), p. 331.

[3] The LO has for decades cooperated closely with the Social Democratic Party (SAP)—a fact that has contributed to the strength of the reformist labor movement in Sweden.

Swedish Municipal Workers' Union was the largest union in the LO.[4] The Central Organization of Salaried Employees (TCO) is the largest central white-collar workers' organization, representing about 75 percent of white-collar workers in both private and public sectors.

The Swedish model is based on the first basic agreement signed by the LO and SAF in 1938, but has, in fact, its original roots in the "December compromise" of 1906 between the SAF and LO.[5] The Saltsjöbaden[6] Agreement of 1938 later laid down procedures for negotiations between employees' and employers' organizations and placed restrictions on industrial action. It constituted the cornerstone of the centralized Swedish model in which strong national organizations negotiated freely without government intervention and assumed responsibility for keeping wages within the limits of macroeconomic balance. Most problems between labor and management were resolved through negotiations and agreements. As a result, there were relatively few laws governing conditions on the labor market until the late 1970s.

The Swedish model was developed by Gösta Rehn and Rudolf Meidner, two economists associated with the LO. Their main proposition was that "labor market policy should no longer be simply a matter of establishing labor exchanges to bring together the unemployed and unfilled jobs, and paying unemployment benefits to those without a job. Instead it should be developed into a preventive policy instrument, part of an integrated model of economic, pay, and labor market policy." In the 1950s and the 1960s these ideas were adopted by the LO and by the ruling Social Democratic Party (SAP). The aims of this integrated model were full employment, price stability, economic growth, and a fair distribution of wages. Instead of the traditional measures used by Keynesian-oriented policymakers, they made a plea for an active labor market policy in order to reach these goals. In the original outline, a central point was that the responsibility for full employment and economic stability should rest with the government, while the unions, together with the employers' organizations, should be responsible for the process of wage formation. Below we summarize the main characteristics of this Rehn–Meidner model and those added in the course of time.[7]

## Centralized Wage Bargaining

Sweden has traditionally been regarded as having one of the most centralized systems of wage bargaining among OECD countries.[8] It was believed that

---

[4] Ahlén, "Swedish Collective Bargaining," pp. 331–32.

[5] It meant that the LO accepted the principle that the employer is entitled to direct and allot work, and to hire labor, including nonorganized labor. In return, the SAF promised that the employers would respect the employees' free right of association and negotiation.

[6] Editor's note: Saltsjöbaden is a town in Sweden.

[7] "Survey: The Swedish Economy," *The Economist,* March 3, 1990, pp. 5–6; and Guy Standing, *Unemployment and Labor Market Flexibility: Sweden* (Geneva: International Labor Office, 1988).

[8] Editor's note: The member countries of the Organization for Economic Cooperation and Development (OECD), located in Paris, are Australia, Austria, Belgium, Canada, Denmark, Finland,

centralized bargaining could deliver a lower aggregate wage increase in line with what the economy could afford. Swedish unions supported this centralized wage bargaining process because it facilitated the policy of wage solidarity (see following subsections). Swedish employers were also in favor of central bargaining, since they believed it would prevent wage inflation and guarantee peace. In fact, they were the driving force behind the first central negotiations, which resulted in a settlement in 1952. At central level, negotiations resulted in *framework agreements,* which set the level of wage-cost increases (i.e., total costs for the factor labor, thus not only wages but also payroll taxes, overtime work, and so forth, and costs of improvement of working conditions or working time reduction) to be granted. Next, the framework agreements were supplemented by industry contracts which specified how the centrally agreed arrangements were to be allocated among employers. Most collective bargaining contracts in Sweden were based on agreements between the SAF and LO or PTK (Bargaining Cartel of Salaried Employees in Industry and Services), and between their counterparts in the national and local government sectors. Finally, companies negotiated with local branches of the unions about the terms as applied to the individual. Throughout the duration of the central contract (1–3 years), the parties pledged to respect the peace obligation, which debarred them from resorting to industrial action to settle disputes over matters regulated in the agreement. In the 1980s, however, centralized wage bargaining came under increasing pressure and eventually broke down.

Throughout the postwar period, the labor market in Sweden has been well known as highly stable and harmonious in comparison with most other European countries. Few working days have been lost because of disputes. However, after the 1980 conflict the Swedish industrial relations model has been the subject of a growing debate. In 1983 the Engineering Employers' Association (VF) signed a separate agreement with the Metal Workers' Union. This impetus for change came from the employers' side. It was the SAF which, in line with the government's wishes, insisted on centralized bargaining in the 1950s, but it was the VF, the leading member association in the SAF, that signaled the break in 1983. The LO and SAF agreed that there would be no centralized negotiations in 1984 (for the first time since 1956). In 1985 and 1986 there was again strong pressure for industry-level bargaining. The 1985 LO-SAF agreement was only a recommendation. In the 1988 bargaining round, full decentralization returned. The LO's role was reduced to coordinating general demands and holding weekly meetings during negotiations to discuss strategies. The demands for decentralized negotiations came chiefly from industries such as metalworking, which had a large export propensity and were highly dependent on the international market. The need to restructure to remain competitive, as well as the current high profits in many of these firms, has created the need to

---

France, Germany, Greece, Iceland, Ireland, Italy, Japan, Luxembourg, the Netherlands, New Zealand, Norway, Portugal, Spain, Sweden, Switzerland, Turkey, the United Kingdom, and the United States.

adjust remuneration to fit market conditions, while encouraging greater productivity. There has always been a sizable element of wage drift,[9] but in recent years wage drift accounted for more than half of the total wage increase. In addition, the LO and SAF failed once again to agree on a national norm for wage increases in 1990, with the unions refusing to restrain wage claims despite the deteriorating economic situation.

Until the current phase of labor shortages and high profits ends, which is unlikely for some time, the likelihood of a return to totally centralized negotiations seems small.[10] Even if the 1991 bargaining round leads toward a central agreement providing for moderate pay rises, they will be undermined by correspondingly higher wage drift. However, decentralized wage bargaining, advocated by the employers, may backfire and create an even bigger upward pressure on wages, as recent bargaining results show. Wage drift has reached record levels in 1990. The unemployment–inflation dilemma has turned out to be the most vulnerable part of the Swedish model. It is not only the employers' new wage policy that confounds wage solidarity: it is also the unions' inner tensions that need resolving.[11]

## "Solidaristic" Wage Policy

The framework agreements determined the room for wage-cost increases. With regard to wages, the wage policy of solidarity played an important role. According to this policy, all employees should receive equal pay for equal work, regardless of the particular financial position of their employer. The interindustry and interenterprise link between productivity and wages should be broken, and this should produce a more equitable distribution of wages. Gradually wage rate differentials should disappear among industries, enterprises, regions, sexes, and age groups. However, as it has worked out in practice, there have been some other consequences as well. Less profitable companies were unable to pay these wages and were forced to reduce their work forces or go out of business altogether. More profitable firms were paying wages below the level that they could actually afford. They could not attract additional labor by paying higher wages, and wage-cost inflation was supposed to be avoided; the excess profits could be used for new investments. Although small wage differentials could inhibit labor mobility, the model's architects argued that in their model narrow wage differentials would actually stimulate mobility. The model has been perceived as a way of accelerating structural adjustment and economic growth. The solidaristic wage policy harmed low-productivity sectors by

---

[9] Editor's note: Wage drift is an increase in the effective rate of pay per unit of labor input, resulting from arrangements outside central agreements. For example, wage drift may occur because of company or plant bargaining, larger differentials for work on the second or third shift, or greater bonus or productivity payments.

[10] Ahlén, "Swedish Collective Bargaining," pp. 334–35.

[11] Ahlén, "Swedish Collective Bargaining," p. 344.

raising the relative wages of workers in these sectors. It favored high-productivity ones by holding back wage growth and speeding up the transfer of employment from old labor-intensive sectors to modern, technologically advanced, capital-intensive sectors. The solidaristic wage policy presupposed a coordination of wage negotiations not only among the LO-affiliated unions but also between the LO and the white-collar confederations.

In the 1980s profit-sharing, productivity-based deals, and employee "convertible loans"[12] have undermined the solidaristic wage policy. Considerable wage drift and profit-sharing schemes are the alternatives for profitable companies to use their high capacity to let their employees share in the firms' profits—both alternatives running counter to the solidaristic wage policy. It is obvious that these consequences of the Swedish wage policy so far have remained unsolved. Even more important in this respect have been the local wage negotiations, which tend to restore wage differentials. Centralized bargaining and the solidaristic wage policy are mutually dependent. However, the LO has now proposed a somewhat modified wage solidarity policy. The guiding principle is to be "equal pay for equal work: different pay for different work," and thus establishes that some pay differentials are fair.[13]

## Active Labor Market Policy

With centralized wage bargaining and a solidaristic wage policy, a special kind of dynamics arose in the economy, namely, a combination of a large demand for and a large supply of labor. Because demand stemmed from high-productivity sectors and supply emanated from low-productivity sectors, matching problems on the labor market could easily occur. To tackle this problem, an active labor market policy was developed. This policy aims at enhancing the mobility of workers who lose their jobs, without relying totally on the price mechanism. It is supposed to perform the role of wage differentials in balancing labor supply and demand and in achieving full employment. A great variety of measures have been developed under the heading of "active labor market policy" (e.g., relocation grants, training or retraining programs, temporary public-sector schemes, and private-sector recruitment subsidies intended to create jobs). This policy stemmed from the idea that the longer people are inactive in the labor market, the more difficult it is to get them back to work. The Swedish model is characterized by the "right to work" model instead of the "right to income" model. Another effect of the model is that the workers would, at least theoretically, find new employment in more viable enterprises and sectors, and higher employment and wage levels would thus be attained in the longer run.

The Swedish model is best known for its active labor market policy. There

---

[12] Editor's note: In British terminology, a "convertible loan" security is a debenture which the holder can convert into ordinary stock shares.

[13] Ahlén, "Swedish Collective Bargaining," p. 343.

is one budget for all measures, and the policy is coordinated by the National Labor Market Board (AMP), in which employers' organizations, employees' organizations, and the government participate. Such an approach guarantees a strong interdependency of all measures. Unemployment is dealt with as follows. First, the labor exchange tries to find a job. It operates with caseloads of 15–30 unemployed persons per member of staff, compared with, for example, 375 in Britain, 370 in West Germany, and 160 in the Netherlands. Unlike most European countries, in Sweden all vacancies and planned layoffs have to be notified to the employment service, so that it has a thorough understanding of the local labor market.[14] If the labor exchange cannot find a job, a training program is often organized. Where workers are declared redundant, hard-to-place workers are sent to high-quality training courses—even *before* they become unemployed in some cases.[15] Thus, economic change is welcomed as an opportunity to provide experienced workers for the industries of the future. If workers have not been placed within six months, employers recruiting them are offered a 50 percent wage subsidy over a six-month period. If this program does not get them a job, workers are entitled to unemployment benefits. These benefits are not open-ended, but are paid for a maximum of 300 days and are subject to a strict work test to discourage scroungers. If a recipient refuses to take a training place or a job, benefits may be stopped immediately.

Sweden has one of the most generous unemployment benefit systems in the world. However, it has also strict eligibility rules. If all these measures fail, the public sector (mainly local authorities) acts as the employer of last resort. It provides work for up to six months, mostly in construction or the caring services. Anyone whose benefit entitlement has run out is entitled to such work by law. This approach contrasts sharply with other European countries. Sweden, however, is not soft touch for the jobless. A vital ingredient of Sweden's success is that it combines the carrot—the promise of training or a job—with a stick.

## A Restrictive Fiscal Policy

Centralized wage bargaining with a solidaristic wage policy and active labor market policy kept unemployment low and aggregate demand high in the economy; thus, the danger of inflation could be round the corner. Therefore another

---

[14] Owing to the fact that notification of vacancies is obligatory for employers, the proportion of all job openings notified to the Public Employment Service is as high as 2/3 in Sweden. Similar laws exist in Belgium, France, Italy, and Spain, though apparently with less effect. The corresponding share varies between 1/10 and 1/6 for Austria, Canada, the Netherlands, and Switzerland. It is 1/4 for France and 1/3 for Australia, Germany, and the United Kingdom. See OECD, *Labor Market Policies in the 1990s* (Paris, 1990), pp. 27 and 89.

[15] Labor market training is not an alternative to work; it is meant to make work possible. In part, its effectiveness depends on the quality of the labor market information on which individual training decisions are based. A large coverage of vacancy information may therefore be crucial.

element of the Swedish model is a restrictive fiscal policy. Budget disequilibria were adjusted in the short term. The Swedish model was known for the high tax rates. (Personal income tax had a top rate of 72 percent; the corporate tax was 57 percent.) Moreover, progressive taxation was essential to finance the Swedish "welfare capitalism," implying a large and growing public sector. In the model, economic growth and investment were to be left to private enterprises. In essence, the model was based on the assumption that, whereas individual firms could be efficient, the market system itself would not be. Although profits were heavily taxed, "excess" profits put into special "investment funds" or "renewal funds" were not taxed, channeling company profits into regional investment, investment in the education and training of workers, or new technology.

## Policy of Selective Economic Growth

As can be deduced from the foregoing points, the Swedish model corrected the results of the free market system. Apart from the points already mentioned, a policy of selective economic growth was used. This policy aimed at the development of subordinated regions and provision of goods that would otherwise not be supplied in sufficient amounts (socially necessary services).

## Scandinavian Inflation Model

The original Rehn–Meidner model was incomplete, insofar as there was no mechanism for determining the level or rate of change of prices or wages. The Scandinavian inflation model was a policy guideline for collective bargaining. The production process was divided into an "exposed," export-oriented *tradable* goods sector and a "sheltered" domestic goods sector. Wages in the exposed sector were supposely set by reference to its productivity growth and internationally determined price increases. The exposed sector acted as a wage leader for the wages in the sheltered sector, with prices being determined as a markup on unit labor costs.[16]

The realism and practical application of the Scandinavian inflation model were undermined during the 1970s by the emergence of the public sector as the new wage leader. Public-sector jobs expanded to include over 35 percent of the work force. In 1987 this model was reformulated by the LO, TCO, and SAF. The new model adds adjustments for international economic factors that the previous model had failed to take into account (factors that affect competitiveness, such as changes in the rate of exchange or in the value of the dollar). The thesis was that the trend toward decentralization had to be reversed, because the system's stability depends on centralized wage bargaining that can permit macro wage flexibility. According to the new model, the economy is divided

---

[16] Standing, *Unemployment*, pp. 46–47.

into three sectors, called "competitive," "private sheltered," and "public sheltered." It specified that bargaining results of the largest industries in the international tradable goods sector should determine pay increases in the rest of the economy and that pay developments in the tradable goods sector should be determined by productivity growth and international price developments in that sector. In this way, pay developments could be kept within the limits the country could afford. The model continues the tradition of sophisticated labor market thinking, but like its predecessor has little practical utility. Locally produced wage drift remains an intractable problem.[17]

## Wage-Earner Funds

The wage-earner funds can be seen as an extension of the solidaristic wage policy. As a consequence of the latter, large profitable companies were gaining extra profits. In 1976 the LO Congress adopted Meidner's proposal for wage-earner funds, to be financed by these extra profits which arose as a result of employees refraining from claiming higher wages in accordance with the principles of solidaristic wage policy. The basic idea was that the capital should remain within the firms but the ownership should successively be transferred to the employees as a collective. Collective profit sharing was seen as a means of making wage restraint more acceptable to workers who might otherwise have seen high profits as a reason for pushing for higher wages. In December 1983 Parliament passed the Employment Investment Fund Bill. Five regional wage-earner funds of very limited size were introduced in 1984. The employers still strongly resist these funds. SAF maintains that profit sharing by the individual is to be preferred. The nonsocialist parties have said they will repeal the legislation once their government returns to office.[18]

## WHAT HAS BEEN ACHIEVED

### Full Employment

Unemployment remains high in many European countries. In Sweden the unemployment rate is well below that of other countries. During the second half of the 1970s it was about 2 percent. It peaked in 1983 (2.9 percent), was a mere 1.4 percent in 1989, and is currently running at about 2 percent. However, skill shortages rose sharply during 1988, reaching their highest level since 1970.[19] The employment–population ratio may serve as an indicator for the utilization of labor resources. This ratio in Sweden, already the highest in the world, has

---

[17] Ahlén, "Swedish Collective Bargaining," and Standing, *Unemployment*.

[18] Richard B. Peterson, "Swedish Collective Bargaining—A Changing Scene," *British Journal of Industrial Relations* 25, no. 1 (March 1987), pp. 31–48; and Standing, *Unemployment*, pp. 139–43.

[19] OECD, *Employment Outlook* (Paris, 1989), p. 21.

continued to grow, while it has fallen in all the main European Community (EC) countries.[20] Sweden probably has the highest rate of labor force participation (82.6 percent in 1988) among major industrial countries. Furthermore, the female labor force participation rate is very high (80.3 percent in 1988). However, when the hours actually worked are taken into account, the utilization rate in Sweden is only a little higher than that of Canada or the United States. This is caused by two factors: (1) Swedish workers are, more often than other workers, "with a job but not at work"; and (2) there are more part-time workers in Sweden.[21] Sickness absenteeism amounts to more than 13 percent for blue-collar workers and about 6 percent for white-collar workers. In addition, absenteeism caused by parental leave and job training must be added.

In spite of the need to improve the adaptability and efficiency of the Swedish labor market, the composition of labor market policy up to 1987 did not give the impression that more emphasis was being put on supply-side-oriented measures. During the 1970s there was a rapid increase in demand-oriented measures.[22] New subsidies were provided to companies to help keep workers in employment. These included financial assistance for stockpiling, in-plant training, and temporary employment subsidies. In 1982, with the return to the government of the Social Democrats, there was a move toward serving the needs of employers directly. A new emphasis was put on "placement efficiency," that is, on a strengthening of employment offices to help fill job vacancies in companies quickly and efficiently. Practice shows that such an approach is effective. It reduces the duration of unfilled vacancies as well as the likelihood of mismatch placements that lead to subsequent unemployment.[23] To counteract rapidly increasing unemployment, a number of labor market policy measures were implemented. From the end of 1982, the number of temporary jobs (relief work) increased; in particular, there was a targeting on youth and disabled workers. For other displaced workers, unemployment benefits had become more significant. Standing concludes that during the 1970s there was a slow erosion of the "right to work" principle and a shift toward the "right to income" principle.[24] This continued into the 1980s, despite strong efforts to reverse the trend.

Sweden's success in achieving full employment and a high level of labor force participation has been due in large measure to its active labor market policy. Also, the tax structure encourages high (part-time) female labor force

---

[20] Richard Layard, "European Unemployment: Cause or Cure?" (Discussion Paper no. 368; London School of Economics, Center for Labor Economics, 1989), p. 19.

[21] Chris de Neubourg, *Unemployment, Labor Slack, and Labor Market Accounting: Theory, Evidence, and Policy* (Amsterdam: North-Holland Publishing Company, 1988), p. 99.

[22] Supply-oriented measures are defined as those designed to improve matching, geographical and occupational mobility, and rehabilitation. Demand-oriented measures are temporary jobs, regional measures, employment for the handicapped, and other employment-creation measures.

[23] Standing, *Unemployment*.

[24] Standing, *Unemployment*, p. 103.

participation, in that married women working part-time are treated most favorably.[25] Other facilities, such as part-time parental leave, child care, and part-time early retirement, also contribute to the high female labor force participation rate.

The special characteristic of Swedish labor market policies as compared with those of other European countries is not the size of the total expenditures, but their composition. Despite the fact that Sweden's overall budget is no higher than that of other European states, the share of active labor market policy in total labor market expenditures is around 70 percent. Around 30 percent is spent on unemployment benefits. In most European countries this division of expenditures is reversed.[26] It has been claimed that Sweden is thus investing in competence, while other countries are investing in unemployment.

## Long-Term Unemployment

From the beginning of 1984, efforts have been made to increase measures designed to counteract long-term unemployment and youth unemployment, and thereby limit the need for relief work and unemployment benefits. A new recruitment grant has been introduced, aiming at facilitating recruitment in the manufacturing industry. In January 1984 the government also introduced the Youth Team Act for 18–19-year-olds who register as unemployed. This guarantees a public-sector job for four hours a day. In principle, the right to a youth team job replaces the right to unemployment benefits. The tendency to direct measures to the long-term unemployed was accentuated when a recruitment grant for employment by county and municipal councils was introduced in January 1985. The reorientation of the labor market policies toward the long-term unemployed also entailed giving preference to the long-term unemployed in placement in ordinary policy measures. Furthermore, special programs and efforts for the long-term unemployed were introduced, such as individual follow-up and counseling; job clubs aimed at strengthening self-confidence, motivation, and job search; cooperation with local trade unions; and so forth.

Some critics argue that the active labor market policy is just unemployment in disguise. However, even if all those on such schemes are included, the total jobless rate is just over 5 percent—still below that of most European countries. In 1988, 3.7 percent of the Swedish labor force was involved in labor market programs. Yet this misses the real point of the measures, namely, to keep the unemployed in touch with the labor market, to improve their chances of employment, and to prevent long-term joblessness. In 1988 only about 8

---

[25] OECD, *Employment Outlook* (Paris, 1990), pp. 163–69.

[26] Since the programs vary with the unemployment situation, the best way to measure a country's commitment to the active labor market policy is to measure expenditures per unemployed person (relative to output per person). This degree of commitment varies considerably, with Sweden doing much more than any other country, and West Germany doing more than any other EC country. [Sweden is not a member of the EC.] See Layard, "European Unemployment."

percent of Sweden's unemployed were jobless for more than a year, compared with 50 percent on average in EC countries. The hysteresis effect is thereby also counteracted.[27] Effects of human capital losses and signaling[28] are minimized. The differences in unemployment rates mainly reflect differences in the duration of unemployment, rather than in the proportion of people who become unemployed. Since 1979 unemployment in the EC countries has grown mainly because of the rise in duration, rather than a rise in inflow.

## Economic Growth and Inflation

Sweden's economic situation, like that of a number of other Western European countries, worsened after the oil crises of 1973 and 1979. Subsidies were pumped into industry (e.g., state-financed inventory building in the shipbuilding and steel sectors) and public-sector projects were expanded. (The local government's service sector was opened up for relief work in the 1970s.) The results were predictable: the budget and external current account went deep in deficit, and inflation rose. In 1982 the reelected socialist government adopted the so-called "third way": export-led economic growth, linked to price and income moderation. The defensive industrial policy was abolished in order to reduce the budget deficit. Also in 1982 the krona[29] was devaluated by 16 percent, and the budget deficit of 13 percent in 1982 turned into a surplus of 1 percent in 1988; exports boomed and unemployment and inflation fell. However, by 1988 relative unit labor costs were more or less at the level observed before the 1982 devaluation. High domestic wage increases were the main cause for the trend.[30] Moreover, since 1985 GDP had grown by an average of 2.3 percent, well below the OECD average of 3.5 percent. The growth figures for 1990 and the forecast for 1991 for Sweden are 0.7 and 0.1 percent, respectively, compared with 2.9 and 2.8 percent for OECD Europe. The change in compensation per employee as well as in unit labor costs in Sweden in the period 1987–91 is higher than in OECD Europe.

Given these figures, it is not surprising that employment growth in Sweden is slower than for OECD Europe. Only with regard to the (standardized) unemployment rate does Sweden perform better than other OECD countries, and this picture does not change in the period 1987–89. It would be interesting to know whether these changes can be attributed to changes in Swedish industrial relations or to the aftermath of the Swedish model as it functioned until the

---

[27] The hysteresis effect denotes cases where the "natural" level of unemployment (a proxy for the unemployment due to market imperfections) is a function of past unemployment. See Olivier J. Blanchard and Lawrence H. Summers, "Hysteresis in Unemployment," *European Economic Review* 31, no. 1–2 (March 1987), pp. 288–95.

[28] Editor's note: In the terminology of labor economics, higher-ability workers "signal" their availability when they compete against lower-ability workers for less-skilled jobs.

[29] Editor's note: The Swedish currency.

[30] OECD, *Economic Surveys: Sweden* (Paris, 1989), p. 14.

early 1980s. It is certain that the changes occurred in a period of declining consensus and decentralization in wage bargaining.

Large wage increases and sluggish productivity growth have pushed up inflation and ended industry's international competitiveness. Swedish industry now invests more abroad than in Sweden—a tendency that undermines the selective economic growth policy, which relies on profitable companies investing in Sweden. The reasons given for this flight of capital out of the country include a need to move nearer to other markets, rising labor costs, labor shortages, high rates of absenteeism, and the taxation system.[31] Sweden's current account deficit is forecast to widen to 4 percent of GDP in 1991. Thus, the devaluation of 1982 brought only temporary relief and concealed low productivity and high production costs. Therefore a new devaluation is not deemed desirable, and a more structural approach is now thought necessary. A labor market policy to increase and improve labor supply could in our view be a part of such a structural approach, which fits well into the Swedish model. For instance, the recently proposed entitlement to at least two weeks' vocational training per year for employees and lower marginal income tax rates could be applied to improve the quality of the labor force, and later retirement could be applied to increase labor supply. Absenteeism through illness could be reduced by making employers more responsible for paying sickness benefits to the workers and by linking the employer's contribution to the sickness benefit fund and the level of sick leave in the enterprise. Better rehabilitation and measures to reduce absenteeism through improvements in working conditions could stimulate labor supply and promote labor mobility.

Swedish inflation has been higher than the OECD average inflation rate for some time. These differences in inflation rates are especially noticeable in the second half of the 1980s. The 1978–87 average inflation rate in Sweden was 8.3 percent against 6.3 percent for the OECD countries. Sweden did not fully succeed in dampening inflation as many other OECD countries did in the early 1980s, and this certainly holds for the second half of the 1980s. The average inflation rate in 1988–90 in Sweden was 8.2 percent, compared with 4.1 percent for the OECD. However, Sweden has undoubtedly achieved a better trade-off between unemployment and inflation (Phillips curve) than most countries, thanks to its active labor market policy.[32] Despite the rise in unemployment, inflation in Sweden is expected to rise to 10 percent in 1991. This suggests a shift in the Phillips curve.

## Labor Market Flexibility

The Swedish labor market shows a significant amount of flexibility. The relationship between the unemployment rate and the vacancy rate (Beveridge curve) is often used as an indicator of the degree of labor market flexibility. In

---

[31] "Survey: The Swedish Economy."
[32] OECD, *Economic Surveys,* pp. 55–56.

most European OECD countries, the Beveridge curve has shifted outward in the last two decades, indicating a rising mismatch between labor demand and supply. In Sweden, this relationship has remained broadly unchanged. Compared internationally, the nonaccelerating inflationary rate of unemployment (NAIRU), long-term unemployment, and youth unemployment are low, and part-time employment is high. Moreover, real-wage rigidity is low and mobility patterns seem favorable.[33]

Labor mobility has two dimensions: employment mobility and job mobility. Employment mobility refers to internal mobility, involving no change in employment. Job mobility refers to external mobility, the move from one enterprise to another. In Sweden internal or functional flexibility has replaced external or numerical flexibility. Training is seen as the top priority by all enterprises, government programs, employers' organizations, and unions. In other European countries the lack of functional flexibility is compensated by more external numerical flexibility. It is the latter that is stressed by the supply-side economists in their proposal for deregulation and greater flexibility. However, research in the Federal Republic of Germany and in France shows that the reduction in employment protection by means of increasing the opportunities for temporary contracts does not result in more employment. Further, the net employment effect of the special government temporary employment programs in Europe is also limited. They merely result in redistribution of unemployment and a shift in the recruitment pattern in the direction of subsidized temporary jobs. Moreover, the countries that have gone the furthest with short-term flexibility may run greater risk that employers will not pay sufficient attention to the source of their long-term flexibility and efficiency, that is, to manpower training.

In Sweden long-term unemployment is avoided and the hysteresis effect is reduced by means of an active labor market policy. This includes the development of training programs with compulsory participation and job guarantees, whereby the government acts as an employer of last resort. Finite unemployment benefits and vacancy registration cover these measures. In 1988 about 70 percent of all unemployed receiving training found a job within six months. It appears also that after training most individuals were able to command higher wages.[34]

## Pay Differentials

The LO's primary objective has been to reduce pay differentials between various groups in the labor market. Wage differentials in Sweden are the lowest in the OECD area.[35] A certain degree of equalization has been achieved, despite

[33] OECD, *Economic Surveys,* and Standing, *Unemployment,* pp. 52–56.

[34] OECD, *Economic Surveys,* p. 82.

[35] Richard B. Freeman, "Labor Market Institutions and Economic Performance," *Economic Policy* 6 (April 1988), pp. 64–80.

the fact that market forces were detrimental to the goal. The wage solidarity policy has also been important in reducing pay differentials between men and women. Nevertheless, the gap is still wide. Recent trends toward more decentralized collective bargaining have been accompanied by a worsening of women's relative pay position. It tends to restore wage differentials. The Swedish labor market is more segregated along gender lines than in most other European countries. Women tend to work in a small number of (part-time) jobs, principally in social services or unskilled manufacturing, while men are found in all categories of employment.

As a consequence of the solidaristic wage policy, the link between profitability and wage levels would be broken and smaller wage differentials would stimulate mobility. The relationship between value added per employee and the percentage of employed (Salter curve) for the Swedish manufacturing sector indeed indicates that the wage profile is independent of profitability, and only a small fraction of employment takes place in firms with low profitability.[36] The Swedish experience, moreover, shows that the narrowing of wage differentials between industries has contributed to the structural adjustment of Swedish industry (e.g., the car and textile industries). The narrowing of wage differentials has also encouraged the growing concentration of employment in large, innovative, relatively profitable companies and has impeded the emergence or growth of small firms, which are a source of employment growth in the longer run.[37]

## Legislation

In the early 1970s, the trade unions were forced to conclude that certain issues of importance to them could not be resolved by means of direct contract negotiations with the SAF. The unions asked the government and Parliament to pass legislation to bring about improvements in areas such as job security and employee participation in decision making. These trade union demands resulted in a number of new laws. The most important was the Act on Employee Participation in Decision Making (MBL), which came into force in 1977. This law required employers to negotiate not only in the area of social affairs but on all major changes in working conditions, including questions of what to produce and how production should be organized. Employers have to give the union access to almost all of the company's economic information. However, the extensive union rights were used primarily to negotiate employment levels and the timing of dismissals.[38] The law became operational through a so-called Development Agreement. The signing of the Development Agreement between the SAF and LO/PTK in April 1982 meant that MBL regulations had been

---

[36] OECD, *Employment Outlook* (1989), pp. 77–78.

[37] Standing, *Unemployment*, pp. 50–51.

[38] Hans Slomp, *Labor Relations in Europe: A History of Issues and Developments* (Westport, Conn.: Greenwood Press, 1990), p. 162.

implemented in all of Sweden's collective bargaining sectors. In the Development Agreement the SAF gained acceptance from the LO and PTK that the law would be implemented at company level.

## THE SWEDISH MODEL: RELEVANT FOR OTHER COUNTRIES?

### The Swedish Model in Discussion

The Swedish model has recently been the subject of more critical scrutiny. High inflation, current account deficits, and high capital exports seem to be the most important problems. In 1990, strikes and a rejection of the proposed economic policy resulted in the resignation of the Social Democratic government. The recent problems shed new light on the question whether the Swedish model can or should be exported. Meidner and Rehn state that the recent problems do not represent the failure of the model, but only the failure of a modified version of the model. The main modifications are a decentralization of wage negotiations, general as opposed to selective expansionist programs, absence of fiscal restraints, and absence of solidaristic wage policy. However, it is also argued that the problems show the failure and the imminent end of this model. Supply-side rigidities and the fixing of unemployment below the NAIRU are responsible.[39] According to this view, the Swedish economy can recover only when taxes are reduced[40] and government expenditure is decreased in order to improve the supply side of the economy. Moreover, decentralization of wage determination and an increase in wage dispersion would improve the quality of labor via wage competition, and an increase in unemployment is needed to take the heat out of the Swedish economy. The adoption of these supply-side policy options will greatly influence the basic features of the Swedish model. An increase in unemployment will influence the active labor market policy, notably the "right to work" principle. Decentralization of wage bargaining endangers both the solidaristic wage policy and the active labor market policy. In evaluating Swedish industrial relations, it should be borne in mind that the Swedish approach follows from a view on unemployment:

> There is no Swedish model that can be accepted or rejected, bought or sold. There is simply an approach—founded on dedicated innovative hard work. Unemploy-

---

[39] Peterson, "Swedish Collective Bargaining"; and "Survey: The Swedish Economy."

[40] After January 1991 the highest income tax rate will stepwise be reduced to 50 percent and the variable corporate tax rate will be replaced by a uniform 30 percent rate. However, the tax base will be broadened to finance this tax cut. Tax revenue losses are to be made up through higher rates on capital, fewer tax deductibles, and a broader application of the value-added tax. The main motives behind this reform are to make the market function more efficiently, to encourage people to work harder and cheat less on taxes, and to revitalize the public sector. See Ahlén, "Swedish Collective Bargaining," p. 342.

ment is in itself a burden on society, and a cost. It represents a valuable production capacity that is wasted. No country is rich enough to afford unemployment.

An increase in unemployment does not comply with such a view.

## Corporatism and Economic Performance

The debate on the Swedish model fits into the discussion on the relationship between corporatism and economic performance which has been the subject of much research and consideration in the 1980s.[41] The results are ambiguous, but point in the direction of a hump-shaped relationship.[42] This implies that both highly centralized and highly decentralized labor market arrangements give better economic performance (i.e., with regard to real-wage flexibility, unemployment, and inflation) than intermediate cases. Despite the poor theoretical basis and the consequently poor measurement of corporatism, empirical results seem to be in favor of a positive relationship between corporatism and macroeconomic performance. This implies that the path toward decentralization may lead to a deterioration in Sweden's economic performance.

The most striking results of the Swedish model concern long-term unemployment. Evidence with regard to OECD countries is provided by Layard.[43] He shows that half of the OECD unemployed have been out of work for over a year; the figure for Sweden is only 8.2 percent. Layard concludes that three elements seem to be important in fighting long-term unemployment: finite benefits, active labor market policy, and centralized wage bargaining. His conclusions are confirmed by Calmfors and Nymoen[44] and Jackman.[45] From these analyses it follows that, whereas the "right to income" policy has led to increasing long-term unemployment, the "right to work" principle has improved the supply side of the economy. Another conclusion is that it is not the level but

---

[41] We are aware of the fact that the term *corporatism* is not unambiguously defined in the literature. However, centralization of wage negotiations, shared perspectives on the goals of economic activity, and explicit attention to the aims of wage-setting seem to be important characteristics of a corporatist society. See Lars Calmfors and John Driffill, "Centralization of Wage Bargaining," *Economic Policy* 6 (April 1988), pp. 13–61; Lars Calmfors and Ragnar Nymoen, "Real Wage Adjustment and Employment Policies in the Nordic Countries," *Economic Policy* 11 (October 1990), pp. 398–448; Freeman, "Labor Market Institutions"; Richard Jackman, Christopher Pissarides, and Savvas Savouri, "Labor Market Policies and Unemployment in the OECD," *Economic Policy* 11 (October 1990), pp. 450–90; and OECD, *Economic Surveys*. Calmfors and Driffill, "Centralization," give an overview of some definitions and the ranking of countries according to these definitions. They show that, whatever definition is used, Sweden is characterized as a corporatist country.

[42] Calmfors and Driffill, "Centralization."

[43] Layard, "European Unemployment."

[44] Calmfors and Nymoen, "Real Wage Adjustment."

[45] Jackman, Pissarides, and Savouri, "Labor Market Policies."

the duration of unemployment benefits that influences economic behavior, and this supports the idea of finite benefits as applied in Sweden.

In our view, the Swedish experience with active labor market policy shows that high rate of long-term unemployment in parts of the OECD is avoidable. One may wonder why the "benefit principle" dominates. There is little to recommend the payment of social security benefits without job opportunities. Passive labor market policies create a labor reserve that cannot be used when necessary. It does not help in relieving either quantitative or qualitative discrepancies on the labor market. Moreover, empirical data on expenditure on labor market policies show that, in countries where employment services are organized around the "employment" principle (as in Sweden, Austria, and Denmark), unemployment is lower.[46] In Sweden, part of the active labor market measures can be classified as supply-side activities enhancing labor market flexibility.[47] We agree with Layard[48] that it is worthwhile for countries to follow Swedish thinking when allocating expenditure on labor market programs.

However, this kind of labor market policy has one drawback, as has been made clear by a recent contribution of Calmfors and Nymoen. They state that, if inflow into labor market programs and inflow into unemployment are not regarded as perfect substitutes by unions and individuals (and if participation in labor market programs is preferred to unemployment), wage adjustments might slow down. Active labor market policy acts as a cushion to relieve the consequences of too high wages and consequently provides insufficient incentives for the unions to adjust wage demands. One of their conclusions makes this point clear: "Our most controversial finding is that accommodative labor market policies, designed to reduce open unemployment, *raise* real wages."[49] This result confirms their statement that labor market programs and open unemployment are not substitutes, and it has important implications for labor market policy. Wage moderation can be seriously hampered by the Swedish approach to unemployment. The results of Calmfors and Nymoen relate to labor market policies in Sweden, Denmark, and Finland, while this result could not be found for Norway.

Adjustments to labor market disequilibria are not, of course, the only indicators of economic performance. For the Swedish system to be viable, long-term developments are important. Calmfors and Driffill[50] distinguish between centralized economies (e.g., Sweden), intermediate economies, and decentralized economies. They show that for 1974–85 both the level and the

---

[46] Jackman, Pissarides, and Savouri, "Labor Market Policies."

[47] In 1989 demand-oriented measures amounted to more than 45 percent of total expenditure on labor-market policy, while supply-side measures accounted for roughly 30 percent and cash unemployment benefits for 24 percent.

[48] Layard, "European Unemployment."

[49] Calmfors and Nymoen, "Real Wage Adjustment," p. 431.

[50] Calmfors and Driffill, "Centralization."

change in the Okun misery index and an alternative performance index for Sweden are lower than the average for the other types of economies.[51] From Freeman[52] it follows that Sweden is ranked 11th of 19 OECD countries with regard to the percentage change of real GDP during 1973–84. Swedish performance is about the same as that of Germany, Denmark, or France. Because of the large growth in employment, real GDP growth per worker is of course less (coming 15th), but real GDP growth has been twice as high as in the United States, while, regarding the level of GDP per worker, Sweden is ranked 8th. Calmfors and Nymoen[53] report a productivity growth for Sweden that shows about the same picture as for Western Europe during 1967–87. From their steady-state wage equations it can be concluded that, of the Nordic countries, wages in Sweden are the most responsive to unemployment. These results indicate that long-term economic performance in Sweden gives no reason to place any doubt about the viability of the model. However, as we have described, this viability depends for a large part on the way corporatism is given shape (i.e., on the way consensus is reached and wages are set). Note that the majority of the research covers 1970–85, while the main problems on which the criticism of the model is based showed up after 1983–85.

## The Swedish Approach and the Wage-Setting Process

For the Swedish model to be effective, consensus is a condition *sine qua non.* This point is much stressed in the literature.[54] Albeda[55] mentions three elements that are characteristic of Swedish labor relations. First, he states, in Sweden there is little polarization and the Social Democrats have been in government since 1932. Only in 1976–82 was there a non-socialist government. Second, Sweden has a very high level of organization on both sides of the labor market. Third, there is (close) cooperation between the trade unions and the Social Democratic Party. Thus, Albeda concludes, this "neo-corporatist" society is very manageable and Sweden is a country with a consensus. In the Swedish model labor market parties not only negotiate about wages, but also make arrangements about employment measures and incomes policy measures. Centralized bargaining seems the only way to reach a workable agreement in such a

---

[51] The Okun misery index is defined as the rate of inflation plus the rate of unemployment. The alternative performance index is measured by the sum of the rate of unemployment plus the current account deficit as a percentage of GDP.

[52] Freeman, "Labor Market Institutions."

[53] Calmfors and Nymoen, "Real Wage Adjustment."

[54] W. Albeda, "The Rebirth of Tripartism in the Netherlands," in *The Challenge of New Technology and Macro Political Change,* ed. William M. Lafferty and Eliezer Rosenstein (International Handbook of Participation in Organizations, vol. 3: Oxford: Oxford University Press, forthcoming 1993); Calmfors and Driffill, "Centralization"; Nils Elvander, "Bargaining Systems, Incomes Policies, and Conflict in the Nordic Countries," in *Current Approaches to Collective Bargaining* (Labor–Management Relations Series, no. 71; Geneva: International Labor Office, 1989), pp. 127–36; and Layard, "European Unemployment."

[55] Albeda, "The Rebirth."

case. Without some kind of centralized bargaining, active labor market policy would be difficult to implement. With decentralized bargaining, parties may assume that other sectors in the economy will take care of prevailing unemployment. They may simply shift the unemployment problem onto the rest of the economy. No sector will make enough room for schooling and job guarantees, shifting the problems onto the government. Moreover, decentralized wage bargaining may also cause problems in a tight labor market (e.g., a wage-price spiral). Central bargaining is a means to internalize the externality that exists when, under decentralized bargaining, the parties ignore the effects of their actions on others.

Evidence from several countries, including the Netherlands[56] and the Nordic countries,[57] shows that centralized wage determination is difficult to arrange and maintain. The Swedish LO blames decentralization for the wage explosion and has urged a return to central bargaining. For centralized bargaining to work well, wages must be set by the sector that is exposed to international competition, and then the rest of the economy must keep in line. However, in Sweden, wage leadership was partly shifted to the public sector. In this environment, centralized bargaining is flawed. The Scandinavian model for setting general wages cannot function fully without a centralized negotiation system. However, the public employer function of the government can be an effective instrument of incomes policy. Experience in Sweden over the last few years suggests that this is almost the only weapon in the incomes policy arsenal that has not been exhausted. But this would imply, for example, that the automatic element in the wage drift for public-sector employees would be dropped.

Elvander also asks whether it is possible that a combination of central agreements on general issues (general wage limits, working hours, and equalization of benefits) on the one hand, and agreements at the sectoral union level on the other, could solve the problem of satisfying overall long-term interests as well as specific national union demands.[58] Our answer would be that, for the Swedish model to survive and to be imported by other countries, ways have to be found that deal with these tensions between the various negotiation levels. Of course, this is more easily said than done, but Swedish experience with more decentralization has not been unambiguously positive.[59] For a country

---

[56] Albeda, "The Rebirth."

[57] Elvander, "Bargaining Systems."

[58] Elvander, "Bargaining Systems."

[59] The point can be illustrated by a quotation from the OECD: "In regard to the negotiation structure, developments through the 1980s have not been propitious, though it may be expected that in the 1989 wage round the trend toward greater decentralization will be stopped . . . The question arises whether higher differentials in recent years have not been more to the advantage of those employed in sectors protected against foreign employment rather than in skill categories associated with a dynamic industrial development. It may be that more centralized negotiations, accompanied by measures to allow wage structures better to reflect underlying demand and supply trends, would significantly improve the outcome of the wage-setting process." OECD, *Economic Surveys*, p. 80.

such as Sweden with its openness, the relation between wage-setting and macroeconomic performance is of great importance. It is not surprising, therefore, that a revision of the Swedish model in the direction of a return to central negotiations is under discussion.[60] The SAF is now talking about a definite end to national bargaining. However, recent developments in wage drift and the deterioration of Swedish economic performance could be important incentives for a continuation of this discussion.

Finally, another problem needs to be pointed out. This deals with the relationship between industrial relations and the structure of the labor force. The core of the Swedish model has been developed in a period of high participation with manufacturing as its main occupation area. However, employment in the service sector has grown, especially during the last two decades, as has the heterogeneity of the labor force. This will hamper organization in large unions and may lead to an increase in the number and variety of unions and create coordination problems if wage-setting is centralized. Moreover, the individual employment relationship itself will change: there will be more temporary contracts, more flexibility, and more part-time labor. Both of these developments may lead to other types of industrial relations than the ones that have existed so long in Sweden.[61]

### Sweden and the European Community

Finally, we want to mention one development that must be kept in mind when discussing the suitability of the Swedish model. After 1992, the European internal market comes into being. This will increase competition (and wage competition) and promote labor mobility. What will happen when some countries adopt a Swedish approach and others do not? Will labor leave the "Swedish" countries in times of high employment and return in times of high unemployment? Sweden has now applied to join the EC. If she becomes a member, she may have to follow labor market policies that will be dictated by European economic performance. A convergence of labor market policies can be forced by economic circumstances.

### CONCLUSION

In our view, the Swedish model has proved its value with regard to labor market policy, especially concerning the duration of unemployment compared with other European countries. The principle of "active" rather than "pas-

---

[60] In February 1990 the Swedish government announced a wage, price, and rent freeze. These measures underline the government's concern about the state of the economy. Although they deviate from the Swedish model of free wage negotiations, the LO has backed the plan. See also Ahlén, "Swedish Collective Bargaining."

[61] Lei Delsen, "European Trade Unions and the Flexible Work Force," *Industrial Relations Journal* 21, no. 4 (Winter 1990), pp. 260–73.

sive'' labor market policy has prevented an increase in long-term unemployment and counteracted hysteresis. In our view, this part of the Swedish model
can be imported by countries that suffer from high long-term unemployment,
and in this sense the Swedish model is (partially) relevant for other countries. It
is a way out of the unemployment trap. Supply-side policies such as training or
retraining programs and a system of finite benefits have increased functional
flexibility. Swedish experience has proved that active labor market policy may
serve as an alternative to deregulation in order to augment the flexibility of the
labor market. Although the Swedish labor market is highly regulated, it is as
flexible as that of the United States[62] or Japan. However, as the recent past
shows, the Swedish model is under attack. It is an open question whether this
model can survive in a setting of decentralized bargains, increasing wage differentials, and an increasingly competitive world.

---

[62] OECD, *Economic Surveys,* p. 83.

## Chapter Nine

# Indicative Planning in France*

*Bernard Cazes*[1]

*In France, in addition to indirect guidance of the economy through monetary and fiscal measures and various kinds of specific intervention, the government endeavors to steer the economy by "indicative" planning. This indicative planning is very different from the comprehensive and detailed control of economic activity pursued in the centrally planned economies to be discussed in Part IV of this book.*

*In French indicative planning, the planning agency attempts to draw up a medium-term plan for the development of the economy, in collaboration with representatives of other government units, business, agriculture, and trade unions. However, this plan is only "indicative"—essentially a forecast—and it is prepared only at the branch level, with no requirements for individual private firms. By at least partially coordinating the production and investment activities of the different branches and the actions of government bodies, the plan tries to reduce uncertainty and risk for individual firms. Although firms will make their own decisions freely in the market, they do so with the benefit of knowledge about the intentions of other parts of the economy and about the government's credit, tax, and regional development policies.*

*In this chapter, an official of the French General Planning Commissariat explains three key functions of French indicative planning: information gathering, dialogue between the government and various interest groups, and coordination among government departments. He then considers to what extent the indicative plan incorporates commitments, of what kind, by what entities, and for how long. He concludes by noting differences between actual French practice and some theoretical interpretations of indicative planning.*

* Reprinted by permission from the *Journal of Comparative Economics* 14, no. 4 (December 1990), pp. 607–20, with the omission of references to foreign language sources and unpublished reports. Copyright © 1990 by Academic Press, Inc. Bernard Cazes is Chief of the Division of Long-Term Studies in the French Commissariat Général du Plan (CGP, General Planning Commissariat).

[1] The opinions expressed in this paper are those of the author and do not necessarily reflect the views of the General Planning Commissariat. This essay was translated from French by Gillian O'Meara.

## THE ORIGINS OF THE FRENCH PLANNING SYSTEM

It may seem odd that by a decree of January 3, 1946, the French government introduced a planning system at a time when planning had strong ultra-left-wing connotations.[2]

There are at least three explanations, two domestic and one international. The first domestic political explanation is provided by Gaston Palewski (Cabinet Director to the then head of government, Charles de Gaulle), who claims in his memoirs that he advised de Gaulle to set up a Planning Office as a kind of countervailing power to the three Communist members of the Cabinet. Second, there is a domestic economic explanation, the most frequently quoted (including by Jean Monnet, France's first Planning Commissioner), which sees the Plan as the key instrument for mobilizing French energies on high-priority goals, namely, the rebuilding and modernization of the French productive apparatus. Third, the Plan was used by the French authorities as an argument in the negotiations with the United States government on financial aid both before and during the Marshall Plan.[3]

This being the case, one might have thought that the institutional mechanism set up by Jean Monnet would last as long as but surely no longer than the presence of Communist ministers in the Cabinet, the decrepitude of the French economy, and the need for Marshall Plan funds. Why did it outlast these characteristics of the early period?

## SOME JUSTIFICATIONS, THEORETICAL AND OTHERWISE, FOR THE PERSISTENCE OF FRENCH PLANNING

To account for the longevity of French planning, in my opinion a reference to negative arguments, what it is not, as well as to positive ones, what it does to the participants in the planning process, is needed.

### Negative Arguments, or, in What Way Does French Planning Differ from a Command Economy?

Clearly, the planning framework that emerged in 1946–47 was not in the least influenced by French interwar debates on the *planisme* of Henri de Man-style revisionist socialists and its feasibility in a capitalist context nor, more importantly, did it have anything in common with the Soviet-type five-year plans, as evidenced by its two permanent characteristics, acceptance of a mixed economy environment and long-term orientation toward an open economy.[4]

---

[2] General de Gaulle, head of the government, signed the decree two weeks prior to leaving office.

[3] Editor's note: Under the Marshall Plan (named for U.S. Secretary of State George C. Marshall), the United States provided aid for Western Europe's recovery after World War II.

[4] Conversely, one could say that any planning that refuses these two principles would tend to be extremely similar to the command plans of Eastern Europe.

In the First Plan (1947–52), one reads: "In our economy, made up of nationalized sectors as well as an extensive free-market sector, the Plan should provide guidance as well as directives. Its means of implementation, while laying down disciplines, should at the same time promote creative initiatives in all sectors and maintain within businesses both justifiable profits and risk-taking, which provide the impetus and necessary sanctions." Unsurprisingly, the reference to the merits of a mixed economy and the implications thereof for the conception of planning were reasserted after 1983, when the architects of the Ninth Plan (1984–88) spoke highly of the "capacity of initiative and invention of entrepreneurs, managers, and innovators, a prime factor of industrial vitality and a crucial weapon in world economic competition."

Given the much deteriorated and obsolete situation of the French economy as of 1946, one might have expected a strong anti-free trade bias in the new planning setup. It is remarkable that the early French planners designed the Monnet (First) Plan as an instrument for restoring France to full participation in world trade in the long run. Again the statements are unequivocal: Our economy is inextricably linked to international trade. Being dependent on foreign markets is the unavoidable risk non-autarkic economies have to face and the price to be paid for a high standard of living based on growing trade with other countries." Such a stance, neatly at variance with the preference normally expected from French officials, especially in the late 1940s, was echoed about 40 years later in the aforementioned Ninth Plan, where protectionism is criticized both for political considerations, including France's commitment to the EEC, and economic arguments, such as that protectionism would generate a "loss of efficiency of the productive apparatus and a significant decrease in the French standard of living."

## Positive Arguments

Negative qualities cannot in themselves help us to understand why the numerous players in the planning process, including government, employers, farmers, and trade unions, found it sufficiently rewarding to participate in that kind of institution for so many years. I suggest that the reason is best formulated in terms of the three functions of planning *à la française,* namely, information gathering, dialogue (*concertation*), and consistency.[5] I maintain that each function can be performed in at least two ways—let us call them radical and middle-of-the-road—so that, in a sense, the history of French planning and, quite probably, of any kind of indicative planning is the history of the choice between these alternative conceptions made by the planners.

**Information Gathering.**   The first function consists of assembling relevant data and research findings of a retrospective or anticipatory nature to form a sound

---

[5] These functions correspond, almost exactly, to what Planning Commissioner Henri Guillaume called "the Plan's three tasks . . . : throwing light on the future; facilitating economic and social debate; appreciating consistency."

and convincing basis for policy analysis and recommendations. It is open to two kinds of radicalism: (1) conceiving the multiyear plan as a comprehensive market research study sufficiently detailed and reliable to ensure that private and public decision makers operate in a low-uncertainty environment; and (2) considering the various time limits used in this first function—the so-called short (up to one year), medium (four to five years), and long term (anything beyond "medium")—as so many dovetailed parts in a continuum between business cycle fine-tuning, structural adjustment policies, and gradual accommodation of in-depth geopolitical, technological, demographic, and other shifts.

Concerning the first vision—planning as an almost uncertainty-free exercise—the increasing volatility of the international environment prompted the planners, especially after 1973, to distinguish clearly between elements such as multiyear projections developed for corporate enlightenment and the plan proper, that is, the quantitative expression of government's medium-term policies and programs. Moreover, they pleaded for a greater awareness of the many risks that might jeopardize the implementation of even the most rational plan—one of the most promising approaches being the drafting of several scenarios based on alternative assumptions of external environment.

What appears to be a fairly obvious message was at that time taken by politicians and social partners alike as a resigned denial of what planning is about, that is, an assertion of will: hence the regrettably successful efforts made in 1975 by the government, employers' federations, and trade unions during the drafting of the Seventh Plan to persuade planners and INSEE[6] model builders to write more sanguine scenarios with more economic growth and less prospective unemployment for 1980, the Plan's terminal year.

As for planning considered as a series of interlocking time frames where the longer term would as a rule take precedence, everyone in the planning community is aware that such a seamless web would be ideal, but that unfortunately, or perhaps fortunately, systemic complexity puts it beyond our reach. This should lead not to a defeatist nihilism, but rather to a greater awareness of what is feasible. Admittedly, long-term planning is necessary to "lessen the effects of not foreseeing major problems, not taking preventive or mitigating steps in time and then having to spend substantial monies to correct the problem," to quote the United States government's contribution to the 1990 OECD survey of public management developments. The planning institution can play quite a useful role in promoting this kind of policy study, particularly cross-sectoral ones that line departments are prone to neglect. On the other hand, a non sequitur between future research and medium-term policy planning is inevitable, if only because any long-range assessment runs the symmetrical risks of disturbing policymakers' complacency by its uncanny foresight or of losing credibility by crying wolf too often. Likewise, the implementation of five-year

---

[8] Editor's note: See Mancur Olson, *The Logic of Collective Action: Public Goods and the Theory of Groups* (Cambridge, Mass.: Harvard University Press, 1965).

plans can never be screened from business cycle shocks, so that a succession of short-term imbalances will often lead to over- or, more likely, underachievement of mid-term goals. Planners thus have the useful but thankless task that Pierre Massé[7] defined quite aptly in the following terms: "Confronted with short-term requirements and desires, the Prime Minister should always have a promoter of medium- and long-term outlooks close at hand."

**Dialogue (*concertation*).** *Concertation,* a key, and tricky, word in French planners' vocabulary, appears as early as the First Plan through a contrast outlined between, on the one hand, "controlled economy (*économie dirigée*) of a bureaucratic or corporatist kind" and, on the other hand, "concerted economy," where problems are settled "through a permanent exchange of ideas between the Government and the public," particularly with regard to the preparation of multiyear plans. This arrangement is also open to two types of radicalism, namely, dialogue broadening and dialogue deepening.

In the early period (1946–47), planning took place in an institutional context characterized by a small number of trade unions, employers' federations, associations, and farmers' organizations that held the monopoly on defending their constituents' interests. The broadening of dialogue implied the inclusion of new partners into the planning process. For instance, in 1980 the government asked that the drafting of the Eighth Plan involve more young people, more women, more inhabitants of the provinces, and, finally, more spokesmen for consumers and public service users—a reasonable intention that was actually very difficult to implement.

As seen from the center (i.e., the planners or the government), this first brand of radicalism makes good sense, for in the wake of the moral revolution of the 1960s many new social actors have emerged, including women's groups, senior citizens' associations, and environmentalists. On the other hand, the more conventional interest groups, especially the trade unions, tend to resent any move toward dialogue broadening, as they feel that they are the real social partners, since unions stem from production relations rather than from "soft" variables such as gender, age, or quality of life. Conversely, they are sometimes bitterly criticized by the new social movements which see them as short-sighted promoters of the interests of male, adult skilled workers, neglecting the problems of jobless, nonunionized people.

Even more ambitiously, deepening implies using dialogue to strengthen the commitment value of a plan, traditionally considered as the *Plan de l'Etat* (the State's Plan), that is, a programmatic statement based on the involvement and resources of the central government. For part of the non-Communist left-wing, a more satisfying conception is the *Plan de la Nation* (the Nation's Plan), whereby nongovernment bodies such as regional authorities, social partners, trade unions, and voluntary associations could commit themselves through

---

[7] Editor's note: Pierre Massé served as head of the General Planning Commissariat.

their participation in the preparation of the plan. A plan based on so-called deepened dialogue, within what was sometimes called *planification démocratique,* certainly looks more consensual, and hence more credible, than a document sponsored by the central government only, even with a blessing of sorts by the Parliament. On the other hand, this second radical variant bristles with difficulties. Elected representatives from the body politic resent the *Plan de la Nation* concept because they feel that political legitimacy based on universal franchise is put on an unduly equal footing with a distinctively inferior representativeness. As for the social partners proper, the inducements of statesman-like responsibilities inherent in their prospective role have not often prevailed over the concern for maintaining the internal cohesiveness of the rank and file. This is the familiar issue of all-encompassing interest groups, in Mancur Olson's terminology.[8]

Within the limits of a dialogue that is bound to be both less than exhaustive (because emergent groups have less visible elites that make for easy co-optation) and of limited depth (since nobody really wishes to be thoroughly committed), government planners still have a lot of homework to do. They must constantly remind politicians and social partners that dialogue is not an end in itself, but only a vital ingredient of policymaking which is all the more efficient if it takes place within a planning context (namely, a comprehensive view and a multiyear time frame), in order to escape the twin sins of free-wheeling dialogue—the neglect of interdependencies and shortsightedness. In other words, it is through its association with dialogue that planning can play the pedagogical role that is often attributed to it: reminding all concerned that there are technical, financial, and socioeconomic constraints that no ideological lyricism can erase, and that community problems are best approached through a joint effort to devise positive-sum game solutions, whereby everyone has something to gain without penalizing other players.

**Consistency.**    This last function is possibly the one which corresponds most closely to the widespread image of planning as an order-promoting agent in a situation that is supposed to spontaneously tend toward anarchy, both in price-regulated market economies and in political life, when powers are fragmented and the reelection constraint is the sole balancing factor. From this economy–politics dichotomy one easily perceives the possible shapes radicalism can take with regard to consistency: one economic and one political. The former consists of expecting the national plan to provide some expression of a societal blueprint (*projet de société*) more or less at variance with current social trends—a vision which incidentally is fairly well in keeping with a preference for deep dialogue toward a *Plan de la Nation.* The latter brand of radicalism sees the planning agency as the focus of a central coordinating power above all

---

[8] Editor's note: See Mancur Olson, *The Logic of Collective Action: Public Goods and the Theory of Groups* (Cambridge, Mass.: Harvard University Press, 1965).

the other departments, including the Treasury, so that the Minister of Planning would become a sort of Prime Minister for medium-term issues.

For French planners the temptation of departmental hegemony has never been strong. They have followed the example set by Jean Monnet, who relied almost fanatically on persuasion and personal influence, of which he had plenty, and who constantly refused any bureaucratic affiliation for the CGP other than a direct link with the Prime Minister. On the other hand, French planners were from the outset highly attracted to grand socioeconomic designs. The message from the Plan Monnet went far beyond a mere catalog of investment projects to be implemented within a given time limit. Seven years after a shattering military defeat and two years after the Liberation, the Plan, with its "modernization and decadence" dilemma, came to represent a national goal. From that time on, one can say that CGP officials have been nostalgic about these early years, during which the Plan embodied the will to live of a whole community. Certain subsequent plans suggest that, albeit in the guise of technical documents, the old urge to provide the French people with a new model of society has not subsided.

Nevertheless, at the same time, the planners did their best to provide a certain consistency to clients who only had a moderate appreciation thereof and to remedy the twin deficiencies of the economic and political markets (i.e., undue concentration on short-term considerations and indifference toward negative as well as positive external effects). In the French experience of planning, the important thing is that nonmarket failures loom as large as the more conventional market-related ones as a justification for the consistency-provision function, even if official documents understandably do not emphasize too heavily political myopia. With the multiplicity of uncoordinated bureaucratic players, hidden behind deceptively homogenous concepts such as the state or central government, and the political cycle, which dictates much too short a time limit for many policy issues, planners' unemployment appears unlikely—even though their clients on the political–administrative side may not appreciate the two services provided free of charge by the national planners[9]:

1. The longitudinal consistency or continuity of a given policy over time, short-term hiccoughs notwithstanding. The most characteristic example is the policy that gave France a powerful electronuclear industry.

2. Cross-sectional consistency within a single policy (e.g., price and structure dimensions of agricultural policy), or across policies (e.g., financing social welfare without jeopardizing job creation).

---

[9] ". . . the state itself is a cluster of often imperfectly coordinated agencies who can benefit from indicative planning as well for the purposes of their own strategic planning," according to Peter Holmes, "Indicative Planning," in *The New Palgrave: A Dictionary of Economics,* ed. John Eatwell, Murray Millgate, and Peter Newman (London: Macmillan, 1987), vol. 2, p. 783.

# PLANNING AS A COMMITMENT: TO WHAT? BY WHOM? FOR HOW LONG?

There is no commitment in a forecast, except perhaps insofar as the scientific reputation of the forecaster is concerned. On the other hand, a plan without any commitment from anybody is hardly worth preparing. Beyond that lies the most difficult issue for any kind of nonimperative planning: commitment to what? by whom? and for how long?

## Commitment to What?

In principle this first question calls for two answers, one global and one specific.

Globally speaking, the plan can be seen as a commitment both to macroeconomic goals and to the strategy needed to reach them in line with assumptions about the future of the international situation. The goals themselves can be conceived as absolute figures, or expressed relatively in terms of differentials vis-à-vis foreign performance, as in the Ninth Plan. Then, apart from macrogoals, the promise of a given plan may concern achievements whose limited character is compensated by their importance or what is vaguely referred to as their strategic significance. This presents two difficulties. First, line departments are understandably, albeit regrettably, prone to using planning priorities to boost their secondary programs, while relying on their political clout to promote what they see as their true priorities. Second, there is the technically and politically complex issue of striking the right balance between the two extreme conceptions of the plan's hard core—on the one hand, where almost everything is given priority so that the concept becomes meaningless, and on the other hand, where the minimum core is too small for its implementation to make a difference.

From that angle, French planning started out with a strong selective and sectoral view of priorities. In the First Plan, so-called basic upstream sectors' investments were given priority as their modernization was considered a precondition of the later development of other activities. As the content of the later plans widened, the notion of priority gradually lost its force. The planning process became so attractive as a discussion forum for policy proposals that the number of investment projects which their bureaucratic proponents wanted to see registered in the next five-year plan increased dramatically. Hence, during the 1960s and early 1970s, the French plans progressively became a list of detailed projects with no clearly discernible pattern. From the mid-1970s onward, there was in fact a reaction against this dilution of planning. Public and budgetary commitments were limited to a small number of well-defined programs, in principle complete with long-term earmarked funding.

## Commitment by Whom?

The issue of who is committed appears apropos of dialogue every time it goes beyond a mere consultation. In the discussion about "State vs. Nation" planning, the grand, abstract concepts could not hide what was really involved, that is, the sharing of responsibility among central and local government, businesses, and the trade unions. Social partners are reluctant to have their hands tied by plan targets of any kind. But it would be wrong to infer that a *Plan de l'Etat* variant is trouble-free. Beyond strictly political reasons, such as the lack of a sizable majority in Parliament, which encourage commitment aversion within governments, policymakers (especially in finance departments, but elsewhere, too) feel that the long-term nature of multiyear goals and programs is a source of embarrassment, as it reduces the elbowroom that they wish to keep in case of political or business cycle shocks. Moreover, the existence of explicit public commitments in a plan could well go against the government, for it would be most surprising if there were no gap whatsoever between set and realized goals—hence, the gradual shrinking of the programmed part of the plans, a process that unsurprisingly started in the mid-1970s.

The only answer to this difficulty possibly lies in an offsetting increase in the contractual part of the plan, as was the case with the Ninth Plan. The state is no longer the only player, as other partners such as regional authorities and public firms (or, rather, nationalized undertakings with a monopoly) agree through contracts concluded with the state to be jointly committed to various national plan targets/programs that happen to fit in with their own priorities.

## Commitment for How Long?

Whatever the scheme used to accommodate multiple, heterogeneous partners, every exercise in planning with uncertainty is loaded with one other unsolved riddle concerning the continuity of the planning process in the implementation phase. The choice is as follows: Should the multiyear plan be drafted once and for all, to be succeeded by another plan of the same duration, or should it be ongoing, with annual reassessments and deadlines continually deferred by one year?

One advantage of discontinuous planning is that every five (or *n*) years an important event pulls the public and bureaucracies alike out of the slumber of day-to-day management, while a so-called revolving plan runs the risk of becoming almost invisible, as it is incrementally adjusted every year. Symmetrically, once-and-for-all planning may give the spurious impression of a fresh start. Moreover, as time passes, its anticipatory value gradually diminishes, so much so that at the end of the period the plan has become very short-term indeed. On the other hand, a revolving plan is almost entirely immune from aging, as there is a quasi-permanent interaction among changes in environment, implementation hazards, and the substance of the plan. Until now, continuous planning has never been put to the test, despite nice comments periodically made about the exemplary value of corporate planning.

## THE TENTH PLAN (1989–92)

The Tenth Plan emerged after two "lean years" in 1986 and 1987, during which the government in office hesitated between abolishing the CGP and transforming it into a so-called *Commissariat à la Strategie* (Office of Strategy). Hereafter I briefly examine its contribution to the renewal of French planning through a number of concepts and issues discussed in this essay.

We have seen how early French planning could be accounted for in terms of a series of factors, including structural rejuvenation and French–United States aid negotiations. Interestingly, while domestic use of the Plan message is more relevant than ever, the international message is also still valid, with the EEC replacing the United States—so much so that just as the length of the Monnet Plan was extended to coincide with the Marshall Plan termination date, the time frame of the Tenth Plan was set to 1992 instead of 1993, as expected with a five-year plan, because the Single European Market was to be completed on January 1, 1993. Moreover, the study of the macroeconomic implications of the French government guidelines to the CGP was carried out by a group of experts chaired by INSEE's Paul Dubois and included macroeconomists from the EEC Commission in Brussels. The group used the EEC's 1988–92 growth forecasts drawn up by the Commission as an international reference scenario.

### The Three Functions

The three functions are still in existence, although they have changed with time. Three innovations are worth mentioning:

- *Throwing a light on the future* involved two different time frames: the year 2000 and beyond, dealt with by a task force headed by the historian E. Le Roy Ladurie; and France in 1992, dealt with by the aforementioned Dubois group.
- *Dialogue (concertation)* took place along the same lines as before, but in a lighter structure (only eight committees). Moreover, two kinds of new partners were included in the circle: private and public European leaders and young people from 18 to 25.
- *Consistency* remains one of the CGP's main concerns, especially in regard to the macroeconomic strategy of the Tenth Plan, which had the dual aims of regaining a high level of employment and preparing the French economy for the European market. Concern for consistency is no less important, however, in sectoral policy, but it has inevitably taken on a new shape, still not clearly perceived, with the political decentralization introduced in 1981. Decentralization considerably increased the

number of decision makers to be coordinated—the clearest example being education, which, even when centralization was at its height, was
never really given any direction.

## The Commitment Value of the Plan

The commitment value of the Plan also has several features that differ from
those of past plans. In the past, the CGP and INSEE carried out the forecasting
technical studies prior to the plan's preparation. This time, the government
drew up a draft plan defining the main lines of the macroeconomic strategy that
would be compatible with France's European policies. The forecasts merely
served to simulate the consequences and the conditions of the feasibility of this
strategy. Over 30 hours of interdepartmental discussion, far more than in the
past, were given to finalizing the draft plan.

The commitment value was just as high where the contractual part of the
Tenth Plan was concerned. Here, the government committed itself to injecting
52 billion francs over five years into the financing of the state's part of the
state–regions' Plan contracts.

The commitment value for the programmed part of the Plan was, however,
lower than previously, as there were no longer any priority budgetary programs. The state capital budget now represents only one third of public capital
expenditure, while large nationalized monopoly firms and local authorities remain big investors. It is perhaps impossible to win on both scores, as Planning
Secretary Lionel Stoléru suggested during the Parliament's discussion on the
draft Plan: "The Plan gains in political credibility, that is, commitment
strength, what it often loses in precision regarding the means of the State." In
this case, past battles for or against programming public expenditure may well
be obsolete.

Finally, the discontinuous-revolving plan controversy is perhaps a thing of
the past, too. There are, after all, fewer macro and sectoral figures to be
revolved, and with the new strategic frame of mind of French planners, one
shifts from cardinal numbers to ordinal ones, from absolute figures to relative
magnitudes.[10] There is nothing to be concerned about, except that strategic
planning is more sophisticated—hence less visible to the public than its former
versions—and its programmatic data and projected targets are compared easily
with actual ones even without slide rules. This is further proof, if proof were
necessary, that planning means making choices.

## CONCLUSION

Indicative planning, like the economy it is part of, cannot escape the division-
of-labor characteristic of modern society—according to which plan practition-
ers put planning into practice and economists interpret their actions through the

---

[10] The inflation objective in the Tenth Plan read as follows: "Aligning the pace of our price
increases with the best European performance on a long-term basis."

scientific paradigms of their disciplines, either on the level of theoretical and applied reflection as do Estrin and Holmes[11] or on a strictly theoretical level as do Frank and Holmes.[12]

I conclude by explaining why I have difficulty finding planning, as it is practiced and justified in France, behind these theoretical analyses. Three points warrant emphasis.

First, optimism or pessimism in the business world—especially in these times of instant information and the globalization of the economy and even of politics—hangs on the Plan and the impact of its forecasts, but also on factors that are external to the Plan: the United States' monthly balance of payments, events in Eastern Europe or in the Soviet Union, the Tokyo stock exchange, and so forth. Consequently, when planners try to capture the attention of businesses to influence their expectations, they come up against the same noise problems as do teachers fighting the attraction of television in their attempts to educate pupils.

Second, the only economic factors that are really taken into account by these theoretical analyses are businesses and their need to exchange information, while the government seems content to play the honorable, albeit a little unobtrusive, role of the Walrasian auctioneer.[13]

Third, the failures that need to be remedied are solely market failures, with the exception of Peter Holmes' phrase cited in footnote 9, when, in fact, non-market failures really do exist. For reasons that I do not consider myself competent to analyze, this second type of failure presents the same structure as the first type, those of the market. This becomes obvious in Musgrave's article on planning, where he clearly explains that public policies should have two qualities, "policy cohesion and allowance for a longer view," adding: "There is no question that a *coherent* set of public policies is needed to complement the market. The invisible hand works, but only part of the way. It is also evident that policy thinking—goals and instruments—must extend beyond the short run into the longer future."[14]

If we accept this idea, it follows that to think about planning theoretically we have to go beyond literature on transaction costs and delve into works, such as those by Mancur Olson, on the links between the institutional framework and growth; and into the literature on rational methods of choice in the nonmarket universe, notably that on evaluation and social experimentation.[15]

---

[11] Saul Estrin and Peter Holmes, *French Planning in Theory and Practice* (London: Allen & Unwin, 1983).

[12] Jeff Frank and Peter Holmes, "A Multiple Equilibrium Model of Indicative Planning," *Journal of Comparative Economics* 14, no. 4 (December 1990), pp. 791–806.

[13] Editor's note: The theory of exchange developed by Léon Walras (1834–1910) compared the market's reconciliation of buyers' and sellers' offers of prices and quantities to the bidding process in an auction.

[14] Richard A. Musgrave, "National Economic Planning: The U.S. Case," *American Economic Review* 67, no. 1 (February 1977), pp. 50–54.

[15] See, for example, Richard Nathan, *Social Science in Government—Uses and Misuses* (New York: Basic Books, 1988).

A second consequence is that the questions that should be asked are different from those suggested by a theoretical approach to information *stricto sensu*. One type of questionnaire, by no means exhaustive, could read as follows:

- Is a formal national plan necessary? After all, it does not appear indispensable in the theories of information and transaction costs, where only the information flow between businesses counts.[16]
- If the answer is positive, do we need to introduce time yardsticks into the plan for the final year, or on a yearly basis? What would its status be? Would these yardsticks be formulated in absolute figures or by comparison with performance on foreign markets? Should they be corrected periodically if they seem to become obsolete?
- What type of decisions would it be advisable to clarify through a planning procedure?
- What is gained by submitting the plan for Parliamentary approval, an approval that is totally superfluous in the aforementioned theoretical approach?
- What is gained by defining the content of the plan through links (we avoid the word dialogue here) with actors other than businesses, for example, unions, government agencies, and voluntary associations?
- Last question: is the idea of indicative planning linked to certain political–cultural patterns? Would it merely die away in another environment? How can we explain that France and Japan remain faithful to indicative planning, while the United States, the United Kingdom, and Germany have never really been tempted by it?

---

[16] It would seem that for Musgrave, too, it is not absolutely necessary to have a national plan to remedy nonmarket failures; here again, the process would seem to count more than the product. Pierre Massé said: "The important thing is not having a plan; it's having done it."

*Chapter Ten*

# Economic Consequences of German Unification*

*Gerhard Pohl[1]*

*The integration of eastern Germany (the former German Democratic Republic, or GDR) into western Germany (the former Federal Republic of Germany, or FRG) is the major economic and political issue for the now united Germany.*

*In a dramatic example of the fall of a Communist state, the GDR's political and economic systems collapsed in 1989. In response, the FRG proposed first a currency union; then a more comprehensive monetary, economic, and social union; and ultimately full political unification. In 1990 the GDR merged with the FRG into a single Germany with the political and economic systems of the FRG.*

*In this chapter, Pohl discusses the weak economic performance of the GDR due to the deficiencies of its socialist centrally planned economic system. Next, he examines the components of the program for economic and political unification. Then he analyzes macroeconomic aspects of unification, including the rates for the conversion of the east German Mark (M) into the west German Deutsche Mark (DM) for current payments and for assets and liabilities; the relationship between wage levels in the two parts of the country; and the reasons for the sharp decline in manufacturing output in eastern Germany. He also considers microeconomic problems in the industrial, agricultural, and services sectors of eastern Germany. Pohl devotes special attention to issues in the privatization of GDR state enterprises. Finally, he appraises the investment program needed to create jobs and infrastructure in eastern Germany in order to narrow the economic and social gap between the western and eastern parts of the country.*

* Reprinted by permission from Gerhard Pohl, *Economic Consequences of German Reunification: Twelve Months after the Big Bang* (Working Paper Series no. 816; Washington, D.C.: World Bank, 1991), with the omission of some tables and references to foreign language sources, unpublished papers, and limited-circulation documents. Gerhard Pohl is Manager of the Private Sector Development and Finance Group, Technical Department, Europe, Central Asia, Middle East, and North Africa Regions, of the World Bank.

[1] The findings, interpretations, and conclusions are those of the author alone, and do not necessarily represent official World Bank policy.

173

*Large government expenditures for the reconstruction of eastern Germany have sharply increased the German budget deficit. Therefore, in an effort to restrain inflation, the German central bank has followed a tight monetary policy. However, high German interest rates strengthen the German DM relative to other West European currencies, weakening the movement toward economic and monetary union in the European Community, as will be explained in Chapter 11.*

## INTRODUCTION

Over the past two years, a political revolution has swept through Eastern Europe. One country after another has taken advantage of the changes in the Soviet Union to sweep away Communist regimes, to introduce democracy and civil liberties, and to restructure their economies into market economies. While political changes have been rapid, the economic restructuring promises to be a long and painful process. The German unification provides an opportunity to learn a few lessons about the immensity of this task in the best of all circumstances: the takeover by a "big brother" who is ready to lend a hand in the reconstruction task, and willing to foot most of the bill.

There are, of course, important differences between the situation of east Germany[2] and its former Comecon partners. They mostly relate to the fact that east Germany has become an integral part of a larger, and much richer, country. In east Germany, external factor mobility (of both labor and capital) plays an important role. In Eastern Europe, there will be little external labor mobility, and even capital flows will only play a secondary role. The adjustment mechanism will be primarily through an exchange rate adjustment, to generate exports to pay for imported investment goods. Most of the investment needed to adapt the outdated human and physical capital stock will have to be generated by domestic saving. East Germans, by contrast, are experiencing an immediate increase in living standards and consumption, financed by large fiscal transfers from west Germany.

Despite these obvious differences, there remain important common factors. East Germany shares with other Eastern European economies a common legacy of socialism and central planning that has led to similarly low productivity, similar poor integration into the world economy, similar technological backwardness, and a consequent need to restructure the economy from the basement to the roof. Eastern European countries also share the common aspiration to become full members of the European Community. Since the macroeconomic adjustments are different, transferable lessons are mostly in the microeconomics of structural change in east Germany. They relate both to the past—a more realistic assessment of the backwardness of socialist econo-

---

[2] The term *east Germany* is used to denote the area of the former German Democratic Republic (GDR) after unification (October 3, 1990). For earlier dates, the terms *GDR* and *East Germany* are used. The Federal Republic of Germany (FRG) denotes West Germany before unification.

mies—and the future, for example, the extent of restructuring required in industry, or lessons about the privatization process.

## THE LEGACY OF THE PAST

If there ever was a "model" socialist economy, it had to be the German Democratic Republic. It boasted the highest living standards among socialist countries and had implemented Stalin's model of "democratic centralism" (and its application to economic organization) most rigorously. The private sector accounted for only 4 percent of economic activity in 1989. As in Czechoslovakia, the government maintained tight control over enterprises, and avoided large macroeconomic imbalances or excessive external borrowing that plagued Poland, Yugoslavia, and Hungary.

The main shortcomings of the GDR economy were the common, systemic weaknesses of command economies: centralization and bureaucratization, excessive information requirements, poor incentives, and lack of individual initiative.[3] Together, they resulted in slow innovation and productivity growth. In order to manage the information overload of a command economy, autarky was pursued at all levels: internationally, within sectoral and regional bureaucracies, and even at the enterprise level. Enterprises tended to be large and self-contained, producing a large share of parts and components in-house, at suboptimal scale and often with inadequate, artisanal methods. Outdated production techniques at the plant level were combined with sectoral monopolies for final products, eliminating competition and stifling innovation and efficiency. Large units were created where there were no economies of scale, for example, in agriculture, but opportunities to reap economies of scale, for example, through specialization and buying-in of components in much of manufacturing were largely missed. Enterprises produced a very large range of products, as external trade was tightly circumscribed. The large range of social services provided directly by enterprises to their workers further reduced efficiency, and turned enterprises into social and political, rather than economic, organizations.

### Productivity and Income Levels

Western analysts have, in the past, widely overestimated the productivity and competitiveness of socialist economies.[4] Western estimates of income levels in

---

[3] For theoretical and empirical discussions of the shortcomings of socialist economies, see, for example, *Collectivist Economic Planning*, ed. F. A. Hayek (London: Routledge & Kegan Paul, 1935); David Granick, *Enterprise Guidance in Eastern Europe* (Princeton, N.J.: Princeton University Press, 1975); and Ed A. Hewett, *Reforming the Soviet Economy* (Washington, D.C.: Brookings Institution, 1988).

[4] Comparing Western and Eastern economic statistics was difficult for a number of reasons: (*a*) socialist countries used different methodologies for national income statistics; (*b*) administratively set prices and absence of competition led to different measures of inflation and real growth; (*c*)

Eastern Europe put East German per capita income at 50–70 percent of U.S. levels, and 43–86 percent of West German levels, depending on the methodology, with purchasing power and physical indicator methods at the upper end of the range. In all these estimates, the GDR is on top, followed by Czechoslovakia, Hungary, the USSR, Poland, and then the poorer southeastern European countries.

Binary purchasing power comparisons between East and West Germany have yielded estimates for East Germany pegging purchasing power GDP in East Germany at 58 percent of West German levels in 1983. The implied purchasing power parity exchange rate was estimated at around 1 : 1 (GDR Mark/ FRG DM). East German labor productivity averaged 49 percent of West German levels, ranging from 41 percent in agriculture to 51 percent in manufacturing and 57 percent in construction. Subsectoral estimates in manufacturing were lowest for process industries (cement, 41 percent; food and beverages, 43 percent) and highest for engineering goods (machinery, 56 percent).

In retrospect, all these comparisons failed to take account of the large, and increasing, difference in product quality between market and planned economies. Despite these shortcomings, the comparisons *within* each set of countries (planned or market) are reasonably reliable. Eastern European economies had similar management systems, resulting in similar investment and production patterns, and the same is true for most industrialized market economies. However, comparisons *across* different systems are hazardous. The planned economies have pursued very different policies, resulting in different, by Western standards highly distorted, production and consumption patterns.

The impact of quality differentials and economically irrational trade patterns became apparent when the veil on the secrets of East German trade statistics was lifted in 1990. Until then, trade statistics were expressed in "valuta mark" (VM), whose value was a mystery.[5] It was revealed that the domes-

---

limited involvement in foreign trade led to a very different economic structure; and (*d*) in some cases, unfavorable statistics were withheld and sometimes falsified. Western analysts have employed a number of techniques in trying to overcome these difficulties and to estimate comparable national income indicators for socialist economies. The simplest approach involved taking Eastern European national income data (based on the material product system—MPS) and adjusting them to Western definitions (GDP or GNP, according to the UN's system of national accounts—SNA), by adding in "non-material" services and depreciation to yield GDP in domestic currency. In the absence of market-determined exchange rates, an estimate had, however, to be made to convert GDP to a common denominator. Three approaches have been used: (*a*) using a purchasing power parity (PPP) exchange rate, derived from price comparisons; (*b*) adjusting official exchange rates or purchasing power parities to reflect market exchange rates; and (*c*) avoiding official national accounts data altogether, by estimating comparable income levels directly from detailed physical output data.

[5] The fiction of 1 VM = 1 DM was maintained in economic relations with West Germany. The official value in terms of a "transferable ruble" was 4.67 VM/TR, and the implicit cross rate with the DM (based again on the official, but equally arbitrary, dollar/ruble exchange rate of 0.65 TR/$) was 1.62 VM/DM in 1988. [Editor's note: The "transferable ruble," an accounting unit used in trade within the Soviet bloc, is discussed in Chapter 23.]

tic currency costs of convertible currency exports were 4.40 M/DM in 1989 rather than 1 : 1 or 1.6 : 1 implied in trade statistics.[6] Domestic resource costs[7] of convertible currency exports had increased sharply during the 1980s (from 2.40 M/DM in 1980 to 2.90 in 1985, and 4.40 in 1989), documenting a rapid loss in external competitiveness. The "equilibrium" market exchange rate—reflecting competitiveness in the tradable goods sector—was more than three-quarters below purchasing power parity. East Germany had fairly high living standards in terms of old fashioned "material" goods (eggs, bricks, or tram tickets), but living standards were low in terms of goods and services that had elsewhere experienced large quality changes (e.g., cars, consumer electronics, and prepared foods). The "Trabant," the symbol of the GDR's predicament, is a case in point: it is at best equivalent to a 1950s vintage West German car.

## Growth and Investment

Official statistics continued to paint a rosy picture of growth and economic development in the GDR—right up to the collapse of the regime. According to official statistics, East German per capita income had gained 66 percent on West Germany over the past three decades, and continued to grow at 4 percent per year (double West German rates) throughout the 1980s. The reality was different. Western estimates—based on microeconomic data—put East German GDP growth at slightly less than 2 percent per year for the 1980s, somewhat higher than in the neighboring socialist "reform" economies. But even this is an overestimate. In reality, productivity and external competitiveness have fallen further behind, as structural change (such as a reduction in agricultural or textile industry employment) remained very limited.

Like other Eastern European countries, the GDR tried to maintain flagging growth in the 1970s through increased external borrowing. Net external debt increased from negligible levels in 1970 to about $11 billion in 1980 and was used primarily to maintain high levels of industrial investment. The borrowing strategy proved unsustainable: external debt increased to three times convertible currency exports by 1979. With the onset of the second oil crisis, the borrowing strategy was reversed: exports were increased at all costs to reduce the outstanding debt. One avenue was fuel substitution: wherever possible, heavily polluting solid fuels were substituted for imported Soviet oil, and surplus oil was exported to the West.

Since income levels in the two parts of Germany were roughly the same before 1945, one can derive the growth rate, according to Western definitions,

---

[6] The underlying market-clearing exchange rate was actually even more unfavorable, since imports were tightly controlled through administrative restrictions, and an easing of these restrictions would have required a further exchange rate adjustment.

[7] Due to domestic price distortions, exports valued at domestic prices are not strictly domestic resource costs. However, for sufficiently broad categories of goods, subsidies and levies cancel out. For all convertible currency exports, costs at (distorted) domestic prices are approximately equal to domestic resource costs (= economic costs in domestic currency).

**TABLE 10–1**    Germany: Official and Reestimated Growth Rates,
1950–1989 (average annual growth rates in percent)

|  | GNP | GNP per Capita |
|---|---|---|
| Federal Republic of Germany | 4.2 | 3.6 |
| German Democratic Republic | | |
| Official Statistics (Net material product) | 5.6 | 5.9 |
| Based on 1989 GNP, at 1 : 1 Mark/DM | 1.6 | 1.9 |
| Based on 1989 GNP, at 4.40 Mark/DM | −2.2 | −1.9 |

SOURCES: FRG and GDR Statistical Yearbooks; Deutsches Institut für Wirtschaftsforschung [German Institut for Economic Research].

by comparing present and past income levels. Table 10–1 gives two measures. The first uses GNP estimates for the two parts in 1989, resulting from the Mark/DM conversion at 1 : 1 (about 52 percent of West German levels).[8] Under this assumption, per capita GNP growth for the GDR was 1.9 percent per year, roughly one half West Germany's rate. An alternative estimate can be derived by taking the GNP for 1989, and applying the implicit Mark/DM exchange rates for GDR exports in 1990 (4.40 M/DM).[9] This yields a far lower income level (15 percent of West Germany's), and an implicit per capita growth rate of *minus* 1.9 percent per year for the past four decades. The higher estimate is based on purchasing power parities (and would not be sustainable without massive fiscal transfers), while the lower estimate reflects international competitiveness in tradable goods, and is comparable to the situation of other Eastern European countries. The achievements of 40 years of socialism are, in comparable Western definitions, at best sluggish growth and perhaps even sustained regression, due to economic and technological isolation.

## Foreign Trade

As in other socialist countries, the external trade of East Germany was carried out exclusively through specialized foreign trade corporations that had a monopoly within their sector or product range and were the principal contact point for foreign buyers and sellers. Trade with member countries of the Council for Mutual Economic Assistance (CMEA, or Comecon) was carried out on the

---

[8] Derived from national accounts calculations for east Germany by the FRG Statistical Office for 1990, and growth rates for 1989/90, estimated by one of the leading German economic research institutes (DIW). Per capita GNP in east Germany in 1990 was 42 percent of west German levels. In view of the sharp decline in GNP in 1990 (−16 percent), the implicit value for 1989 is 52 percent.

[9] This exchange rate would have been unsustainable if the GDR economy had been opened to foreign competition (without massive capital inflows), as this rate reflects tight import restrictions. Moreover, the official GNP figure for 1989, released for the first time in 1990, has been revised downward by 20 percent.

basis of bilateral trade agreements. While raw material prices were based on five-year averages of world market prices, prices for industrial goods were essentially negotiated, since international prices for these (mostly uncompetitive) goods were hard to establish. Use of unrealistic transferable ruble/dollar exchange rates[10] made the share of CMEA trade appear far larger than its actual significance. At realistic ruble exchange rates, reflecting domestic resource costs, less than one half of East German trade was with CMEA members, and the same was true for most other East European economies.

Far more important is the low export-intensity, with per capita exports of around $990 for the GDR—less than Portugal ($1,200), and one fifth of West German levels ($5,500). Despite its orthodox command economy, total and convertible currency exports of the GDR were higher than elsewhere in Eastern Europe (on a per capita basis), reflecting the inherited industrial know-how and the special relationship with West Germany. Intra-German trade was treated in West Germany as domestic trade, with no tariff or other barriers applying to imports from East Germany. Not surprisingly, two thirds of East German exports to the European Community (EC) were to West Germany (although some may have been reexported to the rest of the EC, after entering duty-free via West Germany). Despite this favorable treatment, the share of East Germany in West Germany's imports declined from 1.6 percent in 1980 to 1.4 percent in 1989.

## Summary

Within the group of CMEA countries, the GDR maintained its position as the most developed and industrialized socialist economy. Compared to the "reform" economies, the preservation of orthodox Stalinist economic policies was not a major disadvantage. On two essential counts, growth and hard currency exports, the GDR continued to perform better than Hungary, Poland, or Yugoslavia. Compared to West Germany and other European market economies, the conclusion is very different. As elsewhere in Eastern Europe, the shortcomings of command economies led to inadequate incentives, inefficient organizational patterns, isolation from world markets, and a divorce from the international division of labor and the diffusion of technological progress. The production of increasingly outdated and unwanted products increased at a moderate rate, but in terms of comparable measures of economic growth and welfare, the GDR experienced four decades of virtual stagnation. However, as in other Eastern European countries, living standards and productive potential are significantly higher than suggested by per capita incomes at market-clearing exchange rates, which reflect the distortions of the past, and the high demand for imported investment goods after the sudden opening of these economies.

---

[10] The official cross rate was originally 0.65 TR/$. In 1989, TR/$ cross rates used in national trade statistics ranged from 0.65 in Bulgaria to 1.74 in the GDR, 2.09 in Hungary, and 2.96 in Poland.

## UNIFICATION: THE EVOLVING POLICY FRAMEWORK

Chancellor Kohl's proposal for a currency union, made in early February 1990, was essentially a political decision. Until then, virtually all proposals made by the economics profession envisaged a gradual transition of the GDR toward a market economy, including a step-by-step move toward convertibility, supported by a flexible exchange rate policy.[11] The offer for monetary union was made conditional on the GDR "creating simultaneously the legal prerequisites for introducing a social market economy."

### Monetary and Economic Union

The principal features of the "monetary, economic, and social union" negotiated in May 1990 included:

- Conversion of all current payments at an exchange rate of 1 : 1 (M/DM), roughly maintaining past purchasing power.
- Conversion of all outstanding monetary claims and liabilities at 2 : 1, except for a per capita quota of savings, converted at 1 : 1.
- Adoption, by the GDR, of a market economy, based on private property.
- Introduction of a common legal and regulatory environment, based on the laws of the Federal Republic.
- Introduction of the main features of West German social policies, including free collective bargaining, comprehensive retirement, medical and unemployment insurance, and worker participation in company organs.

The question of the appropriate conversion from Marks to DM created the most heated controversy in the discussions leading to the monetary union. In recent years, the implicit exchange rate for convertible currency exports had deteriorated to 4.4 M/DM (see above) and free market rates (outside the GDR) had been around 12 : 1. A majority of economists and commentators in West Germany, including the Bundesbank (the West German central bank), argued for a 2 : 1 rate as the maximum feasible, while public opinion in East Germany was strongly in favor of a 1 : 1 conversion (implying pretax wages of about one third the West German level). The arguments for a 1 : 1 conversion were based on past purchasing power and productivity comparisons (see above). They also reflected political and social concerns. It was difficult to "sell" reunification to GDR citizens, if that involved perceived large cuts in living standards, while

---

[11] The Council of Economic Advisors of the Federal Republic of Germany did not even mention the possibility of a monetary union in its advisory report on economic reform options for the GDR just two weeks before the proposal was made. However, a few prominent West German economists and politicians of both colors had advocated a rapid monetary union, and the advisory council of the Ministry of Economics had envisaged such an option in December as part of an alternative scenario that would lead to rapid political unification.

much better-off West Germans would not have to share much of their income and wealth.

This still left the question of what to do with outstanding assets and liabilities of enterprises and households. Imported equipment had generally been sold to enterprises at the implicit exchange rate (recently 4.40 M/DM) and was financed by channeling household savings and deposits through the state bank to enterprises. A 1 : 1 conversion would have burdened enterprises with debt up to four times the actual value of imported plant and equipment. The approach finally adopted was currency conversion with monetary reform, not unlike the 1948 currency reform in West Germany: wages, pensions, stipends, rentals, and other current payments were converted at 1 : 1; all past claims were converted at 2 : 1.[12] The resulting conversion was 1 : 1 for current payments, and an average of around 1.8 : 1 for the consolidated balance sheet of the banking system. From a monetary perspective, the conversion was not too different from the Bundesbank proposal of 2 : 1 that also included an (unspecified) adjustment of wages to compensate for losses in purchasing power arising from price adjustments. The currency reform had dramatic consequences for the balance sheets of financial institutions: a substantial part of their liabilities was converted at 1 : 1, while almost all assets were converted at 2 : 1, leaving large negative net worth. An "equalization fund" was set up to cover valuation losses arising from the currency conversion, plus any shortfalls to meet West German capital adequacy rules for banks. These assets are interest-bearing and will be amortized over a period of 40 years.

*Privatization* issues were, together with the "appropriate" exchange rate, among the most contested issues in the discussions on economic union. There was little disagreement about the switch to a market economy, based on private ownership and the legal and regulatory framework of the FRG. There was, however, disagreement on the scope and means of privatization, and the extent of reprivatization (restitution) to former owners. As discussed further below, misperceptions in East Germany about the value of "productive" assets of the GDR explain most of these differences. The monetary union treaty left many details to be resolved later. In the months before the economic union, a number of legal changes had already been introduced to permit private sector activities, to reprivatize small and medium enterprises nationalized in 1972, and to convert state enterprises into independent entities, with ownership vested into a state property fund, the Treuhandanstalt. The law on privatization and reorganization of state property, enacted at the same time as the monetary union treaty, provided for the privatization of all state enterprises and most other state property.

A number of *transitional measures* were agreed on in the treaty to assist enterprises to adjust. These included temporary quantitative restrictions on

---

[12] Except for a per capita quota for savings accounts, converted at 1 : 1 up to a maximum of M 4,000 per adult (equivalent to about four months pre-union wages), M 2,000 for children, and M 6,000 for retired persons. The average conversion rate for savings accounts was about 1.4 : 1.

imports of agricultural products; temporary import duties on certain consumer durables; investment subsidies of 12 percent for the first year and 8 percent for the second year of the economic union; and a reduction of the value-added tax in the Federal Republic for GDR imports. In the event, the temporary import restrictions and import duties proved unenforceable, once border controls were eliminated, and were abolished in the first weeks of the economic union.

The adoption of the West German tax system had the effect of dramatically reducing east German *government revenues,* previously based on high levies on enterprises. The resulting deficit was projected to reach about DM 52 billion (20 percent of GNP) for the first full year after the economic union. Two thirds of the projected deficit was to be financed by budgetary transfers from the Federal Republic and one third through borrowing of the GDR government. Most of the financing of the FRG portion was to be carried out through a "German Unity Fund" of DM 115 billion, covering expenditures during 1990–94. The increase in public sector borrowing for the economic union (the German Unity Fund plus the borrowing by the GDR government in its own name) was estimated at slightly over 2 percent of West German GNP in 1991, and was projected to decline rapidly thereafter.

## Political Unification

Once the desolate status of the East German economy became evident with the implementation of the monetary and economic union on July 1, 1990, political pressures to accelerate the unification multiplied. The unification treaty was negotiated in less than two months and signed on August 31, and went into effect on October 3, 1990. It was complemented by a treaty with the former Allied Powers, settling the external aspects of German unification and reestablishing full sovereignty. The treaty included only a few substantive changes in the laws and institutions of the Federal Republic, but many changes had to be made to legal texts to reflect transitional provisions and extensions of authority to the new territories. Rather than designing entirely new policies and institutions for the transition of eastern Germany to a market economy, special support measures have generally been designed through simple amendments of long-standing FRG policies.[13] The unification treaty accelerated the process of economic integration and provided additional financial assistance. The "German Unity Fund" was to remain the principal source for financial assistance to east Germany, but in addition, federal expenditure programs were now extended to east Germany and the social security systems were merged, providing an open-ended commitment to bear the social costs of economic adjustments.

---

[13] The measures agreed to under the union and unification treaties had also to be consistent with EC laws and regulations. Temporary derogations were granted by the EC for some transitional measures.

**Public Administration.**   The unification treaty extended the restructuring process to the public sector. Public administration in east Germany was remodeled according to the west German federal system, leading to an entirely new government structure. Existing administrative units were transferred to federal, state, and local levels in accordance with west German practice. Qualified personnel were retained only according to needs. Civil service positions are now open to all Germans and appointments are to be made on merit. Since salary scales are lower in the new territories, western German states have made available qualified personnel on a secondment basis. East German government employees will have to pass civil service examinations to obtain tenure.

**Property and Privatization.**   The unification treaty provided further clarification of property and ownership issues. The general principle adopted was that all expropriated property should be restituted to previous owners, whenever possible. Several exceptions were made from this principle, including (*a*) exclusion of property expropriated by Soviet occupation forces during 1945–49 from restitution (including agricultural estates, expropriated during the 1949 land "reform"); (*b*) compensation, in lieu of restitution, whenever property had been substantially changed (e.g., built up), or had been acquired by private citizens *in good faith*; and (*c*) compensation, in lieu of restitution, whenever property is needed for "essential investments" (business, public, or housing), as certified by property restitution agencies.

State property of the GDR has been assigned to various public bodies of the Federal Republic, according to their function. Ownership rights over state enterprises had already been assigned to the privatization agency (Treuhandanstalt). The postal and telecommunications services have been merged, but the east German railways (Reichsbahn) will be merged into the Federal Railways only at a later date, after restructuring (and layoffs).[14] State-owned housing (excluding housing cooperatives) has been transferred to local governments for eventual privatization. Assets that are required for administrative tasks of various government levels have been assigned to them. All other state property (e.g., natural parks, forests) became federal property. Property previously owned by state and local governments is to be returned. All liabilities of the GDR have been transferred into a special fund of the federal government. Privatization proceeds are to be used to reduce these liabilities, with any residual liabilities shared equally between the federal and the new state governments. An eventual positive residual from privatization proceeds (after amortization of past GDR state debts) is to be distributed to residents of eastern Germany (e.g., in form of shares in former state enterprises). It is, however, very unlikely that the privatization of state enterprises will leave a positive residual (see below).

---

[14] The government wants to combine the merger of the railways with a conversion of the Federal Railways into company status, and termination of civil service status for railway employees. This requires, however, an amendment of the constitution.

**Public Finance.**    The financing of the costs of unification was to be raised through borrowing and expenditure reductions in other programs, rather than a tax increase, on the theory that these are exceptional, one-time costs. In view of the DM 115 billion made available through the German Unity Fund, the western states (Länder) refused at first to have the new states participate on equal terms in revenue equalization, but full participation was agreed to after the elections.[15] All federal expenditure programs have been expanded to the new, eastern half of the country. In addition, a number of special assistance programs for the new territories have been agreed (or have been carried over from the first treaty). These include a temporary subsidy for all equipment investments (12 percent in 1991, 8 percent in 1992); temporary special depreciation allowances; inclusion in regional support programs for industrial and high-tech service sector investments (up to 23 percent of investment costs, but limited by budgetary allocations);[16] subsides of up to 90 percent for local government investments in business infrastructure; low-interest credit programs for other local infrastructure investments; low-interest credit programs for housing modernization; and financing for start-up assistance for small and medium-size enterprises. One of the largest items is the open-ended coverage of social security expenditures through the merged social security funds. An additional federal infrastructure investment and assistance program for eastern Germany was approved after the elections in March 1991. The annual financing requirements for east Germany are now estimated at around 4 percent of west German GNP for the next several years, twice the amount projected before the union.

**Social Issues.**    The unification treaty accelerates and concludes the "social union" that had already partly been established with the economic union treaty. The national pension systems are being merged in 1991. Similarly, the health and accident insurance systems (a mixture of compulsory public and alternative private insurance) are being extended to the east during 1991, with lower service fees for a transitional period. Special provisions have been made for partial layoffs and early retirement. Until the end of 1991, enterprises can partially lay off workers (who then receive partial unemployment benefits) to avoid terminations and unemployment.[17] But protection against termination, included in several collective bargaining agreements, has been voided, and

---

[15] Most German taxes are being shared according to preset formulas between the federal, state, and local governments. In addition, a revenue equalization fund redistributes tax revenues among states according to population and "needs." The result is a rather homogeneous distribution of tax revenue to state and local governments, on a per capita basis.

[16] These programs have to meet EC competition policy guidelines, limiting the extent of investment subsidies for regional development programs.

[17] This was again done through a simple (but very liberal) amendment of a long-standing provision of the FRG unemployment insurance, which provides partial unemployment compensation for temporary partial layoffs ("short-time work"). As opposed to west Germany, east German enterprises do not have to guarantee that the reduction in working hours is only temporary.

lapsed in mid-1991. Special preretirement provisions entail a transitional payment of 65 percent of net salaries for a period of up to 3 years for employees over 57 years of age (now reduced to 55 years).

## MACROECONOMIC CONSEQUENCES OF UNIFICATION

### Political Choices

In the discussion of the German unification, its most important features have sometimes been overlooked, particularly in comments made by economists. These essential features are political: the relations between east and west Germany are not any more relations among nations. The citizens of the former GDR have become full and *voting* citizens of an enlarged Federal Republic. With one fifth of the voters, they have a considerable weight in elections, and politicians who want to stay in power better listen to their concerns.

The key example in this regard is the discussion on the "appropriate" exchange rate at the time of the monetary union. The 1 : 1 conversion for current payments, roughly equivalent to a maintenance of purchasing power, has been widely criticized as a mistake. Indeed, it was a mistake, if the standard of judgment is one of self-help and zero solidarity. With a recent effective exchange rate of 4.40 M/DM, the monetary union represents an appreciation of 340 percent. Left to its own devices, east Germany could never hope to compete and maintain macroeconomic stability at a 1 : 1 exchange rate (and wages one third of west Germany's). On the other hand, east Germans are fairly well educated and trained, particularly in technical fields. Many east German scientists, engineers, technicians, and craftsmen have skills equivalent to their west German counterparts, or need only limited additional training. Taken individually, and transferred to west German firms, many are just as productive as their west German counterparts. The low productivity and competitiveness of the GDR economy was a consequence of the *system*. A radical change in that system can be expected to raise productivity rapidly, but even the most hurried implementation will take 2 to 3 years before results will be tangible.

During this transition, the concept of average productivity is virtually meaningless. Some activities and firms are approaching west German productivity levels very rapidly, but others will take years. The essence is that labor (and capital) is extremely heterogeneous during the period of transition. For example, east German workers along the former border are readily finding work in west Germany, at west German wages (half a million are now commuting to the west). For others, the commuting would take too long. Some have skills that can be readily used (e.g., engineers and technicians), but others do not have marketable skills, and need to be retrained (e.g., administrative and commercial personnel, lawyers, Communist Party functionaries, state security employees, and so on). Moreover, productivity changes will not happen smoothly. Productivity will probably take a leap in 2 to 3 years when the initial batch of investment projects will come to fruition.

Lower wages would have saved many old, low productivity jobs, but would have also slowed economic change in east Germany, and would have led to substantial outmigration of those with readily marketable skills. These are exactly the people who are essential for a rapid transformation of the east German economy. The present "high" wages (roughly 50 percent of west German wages, after large wage increases in 1990 and 1991) will eliminate many low productivity jobs and will increase adjustment pressures on firms and the labor market. These wages are feasible only with large fiscal transfers to finance adjustment costs, and to provide incentives to the private sector to switch investments eastward. The low income and the small size of east Germany (relative to west Germany) make this possible.[18]

Two other political factors must be kept in mind in discussing the consequences of the unification. First, the monetary union and political unification treaties—both very complex legal, political, and economic agreements—were negotiated under enormous time pressure, in each case in about six weeks. Compromises were made in some respects in the full knowledge that those were not durable solutions to the problems, and that corrective action would be needed later. Second, politicians inside and outside the government realized keenly that one cannot win elections with promises of hardship[19] or tax increases. The severity of the adjustment problems in east Germany were thus glossed over before the elections. Realism and plans for tax increases were on the table immediately after the elections.

## Macroeconomic Developments

The economic consequences of the sudden switch to a market economy were more severe than expected. Actual developments deviated from earlier expectations in three major ways:

1. East German consumers switched to imported (west German) goods to a far larger extent than expected, "abandoning themselves" as producers.
2. Wage settlements, resulting from collective bargaining agreements, increased wages by one third during 1990, and another third during 1991, raising pretax wages to about one half west German levels by mid-1991.
3. Exports to the Soviet Union, which had been counted upon to maintain employment during the transition, sharply declined with the switch to convertible currency trade in early 1991, and because of the economic dislocation within the Soviet Union.

---

[18] A simple back-of-the-envelope calculation makes the point: at a 1 : 1 conversion of past net wages into DM (equivalent to 40 percent of west German net wages), the cost of the total east German wage bill is about DM 100 billion, or 4.8 percent of west German GNP. A fiscal transfer of that magnitude, while large, is economically feasible, and it would thus be possible to put the entire east German labor force out of work, at 100 percent unemployment compensation.

[19] Except, perhaps, in the case of external aggression. See Winston Churchill's promise of "blood, sweat, and tears."

The first two of these factors were internal to the unification process, and could perhaps have been anticipated. But they were not. The third factor is an unexpected external shock that is increasing adjustment costs, directly through reduction in export earnings, plant closures, and increased unemployment; and indirectly, through sharply lowered expectations about the future of the Soviet market and, consequently, reduced attractiveness of east German enterprises for west German and foreign investors. These unexpected developments have, in turn, affected other variables. The most important was the drastic decline in manufacturing output, which slumped by half immediately after the economic union, and by another third at the end of 1990, when export commitments to the Soviet Union expired.

**Shifting Demand.**   The sharp decline in manufacturing output was the combined effect of the sudden opening to external trade, which made many east German products uncompetitive, and the pent-up demand of east German residents for western goods. Sometimes, quality differences were only perceived, and attributed to the packaging and brand names of Western products,[20] but often, they were real. It had also to do with rapidly shifting demand patterns: people reduced consumption of formerly subsidized items (e.g., restaurant meals) to buy previously unavailable, or high-priced, Western consumer durables (such as audio-visual equipment, cars, furniture, and appliances). The number of registered cars increased by nearly 1 million (23 percent) in the first six months of the union. Consumers also made a large part of their purchases on weekly shopping trips to western Germany as east German retailers were not yet competitive on choice and price. Finally, the switch to modern marketing techniques and Western quality standards led to some temporary adjustment problems.[21] Gradually, these problems are being overcome, and manufacturing output increased for the first time in June 1991. Surveys of manufacturers indicate a 30 percent increase in turnover for the second half of 1991.

**Wages.**   The effect of the high wage settlements resulting from the first "free" collective bargaining round is more difficult to assess since it happened simultaneously with the monetary union, and its incremental impact is thus hard to assess. At the margin, it has made more jobs redundant, thus increasing unemployment. It may also have reduced inflows of private capital and investment. But the extent is difficult to gauge. The higher purchasing power of east German consumers is also increasing consumer spending and tax revenues, creating additional business opportunities and attracting additional investment. The main effect has been to take purchasing power from the pockets of well-heeled west Germans, and put it into the pockets of their poorer eastern brethren.

---

[20] East German citizens had been watching West German TV, including advertising, for decades.

[21] For example, supermarkets simply did not order products without bar-coded product numbers (facilitating automatic checkout and inventory management).

**TABLE 10–2** East Germany: Contract and Effective Wages, 1990–94 (percent of west German wages)

|          | Year          | Contract Wage* | Effective Wage |
|----------|---------------|----------------|----------------|
| Actual:  | 1989          | —              | 33             |
|          | 1990, 2nd half| 50             | 41             |
|          | 1991          | 60             | 47             |
| Projected:| 1992         | 70             | 55             |
|          | 1993          | 80             | 65             |
|          | 1994          | 100            | 80             |

\* Approximate average of sectoral collective bargaining agreements. Only the (pace-setting) metal industry and the textile industry agreements cover the entire four year period 1991–94. Agreements are different in some sectors or regions, for example, the construction industry in east Berlin (70–75 percent in 1991).
SOURCE: German Federation of Employers.

Long-term collective bargaining agreements, concluded in the spring of 1991, provide for an increase of east German wages to about 60 percent of west German *contract* wages in mid-1991, rising to 100 percent of west German contract wages by 1994. However, average *effective* wages are only 47 percent of west German levels in 1991, and are expected to reach 80 percent by 1991, as bonuses and benefits will reach full parity with west Germany only after 1994 (see Table 10–2). The difference in part also reflects job-grading, with a larger percentage of east German employees rated in more junior job categories.[22]

The effects of collective bargaining agreements since the monetary union have been far more important determinants of present wage levels in east Germany than the 1 : 1 currency conversion: wages in mid-1991 are 75 percent higher than a year earlier. It could be argued that the 1990 collective bargaining agreements reflected negotiations between the unions and "agents without principals," that is, managers of state enterprises with nobody fulfilling the role of owners. However, this cannot be said for the 1991 bargaining round: important segments of the east German economy were already privatized (commerce, banking, utilities, some manufacturing) and the ownership function for state enterprises had been clearly lodged in the Treuhandanstalt. Employer associations either believe that the agreed wages are feasible, or are behaving irresponsibly.

**Comecon Trade.** The external shock of reduced Soviet demand hit east Germany in January 1991. Until then, export commitments under the annual bilat-

---

[22] The collective bargaining agreements can be terminated by both sides with three months' notice and could, in theory, be revised downward, if the agreed wages have unacceptable consequences on employment.

eral trade agreement with the Soviet Union were honored, albeit at the cost of large subsidies (totaling DM 4 billion for the second half of 1990). The termination of CMEA barter agreements at the end of 1990 led to a further sizable decline in industrial output, mostly due to the economic dislocations and uncertainty in the Soviet Union. East German imports from Comecon countries had declined already immediately after the monetary union, as demand for domestic goods (using Comecon inputs) collapsed. The Federal Republic has offered to compensate Comecon trade partners for canceled contracts. The effect of the unification on other Eastern European countries has been far less than has been feared. Total (west and east) German imports from Eastern Europe in the second half of 1990 were already substantially higher than in 1989 (+5 percent), reflecting both a switch to west German distribution channels and buoyant west German import demand in the wake of unification.[23] Early reformers benefited most: German imports from Poland increased by 46 percent in 1990, equivalent to 200 percent of past Polish exports to the GDR.[24] Strong double-digit growth of imports from Eastern Europe has continued in 1991.

## Changing Economic Forecasts

The press and some of the outside observers have characterized the aftermath of the unification as a "disaster,"[25] and some have even likened developments in east Germany to the depression of the 1930s.[26] The latter misses the point that only the production of shoddy and unwanted goods is declining, while consumption is leaping at totally unprecedented rates. A better picture of the expected and unexpected consequences can be obtained by comparing successive forecasts of economic developments prepared by one of the "Big Five" German economic research institutes, the DIW (German Institute for Economic Research).[27] Successive DIW forecasts show which consequences of the unification had been correctly forecast, and where errors were made. They also show a swing to pessimism during the winter, when most of the unification news seemed to be bad, and a correction toward more optimistic views, once investment intentions became clearer, and unification was put on sounder fiscal feet after the elections. Actual outcomes in 1991 are now likely to be somewhat more favorable than in the June 1991 forecast.

---

[23] Valuing past CMEA imports into the GDR at the effective exchange rate of 4.4 Mark/DM.

[24] At the TR/$ crossrate used in Polish trade statistics (2.96 TR/$), presumably reflecting Polish costs.

[25] For example, Mr. Pöhl, the President of the Bundesbank (in trying to argue against rapid European monetary union).

[26] For example, George Akerlof, Andrew K. Rose, Janet L. Yellin, and Helga Hessenius, "East Germany in from the Cold: The Economic Aftermath of Unification," *Brookings Papers on Economic Activity,* no. 1, 1991, pp. 1–105.

[27] Fortunately, DIW staff were courageous enough to forecast full-fledged national accounts for east Germany, even before the economic union, and on the basis of rather shaky east German statistics. Other research institutes, the Ministry of Economics, and the Council of Economic Advisors were more prudent and have made only very summary and qualitative forecasts.

On the employment front, the extent of overstaffing has been underestimated. Early projections forecast the maintenance of artificially high labor force participation, particularly among women. This proved wrong. Total labor force participation has rapidly declined to west German levels. The loss of jobs was concentrated in the manufacturing sector, where about one half of all jobs will be lost by the end of 1991. Total working hours have declined even more rapidly than output, yielding considerable productivity gains in 1991, and revealing the extent of hidden unemployment in past work practices. Earlier fears that the large number of terminations at the end of June 1991 (half a million) would lead to further large increases in unemployment have not materialized. Since mid-1991, open unemployment has held constant at about 1 million, while the number of short-time workers has continued to decline rapidly (from a peak of 2 million in April to 1.3 million in September). However, government-financed retraining and employment programs account for a large part of the reduction in short-time work.

Forecasters also failed to foresee the sharp decline in manufacturing output and were too optimistic about the timing of the recovery. Early forecasts have not adequately taken into account that planning and approval of most investments takes some time. Investment activity has remained flat for the first 12 months of the union, but is expected to increase by about 40 percent in the second half of 1991. Early infrastructure investments were concentrated in telecommunications and railway rehabilitation, where lead times were short, but large investment projects are now in advanced planning stages.

Forecasters also underestimated the fiscal consequences of the unification, but by less than has been suggested by the press. At the time of the initial forecast, unification was generally expected for sometime in 1991, and the projections were made on an economic community, rather than a unified country, basis—involving a far lower extent of burden sharing. The earlier forecast included a substantial unidentified "other financing" gap that had not yet been covered by West German government commitments and would have had to be raised by borrowing in the name of the GDR, and would have eventually become a liability of the FRG. Comparisons of the financing agreed under the "German Unity Fund" (covering only part of the forecast fiscal deficit) and later estimates of the total fiscal gap are thus misleading. The main change between the early and mid-1991 forecasts is the fiscal consolidation (through tax increases) of a financing gap, long forecast, but yet uncovered.

The principal items in increased spending are higher transfer payments to unemployed and pensioners, mostly due to higher than expected wages (to which social security benefits are tied); a more pronounced decline in employment (cushioned by a number of one-time social measures, such as generous early retirement benefits); accelerated infrastructure investment programs; and expanded incentives for private investors. Total government expenditures in 1991 are now expected to be less than forecast in mid-1991, because infrastructure investment have taken more time to plan, and labor market developments are somewhat more favorable. The public sector borrowing requirement has also been revised downward, as government revenues have been more buoyant than expected.

## The Costs of Unification

A lot of confusion has arisen about the "costs" of the German unification, and costs and benefits are often liberally confused, or even added up. Strictly speaking, the costs of unification are only what economists would call dead-weight losses, such as transitional unemployment arising from a rapid change in economic policies and signals. Alternatively, one could take into account all costs (expenditures), but then also need to take into account all benefits as well. Different approaches to economic reforms will involve different time paths of cost and benefit streams. Rapid reforms are likely to create larger costs early on, but earlier and larger benefits. More gradual reforms may involve lower costs up-front, but also lower and later benefits. An obvious strategy is to try to minimize deadweight losses, such as transitional unemployment. But even this should be done only to the extent to which it does not reduce benefits, or increase other costs, by a larger margin. A strategy entailing higher transitional unemployment may thus be preferable, if it leads to more rapid restructuring of the economy and higher productivity earlier.[28]

A lower conversion rate at the time of monetary union, and lower subsequent wage settlements, would have clearly involved lower costs for west Germans (and concomitantly lower benefits for east Germans). But the adopted "high cost" solution may yet turn out to be beneficial to west Germans too, if the costs are made up by more rapid productivity growth in west Germany, resulting, for example, from economies of scale in an enlarged domestic market, from a reduction in uneconomic expenditures (e.g., coal mining subsidies or defense expenditures), or from further deregulation (for example, in telecommunications, labor markets, or transport). There are some signs that the large costs of the unification for west German taxpayers may yet lead to a political consensus to tackle longstanding, but politically seemingly immovable, waste and inefficiencies. If it happens, the net benefits from unification may yet be positive for west Germans too.

## MICROECONOMIC CONSEQUENCES OF UNIFICATION

The most important lessons from a microeconomic perspective are that the productivity and competitiveness of state enterprises have turned out to be far worse than expected, and that the restructuring process is taking longer. In the discussions before the monetary union, some economists and policymakers had likened the situation to the 1948 monetary reform in the Federal Republic,

---

[28] Conceptually, this could be measured as discounted incremental national income, resulting from such a strategy. In view of the uniqueness of the reforms, costs and benefits are impossible to quantify accurately.

and expected a rapid increase in production and investment, once the "magic of the market" was permitted to work. That was a misplaced analogy. In 1948, the German economy was a potentially functioning market economy—despite the intervening war years and war-related economic controls—and had already recovered from the collapse at the end of the war. Most importantly, entrepreneurs and managers, fully conversant with market practices, were still in place. Technological progress had continued in the interim, albeit for the wrong purposes. Even the productive capital stock corresponded approximately to 1939 levels, despite war-related damage, due to the massive investments during the war years. A more appropriate comparison is thus 1945–46, but reliable data are not available for West Germany for the immediate post-war period. In the United States, industrial production declined by 55 percent in late 1945. In this perspective, the slump of east German industrial production (by 65 percent) does not look all that exceptional. The recovery will, of course, take longer since it involves not only retooling from wartime to civil production, but the introduction of an entirely new system.

Forty years of command economy have led to a totally ill-adapted and inadequate capital stock and to totally different management and work practices, and entrepreneurs have virtually disappeared. East Germany has the advantage that the legal bases (such as property rights, civil and commercial codes, and company law) were introduced overnight. Moreover, these legal institutions are beginning to function properly within a year or two, due to massive help and training provided by west German professionals (civil servants, accountants, lawyers, judges, and others). After a chaotic start in 1990, considerable progress has also been made in establishing a functioning public administration. This is not only demonstrated by the breathtaking speed of privatization transactions (see below), but across the whole range of government services. Western managers and investors have generally high praise for the training and skills of technical personnel, and the dedication and quick learning of middle-level managers. The most difficult problem is to find competent and experienced top managers.

## Industry

The desolate status of industry is only now being fully appreciated. Earlier expectations, particularly among east German officials, were that the privatization of industry would yield considerable sales revenues, and clauses were inserted into the union and unification treaties, granting east German citizens the residual from the sales bonanza, once enterprise and state debts had been paid off. That residual is probably going to be a negative number. At one half west German wages, almost all east German industrial state enterprises are making losses. The key element in the restructuring of nearly all firms is a reduction in the labor force. As elsewhere in Eastern Europe, early expectations were that one third of the enterprises could become competitive without much restructuring, another third needed extensive rehabilitation, and another third would have to be closed. This has proven wrong. Most manufacturing firms need to lay off around one half of their labor force, with relatively little variation. In a survey of enterprises in mid-1991, expected layoffs due to restructuring ranged from 65 percent in the steel and textile industries to "only" 30 percent in printing and woodworking, with most subsectors in the 40–60 percent range. On the other hand, fewer enterprises will need to be entirely liquidated, but layoffs may be as much as 80–90 percent of the labor force in some cases.

The layoffs are in about equal parts due to true overstaffing, in the sense that the same amount can be readily produced with fewer people, and the far-flung role of socialist firms, catering for many worker needs that can be delivered more efficiently by small and specialized firms. The low level of productivity is not primarily due to low levels of skills and training of the work force (as in poor countries), but due to inadequate incentives, inappropriate organization, and irrational work practices, fostered by a utopian ideology.

The reduction in employment is particularly dramatic (1) in sectors where autarky and autonomous technology development have been pursued, for example, in much of the chemical and steel industries or microelectronics, and (2) in labor-intensive industries which should have been gradually phased out years ago, for example, shipbuilding or textiles. Some of these industries are geographically concentrated and their closure or restructuring will have important consequences for the local labor market: unemployment is likely to be concentrated in a few depressed areas that were until now the pillars of industrial development. Short-term employment prospects are best in construction-related branches (metal and woodworking, cement, etc.) and in industries producing for local markets (food industry, printing). Skill-intensive sectors (machinery, automobiles, electrical, some chemicals) have good longer-term prospects, but need new technology and products.

## Agriculture

The above characterization of the industrial sector applies fully to the agricultural sector as well. It is simply one of the labor-intensive sectors that should have been restructured years ago. Even at the high European agricultural prices, east Germany's agriculture is not competitive with other European producers. At present, about 60 percent of the agricultural cooperatives are operating at a loss (around 30 percent were operating at a loss already before the economic union). The reason is simple: overstaffing. Agricultural employment per 100 hectares (247 acres) was 14 in East Germany, compared to 2 in West Germany—despite the fact that in East Germany 93 percent of the agricultural land was farmed by huge cooperatives and state farms, rather than by too many small family farms (West Germany's agricultural dilemma). Most of the former agricultural production cooperatives have converted to a new legal form, and 10–15 percent are presently being dissolved.

Property issues do not seem to be the major problem. One half of the agricultural land is again private property of cooperative members, another fifth belongs to other private persons, and one quarter is under the administration of the privatization agency. As of mid-1991, property title remains uncertain for only 6 percent of the agricultural land area. The principal problem is that few cooperative members are willing to take the plunge and become agro-entrepreneurs. Most were agricultural workers, and they do not have the confidence that they can survive in a competitive marketplace. Only 3,500 family farms had been created by mid-1991.

The restructuring of agricultural cooperatives will need to be as extensive as for industrial enterprises. The separation of plant and animal production will need to be reversed, the huge production units (up to 5,000 hectares) need to be broken apart, and many nonagricultural units need to be split off from the basic business. Agricultural employment has already been reduced by 30 percent, and one half of the remaining agricultural labor force is on partial unemployment. The agricultural labor force needs to be reduced by at least another 40 percent before farming can become profitable. Fortunately, only one fifth of the cooperative members are landowners. This should help to ease the required reduction in the labor force. A number of west German farmers have taken advantage of the large tracts of land that are becoming available, and have moved their business east.

## Services

The brightest short-term prospects are in commerce and services. The privatization of commerce and service establishments is practically completed (see below), employment in banking and insurance is already growing, and a large number of new businesses are being created (about 400,000 by mid-1991), mostly concentrated in commerce, services, and crafts. The privatization of the health sector is also progressing faster than expected: half of all doctors have already established a private practice, and another third have applied for a license. But most of these services are local services, and they depend on other economic activities for their survival. For business services that could become part of the "economic base," the situation is not much better than in industry or agriculture: they also need a considerable infusion of up-to-date technology and management skills.

Housing reform is not yet under way. Rent controls remain the most important exception from the rapid switch to market principles. As a first measure, maintenance and heating costs have been increased to full-cost recovery in October 1991. This will raise housing costs by about 250 percent and will increase the share of household income devoted to housing from 2.4 percent in mid-1991 to about 8 percent—still less than half the west German average. Ownership for most of the public housing stock has been transferred to local governments for eventual privatization. As long as rents remain far below market values, the incentive to buy is not very strong. Mortgage debt is about DM 50 billion (DM 10,000 per apartment) and could be easily assumed by the future owners. The costs of required renovations to meet Western housing standards are more substantial (DM 40,000 per unit), but far less than the costs of new apartments (around DM 150,000).

## Privatization

Privatization requires both a clear attribution of ownership rights and the creation of a competitive environment to ensure that the new owners and managers behave in a socially desirable manner. In east Germany, this task has been made easier by the wholesale importation of the west German legal and institutional framework. Privatization can thus focus on the more immediate task of bringing in competent management and up-to-date technology. The preferred option is thus the sale of state enterprises to successful west German and foreign firms. However, other privatization techniques are also considered, where appropriate, including management and employee buyouts, particularly for smaller enterprises. Maximizing sales is not the principal or overriding objective. The speed of transition and rapid gains in employment are essential. The quality of the business plan proposed by potential acquirers is thus of overriding importance.

After some initial difficulties, the privatization of state enterprises in east Germany has moved into full gear in early 1991. Since the beginning of 1991, about 300 larger enterprises are being sold by the privatization agency (Treuhandanstalt, or Treuhand for short) *every month*. About one third of the 8,000 state enterprises have been privatized in the first 12 months. An additional 15,000 commercial and service establishments have also been privatized—mostly under leasehold arrangements.

**Organization.**   While Treuhandanstalt had existed for a few months as a state property agency, it was given a clear privatization mandate and organizational structure only in June 1990. The head office in Berlin has direct responsibility for the largest 3,600 enterprises (those with more than 1,500 employees), subsidiaries of large firms, and enterprises in special sectors (utilities, financial institutions, state farms, and department stores). All other enterprises report to 15 regional offices. Managers of the regional offices have full ownership responsibilities for the enterprises under their control and can negotiate sales with acquirers. Only large transactions require approval by the head office. The same principle applies in the head office: some transactions can be approved by department directors, some require approval of one or two executive board members, and only a few large transactions require approval by the full executive board. Special subsidiaries have been created for the privatization of commercial and service establishments and for marketing of real estate.

**Initial Difficulties.**   The monetary reform and the unexpectedly large shift of consumers to imported west German goods created a severe liquidity squeeze for enterprises. Treuhandanstalt had to provide liquidity credits (actually, credit guarantees) to give enterprise managements some breathing space until conditions had settled. Since the old enterprise supervision and control mechanisms had collapsed in the months before the union, Treuhandanstalt had extremely little information on the enterprises under its control. One of the first tasks was to establish a management information system. In the interim, some privatization transactions were concluded, but mostly in reaction to acquisition proposals made by investors. Property restitution claims by former owners also created problems, particularly as long as claims had not yet been filed and registered. Finally, the initial lack of a functioning public administration and the shortcomings of the east German infrastructure (such as the telephone system) hampered privatization for much of the first year.

**Enterprise Management and Control.**   One of the first tasks was to convert all state enterprises to company status ("commercialization"). This happened automatically on July 1, 1990, when the economic laws of the Federal Republic were extended to the GDR. However, since state enterprises did not fulfill registration requirements under FRG company law, they remained in a provisional status until they met these requirements (in particular, approved financial statements, minimum capital, and a functioning management and supervisory board). A special "opening balance sheet law" was enacted to facilitate the transition to FRG accounting standards and other requirements of FRG company law. Treuhand has appointed chairmen for the supervisory boards of the 500 largest companies, who have, in turn, been asked to appoint the other members (in large companies, part of the supervisory board members are elected by employees). The existing management has in most cases remained in place, but on short-term contracts, to permit rapid management transfers at the time of privatization.

To give the larger enterprises and conglomerates an incentive to divest unessential businesses, the "opening balance sheet law" included a number of provisions that require more equity capital for conglomerates than for independent companies. Financial incentives have also been built in to release valuable land that is not required for productive purposes. However, few managers responded to these incentives to restructure and spin off unessential activities. Since many enterprises and conglomerates are heavily indebted, most need some debt relief, and this gave Treuhand an opportunity to restructure large companies or holdings under its powers as *creditor*. Since sales transactions for parts of enterprises (as opposed to subsidiaries with a separate legal personality) are legally quite cumbersome, a special law has been introduced to facilitate splitting former state enterprises into a number of separate companies.

**Privatization Experience.**   While privatization transactions have started immediately after the economic union, the normal legal, economic, and financial preconditions for merger and acquisition activities have been missing for most of the first year. Accounting systems had to be established, financial statements had to be prepared and audited, property rights needed to be clarified, and so on. Moreover, the unsettled economic conditions rendered valuation questions difficult. Real estate markets with settled prices did not yet exist, the future profitability of most enterprises was highly uncertain, and external events, such as the collapse of Comecon trade, quickly turned business plans into useless paper. Since speed was essential, quite a number of corners had to be cut—without, however, jeopardizing the legal validity of transactions or the transparency of the process.

Priority was initially given to a few key sectors, such as energy utilities, and to responses to concrete acquisition proposals made by investors, usually on the basis of direct contacts with enterprise managers, while at the same time Treuhand prepared the information basis for "normal" privatization transactions later on. "First come, first served" was, by necessity, the initial sales strategy. While "large" privatization transactions averaged "only" 70 per month during the second half of 1990, they accelerated to 300–400 per month during 1991, or about 10 times the level of merger and acquisition activity in west Germany.

**Privatization Techniques.**   All possible privatization techniques are being considered, with the overriding objective to ensure a rapid transformation of the economy by fostering individual responsibility and initiative, and bringing in capital, technology, and management and marketing know-how. Most large transactions to date have been *negotiated sales* to west German or foreign firms. A large number of management or employee buyouts have de facto already taken place in the privatization of the commercial sector, and *management buyouts* are also pursued for smaller industrial firms. However, previous managers often cannot cope with the new competitive market environment. *Public share offerings* are not possible for the time being, as none of the firms under Treuhand's control can fulfill the requirements for a stock exchange listing (including audited and approved financial statements for at least three business years). The possibility of future stock market flotations is not excluded, but these will probably be very few. Private placements are, however, possible—for example, in the context of management/employee buyouts.

**Valuation.**   While homogeneous assets, such as land, commercial real estate, or "good will" of shop locations, can be sold through competitive bidding procedures, this is typically not the case with industrial firms. In view of the required deep restructuring, a valuation on the basis of expected future profits is in most cases meaningless. The value of the firm "as is" is in most cases simply the liquidation value of the firm's assets (reflected in the "opening DM balance sheets"), minus the social costs of job redundancies, and is often a negative value. Potential acquirers usually propose rather different business plans, involving different strategies, with different implicit levels of investment and employment. Comparing alternative proposals thus requires an evaluation. The liquidation value (minus costs of layoffs) represents a lower bound of the purchase price. The most useful approach is often a "partial reconstruction" value (i.e., comparing the required incremental investment costs with the cost of an expansion or "green-field" investment elsewhere). This gives a rough estimate of the opportunity costs to the investor that may be the best indicator of the value of the firm to the investor. The value of alternative business plans to Treuhand (and the government) is reflected by appropriate allowances for the number of jobs saved and the volume of investment to be undertaken.

**Enforcing commitments.**   To ensure that business plans are not merely on paper, sales contracts usually contain a few contingency clauses that allow for later adjustments in the purchase price, if the investor does not meet his or her promises. These usually include the volume of investment to be implemented and the number of jobs created or preserved. For example, contracts may include a penalty clause, increasing the sales price by an amount equivalent to one to two years of salary per job, if employment does not reach the levels promised by the acquirer, and similar clauses are being used to enforce investment commitments. Revaluation clauses for land have also frequently been used, particularly if an enterprise had a lot of inner-city land. However, since land prices have now become more settled, land revaluation clauses are employed less often. On the other hand, Treuhand usually retains a considerable part of past liabilities, such as an excessive debt burden, or costs of reducing overstaffing. While the contract usually stipulates a positive price, this may, economically speaking, quite often entail a negative price. Contingent liabilities from environmental risks, such as soil contamination, are also mostly retained by Treuhand, but usually with a small participation ("coinsurance") of the acquirer to keep some incentive to minimize clean-up costs. Beyond this, sales are on an as "seen and inspected" basis, to limit future litigation.

**Foreign Investors.**   While it is a declared objective of the government to attract as many foreign investors as possible, it has not been very successful. Only 5 percent of the sales transactions (but involving 10 percent of the privatized jobs) have been to foreign investors. Part of the reason has been that Treuhand had initially no other choice than to pursue a "first come, first served" policy, and west German investors had a practical advantage in scouting potential deals at the grass roots level. It also reflects language and cultural barriers, as fully one third of all sales to foreign firms involve Austrian and Swiss firms. Foreign investors also tend to be more cautious. In many cases, restructuring will take several years before the companies will be profitable, and investors from some countries have a rather short-term perspective.

## Investment Requirements

The economic success of the German unification depends to a large extent on whether or not a large number of high-productivity jobs can be created within a short period of two to three years. Investment in new equipment and facilities is an important element in raising the productivity of the east German economy, but other elements are just as important, such as better incentives, better organization and management, and selective retraining of the labor force. As discussed earlier, hopes of a quick recovery, similar to the aftermath of the 1948 currency reform, were exaggerated. The east German economy requires far more extensive restructuring, both physically and organizationally. On the other hand, a number of authors have overestimated the investment needed to bring productivity closer in line with west German levels by applying economy-wide capital-output ratios.[29] These authors have overlooked an important characteristic of the capital stock: productivity depends essentially on a relatively small part of the physical capital stock. A large part of the capital stock—not only housing, but a good part of urban, transport, and other infrastructure as well—serves mostly consumption purposes.

Fixed assets of the industrial sector (excluding energy utilities) are only about 11 percent of the net fixed capital stock (but 20 percent of new investment). The reason is the large share of (short-lived) machinery and equipment in the capital stock of the industrial sector. Other sectors are more capital-intensive than manufacturing because of the importance of (long-lived) buildings in their capital stock. This has two consequences for the privatization and restructuring of the east German economy that were not always fully understood. First, the value of the "productive" capital stock is actually rather small. Second, a considerable amount of investment can be postponed to later years (without much effect on productivity), as demand for infrastructure services is to a considerable degree determined by income and wealth (e.g., the number of private cars and urban traffic congestion).

In the negotiations leading to the unification, the GDR negotiators and public opinion did not want to give away the productive capital stock of east Germany, and a clause was inserted in the treaty, granting the east German population a share in the national wealth, once past debt obligations had been met. These demands were in part prompted by GDR statistics, showing the value of the industrial capital stock as GDR Mark 800 billion, or 50,000 per capita. However, this was the gross (undepreciated) value, and the net value (using GDR depreciation schedules) was only 365 billion. Its market value in DM is far less, since GDR depreciation rates were too low, many capital-intensive facilities were uneconomic and obsolete, and imported equipment was accounted for at the implicit exchange rate (4.4 M/DM in 1989). Using west German net capital/GDP relations, one would expect the industrial capital stock to be worth around DM 120 billion. As enterprise debt, after conversion at 2:1, is also around DM 100 billion, the net value of industrial enterprises is rather close to zero, with the actual sign depending on the sharing of past liabilities (enterprise debt, compensation for layoffs, and environmental cleanup) between the privatization agency and the purchasers.

The bulk of valuable assets is in other categories, in particular, housing,

---

[29] For example, Donogh McDonald and Günter Thurmann, "Investment Needs in East Germany," in *German Unification: Economic Issues,* ed. Leslie Lipschitz and Donogh McDonald (Occasional Paper no. 75; Washington, D.C.: International Monetary Fund, 1990), pp. 71–77.

other real estate, infrastructure, and urban land. Most of these assets are not under the control of the privatization agency. They will stay in public hands (infrastructure, hospitals, and public buildings), have been transferred to local governments for eventual privatization (housing), or can be privatized only gradually (urban and agricultural land). While much of the nonindustrial capital stock in east Germany is in poor condition by Western standards, it is nevertheless a valuable asset. Despite its poor condition, the housing stock (without land) may be worth DM 200 billion; and schools, hospitals, and office buildings fulfill their basic functions and can be upgraded with modest rehabilitation and equipment investments. The same applies to a good part of the infrastructure. Insufficient, yes, but far better than none at all. The obsolete telephone system is a case in point. After only nine months and an investment of DM 7 billion, mostly for a digital overlay system, long-distance capacity has increased tenfold, and endless busy signals vanished. In the transport sector, the predominantly north-south railway traffic has been replaced by east-west road transport, adapting rapidly to the totally different postunification transport requirements. Some roads are heavily congested, but rehabilitation and upgrading of existing facilities will give several years of breathing space, until new road and rail projects will come to fruition. The more limited private motorization makes more of the transport capacity available for productive uses, and trucks are fortunately mobile.

In terms of investment, creating high-productivity jobs is primarily a question of (1) replacing and upgrading much of the machinery and equipment in the manufacturing sector; (2) selective upgrading of infrastructure; and (3) adding (rather inexpensive) productivity tools for office workers, such as computers, telephones, fax machines, automated checkout and inventory controls, cash dispensers, and so on. Most of the latter are closely related to the telephone system, and Telekom's DM 55 billion investment program in east Germany will create in a few years the most modern telephone system in Europe. Investments of DM 50 billion are planned for the railways and another DM 60 billion for highways. As approval procedures are to be cut drastically by legislating major projects in all their details, with recourse limited to constitutional issues, construction can begin soon, but completion of major new projects will take at least until 1995. Nevertheless, short-term improvements are possible through removal of selected bottlenecks, and incremental improvements (e.g., computerized signaling).

In the industrial sector, only one half of the existing jobs are likely to be saved through privatization transactions; the rest will be lost to restructuring measures. The investment commitments by acquirers in privatization transactions provide probably the most reliable guide to investment requirements in the industrial sector. Excluding the energy sector, investment commitments average about DM 70,000 per job saved, about the same as the net (depreciated) capital stock per employee in west German industry. Similarly, a survey of firms with investment projects in east Germany indicated that these firms intended to invest about DM 70 billion by the mid-1990s, creating some 400,000 jobs. Excluding utilities, investment costs were given at about DM 100,000 per job[30] by surveyed firms. Two thirds of these firms were in the manufacturing sector, a quarter in services, and the remainder in commerce and construction. The investment plans of these new ventures are about equivalent to those agreed so far under privatization transactions, although there may be some overlap between the two categories, notably in energy and automobiles.

The salvageable 1.5 million industrial jobs may thus require modernization investments of DM 100 billion, while creating another 1 million industrial jobs would require another DM 100 billion, for a total of DM 200 billion. Infrastructure investment programs under preparation add up to another DM 250 billion.[31] These are large, but not unmanageable amounts, if compared to the fiscal transfer of DM 100 billion per year for 1991 and 1992. While investments in the manufacturing sector are estimated at only DM 16 billion in 1991, large increases can be expected for 1992, as projects move beyond the planning stage. If investment continues to increase at 30 percent per year for the next three years, before leveling off (an optimistic but not unfeasible assumption), these investment programs in 1991–95 would total around DM 580 billion, leaving another DM 25 billion per year for investments in housing and private and public services. Most likely, the infrastructure investment programs will take longer than five years to implement, leaving a larger share for housing and service sector investments. The macro consequences would be an unusually high share of investment in GDP, in the 35–40 percent range, and investment in east Germany would be one fifth of the German total.

Creating a productive capital stock, functionally equivalent to that of west Germany, over a period of five years is thus economically feasible. East Germany would still look much poorer, particularly as housing and urban amenities are concerned, but equipment at the place of work is not the problem. The question is, rather, whether the work force will be able to adapt so rapidly to changing demand patterns and job requirements. This could come about either by lowering social protection, to enhance labor market mobility, or by a larger role for government-directed training and employment programs. Given the political constraints, the latter appears more likely, and it has already started in 1991 through creation of rather large training and employment programs, administered by the national employment agency.

## CONCLUSIONS

The experience with the German unification to date raises the question whether there would have been alternative, and better, courses of action. Such options

---

[30] This is about midway between the net (depreciated) value of manufacturing capital per employee in west Germany (DM 70,000) at replacement costs and the gross (undepreciated) value (DM 140,000).

[31] Including (in DM billion) electric power, 50; gas, 20; railways, 50; roads, 60; urban transport, 12; and telephones, 55.

can be considered in three broad areas: (1) the initial conversion rate and, closely connected, wage policies; (2) the wisdom of transferring the economic and legal system of the FRG in its entirety; and (3) the desirability of the adopted mix of adjustment measures, in particular the trade-offs among social assistance, public investment spending, and incentives for private investment.

## Exchange Rate and Wage Policy

If large-scale financial assistance from west Germany were not available, the currency conversion would have been a severe mistake. But such help is available, and unrestricted migration is a political reality. Using a lower exchange rate (such as 2 : 1), without further adjustment in wages, would have implied a gross salary difference of 6 : 1, and a net (after tax) difference of 4 : 1. With such differentials, strong migration would have been likely, depriving eastern Germany of its most productive and entrepreneurial people and creating a large housing shortage in the west. This does not make economic sense, quite apart from the personal and social dislocation of such large-scale migration. Since investment costs for such a large number of new jobs would have been roughly the same in east and west, the migration option imposes additional costs, as housing would have to be built in west Germany. It should be noted again that the 1 : 1 currency conversion was not the determining factor for the present high wages. Rather it is the 1991 collective bargaining agreements which are setting the pace.

It is unlikely that a more gradual unification process would have been an advantage: lower wages would have been desirable only if migration could have been held in check. But the decay of the GDR state and institutions was already so advanced before the economic union that wage restraint would have been difficult, if not impossible, to implement. If migration is not an option (as is the case elsewhere) the argument is exactly the opposite, and the same applies to the wage increases granted on top of the conversion arrangements. In the case of Germany, these large increases have to be seen as part of the costs of moving to a free market overnight. The only alternative would be government-imposed wage restraint. This would go against the very foundations of the German social market economy.

## Big Bang versus Gradual Change

Unification has meant importing the entire economic and legal system of the Federal Republic. In many respects, this rather complex system has proved less than optimal for solving the problems of a sudden transition from a command to a market economy. Some temporary exemptions and transitional measures have been introduced right from the start. Others were added later, as some provisions proved unworkable—in particular the preference given to reprivatization (restitution), which has been softened in 1991 by giving the privatization agency considerable powers to sell enterprises to external investors, even if restitution claims were pending. Similar adverse experiences occurred with the complex and lengthy planning procedures for major public investment projects, such as new highways, rail links, or airports. Legal action is in preparation to shorten the lead times for such projects drastically. These excessively complicated regulatory procedures are one aspect of what has become known as "eurosclerosis." Many of these special procedures for east Germany deserve close consideration for introduction on both sides of the former iron curtain. Beyond the unfinished agenda of deregulation, however, the use of transitional regimes should probably be minimized. Yes, there are very considerable learning costs involved in the adoption of an entire legal system, but any transitional regime would create too much uncertainty and learning costs on both sides.

## Adjustment Measures

The question then remains whether the special incentives have been sufficient and whether the right measures have been introduced. To some extent the answer has already been given: some measures, in particular trade measures protecting the east German market, have proved unworkable and were dropped after a few weeks. Other transition measures proved insufficient or had to be extended. Indeed, it is quite possible that some of the transitional measures will again be prolonged beyond their present terminal date. Apart from public investment programs in infrastructure, most of these measures are either labor-market adjustment measures or incentives to attract private investment. Some economists[32] have argued that general employment subsidies would have been superior [to selective incentives]. That conclusion, however, rests entirely on highly stylized assumptions that are convenient for economic modeling, but very far from reality. Most importantly, labor is not homogeneous during this wrenching transition. Labor subsidies would be spread indiscriminately over sectors and firms with and without adjustment problems. The much-criticized partial unemployment benefits provide much more targeted help to firms with severe adjustment problems and still unclear business prospects. The easier eligibility rules have now been extended to the end of 1991, giving firms some time to decide on their business strategies and labor requirements. Labor subsidies, by contrast, would simply perpetuate past inefficient structures. In view of the large needs to improve infrastructure and urban amenities, employment programs are a useful alternative to unemployment payments.

Investment subsidies have also been criticized on the grounds that they would tend to distort allocation decisions, leading to uneconomically capital-intensive investments. While this may be true in theory, it is doubtful in practice. Investment costs per job are not particularly high in manufacturing, except in a few processing industries in chemicals and basic metals. General

---

[32] For example, Akerlof and others, "East Germany."

investment subsidies that have been granted are fairly low (12 percent); and the additional special subsidies under regional assistance programs are given only for selected purposes, and eligibility criteria (and expenditure ceilings) exclude uneconomically capital-intensive activities.

The question then remains whether a sufficient share of direct government expenditures and private sector incentives have been geared to productive, rather than social, purposes. For the first year of the union, the answer is probably negative, but mostly due to the administrative friction in getting investment going. More could have been done early to get transport and other public infrastructure improvements going, and this would have improved employment earlier. While this may have been a valid point during the first six months of the union, it has now been overtaken by events. Perhaps the best that can be done at present is to sit back and watch the implementation of the "Big Bang" under the present policy framework.

*Chapter Eleven*

# The 1992 Single Market Program of the European Community*

*Anthony H. Wallace*

*The European Community (EC), headquartered in Brussels, Belgium, is the collective designation of the European Coal and Steel Community (ECSC), the European Economic Community (EEC), and the European Atomic Energy Community (Euratom).*

*In 1952, Belgium, the Federal Republic of Germany, France, Italy, Luxembourg, and the Netherlands established the ECSC as a common market—with no internal trade barriers and with a common external tariff—for coal and steel products. An independent supranational authority was thus created. In 1958, the "Rome Treaties" set up the EEC and Euratom, extending the common market to all economic sectors in the EC. In 1973, Denmark, Ireland, and the United Kingdom joined the EC, followed by Greece in 1981, and Spain and Portugal in 1987.*

*In contrast, the European Free Trade Association (EFTA), founded in 1960, removed barriers to trade among member countries but permitted each country to impose its own restrictions on trade with nonmember countries. The current members of EFTA are Austria, Iceland, Norway, Sweden, and Switzerland. (Denmark, Portugal, and the United Kingdom left the EFTA to join the EC.)*

*Membership in the EC has curtailed national sovereignty over foreign trade policy, and thus over protection of domestic economic activity, competition, and national economic development programs.*

*The latest step in EC integration is the Single Market Program (SMP), effective December 31, 1992. It created a unified economic area within which people,*

* Reprinted from *Europe and the United States: Competition and Cooperation in the 1990s* (Study Papers Submitted to the Subcommittee on International Economic Policy and Trade and the Subcommittee on Europe and the Middle East, Committee on Foreign Affairs, U.S. House of Representatives, 102d Cong., 2nd Sess.) (Washington, D.C.: U.S. Government Printing Office, 1992), pp. 64–78, with some rearrangement of material and the omission of references to limited-circulation publications. Anthony H. Wallace, an international trade expert, is an Adjunct Professor in the International Institute of George Mason University.

*goods, capital, and financial services can circulate freely—as occurs across state borders within the United States.*

*In this chapter, Wallace discusses the reasons for adoption of the SMP. Then he explains specific measures affecting the movement of people and goods, standards and testing, government procurement, financial services, telecommunications, transportation, and environmental policy. He identifies three main elements in the SMP: pooling of sovereignty, deregulation at the national level and reregulation at the supranational level, and pressure toward harmonization of national tax systems and rules for business. Also, Wallace examines the SMP's implications for non-EC countries, particularly the United States.*

*Although the SMP advances the EC's integration in regard to goods and factors of production, harmonization of the member countries' monetary and fiscal policies is much more difficult. In 1979, a European Monetary System (EMS) was established to link member countries' exchange rates in an Exchange Rate Mechanism (ERM). Each country in the ERM promised to maintain the value of its currency, relative to other ERM currencies, within a specified range ("band"). A country undertook to sustain this link by the use of monetary policy (affecting interest rates and capital movements) and, if necessary, by direct intervention (through purchases and sales) in foreign exchange markets. Moreover, adjustment of monetary policy has implications also for fiscal policy, the other method of controlling aggregate demand.*

*At a meeting in Maastricht, the Netherlands, in 1991, the leaders of the EC countries agreed to work toward an Economic and Monetary Union (EMU). The EMU would, not later than 1999, create a single EC currency (in place of national currencies) and an EC central bank to manage monetary policy and exchange rate policy for the single currency vis-à-vis non-EC currencies. Although fiscal policy would nominally remain within the province of individual member countries, they would have to coordinate their fiscal policies to support the common monetary policy.*

*Progress toward the EMU stalled when the ERM broke down in 1992. Germany pursued a tight monetary policy to offset its budget deficit from expenditures for the reconstruction of eastern Germany after unification (see Chapter 10). High interest rates in Germany led to a rising value of the German currency relative to other currencies in the ERM. The United Kingdom and Italy decided it was not feasible to keep their exchange rates within the ERM bands, and they depreciated their currencies and suspended their membership in the ERM. Thus, it is uncertain how fast the EC can advance toward monetary integration, with the accompanying coordination of national fiscal policies, of member countries.*

## INTRODUCTION

Implementation of the 1985 blueprint to turn the European Community (EC) into a single market has progressed steadily in spite of a number of developments not foreseen by the framers. Two of these were the pressure for enlargement of the Community coming from some of the European Free Trade Association (EFTA) countries and former eastern bloc countries that desire closer association with the EC. Another unexpected development was the extent to which the EC has had to reexamine and revise the 1992 program in light of concerns expressed by the United States, Japan, and other trading partners. In addition, the specter of recession and the imminent prospect of increased competition between enterprises within and without Europe has led to some foot-dragging, characterized by requests for exceptions, delays in application, and lax enforcement of EC-92 directives on the part of member states. On a more positive note, faster than expected progress in moving toward a single currency and monetary policy (economic and monetary union, or EMU) has served to encourage members to get their economic houses in order for the day when they will no longer be able to insulate themselves from their neighbors.

Because of these developments, the EC will probably not realize the growth and employment gains projected by the Cecchini Report[1] and other analyses as quickly as they had hoped. The United States and other trading partners will find they have to wait a bit longer than expected for totally free access to the single market in important areas such as standards, testing and certification, government procurement, and financial services. This does not mean that the single market project will fail, or that fears of "fortress Europe" will be realized. The EC states have come too far in the process of reducing barriers to go back. Although all 282 directives in the blueprint may not be enacted by the December 1992 deadline, EC-92 is a process which seems certain to accomplish its stated objective. The Europeans will find ways to get around most if not all of the sticking points they have encountered.

As far as the prospects for a fortress, the Commission of the EC is aware that it must work to keep the market as open as possible to reap maximum gains from international trade. What the EC's trading partners must watch for is the extent to which the Commission may, in the implementation process, find it necessary to pay for internal reform with compromises which have the effect of limiting foreign access to the EC market. Any movement away from the White Paper "vision" toward managed trade or interventionist industrial policy at EC level or member-state level could result in a change in the generally favorable U.S. view of the single market project.

## HOW THE PROCESS GOT STARTED

The idea of moving to a single market with freedom of movement of people, goods, capital, and services was part of the vision of the founders of the European Community. The process of reduction of barriers to these four elements started well enough with the establishment of a customs union in 1968. With all internal tariffs and quotas gone, the Community then took another 20 years to begin the business of establishing a single market free of the more subtle barriers that limit trade.

---

[1] Commission of the European Communities, *Research on the "Cost of Non-Europe"* (Brussels, 1988).

Important catalysts which gave the 1992 project momentum included the following:

- Pressure from European business, concerned over the high cost of cross-border operations, and activist groups in the European Parliament forced Brussels to try again to enact market-opening laws that had languished for years.
- The development, through court cases, of the principle of mutual recognition made it possible to avoid the laborious process of harmonization of the legal systems of 12 nations.
- A break in the deadlock over the Community budget in 1988 resolved U.K. concerns about a fair return and promised increased regional aid to those less-developed members worried about problems of transition.
- The unique collection of personalities in the Commission who created an effective game plan (the 1985 White Paper[2]) and gave impetus to the movement to amend the Treaty of Rome, thus breaking the legislative log-jam.

The action of these catalysts, on those who were concerned over the loss of sovereignty a single market might bring and those who feared they would be unable to compete, eased the acceptance of the White Paper and the passage of the Single European Act (SEA) of 1987. By introducing majority voting (instead of the old requirement for unanimity) for most single market measures, the SEA promised speedier implementation of the legal changes proposed in the White Paper. The act also blessed the White Paper and its deadline and managed to inject a bit more democracy into the decision-making process by allowing the Parliament to reject or amend single market proposals under certain conditions.

## PROGRESS TOWARD 1992

In the process of evaluating what has been accomplished in the 1992 program and the impact of that progress on the United States, it is useful to note that the EC has proven to be very flexible in adapting to problems encountered on the way. Where something did not work, for example, rigid harmonization of value-added taxes (VAT) and excise taxes, the Commission came up with an acceptable alternative. Where elements needed to be added to the program (e.g., energy, the environment, and social policy), the Commission moved to establish a "vision" in the form of a charter or green paper (outline of proposed legislation) and then drafted directives to implement the vision. Several proposed directives were considered unnecessary and were dropped.

---

[2] Commission of the European Communities, *Completing the Internal Market* (White Paper from the Commission to the Council; Brussels, 1985).

As of early 1992, only about 50 of the 282 White Paper measures had not been adopted by the Council of Ministers and therefore were not yet EC law. Many of these cover relatively technical areas such as animal and plant health controls and are not "deal breakers." Others, such as several pending controversial social policy directives dealing with working conditions, will, as a result of the December 1991 Maastricht Summit, be dealt with outside of the framework of the White Paper. Procedural delays and the EC's own special version of "log rolling" are holding up some of the initiatives, but the great bulk of single market legislation will be approved at Brussels level by the end of the year. A review of EC-92 accomplishments to date follows.

## Barriers against People

Progress is slow toward the goal of mutual recognition of education and qualifications of professionals and vocational school graduates. Those with lower-level occupations can move freely, but the problem of pension and social benefits transfer has not been resolved. The Commission is using a ground-up approach, providing funding for exchange programs, placement, and cooperative development of training programs.

On the border-security issues, eight nations (the Schengen Group) have agreed (effective January 1, 1992) to remove all checks (for drugs, guns, terrorism, art smuggling, espionage) on people as soon as the Schengen accord is ratified. The United Kingdom, Ireland, Denmark, and Greece are not willing to end all checks on people. The Schengen eight hope to implement their policy through greater police and justice ministry coordination and information exchanges.

The success of this "two-speed" approach to freedom of movement will depend on tighter control of illegal crossing of EC boundaries, a common visa policy, and agreement on procedures for dealing with requests for asylum. At the Maastricht Summit, the 12 agreed that Brussels competence would be limited to establishing a common visa policy. The remaining difficult immigration issues will be resolved through intergovernmental consultations. This may extend the process of fulfilling the White Paper goals considerably and may in the end limit the benefits of the Single Market.

## Barriers against Things

As in the case of movement of people, the idea is to get rid of the checkers on EC internal borders. Convergence of VAT and excise taxes, abolition of Common Agricultural Policy (CAP) monetary compensation amounts, and harmonization of plant and animal health standards are all on the agenda. Mundane things such as collection of trade statistics will be handled in the future by using the new VAT clearance system and other methods. Of considerable interest to the United States and Japan is the way in which the Commission has chosen to end the system of national quotas against non-EC products permitted under

Article 115 of the Rome Treaty. The Commission has, under pressure from auto quota countries, had to compromise. In place of national quotas against Japanese cars, the EC will operate a restraint agreement until 1999.

Some observers are concerned that, as the remaining internal market barriers come down and competition becomes more intense, Brussels may be forced to make similar compromises in other sectors. This might, they contend, result in a perceptible bias against imports from nonmembers and a preference for foreign direct investment.

## Standards, Testing, and Certification

Rather than attempting to harmonize the thousands of product standards in the 12 member states, Brussels has set out essential requirements in directives only for those items for which health and safety are important considerations (toys, some industrial machines, pacemakers, etc.). The European (19-country) standards bodies (CEN, CENELEC and ETSI[3]) are responsible for elaborating Europe-wide technical specifications for these products. For other nonsensitive products where differing national standards are not incompatible, members will be expected to recognize each others' standards. The Council has adopted all of the essential requirements directives outlined in the White Paper. Elaboration of the approximately 4,000 EC-wide technical standards required by these directives will not, however, be completed by the end of 1992. This will delay full realization of the gains of the single market for EC members and pose problems for their foreign trading partners.[4]

U.S. firms have been concerned about limitations on their ability to participate in the standards-setting process of the EC. The U.S. Secretary of Commerce and EC Internal Market Commissioner Bangemann have met frequently since 1988 to assure that U.S. companies get early warning of proposed standards, and a right to comment on these drafts (directly if they are based in Europe, and through the American National Standards Institute and the International Standards Organization if they are not). The EC has also promised to use existing international standards where feasible instead of devising a separate EC standard. The U.S. side is monitoring EC implementation of these commitments closely.

In the area of conformity assessment, the EC is establishing uniform procedures and criteria for its testing labs. U.S. labs seek to be accredited by the EC to test U.S. products that are to be exported to Europe. Without this recognition by the EC, U.S. firms would be forced to test a product twice—

---

[3] The European Committee for Standardization (CEN), the European Committee for Electrotechnical Standardization (CENELEC), and the European Telecommunications Standards Institute (ETSI) are the major standards-setting organizations in Europe.

[4] Until CEN/CENELEC elaborates an EC-wide standard for a particular product, U.S. exporters would still have to deal with an array of differing national standards for that product. This would continue to make it difficult for the U.S. exporter to sell the product throughout the EC.

once in the United States and once in the EC. This duplication would increase costs for the U.S. supplier. The United States and the EC have agreed that the National Institute of Standards and Technology will be the central body responsible for assuring the competence of U.S. testing facilities. In the interim, U.S. labs hope to be approved as subcontractors to EC bodies for specific products.

## Government Procurement

The EC government procurement market (not including defense) totals over $500 billion annually. Before the start of the EC-92 program, 95 percent of this total was supplied by national firms. The French government bought French goods and services, for example, even if they were not the best available in the world market in terms of quality or cost. The cost of this closed procurement market has been estimated at over $25 billion per year.[5] The single market program moved quickly to tighten up older directives on procurement of works and supplies and to open procurement in the formerly "excluded sectors" of energy, telecommunications, transport, and water. A directive dealing with procurement of services is also in the pipeline.

The excluded-sectors directive accomplishes, at least for EC members, what the members of the GATT Government Procurement Code have been trying to do since the end of the Tokyo Round. The EC, however, has taken the position that only those countries which offer reciprocal procurement opportunities can take advantage of this major opening of the EC market. The EC has asked the United States to put more procurement opportunities on the table (state and local government procurement and purchases by private utilities, transport, and communications entities) in order to demonstrate reciprocity. The GATT code covers Federal procurement only. The United States has informed the EC that the Federal government cannot force states and localities to remove Buy-American restrictions on procurement or require private companies such as the regional Bell Companies, electric utilities, and private transport entities to open their procurement in a similar manner.

For U.S. firms bidding on EC contracts, the present situation is even less satisfactory than the former one. The EC reserves the right to reject bids with less than 50 percent EC content, even if they are price-competitive and conform to specifications. There is also a 3 percent price preference for EC bids. Approximately 18 U.S. states interested in participating in the EC procurement market have expressed an interest in reexamining their restrictive procurement provisions. The next step in this process, which is being led by the U.S. Trade Representative (USTR), will be solicitation of specific commitments by states to abolish restrictive provisions. The USTR hopes to be able to put enough

---

[5] Commission of the European Communities, *Research on the "Cost of Non-Europe": Basic Findings. The "Cost of Non-Europe" in Public Sector Procurement* (Brussels, 1988), vol. 5, parts A and B.

state, local, and private procurement "on the table" to meet EC reciprocity requirements. The process has begun, but it raises important issues for the Congress and the states.

## Financial Services

The key to opening up the EC financial services market was the agreement to end controls on cross-border capital movements in mid-1990. Portugal and Greece are allowed more time for transition. In many ways the EC-92 program seeks to emulate what the United States accomplished in its early attempts to create a single market. Trade between countries in Europe after 1992 will resemble the movement of goods among the states in the United States. In certain areas, however, the Europeans have made a conscious effort to do things differently.

In banking, for example, the EC has adopted a directive which will entitle a bank established in one member state to establish branches without restriction in any other member state. That bank will be able to engage in the full range of activities permitted by the directive (the list includes traditional banking functions as well as sale of securities and portfolio management and advice). In addition, the bank will be governed by the laws of the home country.[6]

This system is radically different from the U.S. system of restrictions on branch banking, prohibition of sale of securities, and host state control. In the early days of the second banking directive, the EC insisted on a "mirror image reciprocity" that would have forced the United States to give EC banks operating here more privileges than U.S. law allowed to American banks. The EC realized the intractability of this problem and modified the directive to call for "national treatment" reciprocity. This was one of the first single market areas in which the EC found it necessary to alter the EC-92 game plan in response to a problem with a trading partner.

With the exception of a few large institutions, U.S. banks have not responded to the opening of the EC banking market, especially at the retail level. The major beneficiaries of the "single passport" system will be the more efficient European commercial banks (including those in the EFTA countries such as Switzerland). In the coming banking shake-out in Europe, competition will be fierce and many banks will disappear. In anticipation of this, many European banks are merging.

The other areas of financial services are moving more slowly. In insurance, for example, cross-border sales of commercial fire, theft, and auto insurance are permitted for large risks but not for individuals. Only national companies can insure individuals.[7] There are still significant restrictions on cross-border

---

[6] Some local "conduct of business" rules will govern these branches, e.g., opening and closing hours.

[7] An earlier directive provided the right of establishment to service providers. Therefore, foreign subsidiaries may sell insurance.

sales of life insurance. A directive granting a single passport for life insurance and commercial risk insurance sales is facing stiff opposition, mainly from Germany. U.S. firms see opportunities in Europe, especially in life insurance,[8] but when the market is fully liberalized, U.S. insurers will most certainly seek to establish a presence there.

The area of investment services (rules governing activities of securities firms and stock exchanges) is one of the few EC-92 initiatives which may fail. The directive is currently stalled over the issues of off-market trading[9] and capital adequacy rules for investment firms.

U.S. credit card issuers are concerned about proposed EC rules on protection of personal data. The proposed directive requires consent of all data subjects before data can be used and restricts transfer of personal data to third countries which cannot provide an "adequate level of protection." Member states are divided over the directive, with Germany pushing hard for strict rules. The data protection issue could be an important irritant this year.

The EC is concerned about reciprocity in the U.S. insurance market (some states discriminate against foreign companies in fiduciary requirements and taxation) and about language in the new U.S. banking reform legislation that, if not amended, may force European banks to convert their U.S. branches to subsidiaries at great expense.

## Telecommunications Equipment and Services

The main purpose of the EC-92 telecommunications proposals is to open what has been a virtually closed market[10] enjoyed by the large public and private telecommunications authorities (TAs). The goal is to provide higher quality and greater variety of telecommunications services and equipment by liberalizing the market and providing a more consistent regulatory structure.

Voice communications (90 percent of the market) will remain the preserve of the TAs, at least for the moment. The EC has adopted a series of directives which open procurement of telecommunications terminal equipment, allow competitition in non-voice communications (services such as e-mail, electronic data interchange, and data communications), and set conditions for access by private service providers to the networks of the TAs. Two of these directives were enacted under the provisions of Article 90 of the Treaty of Rome, which

---

[8] There would appear to be considerable scope for sales of life insurance in Europe. Per capita expenditures on life insurance premiums in Europe range from $13 in Portugal to $700 in the United Kingdom (the EC average is $370 compared to $678 in the United States). Source: The Swiss Re Reinsurance Company.

[9] France and Italy support language banning off-market trading in stocks. The United Kingdom, Germany, the Netherlands, and the Commission do not wish to abolish existing curb markets.

[10] In 1984, the United Kingdom privatized British Telecom and allowed a competitor, Mercury, to offer service. The United Kingdom later opened its market wider, and Sprint is currently applying to supply full telephone services.

allows the Commission to take action against public monopolies that abuse their dominant position.[11]

U.S. companies will benefit from procurement liberalization, a move toward common standards, and the opening of the non-voice market. This segment should grow dramatically after deregulation in much the same way the U.S. market grew after the AT&T breakup. Several U.S. firms have moved to establish a presence in Europe to take advantage of the potential. Until the issue of reciprocity under the excluded sectors procurement directive is resolved, the extent of participation of U.S. exporters of equipment and services will be unclear.

## Transport

By phasing out restrictive national rules governing road, rail, sea, and air transport, the Community hopes to reduce cross-border business costs and promote economic growth. In trucking, Brussels seeks to end cabotage restrictions; establish a freely available EC license for cross-border haulage; harmonize truck taxes and excise duties on oil and gas; and standardize truck weights, dimensions, speed limits, driver qualifications, and working conditions. Europe's stagnant rail sector will be revitalized by making the rail system more continent-oriented, upgrading lines for greatly increased use of high-speed trains, harmonizing equipment and infrastructure, and rationalizing freight pricing. Member states will be required to open access to their rail lines to private carriers for a user fee.

Most of the directives in these areas have been passed, but because of member-state reluctance, the Commission has had to include lengthy transition periods. U.S. transport firms established in the EC will be able to take advantage of these sweeping transport deregulation measures, and U.S. firms in general will share in the benefits of a liberalized EC transport sector.

The EC's "open skies" program is an ambitious attempt to end the civil air cartels that have spelled high ticket prices and limited service in Europe for years. Directives that dismantle bilateral traffic-sharing agreements are gradually introducing competition and creating conditions for the entry of new airlines. The EC and its member states seek to rationalize Europe's inefficient and uncoordinated air traffic control system[12] and are developing plans to expand Europe's crowded airports. Resistance on the part of member states, particularly those concerned about the fate of their national airlines under "open skies," has been strong.

---

[11] France and others challenged the Commission's use of Article 90 in the terminal equipment directive in the European Court of Justice and lost. Another directive dealing with telecom services is also being challenged.

[12] Planes in the busy northeast air corridor in the United States can fly as close as 5 miles, while flights in Europe must be separated by as much as 80 miles in dense corridors.

U.S. government civil air negotiators will now have to deal with Brussels (which will be acting in the interests of 12 countries) rather than individual EC states. There will be considerable pressure from the EC to open new gateways in the United States and to allow for "beyond rights" and cabotage. U.S. airlines are better prepared to face the stiff competition which will come with "open skies." U.S. suppliers of air traffic control and communications equipment, terminal systems, and computers should also do well, provided that the procurement market is open.

## Environmental Policy

Under increasing pressure from Green movements all over Europe,[13] the EC has increasingly focused on environmental concerns and sustainable growth issues in pursuing the single market. The 1987 Single European Act gave Brussels competence in this area for the first time, but did not mandate establishment of an EPA-type body to enforce existing and new directives.[14]

The EC approach has been to develop rules governing the production of undesirable elements (air, noise, and water pollution); the development of "safe" nonpolluting products and packaging; and the regulation of toxic waste treatment, shipment, and disposal. Directives requiring procedures to deal with accident hazards and disposal and storage of toxic wastes are already in force. The EC has decided to adopt the U.S. principle of joint and several liability for accidents involving toxic wastes. Brussels has also adopted U.S.-level emission standards for small cars[15] and a tough requirement for large cars, buses, and trucks which poses a major problem for the diesel engine industry. The Commission also seeks to set an EC-wide speed limit (there is strong German opposition to this). There are also directives dealing with landfill techniques, plastic and metal waste, and treatment of nontoxic industrial and municipal waste.

U.S. companies, accustomed to tough EPA standards at home, will face few problems in adjusting to European rules. Firms in the toxic waste treatment and disposal business may find that EC constraints on cross-border shipments of hazardous materials limit opportunities in the Community.

## COMMON THREADS IN THE EC-92 PROCESS

The Brussels bureaucracy has demonstrated considerable resourcefulness and flexibility in pushing through the single market program. Where rigid harmoni-

---

[13] As a result of the 1989 European Parliament election, Green seats increased from 20 to 39. Green candidates received 15 percent of the total European vote in that election.

[14] Assuming the member states can agree on where to locate a European environmental agency, the body will, at least for the first several years, serve only as a collector of statistics.

[15] Passenger cars with a displacement of 1.4 liters or less make up 67 percent of the European fleet.

zation by means of directives proved unworkable, the Commission devised ingenious alternatives, as in the case of indirect taxes. Where member-state fears arose that Brussels would attempt to micromanage social policy, the Commission has backed off. Irreconcilable conflicts have arisen in areas such as border checks on people and animals, voting procedures on sensitive social policy issues, and immigration policy. The Commission has tolerated "opt outs" or "two-speed" formulas to deal with these issues. This approach, while allowing the 12 (and prospective members) to stay together, could result in a watering down of the original vision. Some of the elements which have contributed to the progress so far as discussed below.

## Pooling of Sovereignty

The Commission has been successful in allaying member concerns over loss of sovereignty as the single market process dismantles national regulations. This was accomplished in two ways. The Single European Act and the Maastricht Treaty on European Union now being prepared for ratification have helped to reduce the "democratic deficit," that is, the perception that the people of Europe have no power in Brussels. Secondly, the inherent logic of the single market program has made a profound impression on even the most suspicious members. Lord Cockfield, the author of the White Paper, has aptly described the process as a "pooling of sovereignty" rather than a loss of sovereignty.

## Deregulation at National Level and Reregulation by Brussels

EC-92 works because the dismantling of restrictive national laws that served as barriers to cross-border trade has unleashed powerful market forces. In general, Brussels has chosen carefully the areas to be governed by directive. The reregulation effort seeks to establish general principles only (e.g., the "essential requirements" that form the basis of CEN/CENELEC technical standards). Member states are free to devise their own laws and regulations, provided they incorporate the essential requirements. This strategy has allowed Brussels to put its stamp on subjects which had been jealously guarded by the member states, including taxes, transport regulation, banking rules, and public procurement procedures.

## Convergence

Perhaps the most powerful force contributing to the success to date of the single market effort is the pressure on member states, once market forces have been unleashed, to move toward harmonized direct and indirect taxes, and similar rules governing foreign investment, transport, and environmental pollution. The urge to converge, for example, will make it hard for one member to maintain substantially higher VAT, excise, and company tax rates than other states. Shoppers will be attracted by lower indirect taxes and potential investors will move to the lowest-cost sites. Convergence will probably not work in some areas in which compromise is not feasible, such as ending all border checks on people and goods, or permitting off-market trading in stocks.

### Things to Watch in the Endgame

The most important ongoing issue in the 1992 process will continue to be that of competency, that is, who does what? The principle of subsidiarity[16] has served the Commission well, providing a guide to determining the extent of Brussels involvement in single market areas. The Maastricht Summit resolved serious differences of opinion concerning conduct of immigration and social policies. Another important sovereignty issue concerns voting in the Council of Ministers on single market directives. The Commission is seeking to maximize the use of qualified majority voting, while some members insist on retaining unanimity for certain issues. The Maastricht Summit settled some of these problems. Proposed legislation in the areas of consumer protection, health, education, networks (transport, telecommunications, energy), and some environmental rules will be subject to qualified majority. Unanimity will be retained for culture and industrial policy proposals.

## EFFECTS OF 1992—CHANGES IN THE LANDSCAPE

Even before the first single market directives were adopted, European companies began to anticipate reduced barriers to cross-border trade by engaging in a frenetic round of mergers and acquisitions. From 1984 to 1988 mergers and acquisitions within individual member states rose from 100 to 214, mergers within the EC rose from 29 to 111, and international mergers rose from 29 to 58. A large percentage of the mergers within the EC during the early period were in the food business. Since 1988 there have been a growing number of alliances among small high-tech companies.

Foreign companies have moved rapidly in anticipation of the establishment of a single market. Japanese investment in the EC doubled between 1987 and 1990 and now totals over $60 billion (compared to $150 billion for the United States). Approximately 700 companies in Europe have Japanese ownership of 10 percent or more. About 200 of these are in the United Kingdom where the climate for mergers and acquisitions is most favorable. Sweden and other EFTA countries are also aggressively buying into the EC in the belief that for purposes of standards conformity, rules of origin, and public procurement it will be important to produce inside Community borders.

---

[16] This concept has its origin in the early history of the Christian church, when powerful bishops sought to share power with Rome. In the Treaty on European Union, it means that Brussels will act only if the objectives of a proposed action cannot be achieved by the member states. Community actions are not allowed to go beyond what is necessary to achieve the objectives of the treaty.

As the single market takes shape, the European consumer is also changing. The removal of barriers will stimulate increased travel and relocation for work. Tastes, fashions, and trends will cross borders more rapidly. In some market segments, pan-European life styles will emerge, allowing firms to take advantage of economies of scale in production, marketing, and advertising. EC-92 will not, however, result in the emergence of a lowest common denominator "European culture" with complete homogeneity of tastes.

## HOW U.S. FIRMS ARE DEALING WITH THE SINGLE MARKET

U.S. firms interested in the European market have mastered the details of the 1992 program, have determined which of their product/service areas will benefit most (or be threatened most) by single market directives, and are now implementing their strategies. Because of the way the market is developing, many companies see the need to establish a production, marketing, and research presence in Europe. For semiconductor companies, for example, the combination of EC provisions dealing with the chip rule of origin,[17] dumping, and procurement make it difficult to compete in the EC market as an exporter. U.S. manufacturers of power generation equipment are seeking strategic alliances with EC manufacturers to avoid the restrictive content provisions in the excluded sectors procurement directive. Many U.S. firms see a need to produce locally to avoid difficulties posed for U.S. exports by expected delays in liberalizing the EC standards and testing and certification regimes.

For U.S. firms, the positive aspects of the move to an EC single market outweigh the negative prospects which stem from problems in certain directives and with the implementation process in general. U.S. companies will continue to monitor developments and will seek U.S. government assistance with major problems which may arise in the areas discussed below.

## FORTRESS EUROPE OR NOT? SOME ACID TESTS

There are four problem areas to watch in the future. How they develop will determine to a great extent whether the open market the Europeans are building for themselves will be equally accessible for foreign goods and services. The 1992 directives, taken individually, are not meant to be protectionist and generally do not have that effect. In cases where the United States and other trading partners have found objectionable features in proposed EC legislation, the two sides have generally found an acceptable solution. An important exception is the TV Without Frontiers directive, which retains a local content provi-

---

[17] The EC rule of origin for integrated circuits considers a semiconductor chip to be European (and therefore not subject to the EC's 14 percent tariff) if the process of diffusion (etching the circuitry onto the silicon wafer) takes place in the EC.

sion which the U.S. film industry has found objectionable. In the case of semi-conductors mentioned earlier, individual single market directives were not intended to affect U.S. exports adversely. However, when some of these directives are combined with changes in existing rules (e.g., dumping anticircumvention regulations and rules of origin) they have created the impression in the U.S. industry that a European presence would be necessary to compete in the EC market. This is why Intel chose to invest in an EC production facility. An unknown number of other American businesses have felt the need to take similar steps.

## Implementation of 1992 Directives

An EC directive does not have the force of law in a member state until it is incorporated into national law by the legislature of that state. Only about 50 of the 230 single market directives adopted by the Council have been incorporated into the laws of all 12 member states. Some of those incorporated have been accepted, but with derogations which reduce their effectiveness. Other incorporated directives have not been implemented, necessitating enforcement actions by Brussels. In those areas of great importance to EC trading partners, including government procurement and standards, foot-dragging by member states could greatly reduce the potential benefits of the single market for outsiders.

## Competition Policy

The manner in which the EC implements the merger control regulations will affect the ability of foreign firms to make mergers and acquisitions in Europe. If the directive follows Treaty of Rome articles concerning abuse of dominant position (e.g., no blatant exceptions for national champions) and is not used in a way that discriminates against non-EC enterprises, U.S. firms will have nothing to complain about. The U.S. Justice Department and the EC Commission have recently concluded an antitrust cooperation agreement which provides for greater coordination in antitrust regulation. The agreement calls for increased contacts and exchange of information on investigations of business practices and proposed mergers. EC decisions on whether to block mergers will still be made independently by the Commission's task force on merger controls. Because of this, the agreement contains no dispute settlement mechanism for dealing with a situation in which a merger between two U.S. companies was approved by U.S. authorities but blocked by the Commission.[18]

---

[18] The merger control regulation allows the EC to pass on mergers between two U.S.-headquartered firms if the combined turnover in the EC of these two firms is above a certain threshold (currently ECU 250 million, or $300 million).

### After National Quotas, What?

The way in which the EC has had to deal with national quotas against Japanese auto imports raises serious concerns for EC trading partners. The EC-wide arrangement which replaces those quotas is a grey area measure which may be very hard to displace in 1999, when it is supposed to end. Similar solutions may crop up in other important areas, such as consumer electronics and office products, which are now covered by national restraint measures. The auto arrangement has already raised the issue of how to treat imports of autos made in the United States by Japanese transplants.

### Industrial Policy—An End to National Champions?

The most important area to watch is undoubtedly the continuing tug of war within the EC over implementation of the Commission's "new policy for industry." The two major elements of that policy of concern to U.S. companies are regional and structural aid and cooperative R&D policy. In the area of state aids, there appears to be a major difference between U.S. and EC views on what constitutes an unfair subsidy from the point of view of GATT rules. In R&D policy, U.S. firms will be watching closely to see the extent to which Brussels supports cooperative programs that operate relatively close to the market (i.e., fairly far down the continuum from the basic research programs common in the United States). In addition there is the problem of national industrial policies, such as those promoted by the government of (former Prime Minister) Edith Cresson in France, that may not be consistent with the Commission's stated goal of ending support for white elephants. Concerns over the conduct of industrial policy surfaced at Maastricht, where Germany and the United Kingdom successfully turned back an attempt by France and Italy to shift decisions on EC R&D support to majority voting.

## IMPLICATIONS FOR THE UNITED STATES

Successful completion of the single market program and nonprotectionist implementation of that program will provide great benefits for the United States. A prosperous Europe will buy more from us. The efficiences introduced by the reduction of barriers will lower costs for all firms operating in Europe and result in significant scale economies. European firms will become stronger and more competitive in the EC market as well as in our own backyard.

Major U.S. concerns in the areas of standards, testing and certification, and procurement are moving toward resolution. Industrial policy, data protection, competition policy, and implementation of the Community's social dimension will be among the important EC-U.S. issues of the 90s.

## CONCLUSION

As the European Community nears the end of its massive project to transform the economies of 12 countries into a single market of more than 340 million people, it is worthwhile to assess the progress to date and to measure the potential effects on the Community's trading partners. The process of reducing all barriers to the movement of goods, people, services, and capital—delayed for 20 years by member-state fears over loss of sovereignty, the oil shock, and the recession—began again in the mid-80s. Momentum was provided by pressure from European business, a few landmark court cases, and the leadership of a remarkable group of commissioners in Brussels. These factors made possible the issuance of a plan (the White Paper and its 282 legal changes needed to get to the single market) and the amendment of the EC constitution to allow for majority voting on many of these legal proposals.

What has brought the Community to the present state in which almost all of the important proposals have been adopted has been a demonstration of resourcefulness and flexibility by Brussels and the strength of the market forces released in the process. As restrictive national rules in the areas of public procurement, transportation, financial services, telecommunications, environmental pollution, and standards have been dismantled, the costs of doing business across borders in Europe look set to drop dramatically. This has convinced the member states of the value of "pooling" their sovereignty in order to increase the economic growth and competitiveness of Europe.

There are just a few sticking points to be resolved, including how to implement the goal of free movement of people, animals, and plants across borders, and how to legislate the worker rights proposals in the Social Action Program. Of more concern is the fact that the rate of member-state application of the already-adopted EC-92 directives has lagged and enforcement of some of those directives incorporated in member-state law has been lax.

U.S. firms stand to gain from the progress achieved in moving toward EC-wide standards and liberalized public procurement and in opening up the telecommunications, financial services, and transport sectors. The Community has, after expressions of concern from the United States and other trading partners, revised some EC-92 proposals, including those dealing with banking and standards-setting, testing, and certification. The U.S. film industry has not been successful in getting the EC to remove local content provisions in the TV directive; credit card companies are concerned about proposed rules governing protection of personal data; and chip makers see a "forced investment" policy emerging from EC rules on origin, dumping, and procurement. Many U.S. firms have decided to establish production in Europe to avoid potential problems in implementation of EC product standards and public procurement programs.

Successful completion of the single market program will provide benefits to U.S. companies located in Europe and increase EC demand for U.S. exports, but it will also make EC firms more competitive in the global market. The framers of the EC-92 program did not set out to build a "fortress Europe." Vigilance will be required on the part of the United States, however, to assure that the Community and the member states do not stray from the game plan in important areas such as procurement, support for industry, and competition policy.

## Chapter Twelve

# Japanese Industrial Policy*

## Hugh T. Patrick

*"Industrial policy"* is a broad term. It may have such *"macroeconomic"* objectives as overall economic growth, reduction of unemployment and/or inflation, and adjustment of the balance of payments. But, commonly, industrial policy is more *"microeconomic"* in orientation, focusing on certain industries such as steel or automobile production, or on the development of specific regions of a country. The objectives of industrial policy may be implemented by the use of fiscal instruments, such as subsidies and tariffs; favorable credit arrangements; direct controls, such as import quotas; changes in the rules for market structure and competition; and nationalization of selected industries or firms.

Industrial policy often classifies particular industries, or parts of them, into one of three categories. (1) The government will actively promote the development of some industries, for example, by funding research and development for computers. (2) For other industries, the aim is to stabilize them against a decline threatened by foreign competition, for instance, through import restrictions that protect steel and auto producers. (3) In some cases (for instance, output of clothing and footwear), the government accepts their contraction, but seeks to cushion it by adjustment assistance such as extended unemployment compensation and retraining for workers.

Japan is usually cited as the capitalist regulated market economy in which industrial policy has been pursued most vigorously and most successfully. In this chapter Patrick explains the scope and content of Japanese industrial policy, how it is implemented, and how it has changed as the Japanese economy has evolved. Next, he discusses the disagreement among specialists about the effects of industrial policy on Japan's economic performance. Finally, he draws seven lessons for the United States from Japanese experience with industrial policy.

* Revised (1993) from *Industrial Policy, Economic Growth, and the Competitiveness of U.S. Industry* (Hearings before the Joint Economic Committee, 98th Cong., 1st Sess.) (Washington, D.C.: U.S. Government Printing Office, 1983), part 2, pp. 19–42. Used with permission. Hugh T. Patrick is R. D. Calkins Professor of International Business at Columbia University.

## INTRODUCTION

The United States is once again engaging in an important national debate on the goals, nature, and effectiveness of governmental economic policy and its appropriate role in our economy and society. A potentially likely entrant into the panoply of instruments which make up the economic policy system is industrial policy. Interest in industrial policy has been heightened by perceptions of deep-seated difficulties in the American economy not treatable by traditional policy measures, by perceptions of Japanese industrial success and its competitive challenge to certain important American industries, and by perceptions of the success of Japanese industrial policy. Here, I consider three themes in evaluating Japanese industrial policy and its relevance for American industrial policy.

First, it is important to define the nature and scope of the concept of industrial policy, since the term has been used in so many ways in the contexts of the American economy, the Japanese economy, and indeed other advanced industrial nations and developing nation economies as well.

Second, we need to know, and understand well, Japanese industrial policy—its successes and its failures—before we attempt to derive possible lessons for United States policy. Simplistic and misleading myths and stereotypes abound regarding the Japanese economy and Japanese industrial policy, and we should beware of what may be incorrect "lessons." All too often, perceptions of the Japanese economy are outdated, conditioned excessively by the earlier high-growth era—from the mid-1950s to the early 1970s—when Japanese industrial policy achieved its greatest successes.

Finally, I conclude with some general lessons for possible United States industrial policy that do seem derivable from the Japanese experience.

## THE CONCEPT OF INDUSTRIAL POLICY

Every nation pursues policies which significantly affect both the aggregate productive capacity of the economy and its particular industrial structure. Some policies have these goals explicitly; others have indirect and at times unanticipated impacts on the economic structure. Some policies are macro, others micro.

The term *macroindustrial policy* has been used to describe macro policies, especially incentives to save, to invest, and to engage in R&D, which increase the productive capacity of the economy in the longer run while leaving it to the marketplace to allocate resources among specific industries. Such policies—an important element of supply-side economics—have long characterized Japanese economic policy. A broad definition of macroindustrial policy would include any macro policies to increase the quantity and especially the quality of the factors of production—labor, capital, and natural resources. This would include educational policy and science and technology policy. It is noteworthy that Japan has an elementary and secondary school educational system which produces a substantially higher average level of competence in natural sciences, mathematics, and literacy than in the United States. It also has a college system, predominantly private and of heterogeneous quality, that produces more engineers and especially electrical engineering college graduates than does the United States.

However, industrial policy more typically is defined in *micro* terms: identification of certain specific industries deemed to be of sufficient national importance to merit and receive differentially favorable policy treatment so that those industries have access to resources in degrees and/or timing different than would occur through the normal operations of the marketplace. A range of policy instruments can be used: direct subsidy payments, tax benefits, government-supported financing, protection from imports or promotion of exports, direct government purchases, funding of relevant R&D, special regulatory provisions, and so forth. The central point is the *differential* advantages government policy provides selected, targeted if you will, industries—to their benefit and to the relative disadvantage of all other industries. Those propounding industrial policy as so defined must believe the marketplace is not operating optimally due to market imperfections or outright market failure, so that specific government intervention is warranted.

Even this definition of industrial policy, without reference to its basic objectives, to the policy environment, and to the utilization of specific policy instruments, is quite general. By this definition, the United States pursues an industrial policy in the priority it has given defense and aerospace industries, for example; and the continental Western European nations do so through regional development programs which in practice are keyed to certain basic industries such as steel. The concept of industrial policy can be further refined through examination of the Japanese case.

## JAPANESE INDUSTRIAL POLICY IN CONTEXT

Japanese industrial policy can be characterized as follows: Its goal has been to enhance economic growth by anticipating dynamically efficient allocation of resources by the criterion of world, not just domestic, prices. To this end it has selected certain key industries as essential for preferential treatment. It has provided such treatment through a comprehensive, coordinated package of policy instruments. And it has conducted industrial policy in a generally conducive and supportive domestic policy environment.

It is important to understand that the goals, policy instruments, and policy environment have changed dramatically over the postwar period, and just what those changes have been. The postwar Japanese economy has gone through three phases: a decade of postwar reconstruction following the devastation of World War II; almost two decades, from the mid-1950s to 1973, of superfast GNP growth (about 10 percent annual average); and the two subsequent decades of 4 percent growth in a domestic and world environment of oil crises, dramatic changes in exchange rates, and cyclical economic performance. Industrial policy has evolved from one period to the next.

Well into the second phase, Japan was a low-income, developing country, and pursued trade and industrial policies like many other such countries. Industrial policy played an important role from the beginning, initially with a strong domestic market orientation; reconstruction required special government help for the fertilizer, electric power, coal, steel, and transport industries. As the Japanese high-growth era progressed, industrial policy, and the intellectual rationalizations of it, achieved their heyday. New industries—chemicals, petrochemicals, and other intermediate goods industries—were added to the list for preferential support. Between 1955 and 1973 the Japanese GNP increased almost six times in real terms. By the early 1970s Japan had become the world's third largest industrial economy (following the United States and the USSR), with per capita income comparable to Western Europe. This profound surge of growth transformed the industrial structure and changed substantially the needs and conditions of industrial policy.

Japanese industrial policy as an ideal type came into its own in the high-growth era. It is useful to characterize it first in these ideal-type terms, then to indicate the changes that have taken place in industrial policy in the past two decades, and finally to provide an evaluation of Japanese industrial policy in both its historical and present contexts.

## Japanese Industrial Policy as an Ideal Type

Japanese industrial policy has been pragmatic and economic in its orientation. The basic goal has been to create the productive capacity for rapid growth by accelerating the transfer of resources to the major industries of the future, while smoothing the process of decline of uncompetitive industries, sometimes termed "picking winners and phasing out losers." In principle, "winners" should meet the following criteria: (1) industries of significant size in which Japan would have future comparative advantage as the relative supplies and costs of its factors of production changed with domestic growth and evolving international economic conditions, and as learning curve economies were achieved (infant-industry cases); (2) industries for which domestic and world demand would be highly income-elastic; and (3) industries in which Japan would become internationally price-competitive.

The emphasis of Japanese industrial policy has been on economic growth and economically efficient resource allocation. Economic efficiency has come to be defined in terms of world markets, not (protected) domestic markets, and in terms of competitive prices, high quality, and other nonprice attributes. In contrast, the major goal of American industrial policy has been to maintain the industrial basis for military strength, in terms of quality and quantity, but not of price. The United States has also pursued policies to help specific industries, such as textiles and automobiles, mainly by restrictions on imports. The contrast in policy goals between American military prowess (and the development of comparative advantage and export sales in military hardware) and Japanese economic/commercial strength stands out. As already noted, Western Euro-

pean nations aid various industries, but with such pronounced regional development objectives that they seldom use the term *industrial policy*. The major
exception is France with its nationalization and high-technology policies. While
there may be a major distinction in principle between the Japanese emphasis on
efficient resource allocation and American and Western European emphasis on
the more equitable distribution of income, the political economies in practice
are not so different. Japanese policymakers have continuously provided support for inefficient but politically powerful farmers and small business on income distribution grounds.

Japanese industrial policy has been designed, implemented, and justified
by the Ministry of International Trade and Industry (MITI). MITI was quick to
argue market failure, so-called excessive competition, and hence need for government intervention. Its rationale for industrial policy included the following
themes. The private market mechanism inadequately allocates resources for
long-run growth; MITI officials emphasize instances of market failure (external
economies or diseconomies, public good effects, private underinvestment in
R&D) and Japanese labor and capital market imperfections. One senior MITI
official has argued that Japanese are so locked into their own company (group)
and so competitive vis-à-vis others that they go beyond the bounds of normal
economic behavior and engage in excessive competition—with each other as
much as with foreigners.

MITI officials apparently believed they could anticipate the long-run strategic needs of the economy better than the marketplace, which inevitably has
too short a time horizon and is unwilling to assume enough risk, or quickly
enough. They believed they could anticipate where the market will go, thereby
speeding up its operation. While not so clearly stated, underlying their definition of future key industries is a strategic sense as to what industrial structure
will be required for Japan to be a major economic power 10, 20 years from now.
These include semiconductors, computers, telecommunications, nuclear energy. Since the mid-1970s an objective of Japanese industrial policy has been to
assist in the structural adjustment process of major uncompetitive, declining
industries such as aluminum, petrochemicals, and textiles. The MITI rationale
is pragmatic: In scaling down an industry, it is more efficient to close plants and
achieve economies through (government-encouraged) merger than through
bankruptcy.

The Japanese implementation of industrial policy has several important
elements. First, once an industry was selected for support, MITI put together
(in negotiations with the Ministry of Finance) a comprehensive package of
support: accelerated depreciation allowances, special R&D funding (often
through the industry association) or tax benefits, loans through the Japan Development Bank or other government financial institutions, and so forth. Second, the policy measures try to anticipate and to use the marketplace rather
than replacing it, by providing various incentives to business to allocate resources as desired. Such a policy package based on market incentives to encourage business behavior in desired directions contrasts with the more piece-

meal American approach of reliance on a single instrument in aiding specific industries without building in incentives to alter business behavior, as exemplified by de facto restrictions on imports of textiles or automobiles.

Third, MITI policy encouraged the combination of a competitive environment and of effective economies of plant scale in any chosen industry. Indeed, this was the real success of Japanese industrial policy in the high-growth era of the 1950s and 1960s: rapid, efficient industrialization by enabling sufficient new firms to enter major industries that firms were forced to compete with each other, with the realization that import barriers would ultimately be reduced so that firms would face world, not just domestic, competition. Thus Japan, more rapidly than other nations industrializing behind import barriers, was able to achieve international competitiveness in a number of new important industries, ranging from consumer electronics to steel to automobiles to certain types of semiconductors and computers.

Just how micro has Japanese industrial policy been? Let us consider three levels: an individual large firm; an industry, narrowly or more broadly defined; and a productive sector, such as manufacturing, construction, agriculture, or services. Japanese industrial policy has been at the industry level, usually rather broadly defined. MITI has not chosen individual firms as national champions; it has not particularly favored one large firm over another; while it will help an industry in trouble, it usually will not help an individual firm in trouble of its own making. On the other hand, at the broad sectoral level the cumulative effect of both industrial policy and macro policy was to provide preferential access to resources to business, especially large firms, at the expense of housing, consumer credit, or social infrastructure. Agriculture, a lagging, not a leading growth sector, also received special help. In the United States, on the other hand, resources were preferentially allocated to defense, aerospace, agriculture, and housing. And within industry, it may well be that the macrosystem of tax and other incentives differentially affected specific industries in the United States even more than in Japan; certainly the taxation of corporate profits varies widely by industry in the United States.

The Japanese domestic policy environment has been quite favorable for industrial policy and for economic policy generally. High priority is given in Japanese government policymaking to economic issues, domestic and international. The earlier predominant focus on economic growth and efficiency has evolved into a broader mix of goals, including price stability and social welfare (mainly transfer payments for health and old age). The emphasis has been on private enterprise and the operation (and influencing) of the market mechanism, with the first claim on scarce resources going to business, not government. As the economy has continued to grow and has become very strong, the marketplace has become the driver of business decisions, and the government's role less intrusive and more reactive.

Japanese are very competitive, and there are many areas and problems of conflict in Japan as in other societies. Japanese society is built upon individual participation in groups—the family, the school class, the workplace—and societal norms stress the importance of harmony through cooperation and at least formal consensus. This mutes and makes more subtle the normal conflicts of interest and adversarial relationships of life. Accordingly, labor–management relations and government–business relations are much more cooperative and mutually beneficial than in the adversarial, suspicious, more individualistic American society and its institutions. In Japan these relationships are seen as positive-sum, not zero-sum, games. And business in Japan has benefited sub-stantially from the continuance in power of the pro-business, conservative Liberal-Democratic party ever since 1955. It has also benefited from an easier antitrust environment within which, with MITI approval, targeted industries could form temporary antirecession cartels and high-technology firms could participate in joint R&D projects, and within which various forms of anticom-petitive behavior have seemingly been tolerated.

## Changes in Japanese Industrial Policy in the Past Two Decades

Over the past two decades Japanese industrial policy has changed significantly as Japan has achieved affluence (''caught up with the West''), business has become strong and independent, growth has slowed greatly, the price of energy has risen dramatically, and Japan has adopted a free-trade policy and greatly liberalized most of its imports of manufactures. These have affected substan-tially the goals, policy instruments, and policy environment for industrial policy.

Industrial policy is now much less important in Japan than earlier. The goals of economic policy have widened, with greater emphasis on small busi-ness, environmental concerns, and social welfare. The focus of government attention in the 1980s was upon the macro problems associated with huge budget deficits, and upon ''administrative reform'' (read: reducing budget sub-sidies to agriculture and the Japan National Railways in particular). In the early 1990s, attention shifted to ''structural reform,'' as a result of the appreciation of the yen and the bursting of the speculative stock market and land price bubbles of 1986–90.

MITI still tries to identify and support the industries of the future, espe-cially high-tech industries; theirs is now a vision of an information society. But governmental resources, in fact, now go more to the losers, those in difficulty, than to the potential winners—to the structurally depressed industries hit by high energy costs (aluminum, petrochemicals, etc.), low world demand (ship-building), or high labor costs (textiles, simple assembly operations). Most gov-ernment loans go to small businesses, not to large businesses. And almost all government subsidy payments go to agriculture, not industry.

The variety and power of policy instruments to implement industrial policy have been reduced sharply. Most importantly, in the present world environ-ment and given Japan's commitment to the liberal trading system in principle, MITI is no longer able to impose foreign exchange or import restrictions—tariffs, quotas, nontariff barriers—in order to help new potential ''winner'' industries. The licensing of foreign technology imports came to an end in 1968. Antirecession cartels are no longer effective since imports cannot be restricted.

Direct subsidy payments have never been very important in industrial policy; given the continuing budget pressures, they are unlikely to be important in the future. Special tax benefits are increasingly resisted by the Ministry of Finance, obsessed by the budget deficits. The differential between commercial bank and government lending interest rates has become so narrow for large firms that government loans have far smaller benefit than earlier. Nonetheless, MITI continues to have significant policy instruments at its disposal, particularly its ability to subsidize and encourage commercially oriented R&D in high-technology industries. And in the laws concerning structurally depressed industries enacted in the 1980s, MITI obtained powers to encourage mergers and otherwise help a few selected major industries that were in continuing trouble from losing international competitiveness.

The policy environment for industrial policy has changed a great deal from the earlier, high-growth era. As already noted, there no longer is the overwhelming focus on pell-mell growth; other objectives have become more important. Business is correctly perceived as able to grow on its own, especially given the moderate GNP growth-rate experience of 4 to 5 percent between the mid-1970s and the early 1990s, and projections of somewhat lower growth in the future. Unlike in earlier times, savings have been in ample supply; the problem has been encouraging business to invest, rather than rationing credit to business. Big business now is, and feels, strong and independent; it does not want to be beholden to, or dependent upon, MITI or other government officials.

One of the most important changes in the policy environment is that, since the early 1970s, Japan no longer has been insulated from the rest of the world. Foreign governmental pressures—especially American—intruded upon the cozy domestic arrangements that were so much a part of Japanese industrial policy in the 1950s and 1960s. Japan is a major economy and world trader and indeed the challenger of American and European industrial might, not only in steel and motor vehicles but also in semiconductors, computer hardware (but not software), telecommunications, and other high-technology areas. Japan's actions, policy and otherwise, inevitably invite scrutiny and at times reactions by the United States and others. Japan has truly become an interdependent member of an interdependent world. As one of the three pillars of the liberal international economic order—together with the United States and West European industrial democracies—Japan cannot use trade policy as an instrument of industrial policy. It must reduce trade barriers, not raise them, especially in light of its very large and persisting trade and current account surpluses since the early 1980s.

## Evaluation of Japanese Industrial Policy

In my judgment, industrial policy has been somewhat beneficial for the Japanese economy, but its role and efficacy have been overrated by many. Japan has pursued a relatively coherent industrial policy, though its impact has perhaps been less than meets the eye. MITI has supported a number of specific industries and has had some notable successes. It has some important failures—even aside from the promotion in the 1960s of petroleum- and energy-intensive industries—which were made uncompetitive by the sharp rises in energy prices in the 1970s. And there are a number of industries, such as consumer electronics, automobiles, and indeed, virtually all consumer goods, in which the government did not take any specially supportive role, but which have dramatically succeeded on their own.

It should be recognized that there is no clear consensus among specialists on Japan's political economy regarding the effectiveness of Japanese industrial policy. There are two schools of thought, reflecting honest differences of opinion among respected scholars. Let me describe the schools in perhaps stereotypic form in order to differentiate them. Most specialists would place themselves somewhere between these two extremes.

One school sees Japan as embodying a state-guided capitalist developmental system in which MITI and industrial policy have played a central role. In this view, government leadership has been the key to Japan's economic success, with business a willing follower. An extreme version of this approach is encapsulated in the phrase "Japan Inc.," though most agree that is too simplistic and naive a concept for what is a more complex, multidimensional set of relationships among the triad of Liberal-Democratic party politicians, central government bureaucrats, and big business leaders. Essentially, the responsibility for determining the goals of economic policy and seeing to it they are achieved is attributed to the bureaucracy: politicians reign, but bureaucrats rule.

The other school sees the basic source of Japan's economic growth as lying in a vigorous private sector which, taking advantage of the private market mechanism, energetically, imaginatively, and diligently engaged in business productive investment and commercially oriented research and development and in the saving to finance those activities. Business entrepreneurs were the engine of growth. At the same time, the government is given credit for having pursued macro and industrial policies beneficial to private sector growth. The government helped contribute to a favorable economic environment, as did the postwar international economic system—but the major impetus to growth was from the private, market-oriented sector. Industrial policy may well have helped the growth process, but it did not play a leading or central role.

The Japanese central government bureaucracy is certainly able and powerful; however, it is by no means monolithic. Indeed, Japanese ministries are more entrenched and autonomous than their counterparts in the United States executive branch. Each ministry has its own, at times self-serving, definition of the national interest. Thus the Ministry of Finance, and certainly the Ministry of Agriculture, Forestry and Fisheries, perceive the national interest quite differently than MITI. MITI and the Fair Trade Commission take different positions on antitrust and industrial policy. Moreover, jurisdictional disputes and turf problems are as abundant in Japan as in other national bureaucracies. While MITI has jurisdiction regarding the domestic activities and foreign trade of most industries, other ministries have responsibility for certain important sectors: Ministry of Finance for all the financial institutions; Health and Welfare for medical equipment and pharmaceuticals; Agriculture for food processing; Transport for civil air transport, shipping, trucking, and taxis. Thus, MITI's industrial policy does not and cannot cover all industrial activities.

It is important to recognize that government policies which encourage all industries, as occurred in the 1950s and 1960s through import protection, in effect protect none differentially. The main result is to give priority to business over households. The essence of industrial policy is that it differentiates among industries by providing only certain industries especially large incentives. Research in the early 1980s indicated that the differential impact across industries was substantially less than believed earlier. This finding supports an earlier study on specific tax concessions granted to specific industries. Although specific to each industry, such concessions were so widespread that their differential impact was relatively modest. Japanese industrial policy may have started on a micro basis with specific priorities, and some certainly persisted; but the bandwagon effect became so widespread, especially in trade protection but also in tax concessions, that its effect may have been akin to a macroindustrial policy of helping virtually all industry.

If industrial policy is successful, one might expect an industrial structure to emerge quite different from that which would result from the operation of purely market forces. Yet that has not been the case. The Japanese industrial structure is very similar to that of other industrial nations when adjustments are made for market size, per capita income level, natural resource endowment, and distance from markets. This is not to say that past Japanese industrial policy has not had substantial effects. However, it does suggest that the picture is more complex and less well understood than some would suggest.

The ultimate test of the success of Japanese industrial policy is whether it led to a significantly more rapid GNP growth rate than would have occurred otherwise. This is at the core of the scholarly debate. Japanese industrial policy seems to have anticipated where the market would have taken the industrial structure anyway. That is to say, MITI encouraged certain industries which were among the growth industries of the future to develop sooner than they might have otherwise. If so, the industrial policy may have had some success in accelerating the growth rate. The problem is that we do not yet have detailed, definitive studies which settle once and for all the issue of the degree and nature of the effectiveness of Japanese industrial policy.

Today, the goals of Japanese industrial policy are more diffuse and less well defined than two or three decades ago, and the ability to implement policy weakened. With Japan now at the frontiers in many nonmilitary high-technology sectors, it is considerably more difficult for MITI bureaucrats to pick future "winners." There is no longer the American model of evolving industrial structure to emulate, because Japan caught up to it some time ago.

Nonetheless, we should not underestimate the Japanese government's ability to implement a high-technology industrial policy, and in ways consonant with GATT rules. (It is of course important that Japan not impose import barriers on high-technology products, and that it adhere to the "equal national treatment" rule for American high-technology firms operating in Japan.) Now that capital and skilled labor are abundant, government industrial policy places even greater emphasis on technological innovation by R&D through a variety of incentives and institutional mechanisms. Japanese sources have estimated that the American government spends on the order of 10 times as much for R&D in computers and semiconductors as the Japanese government does, but most has been by the Department of Defense and NASA for military and aerospace programs. In contrast, Japanese government R&D, while far smaller absolutely and as a percentage of GNP than that of the United States, is predominantly applied and commercially oriented. Moreover, established, large Japanese companies benefit from the favorable institutional environment, with the opportunity to cooperate in R&D activities. On the other hand, new, small, high-technology firms suffer from the lack of access to capital, due to the still small venture capital market.

In the 1980s easing the structural adjustment of declining industries became as important a component of Japanese industrial policy as efforts to pick winners. As Japan's comparative advantage continues to evolve—due to the continuing spread of the industrial revolution to the developing nations, to Japan's own future growth, to exchange rate adjustments, and to changing world relative prices of energy and other commodities and products—structural adjustment problems have become more severe in Japan as in all advanced industrial nations. While MITI helped the adjustment process in coal mining and cotton textiles in the late 1950s and early 1960, most of its experience in declining industry programs dates from the late 1970s and continues at present. It is more difficult to persuade firms to contract than to expand—to scrap equipment, reduce capacity, rationalize, merge, change business, or go out of business. The policy mix is different too: more direct subsidies, greater reliance on low interest rate loans, virtually forced merger of firms. The record of industrial policy in helping declining industries is mixed. The policy package for shipbuilding in the early 1980s was effective; capacity was reduced by one third without major bankruptcies.

It is unclear whether declining industry industrial policy has resulted in a more efficient restructuring of firms and industries, or at less social cost, than simply allowing the marketplace to work. Indeed, it is unclear whether MITI policy has anticipated, or simply followed, the adjustment process forced by market conditions. However, viewing the choice as simply that of adjustment via the free market or via MITI is politically naive. These are powerful industries, with large debts to powerful banks. It may well be that the government, for the same domestic political reasons as in the United States and all industrial democracies, has to take some kind of ameliorative action. The MITI programs of structural adjustment of declining industries may not be optimal, but they certainly are preferable to such ad hoc measures as direct government subsidies or new protectionist barriers against competitive imports.

## THE RELEVANCE OF THE JAPANESE EXPERIENCE
## FOR UNITED STATES INDUSTRIAL POLICY

It is important to learn from experience, our own and that of others. Japan is probably the most successful case of industrial policy in recent world economic history. Nonetheless, my "lessons" are mainly cautionary; there are no simple answers or solutions.

First, American policymakers should beware of facile generalizations about the nature and effectiveness of Japanese industrial policy. It is premature to present the case to the jury; the evidence is still far from complete and real consensus has yet to emerge from the specialists. There were many factors at play bringing about Japan's two decades of superfast growth up to 1973, and the still good economic performance of the past two decades relative to the United States and Western Europe. In my judgment, industry-specific industrial policy has had a useful but not the central role in Japan's economic success; it has made less of a policy contribution than macroindustrial policy or aggregate demand policy.

Second, it is even less clear whether Japanese-style industrial policy in its historical or especially in its current manifestations is appropriate for the United States. In what ways and to what extent can an industrial policy system be incorporated into the ideology of American economic policy and help achieve its basic goals, and fit into the existing panoply of policy instruments, institutional arrangements, and governmental administrative structure?

Third, what I have termed *macroindustrial policy* has made a significant contribution to Japanese growth: general tax incentives to business to invest productively and to engage in R&D, and to families to save; and the development of a highly effective public education system. Macroindustrial policy, like industry-specific policy, can and should rely upon the marketplace while using it. Thus, the risks, costs, and inability to appropriate fully its benefits mean government funding of R&D is desirable, in both Japan and the United States. Much of the historic rationale for Japanese industrial policy was the shortage of capital in the high-growth era and an inadequate financial institution framework for allocating capital well. The United States has very well developed financial markets, so has less need of industrial policy. On the other hand, in certain respects, Japanese labor markets and institutions work better than their American counterparts. Certainly any American industrial policy should take into account manpower needs and conditions, and the development of skills.

Fourth, it is easier for a nation to pick potential future winner industries when it is in a follower position. It can study the industrial structure of more advanced nations to learn its potential future competitiveness. However, the United States is at the technological frontiers; no other countries are ahead of us to emulate. I am skeptical as to whether American government bureaucrats, scholars, or other experts can judge better than the marketplace what the industries of the future should be. As just stressed, more general policies— support of basic R&D, improvement of the educational system, general incentives for investment and saving—will probably be more effective in enhancing sustained economic growth than special governmental support of specific new industries.

Fifth, perhaps the most important lessons from Japanese industrial policy are how to deal most effectively with important industries in trouble, needing structural adjustments. The realities of the political economy of any industrial nation, including the United States and Japan, are that the political and social costs of adjustment are too great to rely solely and simply upon the market mechanism. Whether consumers and taxpayers like it or not, something is likely to be done to help American textiles or steel or automobiles. Our policy solutions have tended to be *ad hoc*, and import-restrictive. They have not really provided incentives for management and labor to bring about the changes needed in those industries if they are to be efficient, cost- and price-competitive. Japanese industrial policy for structurally depressed industries may provide a better second-best solution than the second-best solutions we have been using thus far. This probably is the most fruitful aspect of the Japanese experience in industrial policy that the United States can learn from.

Sixth, recent Japanese and American experience suggests that once a country is at the technological frontiers, import restrictions may not be an efficient instrument of industrial policy either for picking winners or for solving the structural problems of industries in trouble. Moreover, protectionism is not an appropriate policy for advanced industrial nations; it is destructive of the international economic system so carefully crafted and nourished ever since 1945. As a less developed follower nation, Japan in the 1950s and early 1960s by general restrictions of industrial imports achieved broad-based industrialization and rapid growth. Perhaps the greatest success of industrial policy was the maintenance and encouragement of vigorously competitive domestic markets which forced firms to become efficient while growing in size. Though, in a narrow sense, the implementation of industrial policy has been weakened by Japan's import liberalization over the past two decades, the industrial sector as a whole was sufficiently developed that it benefited from increased foreign competition in Japanese markets. Resources are being allocated more efficiently in a decade of major structural change in industry.

Seventh, if the United States decides to employ industrial policy to achieve important economic objectives, it can learn from the Japanese methods of implementation. Policy should be long-run in focus, consistent in approach, and mobilize a package of mutually supportive policy instruments. The criterion of effectiveness should be economic efficiency, as measured by cost- and price-competitiveness in world, not just United States, markets. And, since the benefits of industrial policy in the first instance accrue to the owners, managers, and workers of those industries targeted for preferential treatment while the costs are borne by taxpayers and/or consumers, then the beneficiaries should be required to meet performance goals in order to justify the support received.

## Chapter Thirteen

# Japan's Industrial Groups, the *Keiretsu**

## *Dick K. Nanto*

*A distinctive feature of Japanese industrial organization is the importance of large and powerful conglomerate or vertically integrated groups called the* keiretsu. *They are sets of companies linked by long-term association, cross-holdings of stock, extensive mutual business dealings, and sometimes sharing of company name. Among the* keiretsu *are such world-famous names as Toyota, Nissan, Toshiba, Matsushita, and Mitsubishi.*

*In this chapter, Nanto analyzes the different types of* keiretsu, *the ties that bind companies in a group, and the ways in which related enterprises coordinate their activities. He shows how the* keiretsu *contribute to Japan's exports, on the one hand, and make it difficult for foreign firms to operate in the Japanese market, on the other. These export and import effects of the* keiretsu *help explain Japan's trade surpluses with other nations, and thus Japan's "trade friction" with those nations. The United States, for example, has complained that Japan's antitrust laws are not energetically enforced against anticompetitive behavior by the* keiretsu.

## INTRODUCTION

As the Japanese economy has grown, it has developed some fairly distinctive institutions that have only vague parallels in other industralized nations. Japan's *keiretsu*,[1] or industrial groups, are one such institution. These consist of

* Reprinted from *Japan's Economic Challenge* (Study Papers Submitted to the Joint Economic Committee, U.S. Congress, 101st Cong., 2nd Sess.) (Washington, D.C.: U.S. Government Printing Office, 1990), pp. 72–88, with the rearrangement of some material and the omission of a table and references to foreign language sources, unpublished studies, and limited-circulation publications. Dick K. Nanto is a Specialist in Industry and Trade in the Congressional Research Service, Library of Congress.

[1] The *keiretsu* (kay-ret-sue) also are referred to as *zaibatsu* (financial cliques). *Zaibatsu*, however, has a negative connotation and usually refers to Japan's prewar industrial combines characterized by holding companies. At the end of World War II, Japan's four largest *zaibatsu* controlled about a quarter of the paid-in capital of Japan's incorporated business. See Eleanor M. Hadley, *Antitrust in Japan* (Princeton, N.J.: Princeton University Press, 1970).

either vertical or conglomerate groupings of companies that are characterized by long-term association, cross-holdings of stock, extensive business dealings, and, sometimes, sharing of company name. The *keiretsu,* themselves, do not violate Japan's antitrust laws, but their activities can.

The *keiretsu* have been one of the targets of the Structural Impediments Initiative talks between the United States and Japan in 1989–90. The United States claims that the close links among Japanese corporations can "promote preferential group trade, negatively affect foreign direct investment in Japan, and give rise to anticompetitive business practices." The United States also claims that the industrial groups can hinder market access of U.S. firms and allow member companies to generate profits in protected markets at home, thereby enabling them to shave profit margins and gain market share abroad. The long-term, buyer–supplier relationships also can even lock out foreign suppliers with superior products, while the supplier–distributor links can prevent retailers from carrying competing products and can hinder price competition. The cross-holdings of shares also can impede foreign aquisitions of Japanese companies and make trading in stocks of certain companies thin.

Many Japanese see the *keiretsu* as a natural growth of their unique economic developement and one of their greatest strengths in international competition. Along with the elite government ministries, the core companies of the *keiretsu* are the first choice for employment among Japan's top graduates each year. Japanese also point out that Germany has similar business organizations. Hence, it is the United States, not Japan, that is out of step with the rest of the world.

In this study, we examine the types of *keiretsu* organization, discuss briefly Japan's Fair Trade Commission, and outline some implications for the United States.

## TYPES OF INDUSTRIAL GROUPS

Japan's *keiretsu* can be classified into two types: conglomerate[2] and vertical. The conglomerate groups comprise firms in a variety of business activities and usually are centered around trading companies and banks. Firms in a vertical grouping will be centered on a major manufacturer and can include both suppliers and sellers within a specific sector. Vertical groups also can depend on the conglomerate group members for particular functions, such as procurement, financing, and distribution of finished products.

As shown in Figure 13–1, the conglomerate groups include three with origins in the prewar *zaibatsu* (industrial combines)—Mitsubishi, Mitsui, and Sumitomo—and three that are bank centered—Fuyo (Fuji Bank), DKB (Dai-

---

[2] Some authors refer to the conglomerate *keiretsu* as horizontal *keiretsu*. Horizontal integration, however, usually refers to firms producing similar products (e.g., Chrysler's acquisition of American Motors).

**FIGURE 13–1**    Japan's Industrial Groups, the *Keiretsu*

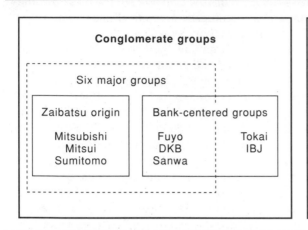

SOURCE: Prepared by the Congressional Research Service.

ichi Kangyo Bank), and Sanwa (Sanwa Bank). For example, the Mitsubishi Group, a descendent from a prewar *zaibatsu,* is centered on the Mitsubishi Corporation (a trading company), Mitsubishi Bank, and Mitsubishi Heavy Industries. The affiliated Mitsubishi companies include 35 firms in insurance, construction, food, textiles, paper, chemicals, petroleum, glass, cement, steel, nonferrous metals, machinery, electronics, transportation machinery, optical instruments, shipping, real estate, and warehousing. As a group, Mitsubishi's sales are about twice the level of those of General Motors, the world's largest industrial corporation.

The vertically integrated groups include 39 blue-chip manufacturers such as Nippon Steel, Toyota, and Matsushita Electric. These groups resemble the business empires found in all industrialized nations of the world.

## Conglomerate Ties

The six major *keiretsu* organized into conglomerates use a variety of methods to tie their enterprises together. These include:

- Cross-holdings of shares.
- Intra-group financing by a common bank.
- Presidential councils.
- Mutual appointments of officers.
- Use of trading companies for marketing and organizing projects.
- Joint investments in new industries.

The *cross-holdings of shares* in Japan stem from three factors. First, when the U.S. occupation authorities after World War II liquidated the Japanese holding companies and forced them to sell their stock, the major buyers with funds to purchase them were other companies. Second, as Japan liberalized its capital markets in the 1960s and 1970s, companies began to fear hostile takeovers from abroad. They protected themselves by having friendly companies serve as stable stockholders. Third, Japan's antimonopoly law proscribes holding companies. Hence, the cross-shareholding substitutes for vertical shareholding possible through holding company structures prevalent in other countries.

The extent of stock cross-holdings among the conglomerate *keiretsu* ranges from about 14 to 22 percent of total paid-up capital. The purposes of the mutual holdings of stock include cementing relationships and precluding hostile takeover attempts. The holdings of stock are rarely sold.[3] The mutual share holdings also reduce pressures on companies to increase short-term profits.

In the *bank-centered keiretsu*, the holding of shares by the bank in the group companies signifies a relationship that also is buttressed by other means. The companies exchange information with the bank and usually deposit large amounts of cash there just to maintain satisfactory relationships. They also, however, make such deposits with other banks, just to ensure that ample credit will be available during periods of tight money and that no single bank will exert undue influence on the corporation.[4]

Given the debate in the United States over the cost of capital for businesses, one question is whether or not the members of a bank-centered *keiretsu* are able to gain access to loans under preferential conditions. Even though interest rates might be the same for inside and outside borrowers with similar credit ratings, member firms probably have received preferential access to available funds during credit crunches. They also can receive favorable terms for repayment and extensions, if necessary. The bank may step in and provide management to a firm that is facing bankruptcy. At one time, *zaibatsu* banks were referred to as "organ" banks or an integral part of the organization.[5] The current surplus of capital in Japan and the ready availability of other sources of finance, however, indicates that the importance of this "captive" bank is diminishing. As long as cheaper sources of capital exist in world financial markets, firms will continue to diversify their borrowing away from their primary bank.

Under the postwar dissolution of the *zaibatsu* and subsequent laws, the *keiretsu* banks were forced to diversify their lending activities. Likewise, borrowing firms began to limit their loans from their primary banks to about 30 percent. Even bank-centered *keiretsu* companies, therefore, borrow from several other banks. However, ties still are strong. In the case of Nihon Dennetsu,

---

[3] Since most companies carry these stocks at their historical value, many Japanese companies have balance sheets in which net worth is considered to be understated.

[4] James C. Abegglen and George Stalk, Jr., *Kaisha, The Japanese Corporation* (New York: Basic Books, 1985), pp. 165–66.

[5] Hadley, *Antitrust in Japan*, p. 157.

a member of the Mitsui *keiretsu*, it had been obliged to consult with Mitsui prior to borrowing money outside the group.

The *presidential councils* comprise the presidents of the leading companies of the group, who meet periodically (usually monthly) to discuss matters of mutual interest. The importance of these councils appears to be diminishing, since in the 1960s such councils met weekly. While the councils claim not to be policy-making bodies for the group (as were the prewar holding companies), they do discuss such topics as economic and financial conditions, promising business activities, research and development, intra-group trademarks, and labor problems. They also can decide on joint investments in new industries, political contributions, public relations, rehabilitation of troubled member companies, and key personnel appointments.

During the recent merger of Mitsubishi Metal and Mitsubishi Mining and Cement, Takeshi Nagano, President of Mitsubishi Metal, said that the merger was not discussed in the Presidential Council for fear of allegations of insider trading. Other *keiretsu* members were informed of the decision personally after the decision had been made.

At the center of several conglomerate *keiretsu* are general *trading companies*.[6] These huge companies operate diverse businesses on their own while providing many services to member firms. They procure raw materials, distribute products, finance some activities, organize diverse projects, and gather and disseminate intelligence. Since trading companies are involved in both importing and exporting, they can absorb considerable foreign exchange risk for the group. The trading company usually is considered to be the lead company or it shares leadership with a bank or other major company in the group. Mitsui & Co. (the trading company), for example, shares leadership with Mitsui Bank and Mitsui Real Estate Development in their *keiretsu*.

Trading companies, moreover, engage in transactions not only for Japanese firms, but also with buyers and sellers in third countries. Such transactions might include, for example, arranging for a sale of a U.S. chemical plant to the Soviet Union or importing Romanian urea into Bangladesh.[7] In the early 1980s, Japanese trading companies handled as much as 10 percent of all U.S. exports. In 1987, the nine leading trading companies reported that 17 percent of their sales were exports from Japan, 19 percent were imports, 20 percent were third-country sales, and 44 percent were domestic sales.[8]

Japan's general trading companies enter into a variety of transactions. Each company will handle as many as 20,000 different products with numerous suppliers. This enables them to arrange multiproduct deals that encompass many facets of a project. An example would be the export of a turnkey petro-

---

[6] Alexander K. Young, *The Sogo Shosha: Japan's Multinational Trading Companies* (Boulder, Colo.: Westview Press, 1979), pp. 9–10.

[7] M. Y. Yoshino and Thomas B. Lifson, *The Invisible Link: Japan's Sogo Shosha and the Organization of Trade* (Cambridge, Mass.: MIT Press, 1986), p. 2.

[8] *Japan Economic Almanac, 1988* (Tokyo: Nihon Keizai Shimbun, 1988), p. 226.

chemical plant to Singapore that required equipment, technology, and consulting services of many different firms.[9] About half of the sales of the nine leading trading companies were in metals and machinery. Other major categories were fuels, chemical products, foodstuffs, and textiles. In 1987, the top nine trading companies in Japan handled 74 percent of all Japan's imports and 42 percent of its exports, and carried even greater shares of certain products, such as steel and grain.

General trading companies wield considerable market power. Through control of key ports and shipping facilities, they can exert pressure on member companies in their buying and selling decisions, and can hinder U.S. exports. Since such a high proportion of Japan's imports are concentrated in the hands of a few firms, moreover, the government is better able to exert "administrative guidance" to dampen imports of particular goods. This has happened in the past in steel and textiles.[10] Most of the imports handled by trading companies, however, are bulk commodities. Hence, they are less influential in either promoting or hindering imports of manufactured goods.

In terms of *new business ventures*, the *keiretsu* often form committees to study promising areas. Mitsubishi, for example, used a study committee to plan how the group would move more rapidly into advanced communications. Mitsui coordinated member company efforts in new media research, and Sumitomo in commercial uses of space.[11]

U.S. businesses have charged that the conglomerate *keiretsu* prefer to buy from other member companies rather than from outsiders, particularly foreign companies. While such intra-group buying appears to be declining, it still can be quite significant, particularly for capital goods. On average, intra-group purchases account for 10 to 20 percent of the purchases by *keiretsu* firms. In 1981, for the six largest firms in the distribution sector, the share of purchases from fellow *keiretsu* firms amounted to 3.1 percent for textiles and clothing; 0.5 percent for agricultural products; 9.9 percent for minerals, metal products, and chemicals; and 21.1 percent for machinery and equipment.[12]

In a 1985 survey of Japan's machinery manufacturers by Japan's Ministry of International Trade and Industry (MITI), 95.1 percent of the respondents said they would pick the superior good whether in-group or imported, while 2.0 percent favored in-group goods even if imports were superior, and 2.9 percent said they favor imports, even if in-group goods were superior. (This last group of respondents were all affiliates of foreign companies.)

The three major U.S. complaints about Japanese conglomerate *keiretsu* are their intra-group trading, control over markets, and cross-shareholding

---

[9] Young, *The Sogo Shosha*, pp. 4–9.

[10] Edward J. Lincoln, *Japan's Unequal Trade* (Washington, D.C.: Brookings Institution, 1990), p. 88.

[11] Clyde V. Prestowitz, Jr., *Trading Places* (New York: Basic Books, 1988), pp. 159–60.

[12] Erich Batzer and Helmut Laumer, *Marketing Strategies and Distribution Channels for Foreign Companies in Japan* (Boulder, Colo.: Westview Press, 1989), p. 111.

which makes hostile takeovers extremely difficult. The conglomerate's trading companies, however, have been used by some exporters to facilitate exports to Japan. The conglomerates no doubt will continue to grow, but future growth will likely come at the expense of the traditional "family" ties. Individual companies in the conglomerates are likely to become more and more independent in the future as they develop their own marketing mechanisms and establish links with firms in other countries and industries.

Two major trends are developing in industries in the three developed markets of the world: North America, Europe, and Japan. The first trend is toward consortia of firms in a specific industry to link together to market products simultaneously in all three markets. General Motors, for example, has ties with Isuzu and Suzuki in Japan and its subsidiaries in Europe.

The second major trend is for corporations to establish networks by which they link with other firms to share technology, jointly develop products, or cover markets. The recent agreement between Mitsubishi and Daimler-Benz conglomerates to cooperate over a wide range of business activities is one such example. The tie-up is expected to spawn joint projects in automobiles, electrical machinery, aerospace technology, and corporate telecommunications networks. Hence, even the largest and most centralized of the conglomerate *keiretsu* is finding it necessary to network with the largest German conglomerate in order to remain competitive in world markets.

As long as markets continue to expand, intra-group trading as a percent of total trade will likely diminish. During a severe recession, however, conglomerate *keiretsu* could implode upon each other. They would likely support fellow conglomerate members in adverse business conditions.

The cross-shareholdings of stock also could diminish. Given the heights reached by the Tokyo stock exchange, some companies are questioning the value of keeping a portfolio with so many shares of other companies, when the value of those stocks has risen so much and those funds could be used for other purposes.

## Vertical Ties

In addition to the *keiretsu* integrated into conglomerates discussed above, numerous vertically integrated groups exist in Japan. Some of these vertically integrated groups also maintain horizontal ties. These independent industrial groups resemble the corporate behemoths elsewhere in the industralized world.

The groups usually are headed by one or more large industrial concerns and are commonly concentrated in one or a few industries. Normally, the affiliated firms maintain vertical buyer-supplier relationships, although ties with horizontal firms also are common. The Nissan Motor Corporation, for example, has links with Fuji Heavy Industries (makers of Subaru automobiles), but its primary relationships are with its 22 upstream suppliers of parts and downstream distribution-related companies, such as Nissan Motor Sales, Nissan Auto Transport, and Nissan Motorist Service. Hence, the relationships go both down the supply chain from manufacturer to raw material provider or component maker and up the distribution system through the wholesaler and retailer.

There are no strict criteria for distinguishing a vertically integrated *keiretsu* from other large vertical groupings. Dodwell Consultants lists as *keiretsu* 39 vertically integrated groups whose sales exceeded 1 trillion yen in 1987. The list includes companies whose brand names boast world-wide recognition: Toyota, Nissan, Honda, Mazda, Sony, Mitsubishi Electric, Hitachi, Toshiba, NEC, Nippon Steel, NTT, and Sharp. Some of the vertically integrated groups also are members of conglomerate *keiretsu*.

As with the conglomerate *keiretsu*, vertical *keiretsu* firms hold each other's shares, exchange information, and cooperate in new ventures. Since the relationship is vertical, however, the closest ties are between buyers and suppliers or between maker and distributor in the group. Under Toyota Motor, for example, stand 22 firms making auto parts or assembling sister products (such as looms). These include Toyota Auto Body, Toyoda Automatic Loom Works, Aichi Steel Works, and Koito Manufacturing. Toyota also owns dealerships, an insurance company, and three ventures in nonautomotive fields. This is similar to General Motors or Ford.

The distinguishing feature of the vertical links in Japan (and one that U.S. firms also are adopting) is the close relationship between the parent company and its suppliers. Such links tend to pervade all Japanese businesses, but are the strongest within the *keiretsu*. Relationships that initially are forged by the mutual buying of each other's stock are expected to continue for a long time. The supplier participates actively with the final manufacturer in designing products, upgrading technology and manufacturing processes, and implementing quality control. The buyer usually is allowed to examine the supplier's books, and cost savings generally are passed on to the final manufacturer to be incorporated into the retail price of the product. The supplier is an integral link in the competitive strategy of a Japanese manufacturer.

The close links also substitute for legal work in Japan. Supplier–buyer contracts often do not contain the detailed contingency clauses common in American contracts. If a problem arises, the relationship of mutual trust allows the companies to work out a satisfactory solution. The long-term nature of the relationship, moreover, means that if one side has to take a loss because of unforeseen difficulties, it may be favored the next time a problem arises. Hence, equity can be attained.

The traditional Japanese system of permanent employment reinforces the vertical *keiretsu* system. Although permanent employment covers only the core employees of a company and only about a third of the total work force, it usually is standard in the *keiretsu* companies. Under permanent employment, new hires are kept on the job until they retire (at age 55 to 60), and their salary rises with their years of service.

The problem with permanent employment is that every company has an organizational structure shaped like a pyramid. Every person hired cannot be promoted continually. Not enough jobs exist in management. The company can solve the problem by growing fast enough to create new managerial jobs as the permanent employees rise in the organization, but eventually every company runs out of positions, even for highly capable individuals.

It is in solving this employment problem that subsidiaries and suppliers in the *keiretsu* play a critical role. The subsidiaries and suppliers usually are required to accept retiring employees from the lead manufacturer. This also helps the supplier, since the retiree usually turns around and deals with people in the parent company whom he formerly supervised. Such personnel transfers add to the difficulty of an outsider firm in breaking into a *keiretsu* buyer–supplier relationship.

Japanese manufacturers also do not change suppliers without first consulting existing ones. If a competing supplier comes in with a lower price or new product, the existing supplier often is given a chance to match it. U.S. automotive parts suppliers, in particular, have complained that they cannot even get specifications for parts from Japanese automakers. They are told that they have to enter the process earlier. The existing suppliers have already been involved in developing those specifications and manufacturing processes.

A supplier also will supply parts under a contract that will have provisions for falling prices, zero defects, and just-in-time delivery. The philosophy of Japanese contracting is that as a company moves out on the experience curve for a given product, the price of that product should fall. Also, manufacturers often require their suppliers to ensure that their products are 100 percent defect-free. Such parts can be delivered directly to the manufacturer's assembly line and are not reinspected or stored. Parts also must be delivered as they are needed on the assembly line. This just-in-time delivery means that the supplier may be required to make several small-lot deliveries at specific times each day.

Such exacting requirements for the supplier mean that the buyer and supplier must have a relationship that goes beyond that specified in the contract. There must be trust, loyalty, a mode of operation that allows for problems to be worked out in a mutually satisfactory manner, enough confidence in the relationship that supplier is willing to invest in new technology, and a sharing of production and cost data that normally might be considered proprietary. Such relationships are difficult to cultivate without closer tries than those developed through arms-length transactions. Hence, in Japan vertical *keiretsu* have developed.

The complaints of outsiders, not just foreigners but including Japanese companies who are not members of the privileged few suppliers, is that breaking into existing buyer–supplier relationships is nearly impossible. The best chance for an outside company to break into the existing buyer–supplier chain is with a unique product. Even a unique component, however, will usually be incorporated into a new, not existing, product. The buying firm will maintain its links with the existing suppliers.[13] Rarely can a new firm break in on the basis of price alone.

---

[13] Batzer and Laumer, *Marketing Strategies*, p. 103.

The size of the *keiretsu*, moreover, makes it easier for the lead companies to establish cartels and divide up markets or exclude outsiders.

## Distribution *Keiretsu*

Vertical *keiretsu* also extend from the manufacturer through distribution and even to retailers. Much like automobile dealership franchises, some Japanese makers maintain exclusive wholesale and retail networks. These are common for automobiles, electrical appliances, cosmetics, confectioneries, and musical instruments. Discipline is maintained in the distribution system through providing capital and rebates. Capital is usually supplied by purchasing large blocks of the wholesaler's stock, holding promissory notes while goods are moved, and other forms of trade credit.[14] Rebates also are provided both to increase profit margins and as sales promotions.

Matsushita Electric Industrial Company, the maker of National and Panasonic brand name products, for example, maintains its 25 percent share of Japan's domestic refrigerator market through 24,000 "National" shops which sell its brand-name products. More than half of Matsushita's home appliance products are still sold through such shops. Similarly, 11,000 shops belong to the Toshiba *keiretsu,* 9,000 to Hitachi, 5,000 each to Sanyo and Sharp, and 3,000 to Sony.

In 1990, Matsushita indicated that in response to U.S. pressures it intends to overhaul its *keiretsu* distribution system for home electrical appliances. The company will abolish special rebates for companies that sell a large volume of its products, and will revise the system by which retailers could make a deposit with Matsushita worth 1 percent of their transactions with the company and receive returns at the same rate as Matsushita stocks (about 20 percent currently). Matsushita also indicated that it would revise its use of officially suggested retail prices.

Japan's antimonopoly law has provisions aimed at most monopoly practices in distributing products from the manufacturer to the customer. Resale price maintenance, exclusive dealing stipulations, and customer restrictions seem to be disallowed in the law, but the sanctions are so weak that the law appears to have little effect. When successful antitrust proceedings are brought against a company, the result is usually a cease and desist order rather than a penalty.

In Japan, vertical restraints generally are treated as unfair business practices rather than as private monopolizations. In 1982, Japan's Fair Trade Commission (JFTC) designated practices it considered to be unfair. These included unjust exclusive dealing, unjust resale price maintenance, and unjust customer relations. Actual examples from the files of the JFTC include firms that stipu-

---

[14] Kozo Yamamura and Jan Vandenberg, "Japan's Rapid-Growth Policy on Trial: The Television Case," in *Law and Trade Issues of the Japanese Economy,* ed. Gary R. Saxonhouse and Kozo Yamamura (Seattle: University of Washington Press, 1986), pp. 243–44.

lated minimum retail prices or maximum wholesale prices, prohibited firms from upsetting a discriminatory price structure, assigned exclusive territories, or required salesmen to deal exclusively in their products. Each of these cases can be explained by standard economic arguments common in the United States and other industrialized countries and not unique to Japanese culture, custom, or tradition.

One allegation made by several U.S. competitors is that Japan's *keiretsu* distribution system allows Japanese companies to generate large profits at home and use those profits to cover their fixed costs, and to charge prices close to variable costs or even less than variable costs in export markets. In theory, such behavior can lead to the dumping of products abroad, particularly when excess production capacity exists in Japan.[15]

The philosophy of many Japanese firms is that a loss can be taken in developing new markets if the potential for long-term profits is high enough. Toyota, for example, took years before it began to turn a profit in the U.S. market. The *keiretsu* distribution system in Japan tends to support such market behavior abroad.

Any change in Japan's vertical *keiretsu* is likely to be marginal and in response to economic as well as political pressures. As Japan's distribution system is modernized, however, the single-brand stores are likely to lose business to the large-scale marketers. In the case of cameras, the discounters, such as Yodobashi Camera in Tokyo, sell in such volume that Japan's camera makers have been forced to deal with them. In the process, the camera makers have lost much of their control over prices. The loosening of import restrictions, moreover, means that Japanese firms will no longer be able to charge higher prices domestically, thereby fattening their profit margins at home in order to shave them abroad.

## THE JAPAN FAIR TRADE COMMISSION

The Japan Fair Trade Commission (JFTC) was created by the U.S. Occupation authorities in 1947 (based on the American model) and serves as Japan's watchdog agency dealing with antitrust laws. Under the antimonopoly law established at the same time, and as elaborated in a 1953 notification by the JFTC, the six categories of business practices considered to be unfair include (1) boycotts and refusals to deal; (2) discrimination in prices, terms, or access to concerted activities; (3) unreasonably high or low prices; (4) exclusive dealing; (5) vertical restrictive agreements including tying and (generally) resale price maintenance; and (6) abuse of a dominant bargaining position.[16]

---

[15] Most recent antidumping cases against Japan deal with industrial materials or products not sold in Japan through a *keiretsu* distribution system.

[16] Richard Caves and Masu Uekusa, "Industrial Organization," in *Asia's New Giant,* ed. Hugh Patrick and Henry Rosovsky (Washington, D.C.: Brookings Institution, 1976), pp. 485–86.

The JFTC uses summary investigation procedures when a violation is not substantial or is limited in scope. In formal investigations with sufficient evidence of a violation, the JFTC will take formal action. Where the evidence is insufficient, the commission usually issues a warning to eliminate the activities in question. Only in exceptional cases will the JFTC file a criminal accusation against a company; the most recent example was against a 1974 oil cartel.[17]

In total, the JFTC handles as many as 500 cases per year. Not all, of course, involve the *keiretsu*. In 1975 and in 1976, it found more than 30 violations of the antimonopoly law (mostly price-fixing agreements). After that, however, violations averaged only about 11 per year, and they dropped to about 5 per year in 1986 and 1987.

The 1977 revision of Japan's Antimonopoly Law allows the JFTC to assess surcharges against violators. The surcharges are based on the sales volume of the firm during the period of violation. In the mid-1980s both the number of violations and the amount of the surcharges declined. Whether this was because of a greater awareness of the antitrust guidelines by businesses or because of more lax enforcement is not possible to determine. Since then, however, the JFTC seems to have become more aggressive. In December 1988, it levied a surcharge of 290 million yen ($2.04 million) on 70 firms for conspiring to fix bids for projects at the U.S. Navy base at Yokosuka. It also punished construction companies for similar activities at the Osaka airport project, and issued a written warning to 36 firms suspected of forming a cartel to import beef.

The contention of the United States is that the JFTC is underbudgeted, understaffed, and lacks enough clout to prevent abuses of monopoly power. The JFTC's staff and budget are about one quarter the level of the combined U.S. antimonopoly force. The JFTC is one of the weakest agencies in the Japanese government. The chairman of its five-man commission usually comes from the Ministry of Finance, and MITI always has a representative there. Neither agency is a strong supporter of antitrust enforcement.

The United States also has pointed out the disincentives for private companies or groups to file antitrust suits in Japan. Such suits are permitted, but they are rare and financial settlements are modest. During the oil crisis in 1973–1974, for example, two consumer groups alleged that the oil companies were overcharging them. They eventually settled for the sums of $985 and $577 after the cases reached the Tokyo High Court. In another case, the consumers rejected a proposed settlement of $1,808, but went on to lose the case on appeal to the Supreme Court.

In the April 5, 1990, Interim Report by the Japanese Delegation to the Japan-U.S. Structural Impediments Initiative (SII), the Japanese government indicated that it intended to strengthen the JFTC and have it enforce the anti-

---

[17] Iyori Hiroshi, "Antitrust and Industrial Policy in Japan: Competition and Cooperation," in *Law and Trade Issues*, pp. 65–66.

monopoly law more strictly. The JFTC is to monitor the transactions among *keiretsu* firms to determine whether or not they are being conducted in a manner that impedes fair competition.

The JFTC, with the assistance of an advisory group, is also to establish guidelines to ensure that transactions among companies in *keiretsu* groups do not discriminate against foreign firms. Furthermore, the JFTC is to publish biennial analyses of the *keiretsu* groups, including supplier–customer transactions, financing arrangements, personal ties, and the role of trading companies in the groups.

The issue of the *keiretsu* has also reached the U.S. operations of Japanese companies. The U.S. Federal Trade Commission has begun a probe of Japanese companies and their parts suppliers operating in the United States. The investigation is to determine whether or not their propensity to buy components from suppliers in which they hold a financial interest illegally discriminates against competing parts makers.

## IMPLICATIONS FOR U.S. POLICY

The *keiretsu* are a fact of life in Japan and are not likely to change significantly in the near future. Over time, however, all such arrangements tend to weaken because member companies grow so large that company policies become difficult to enforce, subsidiaries become financially independent, and the product lines of member firms become so complicated that the parent company can no longer provide meaningful guidance for them. Obviously, however, U.S. firms attempting to enter the Japanese market cannot wait for this process to develop.

To say that Japan's *keiretsu* exist is not to say that competition in Japan is bridled. Among the *keiretsu* companies, competition is ferocious. Companies compete, however, more in product quality and new features, rather than just price. The ferocity of this competition is attested to by the speed of technological innovation and the rapid decline in the cost of production in Japan's manufacturing sector. This makes the *keiretsu* different from government-sanctioned monopolies or other such uncompetitive (and anticompetitive) entities in other nations. Since competition is so fierce, Japan's *keiretsu* companies tend to keep up with world developments in technology, manufacturing processes, and product development.

On a practical level, U.S. firms assessing potential customers in Japan should first look at existing *keiretsu* links. They should examine the number of employees received by suppliers from the buying company and the positions they occupy, the cross-holdings of stock, and the nature of the buyer–supplier relationships already in place. Once the U.S. firm has gauged the extent of the *keiretsu* ties, it has several options.

First, the U.S. firm can focus on those buyers without *keiretsu* ties. These usually will be smaller firms often located outside of Tokyo or they may be entrepreneurial firms such as Sony or Honda. While the entrepreneurial firms may be vertical *keiretsu* themselves, they often are more open to outside products because they have had to battle the entrenched conglomerate *keiretsu* from their inception. Taiwanese exporters pursued this strategy. They began by establishing contacts in second-tier cities such as Osaka and Fukuoka. There, they found companies whose major problem also was trying to compete with the *keiretsu* firms and who were searching for new products that might give them an advantage.

Second, the U.S. firm can attempt to link up with a supplier who is already a member of the *keiretsu* or its supply network. U.S. companies such as Borg Warner and Honeywell have followed this strategy by forming joint ventures or licensing local production. This avenue can achieve short-term results, but it has the long-term danger that the Japanese partner could adopt the technology and improve upon the U.S. firm's product so much that it becomes independent and takes over the market by itself.[18]

A typical joint venture might result in 20 Japanese engineers sent to the U.S. parent company to learn about the American technology and one American engineer sent to Tokyo to help the Japanese partner adopt it. Nowhere in the process are American engineers sent to Tokyo to learn about Japanese technology.

In terms of distribution, a U.S. firm might link up with either a similar company or one in a different sector but servicing the same clientele. Sales of Tiffany products by Mitsukoshi department stores, for example, reached $26 million by 1988. Honda is starting to distribute Chrysler Jeeps in Japan, and Diner's Club worked with the Japan Travel Bureau as its partner at an early stage.

Third, the U.S. firm might establish a relationship with some other part of the buying company. One method is for the American company's engineers to provide the engineering staff in the *keiretsu* company with technical help on an informal basis. This bypasses the purchasing department entirely. After the Japanese engineers begin to feel indebted to the U.S. company's engineers and see how the U.S. product might solve their problems, the U.S. company's engineers then suggest that the Japanese engineers ask their purchasing people to buy the U.S. product. This is a tactic that has been used successfully by European machine tool makers.

A similar strategy is to begin working with the potential buyer long before the buying decisions are made. In May 1990, for example, the Nippon Telegraph and Telephone Corporation announced that AT&T International, Motorola, and Ericsson of Sweden had been selected, along with seven Japanese companies, to develop its next generation mobile-telephone system. When the actual purchases are made, these foreign companies should be able to compete equally with Japanese companies because they will have been in the market

---

[18] See, for example, Robert B. Reich and Eric D. Mankin, "Joint Ventures with Japan Give Away Our Future," *Harvard Business Review* 64, no. 2 (March–April 1986), pp. 78–86.

from the beginning. Similar opportunities are available for U.S. semiconductor suppliers for high-definition TV.[19]

Fourth, if the U.S. firm has deep pockets, it can establish its own subsidiaries and distribution system and confront the *keiretsu* on their home turf. This has been the route followed by companies such as IBM and Coca-Cola.

If U.S. firms perceive that the *keiretsu* system is working to block their sales in Japan, pressures can be brought to bear on the system by the U.S. government. One of the problems, however, is that U.S. firms with complaints often are afraid to bring them to light for fear of jeopardizing their existing market in Japan. Occasionally, egregious cases, such as the case of soda ash[20] or of amorphous metals, will come to light, but alleged violations often go unreported if the risks of complaining are greater than the probable gains.

The United States has not argued that long-term, *keiretsu*-type relationships that make economic sense are wrong. Indeed, relationships based on trust that reduce the need for legal work enhance the efficiency of producers. The existence of *keiretsu*, by themselves, is not the problem. The problem is that the close coordination among group members facilitates violations of antitrust laws and dealings that can exclude U.S. exporters.

In terms of reciprocity and equity, moreover, the ease with which Japanese companies can buy into U.S. firms compared with the difficulty of U.S. firms to do likewise in Japan offends the sense of fairness of many Americans.

U.S. pressures on the system through the SII and other forums are likely to speed up the process of liberalization and can restore some of the power of the JFTC to pursue abuses among *keiretsu* companies. The demands by the United States that the JFTC be strengthened are also supported by the JFTC. During the SII talks, the U.S. Embassy in Japan kept in close contact with the JFTC to ensure that the U.S. demands were reasonable. After the SII talks are completed, oversight and monitoring will be important.

The fastest changes in the *keiretsu* system are likely to occur in distribution. The economic rationale for the vertical buyer–supplier relationships is so strong that such *keiretsu* are unlikely to change much. The conglomerate *keiretsu* are likely to grow rather than to shrink, although coordination among member companies is likely to diminish as individual companies become more independent and networking outside the *keiretsu* system becomes more common.

Recently, in Washington, D.C., Akio Morita, the Chairman of the Sony Corporation, was asked what he thought about the *keiretsu* (referring to the mammoth conglomerate *keiretsu*). His reply was that every firm would like to have a guaranteed market for some of its output. Someday, he would like Sony itself to develop into a *keiretsu*. This seems to be the attitude of most of Japanese big business.

---

[19] Jacob M. Schlesinger, "Japan's NIT Loosens Its 'Family' Ties," *The Wall Street Journal,* May 21, 1990, p. A8.

[20] Prestowitz, *Trading Places,* pp. 162–63.

Japan's Keidanren (Federation of Economic Organizations), a powerful voice representing big business, favors a review of Japan's competition policy and some increased enforcement of the antimonopoly law. It points out, however, that if the law were to be revised without also changing the statutory waivers from applications of the law for selected industries, inequities would develop. They favor establishing the rule of "free in principle, subject to regulation only in exceptional circumstances" and more transparency in administering the law and applying regulatory guidelines. They agree with the United States that governmental administrative guidance should be given in writing, and not just orally.

Keidanren, however, comprises nearly all the *keiretsu* companies in Japan. While it favors a stronger JFTC, it still considers the *keiretsu*, in general, to be a strength of Japan. Stronger antimonopoly enforcement, therefore, is not likely to lead to a demise of the *keiretsu*. Americans might also consider emulating this form of business organization. In a recent article in the *Harvard Business Review* that discusses the future of the computer hardware industry, the author concludes: "To compete in the new digital information industry, U.S. and European companies must expand their alliance into a new industrial architecture. . . . They must build large-scale corporate families that are strategically cohesive, yet entrepreneurial and flexible. They must form uniquely American (or Euro-American) versions of the Japanese *keiretsu*."[21]

## CONCLUSION

As the Japanese economy has grown, it has developed some fairly distinctive institutions that have only vague parallels in other industrialized nations. Japan's *keiretsu*—or industrial groups—are one such institution. Consisting of either vertical or conglomerate groupings of companies, they are characterized by long-term association, cross-holdings of stock, extensive business dealings, and, sometimes, sharing of company name. The *keiretsu*, by themselves, do not violate Japan's antitrust laws, but their activities can.

The conglomerate groups consist of "families" of corporations spanning numerous industries and usually centered on trading companies and/or banks. They include three with origins in the prewar *zaibatsu* (industrial combines)— Mitsubishi, Mitsui, and Sumitomo—and three that are bank centered—Fuyo (Fuji Bank), DKB (Dai-ichi Kangyo Bank), and Sanwa (Sanwa Bank). The extent of stock cross-holdings among the conglomerate *keiretsu* ranges from about 14 to 22 percent of total paid-up capital.

U.S. businesses have charged that the conglomerate *keiretsu* prefer to buy from other member companies rather than from outsiders, particularly foreign companies. While such intra-group buying appears to be declining, it still can

---

[21] Charles H. Ferguson, "Computers and the Coming of the U.S. *Keiretsu*," *Harvard Business Review* 90, no. 4 (July–August 1990), p. 56.

be quite significant, particularly for capital goods. On average, intra-group purchases account for 10 to 20 percent of the purchases by *keiretsu* firms.

The vertically integrated groups include 39 blue-chip manufacturers, such as Nippon Steel, Toyota, and Matsushita Electric. These groups resemble the business empires found in all industrialized nations of the world. As with the conglomerate *keiretsu,* vertical *keiretsu* firms hold each other's shares, exchange information, and cooperate in new ventures. Since the relationship is vertical, however, the closest ties are between buyers and suppliers or between maker and distributor in the group.

The Japan Fair Trade Commission enforces the antitrust laws, which resemble those in the United States. It tends, however, to be understaffed and underbudgeted and recently has not been aggressive in prosecuting alleged antitrust violations. During the late 1980s, it found fewer than 10 violations per year.

American businesses can work around Japan's *keiretsu* system by pursuing several strategies. The system also has been one of the targets of the Structural Impediments Initiative talks between the United States and Japan in 1989–90. Japan has promised to strengthen its antitrust laws and enforcement, but, given the support for the *keiretsu* by Japan's business, government, and political elite, the *keiretsu* are not likely to disappear soon.

*Chapter Fourteen*

---

# The Perceptions and the Reality of Japanese Industrial Relations*

## Haruo Shimada

*As Chapter 12 explains, there is considerable controversy among specialists about the precise contribution of government industrial policy to Japan's economic success. In contrast, there is wide agreement that favorable industrial relations have played an important role in Japan's industrial growth and exports. But this chapter shows that the usual American and European view of Japanese industrial relations is oversimplified and inaccurate.*

*A common misconception is that harmonious labor relations in Japan rest on lifetime job security, compensation according to seniority more than performance, and docile labor unions.*

*Instead, the Japanese reality is that there is less job security and more labor mobility than usually supposed, age–wage profiles are not so different between Japan and the United States, and Japanese labor relations became more harmonious only after a period of bitter strikes.*

*What then are the distinctive positive features of Japanese industrial relations? Shimada believes they include extensive consultation and information-sharing by management with labor, broad training of workers by their companies, the selection of first-line supervisors from experienced workers, the joint effort of management and labor to improve quality—and the strength of domestic and international competition that presses Japanese firms to apply these labor relations practices successfully.*

According to a widely prevalent stereotypic image of Japanese industrial relations in the Western world, the Japanese are a homogeneous and consensual people with industrial relations that are as a consequence harmonious, trustful,

---

* Reprinted by permission from *The Management Challenge: Japanese Views*, ed. Lester C. Thurow (Cambridge, Mass.: MIT Press, 1985), pp. 42–66, with the omission of tables and a chart. Copyright © 1985 by the Massachusetts Institute of Technology. Haruo Shimada is Professor of Economics at Keio University, Japan.

and peaceful. And so industrial relations are highly productive in Japan—as demonstrated by the remarkably successful performance of Japanese industries.

This chapter attempts to correct exaggerations and misunderstandings associated with such a stereotyped image and provide an alternative explanation of the role of industrial relations in the process of Japanese industrial growth.

## THE STEREOTYPED IMAGE OF JAPANESE INDUSTRIAL RELATIONS

The stereotype starts by emphasizing the common social values of Japanese society, that the Japanese are so homogeneous that they share the same culture, ideologies, tastes, historical traditions, and even behavioral patterns. This leads to *harmony, groupism,* and *consensus.* These Japanese social characteristics in turn are used to explain the unique nature of Japanese industrial relations.

Stereotypes of Western industrial relations are by contrast characterized by adversarial labor–management relations instead of harmony, individualism instead of groupism, and conflicts instead of consensus.

There are further to be considered three conspicuous institutional components of the Japanese industrial relations system. First, workers are employed for life within a particular company and are not dismissed even when the level of business activity declines, unless the decline is so deep that the company faces bankruptcy. Inherent in this notion is the worker's attitude: Workers commit themselves to the company for their lifetime in return for lifetime employment. Second, a length-of-service reward system is observed by every company whereby salary levels are determined in accordance with the worker's length of service within the company. Third, in enterprise unionism a union is organized within the realm of an individual enterprise covering both white- and blue-collar workers. Such unions are consequently docile and cooperative with management.

Characterized by these three institutional components, Japanese industrial relations are thought to be unique, although to the eyes of some Westerners they appear to be economically irrational. Japanese labor analysts often reinforce this impression of uniqueness. These analysts assert that the Japanese company retains its employees despite business fluctuations because it is governed more strongly by the principle of group cohesiveness than profit maximization; that the Japanese company can enjoy industrial peace with a docile enterprise union as a bargaining counterpart because both management and labor desire harmony and share common goals and interests arising out of their homogeneous natures; and that the length-of-service reward system serves as an important function of social ordering within a Japanese company.

In what way and under what conditions did such perceptions become the standard stereotype of Japanese industrial relations? During the 1950s when the Japanese economy was recovering from the war, Japanese scholars regarded characteristics of Japanese industrial relations such as the length-of-service reward system and enterprise unionism as undesirable symptoms of undeveloped capitalism.

But starting in the mid-1960s, when the Japanese economy was growing rapidly, the tone of evaluation changed remarkably. An increasing number of Japanese people, including scholars, employers, and even unionists, began praising lifetime employment, the length-of-service reward system, and enterprise unionism as positive factors contributing to economic growth. Indeed, these practices were now often referred to as the "Three Sacred Treasures" of Japanese industrial relations.

In the 1960s many foreign scholars also began to pay attention to Japanese industrial relations and to conduct systematic research. They accumulated evidence and tried to make new interpretations. Some scholars pointed out that Japanese industrial relations are not as consensual or harmonious as alleged by the classical culturalists. On the basis of in-depth fieldwork in industrial plants, one sociologist revealed that beneath the seemingly harmonious groupism there existed elements of strenuous competition, confrontation, and conflicts.

Economists provided new interpretations of the seemingly traditional employment practices by saying that those practices are in fact governed by highly rigorous economic principles of competition and optimization. They tried to explain practices of long-term employment and the length-of-service reward system as outcomes of the long process of human capital accumulation within a firm.

When more data and information were made available, other scholars expressed skepticism about the alleged uniqueness of some of the features of Japanese industrial relations. They maintained that features such as lifetime employment, earnings that increase with the length of service, and local unions are found not only in Japan but also in many other industrial countries. These interpretations commonly imply that the Japanese system is similar to other systems in terms of the functions it performs, although it may appear quite different.

Despite expert findings and interpretations that emphasize commonalities with Western practices rather than differences, it is undeniable that the popular view of Japanese industrial relations as an extension of its society still dominates. This interpretation is not surprising. Probably it reflects the fact that the performance of the Japanese economy has been outstanding among advanced industrial economies. Even if labor relations were functionally equivalent, there must remain something in the Japanese economy that explains the superior performance.

A report on industrial relations published a few years ago by the Organization for Economic Cooperation and Development (OECD) suggests that there must be a fourth pillar that makes the whole system of Japanese industrial relations work effectively. The report suggests that the fourth pillar is a unique value system commonly held by the Japanese people but leaves the real content of such a value system largely unknown.

A report on the Japanese economy published by the Brookings Institution of the United States at about the same time attributes the successful industrial performance to highly biased allocation of resources in favor of industrial production at the expense of the welfare of the working class. In other words, the report stresses, in sharp contrast to the OECD report, "exploitation" and "powerless unions," which were unable to protect workers' interests. This difference in interpretation of basically the same set of observations of the Japanese economy eloquently reflects the lack of well-balanced and reliable information necessary for sound analysis.

Because of increased interest in the performance of the Japanese economy, books such as *Japan as No. 1* by Ezra Vogel, *Theory Z* by William Ouchi, and *The Art of Japanese Management* by Richard Pascal and Anthony Athos[1] gained a phenomenal popularity in both the United States and Japan. In *Theory Z*, for example, Professor Ouchi asserts that American firms do not lack capital or technology. What they lack is the human factor. He maintains that in successful business organizations, there exist "trust," "subtlety," and "intimacy"—elements typically observed in Japanese firms and in some uniquely successful American corporations. Ouchi proposes essentially a restatement of the classical stereotype of mystic Japanese industrial relations.

Books of this type simply reinforce conventional impressions that Japanese companies enjoy a culturally unique system. They are privileged to do so because they are Japanese companies with Japanese workers.

Why does this kind of stereotype persist despite skepticism and criticisms? Again, it is basically due to a lack of well-balanced and reliable information about Japanese industrial relations.

Most foreigners visited Japan after it had entered its stage of miraculous economic growth. They studied mostly successful large business corporations in the private sector. They ignored Japanese experiences in the difficult and painstaking period preceding the era of rapid economic growth, when the crucial conditions and ground for the remarkable growth were in fact prepared. By overlooking this critical period, they failed to understand the causes responsible for triggering Japan's dynamic and successful industrial development in the subsequent period.

Also, by visiting only successful large firms, they ignored a great number of unsuccessful, unstable small firms and problematic public corporations. This bias deprived foreign observers of opportunities to investigate critical elements that generated successful cases and differentiated them from unsuccessful ones. These omissions distorted foreigners' evaluations of Japanese industries by imposing an illusion that Japanese firms are successful because they all enjoy a uniquely Japanese cultural inheritance.

---

[1] Editor's note: Ezra Vogel, *Japan as No. 1* (Cambridge, Mass.: Harvard University Press, 1979); William Ouchi, *Theory Z* (Reading, Mass.: Addison-Wesley, 1981); and Richard Pascal and Anthony Athos, *The Art of Japanese Management* (New York: Warner Books, 1982).

To correct these misperceptions I will proceed in two steps: first, to qualify or correct misunderstandings associated with the popular image of the Three Sacred Treasures and, second, to probe for a more balanced view of the complex system of Japanese industrial relations.

## MYTHS AND THE REALITY OF THREE SACRED TREASURES

I start by qualifying the concept of lifetime employment.[2] In fact there is no lifetime employment system, in its true sense of the word, in Japan. Due to compulsory retirement, workers must leave the company of their primary employment opportunity around the age of 55 to 60. Since the majority of workers retire from the labor market in their late 60s, even the most privileged workers in terms of employment security—the one third of total employees who work for large firms—have to leave their primary employment opportunity five to ten years prior to their actual retirement.

Moreover, when employment is reduced in recessions, it is these older workers who are more likely to be dismissed or sent to subsidiaries. In effect the degree of employment protection given to older workers in the Japanese employment system is much lower than that afforded American workers who can work until they reach the age eligible for full pension benefits.

Labor mobility is also not as low as one might expect from the preconception of an immobile and rigid lifetime employment system. Ten to 20 percent of all employees leave their firm every year. Turnover rates are higher for females than for males and higher for smaller firms than for larger ones. Roughly half of newly hired people have had an occupational experience somewhere else. Recent graduates account for only a quarter to a third of total recruits.

These observations suggest that, quite unlike the stereotype, Japanese employment is in fact fairly flexible and mobile. Had the Japanese labor market not had a flexible and efficient allocative system for labor, the economy could not have attained the vigorous growth it did.

Second, consider what is really meant by the *nenko* ("length-of-service") wage system. Wages that increase with length of service or experience are not unique to Japanese industries. They are seen widely in other industrial countries. In Western industrial countries wage rates increase with promotion. In Japan wage rates that increase with age or experience are also accompanied by increases in the level of skill or status.

Japanese age–wage profiles are quite similar to those of U.S. workers except for the younger groups. It is interesting that relative differentials between white- and blue-collar workers are remarkably similar between the two

---

[2] Editor's note: "Lifetime employment" in Japan applies only to "core" personnel (excluding temporary, "contract," and part-time workers) in larger firms—about a third of the total labor force.

countries, suggesting that age–wage profiles are affected significantly by technological and organizational factors regardless of national differences.

The third element is enterprise unions. More than 90 percent of Japanese unions are organized on the basis of enterprises, and more than 80 percent of unionized workers are organized by such enterprise unions. This organizational form is probably unique to Japanese industrial relations.

However, the functions of these unions are not unique. Their main function is collective bargaining, just like their American counterparts. In fact the trade union law in Japan, which regulates union activities, was patterned after the labor relations law of the United States. If the function of enterprise unionism is to determine the working conditions of its members through collective bargaining, de facto equivalent practices are found quite widely in many other industrial countries. Collective bargaining at the firm level often occurs in the United States, and when it does it is functionally equivalent to what is done in Japan.

What is unique is a system of joint consultation by which management and worker representatives, usually union officials, exchange information on various matters relating to management policies, production plans, working conditions, fringe benefits, and the like.

This system is formally strictly distinguished from collective bargaining. It is the place for consultation and information-sharing and not for bargaining or making collective agreements.

According to a Ministry of Labor survey on labor-management communications conducted in 1977, more than 70 percent of the 5,000 private enterprises surveyed with 100 or more regular employees reported having a joint consultation system. Various surveys reveal that the system is more prevalent and more clearly defined the larger the size of the firm. In other words, the distinction between collective bargaining and joint consultation becomes less clear for smaller firms.

In many firms the consultation meeting is held fairly regularly, generally at least once a month. The issues discussed are mostly those directly related to working conditions, fringe benefits, and personnel matters, whereas issues reserved for managerial decisions such as management policies, financial matters, and investment in the plant are simply explained to labor representatives in most cases.

## AREAS OF MISSING INFORMATION

### Conflicts

Unlike the popular image of harmony and consensus, Japanese society and industrial relations contain ample elements of frustration, confrontation, and conflict—perhaps exemplified by well-publicized violence and struggles that delayed the opening of Tokyo International Airport for more than a decade. Indeed, an examination of modern Japanese society will reveal ample evidence of social strife. Japanese society has been far from a harmonious or consensual society.

Even limiting our focus to the arena of industrial relations, we can point to many incidences of bitter labor struggles, at least up until the mid-1960s. One measure of the degree of industrial conflicts is the number of worker-days lost during a year due to labor disputes. The average for the 1970s in Japan was 1.1 for every 10 worker-years. This is much lower than the 5.1 for the United States or the 5.8 for the United Kingdom for the same period—but much higher than the 0.5 recorded for West Germany.

In retrospect, however, the data give quite a different impression: 1.0 for 1965–69, 1.8 for 1960–64, 2.6 for 1955–59, 4.5 for 1950–54, and 4.6 for the late 1940s. In other words, during the first decade after the war, Japanese industrial relations were quite conflictive. The situation did not change markedly until the late 1950s.

Peaceful industrial relations are not as widespread as they are often depicted and even those peaceful and successful industries such as steel, shipbuilding, autos, and electronics did not enjoy industrial peace until the mid-1960s. Industrial peace is maintained very carefully on a very delicate power balance even for these relatively successful industries.

## Unsuccessful Cases

There are also innumerable cases of business failures side by side with success stories. Many of these unsuccessful cases are characterized by management's poor judgment and leadership, hostile labor–management relations, stagnant organization, poor human resource development, defective financing policies, poor policies for technological change, and inappropriate management of production, cost accounting, and distribution.

Information on these failures is extremely limited even within Japan. This lack precludes a systematic examination of the critical elements and conditions that made some Japanese industries and firms successful.

## Small Firms and Subcontractors

Large Japanese firms such as those in automobiles also use small firms as subcontractors. But information as to actual conditions in these small firms is extremely scarce. Marxist economists often claim that workers in these firms are victims of exploitation. We simply do not know. Nor do we have information on technological innovation, human capital development, competition, and other important aspects of management in these small firms.

## Public Sector

Business corporations in private industries have been studied intensively, but much less attention has been paid to the public sector. Although the size of the public sector is relatively small in the Japanese economy, it nevertheless exerts important influences on the general model of Japanese industrial relations—both as the largest employer in the country and as the prime pattern setter for working conditions. If we had more information about this sector, it would probably show little difference from the public sectors in Western industrialized countries. Differences certainly exist, but they are only a matter of degree. Basic principles and structures of industrial relations and labor markets are largely similar.

As a result, the highly successful segment of the economy that foreigners pay so much attention to in industrial relations is actually a relatively limited sector of the economy. Not all Japanese enjoy successful and trustful industrial relations simply because they were born Japanese.

Even after recognizing this heterogeneity and the complexity of actual industrial relations in Japan and their basic comparability with industrial relations systems of other countries, one may still wish to ask why and how such a successful achievement was possible in a relatively limited section of strategically important industries.

## CRISIS CONSCIOUSNESS IN JAPANESE INDUSTRIAL GROWTH

The Japanese economy survived drastic external shocks in the 1970s chiefly because of powerful fundamentals that were built during the 1960s. The basis for such a development had in turn been laid out during the crisis-ridden 1950s.

One of the serious defects associated with anthropological explanations of Japanese industrial success is the tendency to relate the recent remarkable industrial performance directly by a short circuit with ancient cultural inheritances without paying due attention to what had been done during critical periods preceding the rapid growth.

This tendency is particularly conspicuous in foreign observers, perhaps because of an unfortunate imbalance of available information. Although information available in foreign countries on Japan is relatively abundant for the late 1940s, when Japan was occupied and controlled by the Allied Forces, and the period after the mid-1960s, when the economy started to exhibit phenomenal growth, outside observers have little information about the 1950s, the period during which the critical bases were built for the subsequent growth.

After the termination of the shallow and short-lived Korean War boom, the Japanese economy was faced with a difficult impasse. Although the economy was prepared again to participate in world markets—after dampening the postwar hyperinflation, restoring the free market system, and overcoming the destruction of World War II—it still was far from being able to attain economic independence. Under such circumstances Japan had to seek drastic measures to attain both economic independence and improvements in the standard of living.

Reflecting a national crisis and a popular desire to catch up with advanced Western nations, the country chose the strategy of promoting exports through industrial rationalization.

In any country public consciousness of a national crisis helps mobilize human and physical resources toward some national goal, much more powerfully than is possible in more normal times. The Japanese experience in the 1950s may be viewed as one such example. Interestingly this kind of public consciousness has been relatively long-lived in Japan and often revived in response to various external shocks such as the recent oil shock.

Although a crisis mentality may not have been the most important factor in generating vigorous industrial growth, it certainly was helpful in reinforcing the effects of other factors. Noteworthy is the fact that the basic conditions necessary for the subsequent industrial growth were prepared during this period: technological know-how to improve quality of products, cooperative labor-management relations that are now predominant in export-oriented major industries, information-sharing systems within the internal labor market of corporate organizations, and an industrial structure with an abnormally developed sector of basic material input industries.

## Emphasis on Quality Goods

Management believed that the most important and promising strategy for success was to improve the quality of products. Production of high-quality goods at low cost was thought to be the key to winning international competition, and corporations systematically mobilized their human and physical resources to achieve this goal. The target was pursued by the introduction of foreign technological and managerial know-how, on the one hand, and massive investments to attain rationalization, on the other.

Business corporations eagerly learned industrial engineering techniques from the United States and European countries. They sent their engineering and managerial staffs abroad to learn such techniques. To name just a few well-known examples of technological transfer, we may recall the assistance of ARMCO to Fuji Steel Co., General Electric to Toshiba, Austin to Nissan, and Philips to Matsushita.

Investments for the purpose of rationalization during the 1950s were also large. An outstanding example was the first five-year rationalization plan for the steel industry, which started in 1951. By the completion of this project, major steel corporations had established an integrated mass production system equipped with strip rolling mills. This achievement was succeeded by the second rationalization plan. By the late 1950s the waves of large-scale investments and technological innovation spilled over to key industries—electric power, shipbuilding, petroleum chemicals, autos, and electrical equipment. Such investments were important to using technological innovations.

Simply learning techniques from foreign countries does not help improve production, however. What is important is implementing such techniques and industrial know-how in production. The experience of Japanese automakers is interesting in illuminating this point. Japanese automakers developed a unique system of supplying parts and materials, incorporating both outside suppliers and intrafirm organizations for the purpose of minimizing inventories. The system operates under the principle of "just-in-time" (minimizing inventory), which is most symbolically exemplified by the case of the Toyota method of production.

The basic principle of minimizing inventory is, however, not a new production management technique. But Japanese automakers seriously attempted to construct a complex social and technical system organizing many tiers of subcontracted parts suppliers and various branches of plant organization, following basic principles of production and cost management yet gearing them effectively to specific local conditions. In order to achieve such a goal, the corporation had to secure the maximum degree of understanding and cooperation from its employees and the people in the local community.

Efficient production can be attained only by full utilization of human and physical resources. For this reason full cooperation of workers and unions is crucial to achieving the goal. To secure their motivation and understanding, Japanese corporations took advantage of reshaped labor–management relations and information-sharing systems.

## Fostering New Labor–Management Relations

Labor–management relations up to the mid-1950s were far from peaceful or harmonious. Quite the contrary, they were hostile and adversarial. Labor unions were dominated largely by leftist or communist leaders, and there were a number of strikes.

With high inflation and economic disorder in the years immediately following World War II, unions emerged spontaneously in most large and medium-size enterprises. They often resorted to strikes or even workers' control of production in order to protect workers' security. The *Sanbetsu-Kaigi* (Congress of Industrial Unions), organized in 1946 by communist leaders, quickly gained ascendency in organizing disputes in various sectors of the economy.

Bitter labor disputes swamped almost every major industry until the mid-1950s. There were a 56-day strike of Toshiba unions, a power industry strike in 1946, an attempt at a general strike (quickly banned by the order of the Supreme Commander of Allied Forces) led by public sector workers in 1947, a postal workers' strike, antidismissal disputes at Hitachi, a strike by National Railway workers in the late 1940s, a 63-day strike of coal miners, a Nissan strike in 1953, steel workers' strikes in 1954, and more. An average of 4.6 worker-days was lost for every 10 workers in the late 1940s and 4.5 worker-days in the first half of the 1950s.

Since the mid-1950s, however, there has been a change in the labor movement. Although it is difficult to provide a complete explanation of the causes, certainly critical facets can be described. In many cases, enterprise unions were split in the prolonged bitter struggles under way. Hostility and antagonism developed among various groups of workers. Facing hardships, leftist leaders grew more radical and extreme. Rank-and-file workers, on the contrary, grew increasingly skeptical about the reliability and usefulness of these dogmatic views. Reflecting such rank-and-file views, a second union often gained more popularity than the original one.

It was at this time that in some industries, such as steel, auto, and ship-building, conscious attempts were made to foster new management–labor relations by young and alert labor leaders. They admitted the necessity of planning ahead for future cooperation with management. In response, management helped them with their organizing activities.

Through bitter struggles and painful experiences this new group of labor leaders gradually acquired popularity among increasingly broader segments of key industries. Many recently influential union leaders in major export-oriented industries grew out of this movement.

One such example is the steel industry. In the fall of 1957 the steel industry federation of unions, led by leftist leaders, organized a 98-hour strike, which failed to win any concession from management. In 1959 the union federation organized a 47-day strike selectively at Nippon Kokan and Fuji Co. and was again defeated. As a result, the leftist leadership eventually had to give way to a new, more realistic leadership led by Yoshiji Miyata. In this process of struggle those who were critical of radical leftists gradually but steadily increased. This development was backed up in various forms by management, who wished to develop new and constructive labor–management relations.

National organizations were reorganized. Criticism by four industry federations of unions within *Sōhyō* against the strikes of coal miners and power industry workers in 1952 eventually resulted in the formation of *Zeonrō-Kaigi* (All Japanese Congress of Unions), a confederation of more moderate unions. The top leadership of *Sōhyō* also shifted through the 1954 and 1955 elections from Minoru Takano, who emphasized political unionism involving community actions, to Kaoru Ohta and Akira Iwai, who advocated economic unionism.

The new labor–management relations promoted by these movements, particularly at the levels of the firm and workplace, now provided an arena for intensive and productive interactions between management and labor.

## Development of Information-Sharing Systems

A number of new labor–management devices were developed and put into practice. Three notable examples are the *joint consultation system, the role of first-line supervisor,* and the well-known *quality control* (QC) *circle movement.*

*The joint consultation system* is an important vehicle for communication between management and labor on critical issues affecting the corporation and therefore the workers themselves. Unlike collective bargaining, joint consultation is used not for negotiation but for management and worker representatives to discuss a broad spectrum of issues, ranging from such large topics as investment and production plans to more specific issues such as revisions of housing allowances. In some cases, top management releases highly confidential information to union leaders at such meetings at a relatively early stage of the decision-making process in order to enlist the cooperation of the union. In other cases, worker representatives provide alternative plans to make their standpoint clearer and to seek better understanding from management.

Introduction of the joint consultation system was first proposed by management after the war as a means to counter the workers' control of production advocated by radical labor leaders. It was not, however, until after the mid-1950s, when the new type of labor–management relations were constructed in major manufacturing industries, that the system started to prevail broadly. The campaign of the Japan Productivity Center, founded with U.S. help, was highly instrumental in promoting this trend.

Currently, more than 70 percent of private enterprises with 100 or more employees have adopted the system as a standing organ. Many large firms have a well-developed and well-defined joint consultation system, which is clearly distinguished from collective bargaining; the distinction becomes less clear as the size of the firm gets smaller. Nevertheless, the joint consultation system is an important element in a complex system of information-sharing.

*The role of first-line supervisor* is also important. First-line supervisors have dual roles in Japanese business organizations: they are the lowest-level manager and the highest-level worker—leaders of production teams.

The formalization of the first-line supervisor's role was also developed during the 1950s. Responding to the desire of management to restore systematic order at the workplace level, management attempted various training programs with the backing of the Japan Federation of Employers Associations in the 1950s. The need to establish some systematic order in the workshop was felt even more keenly as industrial rationalization proceeded. Responding to such a need, various attempts were made in many industries to enrich and strengthen the role of first-line supervisors. A well-known example of such developments is the introduction of the foreman system, learned from the United States, into steel corporations (Yawata Co., 1956, and Nippon Kokan Co., 1959).

Although the foreman system was patterned after the U.S. model, the Japanese foreman system has an important practical difference. Japanese foremen almost always are promoted from the ranks of production workers after accumulating long service and broad experience, and consequently they are very well informed about the business organization as a whole. Foremen often perform an integral role in transmitting information back and forth between management and labor and in sharing information among workers themselves in the workshop. By contrast, in the United States the role of foreman is limited partly because many of them acquire the position without necessarily accumulating as much experience as their Japanese counterparts and partly because their role as management is much more emphasized via-à-vis their role as leader of the work group.

The *quality control circle* activities are designed to improve products. They can contribute to quality improvements by finding the best way of combining the abilities and characteristics of members of the work team. In the process of finding out different traits of workers by working and learning together, the activity also served the function of mutual communication and information.

The QC circle movement, which began in the early 1960s, has grown rapidly. There were 33,000 QC circles (400,000 participants) in 1970 and 115,000 (more than a million participants) in 1980. This growth reflects the rapid spillover of information-sharing systems in the workplace through informal group activities developed on the basis of structural reforms of work organizations promoted in the 1950s.

One of the outstanding features, and perhaps the most important feature, of Japanese business corporations is found in their highly internalized system of human capital development for production workers. The practice of long-term employment and internal promotion is not unique to Japanese corporations; it is found widely in large corporations in the United States and European countries. However, the uniqueness associated with the Japanese practice is the relative breadth of occupational experience while serving within the same company. A Japanese production worker typically is rotated among a relatively broader range of different job assignments within a company compared to his European or American counterparts. An important result of this practice is that Japanese workers tend to have greater opportunities to learn about relationships among different jobs. This aspect is constantly reinforced by in-company training and education.

A number of hypotheses have been proposed to explain why this type of employment practice is prevalent in large Japanese corporations. Some attribute it to the fact that many of Japan's leading corporations, which started out by importing foreign technologies in prewar and postwar days, had to develop skilled workers within their internal labor markets since no trained workers were available outside the firms. Others emphasize the role of the postwar social reforms and union movement by which the status of blue-collar workers was elevated appreciably.

These employment practices, and the emphasis on internal training, have provided Japanese workers with a capacity to share information with management and to participate willingly in an effort to improve production.

## Industrial Structure and Industrial Policies

A peculiar feature of the Japanese industrial structure that has contributed importantly to improving productivity is a highly developed sector of intermediate material input industries. Production of intermediate-input materials such as steel and petrochemical products can enjoy economies of scale. This means that the larger the capacity of production, the higher the productivity and thus the cheaper the price. Japan, which has to import most raw materials for industrial production, has sought to overcome this disadvantage by pursuing the benefits of economy of scale. As a consequence Japan has established an industrial structure with an abnormally large sector of intermediate-input industries, equipped with large-scale production facilities.

This structure provides price advantages not only to these intermediate-input industries themselves but also to industries that use the intermediate inputs. Steel is an example of such intermediate inputs. Industries such as auto or shipbuilding can improve their productivity and the quality of their products by taking advantage of cheap high-quality steel sheets. In this regard the oligopolistic yet highly competitive nature of Japanese industrial organization was instrumental in keeping prices low through strenuous competition among producers.

The government also played an integral role by formulating industrial policies designed to guide the formation of this type of industrial structure and to maintain a reasonable degree of competition within industries.

The industrial policies of the Japanese government have attracted broad attention throughout the rest of the world, with a notorious connotation of "Japan, Inc." This image suggests that close ties exist between the government and businesses. Although it is true that the Japanese government exerted strong direct controls over industrial activities during postwar reconstruction, the mode of control shifted with the development of the economy toward utilizing the competitive function of markets. The most significant characteristic of Japanese economic and industrial policies may be found in the fact that the government collects, interprets, and disseminates relevant information to certain sectors of the economy, essentially to pave the way for the market to operate efficiently under given resource constraints. Had the Japanese industrial policies not operated to take advantage of market principles, it would not have been possible for Japan to attain such vigorous growth during the 1960s.

In the case of Japan a unique industrial structure and the mode of coordination necessitated by strenuous competition have contributed appreciably to increasing manufacturing productivity. Although this aspect is often overlooked in the discussion of corporate performance, it may have been the most important factor responsible for productivity improvement of Japanese firms. Notable is the fact that this factor developed during the 1950s.

Several background factors are often cited to explain the remarkable industrial growth of the postwar period: Total physical destruction by the war provided Japanese industries an opportunity to reequip with newer and more productive facilities than those of their competitors; the social and political impact of the defeat in the war was helpful in introducing somewhat idealistic legal frameworks to maintain reasonable competition in labor and product markets and an abundant young and well-educated labor force; and lack of domestic resources made the Japanese look for cheap overseas raw materials and energy resources.

However, without active and positive efforts on the part of entrepreneurs, workers, and policymakers, these background factors may well have worked not as helpful factors but as hindrances. It is on the basis of this powerful industrial achievement that some segments of Japanese firms now enjoy peaceful, harmonious, and productive labor–management relations.

## CONCLUSION

The style of Japanese management and industrial relations may appear to be strongly influenced by peculiarly Japanese humanistic characteristics and cultural inheritances. But in fact there exist many companies in Japan that practice typically Japanese-style management and industrial relations and yet perform only poorly. In other words, style and industrial success are two different matters.

Japan's industrial success has been attained by intentionally constructing with considerable costs and effort the basic conditions necessary for economic success. The structure and organization of production built within the Japanese economy during the preparatory 1950s and the rapid-growth 1960s are a monumental achievement in the industrial history of the world—economically, technologically, and from the viewpoint of social engineering. The success that attracts foreign attention is simply the result of the operation of such a remarkable system. It is neither luck nor miracle, nor is it historical inheritance.

If this is indeed the case, we may find two important policy implications. One is the transferability of such experiences. If industrial success has been achieved through intentional and rational efforts by the Japanese to overcome a perceived crisis rather than destined by humanistic and cultural traits, Japan's experience should contain elements that other countries will find useful. The sharing, however, is not in the form of superficial management styles as such but rather in the sense of how economically and technologically rational choices were realized in actual social and political processes of the society by intentional efforts.

The other relates to the future choices for Japan. To the extent that success was achieved under certain conditions in the past, it will not necessarily be guaranteed for the future. Indeed, in sharp contrast to relatively successful industries such as auto and electronics, basic material industries such as petrochemicals, aluminum, copper, paper, pulp, and various branches of chemical industries are suffering seriously from changes in their external conditions. And even the relatively successful industries, which have acquired a large share in the world market, will not be able to operate without taking into account their impact on affected countries.

Whether the industrial success of Japan can be maintained for the future will depend on whether the Japanese economy and society can adapt effectively to new and different external conditions in the future.

# Suggestions for Further Reading
# for Part II

*Government Intervention in the Market Economy*

Barr, Nicholas. "Economic Theory and the Welfare State: A Survey and Interpretation." *Journal of Economic Literature* 30, no. 2 (June 1992), pp. 741–803.

Helm, Dieter, ed. *The Economic Borders of the State*. New York: Oxford University Press, 1989.

Stiglitz, Joseph E., and others. *The Economic Role of the State*. Oxford: Basil Blackwell, 1989.

Wolf, Charles, Jr. *Markets or Governments: Choosing between Imperfect Alternatives*. Cambridge, Mass.: MIT Press, 1988.

*Great Britain*

Cairncross, Alec. *The British Economy Since 1945: Economic Policy and Performance, 1945–90*. Oxford: Blackwell Publishers, 1992.

Crafts, N. F. R., and N. W. C. Woodward, with the assistance of B. F. Duckham. *The British Economy Since 1945*. Oxford: Clarendon Press, 1991.

Curwen, Peter, ed. *Understanding the U.K. Economy*. New York: St. Martin's Press, 1990.

Foster, C. D. *Privatization, Public Ownership, and the Regulation of Natural Monopoly*. Oxford: Blackwell Publishers, 1992.

Morris, Derek, ed. *The Economic System in the U.K.* 3rd ed. Oxford: Oxford University Press, 1985.

*Sweden*

Bosworth, Barry P., and Alice M. Rivlin, eds. *The Swedish Economy*. Washington, D.C.: Brookings Institution, 1987.

Calmfors, Lars, ed. *Wage Formation and Macroeconomic Policy in the Nordic Countries*. Oxford: Oxford University Press, 1990.

Maccoby, Michael, ed. *Sweden at the Edge: Lessons for American and Swedish Managers*. Philadelphia: University of Pennsylvania Press, 1991.

Milner, Henry. *Sweden: Social Democracy in Practice*. New York: Oxford University Press, 1989.

Persson, Inga, ed. *Generating Equality in the Welfare State: The Swedish Experience*. Oslo: Norwegian University Press, 1990.

*France*

Adams, William J. *Restructuring the French Economy: Government and the Rise of Market Competition since World War II*. Washington, D.C.: Brookings Institution, 1989.

Adams, William J., and Christian Stoffaës, eds. *French Industrial Policy*. Washington, D.C.: Brookings Institution, 1986.

Estrin, Saul, and Peter Holmes. *French Planning in Theory and Practice*. London: George Allen & Unwin, 1983.

Hayward, Jack. *The State and the Market Economy: Industrial Patriotism and Economic Intervention in France*. Brighton, Eng.: Wheatsheaf Books, 1986.

*Germany*

Giersch, Herbert; Karl-Heinz Paqué; and Holger Schmieding. *The Fading Miracle: Four Decades of Market Economy in Germany*. Cambridge, Eng.: Cambridge University Press, 1992.

Leaman, Jeremy. *The Political Economy of West Germany, 1945–85*. New York: St. Martin's Press, 1988.

Smyser, W. R. *The Economy of United Germany: Colossus at the Crossroads*. New York: St. Martin's Press, 1992.

Welfens, Paul J. J., ed. *Economic Aspects of German Unification: National and International Perspectives*. Berlin: Springer-Verlag, 1992.

*European Economic Community*

Britton, Andrew, and David Mayes. *Achieving Monetary Union in Europe*. London: Sage Publications, 1992.

Devinney, Timothy M., and William C. Hightower. *European Markets after 1992*. Lexington, Mass.: D. C. Heath and Co., 1991.

El-Agraa, Ali M., ed. *The Economics of the European Community*. 3rd ed. New York: St. Martin's Press, 1990.

Molle, Willem. *The Economics of European Integration (Theory, Practice, Policy)*. Aldershot, Eng.: Dartmouth Publishing Company, 1990.

Nevin, Edward. *The Economics of Europe*. New York: St. Martin's Press, 1990.

Pinder, John. *European Community: The Building of a Union*. New York: Oxford University Press, 1991.

*Japan*

Aoki, Masahiko. "Toward an Economic Model of the Japanese Firm." *Journal of Economic Literature* 78, no. 1 (March 1990), pp. 1–27.

Calder, Kent E. *Strategic Capitalism: Private Business and Public Purpose in Japan*. Princeton, N.J.: Princeton University Press, 1993.

Gerlach, Michael L. *Alliance Capitalism: The Social Organization of Japanese Business*. Berkeley: University of California Press, 1993.

Ito, Takashi. *The Japanese Economy*. Cambridge, Mass.: MIT Press, 1992.

Johnson, Chalmers; Laura D'Andrea Tyson; and John Zysman. *Politics and Productivity: The Real Story of Why Japan Works*. Cambridge, Mass.: Ballinger Publishing Co., 1989.

Takenaka, Heizo. *Contemporary Japanese Economy and Economic Policy*. Ann Arbor, Mich.: University of Michigan Press, 1991.

Whitehill, Arthur M. *Japanese Management: Tradition and Transition*. London: Routledge, 1991.

*Part III*

---

# Socialist Market Economies

A *socialist market economy* (sometimes called "market socialism" in contrast to "centrally planned socialism") seeks to combine the socialist principles of (1) collective ownership and (2) limited inequality in the distribution of income and wealth with (3) the use of markets and prices to allocate resources and goods. However, around this central core there are various possible arrangements for the combination of planners' and consumers' sovereignty, the method of price formation, the nature of enterprise management, and other features of the economic system.

The first blueprints for a socialist market economy originated in response to the arguments of some prominent economists in the 1920s that rational economic calculation and thus efficient allocation of resources were, in principle, impossible in a socialist economy. The most famous member of this school was Ludwig von Mises, whose views are summarized in Chapter 15.

To refute this conclusion, Oskar Lange developed the model of a socialist market economy presented in Chapter 16. In his model, the prices of consumer goods and labor services are determined directly by market forces, while a government agency attempts by trial and error to set prices for producer goods which equate their supply and demand. (In a variant of this model, proposed by Abba Lerner and others, the prices of producer goods are determined directly by the interplay of the supply and demand of socialist firms in markets for producer goods.) Given these "parametric" prices and some very broad rules, state-appointed enterprise managers decide the outputs and inputs of their firms.

In contrast, in the "participatory" version of a socialist market economy, each firm is managed by its workers. Chapter 17 sketches Jaroslav Vanek's model of such an economy.

Yugoslavia provided the only real-world case of a socialist market economy. Its version included labor-managed enterprises. The organization and decision making of these "self-managed" firms are analyzed in Chapter 18. Chapter 19 then explains and evaluates the economic system in which these worker-managed firms operated. Chapters 18 and 19 also compare the Yugoslav case with the Vanek model in Chapter 17.

*Chapter Fifteen*

---

# Economic Calculation in Socialism*

*Ludwig von Mises*

*Is efficient resource allocation possible in a socialist market economy? No, said Mises in an argument which has since the 1920s influenced the development and critical evaluation of models of socialist economies.*

*Mises asserts that efficiency requires "rational economic calculation" based on prices for goods and services reflecting their relative scarcities. In capitalism, such prices are formed by the supplies and demands of independent sellers and buyers. In socialism, such prices could be generated in a similar manner in a market for consumer goods in which the state is the seller and households are buyers. But since in socialism the state owns the means of production, it would be both the producer and the user for producer goods such as raw materials, fuels, and machinery and equipment. With the state on both the supply side and the demand side for producer goods, there would be no genuine market mechanism with independent sellers and buyers to generate prices reflecting scarcities of supplies relative to demands. The state could arbitrarily assign prices to producer goods, but these prices would not reflect scarcities and therefore could not serve as a basis for efficient resource allocation.*

Without calculation, economic activity is impossible. Since under socialism economic calculation is impossible, under socialism there can be no economic activity in our sense of the word. In small and insignificant things rational action might still persist. But, for the most part, it would no longer be possible to speak of rational production. In the absence of criteria of rationality, production could not be consciously economical.

---

* Reprinted from Ludwig von Mises, *Socialism: An Economic and Sociological Analysis,* translated from the German by Jacques Kahane (London: Jonathan Cape Limited, 1936; 2nd ed.: New Haven, Conn.: Yale University Press, 1951), pp. 119–22, 136–42; used by permission of Liberty Fund, Inc., 8335 Allison Pointe Trail, Suite 300, Indianapolis, IN 46250-1687, 1981. This volume is an expanded translation of *Die Gemeinwirtschaft,* originally published in 1922. Ludwig von Mises was Professor of Economics at the University of Vienna and New York University.

For some time possibly the accumulated tradition of thousands of years of economic freedom would preserve the art of economic administration from complete disintegration. Men would preserve the old processes not because they were rational, but because they were sanctified by tradition. In the meantime, however, changing conditions would make them irrational. They would become uneconomical as the result of changes brought about by the general decline of economic thought. It is true that production would no longer be "anarchical." The command of a supreme authority would govern the business of supply. Instead of the economy of "anarchical" production the senseless order of an irrational machine would be supreme. The wheels would go round, but to no effect.

Let us try to imagine the position of a socialist community. There will be hundreds and thousands of establishments in which work is going on. A minority of these will produce goods ready for use. The majority will produce capital goods and semimanufactures. All these establishments will be closely connected. Each commodity produced will pass through a whole series of such establishments before it is ready for consumption. Yet in the incessant press of all these processes the economic administration will have no real sense of direction. It will have no means of ascertaining whether a given piece of work is really necessary, whether labor and material are not being wasted in completing it. How would it discover which of two processes was the more satisfactory? At best, it could compare the quantity of ultimate products. But only rarely could it compare the expenditure incurred in their production. It would know exactly—or it would imagine it knew—what it wanted to produce. It ought, therefore, to set about obtaining the desired results with the smallest possible expenditure. But to do this it would have to be able to make calculations. And such calculations must be calculations of value. They could not be merely "technical"; they could not be calculations of the objective use-value of goods and services. This is so obvious that it needs no further demonstration.

Under a system based upon private ownership of the means of production, the scale of values is the outcome of the actions of every independent member of society. Everyone plays a two-fold part in its establishment, first as a consumer, second as a producer. As consumer, he establishes the valuation of goods ready for consumption. As producer, he guides production-goods into those uses in which they yield the highest product. In this way, all goods of higher orders[1] also are graded in the way appropriate to them under the existing conditions of production and the demands of society. The interplay of these two processes ensures that the economic principle is observed in both consumption and production. And, in this way, arises the exactly graded system of prices which enables everyone to frame his demand on economic lines.

Under socialism, all this must necessarily be lacking. The economic administration may indeed know exactly what commodities are needed most

---

[1] Editor's note: Producer goods.

urgently. But this is only half the problem. The other half, the valuation of the means of production, it cannot solve. It can ascertain the value of the totality of such instruments. That is obviously equal to the value of the satisfactions they afford. If it calculates the loss that would be incurred by withdrawing them, it can also ascertain the value of single instruments of production. But it cannot assimilate them to a common price denominator, as can be done under a system of economic freedom and money prices.

It is not necessary that socialism should dispense altogether with money. It is possible to conceive arrangements permitting the use of money for the exchange of consumer goods. But since the prices of the various factors of production (including labor) could not be expressed in money, money could play no part in economic calculations.

Suppose, for instance, that the socialist commonwealth was contemplating a new railway line. Would a new railway line be a good thing? If so, which of many possible routes should it cover? Under a system of private ownership we could use money calculations to decide these questions. The new line would cheapen the transportation of certain articles, and, on this basis, we could estimate whether the reduction in transport charges would be great enough to counterweigh the expenditure which the building and running of the line would involve. Such a calculation could be made only in money. We could not do it by comparing various classes of expenditure and savings in kind. If it is out of the question to reduce to a common unit the quantities of various kinds of skilled and unskilled labor, iron, coal, building materials of different kinds, machinery, and the other things which the building and upkeep of railways necessitate, then it is impossible to make them the subject of economic calculation. We can make systematic economic plans only when all the commodities which we have to take into account can be assimilated to money. True, money calculations are incomplete. True, they have profound deficiencies. But we have nothing better to put in their place. And, under sound monetary conditions, they suffice for practical purposes. If we abandon them, economic calculation becomes absolutely impossible.

This is not to say that the socialist community would be entirely at a loss. It would decide for or against the proposed undertaking and issue an edict. But, at best, such a decision would be based on vague valuations. It could not be based on exact calculations of value.

A stationary society could, indeed, dispense with these calculations. For there, economic operations merely repeat themselves. So that, if we assume that the socialist system of production were based upon the last state of the system of economic freedom which it superseded, and that no changes were to take place in the future, we could indeed conceive a rational and economic socialism. But only in theory. A stationary economic system can never exist. Things are continually changing, and the stationary state, although necessary as an aid to speculation, is a theoretical assumption to which there is no counterpart in reality. And, quite apart from this, the maintenance of such a connection with the last state of the exchange economy would be out of the question, since the transition to socialism with its equalization of incomes would necessarily transform the whole "set" of consumption and production. And then we have a socialist community which must cross the whole ocean of possible and imaginable economic permutations without the compass of economic calculation.

All economic change, therefore, would involve operations the value of which could neither be predicted beforehand nor ascertained after they had taken place. Everything would be a leap in the dark. Socialism is the renunciation of rational economy.

\* \* \* \* \*

Some of the younger socialists believe that the socialist community could solve the problem of economic calculation by the creation of an artificial market for the means of production. They admit that it was an error on the part of the older socialists to have sought to realize socialism through the suspension of the market and the abolition of pricing for goods of higher orders; they hold that it was an error to have seen in the suppression of the market and of the price system the essence of the socialist ideal. And they contend that if it is not to degenerate into a meaningless chaos in which the whole of our civilization would disappear, the socialist community, equally with the capitalist community, must create a market in which all goods and services may be priced. On the basis of such arrangements, they think, the socialist community will be able to make its calculations as easily as the capitalist entrepreneurs.

Unfortunately, the supporters of such proposals do not see (or perhaps *will* not see) that it is not possible to divorce the market and its functions in regard to the formation of prices from the working of a society which is based on private property in the means of production and in which, subject to the rules of such a society, the landlords, capitalists, and entrepreneurs can dispose of their property as they think fit. For the motive force of the whole process which gives rise to market prices for the factors of production is the ceaseless search on the part of the capitalists and the entrepreneurs to maximize their profits by serving the consumers' wishes. Without the striving of the entrepreneurs (including the shareholders) for profit, of the landlords for rent, of the capitalists for interest, and of the laborers for wages, the successful functioning of the whole mechanism is not to be thought of. It is only the prospect of profit which directs production into those channels in which the demands of the consumer are best satisfied at least cost. If the prospect of profit disappears, the mechanism of the market loses its mainspring, for it is only this prospect which sets it in motion and maintains it in operation. The market is thus the focal point of the capitalist order of society; it is the essence of capitalism. Only under capitalism, therefore, is it possible; it cannot be "artificially" imitated under socialism.

The advocates of the artificial market, however, are of the opinion that an artificial market can be created by instructing the controllers of the different industrial units to act *as if* they were entrepreneurs in a capitalist state. They argue that even under capitalism the managers of joint stock companies work not for themselves but for the companies, that is to say, for the shareholders. Under socialism, therefore, it would be possible for them to act in exactly the same way as before, with the same circumspection and devotion to duty. The only difference would be that under socialism the product of the manager's labors would go to the community rather than to the shareholders. In such a way, in contrast to all socialists who have written on the subject hitherto, especially the Marxians, they think it would be possible to construct a decentralized, as opposed to a centralized, socialism.

In order to judge properly such proposals, it is necessarily in the first place to realize that these controllers of individual industrial units would have to be appointed. Under capitalism, the managers of the joint stock companies are appointed either directly or indirectly by the shareholders. Insofar as the shareholders give to the managers power to produce by the means of the company's (i.e., the stockholders') stock they are risking their own property or a part of their own property. The speculation (for it is necessary a speculation) may succeed and bring profit; it may, however, misfire and bring about the loss of the whole or a part of the capital concerned. This committing of one's own capital to a business whose outcome is uncertain and to men whose future ability is still a matter of conjecture whatever one may know of their past, is the essence of joint stock company enterprise.

Now it is a complete fallacy to suppose that the problem of economic calculation in a socialist community relates solely to matters which fall into the sphere of the daily business routine of managers of joint stock companies. It is clear that such a belief can only arise from exclusive concentration on the idea of a stationary economic system—a conception which no doubt is useful for the solution of many theoretical problems but which has no counterpart in fact and which, if exclusively regarded, can even be positively misleading. It is clear that under stationary conditions the problem of economic calculation does not really arise. When we think of the stationary society, we think of an economy in which all the factors of production are already used in such a way as, under the given conditions, to provide the maximum of the things which are demanded by consumers. That is to say, under stationary conditions there no longer exists a problem for economic calculation to solve. The essential function of economic calculation has *by hypothesis* already been performed. There is no need for an apparatus of calculation. To use a popular but not altogether satisfactory terminology we can say that the problem of economic calculation is of economic dynamics; it is no problem of economic statics.

The problem of economic calculation is a problem which arises in an economy which is perpetually subject to change, an economy which every day is confronted with new problems which have to be solved. Now in order to solve such problems it is above all necessary that capital should be withdrawn from particular lines of production, from particular undertakings and concerns, and should be applied in other lines of production, in other undertakings and concerns. This is not a matter for the managers of joint stock companies; it is essentially a matter for the capitalists—the capitalists who buy and sell stocks and shares, who make loans and recover them, who make deposits in the banks and draw them out of the banks again, who speculate in all kinds of commodities. It is these operations of speculative capitalists which create those conditions of the money market, the stock exchanges, and the wholesale markets which have to be taken for granted by the manager of the joint stock company, who, according to the socialist writers we are considering, is to be conceived as nothing but the reliable and conscientious servant of the company. It is the speculative capitalists who create the data to which they have to adjust their business and which therefore give direction to their trading operations.

It follows, therefore, that it is a fundamental deficiency of all these socialist constructions which invoke the "artificial market" and artificial competition as a way out of the problem of economic calculation, that they rest on the belief that the market for factors of production is affected only by producers buying and selling commodities. It is not possible to eliminate from such markets the influence of the supply of capital from the capitalists and the demand for capital by the entrepreneurs, without destroying the mechanism itself.

Faced with this difficulty, the socialist is likely to propose that the socialist state as owner of all capital and all means of production should simply direct capital to those undertakings which promise the highest return. The available capital, he will contend, should go to those undertakings which offer the highest rate of profit. But such a state of affairs would simply mean that those managers who were less cautious and more optimistic would receive capital to enlarge their undertakings while more cautious and more skeptical managers would go away empty-handed. Under capitalism, the capitalist decides to whom he will entrust *his own* capital. The beliefs of the managers of joint stock companies regarding the future prospects of their undertakings and the hopes of project makers regarding the profitability of their plans are not in any way decisive. The mechanism of the money market and the capital market decides. This, indeed, is its main task: to serve the economic system as a whole, to judge the profitability of alternative openings, and not blindly to follow what the managers of particular concerns, limited by the narrow horizon of their own undertakings, are tempted to propose.

To understand this completely, it is essential to realize that the capitalist does not just invest his capital in those undertakings which offer high interest or high profit; he attempts rather to strike a balance between his desire for profit and his estimate of the risk of loss. He must exercise foresight. If he does not do so, than he suffers losses—losses that bring it about that his disposition over the factors of production is transferred to the hands of others who know better how to weigh the risks and the prospects of business speculation.

Now if it is to remain socialist, the socialist state cannot leave to other hands that disposition over capital which permits the enlargement of existing undertakings, the contraction of others, and the bringing into being of undertakings that are completely new. And it is scarcely to be assumed that socialists of whatever persuasion would seriously propose that this function should be made over to some group of people who would "simply" have the business of doing what capitalists and speculators do under capitalist conditions, the only difference being that the product of their foresight should not belong to them but to the community. Proposals of this sort may well be made concerning the managers of joint stock companies. They can never be extended to capitalists and speculators, for no socialist would dispute that the function which capitalists and speculators perform under capitalism, namely directing the use of capital goods into that direction in which they best serve the demands of the consumer, is only performed because they are under the incentive to preserve their property and to make profits which increase it or at least allow them to live without diminishing their capital.

It follows, therefore, that the socialist community can do nothing but place the disposition over capital in the hands of the state or, to be exact, in the hands of the men who, as the governing authority, carry out the business of the state. And that signifies elimination of the market, which, indeed, is the fundamental aim of socialism, for the guidance of economic activity by the market implies organization of production and a distribution of the product according to that disposition of the spending power of individual members of society which makes itself felt on the market; that is to say, it implies precisely that which it is the goal of socialism to eliminate.

If the socialists attempt to belittle the significance of the problem of economic calculation in the socialist community, on the ground that the forces of the market do not lead to ethically justifiable arrangements, they simply show that they do not understand the real nature of the problem. It is not a question of whether there shall be produced cannons or clothes, dwelling houses or churches, luxuries or subsistence. In any social order, even under socialism, it can very easily be decided which kind and what number of consumption goods should be produced. No one has ever denied that. But once this decision has been made, there still remains the problem of ascertaining how the existing means of production can be used most effectively to produce these goods in question. In order to solve this problem, it is necessary that there should be economic calculation. And economic calculation can only take place by means of money prices established in the market for production goods in a society resting on private property in the means of production. That is to say, there must exist money prices of land, raw materials, semimanufactures; that is to say, there must be money wages and interest rates.

Thus the alternative is still *either* socialism *or* a market economy.

Chapter Sixteen

# On the Economic Theory of Socialism*

*Oskar Lange*

*In response to Mises's argument that socialism and a genuine market economy were incompatible (Chapter 15), Lange developed the model of a socialist regulated market economy summarized in this chapter.*

*In Lange's model, households, managers of socialist enterprises, and a government agency which he called the Central Planning Board (CPB) share in the decisions guiding the economy.*

*Prices and quantities of consumer goods and services are decided in a market for consumer goods by the demands of households and the supplies of socialist firms. In an analogous way, wages are determined in a labor market by the demands of socialist firms and the supplies of households.*

*The name of Lange's Central Planning Board (CPB) is somewhat misleading. It does not engage in the detailed planning of the bill of goods, resource allocation, and income distribution characteristic of a centrally planned economy (the subject of Part IV of this book). Instead, Lange's CPB has much more limited responsibilities, chiefly involving the pricing of producer (but not consumer) goods and the rate of investment.*

*By trial and error the CPB adjusts the prices of producer goods in an effort to equate the supply and demand for each good. When a shortage is observed, the price is increased; when a surplus occurs, the price is reduced. In this way, the CPB strives for scarcity prices for producer goods.*

*The prices for consumer goods (set directly by the market) and for producer goods (set by the CPB seeking to "imitate the market") are to be considered "parametric," or given, for the managers of socialist enterprises. In the light of these prices, managers determine their inputs and outputs according to two broad rules, without any detailed assignments from the CPB about inputs or outputs.*

* From Oskar Lange and Fred M. Taylor, *On the Economic Theory of Socialism*, ed. Benjamin E. Lippincott (Minneapolis: University of Minnesota Press, 1938), pp. 72–86. © 1938 University of Minnesota, 1966 B. E. Lippincott. Originally published in *Review of Economic Studies* 4, no. 1 (October 1936), pp. 60–66. Reprinted with the permission of the *Review of Economic Studies* and the University of Minnesota Press. Oskar Lange was Professor of Economics at the University of Chicago and Professor of Political Economy at Warsaw University.

*First, managers must combine factors of production so as to minimize the average cost of production for whatever output they choose. Second, they must select that output level at which the marginal cost of the enterprise equals the parametric price. In combination, these two rules secure the most economical production of the optimum output.*

*The CPB also decides the rate of investment for the economy as a whole. It then sets an interest rate on investment funds which equates the demand for them, on the part of socialist managers, to the amount available.*

*Finally, the CPB distributes to the population, the owners of the means of production, a "social dividend."*

In order to discuss the method of allocating resources in a socialist economy we have to state what kind of socialist society we have in mind. The fact of public ownership of the means of production does not in itself determine the system of distributing consumers' goods and of allocating people to various occupations, nor the principles guiding the production of commodities. Let us now assume that freedom of choice in consumption and freedom of choice of occupation are maintained and that the preferences of consumers, as expressed by their demand prices, are the guiding criteria in production and in the allocation of resources. . . .

In the socialist system as described, we have a genuine market (in the institutional sense of the word) for consumers' goods and for the services of labor. But there is no market for capital goods and productive resources outside of labor.[1] The prices of capital goods and productive resources outside of labor are thus prices in the generalized sense, that is, mere indices of alternatives available, fixed for accounting purposes. Let us see how economic equilibrium is determined in such a system. Just as in a competitive individualist regime, the determination of equilibrium consists of two parts: (A) On the basis of *given* indices of alternatives (which are market prices in the case of consumers' goods and the services of labor and accounting prices in all other cases), both the individuals participating in the economic system as consumers and as owners of the services of labor and the managers of production and of the ultimate resources outside of labor (i.e., of capital and of natural resources) make decisions according to certain principles. These managers are assumed to be public officials. (B) The prices (whether market or accounting) are determined by the condition that the quantity of each commodity demanded is equal to the quantity supplied. The conditions determining the decisions under A form the *subjective*, while that under B is the *objective*, equilibrium condition. Finally, we have also a condition (C), expressing the social organization of the economic system. As the productive resources outside of labor are public property, the incomes of the consumers are divorced from the ownership of

---

[1] To simplify the problem, we assume that all means of production are public property. Needless to say, in an actual socialist community there must be a large number of means of production privately owned (e.g., by farmers, artisans, and small-scale entrepreneurs). But this does not introduce any new theoretical problem.

those resources and the form of condition C—social organization— is determined by the *principles of income formation adopted.*

The possibility of determining condition C in different ways gives to a
socialist society considerable freedom in matters of distribution of income. But
the necessity of maintaining freedom in the choice of occupation limits the
arbitrary use of this freedom, for there must be some connection between the
income of a consumer and the services of labor performed by him. It seems,
therefore, convenient to regard the income of consumers as composed of two
parts: one part being the receipts for the labor services performed and the other
part being a social dividend constituting the individual's share in the income
derived from the capital and the natural resources owned by society. We assume that the distribution of the social dividend is based on certain principles,
reserving the content of those principles for later discussion. Thus, condition C
is determinate and determines the incomes of the consumers in terms of prices
of the services of labor and social dividend, which, in turn, may be regarded as
determined by the total yield of capital and of the natural resources and by the
principles adopted in distributing this yield.[2]

A. Let us consider the subjective equilibrium condition in a socialist economy:

1. Freedom of choice in consumption being assumed,[3] this part of the
subjective equilibrium condition of a competitive market applies also to the
market for consumers' goods in a socialist economy. The incomes of the
consumers and the prices of consumers' goods being given, the demand for
consumers' goods is determined.

2. The decisions of the managers of production are no longer guided
by the aim of maximizing profit. Instead, certain rules are imposed on them
by the Central Planning Board which aim at satisfying consumers' preferences in the best way possible. These rules determine the combination of
factors of production and the scale of output.

One rule must impose the choice of the combination of factors which
minimizes the average cost of production. This rule leads to the factors
being combined in such proportion that the marginal productivity of that

---

[2] In formulating condition C, capital accumulation has to be taken into account. Capital accumulation may be done either "corporately" by deducting a certain part of the national income before
the social dividend is distributed, or it may be left to the savings of individuals, or both methods
may be combined. But "corporate" accumulation must certainly be the dominant form of capital
formation in a socialist economy.

[3] Of course there may be also a sector of socialized consumption, the cost of which is met by
taxation. Such a sector exists also in capitalist society and comprises the provision not only of
collective wants, in Cassel's sense, but also of other wants whose social importance is too great to
be left to the free choice of individuals (for instance, free hospital service and free education). But
this problem does not represent any theoretical difficulty and we may disregard it. [Editor's note:
Gustav Cassel, 1866–1945, was a Swedish economic theorist whose writings included *The Theory
of Social Economy* (1st German ed., 1918; English trans., 1923).]

amount of each factor which is worth a unit of money is the same for all factors. This rule is addressed to whoever makes decisions involving the problem of the optimum combination of factors, that is, to managers responsible for running existing plants and to those engaged in building new plants. A second rule determines the scale of output by stating that output has to be fixed so that marginal cost is equal to the price of the product. This rule is addressed to two kinds of persons. First of all, it is addressed to the managers of plants and thus determines the scale of output of each plant and, together with the first rule, its demand for factors of production. The first rule, to whomever addressed, and the second rule when addressed to the managers of plants perform the same function that in a competitive system is carried out by the private producer's aiming to maximize his profit, when the prices of factors and of the product are independent of the amount of each factor used by him and of his scale of output.

The total output of an industry has yet to be determined. This is done by addressing the second rule also to the managers of a whole industry (e.g., to the directors of the National Coal Trust) as a principle to guide them in deciding whether an industry ought to be expanded (by building new plants or enlarging old ones) or contracted (by not replacing plants which are wearing out). Thus each industry has to produce exactly as much of a commodity as can be sold or "accounted for" to other industries at a price which equals the marginal cost incurred *by the industry* in producing this amount. The marginal cost incurred by an industry is the cost to that industry (not to a particular plant) of doing whatever is necessary to produce an additional unit of output, the optimum combination of factors being used. This may include the cost of building new plants or enlarging old ones.[4]

Addressed to the managers of an industry, the second rule performs the function which, under free competition, is carried out by the free entry of firms into an industry or their exodus from it: that is, it determines the output of an industry.[5] The second rule, however, has to be carried out

---

[4] Since in practice such marginal cost is not a continuous function of output, we have to compare the cost of each additional *indivisible input* with the receipts expected from the additional output thus secured. For instance, in a railway system as long as there are unused carriages the cost of putting them into use has to be compared with the additional receipts which may be obtained by doing so. When all the carriages available are used up to capacity, the cost of building and running additional carriages (and locomotives) has to be compared with the additional receipts expected to arise from such action. Finally, the question of building new tracks is decided upon the same principle. Cf. A. P. Lerner, "Statics and Dynamics in Socialist Economics," *Economic Journal* 47, no. 186 (June 1937), pp. 263–67.

[5] The result, however, of following this rule coincides with the result obtained under free competition only in the case of constant returns to the industry (i.e., a homogeneous production function of the first degree). In this case marginal cost incurred by the industry equals average cost. In all other cases, the results diverge, for under free competition the output of an industry is such that

irrespective of whether average cost is covered or not, even if it should involve plants or whole industries in losses.

Both rules can be put in the form of the simple request to use always the method of production (i.e., combination of factors) which minimizes average cost and to produce as much of each service or commodity as will equalize marginal cost and the price of the product, this request being addressed to whoever is responsible for the particular decision to be taken. Thus the output of each plant and industry and the total demand for factors of production by each industry are determined. To enable the managers of production to follow these rules, the prices of the factors and of the products must, of course, be given. In the case of consumers' goods and services of labor, they are determined on a market; in all other cases they are fixed by the Central Planning Board. Those prices being given, the supply of products and the demand for factors are determined.

The reasons for adopting the two rules mentioned are obvious. Since prices are indices of terms on which alternatives are offered, that method of production which will minimize average cost will also minimize the alternatives sacrificed. Thus the first rule means simply that each commodity must be produced with a minimum sacrifice of alternatives. The second rule is a necessary consequence of following consumers' preferences. It means that the marginal significance of each preference which is satisfied has to be equal to the marginal significance of the alternative preferences, the satisfaction of which is sacrificed. If the second rule was not observed certain lower preferences would be satisfied while preferences higher up on the scale would be left unsatisfied.

3. Freedom of choice of occupation being assumed, laborers offer their services to the industry or occupation paying the highest wages. For the publicly owned capital and natural resources a price has to be fixed by the Central Planning Board with the provision that these resources can be directed only to industries which are able to "pay," or rather to "account for," this price. This is a consequence of following the consumers' preferences. The prices of the services of the ultimate productive resources being given, their distribution between the different industries is also determined.

B. The subjective equilibrium condition can be carried out only when prices are *given*. This is also true of the decisions of the managers of production and of the productive resources in public ownership. Only when prices are

---

average cost equals the price of the product, while according to our rule it is marginal cost (incurred by the industry) that ought to be equal to the price. This difference results in profits being made by the industries whose marginal cost exceeds average cost, whereas the industries in which the opposite is the case incur losses. These profits and losses correspond to the taxes and bounties proposed by Professor Pigou in order to bring about under free competition the equality of private and social marginal net product. See A. C. Pigou, *The Economics of Welfare,* 3rd ed. (London: The Macmillan Company, 1929), pp. 223–27.

given can the combination of factors which minimizes average cost, the output which equalizes marginal cost and the price of the product, and the best allocation of the ultimate productive resources be determined. But if there is no market (in the institutional sense of the word) for capital goods or for the ultimate productive resources outside of labor, can their prices be determined objectively? Must not the prices fixed by the Central Planning Board necessarily be quite arbitrary? If so, their arbitrary character would deprive them of any economic significance as indices of the terms on which alternatives are offered. This is, indeed, the opinion of Professor Mises.[6] And the view is shared by Mr. Cole, who says: "A planless economy, in which each entrepreneur takes his decisions apart from the rest, obviously confronts each entrepreneur with a broadly given structure of costs, represented by the current level of wages, rent, and interest. . . . In a planned socialist economy there can be no objective structure of costs. Costs can be imputed to any desired extent. . . . But these imputed costs are not objective, but *fiat* costs determined by the public policy of the State."[7] This view, however, is easily refuted by recalling the very elements of price theory.

Why is there an objective price structure in a competitive market? Because, as a result of the parametric function of prices, there is generally only *one* set of prices which satisfies the objective equilibrium condition, that is, equalizes demand and supply of each commodity. The same objective price structure can be obtained in a socialist economy if the *parametric function of prices* is retained. On a competitive market the parametric function of prices results from the number of competing individuals being too large to enable anyone to influence prices by his own action. In a socialist economy, production and ownership of the productive resources outside of labor being centralized, the managers certainly can and do influence prices by their decisions. Therefore, the parametric function of prices must be imposed on them by the Central Planning Board as an *accounting rule*. All accounting has to be done *as if* prices were independent of the decisions taken. For purposes of accounting, prices must be treated as constant, as they are treated by entrepreneurs in a competitive market.

The technique of attaining this end is very simple: The Central Planning Board has to fix prices and see to it that all managers of plants, industries, and resources do their accounting on the basis of the prices fixed by the Central Planning Board, and not tolerate any use of other accounting. Once the parametric function of prices is adopted as an accounting rule, the price structure is established by the objective equilibrium condition. For each set of prices and consumers' incomes a definite amount of each commodity is supplied and demanded. Condition C determines the incomes of the consumers by the prices

---

[6] "Economic Calculation in the Socialist Commonwealth," reprinted in *Collectivist Economic Planning,* ed. F. A. Hayek (London: Routledge & Kegan Paul, 1935), p. 112.

[7] G. D. H. Cole, *Economic Planning* (New York: Alfred A. Knopf, Inc., 1935), pp. 183–84.

of the services of ultimate productive resources and the principles adopted for the distribution of the social dividend. With those principles given, prices alone are the variables determining the demand and supply of commodities.

The condition that the quantity demanded and supplied has to be equal for each commodity serves to select the equilibrium prices which alone assure the compatibility of all decisions taken. *Any price different from the equilibrium price would show at the end of the accounting period a surplus or a shortage of the commodity in question.* Thus, the accounting prices in a socialist economy, far from being arbitrary, have quite the same objective character as the market prices in a regime of competition. Any mistake made by the Central Planning Board in fixing prices would announce itself in a very objective way—by a physical shortage or surplus of the quantity of the commodity or resources in question—and would have to be corrected in order to keep production running smoothly. As there is generally only one set of prices which satisfies the objective equilibrium condition, both the prices of products and costs[8] are uniquely determined.[9]

Our study of the determination of equilibrium prices in a socialist economy has shown that the process of price determination is quite analogous to that in a competitive market. The Central Planning Board performs the functions of the market. It establishes the rules for combining factors of production and choosing the scale of output of a plant, for determining the output of an industry, for the allocation of resources, and for the parametric use of prices in accounting. Finally, it fixes the prices so as to balance the quantity supplied and demanded of each commodity. It follows that a substitution of planning for the functions of the market is quite possible and workable.

Two problems deserve some special attention. The first relates to the determination of the best distribution of the social dividend. Freedom of choice of occupation assumed, the distribution of the social dividend may affect the amount of services of labor offered to different industries. If certain occupations received a larger social dividend than others, labor would be diverted into the occupations receiving a larger dividend. Therefore, the distribution of the social dividend must be such as not to interfere with the optimum distribution of labor services between the different industries and occupations. The optimum distribution is that which makes the differences of the value of the mar-

---

[8] Hayek maintains that it would be impossible to determine the value of durable instruments of production because, in consequence of changes, "the value of most of the more durable instruments of production has little or no connection with the costs which have been incurred in their production" (*Collectivist Economic Planning,* p. 227). It is quite true that the value of such durable instruments is essentially a capitalized quasi-rent and therefore can be determined only after the price which will be obtained for the product is known (cf. ibid., p. 228). But there is no reason why the price of the product should be any less determinate in a socialist economy than in a competitive market. The managers of the industrial plant in question have simply to take the price fixed by the Central Planning Board as the basis of their calculation. The Central Planning Board would fix this price so as to satisfy the objective equilibrium condition, just as a competitive market does.

[9] However, in certain cases there may be a multiple solution.

ginal product of the services of labor in different industries and occupations equal to the differences in the marginal disutility[10] of working in those industries or occupations.[11] This distribution of the services of labor arises automatically whenever wages are the only source of income. *Therefore, the social dividend must be distributed so as to have no influence whatever on the choice of occupation.* The social dividend paid to an individual must be entirely independent of his choice of occupation. For instance, it can be divided equally per head of population, or distributed according to age or size of family or any other principle which does not affect the choice of occupation.

The other problem is the determination of the rate of interest. We have to distinguish between a short-period and a long-period solution of the problem. For the former, the amount of capital is regarded as constant, and the rate of interest is simply determined by the condition that the demand for capital is equal to the amount available. When the rate of interest is set too low, the socialized banking system would be unable to meet the demand of industries for capital; when the interest rate is set too high, there would be a surplus of capital available for investment. However, in the long period the amount of capital can be increased by accumulation. If the accumulation of capital is performed "corporately" before distributing the social dividend to the individuals, the rate of accumulation can be determined by the Central Planning Board *arbitrarily*. The Central Planning Board will probably aim at accumulating enough to make the marginal *net* productivity of capital zero,[12] this aim being never attained because of technical progress (new labor-saving devices), increase of population, the discovery of new natural resources, and, possibly, because of the shift of demand toward commodities produced by more capital-intensive methods.[13] But the rate, that is, the *speed,* at which accumulation progresses is arbitrary.

The arbitrariness of the rate of capital accumulation "corporately" performed means simply that the decision regarding the rate of accumulation

---

[10] It is only the *relative* disutility of different occupations that counts. The absolute disutility may be zero or even negative. By putting leisure, safety, agreeableness of work, etc., into the preference scales, all labor costs may be expressed as opportunity costs. If a device is adopted, each industry or occupation may be regarded as producing a joint product: the commodity or service in question *and* leisure, safety, agreeableness of work, etc. The services of labor have to be allocated so that the value of this marginal *joint* product is the same in all industries and occupations

[11] If the total amount of labor performed is not limited by legislation or custom regulating the hours of work, etc., the value of the marginal product of the services of labor in each occupation has to be *equal* to the marginal disutility. If any limitational factors are used, it is the marginal *net* product of the services of labor (obtained by deducting from the marginal product the marginal expenditure for the limitational factors) which has to satisfy the condition in the text.

[12] Cf. Knut Wicksell, "Professor Cassel's System of Economics," reprinted in his *Lectures on Political Economy*, ed. L. Robbins (2 vols.; London: Routledge & Kegan Paul, 1934), vol. 1, p. 241.

[13] These changes, however, if very frequent, may act also in the opposite direction and diminish the marginal *net* productivity of capital because of the risk of obsolescence due to them. This is pointed out by A. P. Lerner in "A Note on Socialist Economics," *Review of Economic Studies* 4, no. 1 (October 1936), p. 72.

reflects how the Central Planning Board, and not the consumers, evaluate the optimum time-shape of the income stream. One may argue, of course, that this involves a diminution of consumers' welfare. This difficulty could be overcome only by leaving all accumulation to the saving of individuals.[14] But this is scarcely compatible with the organization of a socialist society.[15] . . .

Having treated the theoretical determination of economic equilibrium in a socialist society, let us see how equilibrium can be determined by a method of *trial and error* similar to that in a competitive market. This method of trial and error is based on the *parametric function of prices*. Let the Central Planning Board start with a given set of prices chosen *at random*. All decisions of the managers of production and of the productive resources in public ownership and also all decisions of individuals as consumers and as suppliers of labor are made on the basis of these prices. As a result of these decisions the quantity demanded and supplied of each commodity is determined. If the quantity demanded of a commodity is not equal to the quantity supplied, the price of that commodity has to be changed. It has to be raised if demand exceeds supply and lowered if the reverse is the case. Thus the Central Planning Board fixes a new set of prices which serves as a basis for new decisions, and which results in a new set of quantities demanded and supplied. Through this process of trial and error equilibrium prices are fully determined. Actually the process of trial and error would, of course, proceed on the basis of the prices *historically given*. Relatively small adjustments of those prices would constantly be made, and there would be no necessity of building up an entirely new price system.

---

[14] This method has been advocated by Barone in "The Ministry of Production in the Collectivist State," in *Collectivist Economic Planning,* ed. F. A. Hayek (London: Routledge & Kegan Paul, 1935), pp. 278–79.

[15] Of course, the consumers remain free to save as much as they want out of the income which is actually paid out to them, and the socialized banks could pay interest on savings. As a matter of fact, in order to prevent hoarding they would have to do so. But *this* rate of interest would not have any necessary connection with the marginal *net* productivity of capital. It would be quite arbitrary.

*Chapter Seventeen*

---

# The Participatory Economy*

## *Jaroslav Vanek*

*In the Lange model of a socialist regulated market economy in Chapter 16, enterprises are run by state-appointed managers following common broad rules drawn from welfare economics. In contrast, Vanek's model of a socialist regulated market economy involves firms owned by society as a whole but managed by the workers of the individual firms.*

*Vanek first explains briefly five key characteristics that define the "participatory economy": worker management, income sharing, payment for the use of society's capital, free markets, and freedom of employment.*

*Next he examines various aspects of the operation of such an economy, including competition, labor relations, stability of employment and prices, income distribution, externalities, and innovation.*

*Vanek concludes that the participatory economy is superior to other economic systems on both economic and noneconomic grounds.*

*Chapters 18 and 19 then compare the experience of Yugoslavia, which has had self-managed enterprises in a socialist regulated market economy, with the Vanek model.*

## CHARACTERISTICS OF THE PARTICIPATORY ECONOMY

\* \* \* \* \*

To use an analogy, we may liken the labor-managed economy—or for that matter, any economy—to a motor vehicle. If we want to become acquainted with the vehicle, we should learn principally about two things: One, what are

---

* Reprinted from Jaroslav Vanek, *The Participatory Economy: An Evolutionary Hypothesis and a Strategy for Development* (Ithaca, N.Y.: Cornell University Press, 1971), pp. 8–14, 21–22, 25–30, 34–38. Copyright © 1971 by Cornell University. Used by permission of the publisher, Cornell University Press. A more detailed and technically rigorous exposition appears in his *The General Theory of Labor-Managed Market Economies* (Ithaca, N.Y.: Cornell University Press, 1970). Jaroslav Vanek is Professor of Economics at Cornell University.

the vehicle's main component parts, and two, what is its moving force? Accordingly, we will first introduce a set of defining characteristics of the labor-managed economy, and then explain what its principal moving force is—that is, the motivation on which economic actions within it are actually taken. Pushing the analogy a step further, we may also ask how the vehicle compares with other vehicles in respect to the main component parts. And going still another step, we may want to learn how the moving force—that is, the motor—compares with that of other vehicles. These other aspects of characterization by comparison will also concern us. . . .

The first of our five defining characteristics is quite obvious. The labor-managed or participatory economy is one based on, or composed of, firms controlled and managed by those working in them. This *participation in management* is by *all* and on the basis of equality, that is, on the principle of one-man one-vote.[1] It is to be carried out in the most efficient manner—in the majority of cases through elected representative bodies and officers: a workers' council, an executive board, and the director of the firm.

Clearly, the exact form of labor management that is most efficient can vary from enterprise to enterprise and from one labor-managed economy to another, and as such need not concern us here. It could not be overemphasized that the participation in control and management derives uniquely and unalterably from *active* participation in the enterprise. Participation in ownership in no way and under no circumstances entails the right to control and manage; whether active participants are also owners of the assets of the firm or whether they contribute to the formation of such assets through undistributed earnings, it is not these contributions but their active participation that entitles them to control and manage.

The second general characteristic is related to and, in a sense, derives from the first. It is *income sharing*. The participants of the labor-managed firm, after they have paid for all material and other costs of operation, share in the income of the enterprise. This sharing is to be equitable, equal for labor of equal intensity and quality, and governed by a democratically agreed-on income-distribution schedule assigning to each job its relative claim on total net income. Of course, not all of net income needs to be distributed to individual participants; a collectively agreed-on share can be used for reserve funds, various types of collective consumption, or investment. In the last-mentioned instance, however, for reasons which will become apparent . . . , it may be preferable to recognize the contributions of savings to the firm's capital formation as individual claims of each participant, and express them in the form of fixed-interest-bearing financial obligations of the firm. Of course, recalling our

---

[1] Alternatively, in a more sophisticated and generally superior voting scheme where the voters are allowed to assign different weights to alternative issues simultaneously to be decided on, each voter is given the same number of points. This reflects the principle of equality of importance among members engaging in the democratic process of decision making.

first defining characteristic, such financial claims cannot under any circumstances carry a right to control or management of the firm.

These considerations of financing bring us to the third basic characteristic of participatory economies. The working community which has the exclusive right to control and manage the activities of the firm does not, as such, have the full ownership—in the traditional sense of the word "ownership"—of the capital assets which it uses. Perhaps the term *usufructus*, the right of enjoying the fruits of material goods, is a more appropriate one. The working community can enjoy the fruits of production in which the plant and equipment were used, but it must pay for this a contractual fee—or rental, or interest on the financial liability brought about by the purchases of such real assets. The community cannot destroy the real assets or sell them and distribute the proceeds as current income. In turn, the lenders of financial capital have no right of control whatsoever over the physical assets of the firm as long as the working community meets its debt-servicing obligations; the same holds for those who may lease physical assets to the firm, as long as the corresponding obligations of the labor-managed firm are met.

Whereas the first three defining characteristics pertain to individual firms, the remaining two bear on the relations among firms and, more generally, among all decision-making units of the participatory economy. The fourth characteristic is that the labor-managed economy must always be a *market economy*. This implies, among other things, that the economy is fully decentralized. All decision-making units, firms, households, associations, and the public sector decide freely and to their best advantage on actions they take, without direct interference from the outside. Economic planning and policy may be implemented through use of indirect policy instruments, discussion, improved information, or more suasion, but never through a direct order to a firm or a group of firms. The economic relations among the above-mentioned decision-making units are settled through the conventional operation of markets, which is perfectly free whenever there are a sufficiently large number of buyers or sellers. Only in situations of monopolistic or monopsonistic tendencies can the public authorities interfere—and then only by fixing of maximum or minimum prices, or, preferably, by rendering the market structure more competitive, either through stimulation of entry or through opening up of the market to international competition. This ought not to be interpreted to mean that values determined by free market operation are desirable in any normative sense; a given society may prefer values different from those established by free competition (e.g., it may desire to make cigarettes prohibitively expensive) but if it does, it must reach its aims through legitimate tools of policy (a high tax on cigarettes or an import duty on imports of tobacco).

We come finally to the fifth basic characteristic. It bears on the human factor which in the participatory economy no longer is a mere factor of production but also—and perhaps primarily—the decision-making and thus creative and entrepreneurial factor. We may refer to the fifth characteristic as *freedom of employment*. It simply indicates that the individual is free to take, not to take, or to leave a particular job. At the same time, the labor-managed firms are free to hire or not to hire a particular man. However, the firms can, as a matter of their collective and democratic decision, limit in various ways their own capacity to expel a member of the community even where strictly economic considerations might call for doing so.

These considerations of freedom of employment—especially the one regarding the right to dismiss—lead us to the second part of identification of the participatory economy. What is the basic motivational force—or in the transposed sense suggested earlier, what is the motor—of the participatory firm and thus of the labor-managed economy as a whole?

In classical capitalism the moving force was the maximization of profit. In the Galbraithian new industrial state it is the self-interest of the upper management stratum of the large corporation,[2] and in Soviet-type systems it is a combination of the fear of penalties attached to plan nonfulfillment and various types of bonuses extended to the plant manager.

In the participatory economy it is a combination of the interests of the members of the labor-managed firms as individuals on the one hand, and as a collective on the other. More specifically, and thinking first of the problem in pecuniary terms, the labor-managed firm's aim is the *maximization of income* for each of its members. Of course, this must be done in conformity with an income-distribution schedule reflecting the comparative shares belonging to each job agreed on democratically in advance; once the schedule is given, the highest income is attained for all participants at each level as soon as it is attained by any single participant.

This pecuniary objective of income maximization can be thought of as the crude form of the moving force of the labor-managed systems. It reflects an important part of the true motivation, and it lends itself to a simple formal analysis of the behavior of the labor-managed firms and of the labor-managed systems as a whole. It does not by any means contain the whole truth, however, and in many concrete situations will not even be seen as the principal objective by the participants of actual labor-managed firms.[3]

The true objective of the participatory firm is complex and multidimensional. If we insisted on reducing it to a single variable, we could not do otherwise than to say that the single variable is the degree of satisfaction of the individuals within the collective. Of course, monetary income may be an im-

---

[2] Editor's note: John Kenneth Galbraith, *The New Industrial State* (Boston: Houghton Mifflin, 1967).

[3] In discussion with practical economists, enterprise directors, or workers in Yugoslavia, the income-maximizing motive will often not be recognized—or will be recognized only after some reflection—and other objectives, such as maximum growth, maximum surplus value, and maximum employment will be given. As an even more extreme point of view—one that certainly cannot be dismissed on *a priori* grounds—some will say that the objective of the participatory firm is simply what the majority of participants wants, there being no single identifiable motive.

portant ingredient of the satisfaction, especially in very poor environments, but it is definitely not the only one. The working collective can, for example, sacrifice some money income in exchange for additional leisure time, lesser intensity of work, better human relations—or even a kinder managing director. If this is so, all the alternatives mentioned must be considered as a part of the participatory firm's objective and thus as a component of the moving force of the labor-managed economy. In fact, the broader interpretation of the motivation base can include even objectives which normally would not be included under the heading of "self-interest," such as giving employment to others in the community, preventing unfavorable external effects of production such as air or water pollution, and many others.

For purposes of the evaluation of the functioning and performance of the participatory economy which we want to carry out in the next section, it will be useful to retain the distinction between the two levels of understanding of motivation in the participatory economy. We may refer to the crudely functioning income-maximizing objective as the *narrow motivation principle* and to the other, truer objective—which embraces a multiplicity of particular objectives—as the *broad motivation principle*.

\* \* \* \* \*

## OPERATION OF THE PARTICIPATORY ECONOMY

Using the image of a vehicle as we did in the preceding section—or to be more specific, a bus—it is possible to ask a number of questions about the efficiency or degree of perfection of its operation. For example, how much transportation service does the bus provide per unit of fuel, labor, or capital invested? What is its maximum speed? Are seats in the front of the bus as comfortable as those in the back? Similarly, economists attempting to evaluate the performance of a given economic system will try to answer comparable questions: How close does the system come to the producible maximum consistent with resources? How fast can it grow—that is, expand its productive resources? How desirable is the income distribution to which it leads?

In this section we will ask about a dozen fundamental questions of this type about the participatory economy and attempt to answer them in a manner intelligible to the general reader. (At times, this will mean simply stating the conclusions of arguments presented in full in my earlier, more technical work on the participatory economy,[4] or providing only partial evidence.) Our answers will allow us to make a summary evaluation of the participatory system. . . . Both in the individual arguments and in the overall conclusion, we will try to evaluate the participatory economy in two ways—on its own, that is, against

---

[4] *The General Theory of Labor-Managed Market Economies* (Ithaca, N.Y.: Cornell University Press, 1970).

an absolute standard of perfection, and in comparison with other economies, especially those found in the majority of countries in the Western world.

* * * * *

Turning now to the question of market concentration and monopolistic tendencies, we may say that in this context the deviation from the optimum in the participatory economy will generally not be considerable. It will certainly be less than in Western capitalist market structures. Several arguments can be offered to substantiate this proposition. First, on strictly psychological and sociological grounds, in self-governing bodies which participate in collective income, there will be a natural tendency to break into the smallest possible operational units (collectives) consistent with economic efficiency. The simple reason for this is the natural desire not to have men functionally remote from one's position participate in decisions and income. Traditional and modern capitalist firms have, by contrast, the well-known tendency to grow without bounds, the interests of the majority of employees being neglected. Very often the capitalist firms will tend to grow even well beyond a size that would be warranted on grounds of efficient operation.

Another argument is more economic and its full development would call for an undue amount of technical analysis; its common sense can be explained, however, without much difficulty. Suppose that a labor-managed firm operates at a level or scale of operation which permits it to be efficient and competitive with other firms in its industry. At that level of operation each worker makes a given income. If now the firm were to double its output—without affecting price significantly—the income per laborer would by and large remain unchanged, assuming that the internal efficiency of the firm were not affected.[5] The conclusion is that under the assumed conditions (which, incidentally, are often encountered in reality) there would be no special desire on the part of the firm to grow because such growth would not improve the income of each worker. And consequently, from this point of view at least, there would be only a slight tendency within the industry to reduce competition—that is, lower the number of firms—once each firm attained its efficient scale of operation. By contrast, under capitalist conditions, doubling of output in our above example would have doubled profits, and this indeed would have served as a powerful incentive to growth and, in many cases, to an eventual complete elimination of competition.

Still another among the several arguments regarding the degree of competition is related to questions of product differentiation, sales promotion, and advertising. Because it concerns such a large number of markets in the real world and also for other reasons, to which we will turn presently, it is probably the most important argument in this general case. The participatory firm differ-

---

[5] Editor's note: For example, suppose that by doubling the number of workers the firm thereby doubled output, sales revenue, and the resulting net income to be shared by twice as many workers.

entiating and promoting its product will, as can be shown[6] in the overwhelming majority of cases, engage in less promotional activity and operate at a lower level of output than a comparable capitalist firm. This leads to the conclusion that other things being equal, differentiated oligopolies (e.g., soft drinks, toothpaste, cigarettes, automobiles, and just about all modern final manufactured goods) under labor management will be much more competitive than capitalist oligopolies as we know them in the Western world. Moreover, and perhaps more important, the participatory alternative will advertise and promote less and thus utilize national resources more efficiently. Especially if we realize that the participatory firm will tend to omit some of the most aggressive forms of promotional activity, and if we recall of what low taste and quality such activity often is and what effects it may have on the minds, outlooks, and values of the public, the comparative advantages of labor management, on this account only, emerge as quite considerable.[7]

To sum up the arguments on competitiveness and market structure: We can say, without exaggeration, that the participatory economy naturally tends to embody the principle of "live and let live" much more than other market economies known to us today. There is far less urge to eliminate one's rival from the market. And this, let it be noted, carries within itself no implication of lesser efficiency. On the contrary, there is every reason to believe that oligopolies will, on the whole, be more efficient under labor management than under capitalism.

Even more obvious—not calling for any refined economics—is the related fact that in the participatory regime, by and large, there is no place for the labor-versus-management conflict. In consequence, the costs to society and to individual firms of strikes and other types of overt economic warfare are eliminated and the moral and mental costs of animosity, anger, and hatred are reduced.

Although this goes beyond the confines of economics, . . . it may be pointed out here that both of the arguments just made are bound to have far-reaching salutary effects on individuals and society. Both the "live and let live" forces of participation and the elimination of the major source of conflict in enterprises will necessarily be reflected in human attitudes and human relations throughout and even outside of the economic world, because people acting in the economic, social, intellectual, family, or religious worlds will, by and large, carry the same habits, prejudices, experiences, and attitudes from one world to another.

We may now return to less abstract considerations, and examine the participatory economy from the point of view of what is usually referred to as macroeconomics. In this field we ask questions about the overall—or global—

---

[6] This slightly involved technical argument is developed in *The General Theory of Labor-Managed Market Economies*, Chap. 6, Section 7.

[7] Cf. Lewis Mumford, *The Myth of the Machine* (New York: Harcourt, Brace & World, 1970).

performance of an economic system. For example, does it guarantee full employment, is it likely to lead to significant fluctuations in income or prices, or is it likely to generate inflationary forces?

Regarding the first question, the answer is that the participatory economy effectively does guarantee full employment. It does so in the sense that the economy normally will operate at, or very near, full employment, and if, as a result of some drastic disturbance, unemployment were to arise, there are forces inherent in the system that will tend to restore full employment. In this respect, the participatory economy has a definite edge over capitalist economies as we know them in the Western world.

A similar advantage, absolute with respect to an absolute standard and relative with respect to other market systems, is that the participatory economy is far less likely to undergo cyclical depressions than are Western market economies, and if such cycles were to occur they would be much less important.

By contrast, and deriving from the same forces, there is more likelihood in the participatory economy to encounter variations, both up and down, in the general price level. But by no means can this disadvantage be so serious as to offset the advantages of lesser or no fluctuations in real income, national product, and employment. No one will doubt that 5 percent of the labor force thrown out of work is incommensurably worse than a 5 percent change in prices.

When it comes to long-range stability of prices, that is, the likelihood of secular inflationary pressures, the labor-managed economy again promises to lead to satisfactory solutions. With no union power to fix wage rates, and a natural tendency of participatory firms to hold employment, prices can move down as easily as they can move up.

This, over long periods, can add up to overall secular price stability if monetary policy is not inflationary. By contrast, in the capitalist economy, where wages and prices are reduced far less willingly than they are increased, secular inflation is a virtual necessity in any economy committed to a full employment policy.

Thus far we have considered the principal aspects of the performance of the labor-managed economy in what we may refer to as its simplified or dehumanized form. Perhaps the second adjective is more descriptive of what we mean. All the results obtained up to this point are inherent in the participatory market economy merely on the assumption that the enterprises maximize income per person, each worker supplying work of equal and constant quality. This assumption is incomplete, and may be termed "dehumanized" because it neglects several key facts about the nature of the participatory economy. The most important among these are: (1) in each firm, people of many different skills are brought together to cooperate, and this raises, among others, problems of income distribution; (2) besides being workers in their firms, the participants also share in the responsibility of management, which involves a good deal more than decisions to maximize income per person; (3) the quality of work is not, in fact, a constant for each person, and the process of participation in decision making coupled with income sharing tends to influence the quality, intensity, and duration of work of each member of the enterprise.

Without going into the technical aspects of the question, it can be said that remuneration and income distribution among different job categories in the labor-managed firm will be influenced by two major sets of forces: (1) market forces and (2) the collective expression of the will and distributional attitudes of the working community. Market forces and, more specifically, competition among firms (both existing and potential entrants into an industry) and individuals will guarantee that there would not be in the economy major differences in remuneration for identical jobs performed with comparable intensity of work. On the other hand, the participatory decision-making process is bound to lead to income-distribution patterns within the enterprise reflecting the will of the collective; and this can be expected to lead to income-distribution patterns somewhat more equal than would result from market forces only.

\* \* \* \* \*

It would be impossible to list all the special effects—or what we may refer to as the special dimensions—of labor management, nor can we present a complete discussion of any single one of them. Nonetheless, we may attempt a brief account of some of the more important of these effects.[8]

We may start at random, selecting an argument of direct relevance to Western industrial societies. It has to do with so-called external diseconomies, such as air or water pollution. The managers of labor-managed firms—that is, workers and employees—who live in the vicinity of their air- or water-polluting plants, are more likely to take care of, or reduce, the undesirable external effects, even at a cost, than capitalist owners who may live thousands of miles away or may never have seen the businesses they own.

Another favorable point is that some laborer-managers may decide to take out some of their incomes in kind, say, in the form of a less strenuous or more hygienic job, where the principle of pecuniary profit maximization in the capitalist firm would not permit such a job improvement. A naïve person may object that this will make the participatory economy produce less real output than the capitalist; but it must be remembered that the building of the pyramids did not maximize social welfare, even if it may have maximized physical output.

For similar reasons, the participatory firm will be more likely to support education, training, and retraining of its members, when a strict profit motive might not suffice to do so. This phenomenon, actually verifiable in Yugoslavia, is of considerable importance for labor force development in the less advanced countries.

Being much more closely related and exposed to local living conditions in the village, town, or borough, the worker-managers of the participatory firms

---

[8] See also *The General Theory of Labor-Managed Market Economies,* Chaps. 13 and 14.

are in a much better position to cope with social ills than are capitalist managers. The latter, who either have no direct exposure to such ills or are expected to maximize returns for the owners, cannot use the weight and resources of their positions.

Still another argument bears on collective consumption of various kinds by the membership of the participatory firm. In many instances, again most frequently in poorer countries, the community of the labor-managed firm may be the only group powerful enough, financially and organizationally, to initiate and carry out projects for collective consumption, such as housing projects, recreation facilities, and even school facilities. While it is true that other—that is, nonparticipatory—firms can do likewise, a strong case can be made to the effect that the participatory ones will be more apt and willing to assume such functions.

This sketch of some of the more important positive factors ought to be complemented by arguments of comparable weight that are negative or unfavorable to labor management. In my opinion, there are only two such arguments—and it is disputable whether even these are actually unfavorable. First, it can be argued that democratic processes of decision making are often slower, more roundabout, and more friction-generating than dictatorial or administrative flat decisions, and this may have unsalutary effects on the economic performance of the enterprise. While there is a good deal of truth in this notion, it also must be recognized that as in political democracy, all is a matter of degree of participation, and the proper degree can itself be sought through democratic procedures. Just as in the political sphere it would be highly inefficient to have a full participation on every small decision, it would be equally inefficient—or at least extremely risky—democratically to delegate full powers in all matters to a director of the firm (or, for that matter, to the president of a country) for 20 years. But the democratic process itself is in a position to strike the proper balance between such extremes. And the balance it strikes, after all, should be efficient in the sense that it is favored by the majority, even if it may imply a slightly lower output and income than might be reached otherwise. The well-being, collective and individual, of the working community is at least as much a positive good as the last five dollars earned or unearned. Also, it may be expected that the democratic decision-making process can be made both more speedy and more efficient, in the sense of leading to results superior to those obtainable by simple majority rule.

The second argument, only a part of which is unfavorable to the participatory solution, is related to the question of inventive and innovative activity. It cannot be denied that with smaller size and a lesser push toward growth in the participatory firm, there will be less possibility to finance *major* invention, innovation, and product development by such firms, as compared to their capitalist counterparts. Of course, a counterargument could be given to the effect that innovation and invention can be assumed by independent labor-managed research firms fully devoted to such activity. But the real counterbalancing argument is that in the context of *minor* inventive and innovative activity, the participatory firm has a distinct advantage. Not only are the workers directly concerned to put into practice improvements they have thought of because they realize the direct benefits that this offers them, but the participatory regime also provides them with appropriate channels of communication, through their elected representatives or otherwise, to have their ideas studied and adopted.

*  *  *  *  *

## Chapter Eighteen

# The Yugoslav Firm*

### Stephen R. Sacks

*Yugoslavia was the only country in which worker-managed firms were the rule rather than the exception. Yugoslavia thus offers a unique case study of the application in practice of principles of self-management explained in Chapter 17.*

*In this chapter Sacks analyzes key features of the Yugoslav firm. One was the separation between ownership by society and control by the workers in the particular enterprise. Another was the arrangement for worker compensation in the form of residual income. The third was the organization of the enterprise into divisions, called* basic organizations of associated labor, *in an effort to make self-management more effective. These divisions within a firm contracted to buy or sell to each other, at agreed internal transfer prices.*

*Sacks then compares Yugoslav experience with predictions of theoretical models of labor-managed enterprises (like the model in Chapter 17) about decisions concerning output, the use of labor and other inputs, and investment. He explains the ways in which Yugoslav practice differed from theoretical models, and the reasons why.*

## INTRODUCTION

Yugoslavia is a small country in southeastern Europe. It has a population of 23 million people and territory about equal to the state of Wyoming. Why does such a small country warrant a chapter in this book? The answer lies in its unique economic system. It is the only country to have implemented the famous Marxist dictum, and long-time socialist battle cry, "Give the factories to the workers." The results are of interest not only to the Yugoslav people but to others all over the world. Socialist countries as diverse as Hungary, Poland,

---

\* Stephen R. Sacks, "The Yugoslav Firm." Revised version copyright © 1988 by Stephen R. Sacks. Used by permission. References to foreign language sources have been omitted. Stephen R. Sacks is Professor of Economics at the University of Connecticut.

China, and the Soviet Union are constantly looking for changes which might improve the performance of their economic systems. Indeed, one might argue that the major "restructuring" being implemented in the Soviet Union by Party Secretary Gorbachev has benefited from Soviet economists' study of Yugoslav successes and failures. And many capitalist countries, including the United Kingdom, West Germany, France, and even the United States, are finding that some sort of worker participation in management is necessary if firms are to operate efficiently. For all of these people the details of how the Yugoslav system works, and its strengths and weaknesses, are of great importance.

Before we look at the details of the Yugoslav economy, it should be pointed out that what we will be studying is not a primarily agricultural country, nor a group of independent artisans and cottage industries. Yugoslavia is a moderately industrialized country, still poor but very much advanced over its level of development at the end of World War II. In the 40 years since then it has grown very rapidly (although unevenly). It is, therefore, not unreasonable for large, modern industrial countries to watch the Yugoslav experiment with interest.

Furthermore, the heart of the Yugoslav economic system, the organizational structure of its enterprises, is used by virtually all of its firms, including very large ones. As we shall discuss below, some Yugoslav firms are indeed very big. Many have tens of thousands of workers and some are as big as firms on the U.S. Fortune 500 list. Thus the system cannot be dismissed as appropriate only for small-scale activities.

One final comment before we examine the characteristics of the Yugoslav economy: Those who study economic systems often say that there is an inevitable trade-off between equality and efficiency, that those systems that lead to a fairly equal distribution of income and wealth (usually socialist systems) are not very efficient, and those that are most efficient (usually capitalist systems) necessarily distribute income very unequally. It seems that we must accept either a wide gap between rich and poor or a lower level of output. A great virtue of the Yugoslav system is that it does rather well on both counts. That is not to say that it achieves complete equality. Indeed, one could argue that exactly identical income for everyone is not desirable. In any case, Yugoslavia does have rich and poor. But because there is virtually no property income (no one owns a factory or a giant apartment building), the gap between top and bottom is smaller than in most capitalist countries. Conversely, because people's incomes do depend on how hard (and how effectively) they work, the efficiency of the system is impressive, relative to most other socialist countries, where centralized planning often results in grossly inefficient decisions. Thus the Yugoslav system, called market socialism, combines some of the best features of both capitalism and socialism. Furthermore, one of its central characteristics, called industrial democracy or worker participation, could just as well be implemented in a capitalist economy. Indeed, there are examples of worker-owned enterprises, some quite large, in the United States as well as in many other capitalist countries.

# YUGOSLAV MARKET SOCIALISM

There are three basic principles of the system of market socialism in Yugoslavia: (1) social ownership of capital, (2) reliance on market forces to coordinate economic activities, and (3) worker self-management. When students discuss the Yugoslav system someone is likely to say, "It's really a type of capitalism." Indeed, it is like capitalism because of the significant role played by the market, but the rules of ownership of capital make the Yugoslav system unequivocally socialist. An individual can own a hammer, a truck, even some machines, but not a whole factory employing dozens or hundreds of workers. Just how much capital can one person own? A hundred dollars worth? A thousand dollars worth? A limit defined in terms of the monetary value of the capital would be very cumbersome to enforce. Instead, the Yugoslav constitution states a limit not in terms of value, but rather in terms of how many people work with the capital. Any enterprise employing more than five workers is part of the social sector and its capital is therefore socially owned.

Social ownership is not the same as government ownership. This subtle distinction is very important to the Yugoslavs. It provides the basis for the second principle of their economic system, the nearly complete absence of central planning. Since enterprises are owned by *society* rather than by the government, the latter has no right to give specific production orders to the enterprise. Unlike the Soviet government, the Yugoslav government does not (and legally cannot) order an enterprise to produce a particular product, use a particular input, or sell to a particular customer. In principle, prices, too, are determined by each enterprise in response to market forces. A market mechanism is, indeed, the basic system for coordination of activities in this economy.

At various times (especially in the early 1970s), the Yugoslavs have been dissatisfied with the market system. Many thought it led to instability, inequality, and inefficient use of resources. The idea of planning is popular, but few Yugoslavs want to return to the central planning system they had just after World War II. Instead of totally abandoning the market mechanism, Yugoslavia has tried to synthesize a unique system which includes both the market and decentralized planning. The fundamental characteristic of the resulting system is numerous independent decision makers exchanging goods and services for money, that is, market transactions. "Self-management agreements" sometimes tie buyers and sellers for a number of years and may set specific criteria for determining prices. Also, relationships between buyers and sellers may be complicated by prices which vary according to specified circumstances, by investment relationships, and by various risk-sharing arrangements. But if this were not *primarily* a market system then the market would have to be, to a substantial extent, *replaced* by planning. It is difficult to argue that there is much *effective* planning in Yugoslavia beyond some thinking ahead by independent actors. In any market system, the participants plan their own future actions and negotiate some of their contracts in advance. General Motors does not decide every morning which cars to produce that day and from whom to buy headlights for that day's production.

There are, of course, many imperfections in the Yugoslav market. They are somewhat further from the textbook pure market system than, say, the United States, which also has many instances of monopoly, oligopoly, price fixing, and output restriction. As in the United States, some of these market imperfections are the result of government actions and others result from enterprise collusion. In the United States, most states set a minimum price for milk, and in Yugoslavia, each republic fixes the price of milk. In the United States, market sharing between firms (I won't make home computers if you don't make mainframes) is likely to be tacit, while in Yugoslavia, explicit agreements are made. There the idea of market sharing and price fixing is popularly acceptable. Indeed, it is official policy to encourage such industry "cooperation."

Government rhetoric is full of references to "harmonization of individual plans" through "iterative searches for consistency" and "*ex ante* coordination of investment plans." But the Yugoslav system of planning, called "polycentric planning" because it relies on numerous centers, each planning for a particular industry or sector, is simply too vague to be useful as a mechanism for coordinating decision making. A good deal of time is devoted to industry meetings where representatives of firms discuss their investment and production plans. But the fact is that the much talked about "self-management agreements" and "social compacts," although supposedly binding, have not been very effective in coordinating economic activities. In the absence of any functional alternative, market forces remain the primary coordinating mechanism. Of course, the central government uses monetary and fiscal policies to influence the economy, but these are macroeconomic tools which affect most industries fairly uniformly and certainly do not involve specific orders to individual firms.

The third basic principle of Yugoslav market socialism is worker self-management. At each firm all the employees elect a worker' council, which is the equivalent of the board of directors in an American company. That does not mean that this group of workers directly manage the enterprise themselves. Day-to-day operating decisions are made by a hierarchy of managers hired by the workers' council. Like American boards of directors, some Yugoslav workers' councils take an active role in supervising the operations of the firm, and some choose to be a rubber stamp for decisions made by management. But in all cases, this worker-elected body has final authority in all decisions. On most significant matters (e.g., an important change in output, a major investment, or the basic wage for each skill level) either the whole council or one of its subcommitees will make the decision.

If you can imagine all of the shares of stock in General Motors divided up equally among the employees of GM and no shares being owned by anyone who is not a GM employee, then you have the fundamental idea of the organization of Yugoslav enterprises. Of course, a number of American firms are employee-owned (Vermont Asbestos, South Bend Lathe, and now National Steel are among the more than 5,000 in the United States), but in Yugoslavia *all* enterprises are self-managed.

Not only do workers have the ultimate decision-making authority in the firm. They also receive any residual profits after all obligations have been met. This does not mean that Yugoslav workers own the factory where they work in the same way that Western capitalists own a company. There are numerous restrictions on what they can do with their capital, including some that are discussed below in the section on investment. But the workers who are entrusted with the socially owned capital in their firm do have a right to the profit earned by virtue of working with that capital. We have, then, several of the basic features needed for an efficient market economy: independent firms choosing inputs, outputs, and prices in order to maximize their own profits. There is reason to believe that Yugoslav firms will respond to market signals (prices and profit) in much the same way as our textbooks predict for capitalist firms. (For more on this topic see the section below on The Theory of the Self-Managed Firm.)

Before the workers can get their share of profit, they must deduct from sales revenue the cost of inputs, certain legal obligations (that are essentially taxes), and their own basic wages.[1] The workers' council then allocates any residual to three uses: reinvestment, collective consumption, and bonuses. The question of how much of profit is reinvested in the firm, a very controversial issue and a very important one, is discussed in some detail below. When the system of market socialism first began to evolve in Yugoslavia, firms were

---

[1] Editor's note: This was the actual effective practice in the Yugoslav firm. However, formally, Yugoslav accounting followed the principle that in a self-managed firm there is no "profit" and workers receive residual incomes rather than "wages." In summary form, Yugoslav accounting showed the following:

Sales revenue of the unit
− Nonlabor costs
= Gross income of the unit
− Taxes paid by the unit
= Net income of the unit
− Investment by the unit (in production facilities and in housing
    and other services for the workers)
= Gross personal incomes of the workers
− Personal taxes
= Net personal incomes of the workers

The gross personal incomes of workers consisted of two parts: (1) a definite "basic" amount for the particular job, paid monthly but deemed an advance against the ultimate total payment; and (2) a variable additional amount paid every three months after the quarterly accounts were drawn up. The two components may be regarded as equivalent, respectively, to a "basic wage" and a "bonus." A legal change that would have made the "basic wage" a cost rather than a residual was proposed, but not adopted, in 1987.

For more details, see, for example, *Workers' Management in Yugoslavia: Recent Developments and Trends,* ed. Najdan Pašić, Stanislaw Grozdanić, and Milorad Radević (Geneva: International Labor Office, 1982), pp. 109–24.

allowed rather little discretion in this matter. Federal laws prescribed minimum and maximum percentages of residual profit to be allocated to each of these three uses. Gradually, over two decades (the 1950s and 1960s) the range between minimum and maximum was widened, giving each enterprise more freedom to make such decisions. During the 1970s there was some reversal of this trend as various restrictions were imposed on size of bonuses and amount of investment, but these restrictions are negotiated among firms in each industry and geographical region rather than being ordered by government. Furthermore, they are easily circumvented.

Collective consumption includes construction of apartments which are rented or sold to members of the firm, subsidized meals at the company cafeteria, vacation hotels at the seacoast, educational expenses for workers and their children, and many other items of that type.

The cash bonuses that constitute the workers' share of profits may be determined in either of two ways. Some firms choose to give equal amounts to all employees, but most firms distribute the money in proportion to salaries. That is, higher paid workers get more than lower paid ones (although in most cases the bonus is the same percentage of wages). Thus the Yugoslavs make no pretense of complete income equality. More skilled people earn more money than those will less skill, both in higher wages and in bigger bonuses. There is also a device that is essentially seniority pay: It is called a return to "past labor" and is intended to reward people for past investment in the firm (which came at the expense of lower bonuses). The idea behind it is that people who have worked for the firm longer should get extra pay because present productivity is partly a result of past investment which required sacrifices by those who were working then. The amount of seniority pay is usually small relative to pay differentials based on skill levels.

## DIVISIONALIZATION OF YUGOSLAV ENTERPRISES[2]

Now that we have an overview of how the Yugoslav system works, we can examine in greater detail a few particularly important issues. One that deserves special emphasis is the internal structure of the firm. For more than three decades, the Yugoslav economy was characterized by a continuing process of decentralization. The centralized command economy of 1945, patterned on the Soviet model, had by the early 1950s begun to develop into a system of self-management by independent enterprises. By 1965 the independence of enterprises from central government control was fairly complete and there had begun to evolve a principle of autonomy for divisions *within* the enterprise. Constitutional amendments in 1971 and the new Law on Associated Labor of 1976 further strengthened this trend. These developments are a logical conse-

---

[2] For more detail on this and other topics discussed in this chapter, see Stephen R. Sacks, *Self-Management and Efficiency: Large Corporations in Yugoslavia* (London: Allen and Unwin, 1983).

quence of the fundamental principle that underlies the philosophy of the entire Yugoslav economic system: Wherever possible, small work units are to be organized as separate, independent entities.

Like the principle of self-management, the idea of breaking a firm up into autonomous subunits is not unique to Yugoslavia. Many American companies are divided into separate divisions. But the Yugoslavs have implemented the principle more completely. Essentially, large corporations are run as though they were sets of smaller firms. An important question, then, is whether this extensive implementation of the principle of self-management by small work units is costly in terms of economic efficiency.

Some people, including many Yugoslavs, argue that firms have been atomized into inefficiently small fragments. Indeed, in 1987 proposals were made in the Yugoslav parliament to change the Law of Associated Labor in ways that would have reversed the trend toward further decentralization, by limiting the autonomy of the subdivisions of the firm. However, by the time the bill was passed in 1988 it had been very much watered down.

When we examine the relationship among its divisions, we find that the Yugoslav firm does bear many of the information and negotiation costs of using an internal market. Each division must devote time and effort to finding out which other divisions are able to produce the inputs it needs and which are able to buy the outputs it makes. Then the divisions must spend time discussing prices until they can agree on how much each will charge. However, these negotiations are easier within the firm than they would be between separate firms, because there is less opportunistic behavior. Therefore, the divisions can write incomplete contracts, relying instead on sharing clauses that allow the kind of adaptive, sequential decision making that is the heart of efficient enterprise operation.

The law specifies that the basic economic unit is not the enterprise but the "basic organization of associated labor," or BOAL, as the divisions are called in Western economics literature. They are the holders of all social sector assets and have final authority in all decision making. They join together to form enterprises, and each division's workers' council appoints representatives to a central council, but the divisions do not delegate much authority to the central management of the enterprise. Important decisions that affect all divisions must be voted on and approved by all of them.

Had the 1987 amendments been passed as originally proposed, some of this divisional authority would have been transferred to the enterprise-wide workers' council, and workers' councils would not have been formed at the divisional level. In that case each division would have had to get approval from the center for any substantial changes in its activities. But the law actually passed leaves the divisions the right to reorganize as they see fit. The only real effect of the 1988 law is that divisions have lost the right to have their own separate bank accounts. They must now transact their business through a single enterprise-wide account.

One of the fundamental principles of enterprise structure is that each worker's income comes from his division, not directly from the enterprise, and that that income depends primarily (although not entirely) on the division's economic performance. Divisions earn income by selling goods and services either outside the firm or to other divisions within the firm. In cases where the output is a result of joint production by several divisions, an effort is made to divide up the revenue according to the contribution of each. Furthermore, every division always has the right to withdraw from the enterprise, subject only to the requirement that it fulfill any commitments to deliver goods to other divisions and compensate them for any harm done by their withdrawal. It is very rare that a division actually leaves a firm, but a few instances are sufficient to prove their independence.

Drawing the dividing lines that define the divisions of a firm presents a problem. The law states that any group of workers whose performance can be measured in terms of value either within the enterprise or on an outside market shall be organized as an independent division. While this principle is conceptually unambiguous, in practice it is often difficult to decide exactly which activities to include in each division. A chain of hotels might be organized with each hotel as a separate division, or each division might include all of the hotels in a geographical region. In manufacturing, a division often includes all the workers involved in a particular product line from raw material to finished product; but it is equally likely that each of the successive stages will be defined as a division. For example, at one shoe producer there might be three divisions, one each for women's shoes, men's shoes, and children's shoes. At another firm one division might make the soles for all the shoes, another the upper parts for all of them, and a third division would sew together the parts for all types of shoes. A Slovenian electronics firm with 27,000 workers is divided into 66 divisions. Most of the divisions correspond to a particular product (for example, motors for home appliances, telephone switchboards, calculators, etc.), but some are defined along functional lines (for example, equipment design, installation, and workers' restaurant).

Administrative services that are provided to all of the divisions of an enterprise are performed by "work communities" rather than by divisions. This includes things like maintenance, bookkeeping, and personnel. Work communities operate under special restrictions: They may not withdraw from the enterprise and they can be dissolved by decision of the divisions. Work communities have no funds of their own, and depend on the divisions to provide money to pay their costs, including personal and collective consumption at a rate equal to the average earned by workers in the divisions. The changes proposed in 1987 would have freed the work communities from domination by the divisions and would have prohibited individual divisions from having their own separate marketing, personnel, and other such services. The work communities would have then had the possibility of earning personal incomes higher than those in the BOALs.

Since the size of divisions is not prescribed by law, they vary quite a lot from one firm to another. In a sample of 67 large industrial enterprises, ranging in size from 1,500 to over 37,000 workers, the number of divisions per firm varied from 6 to 180 and the average division size varied from 88 to 766 workers. Overall, the average size of divisions was 315 employees. Enterprises in the trade sector tend to be about half as large as industrial enterprises and they are divided into about the same number of divisions, resulting in division size averaging 177 workers.

The most obvious advantage of dividing up large enterprises is the improvement in incentives for hard work. The motivational value of a system based on profit sharing among workers is greater when a few hundred, rather than several thousand, others share the results of any extra effort by each worker. Similarly, any collective decision to work harder (or even to maintain the current level of effort) can be more effectively implemented and monitored in a smaller group.

## Internal Prices

Transfer prices are prices paid by one division for goods or services bought from another division in the same firm. Understanding how these prices are determined is crucial for an understanding of the organizational structure of Yugoslav enterprises. Transfer prices result from intensive negotiations between buyer and seller, who are in effect bargaining over their own incomes. They do, in fact, sign a legally binding contract that specifies prices and quantities of the goods or services sold. That these negotiations are not a sham is proved by a few instances where deliveries of goods to sister divisions were halted because agreement on a transfer price had not been reached.

Of fundamental importance for efficient operation of the economy is the question of whether or not production decisions are based on transfer prices. In some cases divisions seem to agree first on quantities and only then on prices. That is, transfer prices appear to affect the distribution of income but not the allocation of resources. However, since both sides are usually aware of outside alternatives, they have a pretty good idea of the transfer prices before output decisions are made and thus it is likely that they do affect production plans. Certainly, last year's prices are known, so one could argue that resource allocation is based on lagged transfer prices.

It is sometimes claimed that the relationship among the divisions in a Yugoslav enterprise is a pure market relationship. Although that is somewhat of an oversimplification, the fact is that in most enterprises intermediate goods and services are sold at transfer prices that approximate, if not exactly equal, market prices. What prevents much deviation is the right of every division to buy and sell outside the firm. If the transfer price were much higher than the price on external markets, the division that uses the service or intermediate product would buy outside. If the transfer price were much lower, the producing division would instead sell on outside markets. There is no central authority within the enterprise that can dictate transfer prices, nor can anyone force a settlement of a dispute. Of course, the central management of the enterprise often is effective in persuading divisions to reach an agreement.

Sometimes transfer prices are explicitly tied to world prices, often with some mechanism that reduces volatility. For example, a Yugoslav aluminum plant agreed to buy bauxite ore from a sister division at a price equal to the six-month average of the prices published in London. In other cases transfer prices are not exactly equal to prices on external markets, but they rise and fall with those outside prices. For instance, at the Sisak steel mill the transfer price for sheet steel sold to another division is pegged at 6 percent below the price on European markets. The 6 percent differential is intended to reflect the conven-

Various other mechanisms are used to set transfer prices. Sometimes outside bids are solicited (with a real possibility that a deal will be struck). Sometimes the private sector provides a benchmark price.[3] Frequently, transfer prices are tied to the price of the firm's final product, so that internal prices move in proportion to that final price. In this last case the annual negotiations are essentially a matter of determining each division's percentage participation in total enterprise income. This is not fundamentally different from negotiating an absolute price. In particular, it allows the possibility that a division will react to a price change by altering its output (the next time an internal contract is negotiated). This income-sharing mechanism means that any change in market conditions will be transmitted rather quickly from a final product to inputs related to it by derived demand, thus tending to strengthen the sense of enterprise solidarity.

Often the price on an external market is taken as a starting point for transfer price negotiations, which then focus on the costs of the seller. From the point of view of overall efficiency, this is particularly desirable in cases where external markets are not perfectly competitive and hence transfer prices equal to market prices would not accurately measure marginal cost. Within the firm both buyer and seller are required to make a complete disclosure of their costs and revenues, as well as of the incomes of their workers, so social pressure tends to push the transfer price to a level that yields a "fair" distribution of profit. This may release the seller from outside competitive pressure to minimize its own costs. But often sufficient pressure to keep on his toes comes from the fact that the division buying the intermediate good must sell a final product on competitive domestic or world markets.

In some situations, of course transfer prices deviate substantially from market prices. This may be because the external price includes some costs of packaging and shipping, which ought to be deducted when the buyer and seller are in close physical proximity. Also, economies of scale in production, ease of billing, and reduced likelihood of bad debts may explain a lower transfer price.

---

[3] See Stephen R. Sacks, "The Private Sector in Yugoslavia." *ACES Bulletin* 20, no. 2 (Summer 1978), pp. 1–11.

Another reason why transfer prices may not equal external prices is that a sense of solidarity develops with sister divisions when there are close, long-term relationships. In some instances social or political pressure causes one division to agree to a transfer price favorable to another so as to improve the financial health of the latter. It is in such cases that the Communist party (called the League of Communists) might play a role. Although it has no formal authority, the Party may exert pressure, through its members who are often in key positions, to take a wider view of the welfare of the firm as a whole, rather than a narrower view of the interests of the individual division. Then the transfer price might hide an intentional transfer of funds. But as long as the participants are aware of market prices, it is clear to them what they are "paying" for enterprise solidarity.

When one division helps finance expansion or modernization of another, the transfer price for transactions between them is likely to be favorable to the lender. However, the law states that a price agreement may not last longer than the period of repayment of such a loan, so this cannot be a basis for long-term distortion of price. Eventually, the price will be renegotiated. Often, the borrower agrees to buy or sell a specific quantity of some intermediate good at a price favorable to the lender and is free to seek a better price outside the enterprise for the remainder of its capacity.

## The Nature of the Yugoslav Firm

The extensive autonomy of the divisions of the Yugoslav enterprise raises a fundamental question: If its divisions have so much independence, what then is a firm? This question continues to perplex Yugoslav economists, one of whom, in discussing proposed legal changes in 1987, asked "What is an enterprise? . . . It is an independent business entity, an independent business agent, . . . and yet it is not and cannot be these things because it does not have its own activities, its own assets, its own income, because all that . . . belongs to the basic organizations of which it is comprised."

The Yugoslav enterprise cannot be defined in terms appropriate for capitalist firms because there is no ownership of a coherent group of assets nor a set of activities controlled by a single command hierarchy. Traditional definitions of the firm as an organization within which the price mechanism does not operate and where there is a structure of authority to give commands, would suggest that each *division* is itself an enterprise. But in Yugoslavia it is usually a *collection of divisions* that is viewed as an enterprise. It is important to make clear that that collection of units does have considerable economic significance.

The significance of the firm stems from the fact that the divisions are not, in fact, entirely independent of one another. The relationship between two divisions that are in the same firm is different from the relationship between two divisions that are not. For one thing, divisions within the same firm are more likely to engage in market-sharing and other forms of collusion. After all, they are joined together because they see some mutual benefit in joint production, marketing or purchasing, or in sharing such common activities as book-keeping and personnel services. Often, a strong desire for stability and a fear of market fluctuations lead them to establish stable supply channels and stable price relationships. They continue to honor and renew agreements with sister divisions even when external prices are somewhat more attractive.

This is not simply a matter of long-term contracts. Any two divisions can make a long-term contract and that by itself does not mean that they become an enterprise. Rather, what binds the subunits of an enterprise together is a strong sense of being a "family." This relationship allows the adaptive, sequential decision making that Oliver Williamson[4] sees as essential to the efficient operation of enterprises. To some extent this results from social and political pressures that encourage unity among the divisions of an enterprise. While each division in principle has the right to buy and sell outside, there is often enough local party and social pressure to deal with a sister division that it will do so as long as the gap between transfer price and external price does not exceed some threshold. Similarly, while each has the right to choose its own outputs, there is likely to be specialization that will lead to market sharing. This may result from either tacit or explicit agreements (for example, I'll make washing machines and you make dishwashers).

The financial ties among the divisions of a Yugoslav firm are difficult to understand. For example, despite their ostensible legal autonomy, divisions often choose to establish mutual liability for debts, primarily because it encourages outsiders to do business with them. This means that, in addition to a general sense of enterprise unity, each division has a more direct interest in the financial health of the others. Although there is no procedure for simply taking money from one division to give to another, there is a tendency to try to reduce (but not necessarily eliminate) any differentials that might exist between personal income levels in different divisions. The obvious mechanism, if there is a substantial differential, would be to adjust transfer prices in favor of the division whose income is lower. But this conflicts with the principle, discussed above, that transfer prices should equal external market prices. There is no simple reconciliation of this conflict.

Sometimes there are explicit transfers of money from one division to another for purposes of modernization or expansion. This raises the very thorny issue of whether, and to what extent, a division that lends capital has a right to share the profits of the division that borrows. The general rule seems to be that the money supplied is treated as a loan that is to be repaid with a rate of interest that is agreed upon in advance. However, both the law and the popular press emphasize the importance of the principles of "pooling resources" and "sharing risks." Indeed, the law specifies that the investor shall be compensated "in proportion to the income realized" by the project. This seems to mean that the

---

[4] See, for example, his *Markets and Hierarchies: Analysis and Antitrust Implications* (New York: Free Press, 1975).

harder the borrowers work, and hence the more successful they are, the greater will be the income of other workers (the lenders) who are not actually working in that division. This sounds uncomfortably close to what Marx would call exploitation.

There are two ways in which this situation can be reconciled with the fundamental socialist principle that prohibits one worker from appropriating the results of the work of another. First, the Yugoslavs consistently refer to the money loaned as the "past labor" of the lender. Thus, by contributing funds that they earned with their own labor, the investors have legitimately earned a right to share in whatever profits come from the joint project.

Second, the law specifies that profit sharing based on contributed capital may not continue on a permanent basis. A repayment schedule must be worked out in advance, and once the initial investment is repaid (with interest), that's the end of the investor's right to a share of the profit. In practice, this is interpreted to mean that until the loan is repaid, the investor is considered to be a contributor to the project and hence has a right to a share of profits *in addition to* the agreed interest and the eventual return of his invested funds.

With increasing divisional autonomy and the virtual elimination of any overall enterprise funds, or central enterprise authority to transfer funds between divisions, the importance of interdivisional lending has increased. One might argue either that profit sharing is more socialistic than the debtor-creditor relationship implied by a fixed rate of return, or that profit sharing means the lender is exploiting the borrower. But in either case the increased mobility of capital that results from the additional incentive to lend seems certain to improve the overall efficiency of resource allocation. Indeed, theoretical studies of self-management have consistently viewed capital immobility as a serious problem. Of course, the variation in the return on interdivisional loans is not the only way in which risk is shared among divisions. Whenever transfer prices are stated as a percentage of the selling price of a final product, all of the divisions have an interest in the price, as well as in the quantity, of the final good sold.

Usually, the real incentive to invest in another division is not the interest earned or direct profit share, but the increased availability of some input or increased demand for the investor's output. This is also true when the investor and borrower are in different enterprises. For example, in one case a shoe manufacturer invested in a slaughterhouse so as to expand the domestic supply of leather, and in another case several television set makers jointly financed a factory that makes cathode ray tubes. It is important to point out that, once founded, the new slaugherhouse, CRT maker, and so on is legally autonomous. It must repay the loans that provided its initial capital according to whatever terms were set, but once it begins operation, technically its capital is its own. Legally, there is nothing to prevent a newly founded division, like any other division, from withdrawing from the enterprise. Indeed, it is this very fact that prevents the founder(s) from imposing exploitative transfer prices. A new division is likely to be established only if it promises to be advantageous to all parties concerned.

One of the most important bonds tying together the divisions in a firm is the enterprise plan. Annually, representatives of every division jointly work out detailed plans (now called self-management agreements) for the coming year. There are also five-year plans, but these are not really operational. Annual plans specify exactly which goods and services each division is to produce; delivery dates and quantities are set; and transfer prices are settled. Once approved by all the constituent divisions, the enterprise plan becomes a set of legally binding contracts. A division's right to withdraw from the enterprise, or to buy or sell outside, is conditional on fulfilling its obligations to the other divisions as specified in the enterprise plan.

The increasing emphasis on economic planning, which has been evident throughout Yugoslav society since 1971, appears to conflict with the principle of autonomy for the divisions. Yet the Yugoslavs deny that there is any conflict: As long as there is no central office (either inside the firm or outside) with authority to impose production orders, each division is merely making its own decisions in consultation with other economic units. It is, in this respect, like French indicative planning, although in this case the plans are more precise and the parties to the agreement actually sign a contract. The underlying principle is that the sharing of information is in itself highly desirable because it enables a market mechanism to work more smoothly. The system is like a set of forward markets where buyers and sellers negotiate quantities and prices in advance so that future relative scarcities become known.

This joint planning is not limited to within firms. In order to avoid bottlenecks and the idle capacity that can result from overinvestment, all of the firms in an industry (along with their suppliers and customers) are expected to formulate self-management agreements for future production plans. The difference between enterprise plans and industry plans is that the former are more detailed and more likely to be fulfilled.

## THE THEORY OF THE SELF-MANAGED FIRM

For many years the unusual system in Yugoslavia has fascinated Western economic theorists. The worker-managed firm is in most respects no different from a textbook capitalist firm, and hence many of the standard neoclassical theoretical results hold (for example, inputs other than labor are used up to the point where their marginal cost equals their marginal value product). However, other characteristics are different (for example, supply elasticity may be very low or even negative). The most complete theoretical study is Jaroslav Vanek's *The General Theory of Labor-Managed Market Economies*.[5] Vanek and others

---

[5] Ithaca, N.Y.: Cornell University Press, 1970.

show that under conditions of perfect competition, a market economy consisting of labor-managed firms will use the same amount of each input and produce the same amount of output as otherwise identical capitalist firms. That is, the self-managed system is no less efficient. There are, however, some important differences, especially under conditions of imperfect competition.

All of the interesting results in the theoretical work stem from the different maximand attributed to the labor-managed enterprise. It is assumed that the firm maximizes profit per worker rather than total profit, as does the textbook capitalist firm.[6] This assumption makes sense, given that the firm is run by the workers' council which is elected by the entire group of workers. It is not, however, the only possible criterion on which to base decisions. One could imagine that concern about the level of unemployment in the community could lead the council to hire (or retain) more employees than is optimal according to that criterion. Or a strong sense of social consciousness may cause them to increase output beyond what is in their own narrow self-interest. Similarly, a sense of unity in the enterprise might focus attention on total profit. Conversely, desire by the present cohort of workers to retain control of the firm might lead them to resist hiring more workers even when additional employees would raise profit per worker. The new workers would threaten that control because Yugoslav law makes no provision for seniority in voting: All workers have equal voice in running the firm. Another possible criterion is stability. If workers are conservative they might resist both increases and decreases in labor input (and hence output), even if that means profit per worker will not be maximized. It has also been hypothesized that firms' behavior is the result of a compound maximand which includes several of these considerations.

Because there are numerous possible criteria for enterprise decision making, the economic literature on the self-managed firm has grown extensively. Most of that literature, however, accepts profit per worker as either the exclusive maximand or one of several criteria. This is analogous to the literature on capitalist firms: We usually assume that the firm maximizes total profit, while admitting that there are also other criteria that may be of even greater significance. John Kenneth Galbraith, for instance, has effectively argued that capitalist firms pay less attention to profits than they do to stability, size, and control of the markets for their inputs and outputs.[7] Just as our awareness of other considerations does not prevent us from assuming profit maximization by capitalist firms, we can admit the various possible criteria for self-managed socialist firms and still learn something by assuming that they maximize profit per worker. The truth of the matter is that Yugoslav firms do try to satisfy

---

[6] Editor's note: In the literature about labor-managed firms, "profit" is sometimes used to refer to (1) sales revenue − (nonlabor costs + taxes), or (2) sales revenue − (nonlabor costs + "basic wages" + taxes). In contrast, in the capitalist firm, all wages are included in costs before profit is calculated.

[7] See, for example, his *The New Industrial State* (Boston: Houghton Mifflin, 1967).

several of the criteria mentioned above, but profit per worker is the one that carries the most weight.

The first significant theoretical work on the Yugoslav self-managed firm, and the basis for much of what came later, was done by Benjamin Ward.[8] He expressed the maximand of the firm as

$$Y = \frac{p_x X - p_k K}{L}$$

where

$Y$ = income per worker[9]
$p_x$ = the price of output $X$
$X$ = the amount produced of output $X$
$p_k$ = the price of capital
$K$ = the amount of capital the firm uses
$L$ = the amount of labor the firm uses

Clearly, all this says is that income per worker equals total revenue from the product the firm produces minus the cost of capital, all divided by the number of workers in the firm. For simplicity, we are assuming that there are only one output and no inputs other than labor and capital. If we rewrite this expression as

$$Y = \frac{p_x X}{L} - \frac{p_k K}{L}$$

we can see that income per worker equals the difference between the value of the average product of labor ($VAP_L$) and the cost of capital per worker. If we make the usual assumptions about labor productivity (increasing and then diminishing marginal productivity) and if the firm is small enough so that its actions don't affect the price of capital, then a graph of these two functions will look like that shown in Figure 18–1. Also drawn is the dividend curve ($Y$), which shows income per worker.[10]

In the short run the amount of capital is fixed, so the only choice to be made is the amount of labor. If the firm wants to maximize income per worker, it must choose the amount of labor input that maximizes the difference between the value of the average product of labor and the cost of capital per worker. In the diagram, that is the point on the horizontal axis ($L_o$) where the vertical distance between the two curves is greatest. Since the dividend curve is noth-

---

[8] "The Firm in Illyria: Market Syndicalism," *American Economic Review* 48, no. 4 (September 1958), pp. 566–89.

[9] Some theorists prefer to divide worker income into fixed wage and profit share. That approach is more realistic but does not affect the implications of the model.

[10] Editor's note: The dinar is the Yugoslav monetary unit.

**FIGURE 18–1**    Choice of Labor Input to Maximize Income per Worker

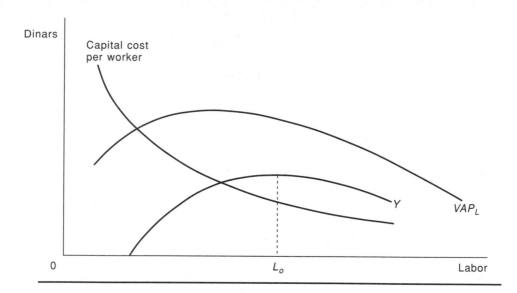

ing but the difference between the other two curves, it peaks at that point. It is zero where revenue per worker equals capital cost per worker. It diminishes beyond the optimum labor input, because beyond $L_o$ the value of the average product of labor declines more rapidly than does the cost of capital per worker.

Not shown in the diagram is the curve representing the value of the marginal product of labor ($VMP_L$). But we know that it must pass through the peak of the dividend curve. As long as $VMP_L$ is more than the dividend, the dividend is increasing, and as soon as $VMP_L$ is less than the dividend, the dividend will fall. That is, if an additional worker adds more to total revenue than he takes as his share of income, he is increasing income per worker. Conversely, if the value of his marginal product is less than the current dividend, then hiring him will reduce the dividend for all the workers.

What we've done so far is to locate the optimum number of workers for the firm to employ, given its production function and the prices of its output and capital. Since labor is the only variable input, this is equivalent to deciding how much output to produce. Now, let's look at what happens in this optimum input (and output) level when the price of the output ($p_x$) changes. When this price increases, the $VAP_L$ curve rises (more revenue from every input level). Where is the new optimum? Again, it is where the two curves are furthest apart, and that means where their slopes are equal. The lower curve (capital cost per worker) doesn't move, so its slope at $L_o$ doesn't change. But as $VAP_L$ shifts up, its slope at every point gets steeper.[11] Therefore, the slopes will be the same (and the two curves will be furthest apart) at a labor input level to the *left* of $L_o$. Conversely, if $p_x$ falls, optimum labor input will be to the *right* of $L_o$. Remember that when labor input rises or falls, so does output. But what are we doing when we figure out the relationship between the price of a product and the amount of it the firm will choose to produce? We're determining the supply curve, and in this case it slopes downward!

If, indeed, it is true that a labor-managed firm will reduce output when the price of its product rises and increase output when the price falls, there is a serious question as to whether, in an economy consisting of such firms, a market mechanism can function properly. If firms' supply curves slope downward, then market equilibria may be unstable. And certainly the whole notion of consumer sovereignty falls apart if firms react perversely to an increase in demand that pushes price up. Either market socialism with labor-managed firms is an unworkable system or this theory provides an inaccurate description of the situation.

The fact is that a more complex (and realistic) model gives rather different results. If we introduce the possibility of several inputs and multiple outputs, we have to consider the labor-managed firm's demand for variable inputs other than labor. Holding labor input constant, any action which increases total profit increases profit per worker. Therefore, the labor-managed firm will use the standard textbook rule of using each such input up to the point where the value of its marginal product equals its price. That is, it will use the same amounts of nonlabor inputs as a capitalist firm. Further, if the firm produces several outputs, then when the price of one product rises, the reduction in labor input may show up as a reduction in the output of some other product. Then, instead of getting a downward-sloping supply curve, we conclude merely that the supply curve will be less elastic than that of a comparable capitalist firm. Whether the supply curve does slope downward or not depends on a number of things, including the relative height and steepness of the marginal productivity curves for labor and nonlabor inputs.[12] This suggests that this socialist market economy will be somewhat less responsive to changes in demand than a textbook capitalist system, but not that it won't work.

Also contributing to the inelasticity of supply is the reluctance of Yugoslavs to fire their fellow workers and their cautiousness about hiring new people. For all these reasons, the operation of the Yugoslav economy tends to support the theoretical prediction: Yugoslav firms are sluggish in adjusting

---

[11] The slope of $VAP_L$ is

$$\frac{d\left(\frac{p_x X}{L}\right)}{dL} = p_x\left(\frac{X'}{L} - \frac{X}{L^2}\right),$$

which increases as $p_x$ increases.

[12] See Jaroslav Vanek, *The General Theory of Labor-Managed Market Economies* (Ithaca, N.Y.: Cornell University Press, 1970), Chap. 3.

output levels, both upward and downward. Consequently, worker income rather than amount of employment absorbs much of the variation in market conditions.

We have so far been looking at firms in perfectly competitive markets. There are two additional theoretical points that should be made in connection with imperfectly competitive firms. First, the theoretical model indicates that in some circumstances the capital/labor ratio will be higher than in comparable capitalist firms. To see this, draw a set of isoquants and some isocost lines that are steeper than in the capitalist case because worker-owners "cost" more than capitalist workers who don't get a profit share. In perfect competition there is no profit, so worker-owners don't "cost" more and the capital/labor ratios are not different. Empirical evidence from the Yugoslav economy confirms this tendency towards capital-intensive production.

Second, we know that in capitalist systems monopoly or oligopoly is likely to lead to restriction of output. What happens if a labor-managed firm knows that its own output decision has an effect on the price of its product? In that case the $VAP_L$ curve[13] will become steeper (additional workers mean more output and hence lower price) and the optimal amount of labor input will be to the left of $L_o$. That is, the firm, like a monopolist in a capitalist system, will produce less.

Now, Vanek claims that there are a number of forces which tend to make labor-managed firms small, so that monopoly power, and its consequent output restriction, are not likely to occur. But empirical study of the Yugoslav economy shows that in fact it is dominated by large firms. There are over 50 firms with more than 10,000 workers each, and about half a dozen have more than 30,000. More than 30 percent of the industrial labor force works in firms with more than 10,000 employees. Measuring size by number of workers, the top 10 Yugoslav firms would rank among the largest 200 firms on the Fortune 500 list. Furthermore, during the 1970s these large corporations increased their share of total economic activity.

## THE PROBLEM OF INVESTMENT IN A SELF-MANAGED ECONOMY

There is a good deal of theoretical literature on investment in a self-managed economy. Much of its concerns a bias which may make workers reluctant to invest their own money in their firm. This, in turn, suggests that the amount of investment undertaken by the labor-managed firm is dependent on whether projects are funded with retained profits, that is, with the money which workers are reluctant to invest, or with outside credit, which presumably they are more willing to spend.

---

[13] If we are talking about imperfect competition, the appropriate term is average value product (AVP) rather than value of the average product (VAP).

In order to understand the logic of investment decisions in Yugoslavia, it is necessary to begin with a basic institutional characteristic: The firm is required by law to maintain the value of its capital. In other words, it must pay into its own business fund each year an amount of money equal to that year's depreciation on its current capital stock. Money in the business fund may be used for investment but may not be distributed for individual consumption. This principle is based on the belief that the capital in every firm belongs to society as a whole and may not be consumed by those who work with it. One way of looking at this is to say that the Yugoslav firm is continually converting physical assets into financial assets: As machinery wears out, the firm sets aside from current revenue an amount of money equal to that depreciation. These financial assets are periodically reconverted into physical assets (for example, when the firm buys a machine), but they may not be distributed as personal income.

Another way to look at this is to say that once the decision is made to undertake a project, the Yugoslav firm is committed to continue perpetually that project, or some other project of equivalent financial magnitude. By contrast, a capitalist firm has in addition the options of (1) allowing an asset to wear out without replacing it, thus gradually ending the project, and (2) selling the asset, without making an equivalent purchase, thus at one stroke ending the project. That is, for the capitalist firm investment involves a continuous decision-making process. On any day an investment decision can be partially or entirely reversed, and the total stock of capital is variable downward as well as upward. For the Yugoslav firm a decision to invest entails a commitment to reinvest, and the amount of capital is variable only upward.

An important implication of this situation has been described in numerous articles by Eirik Furubotn and Svetozar Pejovich.[14] Their argument rests on the fact that workers do not have full ownership rights over the assets of the firm and hence cannot recover the principal amount of an investment in the firm at the end of their time horizon. In individual savings accounts, on the other hand, workers can reclaim the principal as well as interest. Consequently, they will invest in the firm only if the prospective rate of return is higher, by at least a certain amount, than the rate of interest paid on savings accounts.[15]

This bias against reinvesting in the firm money which the workers could put in their pockets or savings accounts has received quite a lot of attention among economists who study economic systems. There is no question but that the theoretical logic behind the bias is correct. However, there are reasons to

---

[14] See, for example, "Property Rights and the Behavior of the Firm in a Socialist State: The Example of Yugoslavia," Chap. 16 in *The Economics of Property Rights,* ed. Eirik Furubotn and Svetozar Pejovich (Cambridge, Mass.: Ballinger, 1974), and "Property Rights, Economic Decentralization, and the Evolution of the Yugoslav Firm, 1965–72," *Journal of Law and Economics* 16, no. 2 (October 1973), pp. 275–302.

[15] For a detailed explanation of the analysis of Furubotn and Pejovich, see Sacks, *Self-Management,* pp. 77–83.

believe that the impact may be offset by certain practical considerations. First, workers may in fact have long time horizons. Second, if workers believe that new equipment is necessary to preserve their jobs in the face of competition, they will vote to invest despite a bias against it. Third, it is important that investment in his firm is virtually the only way a socialist worker can acquire real (as opposed to financial) assets. In situations where inflation is significant (as it nearly always is in Yugoslavia) there is a strong argument for investing in plant and equipment, which pays a return in real goods and services, rather than in financial assets such as savings accounts, which pay a return that is measured in nominal terms and hence eaten away by inflation.

Further, it should be clear that what Furubotn and Pejovich have shown is workers' bias against investing *their own* money in the firm. However, funds that can be borrowed from a bank are quite another matter. If outside funds are available, the amount of investment undertaken by the self-managed firm might not be less than the amount undertaken by a comparable capitalist firm. The extent to which the availability of outside funds will affect investment decisions is the subject of a lively theoretical controversy in the economics journals.[16]

In practice, Yugoslav firms do rely heavily on bank loans to finance investment. However, banks will not lend 100 percent of any project, so every undertaking is at least partially financed with retained earnings of the firm. Perhaps because workers are afraid of losing their jobs in the face of more technologically advanced competitors, or because inflation counteracts the Furubotn-Pejovich bias, Yugoslav firms do reinvest a substantial part of their profits. Investment rates have been erratic, but in comparison to other countries of similar wealth and level of development they are quite high.

## CONCLUSION

The three basic principles of Yugoslav market socialism are social ownership of capital, dependence on a market mechanism to coordinate economic activity, and worker management of enterprises. The distinction between social and government ownership of capital means that enterprises are not subject to central planning. Instead, elected representatives of the workers in each factory, and the management hierarchy hired by them, run the firm in response to price and profit signals. Revenue from the sale of the firm's output is used to pay for inputs, taxes and other obligations, and the workers' basic wages. Any residual funds are divided up among reinvestment, collective consumption, and profit sharing.

An outstanding feature of the Yugoslav system is the divisionalization of enterprises into independent subunits. To a large extent, the income of a

---

[16] See, for example, Eirik Furubotn, "Bank Credit and the Labor-Managed Firm: The Yugoslav Case," Chap. 18 in *The Economics of Property Rights,* ed. Furubotn and Pejovich; and Frank Stephen, "Bank Credit and the Labor-Managed Firm: Comment," *American Economic Review* 70, no. 4 (September 1980), pp. 796–99.

worker is determined by the economic performance of his or her division. The relationship among the divisions of a firm is similar to that of a market, with goods and services sold at transfer prices that approximate the prices on external markets. This means that the enterprise bears some of the transaction costs of using a market (negotiating prices and enforcing contracts). But the sense of unity among the divisions allows the adaptive, sequential decision making that many economists view as the key to efficient operation of a firm.

Theoretical models of the self-managed firm indicate some potential problems. The enterprise's supply curve is likely to be less elastic than that of a comparable capitalist firm. Under perfect competition this economic system can be expected to be efficient, but otherwise a misallocation of resources is likely to result. Investment seems more likely to be a problem. Because workers have limited property rights over the assets of their firms (they get the return but cannot reclaim the principal), there is a bias against investing their own money in the firm. Empirical evidence shows that aggregate investment rates are quite high, so this problem appears not to be very serious.

*Chapter 19*

# Self-Managed Market Socialism and the Yugoslav Economy, 1950–91*

*John P. Burkett[1]*

*Yugoslavia provided the only real-world case of a socialist regulated market economy. But it differed from the models of "market socialism" developed by Lange (Chapter 16) and Vanek (Chapter 17) in the nature and operation of the economic system.*

*For example, in Yugoslavia, private enterprise was important in agriculture, crafts, and many services. Markets were characterized by imperfections, such as inadequate information, oligopoly, and low labor mobility. The activities and success of an enterprise often depended strongly upon its relations with government agencies and with officials of the League of Communists, which controlled all levels of government. In their economic policies and specific actions, government bodies were frequently guided by noneconomic considerations, such as political unity among ethnically diverse areas, the desire for regional autonomy, and "nonalignment" in international affairs. Government intervention was often inconsistent or ineffective.*

*In this chapter Burkett analyzes and evaluates the complex reality of the Yugoslav economic system. He examines the operation of markets for labor, consumer goods, material inputs, financial capital, and foreign exchange. He explains the objectives and instruments of government intervention in these markets. He compares the resulting performance of the Yugoslav economy with the performance of European capitalist regulated market economies and centrally planned economies at about the same level of economic development.*

* John P. Burkett, "Self-Managed Market Socialism and the Yugoslav Economy, 1950–91." Copyright © 1993 by John P. Burkett. Used by permission. References to foreign language sources have been omitted. John P. Burkett is Professor of Economics at the University of Rhode Island.

[1] The author thanks Zvonimir Baletić, Morris Bornstein, Mark S. Ellis, Ante Puljić, Bojana Ristich, and Borislav Škegro for many useful comments on earlier drafts of this study, while retaining sole responsibility for any remaining errors.

*Burkett appraises the extent to which the Yugoslav economy conformed to the five characteristics of a socialist regulated market economy with labor-managed enterprises specified in Vanek's model in Chapter 17.*

*Burkett concludes by analyzing the relationship between the Yugoslav economic system and the disintegration of the country in 1991.*

## THE ORIGIN AND EVOLUTION OF THE YUGOSLAV ECONOMIC SYSTEM

Before World War II Yugoslav communists drew their ideas largely from the writings of Central European Marxists and Russian Bolsheviks, who presumed that under socialism planning would triumph over "the anarchy of the market." The works of the neoclassical economists who conceived market socialism (Barone, Lange, Lerner, Taylor) were not influential in Yugoslavia.[2] The theory of the self-managed (or labor-managed) firm did not yet exist.[3] Thus when the Communist Party of Yugoslavia (CPY) took power at the end of the war, it at first attempted to build a Soviet-type economy, complete with imperative planning, one-man management, and collectivized agriculture.

The first step toward self-managed market socialism was taken as a pragmatic response to problems of external origin. In 1948 tensions between Yugoslavia and the Soviet Union over trade and politics reached a breaking point. Stalin denounced Tito while the Soviet Union and its East European satellites broke off trade with Yugoslavia. Needing to buttress its domestic political support, the Yugoslav government, after a brief attempt to prove itself more Stalinist than Stalin, adopted in 1950 a law under which formal managerial authority over state-owned enterprises was transferred to the workers. All workers in a firm were given the right to vote in referenda on basic issues such as mergers or sales of assets and in biennial elections to choose members of a workers' council, to which responsibility for other decisions was given. The council, typically meeting monthly, elected a management board to supervise day-to-day decisions. Members of the board, 75 percent of whom were sup-

---

[2] The seminal works on market socialism include the following: Enrico Barone, "Il ministro della produzione nello stato colletivista," *Giornale degli economisti* (1908), translated as "The Ministry of Production in the Collectivist State," in *Collectivist Economic Planning*, ed. F. A. Hayek (London: Routledge & Kegan Paul, 1935), pp. 245–90; Oskar Lange, "On the Economic Theory of Socialism," in Oskar Lange and Fred M. Taylor, *On the Economic Theory of Socialism*, ed. Benjamin E. Lippincott (Minneapolis: University of Minnesota Press, 1938), pp. 55–143; Abba P. Lerner, *The Economics of Control* (New York: Macmillan, 1944); Fred M. Taylor, "The Guidance of Production in a Socialist State," *American Economic Review* 19, no. 1 (March 1929), pp. 1–8, reprinted in Lange and Taylor, *On the Economic Theory of Socialism*, pp. 39–54. [See Chapter 16 in this book for a key portion of Lange's article—Editor.]

[3] The theory of self-managed enterprises was first developed by Benjamin Ward, "The Firm in Illyria: Market Syndicalism," *American Economic Review* 48, no. 4 (September 1958), pp. 566–89. A simple exposition is provided by Stephen R. Sacks, "The Yugoslav Firm," in the preceding chapter in this book.

posed to be production workers, were elected annually and could serve no more than two successive terms. Local government bodies retained a role in selecting enterprise directors.[4]

Needing to make the economy more responsive to rapidly changing circumstances of the late 1940s and early 1950s, the government abandoned short-run imperative planning of production, leaving enterprises to decide how best to utilize their plant and equipment. The government retained primary responsibility for investment and foreign trade.[5]

Central allocation of investment and foreign exchange became a focus of regional antagonism.[6] Representatives of the more developed regions (concentrated in Croatia and Slovenia) complained that resources generated on their territories were being diverted to unproductive use in less developed areas (concentrated in Bosnia and Hercegovina, Kosovo, Macedonia, and Montenegro). Representatives of the latter areas complained that the amount of assistance they received was inadequate to narrow the regional disparities in per capita income. To avoid protracted and divisive arguments in federal bodies over investment and foreign exchange allocation, the federal government decided to cede some of its allocative responsibilities to market forces, with the hoped-for side effect of increasing efficiency and enlarging the scope of self-management. Thus in the mid-1960s a second step toward full market socialism was undertaken.

The economic reform of the mid-1960s decentralized the investment mechanism, liberalized the foreign trade regime, and adjusted relative prices. Government investment funds were abolished and their assets transferred to banks, which were to be managed by assemblies of representatives of large investors (firms and government bodies), no one investor having more than 10 percent of the votes. The levies that had formerly fed the government investment funds were abolished, leaving enterprises in control of a larger share of their revenue. The foreign trade regime was liberalized by abolishing export premiums and tax rebates, lowering import tariffs, relaxing import quotas, and easing restrictions on obtaining import licenses. In preparation for the liberalization of foreign trade, domestic prices were restructured so as to more closely resemble world prices. This restructuring entailed raising the prices of raw and semiprocessed

---

[4] Christopher Prout, *Market Socialism in Yugoslavia* (Oxford: Oxford University Press, 1985), Chap. 2.

[5] See Dennison Rusinow, *The Yugoslav Experiment 1948–1974* (London: C. Hurst, 1977), and Fred Singleton, *Twentieth-Century Yugoslavia* (London: Macmillan, 1976).

[6] From 1945 to 1991, Yugoslavia was a federation of six republics: Bosnia and Hercegovina, Croatia, Macedonia, Montenegro, Serbia, and Slovenia. Serbia was further divided into Serbia proper and two autonomous provinces—Kosovo and Vojvodina. Before Yugoslavia was created in 1918, Bosnia and Hercegovina, Croatia, Slovenia, and Vojvodina were part of the Austro-Hungarian empire, while other parts of the country were independent states recently freed from the Ottoman empire. The regions' varied histories have left a legacy of uneven development, cultural differences, and linguistic barriers.

materials, agricultural products, and construction and transportation services relative to those of finished manufacturers.[7]

While the economic reform as a whole represented a step toward self-managed market socialism, one of its features was retrogressive with respect to Jaroslav Vanek's version of such a system: The tax on capital was reduced in 1965 from 6 to 4 percent and later abolished altogether. This contributed to excess demand for, and non-price rationing of, capital.

After the economic reform, systemic change continued, but without on the the whole bringing Yugoslavia closer to pure market socialism and self-management. The ambiguities of subsequent change are illustrated by a constitutional amendment adopted in December 1968 which modified self-management in two respects. First, firms were given greater discretion in choosing managerial structures. In particular, firms were no longer required to have a management board with three quarters of its membership drawn from production workers. The role of production workers in managerial decisions subsequently shrank in many firms. Second, the amendment gave to the workers' council exclusive authority to appoint and dismiss executives, thus curtailing the influence of local governments. The amendment was widely thought to have strengthened the authority of professional managers vis-à-vis both production workers and government bodies, an outcome protested by both the Trade Union Congress and the League of Communists of Yugoslavia (LCY, a new name for the CPY).[8]

The late 1960s were marked not only by a perceived shift in power from production workers and politicians to the managerial elite, but also by rising unemployment and inequality and a falling growth rate for national income. Dissatisfaction with these developments prompted the government to break large enterprises into semiautonomous Basic Organizations of Associated Labor (BOALs) and to introduce a system of multilateral bargaining. Under this system, economic agents—including government organizations, BOALs, enterprises, chambers of commerce, and trade unions—negotiated agreements called social compacts, dealing with, *inter alia*, incomes and prices. Within the framework of the compacts, economic agents entered into legally binding contracts called self-management agreements. To interpret and enforce the agreements, so-called courts of associated labor were created. This system of multilateral bargaining was codified in constitutional amendments adopted in 1971, a new constitution adopted in 1974, and a Law on Associated Labor adopted in 1976.[9]

---

[7] John P. Burkett, *The Effects of Economic Reform in Yugoslavia: Investment and Trade Policy, 1959–1976* (Berkeley: Institute of International Studies, University of California, 1983), pp. 1–9.

[8] Prout, *Market Socialism in Yugoslavia*, Chap. 2.

[9] Laura D'Andrea Tyson, *The Yugoslav Economic System and Its Performance in the 1970s* (Berkeley: Institute of International Studies, University of California, 1980), Chap. 1; Stephen R. Sacks, "The Yugoslav Firm"; David A. Dyker, *Yugoslavia: Socialism, Development and Debt* (London: Routledge, 1990), Chap. 4.

The system of social compacts and self-management agreements proved troublesome in three respects. First, the compacts and agreements took so long to negotiate that they could not counteract market disturbances in a timely manner. Second, bargaining between organized sellers and buyers commonly resulted in less efficient resource allocation than might be with either rational central planning or competitive markets.[10] Third, implementation—left up to decentralized agents—was frequently uneven or poorly coordinated.

Partly because of these problems with social compacts and self-management agreements, Yugoslav economic performance deteriorated in the late 1970s and early 1980s. In response to this deterioration, a comprehensive reexamination of the economic system and policy was undertaken in 1982 by a government-appointed Commission for Problems of Economic Stabilization. The commission's proposals were not entirely consistent, but their main thrust was in favor of a unified market economy. The proposals were endorsed by the Federal Assembly in July 1983 but were not generally implemented.[11] In practice, the system of multilateral bargaining remained largely intact until the late 1980s.

In late 1988 the commitment of the Yugoslav government to self-management and socialism began visibly to crumble. In December of that year the federal parliament adopted a Law on Enterprises, facilitating changes in ownership and management. The law legitimized private and mixed ownership and introduced joint-stock and limited-liability companies. It also abolished BOALs and curtailed self-management, strengthening the authority of directors and capital owners. It was followed in 1989 by laws legitimizing equity shares, capital markets, and sale of social assets to residents and foreigners. In 1990 Prime Minister Ante Marković made privatization a centerpiece of his economic reform program.[12]

Federal laws and programs had diminishing impact as republican governments arrogated increasing authority. The centrifugal forces triumphed in 1991: Croatia and Slovenia declared independence on June 25; Bosnia and Hercegovina and Macedonia soon followed, leaving Montenegro and Serbia alone in the federation. Civil wars ravaged Croatia and Bosnia and Hercegovina while an economic embargo weighed upon the rump federation. It is too soon to say

---

[10] Leif Johansen, "The Bargaining Society and the Inefficiency of Bargaining," *Kyklos* 32, no. 3 (1979), pp. 497–522.

[11] The commission's proposals are reminiscent of the economic reform of the mid-1960s. However, the commission did not stress this comparison, because the reform had been somewhat discredited. For a summary and analysis of the commission's proposals, see John P. Burkett, "Stabilization Measures in Yugoslavia: An Assessment of the Proposals of Yugoslavia's Commission for Problems of Economic Stabilization," in *East European Economies: Slow Growth in the 1980s* (Papers Submitted to the Joint Economic Committee, 99th Cong. 2nd Sess.) (Washington, D.C.: U.S. Government Printing Office, 1986), vol. 3. pp. 561–74.

[12] Organization for Economic Cooperation and Development (OECD), *Yugoslavia 1989/1990* (Paris, 1990), p. 48; Milica Uvalić, *Investment and Property Rights in Yugoslavia: The Long Transition to a Market Economy* (Cambridge, Eng.: Cambridge University Press, 1992), Chap. 9.

what political and economic arrangements may emerge from the third Balkan war. However, it is clear that none of the governments of the successor states of Yugoslavia is committed to market socialism and self-management.

Market socialism and self-management have never been more closely approximated on a national scale then they were in Yugoslavia, 1966–88. Hence, it is tempting and sometimes useful to interpret the Yugoslav experience in the light of models of market socialism and self-management. However, remembering that Yugoslavia's institutions were designed by Marxist politicians rather than by students of Lange or Vanek, we should be alert to possible discrepancies between models and reality. After surveying Yugoslav markets, government intervention, and economic performance, we will assess the extent of these discrepancies, the relevance of the Yugoslav experience for theories of market socialism, and the relation between Yugoslavia's economic system and the country's ultimate disintegration.[13]

Unless otherwise indicated, the following discussion pertains to the mature Yugoslav system, as it existed between from 1966 through 1988.

## MARKETS

Let us examine the markets for labor, consumer goods, material inputs, financial capital, and foreign exchange, in each case discussing first demand, then supply, and finally their balance and price adjustment.

### Labor

In the mid-1980s about 9 million individuals were reportedly employed in Yugoslavia, of whom 69 percent worked in the social sector and the remainder in the private sector. About three quarters of a million Yugoslavs were temporarily employed abroad, mostly in Western Europe.[14]

Within the social sector, the largest number of workers were in industry (39 percent) and trade and construction (10 percent each). Assuming that self-managed firms in the social sector maximized income per worker, we might expect their labor demand to have varied negatively with the price of their products. The expected negative relationship has been statistically verified for

---

[13] Because their survey is focused on Yugoslavia's relationship to self-managed market socialism, it passes over other interesting aspects of the Yugoslav economy. For these, see Dyker, *Yugoslavia: Socialism, Development and Debt;* Branko Horvat, *The Yugoslav Economic System* (White Plains, N.Y.: International Arts and Science Press, 1976); and World Bank, *Yugoslavia: Adjustment Policies and Development Perspectives* (Washington, D.C., 1983).

[14] See OECD, *Yugoslavia 1986/1987* (Paris, 1987), and *Statistički Godišnjak Jugoslavije 1987* (Statistical Yearbook of Yugoslavia 1987) (Belgrade: Savezni Zavod za Statistiku, 1987). The data on private-sector employment are unreliable because some individuals worked in the private sector without registering, while some registered workers—particularly in agriculture—were underemployed.

the Zagreb area, 1968–86.[15] Yet the impulse to adjust employment to maximize income per worker was constrained by three factors. First, solidarity among worker-managers usually precluded layoffs. Thus, employment could generally be reduced only by nonreplacement of workers who resigned or retired. Second, worker-managers sometimes created jobs for relatives and friends, even at the expense of lowering income per worker. Third, the pervasive influence of the political authorities made firms mindful of their priorities. (This point is elaborated below in the section on government intervention.) The limited tolerance of the political authorities for unemployment, conspicuous inequality, idle capacity, and income-inflation appears to have pushed employment beyond the levels that would be chosen in the absence of political pressures.

Some social-sector employers were large relative to their labor markets, five having more than 50,000 workers each and the 500 largest (in terms of revenue) accounting for 62 percent of social-sector employment. This high market concentration could adversely affect workers' interests under some systems but did not do so in Yugoslavia. Large capitalist employers might use their oligopsonistic power to hold down incomes by limiting employment; but labor-managed firms have no reason to do so. The concentration of employment in a few enterprises could limit the range of choice of working environments; however, the division of large enterprises into BOALs alleviated this problem.

Within the social sector, employment was provided not only by labor-managed firms, but also by government agencies. The latter's demand for labor depended primarily on administrative needs and secondarily on macroeconomic objectives.

Within the private sector, agriculture provided 81 percent of the employment. The responsiveness of labor demand to prices and wages may have been curtailed by laws forbidding private firms from employing more than 10 workers. However, most private firms employed fewer than the legal maximum, leaving room to expand when price and wage movements warranted. Entry of new firms further increased employment.

Foreign demand for Yugoslav labor varied with business conditions in Western Europe and developing countries. In the early 1970s labor shortages in Western Europe were filled by *gastarbeiters* (guest workers) drawn from neighboring countries, including Yugoslavia. Later, as West European labor markets grew more slack, the *gastarbeiters* were forced to return home. The number of Yugoslavs employed in West Germany declined from 535,000 in 1973 to 350,000 in 1985. When developing countries were enjoying favorable terms of trade and able to borrow freely, they employed a large number of Yugoslav specialists and construction workers. Later, unfavorable terms of trade and

---

[15] Michael L. Wyzan and John C. Leadley, "Local Labor Markets under Yugoslav Self-Management," *Advances in the Economic Analysis of Participatory and Labor-Managed Firms* 4 (1992), pp. 137–56.

heavy external debts reduced the demand of these countries for foreign labor. The total number of Yugoslavs employed abroad declined from 1,100,000 in 1973 to 710,000 in 1985.

The supply of labor in any country depends on the size and composition of the population and on parameters that influence household decisions. From 1975 to 1986 the population of Yugoslavia grew at an annual rate of 0.8 percent. The age structure of the population was such that the potential labor force grew 1.0 percent a year, little faster than the population. These growth rates were similar to those in other South European countries. More unusual was Yugoslavia's strong regional dispersion of growth rates. The population growth rates for 1975–86 ranged from 0.3 percent in Croatia to 2.3 percent in Kosovo.[16]

The parameters influencing labor supply behavior include wages, prices, taxes, the availability of consumer goods and assets that can serve as a store of value, and the provisions for working parents. Real incomes rose steadily through 1978, declined through 1984, and stagnated thereafter, with an uncertain effect on labor supply. Inflation, which was chronic, would normally reduce the real value of financial assets, increasing the labor supply. However, Yugoslavs held a large fraction of financial assets in foreign exchange, the purchasing power of which was unaffected when inflation was matched by depreciation of the dinar (the Yugoslav currency).

Personal income tax rates were so low for most people that they cannot have had a major influence on labor supply. Tax was paid on income above three times the average level in the relevant republic or province. The rate rose from 3 to 80 percent, but the top rate applied to very few people.

If consumer goods are unavailable, people may see little point in earning money, particularly if no suitable stores of value are available. The availability of consumer goods, more erratic in Yugoslavia than in developed capitalist countries, varied over time, deteriorating in the early 1980s as imports were curbed and domestic goods were diverted to export markets, but improving in the mid-1980s as consumer purchasing power declined. Even when shelves in social-sector stores were bare, goods were available from private-sector vendors. Yugoslavs considered foreign exchange and real estate acceptable stores of value; hence temporary shortages of consumer goods were not likely to reduce labor supply appreciably.

Provisions for working parents were generous by U.S. standards. Mothers were eligible for a year of maternity leave. Publicly supported nurseries accepted children at an early age. Thanks to the persistence of extended-family households, grandparents were frequently available for babysitting. As of 1986 the share of women in social-sector employment was 38.3 percent for Yugoslavia as a whole. The share varied regionally from 22.3 percent in Kosovo,

---

[16] See Emile Primorac and M. F. Charette, "Regional Aspects of Youth Unemployment in Yugoslavia," *Economic Analysis and Workers' Management 21*, no. 1 (1987), pp. 193–219, and OECD, *Yugoslavia 1986/87*, pp. 94–96.

where traditional Moslem attitudes still prevailed, to 45.9 percent in Slovenia. It varied by industry as well, from 9.8 percent in construction to 75.8 percent in health and social services.

Unions may affect the terms on which labor is supplied. Close to 6 million Yugoslavs belonged to the Federation of Unions. However, this body was not ordinarily a major economic force. In the social sector, labor management deprived unions of much of their *raison d'être*. In the private sector, family and social ties among workers and employers in minuscule firms had the same effect. In any case, the unions—led by the LCY—could not be considered an independent force.

Strikes were tolerated and became frequent after real incomes fell 28 percent from 1978 to 1984. (There were nearly 1,000 strikes in the first nine months of 1987).[17] Among frequent causes of strikes were workers' opposition to incomes policy, workers' distrust of their elected managers, and disputes among BOALs over whose pay was to be docked when the joint earnings of several BOALs fell.

Imbalances between demand and supply in the labor market appear as unemployment and job vacancies. Approximately 1 million individuals were registered as unemployed in the mid-1980s, although some of these were attending school or working while seeking another job. Some 700,000 were genuinely jobless and actively seeking work.[18] To these might be added an unknown number of discouraged workers.

When the number of firms and the size of their capital stock are given, their demand for labor need not equal the supply. Unemployed workers may be willing to work for less than the going rate of pay, but labor-managed firms, unlike textbook capitalist firms, will not willingly hire them if doing so entails lowering income per worker.[19]

Entry of new firms and accumulation of capital could reduce unemployment to frictional levels, but Yugoslavia made little visible progress in this direction. One reason why unemployment persisted despite entry of new firms, even in periods of rapid capital accumulation, was that the creation of well-paid industrial jobs drew migrants out of the low-income private agricultural sector, replenishing the pool of urban unemployed.[20] Unlike the Soviet Union or China, Yugoslavia did not forcibly stop the migration. In this respect Yugoslavia more closely resembled a developing capitalist country than a centrally planned economy.

---

[17] Strike data come from "Restless Slav Soldiers," *The Economist*, October 3, 1987, p. 18.

[18] OECD, *Yugoslavia 1986/1987*, p. 11.

[19] The textbook capitalist firm employs just enough labor so that labor's marginal value product equals a market-clearing wage. However, persistent unemployment in capitalist countries and the theory of efficiency wages suggest that real-world capitalist firms may elect to pay a wage above market-clearing levels so as to make the threat of firing a spur to productivity.

[20] Will Bartlett, "Migration and Unemployment in Yugoslavia, 1958–1977" (Working Paper no. 90; Florence: European University Institute, 1984).

The incidence of unemployment was uneven. Unemployment was concentrated among new entrants to the labor market because layoffs were rare. Many of the new entrants were highly educated young people; thus the cost of unemployment in terms of lost output was substantial. New entrants were not eligible for unemployment insurance, so they typically depended on relatives for support. Some young people extended their education to receive student stipends while looking for work.

Unemployment was concentrated in the less developed republics and provinces, in part because that is where population growth rates were highest. The ratio of registered unemployed to employed ranged from .018 in Solvenia to .491 in Kosovo. (These figures must be taken with a grain of salt because some individuals registered as unemployed in one republic or province may have been employed in another.)

In 1986, there were about 88,430 jobs vacancies in Yugoslavia—that is, about 1 for every 12 job seekers. The ratio of vacancies to job seekers ranged from .013 in Kosovo to .666 in Slovenia. Unemployment and vacancies coexisted because the unemployed were not in the right locations, did not have the appropriate skills, or were not aware of the vacancies.[21]

Earnings as well as unemployment and vacancy rates varied among republics and provinces. The inter-regional coefficient of variation for income of unskilled workers hovered around .10 from 1963 to 1984, showing no secular tendency to rise or fall.[22] Linguistic and cultural differences retarded the flow of labor from regions with high unemployment, few vacancies, and low incomes to those with low unemployment, many vacancies, and high incomes.

In a labor-managed market economy, firms in which labor has a high marginal product and enjoys a high income have no incentive to hire workers away from firms in which labor has a lower marginal product and a lower income. Due to this labor market imperfection (and a capital market imperfection discussed below), inequalities of incomes and marginal products may persist unless eliminated by the entry of new firms in high-income industries.[23]

## Consumer Goods

Demand for consumer goods, like the supply of labor, depends on population size and composition and on the parameters influencing household decisions. Having examined the population trends and some of the parameters above, we

---

[21] OECD, *Yugoslavia 1986/1987*, pp. 10–11.

[22] The coefficient of variation is a measure of dispersion, defined as the ratio of the standard deviation to the mean. Time series for the coefficient of variation for incomes of unskilled workers are reported in John P. Burkett and Borislav Škegro, "Are Economic Fractures Widening?" in *Yugoslavia: A Fractured Federalism,* ed. Dennison Rusinow (Washington, D.C.: Wilson Center, 1988), pp. 142–55.

[23] Saul Estrin and Jan Svejnar, "Explanations of Earnings in Yugoslavia: The Capital and Labor Schools Compared," *Economic Analysis and Workers' Management* 19, no. 1 (1985), pp. 1–11.

need only add a few comments. Because of unemployment, labor income was a parameter rather than a decision variable for many households. Because consumer credit was rationed, consumption was commonly constrained by liquidity rather than by prospective income. Because little wealth was held in dinar-denominated financial assets, the real balance effect was muted. Consumer demand thus depended primarily on current disposable income and the supply of credit. In the 1980s real incomes declined faster than employment rose, causing a fall in real personal income and consumer demand.[24]

Foreign demand for Yugoslav-produced consumer goods varied with the robustness of foreign economies and their degree of protectionism. Yugoslav economists feared that the Common Market in Western Europe and the Council for Mutual Economic Assistance in Eastern Europe might divert trade opportunities from nonmembers such as Yugoslavia.[25] Nonetheless, foreigners bought substantial amounts of Yugoslav-produced clothing and footwear, food, furniture, medicines, beverages, and tobacco. Among Yugoslavia's biggest customers for consumer goods were East and West Germany, the Soviet Union, and the United States. The problems of selling to East Germany and the Soviet Union, on the one hand, and West Germany and the United States, on the other, were different. The socialist trade partners tended to be more insistent on bilateral trade balance, while the capitalist trade partners tended to be fussier about product quality.

The supply of consumer goods comprised products of the social and private sectors and imported goods. The social-sector producers were dominant in industry, where market concentration was high. Data on the incidence of monopoly and oligopoly in consumer-oriented industries are set out in Table 19–1. Even in markets where there were as many as eight producers, regional barriers to trade may have meant there was only one supplier in each republic or province. A law against monopolies was adopted in 1974 but was not enforced.[26]

In view of the high degree of market concentration, one might guess that the price and quantity of industrial consumer goods were determined by monopolistic or oligopolistic firms pursuing high incomes per worker, constrained only by technology and the prices of material inputs. However, producers operated under three additional constraints. First, they were rationed in the markets for some inputs—notably capital and imported materials. Second, output prices were subject to various forms of government regulation that effectively flattened the demand curve facing producers (except when the regu-

---

[24] OECD, *Yugoslavia 1986/1987*, pp. 9–13.

[25] In the 1980s the Common Market accorded Yugoslavia's manufactures liberal treatment while maintaining protective barriers against its agricultural products. See Mark S. Ellis, "Yugoslavia's Exports to the European Economic Community—An Analysis of the 1980 Cooperation Agreement," *Economic Analysis and Workers Management* 21, no. 1 (1987), pp. 49–94.

[26] OECD, *Yugoslavia 1984/85* (Paris, 1985), p. 50.

**TABLE 19–1**   Incidence of Monopoly and Oligopoly in Consumer-Oriented
Industries, 1985

| | *Number of Divisions** | | |
| *Industry* | *Total* | *With One Producer* | *With Eight or Fewer Pro-ducers* |
| --- | --- | --- | --- |
| Final wood products | 112 | 4 | 38 |
| Finished textile products | 101 | 7 | 36 |
| Leather footwear and accessories | 50 | 2 | 14 |
| Food products | 221 | 22 | 90 |
| Beverages | 24 | 2 | 10 |
| Final tobacco products | 4 | 1 | 3 |

* Editor's note: In the Yugoslav industrial classification, *divisions* are disaggregated product subgroups, for example, types of food products or beverages.

SOURCE: *Industrijski proizvodi 1985* (Statistički Bilten 1589) [*Industrial Products 1985* (Statistical Bulletin 1589)] (Belgrade: Savezni Zavod za Statistiku, 1987).

latory bodies raised prices to alleviate shortages). Third, the political authorities had limited tolerance for monopolistic restraint on output and employment.

As a result of these constraints, the output of many firms was determined by input availability rather than consumer demand. The automobile industry illustrates the point. One producer, Crvena Zastava (Red Flag), accounted for 72 percent of domestic production. Despite the high degree of market concentration, output was limited by capacity, materials, and energy, not by demand.[27] In 1983 automobile workers on average were idle 12.1 hours a month due to a lack of materials, energy, and the like. Customers waited months for new cars after making down payments. Low-mileage secondhand cars sold for about the same price as new ones, despite the higher proportion of "lemons" among the former.

Private enterprises were common in agriculture, crafts, transportation, construction, and food, lodging, and tourist services. Due to the limits on employment, all private enterprises were small-scale producers. How closely private-sector markets approximated perfect competition depended mainly on the availability of information. Agricultural markets were highly competitive because information was easy to collect. Walking from booth to booth in a farmer's market, one could quickly gather information on the asking price, quantity, and quality of produce. After a little haggling, farmers and customers

---

[27] "The Passenger Car Industry," *Yugoslav Survey* 27, no. 2 (1986), pp. 89–104.

agreed on something close to a competitive equilibrium price. In some other private-sector markets, information was hard to obtain. Through friends and relations, customers could locate one or two plumbers, electricians, and the like. But it was hard to form an accurate estimate of a market-clearing price for their services. Sometimes services were performed more on the basis of reciprocity than of exchange.

The supply of imported consumer goods depended on government policy, which we will discuss below. Here we note simply that the government usually rationed foreign exchange and gave lowest priority to consumer goods. Food, beverages, and tobacco—which account for most important consumer goods—amounted to only 3.2 percent of total imports in 1985. When foreign exchange shortages were severe, imported consumer goods vanished from shelves.[28] Major suppliers of consumer goods included Brazil, the Soviet Union, the United States, and West Germany.

Imbalances between the supply and demand for consumer goods, including both shortage and slack, were common. Shortage was manifest in queues, waiting lists, and bare shelves. Slack was manifest in large inventories, idle capacity, and intensive advertising. Shortage and slack coexisted because of mismatches between the commodity composition of demand and supply and because of regional barriers to trade, both due in part to price controls. An example of the effect of price controls is found in the bread market. By law, the price of whole-wheat bread was lower than that of white bread. The ratio of whole-wheat to white bread in a baker's output was subject to a legally fixed minimum, but this ratio did not match the ratio in demand at the legally determined prices. Stores commonly sold out of whole-wheat bread early in the morning and were left with stale white bread when they closed in the evening.

Prices under the control of republican, provincial, and local authorities varied widely and induced barriers to inter-regional trade. For example, prices of regulated fruits and vegetables differed across regions by up to 78 percent, with predictable consequences:

> For produce in excess supply (e.g., grapes), regions with higher prices erect barriers to imports from those with lower prices. Fruit sometimes spoils in one area while it is unavailable in another. For products in excess demand (e.g., grain, potatoes), regions with low prices set up barriers to export to those with higher prices. For example, in 1982 the authorities of Bosnia and Hercegovina searched trucks headed toward Slovenia in an effort to interdict wheat exports.[29]

---

[28] OECD, *Yugoslavia 1986/1987*, pp. 70–71. Despite occasionally empty shelves, Yugoslav consumers were usually better supplied with imported goods than were their counterparts in some centrally planned economies. *Gastarbeiters* and vacationers returning from Western Europe brought a greater volume of consumer goods into Yugoslavia than into more closed centrally planned economies. According to one joke, a Yugoslav complains to an American and a Russian companion, "Nema banana" (There are no bananas). The American asks, "What does *nema* mean?" The Russian asks, "What does *banana* mean?"

[29] Burkett and Škegro, "Are Economic Fractures Widening?" p. 143.

Apart from price controls, another barrier to inter-regional trade was the underdeveloped condition of transportation. Freight trains moved as slowly in the 1980s as they did before World War II. In the absence of a federal highway program, road-building reflected and exacerbated regional divisions. Highway connections within each republic (and sometimes between a republic and a foreign country) were better than among republics. Coastal shipping was negligible. Transport costs were substantially higher than in other comparable European countries.[30]

Such regional trade barriers were chronic, antedating the economic and political crises of the 1980s. Indeed, trade barriers were probably even more formidable in pre-World War II, capitalist Yugoslavia. Long-run changes in trade barriers are most clearly revealed by trends in regional variation of prices of homogeneous tradable goods. The prices of five such goods—potatoes, beans, prunes, firewood, and laundry soap—are available from 1926 to 1988 (except for a hiatus around World War II) for 10 Yugoslav cities—Banja Luka and Sarajevo in Bosnia, Split and Zagreb in Croatia, Skoplje in Macedonia, Centinje (Titgrad) in Montenegro, Belgrade, Niš, and Novi Sad in Serbia, and Ljubljana in Slovenia.[31] From the 10 local prices we can compute a coefficient of variation (CV) for each year and good. The CV for each good is higher on average before World War II than after, but increases in the late 1980s.

To obtain a summary indicator of regional price dispersion, we calculate the mean of the 10 *CVs* and plot it in Figure 19–1. From this figure we see that price dispersion was generally higher in the capitalist period (1926–39) than in the following socialist period (1953–88), but rose sharply at the close of the latter. Thus the data provide no basis for blaming socialism for the balkanization of markets for consumer goods.

Relative prices were substantially different in post-war Yugoslavia than in the United States. Some of the differences at a disaggregated level are attributable to a Yugoslav policy of imposing price controls on commodities consumed by the poor and taxes on those consumed by the rich. For example, in Yugoslavia milk, bread, and cigarettes were cheap relative to butter, meat, and cigars.

At a more aggregate level, other differences in relative prices appear. By American standards Yugoslav prices of housing, medical care, recreation, and education were relatively low, while those of food, beverages, tobacco, clothing, footwear, home furnishings, and private transportation were high. However, these aggregate-level differences were not significantly greater than those which can be attributed to differences between the two countries in per capita income and population. (Nontraded goods and services tend to be relatively cheap in poorer and more populous countries.) Thus Yugoslav and U.S. policies and systems did not contribute significantly to relative price differences at

---

[30] OECD: *Yugoslavia 1984/1985* (Paris, 1984), and *Yugoslavia 1989/1990*.

[31] Price data are taken from *Jugoslavia 1918–1988: Statistički godišnjak* [Yugoslavia 1918–1988: Statistical Yearbook] (Belgrade: Savezni Zavod za Statistiku, 1989).

**FIGURE 19–1**    Regional Price Dispersion in Yugoslavia, 1926–1988: Mean Coefficient of Variation of Prices of Five Consumer Goods

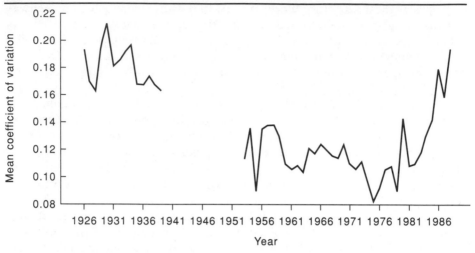

the aggregate level. In contrast, differences in policy and system did contribute significantly to aggregate-level relative price differences between Hungary, Poland, and Romania, on the one hand, and the United States, on the other. Thus, insofar as aggregate-level relative prices are concerned, Yugoslavia was more like a capitalist economy than a centrally planned socialist economy.[32]

## Material Inputs

Demand for material inputs (materials, fuels, machinery, land), expressed by firms in the social and private sectors and by foreign firms, depended on the nature of the firms' budget constraints. Insofar as firms faced hard budget constraints—that is, the necessity of financing purchases from sales at given prices—their demand necessarily depended on prices of inputs and outputs. However, social-sector firms generally faced soft budget constraints in the sense that they anticipated subsidies or price adjustments when they were insolvent but otherwise inoffensive to the political authorities.[33] As a result, demand by social-sector firms was insensitive to prices and in some cases apparently boundless.

---

[32] John P. Burkett, "Determinants of Distance between Price Vectors" (unpublished manuscript). The data are derived from Irving B. Kravis, Alan Heston, and Robert Summers, *World Product and Income: International Comparisons of Real Gross Product* (Baltimore: Johns Hopkins University Press, 1982).

[33] The concepts of hard and soft budget constraints are elaborated in János Kornai, *Economics of Shortage* (Amsterdam: North-Holland Publishing Company, 1980), and "The Soft Budget Constraint," *Kyklos* 39, no. 1 (1986), pp. 3–30. The concepts are applied in the Yugoslav context by Evan Kraft and Milan Vodopivec, "How Soft Is the Budget Constraint for Yugoslav Firms?" *Journal of Comparative Economics* 16, no. 3 (September 1992), pp. 432–55.

The insensitivity of social-sector firms to prices was egregious in the aftermath of oil price increases in 1974 and 1979. Oil-burning power stations found it easier to obtain financial relief than to reduce oil consumption by switching to cheaper fuels or adopting fuel conservation measures. Partly as a result, the ratio of energy consumption to national product was practically unchanged between 1974 and the early 1980s.[34]

The insatiable appetite of some social-sector firms is illustrated by the case of Agrokomerc, a large Bosnian-based processor of agricultural products. Not content with the inputs it could purchase with current revenue, it issued uncovered promissory notes to purchase inputs valued at several hundred billion dinars (several hundred million dollars at 1987 exchange rates). When its financial skullduggery was revealed in 1987, its general manager was expelled from the central committee of the LCY and arrested on fraud charges.[35] His fate may mean that an astute manager should have exercised more self-restraint in issuing promissory notes or merely been more careful in picking political patrons. Enterprises with politically ascendant patrons commonly got away with issuing uncovered promissory notes, although perhaps not on the scale of Agrokomerc.

Private-sector demand for material inputs depends on the prices of private-sector products, wage rates, and of course the prices of the producer goods themselves. Because the private sector was concentrated in agriculture, its demand for material inputs was mainly for farm machinery, fertilizers, fuels, and land. No agricultural household could legally own land in excess of 10 hectares (20 in some mountainous regions). (One hectare equals 2.47 acres.)

Among the largest foreign buyers of Yugoslav-produced material inputs were the Soviet Union and East and West Germany. The sluggish growth of these economies in the 1980s made it difficult for Yugoslavia to expand rapidly its exports of producer goods. Foreigners were prohibited from purchasing land in Yugoslavia, although long-term leases were permitted.

Excess demand for material inputs was common. In the mid-1980s power plants, sugar mills, slaughterhouses, and automobile factories operated at a fraction of capacity for lack of material inputs.[36] Agriculture was sometimes constrained at harvest time by fuel shortages. Price controls and the price insensitivity of social-sector firms prevented prices from clearing markets. The authorities set low relative prices for material inputs in hopes of stimulating growth of processing industries.

## Financial Capital

In financial markets demand was expressed by social- and private-sector firms, households, and government bodies. Social-sector firms' demand for loans,

---

[34] John P. Burkett, "Search, Selection, and Shortage in an Industry Composed of Labor-Managed Firms," *Journal of Comparative Economics* 10, no. 1 (March 1986), pp. 26–40.

[35] "Yugoslavia's IOUs," *The Economist,* September 26, 1987, pp. 79–80.

[36] OECD, *Yugoslavia 1984/1985,* p. 46.

like their demand for producer goods, was practically boundless, and for similar reasons. A firm did not worry much about repaying loans because its political patrons could arrange to have debt forgiven or rolled over indefinitely. Private-sector firms and households, unlike social-sector firms, faced hard budget constraints. Hence they had to weigh the expected rate of return to investment against the rate of interest. However, the real rate of interest was usually well below zero; thus even projects with a negative rate of return were worth undertaking. As a result, private-sector demand for loans was also practically unlimited. Government bodies borrowed from the National Bank of Yugoslavia (NBY) when their expenditure exceeded revenue.

The supply of credit depended on firms, households, and the banking system. Firms, households, and government bodies maintained dinar bank accounts for transaction purposes. Households also maintained foreign exchange accounts as stores of value. Banks re-lent these funds, subject to regulations imposed by the NBY. Apart from credit extended through the banking system, there was a large volume of direct inter-enterprise credit, induced in part by negative real interest rates paid on bank deposits. Enterprises with money to lend often could get a higher interest rate if they bypassed the banking system.

Excess demand for credit was common. Interest rates did not rise to market-clearing levels because banks were controlled by social-sector firms (large borrowers) and government bodies, which preferred cheap credit rationed according to rules of their own choosing. Because the use of capital was subsidized and rationed, the allocation of capital was an important determinant of income distribution.[37]

## Foreign Exchange

In foreign exchange markets the suppliers included exporters, Yugoslavs working abroad, foreign tourists in Yugoslavia, and recipients of foreign loans. On the demand side were importers, Yugoslavs preparing to travel abroad, firms and government bodies with foreign debts to pay off, and households seeking a liquid store of value or wishing to buy goods that were available only in exchange for foreign currencies. Eleven authorized banks bought and sold foreign currencies at rates controlled by the NBY. At these official prices there was usually excess demand and rationing of foreign currencies. Starting in 1986 exporters were required to sell all of their foreign exchange earnings to the banks. When selling foreign exchange, banks were required to give priority to customers servicing debt obligations and importing inputs for export-oriented industries. Because foreign currencies were underpriced and because banks were regionally based, the market for foreign currencies was regionally seg-

---

[37] Estrin and Svejnar, "Explanations of Earnings in Yugoslavia," make an interesting attempt to measure the capital rents appropriated by workers in various industries. Their estimates of capital rents per worker are negatively correlated with other income per worker, suggesting the existence of income-leveling mechanisms.

mented. On the black market the dinar price of dollars, German marks, and other "hard" currencies averaged about 10 percent higher than the official price. The spread between official and black market rates was smallest during the summer tourist season and around the time of holidays (chiefly Christmas and Easter) for which *gastarbeiters* returned home.

## GOVERNMENT INTERVENTION

Let us examine the identity, instruments, and objectives of government policy-makers. Policy-making authority was widely dispersed. At the federal level, ultimate policy-making authority rested in principle with an Assembly comprised of two chambers, one for representatives of republics and provinces and one for delegates from industrial branches. The constitution required the Assembly to adopt important measures by unanimous vote of republican and provincial delegations, except when the Federal Executive Council (FEC) proposed "temporary" measures, which could be passed by majority vote of the delegates. Each December or January the Assembly adopted a resolution concerning economic policy for the coming year.[38]

Implementation of the resolution was the responsibility of the FEC and the NBY. These and all other federal bodies were staffed so as to ensure representation of each republic and province. The policy instruments of the FEC included tax rates, government expenditure, price and incomes controls, and foreign trade regulations. Its power was enhanced by its role as a broker of deals codified in social compacts and self-management agreements. The NBY's instruments included reserve requirements, discount rates, and extension of selective credits to priority sectors. (In the absence of a bond market, open market operations were not feasible.)[39]

Below the federal level were republican and provincial governments, where decision making was concentrated in the 1980s. These not only managed the affairs of their regions and oversaw county and city governments, but also selected representatives to federal bodies and enforced their interpretations of federal laws. The combination of geographic decentralization and intra-regional centralization led some Yugoslavs to say, half in jest and half in sorrow, that their economy was feudal.

---

[38] For more information on the Yugoslav political system, see Steven L. Burg, *Conflict and Cohesion in Socialist Yugoslavia: Political Decision Making Since 1966* (Princeton: Princeton University Press, 1983), and "Elite Conflict in Post-Tito Yugoslavia," *Soviet Studies* 38, no. 2 (April 1986), pp. 170–93; and Susan L. Woodward, "Orthodoxy and Solidarity: Competing Claims and International Adjustment in Yugoslavia," *International Organization* 40, no. 2 (Spring 1986), pp. 505–45.

[39] See Shirley J. Gedeon, "The Post-Keynesian Theory of Money: A Summary and an Eastern European Example," *Journal of Post-Keynesian Economics* 8, no. 2 (Winter 1985–86) pp. 208–21, and "Monetary Disequilibrium and Bank Reform Proposals in Yugoslavia: Paternalism and the Economy," *Soviet Studies* 39, no. 2 (April 1987), pp. 281–91.

The LCY played a leading role in all government bodies. When it functioned as a centralized party, it could coordinate the actions of nominally independent government bodies. Until 1969 a relatively high degree of unity was maintained through central appointment of leading cadres, but after that date the power to appoint party functionaries devolved to the republican and provincial levels. President Tito continued to serve as a supreme arbiter until his death in 1980. Afterward, in the opinion of many observers, the LCY functioned as a federation of regionally based parties. In 1989 the Central Committee of the LCY was dissolved and the republican leagues went their separate ways.

The economic role of government bodies went beyond enterprise regulation and macroeconomic management as these are understood in capitalist countries. Government bodies protected from the rigors of competition those enterprises that stayed ''on line''—that is, compliant with the desires of political leaders. But the same bodies could make much trouble for an errant enterprise by simply enforcing the bewildering array of inconsistent and widely ignored regulations to which all enterprises were nominally subject. In short, the political authorities directed the economy by what may be called, with apologies to Adam Smith, invisible hand-holding and arm-twisting. An insider aptly characterized the Yugoslav system as a mixture of anarchy and totalitarianism.[40]

Turning from the instruments to the objectives of policymakers, we must first note that economic goals were often subordinate to other concerns. At the federal level the overriding concern frequently was maintaining Yugoslavia's precarious independence and unity. At lower levels, primary objectives varied regionally. The first concern of Croatian and Slovene policymakers often was to keep the federal authorities at arm's length. Policymakers in Serbia proper, Kosovo, and Vojvodina were frequently preoccupied with struggles over how much autonomy should be accorded to autonomous provinces. Policymakers in Bosnia and Hercegovina, Montenegro, and Macedonia probably gave higher priority to certain economic objectives, principally the industrialization of their comparatively backward republics.

The pursuit of noneconomic goals sometimes had economic consequences. Seeking to maintain Yugoslavia's position as an independent non-aligned country, federal authorities encouraged a roughly equal tripartite division of trade among centrally planned, developed capitalist, and third world countries. Promoting its own autonomy and status, each republic built its own steel mill. Such practices—examples of which could be multiplied—probably resulted in loss of economies of scale in marketing and production.

When federal policymakers took time to consider economic affairs, their dominant concern, like that of policymakers in the less developed republics, was industrialization. Federal policy resolutions usually set higher growth rate

---

[40] A Yugoslav industrial expert quoted in *The Economist,* August 11, 1979, pp. 42–45.

targets for industry than for agriculture or services. (Concern about the environmental impact of industralization was minimal. The prevailing attitude was that environmental protection was a luxury to be deferred until a higher level of development was attained.[41]) In the 1980s high priority was given to increasing exports and restraining imports so as to reduce Yugoslavia's large external debt.

The fullest statement of federal objectives was contained in the Assembly's annual policy resolutions. Among the targets typically set by these resolutions were growth rates for social product,[42] gross investment in fixed assets, employment in the social sector, living standards, industrial production, agricultural production, exports, imports, the money supply, housing construction, and production of selected fuels and foods. While the setting of macroeconomic targets (e.g., employment and money supply) is a common practice in contemporary market economies, the setting of specific targets for critical products (e.g., coal and wheat) is rather unusual and may be best explained as a holdover from material-balance planning as practiced in the first years of Yugoslav socialism.

## PERFORMANCE

The economic performance of a country is determined not only by its economic system but also by its environment and its leaders' policies. To isolate the effects of the system, we should compare Yugoslavia to other countries that had similar environments and policies but different economic systems. Unfortunately, no very close matches exist. We shall have to make do with comparisons of Yugoslavia in the heyday of self-management to its own past and to broadly similar South and East European countries.

As was indicated in the introduction, the Yugoslav economy has passed through three phases within the era during which the political authorities espoused self-management: (1) decentralized production decisions combined with centralized investment and foreign trade decisions in the 1950s and early 1960s; (2) a market-oriented economy with only sporadic central intervention in the late 1960s and early 1970s; and (3) a system of multilateral bargaining codified in the 1974 constitution and abandoned in 1989. Indicators of economic performance in these three phases appear in Table 19–2, from which we can see that employment, fixed assets, and output grew more slowly in the second period than in the first. (The decline in the growth rate of fixed assets occurred despite an increase in the share of investment in social product, because the rising capital-output ratio increased the share of depreciation in social product.)

---

[41] Nenad Starc, "Development of Project Appraisal Methodology in Air Polluting Industries in Eastern Europe," in *Environmental Consequences of Energy Production: Problems and Prospects,* ed. Shyamul K. Majumdar, Fred J. Brenner, and E. Willard Miller (Easton, Pa.: Pennsylvania Academy of Science, 1987), pp. 198–211.

[42] *Social product* is a measure of output, similar to gross domestic product, but omitting some services.

**TABLE 19–2**    Yugoslav Economic Performance in Three Periods, 1950–1988
(in percent)

| Performance Indicator | 1950–1965 | 1966–1973 | 1974–1988 |
|---|---|---|---|
| Growth rate of employment in social sector | 4.3 | 2.7 | 3.1 |
| Growth rate of fixed assets in social sector | 8.7* | 8.0 | 5.0 |
| Share of gross investment in social product | 29.5* | 30.1 | 29.2 |
| Growth rate of total social product | 6.6 | 5.5 | 2.5 |
| Growth rate of social product in social sector | 7.5 | 6.2 | 2.8 |
| Growth rate of output per worker in social sector | 3.2 | 3.5 | −0.3 |
| Exports as a percent of imports | 65.8 | 67.1 | 70.8 |
| Inflation rate for retail prices | 5.8* | 11.0 | 48.4 |

* 1952–65.

SOURCES: *Statistički Godišnjak Jugoslavije* [Statistical Yearbook of Yugoslavia] for 1973, 1977, 1982, 1987, and 1990 (Belgrade: Savezni Zavod za Statistiku, 1973, 1977, 1982, 1987, and 1990).

The inflation rate nearly doubled from the first to the second period. The only positive developments were slight increases in the trade balance and the growth rate of output per worker. From the second to the third period employment growth accelerated, while the growth of fixed assets and output slowed. Output per worker stopped growing and even declined slightly. The trade balance improved a little while the inflation rate more than quadrupled.

Nonsystemic factors bear partial responsibility for the deterioration of performance. These nonsystemic factors include the increase in oil prices in 1974 and 1979, the ensuing decline in West European demand for imports and *gastarbeiters,* the tightening of world financial markets in the 1980s, and the depletion of opportunities for technology transfer.[43] However, econometric experiments in counterfactual history suggest that the economic reform of the mid-1960s also bears partial responsibility for the deterioration of perfor-

---

[43] Opportunities for technology transfer decrease as a country raises its technological level relative to that of the technological leaders. Until the mid-1970s Yugoslavia appears to have been catching up with the leaders. The growth rate of total factor productivity has been estimated to have been around 4.8 percent per year in Yugoslavia during 1955–74. See Andre Sapir, "Economic Growth and Factor Substitution: What Happened to the Yugoslav Miracle?" *Economic Journal* 90, no. 358 (June 1980), pp. 294–313. The long-term growth rates of total factor productivity in the United States and the Soviet Union have been estimated at around 2.3 percent by Martin Weitzman, "Soviet Postwar Economic Growth and Capital-Labor Substitution," *American Economic Review* 60, no. 4 (September 1970), pp. 676–92, or less by E. Bairam, "Soviet Postwar Industrial Growth and Capital-Labor Substitution: An Empirical Note," *Economics Letters* 24, no. 4 (1987), pp. 331–34. If these estimates are comparable, we may infer that the ratio of the Yugoslav technology level to that of the United States or the Soviet Union rose by about 2.5 percent or more per year until the mid-1970s. Preliminary evidence suggests that the Yugoslav rate of technological progress has since declined.

mance.[44] Considering the inefficiency of most bargaining processes, it would not be surprising if the system formalized in the 1974 constitution were partially to blame as well.

Table 19–3 contains data for Yugoslavia, five centrally planned socialist countries of Eastern Europe (Bulgaria, Hungary, Poland, Romania, and the USSR),[45] and five capitalist economies of Southern Europe (Greece, Italy, Portugal, Spain, and Turkey). These countries were at roughly similar levels of economic development circa 1980, as indicated by per capita gross domestic product (GDP) data shown in the first row of Table 19–3. Hence we might expect differences in performance to be largely the result of differences in policy and system.

The second and third rows of Table 19–3 display data on two indicators of basic-needs fulfillment: life expectancy and literacy. Life expectancy in Yugoslavia was within the ranges found in the centrally planned and capitalist countries. The literacy rate in Yugoslavia was below the range found in the centrally planned economies but within the range found in capitalist countries.

The fourth row of Table 19–3 displays data on the average annual growth rate of per capita real GDP.[46] There are not enough of these data to permit clear comparisons of the growth rates of Yugoslavia and centrally planned economies.[47] However, the growth rate for Yugoslavia was within the range found in the capitalist countries.

The fifth and sixth rows of Table 19–3 display data on two dimensions of macroeconomic performance—inflation and unemployment. The average

---

[44] See Burkett, *The Effects of Economic Reform in Yugoslavia,* and Sapir, "Economic Growth and Factor Substitution."

[45] Bulgaria, Hungary, Poland, Romania, and the USSR were all centrally planned economies in the 1950s. Hungary, Poland, and the USSR introduced elements of market socialism in 1968, 1981, and 1986, respectively. Poland and Hungary took steps toward self-management in 1982 and 1985. For a survey of the evolution of these countries, see János Kornai, *The Socialist System: The Political Economy of Communism* (Princeton: Princeton University Press, 1992), especially Chapters 20–21.

[46] These are the latest estimates based on measurements of national GDPs at purchasing power parity. They should be more accurate than those based on measurement of GDPs at market exchange rates, which do not reflect prices of nontraded goods. See Robert Summers and Alan Heston, "The Penn World Table (Mark 5): An Expanded Set of International Comparisons, 1950–1988," *Quarterly Journal of Economics* 106, no. 2 (May 1991), pp. 327–68.

[47] The data in Heston and Summers (1991) cover only four socialist countries: China (1960–88), Hungary (1973–88), Poland (1980–87), and Yugoslavia (1960–87). GDP per capita rose more rapidly in China than in Yugoslavia, perhaps because China had more catching up to do. Growth was more rapid in Hungary than in Yugoslavia, 1973–88, during most of which period self-management was less developed in Hungary than Yugoslavia. GDP per capita stagnated in Yugoslavia and fell in Poland, 1980–87, during most of which period Poland as well as Yugoslavia had elements of self-managed market socialism. Cruder data for 1965–84 indicate that the average annual growth rate of per capita output (in percent) was higher in Yugoslavia (4.3) than in Poland (1.5) and Romania (3.5) but lower than in Hungary (6.3). See *Statistički Kalendar Jugoslavije 1987* [Statistical Almanac of Yugoslavia 1987] (Belgrade: Savezni Zavod za Statistiku, 1987), pp. 197–99.

**TABLE 19–3**    Economic Performance of Yugoslavia and Selected Other European
Countries

| Performance Indicator | Yugoslavia | Bulgaria | Hungary |
|---|---|---|---|
| Gross domestic product per capita, 1980 ($) | 3,318 | 3,437 | 3,861 |
| Life expectancy, circa 1984 (years) | 69 | 71 | 70 |
| Adult literacy, circa 1980 (%) | 83.5 | 90.6 | 98.9 |
| Growth rate of per capita GDP, 1960–88 (%) | 3.8[a] | — | 3.2[b] |
| Inflation rate, 1963–88 (%) | 32.7 | 1.3[c] | 4.4 |
| Unemployment rate, 1986 (%) | 10.5 | — | — |
| Sulphur dioxide emission (kg. per $1,000 of GDP) | 17.9 | 32.4 | 36.4 |

[a] 1960–87. [b] 1973–88. [c] 1963–87. [d] 1963–82.

SOURCES: Gross domestic product per capita is given in Robert Summers and Alan Heston, "Improved International Comparisons of Real Product and Its Composition: 1950–1980," *Review of Income and Wealth* 30 no. 2 (June 1984), pp. 207–64. Life expectancy is reported in *Statistički Kalendar Jugoslavije, 1987* [Statistical Almanac of Yugoslavia, 1987] (Belgrade: Savezni Zavod za Statistiku, 1987), pp. 197–99. Adult literacy is reported in United Nations Conference on Trade and Development, *Handbook of International Trade and Development Statistics, 1985 Supplement* (New York, 1985), pp. 504–08. Growth rates of per capita GDP are derived from Robert Summers and Alan Heston, "The Penn World Table (Mark 5): An Expanded Set of International Comparisons, 1950–1988," *Quarterly Journal of Economics* 106, no. 2 (May 1991), pp. 327–68. Inflation rates are calculated from consumer price indices given in United Nations, *Statistical Yearbook*, for

annual inflation rate for Yugoslavia was above the rates in the centrally planned economies and at the upper end of the range found in the capitalist economies.

Unemployment rates are difficult to compare across countries. The Yugoslav unemployment rate given in Table 19–3 is exaggerated by the inclusion of employed job-seekers with the unemployed. Correcting for this bias would reduce the Yugoslav unemployment rate to about 7 percent. No unemployment statistics are available for the centrally planned economies, but it is safe to say that open unemployment was lower in these countries than in Yugoslavia. The unemployment rates in the capitalist countries bracketed the unadjusted figure for Yugoslavia and exceeded the adjusted figure.

The last row of Table 19–3 shows data on the emission of sulphur dioxide, one of the most important pollutants and the only one for which internationally comparable data are available. Sulphur dioxide emissions per dollar of GDP were lower in Yugoslavia than in the centrally planned economies, but within the range found in the capitalist countries. Noting that the primary emitters of sulphur dioxide were power plants, we may account for the emissions per dollar of GDP by examining data on emissions per unit of energy consumption and on energy consumption per dollar of GDP. Yugoslav emissions per unit of energy consumption were within the ranges observed in both the centrally

| Poland | Romania | USSR | Greece | Italy | Portugal | Spain | Turkey |
|--------|---------|------|--------|-------|----------|-------|--------|
| 3509 | 2766 | 3943 | 3946 | 4661 | 3092 | 4264 | 2069 |
| 71 | 71 | 67 | 75 | 77 | 74 | 77 | 64 |
| 98.8 | 89.0 | 99.8 | 84.4 | 93.9 | 71.0 | 92.6 | 68.8 |
| — | — | — | 4.1 | 3.6 | 4.4 | 3.7 | 2.8 |
| 11.7 | 0.8[d] | 0.4 | 12.4 | 9.9 | 12.2 | 11.1 | 33.0 |
| — | — | — | 9.0 | 10.1 | 10.3 | 21.5 | 17.3 |
| 23.3 | 32.6 | — | 19.1 | 18.5 | 5.9 | 13.4 | 11.6 |

1972, 1982, and 1988/89 (New York, 1973, 1985, and 1992) and United Nations, *Monthly Bulletin of Statistics,* July 1991. The consumer price index for Portugal was first recorded for 1976. I have extended the Portuguese series back to 1963 using a cost-of-living index for Lisbon reported in B. R. Mitchell, *International Historical Statistics: Europe, 1750–1988* (3rd ed.; New York: Stockton Press, 1991), pp. 849–50. The unemployment rate for Italy is from United Nations, *Monthly Bulletin of Statistics,* July 1987, pp. 17–20. For other countries the unemployment data are from United Nations, Economic Commission for Europe, *Economic Survey of Europe 1986–87* (Geneva, 1987), p. 58. Sulphur dioxide emissions for 1978 are reported in Nenad Starc, "Development of Project Appraisal Methodology in Air Polluting Industries in Eastern Europe," in *Environmental Consequences of Energy Production: Problems and Prospects,* ed. Shyamul K. Majumdar, Fred J. Brenner, and E. Willard Miller (Easton, Pa.: Pennsylvania Academy of Science, 1987), pp. 198–211.

planned and the capitalist economies.[48] Yugoslavia made no special effort to reduce emissions per unit of energy consumption. No regulations on sulphur dioxide emissions were adopted, and none of Yugoslavia's coal-fired power plants used desulphurization devices.[49] Yugoslav energy consumption per dollar of GDP was lower than that in the centrally planned economies but within the range found in the capitalist economies.

## THEORIES OF MARKET SOCIALISM AND THE EXPERIENCE OF YUGOSLAVIA

The five defining characteristics of Vanek's version of market socialism are: equal participation in management, income sharing, payment for use of capital, free markets, and freedom of employment.[50] In Yugoslavia, participation in

---

[48] Data on energy consumption come from *Statistički Kalendar Jugoslavije 1982* [Statistical Almanac of Yugoslavia 1982] (Belgrade: Savezni Zavod za Statistiku, 1982), pp. 197–99.

[49] Starc, "Development of Project Appraisal Methodology in Polluting Industries in Eastern Europe."

[50] Jaroslav Vanek, *The Participatory Economy: An Evolutionary Hypothesis and a Strategy for Development* (Ithaca, N.Y.: Cornell University Press, 1971).

management, income sharing, and freedom of employment were the norm, but payment for capital and free markets were not.[51] As we have seen, real interest rates were negative and the tax on capital was abolished. In effect society paid enterprises to use capital rather than vice versa. Markets were subject to a vast number of rapidly changing, contradictory, and unevenly enforced regulations. To survive in this environment enterprise directors had to oblige the politicians who influenced capital allocation and decided which regulations to enforce against whom.

János Kornai has observed that a state-owned firm in Hungary operated "in a condition of dual dependence": vertical dependence on the state and horizontal dependence on suppliers and customers.[52] The same could have been said of socially owned firms in Yugoslavia. However, the state in Yugoslavia as compared to that in Hungary was more fragmented and more inclined to fire-fighting than to planning. A Yugoslav firm subject to inconsistent regulations may have had more autonomy than a Hungarian firm subject to consistent regulations, but its autonomy was not of the sort enjoyed by a firm in a free market economy.[53]

Turning from structural characteristics to behavior, we may start by asking whether Yugoslav firms maximized income per worker. Two bases for doubt exist. First, incomes policy from time to time imposed a binding constraint on income per worker. During these periods, enterprises which otherwise would have maximized income per worker had to pursue some secondary objective— say, minimizing effort per worker or maximizing investment per worker.

The second and more fundamental basis for doubt is that maximization problems are well defined only if information about constraints (or at least information about the cost of such information) is freely available.[54] Free availability of information may be a useful simplifying assumption when considering a firm operating in a free market where the only relevant information concerns parametric prices and established technologies. However, free availability of information is a far-fetched notion when applied to a firm operating in an environment as politicized as that of socialist Yugoslavia. To formulate, let alone solve, the problem of maximizing income per worker, a Yugoslav enterprise director would have needed to know not only all relevant prices and regulations, but also the attitudes of the political authorities who decided which

---

[51] In practice, the extent of workers' participation in management varies from firm to firm. Of course the same is true of stockholders' participation in management of capitalist firms.

[52] "The Hungarian Reform Process: Visions, Hopes, and Reality," *Journal of Economic Literature* 24, no. 4 (December 1986), pp. 1693–97.

[53] Firms must oblige politicians even in some capitalist countries, particularly in the Third World. For examples, see "The Qualities in Common" and "New Stars from the East and South," *The Economist,* December 26, 1987, pp. 86–88. However, I have the impression that in less developed capitalist countries politicians are often primarily interested in bribes, whereas in Yugoslavia and Hungary they were mainly interested in "on-line" behavior.

[54] Sidney G. Winter, "Economic 'Natural Selection' and the Theory of the Firm," *Yale Economic Essays* 4, no. 1 (1964), pp. 229–30.

regulations to enforce against whom. What were the authorities' tolerance levels for unemployment, inflation, inequality, corruption, and so forth? Information on these matters was not, even to a first approximation, freely available, nor was there information about the cost of such information. Enterprise directors wined and dined politicians in hopes of eliciting such information, but the payoff was uncertain. If the problem of maximizing income per worker was not well defined in the Yugoslav environment, then Yugoslav enterprises could only "satisfice"—that is, follow rules of thumb that had yielded satisfactory results in the past, while searching for alternative rules that might yield better results.[55]

Bearing in mind that the Yugoslav economy had only three out of five of the characteristics postulated by Vanek and that Yugoslav firms were unlikely to consistently maximize income per worker, we should not be surprised if the performance of the Yugoslav economy did not match expectations for a labor-managed market economy. It is an interesting but difficult task to distinguish deviations in performance due to flaws in Vanek's reasoning from those due to discrepancies between Vanek's postulates and Yugoslav reality. Let us try to make the distinction in five areas where Vanek expects a labor-managed market economy to outperform capitalist economies.

First, Vanek argues that firms in a labor-managed economy would be small enough to make markets competitive. However, as we have seen, many product markets in Yugoslavia were dominated by a few large firms. Even some of the differentiated oligopolies, where Vanek expects labor-management to contribute most to competitiveness, were highly concentrated. The high degree of concentration found in some markets was due in large part to the small size of the country and the fondness of politicians for building factories on a monumental scale. Vanek's reasoning may be correct, but we will not have practical proof of it until a larger and less politicized economy adopts labor management.

Second, Vanek argues that a labor-managed market economy would eliminate strikes and other costly forms of economic conflict. But Yugoslav experience shows that fusing labor with management does not eliminate intra-enterprise conflict. BOAL may clash with BOAL; workers may feel betrayed by their elected representatives; an indispensable minority of workers may rebel against majority rule. Even when intra-enterprise relations are harmonious, strikes may be directed against incomes policies or regulations that impose costs on enterprise members. Vanek's error is to suppose that conflict between labor and capital—doubtlessly the predominant cause of industrial strife in capitalist economies—is the only possible one. A labor-managed socialist economy may have its own sources of industrial strife.

Third, Vanek asserts that recessions would be less frequent and severe in a labor-managed market economy than in a capitalist economy. This claim is

---

[55] Burkett, "Search, Selection, and Shortage in an Industry Composed of Labor-Managed Firms."

consistent with Yugoslav experience. Indeed between 1960 and 1987 there was never a year-to-year fall in Yugoslav industrial production, a record that few capitalist economies could match.[56] This stability was due in part to the reluctance of labor-managed firms to lay off workers and in part to the Yugoslav government's consistent emphasis on industrial growth.

Fourth, Vanek hypothesizes that a labor-managed market economy would be less inflation-prone than capitalist economies. However, as we have seen, the Yugoslav inflation rate was at the upper end of the range found in South European capitalist countries. The discrepancy between Vanek's expectation and Yugoslav reality is due in part to an erroneous assumption about capitalist economies and in part to deviations of the Yugoslav system from Vanek's conception of labor management. Vanek assumes that under capitalism there is a trade-off between inflation and unemployment and that policymakers adopt inflationary policies in pursuit of full employment. This assumption was shared by many economists in 1971, when Vanek advanced his hypothesis. Since then, however, policymakers in major capitalist countries have come to believe that there is no usable long-run trade-off between inflation and unemployment. The restrictive monetary policies adopted by these policymakers have sharply reduced inflation.

Both the underpricing of capital and political patronage contributed to inflation. The former was associated with negative real interest rates on bank deposits, which caused disintermediation—that is, withdrawal of funds from banks—and stimulated inter-enterprise credits. To the extent that credit flows bypassed the banking system, the NBY lost control over the money supply.

Political patronage to firms further stimulated the growth of inter-enterprise credit. As noted, Yugoslav firms with powerful political patrons showed little restraint in issuing IOUs in payment for goods. Their suppliers were willing to accept the IOUs because the issuer's patron stood behind them. The patrons were organized in rival regional groups. Each group hoped to expand its claim on national resources by monetizing the IOUs issued by its firms. Under the circumstances, the NBY had only a limited ability to restrain the growth of means of payment.

Fifth, Vanek argues that labor management has an advantage over capitalism in controlling pollution because workers, unlike capitalists, must live near their factories, breathing their smoke and drinking water tainted with their

---

[56] Industrial production fell about 1 percent from 1987 to 1988, marking the onset of what proved to be the terminal crisis of Yugoslav socialism. By the first quarter of 1991 industrial production was 20 percent below its 1985 level. The data on industrial production are reported in OECD, *Main Economic Indicators* (Paris, various issues). While Yugoslav industrial production exhibited no year-to-year falls, it did exhibit growth cycles of substantial amplitude. These cycles were weakly correlated with, and lagged behind, those of OECD Europe. See Branko Horvat, "Business Cycles in Yugoslavia," *Eastern European Economics* 9, nos. 3–4 (Spring–Summer 1971), pp. 1–259; and OECD, *OECD Leading Indicators and Business Cycles in Member Countries 1960–1985* (Main Economic Indicators, Sources and Methods, no. 39; Paris, 1987).

effluents. If sulphur dioxide emissions are indicative of overall pollution levels, then Vanek's conclusion is false as applied to Yugoslavia. The discrepancy between Vanek's expectation and the relative performance of Yugoslavia and capitalist economies is due to three factors overlooked by Vanek:

1. Many pollutants quickly diffuse over a wide area, with the result that people living near the source of pollution bear only a small part of its costs. Sulphur dioxide in particular is an airborne pollutant that can inflict its damage thousands of miles from its point of emission. The incentives to adopt costly pollution control measures may be inadequate regardless of whether the decision makers are workers living in the vicinity of their factory or capitalists living far away.

2. The insidious effects of many pollutants first come to the attention of educated elites. Understanding that sulphur dioxide causes acid rain and hence deforestation is only now spreading out of the scientific community. Thus informational considerations make it doubtful that workers' management reduces pollution.

3. When enterprise managers do not take the initiative in controlling pollution, public authorities may do so. Legislation has played an important role in controlling pollution in capitalist countries. It did not play a role in Yugoslavia because legislators there had other priorities. Efforts to deal with externalities extending across republican boundaries often succumbed to nationalist bickering.[57]

## THE DISINTEGRATION OF YUGOSLAVIA

What was the relationship between the Yugoslav economic system as it developed between 1950 and 1988 and the disintegration of the country in 1991? Was the disintegration a delayed effect of the system? Did the breakdown of political commitment to the system and the rise of pro-capitalist parties cause the disintegration? Or was the relationship less direct?

Definitive answers to such questions might elude even a generously funded interdisciplinary research institute. However, tentative answers are within the reach of anyone willing to compare Yugoslavia with other multinational states.

Three multinational Communist states, each with a different stance toward market socialism and self-management, disintegrated in 1991–92: Czechoslovakia, the USSR, and Yugoslavia. Czechoslovakia remained a centrally planned economy until the 1989 revolution brought pro-capitalist parties to power. The

---

[57] Yugoslav environmentalists were most successful when they confronted a localized pollution problem and were able to enlist the support of enterprises catering to foreign tourists, as in the case of Lake Palić. They were least successful when pollution problems crossed republican boundaries, as in the case of the Sava River. On this point, see Barbara Jančar, "Ecology and Self-Management: A Balance-Sheet for the 1980s," in *Yugoslavia in Transition*, ed. John B. Allcock, John J. Horton, and Marko Milivojević (New York: Berg Publishers, 1992), pp. 337–64.

country never adopted market socialism or self-management. It split into the Czech Republic and Slovakia on January 1, 1993. The USSR remained a centrally planned economy until Mikhail Gorbachev started his ill-fated economic and political experiments in the late 1980s. While the rhetoric of *perestroika* included references to self-management and market socialism, nothing resembling a coherent system of self-managed market socialism took root prior to the dissolution of the Union in December 1991. Thus Yugoslavia was the only one of the three countries in which significant elements of self-managed market socialism were well established prior to disintegration. Self-managed market socialism evidently is not a necessary condition for disintegration. It may or may not be sufficient; one case makes inconclusive evidence.

Pro-capitalist forces were gaining ground when Czechoslovakia, the USSR, and Yugoslavia disintegrated. However, privatization had not proceeded far before disintegration occurred. Thus capitalism does not appear to be a necessary condition for disintegration. Capitalism plainly is not sufficient to cause disintegration of multinational states, since Belgium, Canada, and Switzerland still cohere.

An indirect connection between Yugoslavia's economic system and the county's disintegration is suggested by the tendency in Communist states for party discipline and central authority to decay over time, providing opportunities for subordinates to assert themselves.[58] The forms of decentralization vary with local traditions and conditions.[59] In countries where the central authorities need to make a populist or anti-bureaucratic appeal, they may introduce self-management. Where the authorities lose confidence in their ability to plan, they may introduce markets. Self-management and market socialism may turn out to be transitional forms in the restoration of capitalism. In multinational states, the Communist Party may split into factions espousing rival nationalisms. These conditions happened to coincide in Yugoslavia. Thus the drift from central planning through elements of self-managed market socialism toward capitalism and the rise of secessionist movements can be viewed as joint products, under Balkan conditions, of the decay of Communist authority.

## CONCLUSIONS AND PROSPECTS

Yugoslavia adopted three out of five institutions proclaimed by Vanek as characteristic of labor-managed market socialism, albeit for political reasons remote from Vanek's theoretical case for such a system. These institutions operated most freely following the 1965 economic reform. Unfortunately, the perfor-

---

[58] The decay of central authority in Communist states has parallels in other systems. A classic account of the decay of Bedouin dynasties is given by Ibn Khaldûn, *The Muqaddimah: An Introduction to History,* trans. Franz Rosenthal (Princeton: Princeton University Press, 1967).

[59] On the rise of pluralism in other Communist countries, see Kornai, *The Socialist System,* Chap. 18.

mance of the Yugoslav economy deteriorated after the reform and probably in part because of it.

Yugoslavia's post-reform economic performance, compared to that of either centrally planned or capitalist economies, exhibited a mixture of strengths and weaknesses. Compared to East European centrally planned economies, Yugoslavia performed poorly in the areas of literacy, inflation, and unemployment; unexceptionally with respect to life expectancy and growth; and outstandingly in terms of pollution control, or—more precisely—energy conservation. Compared to the performance of South European capitalist economies, that of Yugoslavia was poor in inflation; unexceptional in the areas of life expectancy, literacy, growth, and pollution; and probably superior in terms of unemployment.

Out of five areas in which Vanek expects a labor-managed market economy to outperform capitalist economies, Yugoslavia showed superior performance in only one—avoiding recessions. In the four remaining areas Yugoslav performance was disappointing, in part because Vanek's expectations for a labor-managed market economy are exaggerated and in part because Yugoslavia did not adopt two features of Vanek's model—free markets and a market-clearing price for capital.

Yugoslavia could probably have made its economy more competitive, more efficient, and less inflation-prone by ending the patronage relations between political authorities and firms and raising the price of capital to something like a market-clearing level. Why, then, did it not do so? An obvious answer is that the political authorities opposed changes that would curb their influence. This answer is correct but incomplete. A fuller answer must take into account the interests of workers in social-sector firms.

Ending the patronage relationship and pricing capital at near market-clearing levels would have made workers true residual income claimants and risk bearers. These would have been onerous roles for two reasons. First, workers—unlike shareholders—cannot easily reduce their risks because they hold no diversifiable portfolios. Second, workers in a labor-managed market economy—unlike their counterparts in a textbook capitalist economy—cannot easily find alternative employment because their labor markets do not clear in the short run.

Workers might have been more willing to give up their partrons' protection and subsidized capital if alternative means of shifting risk had been available. Two possibilities, consistent with self-management, come to mind: income insurance and contingent contracts. However, the feasibility of these alternatives is doubtful.

Income insurance is problematic for two reasons. First, to surmount problems of moral hazard, insurers would have to be able to distinguish avoidable and unavoidable losses. Second, to assure their solvency, insurers would have to limit their liability for widespread losses due to macroeconomic disturbances. Contingent financial contracts could in principle shift most risks from workers to lenders. However, the transaction costs of preparing and enforcing such detailed contracts would be prohibitive.[60] In the absence of income insurance and contingent contracts, risk-averse workers could have reasonably preferred the Yugoslav patronage system to pure labor-managed market socialism.

The Yugoslav patronage system probably could have been refined so as to perform a little better while retaining important elements of self-managed market socialism. However, by the late 1980s many Yugoslavs had grown weary of constant institutional tinkering in search of a third way between centrally planned socialism and capitalism. Some suspected that the third way led to the third world. When the centrally planned economies began to collapse at the end of the decade, capitalism appeared to many Yugoslavs as the only remaining alternative.

What are the economic prospects for the successor states of Yugoslavia? Replacing one medium-sized country with five or more small ones may be cheap or costly, depending on how it is done. Small countries can prosper—witness Luxembourg and Lichtenstein. However, their prosperity is critically dependent on peace and free trade with neighboring countries. Unfortunately the disintegration of Yugoslavia has been anything but peaceful. Over 100,000 people are believed to have been killed. Countless young men have left their jobs to join militias or seek refuge abroad. Employment in the economic sector fell 9 percent from 1990 to 1991. The shelling of cities has caused untold destruction of factories, houses, and offices. International and inter-regional trade has been badly disrupted. From 1990 to 1991 the volume of imports fell 25 percent, the number of nights spent by foreign tourists in Yugoslavia fell 87 percent, and the volume of goods transported over Yugoslav roads fell 30 percent. Inevitably, the loss of manpower, the destruction of physical capital, and the disruption of trade have thrown the economy into a tailspin. From 1990 to 1991 industrial production fell 20 percent.[61] Further economic decline is likely.

The republics seceding from Yugoslavia may have hoped to enter the more prosperous European Community. However, the Community is unlikely to admit them until they are at peace and have accorded their minorities the rights characteristic of European democracies. Thus, until the warring parties reach a compromise, put down their arms, return to work, and resume trade, no economic system can bring prosperity to the Balkans.

---

[60] Jacques H. Drèze, *Labor Management, Contracts, and Capital Markets: A General Equilibrium Approach* (New York: Basil Blackwell, 1989).

[61] *Indeks* [Belgrade], no. 3, 1992.

# Suggestions for Further Reading
# for Part III

## Market Socialism

Le Grand, Julian, and Saul Estrin, eds. *Market Socialism*. Oxford: Clarendon Press, 1989.

Yunker, James A. *Socialism Revised and Modernized: The Case for Pragmatic Market Socialism*. New York: Praeger Publishers, 1992.

## Labor-Managed Enterprises

Ireland, Norman J. *The Economics of Labor-Managed Enterprises*. London: Croom Helm, 1982.

Jackall, Robert, and Henry M. Levin, eds. *Worker Cooperatives in America*. Berkeley, Calif.: University of California Press, 1984.

Mellor, Mary, *Worker Cooperatives in Theory and Practice*. Milton Keynes, England, and Philadelphia: Open University Press, 1988.

Stephen, Frank H. *The Economic Analysis of Producers' Cooperatives*. London: Macmillan, 1984.

———, ed. *The Performance of Labor-Managed Firms*. London: Macmillan, 1982.

Whyte, William F., and Kathleen K. Whyte. *Making Mondragon: The Growth and Dynamics of the Worker Cooperative Complex*. Ithaca, N.Y.: ILR Press, 1988.

## Yugoslavia

Allcock, John B.; John H. Horton; and Marko Milivojevic, eds. *Yugoslavia in Transition: Choices and Constraints*. New York: Berg Publishers, 1992.

Dyker, David A. *Yugoslavia: Socialism, Development, and Debt*. London: Routledge, 1990.

Flakierski, Henryk. *The Economic System and Income Distribution in Yugoslavia*. Armonk, N.Y.: M. E. Sharpe, Inc., 1989.

Lydall, Harold. *Yugoslav Socialism: Theory and Practice*. Oxford: Clarendon Press, 1984.

———. *Yugoslavia in Crisis*. Oxford: Clarendon Press, 1989.

Uvalić, Milica. *Investment and Property Rights in Yugoslavia: The Long Transition to a Market Economy*. Cambridge, England: Cambridge University Press, 1992.

# Part IV

# Socialist Planned Economies and Their Reform

Socialist centrally planned economies (SCPEs) have three main features. (1) Most of the means of production are owned collectively. (2) Government agencies engage in comprehensive and detailed planning and control of most aspects of economic life, in response to planners', rather than consumers', sovereignty. (3) Resources are allocated primarily by administrative "commands" in real (physical) terms—such as production assignments, allocation orders, and rationing—rather than chiefly by markets and prices.

Many SCPEs are now undergoing dramatic reforms affecting property ownership, resource allocation, and income distribution that introduce elements of capitalist regulated market economies.

Chapter 20 explains the key characteristics of SCPEs, their advantages and disadvantages, and efforts to change them through economic reforms.

Chapter 21 analyzes measures to transform SCPEs, such as macroeconomic stabilization, liberalization of markets and prices, restructuring or privatization of state enterprises, and changes in the role of the state in the economy.

Chapter 22 discusses special problems in the reform of agriculture in SCPEs, including curtailment of food subsidies, decollectivization, and reorganization of supply, processing, and marketing activities related to farming.

Chapter 23 is a detailed case study of the nature and operation of the Soviet centrally planned economy, which served as the prototype for other Communist countries. Chapter 24 then examines economic reforms in the successor states of the former USSR.

The next three chapters concern economic reforms in Eastern Europe. (Sometimes the terms *Central Europe* and *Eastern Europe* are used to distinguish a northern tier of Poland, Czechoslovakia, and Hungary in "Central" Europe and a southern tier of Romania and Bulgaria in "Eastern" Europe.) Chapter 25 analyzes privatization and its links to other dimensions of economic reform, such as macroeconomic adjustment, marketization, restructuring, and integration with the world economy. Chapters 26 and 27 present, respectively, a West European and an East European view of the main problems of economic reform in Eastern Europe.

Chapters 28 and 29 consider economic reforms in China. Chapter 28 provides a comprehensive survey and appraisal of China's economic reforms in agriculture, industry, finance, labor, and foreign economic relations. Chapter 29 discusses six key lessons of China's economic reform experience, and their possible applicability in other countries.

*Chapter Twenty*

# The Traditional Centrally Planned Economy and Its Reform*

*Alan A. Brown*

*and*

*Egon Neuberger*

*This chapter provides a comprehensive explanation of the key features of a centrally planned economy (CPE), its advantages and disadvantages, and efforts to change it through economic reforms.*

*The CPE's main objectives are rapid growth and structural change (namely, industrialization) through centralized control of economic activity based on public ownership of the means of production. As a result, the CPE has distinctive features such as a clear set of national priorities, detailed planning of production and distribution in physical terms, and administrative orders to implement ambitious plan assignments for enterprises. Central planning also involves vertical rather than horizontal coordination of economic activity, discontinuous planning, and multiple performance criteria.*

*Central planning can mobilize resources of labor and capital, modify the social structure and the income distribution, alter branch and regional development rates, stabilize prices and wages, and attenuate the effects on the domestic economy from changes in the world economy.*

*But the CPE suffers from many kinds of inefficiency in central planning and administration, from domestic prices and foreign exchange rates that do not reflect relative scarcities, and from ineffective incentive systems. The deficiences of*

* This essay is a revised and considerably expanded version of Alan A. Brown and Egon Neuberger, "Basic Features of a Centrally Planned Economy," in *International Trade and Central Planning: An Analysis of Economic Interactions*, ed. Alan A. Brown and Egon Neuberger (Berkeley and Los Angeles: University of California Press, 1968), pp. 405–14. Original version copyright © 1968 by the Regents of the University of California; reprinted by permission of the University of California Press. New material copyright © 1993 by Alan A. Brown and Egon Neuberger; used with permission. Alan A. Brown is Professor of Economics at the University of Windsor (Canada), and Egon Neuberger is Leading Professor of Economics at the State University of New York at Stony Brook.

*central planning are only partly compensated for by selective violation of instructions in the state sector and by an unplanned "second" economy operating in addition to centrally planned activities.*

*As an economy grows and matures, it moves from an "extensive" phase of development relying primarily on the increase of factor inputs, to an "intensive" phase requiring increases in factor productivity. In the latter phase, the shortcomings of central planning become more apparent, and pressure mounts for economic reforms that decentralize, marketize, and privatize the economic system.*

We may identify the basic features of a traditional, Soviet-type centrally planned economy (CPE) in terms of its objectives and modi operandi. These are considered in sequence under five major headings: objectives and key elements, command economy and planning mechanisms, desired effects, undesired consequences, and adjustment mechanisms. This type of pure model of a Soviet-type CPE represents a relatively satisfactory simplified description of actual economies for a long period of time (from the 1930s to 1980s in the Soviet Union). The model was also adopted after World War II in the countries of Eastern Europe, as well as in China, North Korea, and North Vietnam, and subsequently in Cuba. In Yugoslavia, the model was abandoned in the early 1950s, and in Hungary a series of major modifications were initiated in the late 1960s.

Starting in the late 1970s, there has been accelerating pressure for reforms in other CPEs. These reforms attempted to institute a significantly modified CPE (MCPE), moving toward some type of market socialism. In the late 1980s, this attempt was abandoned and most CPEs shifted to a much more drastic path of reform. Many of the European CPEs, including Russia, adopted programs to transform the CPE or MCPE into a true market economy. In the section on Economic Reforms and Systemic Transformation, we discuss the reasons for reforms, obstacles to reforms (legacies of the CPE), the nature of the partial reforms, and the economics of systemic transformation from CPE to market economy.

## OBJECTIVES AND KEY ELEMENTS

### Objectives[1]

**Rapid Growth and Industralization.**    Planners in traditional CPEs aim at a very high rate of economic growth, as a rule much higher than the rate maintained in market-type economies (MTEs). Not all economic sectors, however, are promoted equally; the result is unbalanced growth. Expansion of industrial sectors is stressed—more specifically, producers' goods and particularly certain heavy industries, such as mining, metallurgy, and machinery production. Attempts to

---

[1] Although preference functions are obviously multidimensional, we attempt to call attention here only to those goals explicitly and strongly stressed by planners.

satisfy an ever-increasing demand for industrial inputs lead to a chronic neglect of agriculture, a trend enhanced by the planners' ideological orientation (i.e., their mistrust and fear of the peasantry). Unbalanced industrial growth is generally pursued without regard for the relative resource endowment of individual CPEs.

**Centralization.**   This term is a shorthand expression that includes both *centralized planning* and *centralized control* of economic activities. Thus, centralization means, on the one hand, that important planning decisions are reserved to the system's directors (to use Abram Bergson's felicitous expression), and, on the other, that decisions are communicated to operational units by direct commands or directives. Centralization implies both concentration of decision-making authority in the center, and a system-wide, hierarchical use of this authority. Of course, effective centralization also implies that the system's directors are able to control the implementation of their decisions by motivating all agents to comply. This requires a system of appropriate positive and/or negative centralized incentives. Centralization, it may be added, is at once an important policy objective and a modus operandi of the system (via certain mechanisms to be discussed below). The planners have a revealed preference for centralization *per se*, pursuing it even at the expense of growth.

**Social Ownership.**   For the most part there is public ownership of the means of production. Manufacturing industry, mining, transportation and communication, banking and finance, and domestic wholesale trade and most of retail trade are nationalized. Foreign trade is a state monopoly. In agriculture, most of the land is owned by the state or by state-controlled, large-scale cooperatives. While social ownership represents one of the independent ideological objectives, it is also a means of achieving the goal of centralization, since ownership is an important source of decision-making power.

## Key Elements

The basic goals of rapid growth, centralization, and social ownership provide direction to the system. The following five key elements represent a relatively complete shorthand description of the CPE.

**Command Economy.**   This involves centralized *bureaucratic* management of the economy with detailed physical planning and supply. (This key element is discussed in much greater detail below.)

**Pressure Economy.**   The key objective of rapid growth leads to increasingly ambitious plans, even when these are not justified by economic conditions; for example, the creation of taut plans which mandate excessively high increases of outputs, given the low levels of inputs and inventories. The underlying rationale is that the pressure will force everyone to work harder than under equilibrium plans. The pressure economy also involves high rates of forced saving (i.e., severely limited consumption) in order to finance massive investments.

**Priority Economy.**   Planning is based on priorities reflecting the dominance of political and ideological criteria over economic considerations in the overall formulation of economic policy; for example, primacy of industry over agriculture, of producer goods over consumer goods, and of material goods over services—except for high priority of education, especially technical education of the labor force.

**Extensive Development.**   This is a method of achieving rapid growth of output by means of massive infusions of labor and capital inputs rather than by "intensive development" (i.e., increasing the productivity of labor and capital, through improved technology, organization, or motivation). In the Soviet Union, as in other CPEs, this was accomplished by massive migrations of labor from agriculture to industry, by major increases in female labor participation rates, and by very large investment resources created by the pressure economy.

**Closed Economy.**   Domestic economic considerations predominate over the exigencies of foreign trade—foreign trade plans being merely addenda to domestic plans. The import plan is mainly based on shortages in the domestic production plan, while the export plan, consisting mainly of domestic surpluses, is designed to earn the foreign exchange needed to pay for imports. This approach reflects the underlying philosophy of "trade aversion" (i.e., that trade is a necessary evil), which ignores the potential gains from trade through specialization. The closed economy is an instrument of both aspects of centralization: central control and central planning.

    In sum, the three basic objectives (rapid growth, centralization, and social ownership), along with the first key element (the command economy) constitute the defining features of the CPE economic system. (Frequently, a shorthand reference to a CPE is "command economy.") The other four key elements represent important features of CPE development strategy. In addition, they also significantly influence economic policy pursued by the system's directors intent on preserving the CPE.


## COMMAND ECONOMY AND PLANNING MECHANISMS

Rapid growth (along with industralization) is usually stressed as an attraction of CPEs for less developed countries. The other two main objectives, centralization and social ownership, are generally considered necessary conditions for the existence of a CPE, since they give the system's directors direct, overall control over decision making. With social ownership, they do not have to persuade or manipulate the private owners of the means of production. Every economic system requires certain mechanisms, or institutional devices, to achieve its basic goals. Before discussing the planning mechanisms of the CPE, we first outline the complex features of the command economy, which is often identified in the literature as the sine qua non of the CPE.

We can focus on the command economy by analyzing the CPE in terms of the DIM (decision making, information, motivation) framework.[2] According to this framework, an economic system is a socially established mechanism for resolving economic decisions on production, consumption, and distribution. It consists of the allocation of decision-making authority among participants (the decision-making structure), the channels and manner in which they exchange information (the information structure), and the manner in which decision-making authority is exercised to secure compliance with decisions (the motivation structure). As for the critical coordination mechanism (which may be the market, the plan, tradition, or a combination of these), it provides the information necessary to assure consistency among the decisions of the agents to whom the decision-making structure allocates certain authority. For the coordination mechanism to be effective, there must exist an appropriate motivation structure.

The decision-making structure of the command economy is centralized (i.e., concentrated and hierarchical). At the top of the pyramid is the leadership of the ruling party which sets the overall goals and parameters within which the central planners organize the economy. The central planning board (CPB) develops both long-term and short-term economic plans that rule the economy. All details of the central plan, which are legally binding once the plan is approved, are transmitted first through functional ministries (e.g., the ministry of finance or ministry of foreign trade) and branch ministries (e.g., the ministry of metallurgy, ministry of machine tool building, or ministry of textile industry), then through various regional and/or functional intermediate authorities, down to the enterprises (which are established only by government organs). In order to make the administration of plans easier, the enterprises are usually larger than they would be in a MTE at the same level of development.

Economic planning in a command economy serves as a means of coordinating economic activity; it is considered a substitute for the "anarchy of the market." Economic plans contain macroeconomic and microeconomic decisions. The CPB decides the distribution of national income into investment, consumption, and government services, including defense. In principle, central plans are based on long-run macroeconomic considerations rather than short-run microeconomic principles. Profit maximization, or maximization of current consumer satisfactions, are both rejected as guidelines for plan construction. Instead the plans are designed to foster rapid economic growth (particularly in

---

[2] The DIM approach is developed in Egon Neuberger and William J. Duffy, *Comparative Economic Systems: A Decision-Making Approach* (Boston: Allyn & Bacon, 1976).

high-priority sectors), to safeguard centralization, and to avoid reliance on private ownership (along with the market mechanism).

The command economy with its central plan requires that all authority is retained by the center, which goes beyond Lenin's celebrated principle of seizing the "commanding heights" of the economy. This, in turn, implies that the information structure also be centralized; that is, the vertical flows of information to and from the center predominate. Similarly, the motivation structure must be centralized, that is, designed and administered, as much as possible, by the center. In sum, the coordination mechanism of the command economy, in principle, requires utmost centralization of each systemic structure.

In order for the CPB to manage the economy, certain planning mechanisms have been developed. We may identify three primary mechanisms (vertical coordination and control, system of material balances, and taut planning) and three secondary mechanisms (discontinuous planning, discontinuous incentives, and multiple criteria).

## Primary Planning Mechanisms

**Vertical Coordination and Control.**    The system relies predominantly on vertical channels of communication and control as a basic method of centralization. Vertical channels involve the communication of information regarding supplies of factors of production, technology, demands for products, plan fulfillment or bottlenecks, etc., from lower levels of the hierarchy to higher levels; and the communication of commands from the center down. This emphasis on direct orders from above reflects an effort by the planners to reduce dependence on "horizontal channels" (i.e., spontaneous, direct communications among operational units) in order to safeguard direct central control.

This mechanism manifests itself in a threefold separation of economic activities: (1) Among different sectors of the economy (intersectoral separation); for example, lack of direct contact between a steel plant and a machine tool plant to arrange the sale of steel products, which instead is done by their superiors. (2) Among the enterprises in a given sector (interfirm separation); for example, no communication between two firms within the machinery industry to reach an agreement to coordinate plans for specialization in certain types of products. (3) Among departments within given administrative or producing units, as within a ministry or firm (interdepartmental separation); for example, one ministerial department in charge of exports, and another of imports, with each department controlled by its hierarchical superior.

**System of Material Balances.**    This is a technique to achieve consistency among the various plans. It has two important aspects.

The first is *physical planning,* the balancing of equations in physical units, rather than in monetary units (e.g., tons rather than rubles), in an attempt to assure that the various part of the national plan fit together well enough to avoid severe shortages or surpluses. For example, in principle, there should be just enough coal produced to meet the planned needs of all industries and house-holds. Then the coal import and export plans are established after the domestic production plans, according to prevailing shortages and surpluses. In practice, the key requirement is that a flow of supplies is assured only to high-priority sectors. The use of physical units is necessary since prices in CPEs are not equilibrium prices, and their use in allocation would lead to unsatisfactory results.

The second is *sequential planning,* the use of successive approximations rather than simultaneous equations to facilitate the planning process. If plan-ners could develop a sufficiently detailed and up-to-date input–output table, and had the computer power to invert such a huge matrix and solve the neces-sary equations, the results would be superior to those obtained by sequential planning. Since neither of these conditions exists, the input–output approach is not feasible for detailed planning on an economywide basis.

**Taut Planning.**   This mechanism is a key feature of the pressure economy, which aims at the swiftest possible central mobilization of all available re-sources—by means of continual sellers' markets—to facilitate rapid growth. In addition to its mobilization features, taut planning is considered to be a useful technique to motivate managers of operational units. We may distinguish three aspects of taut planning. (1) Output (target) maximization: Given certain quan-tities of inputs and technological production functions, plans are drawn up not on the basis of the most likely expectations, but instead according to forecasts that are more optimistic than facts would warrant. (2) Input (or input coeffi-cient) minimization: For a specific output target and production function, plan-ners set input requirements (labor, capital, and materials) at the lowest, most optimistic levels, or even below. (3) Inventory minimization: Planners also set inventory levels lower than required by a given production technique.

## Secondary Planning Mechanisms

**Discontinuous Planning.**   This is a device by which plans are kept unchanged for fairly long periods of time (e.g., a month, a year, or five years), and changes to reflect changed circumstances are strongly resisted. Planners in CPEs try to keep these planning periods as long as possible, by sanctioning plan revisions only infrequently and discontinuously, in order to minimize the burden of planning. Each time a new plan (e.g., a one-year or five-year plan) is intro-duced, a very large amount of work is required from the operational units at every level of the planning hierarchy to provide new information, as well as by the CPB and any other unit involved in making the calculations necessary to produce a new plan.

**Discontinuous Incentives.**   There is a sharp line of demarcation in the incen-tive system between success and failure. The purpose is to encourage fulfill-ment of a centrally specified output pattern. To achieve this purpose, the incentive system is designed to offer rewards only if the plans (particularly the physical output plan) are fulfilled 100 percent. Failure is defined as falling short of the established quotas. Consequently, little attention is paid to differences of degree. While plan overfulfillment is encouraged, enterprise managers are reluctant to do "too well," since their future plan targets are likely to be raised. This is the so-called *ratchet principle* in planning: Overfulfillment will lead to higher plan targets, while underfulfillment does not lower them.

**Multiple Criteria.**   There is no single common standard of value, whether in the planning process (e.g., prices) or in the evaluation control mechanism (e.g., profits).

The tendency to postulate output targets and input norms in physical, nonadditive, and heterogenous units (e.g., 1,000 lathes and 2,000 milling machines, or 100 hours of skilled hours and 1,000 tons of steel, rather than in terms of the number of rubles), is related to the system of material balances (i.e., physical rather than value planning).

Multiple criteria are also used to assess the fulfillment of plans, that is, to measure the performance of operational units. For example, an enterprise might be evaluated on the basis of the number of shoes produced, the productivity of labor in the production of shoes, the saving of electricity in the production of the shoes, as well as the amount of profit earned.

The use of noncomparable multiple criteria is a means of safeguarding central control in the absence of a single satisfactory criterion. However, they also place a severe burden on both the information and motivation structures. They lead to a proliferation of instructions and of reports to the planners regarding the fulfillment of the various criteria. They also motivate enterprise managers to place emphasis on those criteria that weigh most heavily in the evaluation process and neglect all other considerations, especially if they are not clearly specified (e.g., maintenance of equipment).

An extreme example of problems caused by the use of the physical output (rather than value of output) criterion in the CPE is illustrated by a famous cartoon that appeared in a Soviet humor magazine. It shows a mammoth nail being picked up by a crane. The caption explains that the enterprise has fulfilled the plan requiring it to produce one ton of nails: It did, by producing one nail weighing a ton!

## DESIRED EFFECTS[3]

The CPE is able, at least theoretically, to produce certain effects that, given the preferences of the system's directors, are considered desirable. It should be noted that, in practice, some of these effects are attenuated or altogether negated for reasons to be discussed as we proceed.

---

[3] The most comprehensive treatment may be found in P. J. D. Wiles, *The Poltical Economy of Communism* (Cambridge, Mass.: Harvard University Press, 1962), pp. 253–63, where many of the points listed below are discussed at length.

## Socioeconomic Reorganization

**Formation of a New Elite.**   The system is able to orient the whole country toward the goal of economic development, replacing those uninterested in (or hostile to) rapid growth, centralization, and social ownership with a new elite of greater reliability. The new cadres are fully committed to the fundamental objectives of the system. This is accomplished by substituting a new ruling ideology for the old, and shifting power to adherents of the new ideology. The change is aided by the key elements cited above, especially by the command economy.

**Income Distribution.**   Social ownership makes economic development possible without resort to a highly unequal income distribution, a precondition usually considered necessary to attain a sufficiently high level of investment from private voluntary saving. In practice, however, the wage differentials needed for incentive purposes and the lack of progressive taxes combine to widen the dispersion of disposable income in CPEs. A major problem in measuring income distribution in CPEs is that the distribution of money income tends to diverge significantly from the distribution of real goods and services. A large proportion of scarce goods and services is allocated outside the market (e.g., subsidized or free allocation of housing, food, vacations, travel abroad; as well as by formal and informal rationing). Money incomes are thus augmented according to social position or political criteria. Most of these transactions do not appear in the official income statistics.

**Population Policy.**   The CPE, by focusing on economic development and giving power to a new elite imbued with a development ideology, should be in a strong position to deal with one of the most crucial issues facing underdeveloped countries—the problem of population growth. But none of the key elements of the system deals directly with the question. Some CPEs have periodically instituted more or less vigorous population policies (this is particularly true in China), but none of the countries that have adopted the CPE has developed a consistent long-term population policy.

## Mobilization of Inputs

**Capital Formation.**   Given the objectives of CPEs (rapid growth, centralization, and social ownership), the key elements (especially the command economy and the pressure economy) are used to impose very high rates of forced saving and investment, with the corollary effect of greater capital formation than in MTEs.

**Labor Recruitment.**   Extensive development and the priority economy, in particular, facilitate the utilization of relatively abundant agricultural labor and unemployed urban labor, as well as the recruitment of women into the labor force.

**Labor Training.**   Another desirable effect is the improvement of the educational levels and vocational skills of the population. This is promoted according to the objectives of the CPE not only to maintain high growth but also to increase ideologically sanctioned social mobility. Since education is a primary means of achieving this social mobility, it is facilitated by the priority economy.

## Acceleration and Channeling of Economic Development

**Growth of GNP.**   The pressure economy, the priority economy, and extensive development are jointly utilized to achieve a rapid increase of the gross national product, although not necessarily of the standard of living.

**Direction of Development.**   An important function of the priority economy and the command economy is the power they give to the system's directors to shape the development of the economy as they deem most appropriate. For example, the CPE leads itself to the transformation of a primarily underdeveloped, agricultural economy into a more advanced industrial one (as happened in less developed CPEs, such as China, the Soviet Union in its early stages, Romania, and Bulgaria), or to a shift from consumer goods industries to heavy industry (as was the case in Czechoslovakia). This policy is implemented by concentrating the lion's share of investment resources, skilled labor, and raw materials in the favored sectors. While the system's directors may succeed in changing the direction and pace of development, the net results of these policies are not always positive. (For example, Czechoslovakia, one of Europe's wealthier economies before World War II, later became one of the poorer ones. Czechoslovakia lost its leadership in certain consumer goods industries. At the same time, it developed some heavy industries for which it did not have a raw material base, especially ferrous metallurgy.)

**Regional Development.**   Attempts to bring the less developed regions of the country to the more developed level—with a corollary tendency toward greater sociopolitical cohesiveness—are also promoted, given the objectives (centralization and social ownership) and the key elements (especially, the command economy and the priority economy).

## Alleviation of Market Imperfections

**Externalities.**   The ability to internalize external economies and diseconomies, while clearly a theoretical effect of the CPE—particularly of the objectives (centralization and social ownership) and of some key elements (the command and priority economies)—is not easily realized in practice. Central planning organs are not monolithic units and do not have the necessary data and tools to assess externalities accurately.

In terms of the DIM approach, there are two basic problems. First, most of the de facto decisions are not made by a single planning authority, characterized by organizational unity, but rather by various ministries or even units lower in the planning hierarchy, so that the action by one unit does not take into account externalities which affect other units (e.g., the ministry of the chemical industry does not include in its calculations the pollution caused by one of its plants which causes diseconomies to enterprises and people downriver from the plant). Second, the price system does not reflect scarcities, and there is no systematic use of cost–benefit analysis to calculate deviations from social costs caused by external economies or diseconomies.

**Restrictive Influences.**   Centralization and social ownership, along with the command economy and the pressure economy, could be used to some extent to reduce monopolistic misallocation of resources, as well as to assure fuller utilization of all available resources by tightly controlling managerial power and severely limiting trade-union interference.

**Technological Progress.**   Control over management and labor and the absence of artificial monopolies based on patents should foster a more rapid diffusion of existing technological knowledge. This desirable effect is also related to the objectives of the CPE, as well as to certain features of the command and priority economies. However, other elements of the system—such as the pressure economy, the closed economy, and extensive development—tend to work in the opposite direction.

## Promotion of Economic Stability

**Price–Wage Stabilization.**   Elements of the CPE (the command economy and the closed economy) enable the system's directors to control undesirable price and wage fluctuations. Since central planners set not only prices of all important products but also wages, they can maintain price and wage stability if there are temporary inflationary pressures. In addition, if severe long-term inflationary pressures do build up periodically, they can be prevented from affecting resource allocation, in part through control of the wage–price spiral (which can prevent a rise in prices leading to a rise in wages, and therefore further price increases). Of course, postponing price and wage adjustments to avoid revisions of the long-term plans also has a serious disadvantage: The price signals become increasingly meaningless indicators of prevailing scarcity relations.

**Insulation from International Business Cycles.**   CPEs also have more power than MTEs to prevent, at least for short periods of time, external cyclical pressures and disturbances in the balance of payments from dominating domestic economic policies. This is a primary effect not only of the closed economy but also of the command economy. The system's directors do not feel the need to engage in a stop–go policy of investment and growth. As for the banks, given the very limited interaction between money and resource allocation, they have neither the authority nor the responsibility to make the enterprises responsive to external disturbances. To be sure, external disturbances have a stronger impact on small CPEs, where the relatively heavy dependence on foreign trade tends to moderate the emphasis on the closed economy.

## UNDESIRED CONSEQUENCES

We turn now to various undesired consequences of CPEs, rooted in the objectives, key elements, and specific features of the planning system. Although these undesired consequences are interrelated, we may separate them for analytical purposes into four major categories: administrative inefficiencies, unreliable valuation criteria, microeconomic inefficiencies, and macroeconomic problems.

### Administrative Inefficiencies

**Formal Organization.**  In its traditional form, the CPE is hypercentralized (i.e., its centralization interferes with economic efficiency, and ultimately with the objective of rapid growth) and rigidly organized. Its features, which are embedded in the bureaucratic framework of the command economy, lead to various maladjustments. The absence of flexibility pervades all sectors of the economy, from the CPB to every subordinate level. It prevents the producing enterprises from adjusting to changes in production methods or to changing scarcities of various inputs. The hypercentralized supply system does not provide the correct amount of supplies at the right time and right place. Thus, cumulative shortages can arise because of the unavailability of crucial inputs through legal channels, regardless of prices that firms may be willing to pay. This hypercentralization is even more of a burden in foreign trade, where flexible responses are necessary to take advantage of rapidly changing world market conditions, and to keep abreast of major trends in the international economy.

First among the specific problems is an overemphasis on vertical coordination and control channels (and a corresponding neglect of horizontal links among the enterprises), which increases the need for more information in the formulation and implementation of plans. This, along with discontinuities in planning, leads to (a) lags in administrative response, (b) the neglect of special requirements or atypical conditions, and (c) cumulative shortages. The higher up information must travel before a decision can be made, the longer will be the response time. It is also more likely that the information will be filtered or altered. Furthermore, if coordination is restricted to high levels of the hierarchy, then few decision makers must control a large number of operating units, and they cannot pay attention to special or atypical conditions. By necessity, many decisions have to be in terms of highly aggregated averages. The problems of the hypercentralized bureaucracy are aggravated by taut planning (e.g., keeping reserves as low as possible), which increases the likelihood that shortages will become cumulative, and their impact will not be recognized in time or their existence will be ignored. In sum, the planning mechanisms not only create recurrent bottlenecks but also generate further repercussions.

**Informal Bargaining.**   On close inspection, it appears that the CPE, in spite of its highly centralized formal organization, is not a system of rational decision making by an omniscient and monolithic unit. Although vertical command channels are overemphasized officially, the formulation and implementation of plans are pervaded at all levels by bargaining. Results more often reflect the power of individuals than the intrinsic strength of their case.

Anticipating, as it were, the criticisms of the reformers in the 1980s (to be discussed below), Professor Haberler remarked some 25 years ago: "The notion that there are no 'vested interests' in the CPEs . . . seems to me a myth. Vested interests firmly lodged in the rigid structure of bureaucracy constitute a formidable obstacle to change and reform."[4] Thus, our attempt to explain or predict the behavior of CPE planners and other decision makers may be better served by tools of game theory than by traditional economic theories of resource allocation.

## Unreliable Valuation Criteria

**Domestic Prices.**   There are nonsystematic aberrations of domestic prices both from prevailing scarcity ratios and from planners' preferences, primarily because several features of the system tend to immobilize the market mechanism. Without a trial-and-error method, it would be difficult to establish a set of economically meaningful prices for even a handful of basic commodities (e.g., by deriving synthetic or "shadow" prices by means of mathematical programming); and, in any case, the problem of the lack of price flexibility would remain. In a centralized economic system, interrelated price adjustments or general price reforms are too costly and can be undertaken only at infrequent intervals. Several key elements of the system—the command economy, the priority economy, and the closed economy—militate against rational pricing in a CPE.

The inability of the planners to formulate economically meaningful and sufficiently flexible prices may also be directly attributed to certain specific planning mechanisms. First, the emphasis on vertical channels and the corresponding neglect of horizontal connections among operational units slow the transmission and reduce the reliability of information. Second, material balanc-

---

[4] Gottfried Haberler, "Theoretical Reflections on the Trade of Socialist Economies," in *International Trade and Central Planning*, p. 37.

ing, with its stress on quota fulfillment in physical terms, relegates financial accounting to a subsidiary role in the planning process. Third, taut planning and its corollary, periodic supply shortages, inhibit equilibrium pricing.

**Exchange Rates.**   Closely connected with irrational domestic prices is the system of generally arbitrary exchange rates. Both the command economy and the priority economy are to blame, although the closed-economy element is chiefly responsible. While foreign trade decisions are not made primarily on the basis of official exchange rates, the lack of reliable and explicit comparisons between external prices and internal costs tends to interfere with planning as well as with control. Arbitrary exchange rates, like irrational domestic prices, are a contributory cause of both microeconomic and macroeconomic inefficiencies.

## Microeconomic Inefficiencies

**Incentive System.**   Within the pressure economy and the command economy, multiple criteria and discontinuous incentives give rise to a series of problems at the microeconomic level. Both of these aspects of the planning system tend to make incentives dysfunctional.

First, *multiple criteria* provide managers of enterprises with the possibility of structuring the fulfillment of plans in a way that maximizes their benefits (e.g., bonuses or promotions), but does not necessarily correspond to the intentions of the planners. Possibly even more serious is the problem arising from the inability of the planners to establish criteria that cover all aspects of their objectives. For example, if planners do not establish a quantitative criterion for the maintenance of equipment, then managers, trying to maximize their bonuses in the short run, may completely neglect this critical long-term aspect of enterprise productivity. Multiple criteria also provide a strong incentive for outright cheating or *simulation* of plan fulfillment. For example, enterprises may select a product mix that is easiest to fulfill, even though it may be very different from that envisioned by the planners. This is the so-called assortment problem. The anecdotal example of fulfilling the plan by producing a single nail weighing one ton, as mentioned earlier, is a caricature of this problem.

Second, *discontinuous incentives* (a penalty for fulfilling the plan at any level less than 100 percent, and a reward for fulfilling it at 100 percent) make the difference of 1 percent in plan fulfillment so large that it may lead managers to adopt an all-or-nothing philosophy. This is reflected in "storming" and illicit hoarding.

*Storming* (as it is called in the Soviet and East European literature) is the spurt of activity before the end of each planning period (monthly, quarterly, or annual) in an attempt to achieve 100 percent fulfillment, with a subsequent period of slack until the next target date approaches. During the storming period, when the pressure to produce is very high, the quality of the output is likely to be very low.

Discontinuous incentives encourage illicit *hoarding*. If enterprises know that they cannot fulfill the plan in a given period (and the penalty for, say, 97 percent fulfillment versus 99 percent fulfillment is less than the penalty for failing to fulfill the plan by 100 percent), they tend to hoard both inputs and unfinished outputs until the next period. This way, they can increase the probability that they can fulfill their subsequent plan by 100 percent. This creates a cyclical pattern of production, which is socially undesirable, but there is no incentive for the enterprises to take into account the difficulties caused for other enterprises or for final consumers. Thus, the system of discontinuous incentives results in an uneven process of production, with periodic supply bottlenecks, as well as a deterioration of product quality.

**Productivity.**   Extensive development, the pressure economy, the closed economy, and the command economy are jointly responsible for various microeconomic inefficiencies: slow rate of technological innovation in both products and processes, poor quality of output, and low productivity of labor and capital (e.g., long gestation period, inefficient choice or location of investment, and low capacity utilization because of supply bottlenecks and inadequate charges for capital use). At the same time, excessive inventories of unneeded inputs and unsold outputs accumulate.

**Firm Size and Specialization.**   Elements of the command economy, the pressure economy, the priority economy, and the closed economy lead to a pattern of interfirm relationships with a bias toward enterprises that are too large and not sufficiently specialized. The bias toward "gigantism" leads to plants that are larger than justified by economic criteria, thus resulting in higher cost of intraplant movement of products and of transporting goods to markets. Various features of the CPE, especially the centralized supply system, lead enterprises to aim at narrow self-sufficiency, producing many commodities in small series, and engaging in subcontracting as little as possible. The twin biases toward gigantism and self-sufficiency lead toward regional monopolies, rather than optimal allocation at the national level.

## Macroeconomic Problems

**Consumer Satisfaction.**   The objectives, as well as all the key elements, tend to keep consumer satisfaction at relatively low levels. The high rates of forced saving, imposed in order to provide the necessary capital under extensive development, leave less available for consumption. The priority given to defense and heavy industries leaves agriculture and consumer goods industries at a distinct disadvantage. A particularly important problem in maximizing consumer satisfaction is the relative neglect of service industries. The problems of poor quality; wrong assortment in terms of type, size, and style; and poor regional distribution leading to the unavailability of products in certain localities—all add to the low level of consumer satisfaction.

**Hidden Unemployment.**    The reaction to the pressure economy, the neglect of agriculture under the priority economy, the incentive structure under the command economy, as well as the official government policy of full employment lead to a large amount of hidden unemployment of labor and to underemployment of capital equipment and materials. Under the command economy, firms facing unrealistic plan targets tend to hoard labor and capital. Although this practice is illegal, it is tolerated as long as the output plans are met. The priority treatment of industry and neglect of agriculture encourage excessive rural-to-urban migration. The result is that hidden unemployment is transferred from the countryside to large industrial enterprises.

**Agriculture.**    The past collectivization of agriculture and the low priority assigned to it subsequently (keeping agricultural incomes low and making life miserable for peasants)—the consequences of social ownership and the priority economy—have caused an exodus of the best workers from agriculture. While this neglect of agriculture makes extensive development possible and allows increases in industrial output, it has several negative consequences. In addition to leading to low consumer satisfaction, it reduces long-term agricultural performance and increases social problems in overcrowded cities. An important secondary effect of the relative neglect of agriculture is the pressure on the balance of payments. The CPE is forced to use more scarce foreign exchange to import agricultural products than it would if it encouraged agriculture.

**International Specialization.**    The closed economy, the command economy, and the priority economy are responsible for the relative neglect of traditional export industries and the failure to develop new specialized exports based on present or prospective comparative advantage. As a result, CPEs become dependent on the export of commodities that happen to be in temporary excess in the domestic economy. Similarly, the lack of an optimal long-term import policy leads to the import of commodities in temporary short supply, rather than those in which the country has a comparative disadvantage.

## ADJUSTMENT MECHANISMS

CPEs employ, or tolerate, certain adjustment mechanisms to deal with the undesirable consequences discussed above. These mechanisms may be divided into *external* and *internal safety valves*. The external safety valves of *ad hoc* imports are often used to alleviate planning errors or unforeseen disturbances. Domestic safety valves include the semilegal (or illegal, but widespread and generally tolerated) mechanisms whose function is to introduce a measure of flexibility—by means of informal decentralization—into the rigidly centralized system. Two allied devices, selective violation of instructions and priority planning, are widely used to cope with some of the undesired consequences. In addition, a much more fundamental safety valve, which is of particular importance for the reformed or modified CPE, is the *second economy*.

**Selective Violation of Instructions.**   Informally, planning authorities are inclined to overlook a case of the neglect of certain instructions by enterprises so long as the more important instructions are observed (chiefly, the fulfillment of physical output plans). There is, as it were, a hierarchy among instructions, the more important ones being safeguarded at the expense of the less important.

**Priority Planning.**   There is a similar hierarchy among various branches of production, that is, among products of different industries. Thus, priority planning is a means of assuring fulfillments, or overfulfillments, of high-priority output targets—ranking high in the preferences of the system's directors. This occurs at the expense of low-priority goods—commodities that the directors consider to be more expendable, at least in the short run (traditionally, agricultural products and consumer goods).

**Second Economy.**[5]   This is now widely regarded as the most significant adjustment mechanism. Starting with a conceptual clarification, we note that the second economy in CPEs is more broadly defined than the "shadow economy" in MTEs, since the latter is usually restricted to illegal economic activities. In contrast, the second economy in a CPE includes all private economic activities, whether legal or illegal. This implies a system-bound distinction between the first and the second economy. The objective of social ownership is preserved in the first economy, but in the second economy social ownership is formally or informally abandoned. The formal part of the second economy is the officially sanctioned private sector, while the informal private sector is analogous to the selective violations of instructions. Whether formal or informal, the activities of the second economy are largely outside the command economy. In spite of ideological objections, CPEs have tolerated the second economy because it helped to alleviate some of the most serious undesired consequences of the system, especially by providing a significant proportion of certain agricultural products as well as industrial consumer goods and services. Over time, the second economy has acquired increasing importance in the analysis of the *real* (not the *ideal* type) CPE and, particularly, in the evolution of economic reforms.

---

[5] See Gregory Grossman's pioneering contribution, "The 'Second Economy' of the USSR," *Problems of Communism* 26, no. 5 (September–October 1977), pp. 25–40. For recent references and further discussion, see Gregory Grossman, *The Second Economy in the USSR and Eastern Europe: A Bibliography* (Berkeley-Duke Occasional Papers on the Second Economy of the USSR, no. 1; Berkeley, Calif., and Durham, N.C.: Departments of Economics, University of California and Duke University, 1985), and other papers in this series.

## ECONOMIC REFORMS AND SYSTEMIC TRANSFORMATION

### Why Reforms?[6]

Over time, the leaders of most of the CPEs discovered that the undesired consequences became more serious, while the adjustment mechanisms became less effective in solving the basic problems engendered by the CPE. In other words, they have discovered that the CPE is not a "model for all seasons."

Just as both Karl Marx and Joseph Schumpeter have argued that the capitalist system digs its own grave—both by its successes, which make it less necessary, and by its failures, which make it less desirable—we shall argue that the CPE does likewise.

As an economy develops, the problems faced by the system's directors change greatly. There is a shift from radical, discrete transformations of the economy which are useful in the "take-off" phase of industrialization, to more complex, interrelated structural changes required for sustained growth and development in a more mature economy. The greater sophistication of government leaders and technicians makes them more impatient with the crudeness of the CPE model, and the larger supply of trained and politically reliable (or at least neutral) managers and staff personnel makes decentralization seem more feasible.

The increases in income and the sophistication of population lead to a demand for better quality and a greater variety of consumer goods, as well as a highly embarrassing accumulation of stocks of goods which these consumers will not buy. The effectiveness of appeals to ideological fervor and of promises of future pies in the sky diminishes, and the use of the CPE's key elements (command, pressure, and priority economies, as well as extensive development and closed economy) become counterproductive.

Methods that may be effective in the short run tend to outlive their usefulness in the long run. As pointed out by numerous economists, the CPE resembles a war economy, and as such it did fulfill certain needs. But in general, war economies have functioned only for relatively brief periods of time. If such a system is operated for more prolonged periods, the shock-absorbing capacity of its low-priority sectors—because of their continued neglect—tends to be whittled away. This, coupled with the political necessity to provide more for the consumer, leads to an ironic situation—even a farmer cannot indefinitely starve his draft animals and expect them to carry increasing loads.

There arise feedback effects among environmental changes, policy responses, and systemic modifications. If the system's directors try to ignore

---

[6] This section and the following section on legacies are based on Egon Neuberger, "Central Planning and Its Legacies: Implications for Foreign Trade," in *International Trade and Central Planning*, pp. 349–77; and Alan A. Brown and Richard Y. C. Yin, "Communist Economics: Reforms vs. Orthodoxy," *Communist Affairs* 3, no. 1 (January–February 1965), pp. 3–9.

significant changes that take place during the process of development under the CPE, then they are eventually confronted with a system which is less and less desirable.

The rate of growth of national income, one of the fundamental objectives of CPEs, has been substantially reduced over time. There are various reasons for a slowdown. The objectives of centralization and social ownership, as well as the key elements of the CPE, contribute to both static and dynamic inefficiencies, and eventually to a decline in the growth rate.

A major factor behind the falling rate of growth is the increase in the demand for capital, while its supply decreases. A rise in capital–output ratios requires an increased rate of investment to maintain a given rate of growth in output. The pressing demands of the population for more and better goods and services creates increasing demands for a reduction in the rate of investment and a shift in the allocation of investment resources toward the former "buffer sectors" (agriculture, housing, consumer goods industries, and services).

The increased complexity of planning also raises the necessary inputs into information, without increasing informational efficiency. According to calculations by Soviet academicians, planning became 1,600 times more complex during the first 25 years of Soviet central planning; and "the cost of planning tends to increase as the square of output."[7]

Planning becomes more complex as the economic interconnections grow, and as a result of economic development. It is easier to plan fewer and relatively homogeneous products, such as electricity, fuels, and steel than more heterogenous products, such as the output of the chemical or electronic industries. As CPEs develop, the possibility of living off borrowed technology is reduced, and research and development become essential on a much broader front than earlier.

The benefits of extensive development by massive infusions of unskilled labor decline sharply. In fact, extensive development cannot be a long-term strategy of development; CPEs tend to move from labor surplus to labor shortage. Also, the motivation structure and organizational unity of enterprises become more important.

In particular, agriculture and foreign trade are two sectors of the economy that are least suited to the super-centralized command economy of the CPE. In both of these sectors it is very difficult to predict conditions accurately and to supervise performance centrally. Without accurate predictions, the need for frequent replanning is increased, and the more centralized the planning system, the more time-consuming and costly is replanning. At the same time, central planning without effective supervision or control offers little advantage, since the plan is then merely a paper plan.

Not surprisingly, a perennial problem sector of CPEs has been agriculture. LDCs, before they adopted central planning, generally had thriving agriculture

---

[7] *Izvestiia,* May 15, 1963.

with export surpluses. Establishment of CPEs created long-term stagnation of output and a consequent need for agricultural imports. Difficulties have also multiplied in foreign trade, especially as some CPEs have acquired huge foreign debts. The objectives of centralization and social ownership, as well as the key elements of the priority economy, the closed economy, and the command economy, have all contributed to the recurrent crises in both agriculture and foreign trade.

The gains from foreign trade generally depend on the flexibility of the trader, and the command economy is not known for its flexibility. The adjustment mechanisms of the CPE might solve a short-term problem in one area but they tend to create other cumulative problems. For example, substantial reliance on imports, both to alleviate planning errors and to support rapid industrialization, coupled with the planners' traditional aversion to foreign trade, tend to set in motion several dynamic interactions. What evolves is not an increasing trend toward self-sufficiency but an unstable equilibrium in which the priorities keep shifting, introducing ambiguity into the priority economy. Willy-nilly, the importance of foreign trade in CPEs has increased with a simultaneous tendency toward a decline in the gains from trade or a worsening of the terms of trade. This has led to the paradox of trading more and enjoying it less.[8]

The problems connected with foreign trade are especially significant for the smaller CPEs that must take advantage of international specialization according to existing or potential comparative advantage. The closed economy makes it impossible to utilize economies of scale since domestic markets are too small. This makes these countries more receptive to proposals for reform. The exigencies of foreign trade have become the wedge for far-reaching changes in the economic system.

## Obstacles to Reforms—The Legacies of the CPE

Once the system's directors recognize the need to replace the CPE with a more decentralized and market-oriented economy, they are confronted with the legacies of the CPE. There are, of course, both positive and negative legacies of the CPE. However, for the purposes of discussing the obstacles to reforms, only the negative legacies are relevant.

Conflicts arise among members of the group we have called the system's directors regarding the priorities among the objectives. In addition, there are also conflicts between the system's directors and middle-level bureaucrats engaged in planning and control and other economic actors (e.g., managers, workers, and consumers). When neither ideology nor the command structure succeeds in eliminating conflicts among individual objectives, CPEs have no consistent institutional mechanisms for achieving organizational unity.

---

[8] For a techical discussion, see Alan A. Brown, "Towards a Theory of Centrally Planned Foreign Trade," in *International Trade and Central Planning,* pp. 57–101.

Apart from conflict about objectives, some of the key elements of the CPE also become formidable obstacles to reforms. The various features of the command economy, as well as the priority economy and the pressure economy, have been stressed as obstacles by reformers, although their emphasis has varied. For example, Kornai has, in particular, concentrated on the pressure economy, which he refers to as the "shortage economy," while other reformers have generally emphasized the problems of the command economy.[9] To be sure, the need for changing from extensive development and the closed economy have also received their share of critical comments.

The command economy and pressure economy of the CPE lead to sellers' markets; managers are motivated to meet production goals and not to sell the products. This results in a situation where enterprises pay little attention to quality, to timely deliveries, or to aftersale servicing of their products. Monetary fines are not very effective instruments for countering this attitude, since fines do not affect managers' incomes significantly. This makes contracts much less effective than they are in market economies.

Another legacy of the pressure economy is the danger of inflation. CPEs suffer from chronic shortages; there are widespread excess demand and hidden inflation. When attempts are made to relax the controls of the command economy, open inflation threatens. There is a strong temptation to impose stringent price controls. The imposition of such controls delays the introduction of a new market system or provides an excuse to suppress the market and return to the formal and informal planning mechanisms of the CPE. Briefly, attempts to get rid of the pressure economy may lead to a reform oscillation: Shortages strengthen the desire to decentralize (and increase the role of the market), but this in turn may lead to inflation which encourages recentralization.

In general, the CPE breeds an interventionist psychology and an opposition to, and a misunderstanding of, the operation of a market system. This results in the introduction of half-measures, which tend to create more problems than solutions and thereby strengthen the hand of all those opposed to giving up the key elements of the CPE.

The priority economy, pressure economy, and command economy elements combine to yield a legacy of investment projects that have not proved to be economically sound. When this legacy is combined with an unwillingness to admit mistakes, especially big mistakes, the successor system inherits "white elephants" that are continually nurtured at the expense of the rest of the economy. The need to devote investment resources to these white elephants, and their absorption of scarce managerial and technical talent, make it more difficult to develop more productive sectors of the economy.

The closed economy element of the CPE leaves the successor system without a viable export sector, while the priority economy leaves it with a

---

[9] János Kornai, "The Hungarian Reform Process: Visions, Hopes, and Reality," *Journal of Economic Literature* 24, no. 4 (December 1986), pp. 1687–1737.

highly unbalanced investment structure. The concentration of investment resources in the priority sectors in the CPE imposes the burden of having to make
major investments in material and human resources for the former buffer sectors, such as agriculture, housing, and consumer goods industries.

Vested interests, not surprisingly, contribute the most tenacious obstacles
to economic reforms, and even more to the complete transformation of the
economic system. This legacy has various distinct roots. Powerful opposition
to reforms is based on the vested interests of bureaucrats (party functionaries
and planners who find much of their *raison d' être* and much of their power in
meddling in economic affairs) and enterprise managers (who have learned the
ropes and developed ways to beat the system). These individuals have little to
gain and much to lose from the abandonment of a system that has enabled them
to rise to leading roles in their respective hierarchies. This critical obstacle to
reform was emphasized already by Nikita Khrushchev who compared "some
officials" to blind horses, who "put on steel blinkers; they do everything as
they were taught in their day. A material appears which is superior to steel and
is cheaper, but they keep on shouting, 'steel, steel.'"[10]

Workers represent another major vested interest. They may or may not
particularly like the system, but they feel threatened by the uncertainties of
drastic changes. They fear the possible loss of their jobs; the danger of having
to work harder without an increase in real wages; and the price adjustments,
likely to accompany the transition, that may lower their real wages. Also, any
reform is likely to be imposed from above, and the workers have good reason to
mistrust government actions.

Another vested interest is represented by consumers, who have ambivalent feelings toward changing the CPE. While they look forward to improved
supply and quality of products and services, they fear price increases of necessities (e.g., housing, food, and public transportation), resulting from reduced
subsidies. This fear is particularly pronounced among lower-income groups,
especially pensioners.

A crucial legacy of the CPE is the absence of entrepreneurs who know
where to look for profitable ventures and how to carry them out; such talents
are not developed in the command economy. Profitability has to be weighed
against risk and uncertainty. This requires judgment and personal initiative, but
not the kind needed in the priority economy. Nor is there much opportunity in a
CPE for market research based on meaningful prices and exchange rates—
these are absent in a pressure economy. The scarcity of innovative entrepreneurs in the CPE is not due to inferior training or underfunding of higher
education. What is lacking is not technical competence, but rather the motivation to increase productivity as a way to cut costs, and to improve product
quality, since the rewards go to those who can increase output, regardless of

---

[10] *New York Times,* November 21, 1962.

cost considerations. Finally, the closed economy tends to foster a "vent-of-surplus" mentality in exports and the ability to secure imports that are in short supply regardless of price. But reforms require entrepreneurs who can create new channels in international trade, and who can provide sales and service facilities. Such entrepreneurs are scarce in CPEs.

In sum, when and if a successor system is established, it inherits from the CPE not entrepreneurs, but managers who are not trained to be independent, cost conscious, and new-product oriented. Neither are they particularly concerned with financial liquidity or solvency, nor are they likely to be experienced in those skills essential to selling in a competitive world market or in competitive buyers' market at home. They are likely to be oriented toward short-run goals, and not interested in the more difficult problem of trade-offs between profit and risk.

## From Economic Reforms to Systemic Transformation

Increasing dissatisfaction with the performance of the traditional CPE led to many attempts to reform it and replace it with a modified CPE (MCPE). The MCPE represents an effort to maintain the supremacy of the central plan and social ownership, while introducing some components of the market into the command economy, and abandoning or seriously weakening the other four key elements of the CPE (priority economy, pressure economy, closed economy, and extensive development).

Although minor reforms began after the death of Stalin in 1953, the first real attempt to introduce a MCPE was the Hungarian "New Economic Mechanism" in 1968. Some of its features were adopted in other CPEs, such as Poland.[11] The MCPE consisted of limited efforts to replace some coordinating functions of the central plan with those of the market. For example, some prices were determined by firms themselves in response to market conditions, and centrally set prices were altered more frequently in response to changes in cost or demand. Enterprises gained greater authority to determine the level and composition of outputs and inputs, and to obtain inputs and place outputs through negotiations with other firms. Instead of gross output, the chief indicator of enterprise performance became profit or value added.

In terms of the economic system's *objectives*, these changes meant a loosening of centralization in order to promote rapid economic growth. However, although political leaders were willing to trade one of the three basic objectives of the CPE (centralization) for another (rapid growth), challenges to the third objective (social ownership) remained insignificant until the late 1980s.

---

[11] We do not consider here Yugoslavia, where a socialist market economy was established following Tito's break with Stalin in 1948, or Czechoslovakia, where the attempt to give up the CPE was aborted in 1968.

As for the *key elements,* reforms remained piecemeal and, at best, limited. The system's directors in some CPEs agreed to give up the most egregious feature of the command economy, detailed compulsory plans, but they could not jettison the planning mechanisms without first creating a true market system. None of the planning mechanisms described above—primary (vertical coordination and control, material-balance system, and taut planning) or secondary (discontinuous planning, discontinuous incentives, and multiple criteria)—disappeared entirely, although their role diminished. Along the same lines, there was reduced reliance on the pressure economy, on the rigid preference-ordering of the priority economy, and on the trade aversion of the closed economy.

Finally, CPEs could no longer rely on massive reserves of labor (e.g., excess agricultural labor and women not yet in the labor force) and of capital needed to pursue the key element of extensive development. At the same time, none of the CPEs and MCPEs could switch over to an intensive development strategy, because they experienced a decline in productivity after the 1960s. The partial nature and incomplete extent of the changes explain (1) why the MCPE was only a modified CPE, and (2) why it could not succeed and was replaced by a move toward a market economy.

The performance of economies which maintained the key features of the CPE (such as Romania, Albania, Cuba, North Korea, and Vietnam) deteriorated over time. Because of the organic nature of the economic system, the attempts by MCPEs to give up the key elements of the CPE, without incorporating the necessary ingredients of a true market system, did not produce adequate results either. Thus, by the late 1980s, the leaders of MCPEs and some CPEs recognized that their economies were not functioning satisfactorily. MCPEs such as Hungary and Poland shifted their efforts from piecemeal reforms improving the MCPE to comprehensive reforms aimed at creating a market economy. Some CPEs (e.g., Cuba and North Korea) tried to maintain the CPE, but other CPEs (e.g., Czechoslovakia and Russia) moved toward transforming their countries into market economies.

This systemic transformation, with large-scale privatization of retail trade, industry, agriculture, and other economic activities, required a repudiation of the third key objective of the CPE—pervasive social ownership. Prior to that, social ownership of what Lenin had called "commanding heights" (e.g., mining, heavy industry, transportation, banking, and foreign trade), and of most other means of production, was considered a sine qua non of the economic system in CPEs and MCPEs. Private property was tolerated for small firms in areas far removed from the "commanding heights."

We argue that a fundamental shift in attitude toward property rights and toward control of the economy by markets rather than plans may be regarded as a watershed. It separates earlier attempts in MCPEs to establish socialist market economies from current efforts to create market economies with private enterprise as the spearhead for economic development.

## Problems of Transformation

By "economic transformation" we mean a set of complementary reforms designed to replace all the key elements and mechanisms of the CPE with the market system. These necessary reforms fall into four major categories: (1) privatization, (2) marketization, (3) stabilization, and (4) institution-building (i.e., the establishment of a legal and institutional framework for a market system).

**Privatization.**   Privatization is qualitatively different from the previous toleration of limited private ownership in CPEs or MCPEs, since it welcomes private ownership as the primary form of economic organization and even includes parts of the "commanding heights."

Privatization is one of the most contentious and difficult areas of transformation: Serious questions have been raised about such issues as the following:

1. Which branches of the economy (or firms in them) should be privatized, and in what sequence and at what speed?

2. The choice of methods of divestiture of state assets (for instance, to what extent to sell firms, as in Hungary; to issue vouchers to the population, as in Czechoslovakia and Russia; or to reserve some stock shares for employees of firms, as in Poland).

3. The nature and timing of restructuring of state enterprises—for example, industrial restructuring (breaking up very large firms); financial restructuring (writing off bad debts); and physical restructuring (replacing obsolete equipment). In each case, should state agencies restructure firms before privatization, or should the task be left to new private owners?

4. Conditions of sale: Whether to grant concessions to buyers in return for guarantees (*a*) to protect workers' rights to jobs in the firm and (*b*) to engage in sufficient investment to assure the firm's competitive viability, as in the former East Germany.

**Marketization.**   Marketization requires replacement of the plan by a market system for goods and services, and also for factors of production, as the basic coordination and allocation mechanism. The primary task is to reform the price mechanism by replacing the CPE's irrational prices—which often do not reflect either prevailing scarcity ratios or even planners' preferences—by market-clearing prices in both goods and factor markets (including financial markets). The secondary task is to reform the financial system and the conduct of foreign trade, including the establishment of currency convertibility.

While price reform is essential, it is also difficult in many areas where prices are too far out of equilibrium and their importance to income distribution or to production is very great (for example, in the cases of basic food products, housing, and energy).

As noted below, both privatization and marketization depend crucially on the creation of an appropriate institutional framework.

**Stabilization.**   To permit a market system to function effectively, it is essential to stabilize the economy. The processes of marketization and price liberalization release the previously disguised disequilibria of the pressure economy. For example, repressed inflation becomes open inflation, which absorbs some of the "monetary overhang" of unwanted cash holdings built up in the past due to shortages of desirable goods at controlled prices. Existing budget and trade deficits tend to intensify during the transition period, because the financial discipline necessary to control them is usually too severe to be politically acceptable.

Without rigorous stabilization measures, inflationary pressures can start a hyperinflationary price–wage spiral. One of the legacies of CPEs is the absence of macroeconomic stabilization tools, chiefly instruments of monetary policy, such as open market operations and changes in the discount rate or reserve requirements. While stabilization is essential to the success of the transformation process, it is also very painful and politically difficult to implement. The Phillips curve, depicting trade-offs between inflation and unemployment, shifts dramatically outward during the transformation, and both inflation and unemployment can increase to unacceptable rates.

**Institution Building.**   An effective transformation to a market economy requires completely new legal, institutional, and fiscal structures. A statutory framework to protect property rights and contracts must be established. New institutions must be founded for banking (such as commercial banks) and capital markets (such as investment banks and stock exchanges). A new fiscal system should be created to replace the CPE's confiscatory taxes on profit-making firms and automatic subsidies to loss-makers.

New institutions and programs are also necessary to provide unemployment insurance, job retraining, and income maintenance, substituting a much stronger and comprehensive social safety net in place of the CPE's use of unproductive employment (disguised unemployment) for job security.

New governments have a choice: either they may develop their own legal and institutional framework, or they may adopt an existing one, with appropriate modifications, from a market economy. While the latter alternative saves a lot of time, and may offer a more efficient path (especially in attracting foreign investment), the former is likely to have greater appeal to new governments and newly empowered parliaments asserting nationalism.

Even more challenging than the creation of a new legal and institutional framework are the retraining of the existing managerial, legal, and administrative bureaucracies and the education and training of new professionals. Without properly trained people, new institutions will not operate successfully.

## CONCLUSION

We have provided a thumbnail sketch of the traditional CPE, some of the reasons for its demise, its legacies, why earlier partial reforms did not work, and the problems involved in more recent efforts to transform the CPE or MCPE into a market economy.

We end with a few general remarks on the transformation process. One of the most difficult aspects of this process is the coordination and timing of the various component reforms. To prevent systemic collapse, the dismantling of the old system should be harmonized with the establishment of new systemic components. During the transition, policymakers face a set of interrelated problems:

1. Transforming a country from a planned to a market economy cannot be accomplished overnight. Because all of the required reforms cannot be implemented simultaneously, the sequencing of reforms is a key problem in the transition.

2. However, given the organic nature of the economic system, short-term results of partial reforms may be even worse than the status quo. (This was one of the painful lessons of earlier partial reforms—for instance, when some decentralization of decision making to enterprises occurred without rational scarcity prices to guide them.)

3. The political aspects of transformation interact with the economic variables. It is reasonable to expect a worsening of economic conditions in the short term, before the new system can function sufficiently well to bring about a longer-term improvement. However, the population may not be prepared to accept the intensity and duration of the pain of this transformation. Hence, policymakers must consider the political impact when they formulate a set of transformation plans.

4. Furthermore, in the absence of previous attempts to transform a planned economy into a market economy, reformers lack theoretical models or empirical experience to follow.

In sum, there are enormous problems whether the transformation strategy chosen is one of gradual transformation or "shock therapy." Neither extreme is politically or institutionally feasible, and some type of mixed strategy is, in fact, invariably adopted. Also, in the transformation of CPEs, the straight line may not always be a realistic path between plan and market. Some backtracking, through partial reversals of measures, may be necessary to transform a CPE or MCPE into a true market economy that is both economically and politically viable.

# Chapter Twenty-one

# The Process of Socialist Economic Transformation*

*Stanley Fischer*

*and*

*Alan Gelb*[1]

*The authors first compare the East European countries and the former USSR in regard to two sets of "initial conditions" at the start of the reform process that indicate its probable difficulty—the degree of centralization of economic decision making and the extent of internal and external macroeconomic imbalances. Next they analyze the main elements of reform: macroeconomic stabilization; liberalization of prices, domestic markets for goods and factors of production, and foreign trade; restructuring or privatization of state enterprises; and changing the role of the state from detailed administrative control of a socialist centrally planned economy to provision of the legal and regulatory framework for a market economy. Then they recommend a sequence for different reform measures over a 10-year period. They conclude by considering the role of foreign assistance and the interplay of domestic economic and political factors in the reform process.*

In the metaphor of Vaclav Klaus, the Finance Minister of Czechoslovakia: "I like to compare the transformation process with chess playing. When we want to play chess, we must know how to play. We must know how to move various pieces on the chessboard. We must know the basic opening strategies. But it's

*Reprinted by permission from the *Journal of Economic Perspectives* 5, no. 4 (Fall 1991), pp. 91–105, with the omission of references to unpublished papers. Stanley Fischer is Professor of Economics at the Massachusetts Institute of Technology and was Chief Economist at the World Bank when work on this paper was begun. Alan Gelb is Chief of the Socialist Economies Unit in the Country Economics Department of the World Bank.

[1] Opinions expressed are those of the authors, and are not official views of the World Bank. The authors are indebted to Bela Balassa, Olivier Blanchard, Rudiger Dornbusch, and Imre Tarafas for helpful comments. An earlier version of the paper was presented at the May 1991 conference on "The Economic Contest between Communism and Capitalism: What's Ahead?" at the State University of New York at Buffalo Institute for the Study of Free Enterprise Systems.

not possible to know the situation on the chessboard after the fifteenth or twenty-fifth move."[2] In this study we consider the reform process in those Central and East European countries that have made the decision to move from a more or a less planned socialist system to a private market economy, one in which private ownership predominates and most resources are allocated through markets. Because the reform process is both complex and intertwined with political factors—especially the shift toward representative democracy— and because there are substantial differences among the reforming countries, no single detailed road map can guide the way to the new systems. Rather, the study sets out general considerations that provide a framework for reform, and relates the choices to some initial conditions of the various reforming countries. (The framework applies also to the Soviet Union, or in the event of its disintegration, to its successor states as they move to market systems.)

## INITIAL CONDITIONS FOR REFORM

The countries of Central and Eastern Europe are in many respects similar. Income per person, although difficult to measure precisely,[3] is probably in the middle income range from a global perspective, about the same as Brazil, Mexico, or Turkey. Incomes at the start of the reform process were relatively evenly distributed, like those in Scandinavia. The socialist model of development emphasized heavy industry and large monopolistic firms which facilitated central control; most of their international trade was shaped by state agreements, rather than market considerations. Broadly speaking, it is also true that all the countries are moving toward increased political pluralism. However, there were also important differences among the countries when the reform process began. Two key differences are illustrated for six countries in Figure 21–1: the extent of macroeconomic imbalance, both internal and external; and the degree of decentralization of economic management and use of product markets rather than planning.

Countries closer to macroeconomic equilibrium (Czechoslovakia, Hungary) could concentrate on structural reforms leading to a market system. Those needing urgent stabilization (Poland, Yugoslavia) faced the difficult task of combining stabilization with structural reforms, in a situation in which conventional indirect fiscal and monetary policy tools were not available. Domestic macro-imbalances in socialist economies stemmed from both budgetary imbalances and "soft" budget constraints on state enterprises. These imbalances involved open inflation in some countries (for example, Poland), or the involuntary accumulation of financial assets (a monetary overhang) in coun-

---

[2] Vaclav Klaus, "A Perspective on Economic Transition in Czechoslovakia and Eastern Europe," *Proceedings of the World Bank Annual Conference on Development Economics, 1990* (Washington, D.C.: World Bank, 1990), pp. 13–18.

[3] Abram Bergson, "The USSR before the Fall: How Poor and Why," *Journal of Economic Perspectives* 5, no. 4 (Fall 1991), pp. 29–44.

**FIGURE 21–1**    Initial Conditions for Socialist Reform Process

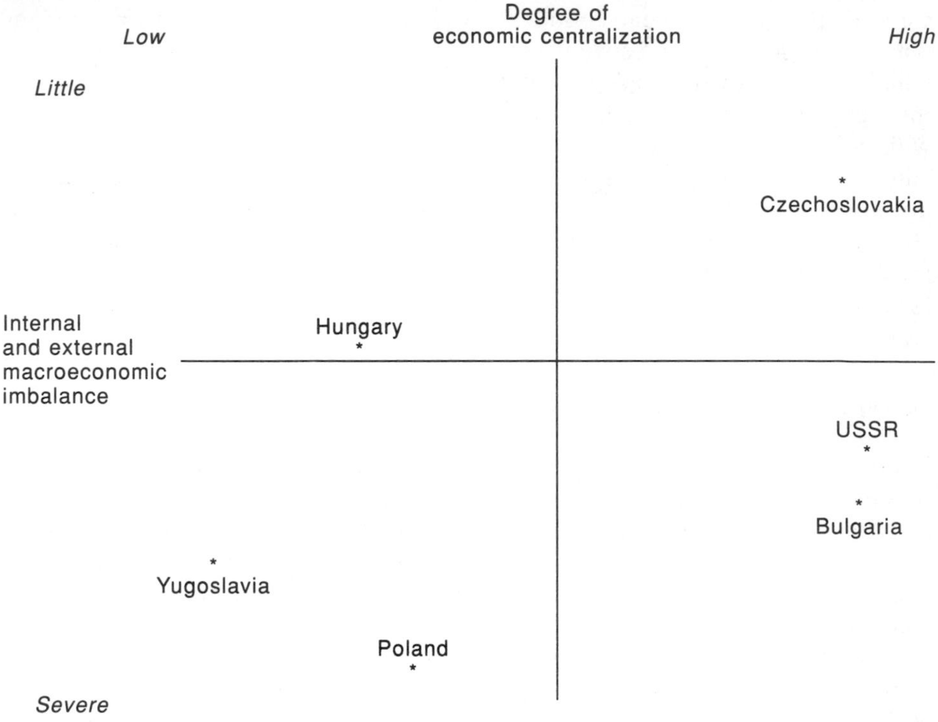

Degree of
economic centralization

Low · · · · · High

Little

                                                                    *
                                                            Czechoslovakia

Internal                              Hungary
and external                             *
macroeconomic
imbalance
                                                                    USSR
                                                                     *

                                                                     *
                                                                  Bulgaria

                        *
                   Yugoslavia

                          Poland
                            *

Severe

tries where other private assets were restricted and with extensive rationing of acceptable goods (the Soviet Union). In either case, structural reforms would not be effective unless aggregate demand and inflation were brought under control.

At the start of the reforms, as shown on the horizontal axis in Figure 21–1, Czechoslovakia, the Soviet Union, and Bulgaria had relatively centralized economies, with a planned material supply system playing a major role and with enterprise management subject to the constant intervention of ministries.[4] By contrast, Yugoslavia had long been the most decentralized of the socialist countries, with Hungary (since 1968) and Poland (since 1981) progressively moving the distribution of products onto a market basis and according greater autonomy to firms.[5]

---

[4] For descriptions of the Soviet and Chinese patterns of management, see, respectively, Ed A. Hewett, *Reforming the Soviet Economy: Equality versus Efficiency* (Washington, D.C.: Brookings Institution, 1988), and Gene Tidrick and Chen Jiyuan, *China's Industrial Reforms* (New York: Oxford University Press, 1987).

[5] China is an interesting and distinctive case. It adopted a two-tier approach to decentralization and markets, in which state firms and the material supply system coexisted with a growing nonstate

This combination of decentralization with limited private ownership has resulted in self-management of the capital within firms. In addition to the dominant role of the self-managed sector in Yugoslavia, some 70 percent of Hungarian and Polish firms became self-managed.

"Socialism without planning" tends to render balance-sheet constraints on firms ineffective, in part because the ownership of firms is uncertain. More importantly, the *soft budget constraint* is a result of government commitment to full employment, interpreted as requiring the preservation of existing jobs. Governments in these economies use taxes and subsidies to redistribute income among firms, and to prevent money-losing firms from going out of business. Together with price controls, this results in chronic scarcities of goods and factors, caused both by expansionist management unconstrained by the need to make a profit, and workers seeking higher pay without fear of layoffs and unemployment and without incentives to prevent the decapitalization of firms.[6]

In some respects, a decentralized socialist economy starts off the transition to a private market economy with advantages. Agents are more familiar with markets, and their response to market incentives is therefore likely to be faster. Also, a larger share of the exports of the less centralized countries went to Western markets, and was thus subject to global competition and international standards. For reasons outlined below, the ability to increase exports rapidly to Western markets must be an important determinant of the speed with which reform can show results.

On the negative side, reformers in a decentralized economy have to reestablish bottom-line discipline over powerful and previously relatively independent firms, subjecting them to market discipline by reducing cross-subsidies and/or by offering them the opportunity to privatize themselves, or directly asserting the state's ownership rights and recentralizing decision-making power. But removing acquired rights is not easy, especially as a shift toward democracy requires maintenance of a reasonable degree of consensus.

A blend of carrot and stick is evolving in reforming countries. Carrots appeal to those in potentially profitable firms; they include the prospect for privatized firms of exemption from wage curbs applied to socially owned firms, or cheap shares for employees. There are also schemes to encourage and fund *spontaneous privatizations,* a process initiated by the management of a firm whereby the firm is sold, or its assets are leased, frequently to a private corpo-

---

sector, largely in agriculture and rural industry. The nonstate sector traded increasingly on a market basis but with different prices for similar commodities. China also experimented in its reform process, with some provinces and special zones moving far more rapidly than others toward markets and pluralistic forms of ownership. See *China's Rural Industry,* ed. William Byrd and Lin Qingsong (New York: Oxford University Press, 1990).

[6] János Kornai, *The Road to a Free Economy* (New York: W. W. Norton, 1990), and Manuel Hinds, "Issues in the Introduction of Market Forces in Eastern European Economies," in *Managing Inflation in Socialist Economies in Transition,* ed. Simon Commander (Washington, D.C.: World Bank, 1991), pp. 121–53.

ration in which the managers and possibly workers have an interest. Spontaneous privatization emerged in Hungary and Poland, and somewhat later in Yugoslavia; it is also taking place in the Soviet Union. Sticks threaten the
loss-making firms; for example, by liquidation of the firm or dissolution of its
worker council if debts, dividends, or an annual fee for the use of state capital
are not paid.

An economy starting out from a centralized system should make great
efforts to define ownership rights clearly and to assign them as rapidly as
possible to agents or institutions outside the enterprises. We do not argue
against some employee shareholding or, as in West Germany, representation
on boards, but there is a need for an independent locus of control. If still-
centralized countries try to reform by first moving to market socialism, they
will have to give ownership rights to workers and then reclaim those rights, a
path which is both difficult and undesirable.

## ELEMENTS OF REFORM

The move to a private market economy requires political changes that recognize the value of diversity and individual initiative, and that require a substantial social and political consensus. This consensus seems now to exist in Poland, Hungary, and Czechoslovakia, but not yet in Romania or—prior to the
failure of the August 1991 coup—in the Soviet Union. This section discusses
the needed changes in the role and organization of government, and in economic structure and behavior. The sequencing of these changes is discussed
later in this study.

### Macroeconomic Stabilization and Control

Following the recent experiences of Poland and pre-1991 Yugoslavia, as well as
stabilizations in market countries with large public sectors, it is clear that
tightening fiscal and credit policies reduces inflation and the current account
deficit in socialist as well as in market economies. However, there are some
differences, which reflect the different microeconomic incentive structures in
the two systems.

Macroeconomic stabilization policies in socialist countries cannot rely on
the same responses as those in a market economy. For example, an increase in
interest rates may encourage household savings, but in the absence of tight
budget constraints, firms may simply refinance growing interest charges in a
giant Ponzi scheme that delays reform and then renders it extremely costly. (In
a market economy, the tendency of weak firms to borrow at very high interest
rates leads lenders to ration credit at market interest rates.) Until bankruptcy
becomes a credible threat, a range of direct controls will therefore be needed to
reinforce indirect measures. These can include the elimination of subsidies that
offset the losses of firms, public-sector wage controls, and credit ceilings ad-

ministered by the central bank. Since large socialist firms tend to be closely linked in oligopolistic interdependencies, direct control of credit must be supplemented with control and monitoring of inter-enterprise credit. Yugoslavia instituted a centralized reporting system covering both bank and inter-enterprise credit, and late payments on either could trigger intervention and bankruptcy.

Stabilization may also require addressing the *monetary overhang,* which is the amount of money consumers have kept on hand because there has been nothing to buy with it. The overhang in the Soviet Union was estimated at about half of household deposits in early 1991. There are several broad options: a currency reform which freezes or confiscates financial balances above certain levels; inflation, incompletely compensated by interest rates; raising interest rates to encourage voluntary holding of all financial assets; and the sale of state property to the public to sop up some of the overhang.

A confiscatory reform is problematic, especially if a broad theme of the reform is to secure private property rights. But in some cases, it can be politically justified as the result of the mistakes of the previous governments and (as argued in the USSR in April 1991) the allegedly dubious nature of activities which had allowed individuals to build up private wealth. The inflationary route was taken in Poland and Yugoslavia at the end of 1989 and also in the Soviet Union in 1991, but it is crucial in such cases to prevent a one-time increase in the price level from turning into a process of continuing inflation.

Selling public assets is most compatible with the desired direction of reform. Small enterprises and premises for businesses and retail shops can be sold fairly rapidly. Housing can also be sold, though this would need accompanying measures to raise the cost and reduce the security of renting, and these, in turn, would require adjustment of pay levels to reflect higher rents. In fact, because rents are usually far below maintenance costs, even giving housing away would improve the budget on a flow basis. Since the speed of privatization is likely to be slower than the desirable speed of stabilization, a possible strategy (not yet used) is to combine privatization with a currency reform by freezing balances above a certain level and permitting their later use to purchase assets that are being privatized.

Consider now, external balance and exchange rates. The experience of 1990 shows that changes in exchange rates can be effective in switching expenditures and output in socialist economies, provided that domestic prices are adjusted or allowed to adjust to create a link between world and domestic prices for tradables. However, all the reforming countries in Eastern Europe (except Yugoslavia) belonged to the Comecon trading system,[7] through which they traded at essentially arbitrary prices with each other and the Soviet Union. The dissolution of Comecon at the start of 1991 created major trade and domestic dislocations for all its former members.

---

[7] Editor's note: The official name was the Council for Mutual Economic Assistance (CMEA).

In sum, macroeconomic measures can help to reduce budget and trade deficits in reforming socialist economies. But given their economic rigidities and narrow markets, the response of socialist systems is likely to be less rapid and more costly in terms of output than is typical in market economies. Rapid systemic and structural changes are needed to ensure that macroeconomic stabilization is sustained.

## Price and Market Reform

Given the number of commodities—approximately 25 million in the Soviet Union—and the interdependence of prices, a planned transition to rational market-oriented product prices would be incredibly complex and protracted. Fortunately, the rational price system needed to guide autonomous enterprises is already known: it is world prices. Opening the economy to foreign trade is the best way of ensuring a rational price system. It does this in part by exposing domestic producers to foreign competition, which is particularly important in economies where industries are monopolized to a much greater extent than elsewhere. Trade liberalization at an appropriate exchange rate also creates the right incentives for potential exporters. It further offers the prospect of faster quality improvements through a range of licensing, processing, marketing, and other joint venture arrangements with foreign firms.

The trade liberalization route to price reform is certainly available for the countries of Central and Eastern Europe. In practice, of course, some distorting tariffs may remain; the reforming socialist governments are not more likely to move to completely free trade than are other governments.

Open foreign trade provides a rational price system for traded goods, but not for nontraded goods. And until the capital account of the balance of payments is opened, interest rates and asset prices can also diverge from world levels.

Price liberalization has been shown to cause a rapid increase in the availability of products. Price liberalization is also necessary for the credible long-term hardening of budget constraints. Until prices are rational, profits and losses are not necessarily good indicators of efficiency, and are therefore not a good guide to decisions on which firms should be closed and which—including those yet to be born—should expand.

Because of past patterns of industrial organization, price liberalization will not be sufficient to develop competitive markets. Domestic deregulation has to take place if firms are to respond appropriately to price signals, along with the demonopolization of transport, distribution, and trade systems and the breakup of large conglomerates. Demonopolization should be approached with an international perspective, especially for the smaller countries. As a method of enhancing competition, the opening up of trade is likely to be preferable to fragmenting firms as a way of achieving competition on the domestic market.

At the start of the reform process, about half the exports of the Eastern European nations went to countries in the Comecon or CMEA system, with the smaller countries mostly exporting manufactured goods and importing energy and raw materials from the USSR.[8] Therefore, except for the USSR, the January 1991 reform of the CMEA system toward multilateral, market-based, trading (which is a logical complement to internal reforms) raised the problem that each reforming country's exports had to compete in previously sheltered markets with superior Western products. Combined with the rapid decline of Soviet demand in 1991 and the shortage of hard currency to make payments, this trade shift severely reduced the exports of most of the reforming economies. In addition, Comecon pricing implicitly subsidized most of the East European countries. Recent OECD estimates are that the implicit subsidy lost through trade liberalization will be more than 4 percent of GDP for a representative country in Eastern Europe.

Although experience in 1990 offers evidence that some countries (such as Poland) can indeed raise their exports to the West rapidly, CMEA trade reform has had high short-run costs, and is probably responsible for much of the drop in measured GDP that followed reform. Similar disruptive effects will occur within the Soviet Union if its disintegration is not accompanied by trade and payment arrangements that allow a phased transition in trade patterns. In the longer run, of course, the reforms will have a positive effect on the economies of its members.

The liberation of labor and capital markets is also important. Labor market reform requires measures to make it easier to hire and fire labor, the relaxation of central wage regulation, the introduction of unemployment insurance, and the establishment of institutions (including employment agencies) to encourage labor mobility. Capital market reform involves the development of financial markets and private-sector financial institutions, including banks.

Freeing input markets should not be an early priority, however. Wage regulation cannot be eliminated until enterprise reform and privatization have proceeded some distance, because there is no countervailing interest to balance pressures for wage increases until budget constraints become harder. For this reason, tax-based wage policies have been implemented in the reforming countries, to limit either the total wage bill or the average wage per firm.

Even more so than other sectors, financial markets depend on underlying legal and information systems and skills that barely exist at the start of reform. Further, the problems of existing loan portfolios, which are in most cases believed to be very substantial, have to be addressed before a sound banking system—and liberalized financial markets—can emerge.

## Enterprise Reform

Enterprise reform, which requires the imposition of bottom-line discipline, definition and change of ownership, and reform of management, is the heart of

---

[8] As noted above, Yugoslavia was not a member of the CMEA.

the transformation process. The ownership issue is a political minefield. Workers in worker-managed firms believe they have substantial claims on the firms. Spontaneous privatizations taking the form of insider sales of firms by and to former managers and bureaucrats, many of them former Communists, create inequities. Political reaction against initial bursts of spontaneous privatization in Hungary and Poland resulted in this suspension. Nationalist sentiment puts limits on the role of foreign ownership.

The two phases of enterprise reform are *restructuring* and *privatization*. Opinions differ on which should come first. The period that has been suggested as appropriate for privatizing a major part of industry ranges from 3 to 30 years in various studies.[9]

Given that privatization will take years, and that many firms in reforming countries are currently run by ministries, the first stage of enterprise reform should take the form of *corporatization* (or, in the even less elegant Soviet term, *destatization*). In this phase, firms are moved out of the control of ministries and set up as corporations with their own boards of directors. They thus are put in a legal framework in which they can begin to operate as commercial enterprises.

Slow privatizers argue that firms should be sold off gradually after restructuring, in a more rational price system, after the new rules of economic behavior begin to emerge, and after a real business class has had time to develop to exercise the ownership function. Slow privatizers cite the need for ''real owners,'' private agents with a long-term view and sufficient equity in a given firm to give a strong measure of control. They emphasize the danger of severe economic dislocation if too much change is attempted quickly.

Fast privatizers respond that traditional methods for privatization are inadequate in view of the number of state enterprises and their size. Worldwide, less than 1,000 firms were privatized between 1980 and 1987. But Hungary has about 2,000 state enterprises and Poland 7,500, to cite just two countries.[10] It is widely accepted that more rapid privatization reduces the expected total sales revenue to the state, but fast privatizers argue that the benefits of a rapid and irreversible shift to private production outweigh the costs of reduced state revenue. They believe that comprehensive and rapid ownership reform is necessary to increase efficiency, and to head off the formation of interest groups representing adversely affected segments of society, such as potentially laid-off

---

[9] China's rural reform, in which communes were to some extent privatized to their members, stands as the most impressive example of property rights reform among socialist countries. The introduction of the household responsibility system—a halfway house to privatization—has been shown to have been responsible for most of the increase in agricultural output associated with the Chinese reforms. See Justin Y. Lin, "Rural Reforms and Agricultural Growth in China," *American Economic Review* 82, no. 1 (March 1992), pp. 34–51. Such reforms are probably far more difficult in an industrial setting, and in a pluralistic political system.

[10] In the context of Hungary, Kornai, *The Road,* argues for slower privatization, whereas the Blue Ribbon Commission, *Action Program for Hungary in Transformation to Freedom and Prosperity* (Indianapolis, Ind.: Hudson Institute, 1990), argues for faster privatization.

workers and redundant bureaucrats. In the end, they believe, higher tax revenues from a more efficient economy offset any loss of revenue from rapid privatization.

Schemes to achieve the goal of rapid privatization typically involve a broad distribution of shares, or vouchers with which shares can be bought, across the population. Most proposals recognize that widely dispersed ownership does not provide a basis for effective control, and therefore include a mechanism to create a group to monitor the management of individual companies. Some offer employees preferential access to a block of shares, both to obtain their support for the process and as an efficiency incentive.

Consider two approaches. First, create holding companies to be dominant shareholders, sufficient in number to ensure competition among them. The state can retain a bloc of shares for later sale or distribution to citizens and it can also offer citizens a diversified portfolio of shares in the holding companies. The difficulty is to ensure that the dominant shareholders operate like private owners, when they are not—unless of course, they consist of foreign owners who have sufficient wealth to buy the shares.

Second, distribute shares of each enterprise or share vouchers equally across the population and start trading arrangements to enable dominant ownership groups to emerge. Without an adequate information base, no stock market established at an early stage of reform would offer a useful basis for valuation or any indication of desirable investment patterns. The purpose of the initial exchanges is, however, quite different—to enable an effective ownership group to emerge. Whether that would actually happen, and whether the large inequities that are likely to arise will prove acceptable, are as yet unanswered questions.[11]

A variety of approaches is likely to be adopted in practice. Consider, first, firms in potentially competitive sectors, and suppose that price reform, trade reform, and macroeconomic stabilization have progressed sufficiently to make reasonable viability judgments possible. Small weak firms should be closed and their assets and premises sold off. Small, stronger firms could be (and have been) privatized rapidly, possibly being sold to all or some of the existing employees, with the state offering seller finance. It seems doubtful that the private sector could handle restructuring of very large, weak industries, so the state will need to restructure or close them.

The larger firms with potential are the crux of the privatization problem. Many could be privatized relatively rapidly, at least in part. Foreign investors could either take on the role of dominant shareholder (possibly temporarily) or

---

[11] See David Lipton and Jeffrey Sachs, "Privatization in Eastern Europe: The Case of Poland," *Brookings Papers on Economic Activity,* 1990, no. 2, pp. 293–333, for the presentation of a rapid privatization scheme for Poland, involving the distribution of shares. In June 1991 the Polish government announced that it would privatize by setting up mutual funds, with adult citizens to be given shares in the mutual funds. Mongolia's privatization plan, by contrast, relies on direct distribution of share vouchers.

could manage the firm on contract for a domestic holding company. Shares in such firms could be distributed under the schemes discussed above.

Given the scarcity of domestic owners it is likely that holding companies will play an important ownership role in the transition. Holding companies may later be fully privatized; or they could be converted into pension funds. Foreign management may be a useful intermediate stage. So might foreign ownership, although it has political limits and it would be inappropriate to sell national assets too cheaply out of very short-term considerations.

Banks are different. Banks can be expected to function as market institutions only after the economy has settled down sufficiently to enable loan portfolios to be kept reasonably clean. This raises sequencing issues, such as how to finance the emerging private sector. These issues are addressed below. Other important questions to be considered are the ownership of banks (they should not be owned by client firms) and whether banks should have an ownership role in firms, as in Germany and Japan. Some entry of foreign banks, including as managers of domestic institutions or as consultants, is likely to be useful in the transition.

## The Role of the State

Redefining the previously all-encompassing role of the state is one of the greatest challenges for reform. Institutions and professions taken for granted in market economies have to be re-created and reformed to support markets. A secure legal environment has to be created to protect property rights and regulate commercial relations. Accounting and audit systems are needed to organize and monitor information. Complementing the system reforms are needed investments in human capital, in areas such as accounting, credit and market analysis, and bank inspection. Management skills have to be upgraded and modernized, especially in finance and marketing. In some areas, such as financial markets, reform may require a greater state role than before.

Such inevitably lengthy reform processes constrain the efficiency and speed of reform. For example, in the United States it takes a minimum of five years to train an examiner capable—perhaps—of dealing with the smallest and simplest bank. These reforms also constitute an area in which foreign assistance may be especially useful. In fact, one view is that a reforming economy can take over and adapt a complete legal and regulatory system from a market economy with historic and cultural ties. For example, Hungary and Czechoslovakia might adopt and adapt the Austrian framework. East Germany, of course, simply adopted the institutions of West Germany. Given their desire for close trade ties with and eventual membership in the European Community, it makes sense for the reforming countries to take over or align with Community regulations and codes.[12]

Reforming governments need urgently to introduce broad-based taxes and to develop the capacity for tax administration, rather than continue to depend

---

[12] We are indebted to Richard Portes for this point.

on profit remittances from state enterprises. The reforming governments will also have to institute a social safety net, especially for those affected by the new phenomenon of open unemployment.

## THE SEQUENCING OF REFORMS

A linear sequence of individual policy changes is not the right concept when considering comprehensive system reform. The problem is better thought of as one of introducing groups of complementary policy reforms, sequentially. The details of the reform path to be followed by a country depend on the state of the economy, on the tolerance of the population for the disruptions that are sure to accompany the reform process, and on the political situation in each country. Nonetheless, we will outline a prototype reform process for a representative Eastern Europe country, with initial conditions somewhere between those of Poland and Czechoslovakia. The process is summarized in Figure 21–2.

The initial bundle of reforms is massive, including macroeconomic stabilization, price reform, trade reform, small-scale privatization, new regulations for private investment, the creation of emergency unemployment insurance, and the start of work on new tax, legal, and regulatory institutions.

For countries with severe internal and external imbalances, macroeconomic stabilization has to be the initial priority. For Poland, stabilization and a move toward a market system included sharp cuts in firm-specific subsidies and tight credit limits. It also included a major trade liberalization at a heavily depreciated exchange rate. In high inflation countries, it may be necessary in the initial phase of stabilization to fix the nominal exchange rate to provide a nominal anchor for the price level. While pegging of the exchange rate makes it possible to reduce inflation from very high levels within a few months, stabilization can be assured only by following consistent macroeconomic policies over periods of years.

Price reform, trade reform, and small-scale privatization have already been discussed. Along with providing rules for treatment of foreign investment, current account convertibility—which means essentially unrestricted access to foreign exchange for current account transactions—is desirable as an early part of the reform program. Reserves have to be adequate before liberalizing the current account at a fixed rate. Poland's reserves had been augmented by standby agreements, and it enjoyed a *de facto* moratorium on debt service. Yugoslavia had accumulated reserves prior to initiating its major reforms. Countries in the position of Bulgaria, with essentially no reserves, have little option but to float their exchange rate and rely on monetary and fiscal policy to anchor nominal prices.[13] The more advanced reformers have moved quite far in these areas of price reform, and world prices now play a substantial role in their

---

[13] Countries lacking reserves may use a dual exchange rate system for a transitional period, but import licensing should not apply to free-rate transactions. Capital account convertibility should come later than current account convertibility, when expectations of stability have been established.

**FIGURE 21–2**    Phasing of Reform

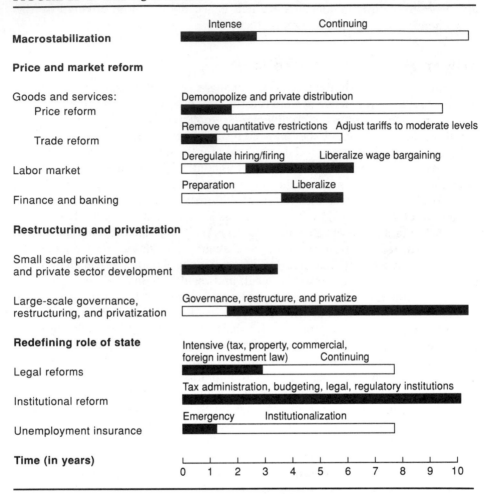

economies. Creating an unemployment insurance system allows social protection to be shifted off the shoulders of firms, thereby facilitating resource reallocation.

Factor markets can be fully liberalized only later. Wage-setting cannot be left to the market early in the reform process, because socially owned firms are not operating under correct price and management signals. At the same time, wages must respond to inflation and changing relative prices. Wage guidelines or formulae, such as partial indexation, have to be used initially in non-privately owned firms. Wage determination can increasingly be left to the market as firms are restructured and privatized. Realistic interest rates are needed to attract depositors into the banking system and to provide a reasonable measure of the cost of financial resources to firms. But it will not be possible to leave interest rate determination to the market until far into the restructuring process.

Although eliminating regulatory discrimination against the private sector and privatization of small firms can start immediately, the privatization of large enterprises raises more difficult problems, and no country has yet moved far in this direction. Hungary's plans rely on a blend of regulated spontaneous privatization and direct sales; Poland and Czechoslovakia will implement versions of the voucher distribution system. The unfolding example of the former East Germany suggests that preparation for the restructuring and privatization of most larger firms is likely to take several years and the execution to take much longer. Thus, preparatory steps such as clarification of ownership rights and corporatization, moving responsibility to boards of directors, should be taken as rapidly as possible.

Preparation for banking system reforms can begin immediately, with the establishment of suitable accounting and asset valuation standards; reform of banking, contract, enterprise, and bankruptcy laws; and the drafting of prudential regulations, as well as staff training. Next come audits of firms and banks and asset valuations, followed by portfolio restructuring (the counterpart to enterprise restructuring), allocation of losses, and recapitalization. Centers of financial expertise can be usefully developed in the banks, for outside firms to begin drawing upon. Only after this process is complete can a market-based banking system emerge and interest rates be liberalized.

From a technical perspective, equity markets can probably be created quite near the start of the reform process. But apart from a possible role in consolidating claims on privatized companies, they will only be a facade. Valuation and information deficiencies will prevent them from playing a significant role in the allocation of resources, at least until the banking system has been restructured.

The need for financial sector reform not to outrun enterprise reform raises the question of how the emerging private sector is to obtain financial services in the interim. One solution is a two-track strategy for the banking system, with private sector service departments in all major banks, initially on a small scale. Assets would be separated between privately and publicly owned entities, and new loans would be separated from old.

Many of the changes required to reorient the role of the state have already been initiated in the reforming countries. Laws and regulations are in the process of intensive revision, but even the more advanced reformers will require time to reshape their institutions and develop the necessary base of skills. The basic lesson in sequencing of reforms is that virtually all the reforms, or at least their planning, have to start quickly, even though implementation may take a decade.

## CONCLUSION

Western nations can make four important contributions to the process of reform. Access to the markets of industrial countries is vital for a rapid return to growth. Intensive and well-coordinated technical assistance, particularly at the direct firm level, can be very useful. Debt relief and access to capital to finance restructuring can provide a cushion during the transformation process. Finally, aid efforts should be coordinated, to avoid stretching the implementation capacities of the reforming governments.

However much outside assistance it receives, every country will face many choices concerning its reform path. Some of these involve the target of reform, that is, the precise shape of the private market economy. Economic theory offers relatively little guidance on some important questions, such as the distribution of wealth across the population, the role of foreign ownership and control, and the extent to which the state should play an active role. Difficult choices are also faced in the choice among alternative national models in areas such as banking, taxation, and antitrust regulation.

The most important strategic choices arise, however, out of the interplay between economics and politics. System-wide reform is an intensely political process: indeed, the main differences among reform strategies largely reflect differing views of what will be politically sustainable. The time needed to reform institutions, create skills, and value assets argues for a measured pace of reform. But a slower pace has costs, including prolonged uncertainty and probably a longer period of poor economic performance, during which opposition can coalesce to block the reform process. A rapid approach, in which markets are liberalized even before adequate preparatory steps, avoids the dangers of delay, but raises the potential for chaos.

Technocractic solutions for optimal transitions cannot be designed without taking account of the political constraints. And once a strategy is chosen, economists have to be on the lookout in the emerging reality for inconsistencies, risks, and dead-ends, and to seek to defuse such problems before they become serious enough to undermine reform.

*Chapter Twenty-two*

---

# Agriculture and the Transition to the Market*

*Karen Brooks,*

*J. Luis Guasch,*

*Avishay Braverman,*

*and*

*Csaba Csaki*

*In Eastern Europe and the former USSR, economic reform in agriculture involves special problems, such as elimination of highly subsidized food prices, decollectivization, and reorganization of activities that supply inputs to agriculture and that process and market output of agriculture.*

*This chapter first explains conditions in agriculture on the eve of reform, including agriculture's role in employment and GNP, the interaction of socialist and private farming, incentives and productivity, and the relationship between farm prices and retail prices.*

*Then the authors examine reform measures for macroeconomic stabilization, price liberalization, and redistribution of agricultural land. They conclude that, despite serious difficulties, some significant progress in the reform of agriculture is evident.*

Agricultural sectors in Eastern and Central Europe are large, and a substantial number of people are directly affected by changes in producer prices, farm employment, and land ownership. Retail food markets are among the most

---

* Reprinted by permission from the *Journal of Economic Perspectives* 5, no. 4 (Fall 1991), pp. 149–61, with the omission of tables. Karen Brooks is Economist, Agricultural Policies Division, World Bank, and Assistant Professor of Agricultural and Applied Economics, University of Minnesota. J. Luis Guasch is Professor of Economics, University of California, San Diego, and Economist, Trade, Finance, and Industry Division, Technical Department, Latin America and the Caribbean Region, World Bank. Avishay Braverman is President, Ben Gurion University of the Negev, Beersheva, Israel. Csaba Csaki is Rector and Professor of Agricultural Economics, Budapest University of Economic Sciences, Hungary.

distorted in the pre-transition economies, and the needed adjustments are correspondingly large. The decollectivization of agriculture and return of land to former owners are among the most dramatic and emotive elements of the economic transition.

Food, moreover, is highly politicized. Citizens of Eastern Europe and the USSR were for decades offered stable, subsidized food prices and a steadily improving diet as an indicator of the superiority of socialism over capitalism, and compensation for deficiencies in other aspects of material life. It is paradoxical that food assumed this political importance, since the economic organization of agriculture in socialist economies was particularly ill-suited for production of cheap food.

The agricultural transition requires substantial adjustments on the demand and on the supply sides of the food economy. Institutional and technological change on the supply side must bring down traditionally high costs of production and increase efficiency and quality. Price liberalization confronts consumers with the real costs of food, and these costs are for some commodities two and three times the former subsidized prices. Domestic demand is reduced by the removal of food subsidies, and producers lose the protection that insulated them from competitors on world markets. Such price liberalization is well under way in Poland, Czechoslovakia, Hungary, Romania, and Bulgaria.[1] The demand side adjustment, although still incomplete, has been swift and less painful for consumers than many people had feared. The supply adjustment is slower, and complicated by depressed demand on both domestic and foreign markets.

Decollectivization and distribution of property rights in land are an important component of the supply adjustment, and merit careful attention. The essence of the agricultural transition, however, is the withdrawal of the state from its traditional role as residual claimant of (positive and negative) rents to the use of agricultural resources. That role will pass in stages to owners of land, where it ordinarily resides in a market economy. A discussion of the new land laws and distribution of land would be incomprehensible without attention to conditions that shape the value of land, the income that owners can earn from it, and the decisions that private owners make regarding land management.

The macroeconomic stabilization, associated liberalization of prices and interest rates, and depressed demand on domestic and foreign markets create an atmosphere of acute economic uncertainty and declining farm incomes that forms the context for the distribution of agricultural land. Romania leads with swift implementation of a land law passed in February 1991. Many owners expect to take possession of their land after the harvest in fall of 1991, although few report plans to remove their lands from collective production next season. The Bulgarian land law was also passed in February 1991, but implementation

---

[1] Yugoslav food prices were less controlled even prior to the current period than was the case in other East and Central European countries.

has been delayed and the approach taken implies a more lengthy process. Land laws in Hungary and Czechoslovakia were passed in April and May of 1991, respectively. In this study we place the agricultural transition in its larger context, and treat the distribution of land more briefly.

## CONDITIONS AT THE OUTSET OF THE TRANSITION

The countries of Eastern and Central Europe comprise a large and diverse agricultural region. In the northern tier—in Poland, the Czech and Slovak Federal Republic, and the former GDR—grains (except for maize), roots, and specialty crops dominate the field crops, and imports augment domestic production of feed to sustain a large livestock industry. In Hungary, Romania, and northern Yugoslavia moisture and warmth are adequate for maize and oilseeds, and mixed grain/livestock farming predominates. Farther south in Yugoslavia and Bulgaria irrigation becomes more important, as do viticulture, orchards, and tobacco production. If the Soviet Union is included, the agroclimatic range of Eastern and Central Europe is replicated, and augmented by the largest area of irrigated agriculture in the world, in Soviet Central Asia.

To draw lessons that transcend the particularities of the individual countries, we create a stylized country with the general features of each, but the particular uniqueness of none. We take this country through an agricultural transition, indicating how various initial conditions affect the path of transition.

Agricultural production in the stylized country was collectivized. Approximately one third of farms were state farms, and two thirds were collective farms (cooperatives), but there was in practice little difference between the two. Many members of collective farms in theory retained title to collectively managed land, but ownership rights in the past were so attenuated as to be meaningless. (The exception to this pattern is the USSR, where all land was nationalized.) On both state and collective farms, workers had a high degree of job and wage security, little responsibility for the financial performance of the farm, and little incentive to improve productivity. Both types of farms were protected from bankruptcy by a soft budget constraint.

Farm employees managed a household plot of about one half hectare[2] in addition to their work on the large farm. The structure of production was thus dual, with very large units of 2,000 and 3,000 hectares plus many mini-farms. The private and socialist sectors were intimately linked in one agricultural system, and each would have faced significantly higher costs of production if forced to function independently of the other. For example, the socialized sector contracted out labor-intensive tasks to the private households, and they, in turn, relied on the larger farms for provision of many inputs for which markets did not exist.

---

[2] Editor's note: 1 hectare equals 2.47 acres.

This dual structure and the constraints on private landholding that produced it had the greatest impact on the livestock sector. The highest value that many households could extract from their tiny plots was in livestock products, but they could not grow feed on a half hectare. The large farms rarely had the flexibility or incentive to make high-quality pasture available for private use, and the livestock sector, both collective and private, became dependent on concentrate feed. The livestock sector faces the most extreme adjustment on both the demand and the supply sides.

Agriculture employed 25 percent of the work force, and produced 20 percent of GNP in this country. In developed market economies, agriculture is capital-intensive and the share of agriculture in the labor force is smaller than its contribution to GNP. In our stylized country, capital investment in agricultural production has also been substantial. Investment was in part necessitated by the political decision to replace small-scale private agriculture by large-scale collective agriculture, with the resulting need for land reclamation, large buildings, and large machines. Although the investment increased output and domestic self-sufficiency in food, only rarely was it guided by a calculus of economic returns. The capital/labor ratio in socialist agriculture is lower than in developed market economies, but this reflects inefficiency of investment, rather than its lack.

Poor incentives and relatively low capital stock per worker in the stylized economy reduced labor productivity. Severe price distortions make it difficult to measure agricultural labor productivity and the contribution of agriculture to GNP, but it is likely that labor productivity was lower than in industry. Agricultural wages were in rough parity with those of other sectors. When earnings from private plots were taken into account, agricultural incomes exceeded those of other workers on average. High wages were sustained by regular increases in controlled prices paid to farms for agricultural products, plus recurrent loans and grants.

Yields of grains and field crops per hectare were not as high as in Western Europe, where farmers receive the support of the Common Agricultural Policy, but they equaled yields of major commercial exporters in other parts of the world. Fertilizer use per hectare was lower than in Western Europe, but higher than in North America. Use of other agricultural chemicals was quite low, but poor storage and management practices resulted in environmental damage and health problems even at low levels of application. Technical productivity in the livestock sector was lower than in crops. Lags in breeding and protein-deficient feed rations reduced productivity. Milk yields per cow lagged those of Western Europe by about one third.

Use of labor, fertilizer, and feed grain was high per unit output, reducing efficiency and raising costs of production. With the drastic realignment of exchange rates at the outset of the transition, costs of production and prices received by farms no longer look high in comparison with world trading prices. With the increased ability to compare domestic prices to world trading prices that a reasonable exchange rate brings, it appears that agricultural producers are substantially discriminated against, since semicontrolled producer prices lag world prices. For example, most Romanian wheat will be purchased this season at \$35 per ton at the market and interbank exchange rate of 200 lei to the dollar. (The official exchange rate is still 60 lei to the dollar.)

These costs and prices, however, still embody distortions in input prices, since fertilizer, energy, and machinery are not yet priced at world trading prices. Part of the distress of the early transition is caused by the more rapid approach of input prices to world levels and slower adjustment of producer prices. As the economies make their ways in fits and starts to a price structure more consistent with world trading prices, it appears that agricultural incomes will increase less than the general price level. This is not necessarily a manifestation of a textbook type of urban bias, although some of the instruments for restraining agricultural earnings, such as Bulgaria's ban on the export of some food products, are standard tools for the transfer of income from rural to urban people.[3] Falling farm incomes now are a symptom of partial liberalization, but they also signal the needed longer-term adjustment: more efficient production of products for which domestic and foreign demand exists under the new price structure.

Agroindustry in our stylized country was highly concentrated, and food processing, distribution, and input supply were managed by several large state monopolies. With pervasive excess demand for food, processors paid little regard to product definition and quality.

The stylized country was a middle-income country, with per capita GNP of about \$6,000, using the purchasing power parity methodology, and \$2,500, using the exchange rate methodology. In recent years, the country sustained aggregate consumption despite declining aggregate growth, by borrowing heavily abroad. Agriculture's contribution to the growth in net foreign indebtedness derived from increased demand for imported feed grains, and diversion of food from export markets to (subsidized) domestic consumption.

Per capita consumption of food was comparable to countries with income levels considerably higher. Caloric consumption was the same as that in market economies with high levels of income, and consumption of meat exceeded that in many more prosperous market economies. This consumption pattern was a result of food subsidies, particularly for livestock products. Retail food prices changed little in nominal terms for several decades, despite growth in nominal incomes. Real food prices (at official prices) thus declined. Since markets did not clear at these official prices, the actual prices that people paid were higher than official prices. Consumers' expectations about what they should be able to purchase, however, were formed on the the basis of official prices.

The most highly subsidized food items were meat and dairy products, and official prices for these products were approximately half the cost of delivery.

---

[3] Avishay Braverman and J. Luis Guasch, "Agricultural Reform in Developing Countries: Reflections for Eastern Europe," *American Journal of Agricultural Economics* 72, no. 5 (December 1990), pp. 1243–51.

Subsidization of items with low-income elasticities is often considered to benefit poorer people, but the most highly subsidized items in the stylized economy
were those with high-income elasticities. The food price subsidy delivered
more benefits to the wealthier groups who consumed more of the most highly
subsidized products, and fewer benefits to poorer people.

Each country camouflaged the growing gap between costs of consumption
and production by passing the costs to the state through subsidies, and increasing imports or reducing exports of food. The increase in consumption of food
and other goods that came with the post-Stalin thaw was one that the underlying productive economies could not deliver on a sustained basis. The degree of
subsidization varied by country and its impact on the macroeconomy also
varied, but in each case the burden of food subsidies was very high. Subsidized
sausage for the relatively wealthy cut into budgetary funds available for investment in education, health care, physical infrastructure, and environmental protection.

## THE TRANSITION

Thus, the agricultural sector on the eve of the transition was characterized by
(a) large inefficient farms with high costs of production (primarily fertilizer,
labor, and feed); (b) high levels of food consumption relative to market economies of comparable prosperity; (c) subsidized food prices; (d) excess demand
for food at those prices; (e) macroeconomic imbalance, including budget deficit
and foreign debt; and (f) pervasive monopoly in food processing and distribution.

The macroeconomic imbalance in the stylized country was substantial, and
the transition is initiated by a program of stabilization. Fiscal outlays are reduced, the money supply tightened, and the overvalued currency devalued.[4]

The macroeconomic stabilization affects the agricultural sector in several
ways.[5] The food subsidy, at approximately 5 percent of GNP, is a visible target
for significant fiscal savings. Although governments throughout the region
approached removal of food subsidies with great trepidation, all (except for
the USSR) have by now eliminated direct consumer food subsidies. Partial
direct income compensation accompanied the removal of subsidies. Without
the subsidy, meat prices approximately double, and food prices rise on
average by 50 percent. Demand for food declines due to the partial compensation, and consumers purchase less and different food at the higher relative
prices. The price increase does not reduce caloric intake on average, but
does induce shifts away from more expensive foods, particularly meat and
cheese.

---

[4] For an exposition of the programs of stabilization and reform more generally, see Olivier
Blanchard and others, *Reform in Eastern Europe* (Cambridge, Mass.: MIT Press, 1991).

[5] For parallels in other regions' adjustment processes, see *Structural Adjustment and Agriculture: Theory and Practice in Africa and Latin America,* ed. Simon Commander (London: Overseas
Development Institute, 1989).

The price liberalization frees processors with market power to act like monopolists, and many respond by raising prices to consumers and pressuring producer prices. The price increase that accompanies liberalization is thus in part due to removal of subsidies, and in part due to the exercise of market power.

The price liberalization does not raise prices that producers receive. In an open market economy, devaluation will raise agricultural producers' prices, since most food and fiber is tradable. However, this economy is not fully open yet, and transmission of changes in world prices and exchange rates is weak. Moreover, producer prices in the past exceeded retail prices by the amount of the subsidy. The increase in retail prices removes the wedge that formerly divided them from producer prices without appreciably affecting farm-level prices. In fact, the formal freeing of retail food prices is sometimes accompanied by retention of controls at the wholesale level, as governments try to insure themselves against too rapid a rise in food prices. Processors' market power allows them to pass controls back to producers. Partial decontrol is reported in Romania and Bulgaria, although statistical monitoring of price movements is weak now.

Producers are unable to push the former volume of production through markets at lower prices, since for products requiring processing, they cannot bypass the processing monopolies. Producers are thus hostage to the pace of change in the processing, marketing, and distribution of food and fiber. The hope of a quick improvement in agriculture that will facilitate change in other sectors is illusory unless a concerted effort to increase competition and the technological performance of food processing and marketing brings early results.

Excess supply appears at the farm level. Some of this can be exported, and it is more competitive than in the past, due to the devaluation. Institutional linkage between producers and international markets, however, is weak, and product definitions and quality are not conducive to quick switching between domestic and export markets. Producers face higher costs for fertilizer and imported animal feed, and the combination of higher costs and reduced demand puts pressure on farm income.

The crucial variables in determining the impact of macroeconomic stabilization on the agricultural sector are the relative magnitude of the food subsidy; the amount of excess demand for food before liberalization; the degree of concentration in processing; and the openness of international markets to products redirected from domestic markets. If the food subsidy is small, if its removal approximately absorbs excess demand, and if processors have limited market power, the adjustment process will be less disruptive for producers. However, if the shock to the demand side is large and the economy shifts abruptly from excess demand to excess supply, producers will face a substantial adjustment. The adjustment will be particularly difficult if exports cannot be readily expanded. [In Eastern and Central Europe] agriculture, like other sectors, has been hard hit by the disruption of trade with the USSR and the Middle East.

Problems in food processing are apparent even prior to the transition, and many participants in the food economy have argued for increased investment to modernize food processing. The investment is sought from both domestic and external sources, and the goal of the investment is usually construction of new plants and/or purchase of more modern equipment. A visitor assessing the "needs" of food processors of Eastern and Central Europe can amass requests amounting to several billion dollars in a few weeks in the field.

Few of these, when viewed as commercial investments rather than as "basic needs," pass careful scrutiny. Unless price liberalization is well under way and changes in food demand are better understood, new investment in food processing is likely to respond to the wrong signals. It will be devoted to the wrong commodities, will be placed in the wrong locations, and will purchase technology inappropriate for the post-transition factor costs.

Some kinds of food processing stand out as particularly poor targets for investment in the early period. Plants that operate wholly or in part with imported raw materials but sell their products on the domestic market, such as oilseed crushers, will be particularly hard hit as foreign exchange risk is passed to them but domestic prices lag world prices. Meat processors and dairy plants in areas dependent on subsidized imported feed are poor targets. Investment in simple packaging technology and materials for products with export markets can be relatively safe and productive. The focus of change in food processing in the early period of the transition should be to augment competition through dismantling monopolistic processing trusts and expanding small-scale private transport. New investment should promote competition rather than simply expand or modernize processing capacity. After the price liberalization has settled down, alternative investments in food processing will be easier to assess.

If producers have poor access to markets because reorganization of processing and distribution is stalled, they will demand direct government subsidies to forestall declines in farm income. Governments will be pressured to embark upon programs of price support that they can ill afford. Tariffs are costless to the budget, but have obvious implications for inflation. Moreover, if producers' difficulties stem in part from lack of domestic competition in processing and marketing, tariffs will not address the basic problem, and may worsen it. Poland, which has led in many aspects of the economic transition, imposed agricultural tariffs in May 1991 to protect the troubled dairy industry.[6]

Given the inherited concentration in food processing, a concerted demand for tariff protection against imported food is a predictable feature of the political economy of agriculture during the transition. Producers may well be drawn into alliance with processors when their longer-term interests are not well served by protection of processors' monopolies.

---

[6] On the Polish experience in the early transition, see Polish-European Community-World Bank Task Force, *An Agricultural Strategy for Poland* (Washington, D.C.: World Bank, 1990).

## DISTRIBUTION OF AGRICULTURAL LAND

In Czechoslovakia, Hungary, Romania, and Bulgaria, recognition of rights of landowners prior to collectivization has been universal.[7] Debate on the legal foundation for reaffirming property rights in land proceeded throughout the region in 1990, and until late in the process it was not obvious that restitution would be the outcome. Parliaments passed land laws in Romania and Bulgaria in February 1991, in April in Hungary, and in May in Czechoslovakia. Each of these laws recognizes the rights of landowners just prior to collectivization, and sets up a procedure for reinstating the property right.

Since most agricultural land is being returned to people perceived to be rightful owners, recipients do not pay, and the land distribution has little impact on macroeconomic balances. In the parts of the Soviet Union in which land was nationalized in 1917 and collectivized between 1929 and 1933, it is difficult to imagine how rights of former landowners could be reinstated. The course of decollectivization is thus likely to be quite different in much of the USSR.

The Romanian land program embodies the judgment that costs of delay are greater than those of moving ahead before all complications are foreseen and forestalled. Local land commissions in each district were established quickly after passage of the law, and began receiving claims. Households can claim a maximum of 10 hectares, and can submit a variety of evidence to support their claims. The period of submission and judgment of claims ended on May 20, 1991. When possible, claimants will be given the land actually owned prior to collectivization. When this is not feasible, a piece of equivalent size and quality will be returned. When the original land was broken into parcels, the parcelization is deliberately duplicated in the returned land; many households in the Danubian plain will receive four or five hectares divided into several parcels. Holdings in the hill areas will be larger, and broken into more parcels.

Romanians who receive land through restitution of their rights can sell it immediately if they so choose, or buy more up to a maximum holding of 100 hectares per household. Family members and neighbors have rights of first refusal on farm land for sale, a restriction on free sale that is intended to address the fragmentation problem. Since in the densely settled areas of intense agriculture almost all land will be distributed through restitution, an active land market could develop rather quickly.

There appears to be little intent in the law or its implementation to create farms of an optimal size, or to look forward to how farming will take place after the land is distributed. This at first appears economically myopic, but may in fact show a more profound sophistication. The Romanian approach to the land distribution is more like a voucher scheme than a land reform, since it widely disperses claims to the land, but carries little expectation that people will work the land in the units they receive. A small number of people receiving large

---

[7] This section is based on field interviews during May 1991. The interviews were part of an ongoing study organized by the World Bank and partners in member countries. The study analyzes changes in land tenure and use in Romania, Hungary, Bulgaria, and Poland.

holdings (for example, 8 to 10 hectares) plan to manage them as households. Most people plan to keep the land in collective management this season and next. The distribution thus opens a trading period during which households can buy and sell their land, consolidate holdings, and prepare to leave the collective when the infrastructure for individual management is more developed and the economic outlook for the sector has improved. In the meantime, the collective will continue to work the land, and landowners will receive a share of returns to land proportionate to their share of the farm's total area.

The land law in Bulgaria was also passed in February 1991, but political stalemate and administrative inertia delayed its implementation. The National Land Commission, the main administrative organ of implementation, was not appointed until May 31, 1991, and appointment of local land commissions was attendant upon the formation of the national commission. As a consequence, people who wanted to claim land in the first half of 1991 had nowhere to take their claims. Many of the records showing who brought land into the collectives are held by the farms, and even managers who wanted to speed the restitution of land rights could not submit them to nonexistent local commissions.

Administrative delay has hindered the implementation of the Bulgarian law. The philosophy of land distribution embodied in the law and the implementing regulations is slow by nature. Rather than relying on market trades to improve a quick and imperfect distribution of rights, the Bulgarian approach attempts construction of appropriate holdings through administrative assignment. Local land commissions accept and adjudicate claims, and when a substantial number of claims have been verified, turn them over to a team of specialists who draw up a local map of the allocated holdings.

The Bulgarian law prohibits purchase and sale of land by private individuals for three years, thus precluding market-based solutions to the land fragmentation problem.[8] In many places the amount of land that can be restored is only a proportion of that claimed, since development has changed the contours and use of land, and agricultural area has declined. In these areas all claims will be prorated by proportionate adjustment. The effort to achieve justice and economic efficiency through administrative meticulousness can be contrasted with the Romanian priority on speed. The costs and benefits of each approach are not yet clear. The slower distribution of land in Bulgaria and the severity of the agricultural contraction suggest that in Bulgaria, as in Romania, management of the land will remain largely collective in the coming seasons despite the change in property rights.

In Hungary, the initial attempt to return agricultural land to prior owners in 1990 was struck down by the Constitutional Court, with the ruling that restitution of ownership of agricultural land must be considered along with that of other assets. In April 1991, landowners, along with dispossessed owners of

---

[8] The economic implications of this restriction have received attention, and amendment of the provision is under debate. As this is written in July 1991, the restriction remains.

other property, were granted vouchers redeemable for agricultural land or other assets. Landowners who continued to hold title to lands managed by the cooperative are granted the return of their managerial rights unconditionally. In Hungary, thus, the restitution for those who relinquished title is essentially monetary, and the impact on demand for land depends on economic agents' assessment of the value of land compared to other assets.

In Czechoslovakia, the law mandating return of agricultural land to prior owners who will cultivate it passed only in late May 1991, and at the time of passage, little interest in claiming land was reported. In Czechoslovakia the agricultural sector is a relatively small part of the national economy, due largely to the industrial development of the Czech republic and its dominance in the aggregate measures. Agriculture is more important in Slovakia. Food markets approximately cleared even prior to the price liberalization, and few citizens of the country perceive that they have had or now have a "food problem." Thus recognition of the need to change the inherited structure of agricultural production has been late in coming, although a fully open trade regime would demonstrate its high cost relative to world levels.

The agricultural contraction is just beginning in Czechoslovakia, and difficulties in marketing meat and milk are pulling farm incomes down. Pressure for change in increasing, but it is early yet to predict whether the form of change will be protection of the old structure, or the start of decollectivization. Since the agricultural sector is a smaller share of the Czechoslovak economy, and given the complications of federal politics, pressures for protection and subsidy will be great.

In Poland, the state sector owns only about 20 percent of agricultural land, since the remainder of land was never collectivized and remains in fragmented private ownership. Although the proportion of marketed output that originated in the state sector was greater than its share of land ownership, the excess supply of food occasioned by the Polish "big bang" diminished the perceived urgency to reorganize state farms. Those most agitated about the fate of state farms were their employees. The disposition of land in state farms throughout the East and Central European region has lagged and followed a different course than that of land held by collective farms.

In summary, the land distribution programs in practice are quite diverse, and are not what most people outside the region expected. In surveying the economic options, few outside economists would have chosen physical restitution of rights to prior owners as the preferred solution. The economic difficulties are evident. The restitution approach does have some redeeming features to complement its apparent political appeal, and counter some of the economic problems it raises. Had land been distributed without payment to the agricultural work force with no higher principle than "land to the tiller," it would have been easy to exclude rural people from further distribution of state-owned assets. Since landowners have instead received back property judged to have been rightly theirs all along, there can be little justification for excluding rural people from a fair share of assets accumulated by the state. Thus, when privatization swings into full force through vouchers or distributed shares, rural people will be integrated into the new capital markets.[9]

## CONCLUSION

The agricultural transition is an essential part of stabilization and adjustment in Eastern and Central Europe because agricultural sectors are large and food is important. Decollectivization is a highly visible component of the agricultural transition, yet the course of decollectivization is strongly influenced by the economic environment in which it proceeds. The economic environment is at present dominated by depressed demand, economic uncertainty, and interest rates higher than agricultural producers in the region have ever seen. The emerging private sector is particularly vulnerable; it is poorly endowed with inherited capital and still has poor access to markets for inputs and outputs. Many producers are therefore choosing to delay their emergence into fully private individual production, and are instead staying with cooperatives until the economic force of the agricultural contraction weakens.

Despite the very clear difficulties, significant progress in the agricultural transition is evident. Liberalization of food prices is not yet everywhere complete, but has proceeded with surprising speed and social acceptance. Redefinition of property rights in land, the first step in decollectivization, is under way. Progress already achieved in Eastern and Central Europe provides instructive lessons and cautious optimism for the USSR. The international community has shown its readiness to support the agricultural transition with capital and technical assistance. The effectiveness of each would be enhanced if the generosity extended to market access.

---

[9] For discussion of privatization more generally, see John Vickers and George Yarrow, "Economic Perspectives on Privatization," *Journal of Economic Perspectives* 5, no. 2 (Spring 1991), pp. 111–32.

## Chapter Twenty-three

# The Soviet Centrally
# Planned Economy*

*Morris Bornstein*

*Actual economies commonly differ in significant respects from the theoretical models of economic systems that they illustrate. For example, a simplified model of a socialist centrally planned economy may specify complete public ownership of, and enterprise with, the means of production, as well as resource allocation exclusively by administrative orders. Furthermore, it is often assumed that planners have both full information at the stage of plan construction and the full cooperation of managers and workers at the stage of plan implementation. In contrast, in an actual centrally planned economy, one finds some nonstate ownership and enterprise, a significant role for markets and prices in resource allocation, imperfect planning, and nonfulfillment of plans.*

*This chapter provides a comprehensive picture of the socialist centrally administered economy of the USSR as it operated in 1990, before the country split apart. First, it explains the nature and relative importance of the state, cooperative, and private sectors. Next it analyzes how output, supply, investment, finance, and foreign trade were planned. Then the role and formation of different kinds of producer and consumer prices are discussed. This chapter also shows how Soviet enterprise managers tried to achieve good performance—initially by seeking easier plan assignments and subsequently by using considerable ingenuity to fulfill the demanding assignments they nevertheless received. The operation of labor markets, the determination of wages, and the sources of nonwage income are examined. Finally, the issue of economic reform is discussed.*

This chapter explains and evaluates the most important characteristics of the Soviet centrally planned economic system. The first part covers the organization of production, investment, and distribution. The next part discusses the planning of output, supply, investment, finance, and foreign trade. In the third part the various facets of the price system and the resulting roles for market forces are examined. The fourth part deals with enterprise management. The allocation and compensation of labor, and the receipt of nonlabor incomes, are considered in the fifth part. The last part discusses economic system reforms in the Soviet Union.[1]

## ECONOMIC ORGANIZATION

From the standpoints of ownership and enterprise, the Soviet economy consisted of three rather different and unequal sectors: state, cooperative, and private. The first two sectors were sometimes called "socialized" because both of them involved "collective" activity—in contrast to individual enterpreneurship in the private sector.[2]

### State Sector

In the USSR the state owned all natural resources, including land, and most of the reproducible capital, such as buildings, machinery and equipment, and inventories. The state conducted virtually all activity in industry, construction, transport and communications, health, and education. But the state sector's share was smaller in agriculture, retail trade, and housing.

In agriculture, for example, the state sector had 53 percent of the sown area; the cooperative sector, 44 percent; and the private sector, 3 percent. Their respective percentage shares of cattle herds were 37, 43, and 20. The

---

[1] Thus, the essay does not deal with the historical evolution of the Soviet economic system or the assessment of Soviet economic growth. On the former, see, for instance, Alec Nove, *An Economic History of the USSR* (London: Pelican Books, 1982); Eugène Zaleski, *Planning for Economic Growth in the Soviet Union, 1918–1932*, translated from the French and edited by Marie-Christine MacAndrew and G. Warren Nutter (Chapel Hill, N.C.: University of North Carolina Press, 1971); and Eugène Zaleski, *Stalinist Planning for Economic Growth, 1933–1952*, translated from the French and edited by Marie-Christine MacAndrew and John H. Moore (Chapel Hill, N.C.: University of North Carolina Press, 1980). On Soviet economic growth, see, for example, Abram Bergson, *Soviet Post-War Economic Development* (Stockholm: Almqvist & Wiksell International, 1974); *USSR: Measures of Economic Growth and Development, 1950–1980* (Studies Prepared for the Use of the Joint Economic Committee, 97th Cong., 2nd Sess.) (Washington, D.C.: U.S. Government Printing Office, 1982); and Gur Ofer, "Soviet Economic Growth: 1928–1985," *Journal of Economic Literature* 25, no. 4 (December 1987), pp. 1767–1833.

[2] The Soviet economy was officially considered "socialist," rather than "communist," in the senses defined by Marx and Engels. They distinguished between socialism and communism with the formula—under socialism: from each according to his ability, to each according to his labor; under communism: from each according to his ability, to each according to his need. Thus, in their view, capitalism is to be followed by a long "stage" of socialism, and communism cannot be established until (1) "abundance" has been achieved and (2) the psychology of people has changed so that they are willing to work for the good of society without regard to their compensation. Since both scarcity and the use of individual material incentives are to disappear with the arrival of communism, so also, presumably, will the use of money, prices, and wages.

**FIGURE 23–1**   Administrative Organization of the State Sector

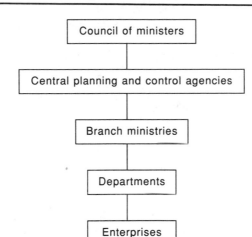

state and cooperative sectors each produced about half of total grain output. The state, cooperative, and private sectors each accounted for about one third of total production of meat.

In total trade, the respective percentage shares of the state, cooperative, and private sectors were 71, 26, and 3. However, the private sector's share was much larger for various unprocessed food products such as fruits and vegetables, poultry, and eggs.

Finally, the state owned three fourths of total urban housing space and one fourth of total rural housing space—with the remainder in each case privately owned.

The administrative organization of the state sector was extensive and complex for two reasons. First, the Soviet economy was very large in terms of population (about 291 million, one sixth more than that of the United States); area (8.5 million square miles, triple that of the continental United States); and GNP (about half that of the United States). Second, the Soviet regime was committed to a high degree of centralized control over resource use in this large and changing industrialized economy.

Thus, a complete organization chart for only the central government economic apparatus would require a large wall poster, or several photographically reduced pages in a book.[3] In a simplified way, one may consider this apparatus to have five main levels (see Figure 23–1).

---

[3] Such charts are presented in Paul K. Cook. "The Political Setting," in *Soviet Economy in the 1980s: Problems and Prospects* (Selected Papers Submitted to the Joint Economic Committee, 97th Cong., 2nd Sess.) (Washington, D.C.: U.S. Government Printing Office, 1983), part 1, pp. 18–21.

At Level 1 was the Council of Ministers of the USSR. Its "supercabinet" of very top officials was called the "Presidium."

Level 2 consisted of two sets of central agencies engaged in planning and controlling various types of activities across the entire economy. One set included a number of State Committees[4]—for instance, for Planning, Material and Technical Supply, Construction, Prices, Labor and Social Problems, and Science and Technology. The second set comprised such organizations as the Ministry of Finance, the State Bank, and the Central Statistical Administration.

At Level 3 were more than 50 "branch" ministries responsible for production, distribution, and investment for particular categories of output. These included about a dozen ministries for different kinds of machine building and about a dozen ministries for different types of construction work.

Because of the large number of enterprises in each branch ministry, they were grouped within the ministry, by geographical location or type of output, into departments that constituted Level 4. These departments were traditionally called "main administrations." Beginning in 1973, in various, especially industrial, ministries these departments were put on a separate accounting basis (*khozraschet,* discussed later in connection with enterprise management) and were renamed "industrial associations."

At the bottom of the organizational pyramid was the producing, construction, or trading enterprise. For example, there were about 46,000 enterprises in industry, 23,000 state farms, and 32,000 state construction organizations. In general, the enterprise might be considered Level 5 in this simplified hierarchical scheme. However, in industry the situation was more complicated because about 17,000 enterprises (of the 46,000) belonged to "production associations" or "science-production associations," each of which on the average comprised 4 enterprises. In this case, the association constituted Level 5 and the component enterprise a still lower Level 6.

The administrative organization of the state sector had a regional dimension. The USSR was a federation of 15 Union Republics, each with its own economic administrative structure that corresponded in many respects to the central structure. About half of the national branch ministries—for example, those concerned with construction, the light and food industries, and domestic trade—were of the "union-republic" type, operating through counterpart ministries in the union-republic governments. The other national branch ministries—including those for machine building, equipment, and electronics—were of the "all-union" type, without regional counterparts.

Finally, the government administrative structure was paralleled by that of the Communist party, which controlled the government at all levels. The Cen-

---

[4] Although the Russian word *komitet* is usually translated as "committee," this was somewhat misleading in the case of a Soviet State Committee. It was not a small group of representatives from several organizations. Instead, it was a separate government agency with many sections, a large staff, and specific operational responsibilities. Therefore, "commission" or "board" is a closer English-language equivalent.

tral Party Secretariat included, for instance, departments for planning and finance, agriculture, construction, machine building, the chemical industry, the defense industry, heavy industry, the light and food industries, trade, and transport and communications. Party units existed in, and participated in the control of, all of the levels of the organizational pyramid.

## Cooperative Sector

The cooperative sector included collective farms and consumer cooperatives. Although their formal ownership was nonstate, the extent and activities of both were closely controlled by state agencies.

There were about 26,000 collective farms. These farms accounted for about 44 percent of the total area sown to crops and 37 percent of the cattle herds. They produced the following approximate percentage shares of important products: grain, 50; cotton, 65; sugar beets, 90; sunflowers (the main source of vegetable oil), 73; potatoes, 20; other vegetables, 24; meat, 30; and milk, 38.

Each farm's members collectively owned its buildings; livestock; machinery, equipment, trucks, and tools; and inventories of seed, fodder, and agricultural chemicals like fertilizers, pesticides, and herbicides. The members participated in the election of the farm's management. They worked in teams of various sizes to cultivate the collectively held land (which, as noted above, belonged to the state) and to raise the collectively owned animals.

Until the mid-1960s, farm members were compensated for their collective work by unequal residual shares of the farm's income, under a scheme similar in principle to that of the labor-managed enterprise[5] and the Chinese commune.[6]

Each farm task (planting a field, milking cows, and so on) was assigned a certain number of "work-day" points—commonly from ½ to 2½ points for one day's work—depending upon the skill and effort involved. However, only after the harvest did farm members learn the value of their accumulated points in kind (e.g., in grain) or in money. The in-kind work-day payment fund consisted of output that remained after (1) deliveries to the state, (2) sales on the collective farm market (in the case of food products not requiring industrial processing), and (3) allocations for fodder and seed. The money work-day payment fund was established by deducting from the farm's revenue (from sales to the state and on the market) (1) the cost of purchased off-farm inputs such as chemicals and fuels, (2) taxes, and (3) farm income reinvested in buildings, machinery, and equipment. The total number of work-day points earned by all farm members was then divided into the in-kind fund and into the money fund to determine the value of one point in kind (e.g., in kilograms of grain) and

---

[5] Editor's note: See Chapters 17 and 18.
[6] Editor's note: See Chapter 28.

in rubles, respectively. The farm management calculated the amount due each member by multiplying the value of one point in kind and in money by the number of points the peasant had earned. (Because this calculation could be made only after the harvest, the farmer received small monthly advances against the eventual annual amounts in kind and in money.)

The peasant's compensation as a collective farm member, therefore, was an uncertain residual that varied with the size of the harvest, the delivery quotas and prices set by the state, and the farm's reinvestment program, as well as the peasant's work. Moreover, on many farms the peasant's compensation, in money and in kind, was very low, both in absolute terms and relative to urban incomes. Thus, the peasant's private plot (see below) was often essential to augment his income from collective work.

In 1966, the Soviet government dramatically changed this compensation scheme for collective farm work. In place of the uncertain residual share, it introduced regular monthly pay in money for collective farmers, at the same daily wage for a particular job paid on nearby state farms. Although collective farm members no longer received payments in kind, they could use part of their pay to buy from the farm grain for their own use and feed for their private animals.

These and other changes, such as the provision of state pensions and the issuance of internal passports to collective farmers, sharply reduced the differences between collective farm members and state farm workers.

Although the collective farms were formally cooperatives, the state controlled them closely in many ways. For each farm the state fixed quotas for deliveries of various products at prices set by the state. The state determined the quantities and prices of the farm's current nonlabor inputs, such as fuels and chemicals, and its capital inputs, such as machinery and equipment. As noted, the state set the wage rates. Finally, although the farm's members formally elected its management, in fact the decision was made by local Communist party and government officials.

Retail trade was conducted in urban areas by state stores, and in rural areas by consumer cooperatives which were nominally subject to committees elected by the rural families that were their members. However, the consumer cooperatives were fully controlled by the state, which determined the number and location of shops, the assortment and quantities of goods and services offered, their prices, the size and wages of their staff, and so forth.

## Private Sector

In the Soviet Union there were various forms of private property. Individuals could own consumer goods such as clothing, jewelry, television sets, refrigerators, and so on; tools; automobiles; apartments or detached houses; and livestock. Individuals could also own financial assets such as savings accounts in the State Bank, government lottery bonds, and currency. Private wealth in physical property or money could legally be inherited.

The most important legal private business activity was the private plot in agriculture. It was sometimes called "individual subsidiary" or "auxiliary household" agriculture to indicate (1) that it was not "socialized" like state or cooperative farming and (2) that it was a supplementary activity undertaken in addition to an agricultural or nonagricultural job in the state or cooperative sectors. State farm employees and collective farm members were allocated (without a rental charge) plots on their farms on which to build houses, keep animals, and tend gardens. Also, some urban residents had small plots at the edge of town.

Private plots ranged in size from less than half an acre to somewhat more than an acre. They accounted for about 3 percent of the total sown area, but they produced one third of total meat and milk output, almost two thirds of all potatoes, and two fifths of the fruit and vegetables. These shares for private plots in total output reflected: the operators' decisions to specialize primarily in high-value labor-intensive crops; work on the plots by children and retired family members as well as by full-time workers in their spare time; and the availability of livestock feed from outside the plot. Most of the concentrated feed for private livestock was produced in the socialized sectors, and private livestock often grazed on the common pastures of collective and state farms and on otherwise unused land, such as along roads.

The state controlled the private plots through limits on their size and the maximum number of cattle, regulations about the sale of feed for private livestock, and requirements for a minimum amount of work by able-bodied family members in their "primary" jobs in socialized activities.

Part of the output from private plots was consumed by the family, and the remainder was sold to the state or on the collective farm market. For many farm families, income from the private plot, in kind and in money, was an important supplement to their wages.

About 20 percent of new housing construction was done privately, with materials acquired from the state and the labor of the future owners, their friends, and moonlighting construction workers.

Soviet law also permitted some private activity in addition to regular jobs in certain professions, such as by physicians and teachers; in the provision of household, repair, and personal services; in a few arts and crafts; and in some other special, minor occupations, such as trapping fur-bearing animals.

However, the employment of one person by another was prohibited (except in the uncommon case of household help). Buying, selling, and trading of personal property could legally be done directly or through state "commission" shops. But any purchase with the intent of resale at a profit was considered illegal "speculation." It was also against the law for a person to rent to others an automobile or apartment, or to lend money at interest.

There was considerable evidence of a variety of illegal private economic activities in the USSR which were sometimes called the "second" economy. But it is more useful to distinguish between a "first" economy that was centrally planned and administered, and a "second" economy that consisted of several kinds of "unplanned" activities. The latter included (1) legal private activities, (2) illegal private activities, and (3) illegal activities of state enterprises and collective farms, seeking to fulfill plan assignments. The common characteristic of all of these second economy activities was that they occurred in response to shortages arising from plan priorities or from the nonimplementation of plans in the first economy.

The next section examines the central planning process in the USSR. Illegal activity by state enterprise managers is considered below.

## ECONOMIC PLANNING

Economic planning is a broad and complex process of explicit administrative guidance of production, distribution, investment, and consumption. Planning is a continuous process for two reasons. First, plans are commonly revised during the course of their implementation. Second, while planning agencies are supervising the execution of the plan for the current period, they are also preparing the plan for the next period.

In highly simplified theoretical models of planning, the work is done by a single "central planning board." In practice in the Soviet Union (and other centrally administered economies), planning was carried out by a number of specialized agencies responsible for different aspects, such as output, supply, investment, finance, labor, and technology. For example, the State Planning Committee was primarily concerned with output and investment plans. The State Committee for Material and Technical Supply allocated and monitored flows of producer goods. The State Bank planned and supervised money flows among enterprises, and between enterprises and households. Its subordinate Construction Bank financed investment, and its Foreign Trade Bank handled external financial transactions. The State Committee for Science and Technology participated in decisions on research and development, investment, production, and foreign trade. Hence, the planning process involved a great deal of coordination among different agencies with particular responsibilities.

The following sections discuss, in turn, Soviet central planning of output and supply, investment, financial flows, and foreign economic relations. The focus is on the "operational" annual national economic plans. In addition, there were much less detailed five-year plans that set forth major goals and priorities of the Soviet regime and provided a framework for the annual plans. Also, some planning—especially for aspects of consumer goods production, housing construction, and labor use—was done on a regional (republic, province, or local) basis.

### Output and Supply

In the spring of each year, work began on the preparation of output and supply plans for the next calendar year. The intricate process consisted of a number of overlapping stages, which may be depicted in a somewhat simplified way as follows.[7]

**Directives.**   In April, usually, the Council of Ministers, guided by the Communist party leadership and secretariat, established a set of aggregate growth targets for the main types of output (machine building, agriculture, and so forth) and activities (investment, retail sales, and so forth) of the economy. These aggregate targets reflected, on the one hand, the goals of the five-year plan, and, on the other hand, the State Planning Committee's assessment of what was possible in view of the actual performance of the economy in the past year or so. On the basis of these directives, the State Planning Committee, in consultation with other central agencies, then prepared a set of "control figures" constituting initial aggregate plan assignments for the branch ministries.

**Input Claims.**   In the early summer, each branch ministry disaggregated its preliminary output assignments among its departments. The latter, in turn, distributed their assignments among their component enterprises (or production associations). Each level then submitted to the next higher level requests for authorization to use labor, materials, fuels, machinery, and other inputs in the amounts claimed to be necessary to achieve the proposed output assignments.

**Bargaining.**   In the late summer, bargaining occurred between the enterprise and the department, between the department and the ministry, and between the ministry and the central agencies over the combination of output assignments and input authorizations for each level. The lower level commonly sought an "easier" plan—with more inputs relative to outputs—through more generous input authorizations, more modest output assignments, or both.

**Balancing.**   In the fall, the State Planning Committee and other concerned agencies undertook to balance the revised output assignments and input authorizations of the numerous branch ministries into a consistent national economic plan.

**Approval.**   The national economic plan was submitted to the Council of Ministers for approval in November, and a summary of it was then ratified in December at a meeting of the Supreme Soviet, the central legislature of the USSR.

**Disaggregation.**   In December or January, the ministry sent to the department, and the department in turn sent to the enterprise, the unit's approved plan for the new year.

---

[7] For a detailed account of Soviet planning of output and supply, see Fyodor I. Kushnirsky, *Soviet Economic Planning, 1965–1980* (Boulder, Colo.: Westview Press, 1982).

In the planning process, the critical link between input authorizations and output assignments for an enterprise was a set of input norms. These technological coefficients stated how many units of labor, machine time, and materials and components of various kinds should be necessary to produce one unit of output. These norms were initially based on statistical studies of past experience, but they were often revised ("tightened") to reflect expected gains in productivity, in the technical sense of reductions in the amount of labor time, machine time, or materials required per unit of output.

A major task of planning was to achieve internal consistency between planned supplies and planned demands for commodities. For this purpose, a large number of "material balances" were constructed for a wide variety of raw and semifinished materials, fuels, machinery, and equipment. Each balance was expressed in a relevant physical unit—for example, electricity in kilowatt hours, steel in tons, cloth in square meters, and so forth. The balance identified and summed the planned sources and uses of supply during the period.

Figure 23–2 shows a simplified version of such a balance. On the sources side are current production and imports during the period, and stocks at the beginning of the period. These stocks include producers' inventories of goods that are finished but unshipped, users' inventories of incoming materials, and reserves under the control of a central agency called the State Committee for Material Reserves. One possible use of the commodity is as an input into the production of another commodity, for example, the use of coal in the production of steel. Among the possible final domestic uses are household consumption (cloth sold to households), government consumption (fuel for the armed forces), and investment (equipment installed in a new factory). Some output may be exported. Finally, some of the supply available during the period will be in stocks, of the three types mentioned, at the end of the year.

It would be lucky, although unlikely, for planners to find total sources and total uses in a particular material balance to be equal on the first try. Because of the Soviet tendency toward "taut" planning, typically total uses initially exceeded total availabilities, and equality had to be sought through increases in sources, decreases in uses, or both. However, any change had repercussions to be evaluated and weighed against the alternatives.

**FIGURE 23–2**   Simplified Material Balance for a Commodity January 1, 19__–December 31, 19__ (millions of units)

| Sources of Supply | Uses of Supply |
|---|---|
| Current production | Intermediate inputs |
| Imports | Final domestic uses |
| Stocks on January 1 | Exports |
|  | Stocks on December 31 |
| Total available | Total required |

For example, on the uses side, a cut in the amount for intermediate inputs would, *ceteris paribus,* decrease the output of other goods made with the commodity. This would cause reductions in the current production entries on the sources side of the material balances for the other goods. A decrease in exports would adversely affect the balance of payments. Adequate stocks were necessary to assure uninterrupted production. And the final uses of consumption and investment by the state, cooperative, and private sectors had priorities assigned by the political authorities.

On the sources side, an increase in current production might seem a tempting solution, but it would divert resources from other activities into the manufacture of this item. Imports might require scarce foreign currency. It was unlikely that stocks at the beginning of the period, only a few months away, could be increased much.

Hence, there were difficult decisions involving other material balances and various agencies concerned with related activities (retail trade, investment, defense, foreign trade, and so forth). Equality between total sources and total uses in a material balance usually was achieved through changes in the amounts for entries on both the sources side and the uses side.

To decrease the adjustments needed in other material balances, planning agencies might tighten input norms linking balances. For instance, when the current production entry on the sources side was raised, producers might not be given a proportional increase in input authorizations. Or when the intermediate inputs entry on the uses side was cut, the output assignments of using firms might not be reduced proportionally. In either case, greater technical efficiency in resource use was ordered.

After the material balances were approved, offices of the State Committee for Material and Technical Supply matched up supplying enterprises and customer enterprises. The partners then worked out with each other detailed contracts covering the deliveries of specific items by type, model, quality grade, color, shipment dates, and so forth.

In addition to material balances, various other techniques—such as input–output tables, mathematical programming, and econometrics—were employed in supplementary ways at different levels and stages in the planning of output and supply.

Input–output tables show how (1) the total output of each "industry" and (2) the supplies of "primary" inputs of labor, capital stock, land, and imports are used—either as intermediate inputs in production or directly for some final demand like consumption, investment, defense, or exports. For this purpose, the production of the Soviet economy was divided into about 250 "industries," with each considered both as a supplier to the others and as a customer of the others (respectively, as a row and as a column in the table). With input–output tables, planners could obtain an overall picture of the economy and explore the implications of alternative broad paths for its development. But these tables were not suitable for the detailed current planning of output and supply. First, input–output tables had far too aggregated a classification of production (about 250 industries versus material balances for more than 50,000 product groups). Second, when alternative output programs were examined through input–output tables, both fixed technological coefficients and constant returns to scale were assumed. In contrast, planners were not bound by these restrictive conditions when they adjusted material balances.

Linear (and to a much smaller extent nonlinear) programming was used in the Soviet Union in such planning tasks as choosing among alternative technologies, distributing output assignments among enterprises, and matching supplier and customer enterprises to reduce transportation costs.

Finally, econometric techniques were employed in a limited way, for instance, to estimate production functions and consumption functions from time series data.

## Investment

There were three main types of investment decisions in Soviet planning. First, the share of investment (or "accumulation") in the national product was determined by the political leadership with advice from the State Planning Committee. Second, the total amount of investment was distributed among sectors, industries, and regions. This decision was made by the State Planning Committee, with the approval of the political leadership, through the use of marginal capital–output ratios which indicated the amount of investment needed for a given increase in output. The third decision involved the investment in a particular new plant. This decision concerned the relative proportions of its capital and labor inputs, and was sometimes called the "choice of techniques," namely, alternative production methods.

In Soviet parlance, the first two investment decisions, comprising a combination of political judgments and economic analysis, were considered "planning" (*planirovanie*), while the third decision, entailing engineering–economic calculations, was labeled "project design" (*proektirovanie*). The last decision will be explained further.[8]

A project–design organization of a ministry was given the following information: the approximate location of the new plant (in a particular province or city), the desired annual outputs of specific products, and a set of input prices. These prices covered capital inputs for construction, machinery, and equipment to build the plant, and current inputs of labor, materials, fuels, and power to operate it thereafter. The project-design unit was to cost out alternative possible "variants" of the plant which differed in regard to the amount and types of construction, machinery, equipment, labor, fuels, etc. Then, with both

---

[8] Investment planning is discussed at length in David A. Dyker, *The Process of Investment in the Soviet Union* (Cambridge, England: Cambridge University Press, 1983).

initial capital costs and subsequent operating costs considered, the "minimum-cost" variant was to be identified.

The general rule was to choose the variant for which

$$C + E^*K = \text{minimum}$$

where

$C$ = the annual operating cost
$K$ = the initial investment cost
$E^*$ = the "normative coefficient of effectiveness" (NCE)

The NCE was an imputed capital charge, usually 12 percent, used to obtain an annual amount for capital costs. The NCE was an entirely notional figure for planning purposes. Its value did not correspond to the estimated annual rate of depreciation of the project's capital stock, or to the tax on assets to be paid by the plant once it was built and in operation.

Suppose the respective values (in millions of rubles) of C and K are 5 and 100 for one variant (i.e., plant design) and 8 and 85 for another variant with less capital-intensive but more labor-intensive methods of producing the same final output. With $E^* = .12$, the calculated "full" cost for Variant 1 is $5 + .12(100) = 17.0$, and that for Variant 2 is $8 + .12(85) = 18.2$. Hence, the more capital-intensive Variant 1 should be chosen.[9]

This approach to the choice of variants was criticized by Soviet economists on two main grounds. First, the value arbitrarily assigned to the NCE (usually 12 percent but less in some cases) was judged to understate the scarcity of capital in the Soviet economy. (As the reader can confirm, in the above example if $E^*$ were set at 21 instead of 12 percent, the less capital-intensive Variant 2 would have been chosen.) Second, the various prices used for construction, machinery and equipment, fuels, and so on, did not reflect their relative scarcities, as explained below. Thus the variant chosen as "minimum-cost" might not actually have been the most economical.

## Finance

As in other economies, money served in the Soviet Union as a unit of account, a means of payment, and a store of value. The Soviet monetary unit is the ruble, divided into 100 kopecks. Currency circulated almost exclusively in transactions between enterprises and households (e.g., for wages and retail sales) and among households. Payments between enterprises were made by transfers between their bank accounts. Bank money was converted into currency when enterprises drew cash for monthly wage payments, and currency was trans-

---

[9] More complicated versions of this formula, with a time-discount factor, were used to compare variants which differed in regard to the length of time to build the plant and/or its estimated useful life.

formed into bank money when retail stores deposited their daily receipts. Few households had checking accounts, although almost everyone had a savings account.

The task of financial planning in the Soviet economy was to assure that individual enterprises and households in the aggregate had enough (but not too much) money to buy the goods and services intended for them in state output and supply plans. For this purpose, central agencies constructed several financial plans, including the state budget, the credit plan, the cash plan, and the balance of incomes and outlays of households.

Through the revenues of the state budget, the Ministry of Finance took money, representing a potential claim over resources, away from households and enterprises. The two main sources of budget revenue were the turnover tax and taxes on profits of state enterprises, accounting respectively for about 25 and 30 percent of total revenues. The remainder of budget revenue came from a number of lesser sources, for example, personal income taxes and social insurance charges on state enterprise payrolls—respectively, about 8 and 6 percent of total budget revenues.

Despite the name, the Soviet turnover tax was neither a general sales tax of the kind collected by most states and some cities in the United States, nor a general value-added tax of the type widely used in Western Europe. Instead, the turnover tax was an excise tax, levied chiefly on consumer goods at highly differentiated rates and included in the prices of the products.

Personal income taxes (withheld from wages) were relatively low, reaching a maximum of 13 percent on most kinds of income.

Through budget expenditures, the Ministry of Finance provided funds for activities that were scheduled to use resources for which they could not pay from sales revenue. These activities included investment projects (like the construction of new factories, mines, and roads) and collective services (such as health, education, and defense). By far the largest budget expenditure category, with almost 60 percent of the total, was "financing the national economy," which comprised investment grants and some operating subsidies for current production. Next, with about one third of the total, was "social-cultural measures and science," covering education, research and development, health, and welfare programs like pensions, illness benefits, child allowances, and so forth.

The explicit "defense" category in the budget accounted for only about 5 percent of total reported budget expenditures. However, the coverage of this category was not explained, and Western analysts believed that substantial expenditures of a military character were also made under budget categories such as "financing the national economy" and the science component of "education and science."[10]

---

[10] For a detailed treatment of budget revenues and expenditures, see, for instance, Raymond Hutchings, *The Soviet Budget* (Albany, N.Y.: State University of New York Press, 1983).

The other important financial planning and control agency was the State Bank. Like central banks in Western capitalist regulated market economies, the Soviet State Bank issued the currency, held official reserves of gold and foreign exchange, and acted as fiscal agent for the Ministry of Finance by receiving tax revenues, holding government funds, and disbursing budget expenditures. However, unlike Western central banks, the Soviet State Bank did not control a network of independent commercial banks through instruments of monetary policy such as reserve requirements, discount rates, and open market operations. Instead, the State Bank—together with its subordinate Construction Bank, Foreign Trade Bank, and savings bank units—had a monopoly over banking services in the Soviet Union, providing them directly to enterprises and households through thousands of branch offices.

The State Bank regulated financial operations of enterprises in three ways. As noted, on behalf of the Ministry of Finance, the State Bank disbursed budget grants for investment, as well as some operating subsidies. Second, the State Bank lent to enterprises (at nominal interest rates, usually 3 to 4 percent) working capital necessary for their planned activities. Enterprises were dependent on State Bank credit, because they were endowed with a relatively small amount of "own" working capital when they were established, and because inter-enterprise credit was forbidden. Third, enterprises had to keep all their funds in their State Bank accounts, from which they made bank transfers to other enterprises and drew currency for wage payments. The State Bank was thus able to monitor all of the enterprise's receipts and payments, verifying whether they were in accordance with the enterprise plan. This kind of financial supervision was called "control by the ruble."

As part of its planning and control of financial flows, the State Bank prepared a "credit plan" for loans to (and repayments by) state and cooperative enterprises, and a "cash plan" covering the flow of currency among the State Bank, enterprises, and households.

Another important financial plan was the balance of incomes and outlays of households. For the (quarterly or annual) period, this balance showed the composition and total of sources of household money income, and its uses. The major sources included (1) wages from state and cooperative enterprises, (2) income from private sector activity, (3) interest on savings deposits, and (4) transfer payments such as pensions, student stipends, and child allowances. The chief uses were (1) purchases at state and cooperative retail outlets, (2) purchases on the collective farm market and through other "second" economy channels, and (3) saving in the form of additions to savings deposits and currency holdings.[11]

Ideally, total money incomes of households should have been absorbed by a combination of retail purchases and voluntary saving. However, there was

---

[11] As already noted, personal income taxes were withheld from wages, and turnover taxes were included in the prices of state and cooperative purchases.

evidence that in the Soviet Union total money incomes exceeded retail purchases plus voluntary saving. Hence, there was also involuntary saving (in
savings accounts and in cash hoards) by households with excess money they
could not exchange for desired goods and services at the prevailing prices. The
value of household aggregate demand for consumer goods and services exceeded the value of their aggregate supply. This excess aggregate demand was
not automatically absorbed by larger quantities and/or higher prices in state
and cooperative retail trade. Planned quantities were restricted by state priorities, and state and cooperative retail prices for many goods and services were
set and rigidly controlled below the market-clearing levels (see below). The
inflationary pressure was thus "repressed," rather than "open." But the excess demand was reflected, for example, in shortages revealed by empty
shelves and queues for various categories of consumer goods and services at
state and cooperative shops. Only a small part of the excess demand could spill
over to, and be soaked up by, the "second" economy, which was able to
supply only a relatively small range and volume of goods and services.

## Foreign Trade

Policymaking and planning for Soviet foreign trade were done by the State
Planning Committee, other State Committees—such as those for Foreign Economic Relations (involved with foreign aid programs) and for Science and
Technology (concerned with technology transfer)—the Foreign Trade Bank
unit of the State Bank, and the Ministry of Foreign Trade.[12]

The actual export and import operations were carried out by more than 60
foreign trade organizations (FTOs), which acted as intermediaries between
Soviet enterprises and foreign firms. The FTOs bought export goods from
Soviet producing enterprises and resold them to foreign customers, and bought
imports from foreign suppliers and resold them to Soviet user enterprises.
About half of the FTOs were in the Ministry of Foreign Trade, a dozen belonged to the State Committee for Foreign Economic Relations, and the rest
were subordinated to a number of different agencies (for instance, the film
export organization was under the State Committee on Cinematography).

Four main types of plans steered foreign trade activities. First, imports and
exports were specifically identified as sources and uses, respectively, in the
material balances for output and supply discussed above. Second, a separate
export and import plan set the quantities and value of trade by trading-partner
country. This plan was then disaggregated into assignments for the individual
FTOs that dealt with foreign firms. Third, there was a special plan for the
quantities, value, and destinations of deliveries of equipment and materials for
projects built abroad with Soviet technical assistance by units of the State

---

[12] The planning and conduct of Soviet foreign trade are discussed in H. Stephen Gardner, *Soviet
Foreign Trade: The Decision Process* (Boston: Kluwer-Nijhoff Publishing, 1983).

Committee for Foreign Economic Relations. Fourth, a balance-of-payments plan was compiled, with separate sections for transactions in convertible currencies, in inconvertible currencies of capitalist market economies, and in special accounts with centrally planned economies in the Council for Mutual Economic Assistance (CMEA).[13] Each of these sections of the balance-of-payments plan covered receipts and payments for commodity trade, services, and capital movements.

The Soviet ruble itself was an inconvertible currency in several senses. First, it could not be freely converted into foreign currencies at the State Bank. Second, it could not be freely exchanged for goods even inside the Soviet Union, because most producer goods were administratively rationed and many consumer goods were not readily available at the official prices. Finally, even when goods could be obtained for money in the USSR, they could not be freely exported, since exports (and imports) were controlled by the foreign trade plans.

(Foreign trade prices and exchange rates are discussed later.)

## Implementation of Plans

Planning theorists sometimes evaluate the results of central planning in terms of several degrees of increasingly sophisticated ideal achievement—consistency, feasibility, efficiency, and optimality—each of which is a prerequisite for the next.

A "consistent" plan attains a "statistical" equilibrium in which component parts sum to their total and any particular flow (e.g., castings from the steel industry into machinery production) has the same magnitude wherever it appears (rather than one amount in the steel industry plan and another in the machinery industry plan). A "feasible" plan not only is consistent on paper but can actually be carried out by the economy during the period because the necessary inputs (labor, land, capital stock, inventories, and imports) are all available and because the technological coefficients linking inputs and outputs are attainable. Among feasible plans, a plan is judged "efficient" if planners are unable, by reallocating available resources, to increase one type of output without reducing another. Finally, an "optimal" plan is that one, of various efficient plans, which is most desirable according to the ruling social preferences. In the Soviet context, the optimal plan would be chosen by the Communist party leadership from a set of alternative efficient plans.

It is questionable whether Soviet planning achieved even consistency (the weakest of the four conditions just explained), as an examination of the material balance approach to the planning of output and supply shows. In the limited time available to them to construct some 50,000 material balances, Soviet plan-

---

[13] In addition to the Soviet Union, CMEA included Bulgaria, Czechoslovakia, the German Democratic Republic, Hungary, Poland, Romania, Mongolia, Cuba, and Vietnam.

ners were unable to make all of the associated sequential adjustments necessary to achieve a consistent set of figures in numerous related material balances.

A change in one balance is likely to call logically for changes in various other balances. For instance, a change in the entry for the intermediate inputs-use in the balance of Commodity 1, used in the production of Commodity 2, implies changes in the entries for the current production source and also the intermediate inputs-use in the balance for Commodity 2. The sequence can then continue in the same way in the balances for Commodities 3, 4, . . . , $n$.

But the planners were able to adjust through, say, only six of the relevant dozen rounds before the material balances had to be completed. As a result, for example, the intermediate inputs-use entry in the material balance for steel castings included an amount destined for a particular branch of the machinery industry that was too small to permit the amount of current production shown on the sources side of the material balance for that kind of machinery. This, in turn, had further repercussions for the amount of equipment that could be made with the likely reduced amount of machinery, the products to be made in plants that would use the equipment, and so on.

Because of the shortages that resulted from these inconsistencies, Soviet plans were often not feasible, as shown by many reports in the Soviet press of widespread and recurrent underfulfillments of plan assignments. In turn, these unfeasible plans were not efficient. Finally, since Soviet planners found it so difficult to generate one consistent set of material balances in the time available, they could not offer the political leadership a choice among various alternative consistent, feasible, and efficient plans—as would ideally have been desired.

As Soviet plan assignments were at least ambitious ("taut") and often unfeasible, their fulfillment was not routinely assumed. Instead, various organizations exercised complementary supervision over the implementation of plan assignments. Within the branch ministry, the ministry monitored the departments, which oversaw the enterprises. In addition, external supervision was performed by a number of agencies. The State Planning Committee followed the extent of plan fulfillment, with the assistance of detailed periodic reports compiled by the Central Statistical Administration. The Ministry of Finance reviewed enterprise activities in the course of collecting taxes on their profits (which in turn depended on sales revenue and costs) and turnover taxes on consumer goods, and of providing budget grants for investment and current operations. The State Bank monitored enterprise deposits from sales revenue and withdrawals for payments of wages and purchases of materials, components, machinery, and equipment. The Committee of People's Control, a government inspection agency, searched for evidence of mismanagement, waste, and dishonesty in the use of state property and funds. Finally, Communist party units throughout the economy were expected to help identify and correct the causes of nonfulfillment of plans.

During the period covered by a plan, the initial assignments for production, supply, investment, financial flows, and so on, might be altered, perhaps often, for two reasons. One was that superior agencies recognized that these assignments were unfeasible. The second was that some plan assignments, though feasible, were no longer considered desirable, because of changes, since the plan was approved, in political priorities (e.g., for military programs) or in conditions abroad (e.g., new opportunities for foreign aid activities).

Soviet official reports on the extent of fulfillment of quarterly, annual, and five-year plans were difficult to evaluate because of revisions in plan assignments during the period of the plan. Claims of fulfillment (say, by 96, 100, or 101 percent) of plan assignments might refer not to the original assignment at the beginning of the plan period, but to a revised, lower assignment made subsequently, perhaps toward the end of the plan period.

## PRICE SYSTEM

Prices performed several functions in the Soviet economic system:

First, they served as measures of relative importance in a common money unit (rubles) for the aggregation and comparison of goods and services that could not be combined in physical terms—such as tons of coal, kilowatt hours of electricity, square meters of factory construction, numbers of intercontinental ballistic missiles, and so forth. Prices were necessary also to calculate enterprise sales revenue from various products; the costs of inputs of labor, components, fuels, materials, and machine time; and profits as the excess of revenue over costs. Prices were essential for the compilation of the national income and product, the balance of payments, and other social accounts.

Second, prices played an important role in the distribution of personal income, as Soviet households received money wages (and other incomes, such as transfer payments) which they spent to buy goods and services at retail prices.

Third, although in the Soviet economy resources were allocated primarily by planning, prices could affect resource allocation. Prices guided production in the private sector. They also could influence some lower-level allocation decisions in the state sector. For example, enterprise managers seeking to increase sales revenue tried to produce more of the higher-priced, and less of the lower-priced, items in their product mix—subject to the constraints of the minimum amounts specified in their enterprise "assortment" plans. Also, in an effort to reduce costs, enterprise managers endeavored to substitute lower-priced for higher-priced inputs—subject to the amounts of particular inputs available to them.

Prices in the state and cooperative sectors were set by government agencies, chiefly by the State Committee for Prices, while prices in the private sector were determined by the market. The following sections explain briefly the various kinds of commodity prices that constituted subsystems of the So-

viet price system: industrial wholesale prices, agricultural procurement prices,
state retail prices, collective farm market prices, and foreign trade prices.[14]
Wages—the prices for labor services—are covered in a later section.

## Industrial Wholesale Prices

Industrial wholesale prices were used in transactions between state enterprises
for nonagricultural products. There were two types of industrial wholesale
prices. The seller enterprise received an "enterprise wholesale price" for its
output. The buyer enterprise paid for its purchases an "industry wholesale
price" that could exceed the enterprise wholesale price because it included one
or more of the following: (1) a markup for the services of the sales organization
of the producer enterprise's ministry; (2) freight charges, if these were included
in the price because they were paid by the seller, rather than billed by the
transport network to the buyer; and (3) turnover taxes levied on a few producer
goods, such as petroleum products. The following discussion deals only with
enterprise wholesale prices.

These prices were set, usually by the State Committee for Prices, as the
sum of (1) the planned branch average cost of production and (2) an arbitrary
profit markup.

The cost component was the weighted average cost of production per unit
of the total output of all the enterprises in the branch ministry making the
product. These calculations included the costs of labor, materials, components,
fuels and power, and depreciation, but not charges for the use of land or
capital.

On the average for all state enterprises, more than half of total profit was
taxed away by the state (as explained above in the section on finance). The
remainder was retained by the enterprise for bonuses; housing, child care, and
recreational facilities for its personnel; and small investments in the modernization of production. The enterprise plan (see below) specified in a differentiated
way for each enterprise the amount of profit it was to retain and the distribution
of this amount among the three uses.

Industrial wholesale prices set in this way had several deficiencies. Their
coverage of costs was incomplete because of the omission of charges for land
and capital. The arbitrary profit markup did not accurately capture these factor
costs. The resulting prices did not reflect relative scarcities or balance supply
and demand for different products. Instead, the goods were administratively
allocated to users by the central supply agencies. Finally, because they did not
correspond to relative scarcities, these prices were misleading measures of the
relative importance of different goods in enterprise calculations of sales revenue, costs, and profit, and in national plans and macroeconomic balances.

---

[14] For a more detailed analysis, see Morris Bornstein, "Soviet Price Policies," *Soviet Economy*
3, no. 2 (April–June 1987), pp. 96–134.

## Agricultural Procurement Prices

Agricultural procurement prices were paid by enterprises of the Ministry of Procurement for products delivered by state farms and collective farms. The procurement enterprises subsequently sold these products, at industrial wholesale prices, either to the light and food industries for processing (as in the case of grain, cattle, and cotton, for example) or to the trade network for sale to households without further processing (as in the case of fruits, vegetables, and eggs, for instance).

Agricultural procurement prices were set as the sum of (1) the planned average cost of production and (2) an arbitrary profit markup. Because of the great diversity of natural conditions (soil, topography, temperature, and rainfall) for Soviet farms, for each product the agricultural procurement price was differentiated by geographical zones, with lower prices in the lower-cost regions. In this way, the government captured most of the "differential rent" that would have accrued to farms in good natural conditions if they received a price based on costs in the worst production conditions.

One shortcoming of Soviet agricultural procurement prices was that they commonly were set too low to cover costs, including reasonable wages for farm personnel, and provide profits sufficient to finance the investments the farms should have made in buildings, equipment, and animal herds. Also, the zonal differentiation of prices imperfectly reflected the extent of regional variations in the costs for different products.

## State Retail Prices

Purchases in state and cooperative retail outlets were made at state retail prices. Soviet households did not exercise "consumer sovereignty" over what was to be produced for sale in these outlets. State agencies determined both the quantities offered and their prices. But households did have "consumer choice" regarding how, in the light of their tastes, to spend their money incomes on the available goods at the prevailing prices (and what part of their money incomes to save).

In this kind of controlled market for consumer goods, the nominal general principle was to try to set state retail prices so as to "clear the market" by balancing household demand with state supply. A market-clearing price would be high enough to "ration" the available supply of a good among households by price, rather than by some other means such as administrative allocation. There would be no unsatisfied effective demand on the part of households desiring the item and able to pay for it. In turn, the market-clearing price would be low enough that all planned sales of the commodity would be accomplished, with no excess stocks above planned inventories.

Such a state retail price could be set as the sum of three components—(1) the industrial wholesale price, covering the producers' cost and profit in making the good; (2) the "trade markup," for the cost and profit of the wholesale and retail trade network in distributing the good; and (3) the turnover tax, a differentiated excise tax discussed in the section on finance above.

In Figure 23–3 suppose that the supply of this good during the period is planned at *OS* units and the planners' estimate of household demand for the good during the period at different relevant prices is shown by the demand curve *DD*. Then the market-clearing price will be *OC* rubles, corresponding to point *E* on the demand curve. The supply curve *SE* is vertical because supply, fixed by the plan, is completely inelastic with respect to the retail price. Suppose further that, per unit of the good, the industrial wholesale price is *OA* rubles and the trade markup is the additional amount *OB* − *OA* rubles. Then the turnover tax per unit should be equal to *OC* − *OB* rubles, just enough to bring the price to *OC* rubles.

However, in Soviet practice many state retail prices did not clear the market by balancing household demand with state supply.

First, pricing agencies might aim for a market-clearing price that equates estimated household demand with planned state supply, but then find that actual demand and/or supply differed from those used in pricing calculations. For instance, with reference to Figure 23–3 a price of *OC* rubles will be too low to clear the market if the actual demand curve lies above *DD* and/or if the actual supply is less than *OS* units. The former could occur if household incomes are larger, or tastes for this good are stronger, than estimated. The latter could happen because the output plan for the good was not fulfilled.

Second, some prices were intentionally set below a market-clearing level because planning agencies (and their political superiors) did not want all of the

**FIGURE 23–3**   Composition of State Retail Price

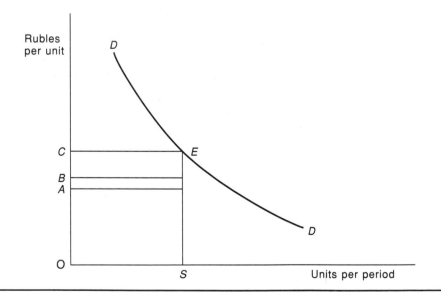

supply to go only to the high-income households which alone could afford to buy a very scarce commodity at a market-clearing price. When social policy precluded distribution through a combination of retail prices and money incomes, nonprice rationing mechanisms were used. At the below-market-clearing price there were shortages, and supply was distributed, with payment at the official price, through formal administrative allocation (as in the case of rentals of new state apartments) or through the willingness of households to queue outside shops (as in the case of meat).[15]

## Collective Farm Market Prices

On the collective farm markets, the supply came from the production of private plots and from the output of collective farms after they met their delivery quotas to state procurement enterprises. In these markets, prices were set by supply and demand and varied from day to day and from market to market. These prices often exceeded state retail prices for the same products by 50 to 100 percent. One reason was shortages at state stores when prices there were below the market-clearing level. Another was the willingness of buyers to pay a premium for better quality and greater freshness of products on the collective farm market, compared to what was available in state stores.

## Foreign Trade Prices

Soviet foreign trade organizations bought from and sold to Soviet enterprises at industrial wholesale prices. But these prices, which did not reflect relative scarcities even in the Soviet economy, could not be used in trade with foreign countries. Instead, separate "foreign trade" prices were necessary.

Soviet trade with market economies was conducted at world market prices expressed in world trading currencies such as the U.S. dollar, the British pound, and the West German mark.

Soviet trade with other CMEA countries was carried on at CMEA "contract" prices. The general rule was that the CMEA contract price for a product should be based on an average of world market prices for it in the preceding five years, although there were various complications in the application of the rule and some exceptions to it.

As a result of these pricing practices and the inconvertibility of the ruble (discussed above), the arbitrary Soviet official exchange rates between the ruble and other currencies set by the Soviet State Bank had limited operational significance. These rates were not expected to reflect the relative purchasing powers of currencies or to equilibrate the balance of payments.

---

[15] Some state retail prices, especially for food products such as bread and meat, were below the sum of the industrial wholesale price and the trade markup. The retail price therefore included a subsidy rather than a turnover tax.

These official exchange rates were used in Soviet foreign trade statistics to translate trade figures in various foreign currencies into special "foreign trade" (*valuta*) rubles different from domestic rubles. For example, if the Soviet official exchange rate between the U.S. dollar and the ruble was $1.50 = 1 ruble, trade of 150 million dollars was reported as 100 million foreign-trade rubles. The official exchange rates were also employed to express CMEA contract prices and trade in "transferable" rubles (TRs) that were equivalent to foreign trade rubles. For instance, if the Soviet official exchange rate was 3.5 West German marks = 1 ruble, a CMEA contract price based on a world market price of 3,500 West German marks was expressed as 1,000 TRs.[16]

Only a narrow range of noncommodity transactions actually involved the exchange of foreign currencies for rubles at the Soviet official rates. This occurred, for example, when foreign visitors exchanged convertible currencies for ruble notes upon arrival at the airport in Moscow.

## ENTERPRISE MANAGEMENT

The management of a Soviet industrial enterprise included the director; the executives in charge of the sections for material supply, labor, production, accounting, and so forth; the superintendents of production shops; and the foremen who were first-line supervisors. The head of the Communist party group in the enterprise had an influential advisory role in managerial decisions. Finally, the chairman of the trade-union unit in the enterprise shared such managerial responsibilities as eliciting worker effort and enforcing labor discipline.[17]

The following sections explain the tasks of the enterprise management, its incentives to accomplish them, and some of the methods it used in pursuit of good performance.[18]

### The Enterprise Plan

The Soviet enterprise operated on an "economic accountability" (*khoziaistvennyi raschet,* or *khozaraschet*) basis which had four main features. (1) The enterprise was set up as a legally separate entity endowed with its own fixed

---

[16] However, the name "transferable" ruble (TR) was somewhat misleading because a country holding TR balances could not freely use or transfer them. For example, if Hungary acquired a TR balance from a trade surplus with Czechoslovakia, Hungary could not use the TR balance to buy goods in the USSR or to settle part or all of a deficit in its trade with another CMEA country, say Romania. Instead, Hungary had to arrange to use up the TR balance by running a trade deficit of the necessary amount with Czechoslovakia in the next plan period. Thus, the TR was only a unit of account, and CMEA was not a payments union for clearing trade balances through mutual offsets.

[17] Trade unions are discussed further in a later section.

[18] On Soviet enterprise management, see, for example, William J. Conyngham, *The Modernization of Soviet Industrial Management* (Cambridge, England: Cambridge University Press, 1982).

and working capital provided by budget grants. (2) The enterprise had its own account in the State Bank, and borrowed additional working capital from it (as discussed in the section on finance above). (3) The enterprise concluded purchase and sale contracts with suppliers and customers, in accordance with the supply plans given to the various enterprises. (4) The enterprise was expected to earn a profit, from an excess of sales revenue over costs, and to surrender most of the profit in taxes to the Ministry of Finance.

The enterprise received from the next higher administrative level in its ministry comprehensive and highly detailed annual, quarterly, and monthly plans, partly in physical units and partly in money terms. These "technical-industrial-financial" plans specified the following:

1. The quantities of output by major types (the "assortment") and the corresponding value of sales at the centrally set industrial wholesale prices.

2. The amounts of materials, components, and fuels allocated to the enterprise (for which it paid at industrial wholesale prices).

3. The authorized number of workers, distributed by major categories (production, technical, administrative, and so on); the total wage fund to pay them at the centrally set wage rates (see below); and the growth of labor productivity (measured as the value of output per worker).

4. Profits and the rate of profit in relation to assets.

5. Payments from and to the budget.

6. The amount of capital investment in construction and equipment; the distribution of investment by specific projects and the schedule for their completion; and the new technology to be introduced thereby.

As discussed above, these plans were demanding. It was difficult, sometimes impossible, for the enterprise management to achieve its production and investment assignments with the resources allocated to it. Moreover, some of the allocated resources might not, in fact, be available.

## Managerial Incentives

Managers had two main kinds of incentives to strive to fulfill these hard plan assignments.

Their "material" incentives included relatively high salaries in their jobs and the prospect of substantial bonuses for fulfillment (and greater bonuses for overfulfillment) of plan assignments. Good performance might also be rewarded by promotion to a better post, while poor results could lead to a demotion.

The "nonmaterial" incentives of managers comprised power from the command over people, property, and money; personal satisfaction from successful solutions to challenging problems; and perhaps public recognition, for instance in the newspapers.

## Efforts at Good Performance

To obtain these material and nonmaterial rewards, enterprise managers strove to get easier plan assignments in the stage of plan construction and to fulfill the nonetheless tough plans given them in the stage of plan implementation.

In the first stage, the enterprise management bargained with its hierarchical superiors for plan assignments with smaller increases in output and/or larger increases in inputs, compared with the preceding period. As part of the bargaining process, the management understated the enterprise's production potential. For example, the management claimed that many of its machines were prone to break down, with long repair periods. It asserted that it could not make a unit of the product with the amount of labor, materials, and machine time stated in the input norm. It underreported the amount of materials, components, and fuels on hand, in order to have concealed "reserves."

Also, the management tried to avoid output assignments that increased the enterprise's specialization in later stages of production. The management preferred to manufacture components inside the enterprise rather than to become dependent for them on outside suppliers that might fail to make scheduled deliveries because the supplers' output plans were too ambitious.

The management furthermore resisted innovation in the products the enterprise was to manufacture or in the production methods it was to use. Such innovation appeared risky to the management, because commonly it involved new outside sources of supply for materials and parts, the need to retrain personnel or hire additional skilled workers in a tight labor market, and the timely installation of more advanced machinery and equipment. It was easier for the management to produce more of the same assortment of output by the same methods than to undertake product innovation or process innovation.

From past experience, the administrative level above the enterprise was well aware that enterprise managers tried for "softer" plans. While the higher level might make some concessions during the bargaining process, it nonetheless gave the enterprise an exacting plan which the management of the enterprise had to exert itself to fulfill.

In the stage of plan implementation, the biggest single problem facing the management was to secure material inputs administratively allocated to the enterprise but in fact not available because of shortfalls in the production of suppliers. To obtain scarce supplies, enterprise managers engaged in unplanned "second" economy activities, such as the use of "expediters" to barter materials with other enterprises.

When specific materials could not be obtained even by these illegal means, the management might substitute other materials that were available, for example, metal sheets thinner than those prescribed in the quality specifications for the product. The use of inferior materials or components was likely to reduce the service life of the product, but the buyer might not learn of the substitution and the consequences for some months or years.

Another method of response to input shortages was the substitution of output through changes in the product-mix. For instance, a clothing factory unable to get all of the scheduled supply of cloth might make more of the smaller, and less of the larger sizes, in order to produce more garments.

Finally, when such measures prove insufficient, the management might file false reports, claiming that it accomplished plan assignments for output or investment that were in fact not fulfilled. However, two factors constrained such false reporting. First, the management might get caught by one of the several supervisory agencies monitoring its activities (see the section on plan implementation above). Second, plan assignments for the next period would involve an increase over the results for the current period (a relationship sometimes called the "ratchet" effect). Hence, overreporting could lead to future plan assignments even more difficult to accomplish.

# LABOR

The Soviet Union had a controlled labor market in which the state created jobs and set their wages, and people sought the best positions they could get subject to some important constraints. The following sections explain in turn the main features of the labor market; the wage system; and nonwage sources of household income, such as transfer payments in money and public services in kind.[19]

## Labor Market

The State Planning Committee, in conjunction with the State Committee on Labor and Social Problems and other organizations, prepared "balances" showing the estimated supplies of labor of different kinds in various geographical areas and the desired use of these workers by branches of the economy. The labor plans for the period were successively disaggregated until the individual enterprise was told the total number of employees it was authorized to have, and the distribution of this total by broad categories such as production, technical, clerical, and administrative personnel.

Able-bodied people of working age in the Soviet Union were normally expected to hold jobs, unless they were full-time students, members of the armed forces, or in prison. About 90 percent of the labor force was employed. People were free to find their jobs except in certain cases of compulsory assignment for a few years. One example was conscription for obligatory military

---

[19] On labor and household incomes in the Soviet Union, see, for example, *Labor and Employment in the USSR,* ed. David Lane (New York: New York University Press, 1986); Bruno Granicelli, *Soviet Management and Labor Relations* (Boston: Allen and Unwin, 1988); J. L. Porket, *Work, Employment, and Unemployment in the Soviet Union* (London: Macmillan, 1989); and Silvana Malle, *Employment Planning in the Soviet Union* (New York: St. Martin's Press, 1990).

service. Another was the assignment of new graduates of technical schools and universities to their first jobs for three years. In this way the state filled, for instance, less desirable teaching and health care positions in rural and remote areas. After completing the period of compulsory duty, a person could leave to seek another job.

Aside from these special cases of administrative assignment, labor planning agencies relied on three main methods to channel workers into the jobs created by state plans. One was the system of differential wages discussed in the next section. The second was the control of occupational training. The third was placement services.

Labor and educational planning agencies determined the quantity and type of opportunities for postsecondary education. The number of places was far less than the number of applicants, and many young people failed to gain acceptance to the training program they desired, or even to another. In principle, admission quotas to different educational programs were related to expected labor needs when students graduated. For example, the number of students accepted for a five-year program in chemical engineering was linked to the estimated number of new chemical engineers required five years later. However, in practice the connection between education and future job openings was somewhat looser, because planners did not have full knowledge of future labor needs and because the capacities of the various parts of the educational system could not be easily changed.

Job placement centers undertook to match enterprises with vacancies and workers seeking first or new jobs. In addition, a special organization recruited people in the developed Western parts of the USSR for work in construction projects, mining, and other activities in Siberia, the Far East, and the Far North.

There were several constraints on an individual's job search. One was his or her occupational qualifications, acquired through postsecondary education or on-the-job training. Another was state control, through the issuance or denial of a residence permit, of the city in which a person might legally live and work. Finally, the choice of employment, or a change in it, was influenced by the general shortage of housing (at the extremely low official rents) and by the fact that part of the housing stock was held by enterprises for the use of their employees.

Soviet planning agencies found it particularly difficult to fill some jobs, for instance in heavy or unpleasant work and in the climatically harsh areas of the country, such as Eastern Siberia and the Far North. Planners were also concerned about excessive labor mobility. People quit jobs because they wanted higher wages, better working conditions (including child care facilities provided by the enterprise), or different housing. Planners disliked "unplanned" job turnover at the initiative of the workers, for several reasons. One was the loss of labor input and thus output during the interval, often one to two months, between jobs. Another was that the worker's labor productivity was likely to be below average for a month or two both at the end of the old job and at the beginning of the new one. Finally, retraining costs might be involved.

In addition to frictional unemployment of people between jobs, there was some evidence of structural unemployment in the Soviet Union, for example, of women seeking positions in light industry or services in regions where the available vacancies were in construction or mining. However, the Soviet Union did not experience cyclical unemployment due to periodic contractions in aggregate demand such as those observed in market economies. In the USSR there were no arrangements for unemployment compensation, because the state asserted that its plans created enough jobs for the labor force and that people unwilling to take existing vacant positions therefore were voluntarily idle.[20]

## Wage System

The wage for a job in the Soviet Union was determined by a number of factors. One was the occupation; for instance, an engineer's wage was double that of a retail clerk. Another factor was the skill grade distinguishing, for example, more from less qualified machinists. The top grade (of usually six to eight grades) often got 50 to 100 percent more than the bottom grade. Third, there was an allowance of 10 to 35 percent for hot, heavy, or underground work. Fourth, for the same work (say, as a junior electrician) the wage was greater in higher-priority branches such as machine building than in lower-priority branches such as retail trade. Finally, there were regional supplements of 10 to 100 percent for work in more remote and/or climatically unattractive areas.

This wage structure represented in part an effort to apply the principle of "equal pay for each work," taking into account knowledge, skill, responsibility, and so on. In addition, the wage structure recognized the relationship between the demand and supply for labor in particular jobs.

However, actual earnings might differ from the specified wages. First, managerial personnel received bonuses for fulfilling plan assignments. Also, workers could get specific rewards for exceeding output quotas, economizing on inputs of certain materials, or making suggestions for improvements in production methods. Finally, managers competing in a tight labor market to get, or keep, scarce skilled workers might evade wage regulations, for instance by classifying workers into higher pay grades than their qualifications justified.

Almost all Soviet workers belonged to the corresponding branch trade union. But these unions did not bargain over wages, hours, or fringe benefits. The main responsibility of union officials was to help management get workers to perform their tasks well. However, union representatives did assist workers

---

[20] See Paul R. Gregory and Irwin L. Collier, Jr., "Unemployment in the Soviet Union: Evidence from the Soviet Interview Project," *American Economic Review* 78, no. 4 (September 1988), pp. 613–32.

in pursuing, with enterprise management, grievances about the application of rules and work norms to individuals, as well as problems concerning job safety, food service, child care facilities, and so forth.

## Nonwage Incomes

Nonwage incomes in the Soviet Union were of two types. Some were for factor services, such as interest on savings deposits and incomes (in money and in kind) from "second" economy activities, like the private plot. Nonfactor incomes included cash transfer payments and income in kind from public services, from instance of education and health, provided at no charge.

According to Soviet official statistics, based on sample surveys of family budgets, transfer payments in money and public services in kind together constituted on the average one fourth of the family income of an industrial worker and one fifth of the family income of a collective farmer. (However, because the coverage and valuation of the public services component were not fully explained, it is best to regard these figures only as rough evidence of the significance of transfer payments and public services as sources of family real income.)

The largest cash transfer payments category was old-age pensions. Normally, men were eligible for retirement pensions at age 60 after a minimum of 25 years of employment, and the corresponding figures for women were 55 and 20. There were lower retirement ages and minimum employment periods for certain occupational groups, such as miners working underground. About one third of all pensioners worked part-time.

Other transfer payments included survivor pensions for dependents upon the death of a worker, disability pensions, sickness benefits, paid maternity leaves, child allowances, and family income supplements to families whose income fell below a minimum level.

There were no tuition fees at any level of Soviet education. Entrance to higher education in universities or technical institutions was very competitive. On the average only one applicant in three obtained a place. Once admitted, a student commonly received a stipend for subsistence expenses. The size of the grant depended on the field of specialization, the year of study, and the student's grades.

Soviet state health care was free, though some people chose to pay for treatment by physicians or dentists who practiced at home in their spare time. Prescription drugs were sold at highly subsidized prices.

In the USSR few statistics about income distribution were published. However, it appears that the initial distribution of wage income was less unequal than in developed capitalist market economies. The extent of inequality in the distribution of real income was subsequently reduced by transfer payments, public services, and retail pricing policies that involved subsidies on rent and many foods and large turnover taxes on consumer durables and high-fashion goods bought by upper-income groups. The personal income tax was not sufficiently progressive to play an important role in this respect.


## ECONOMIC REFORM

The centrally administered Soviet economic system had some serious shortcomings. Plans for output, supply, investment, and finance were based on incomplete and sometimes inaccurate information. As a result these plans were often unfeasible, as revealed by evidence of bottlenecks, shortages, idle capacity, undesired inventories, and other forms of inefficiency and waste. Because industrial wholesale prices did not reflect relative scarcities of material inputs and outputs, these prices could not play a major role in resource allocation. Also, these prices gave economically misleading measures of relative importance in calculations at the enterprise and higher levels.

Soviet enterprise managers strove to maximize total output and sales, in physical or money terms, at the expense of cost and quality. Excess demand for producer and consumer goods created sellers' market conditions in which buyers accepted poor quality products or substituted an available item for the one really desired. Also, enterprise managers resisted assignments for the modernization of products or processes. They considered such innovation riskier than making customary items by familiar methods, as well as unnecessary when output could easily be sold, without regard to cost, at the centrally fixed prices.

These systemic features had significant adverse consequences for the productivity of labor and capital, technological progress, the growth of national product, and the improvement of the population's living conditions in the USSR.[21] As a result, various proposals for changes in the economic system were made by Soviet economists and officials.

Some favored an "administrative decentralization" approach that involved some devolution of authority over selected decisions from higher to lower tiers in the administrative hierarchy, for example, from the central agencies to branch ministries, from these ministries to their departments, and possibly from the departments to the enterprises. The aim was to transfer to lower levels some of the more detailed decisions regarding the composition of output and production methods. Possessing more information on these subjects, the lower level could make more sensible and more timely decisions about them—though within the constraints of global output assignments and input authorizations from the next higher level. Such a shift would also reduce the burden of

---

[21] For a more detailed appraisal of the Soviet economic system, see Richard E. Ericson, "The Classical Soviet-Type Economy: Nature of the System and Implications for Reform," *Journal of Economic Perspectives* 5, no. 4 (Fall 1991), pp. 11–27.

decision making at higher levels, freeing them to concentrate on their nondele-gable responsibilities for more important questions.

Other advocates of economic reform supported an "economic decentral-ization" approach that envisioned a greater role for market forces in determin-ing the composition of output, the allocation of resources, and the distribution of income. The activities of different enterprises would be coordinated to a greater extent by direct "horizontal" market links, with a reduction in the role of "vertical" commands through the administrative hierarchy. Supply and de-mand, operating through more flexible prices, would guide decisions on outputs and inputs. Profit—the "synthetic" indicator simultaneously encompassing all aspects of enterprise activity—could then become the appropriate measure of an enterprise's contribution to the economy, and the basis for bonuses to its personnel.

In the USSR, administrative decentralization was resisted by the officials of organizations that would thereby lose power over activities they controlled.

Economic decentralization was opposed for this and other reasons. The objection on ideological grounds was that "socialism" involved not only public ownership of the means of production but also comprehensive and detailed central planning and administrative control of output, investment, prices, and income distribution. Also, with widespread shortages at administratively set prices, any "rationalization" of the price system to reflect more closely the relationship of supply and demand would entail large price increases, which in turn might require substantial increments in wages. Finally, if emphasis on profitability led enterprises to lay off (or not hire) excess workers, unemploy-ment would rise.

In the face of such opposition, economic reform made little headway in the USSR, as the following examples illustrate.

A set of measures introduced in 1965 ostensibly expanded the authority of enterprise management by reducing the number of performance indicators as-signed in enterprise plans and establishing arrangements for the retention and use of part of the enterprise's profit. But the administrative levels above the enterprise continued, in fact, to control all of the decisions nominally turned over to the enterprise. After a few years, this "economic reform" was seldom mentioned in Soviet publications.[22]

The creation, beginning in 1973, of production associations as a level be-tween the department and the enterprise was a centralizing, rather than a decentralizing, step. The department did not surrender power to the production associations, which instead got some of the authority previously exercised by their component enterprises.[23]

---

[22] Gertrude E. Schroeder, "Soviet Economic Reform at an Impasse," *Problems of Communism* 20, no. 4 (July–August 1971), pp. 36–46.

[23] Alice C. Gorlin, "Industrial Reorganization: The Associations," in *Soviet Economy in a New Perspective* (A Compendium of Papers Submitted to the Joint Economic Committee, 94th Cong., 2nd Sess.) (Washington, D.C.: U.S. Government Printing Office, 1976), pp. 162–88.

In 1979 the Soviet government introduced a program to "improve the economic mechanism." It involved a variety of measures affecting aspects of planning, performance indicators, incentives, and finance. But the program was not an "economic reform." Rather, it was an effort to strengthen the effective control by central planning agencies and ministries over the operations and results of the Soviet economy. However, this program was incompletely and unsatisfactorily implemented, and little was changed in the Soviet centrally administered economy.[24]

During 1986–91 the Gorbachev regime adopted a variety of economic reform measures. In the state sector, they included administrative reorganizations; a reduction in detailed central planning and administrative orders; an increase in enterprise management's authority over outputs, inputs, and wages; and opportunities for some enterprises to engage more directly in foreign trade. The government also permitted the expansion of cooperative and individual business activity, chiefly in agriculture and services. Legislation affecting property rights was passed. Some centrally set prices were raised and others were decontrolled. However, the Gorbachev regime's economic reform measures were partial rather than comprehensive, sometimes mutually inconsistent, frequently revised, and often weakly implemented.[25] Therefore, they failed to achieve fundamental changes in the economic system or to arrest the decline in Soviet economic performance before the breakup of the USSR after an unsuccessful coup attempt against Gorbachev in 1991.

---

[24] Morris Bornstein, "Improving the Soviet Economic Mechanism," *Soviet Studies* 37, no. 1 (January 1985), pp. 1–30.

[25] See Gertrude E. Schroeder, "Anatomy of Gorbachev's Economic Reform," *Soviet Economy* 3, no. 3 (July–September 1987), pp. 219–41; Ed A. Hewett, *Reforming the Soviet Economy: Equality versus Efficiency* (Washington, D.C.: Brookings Institution, 1988); Padma Desai, *Perestroika in Perspective; The Design and Dilemmas of Soviet Reform* (Princeton, N.J.: Princeton University Press, 1989); Gur Ofer, "Budget Deficit, Market Disequilibrium, and Soviet Economic Reforms," *Soviet Economy* 5, no. 2 (April–June 1989), p. 107–61; Anthony Jones and William Moskoff, *Ko-ops: The Rebirth of Entrepreneurship in the Soviet Union* (Bloomington, Ind.: Indiana University Press, 1991); Anders Aslund, *Gorbachev's Struggle for Economic Reform*, 2nd ed. (Ithaca, N.Y.: Cornell University Press, 1991); and Marshall I. Goldman, *What Went Wrong with Perestroika* (New York: W. W. Norton, 1991).

## Chapter Twenty-four

# Post-Soviet Economic Reforms in Perspective*

## *Gertrude E. Schroeder*

*The 15 sovereign states that replaced the Soviet Union in 1991 have begun a long and difficult transformation from socialist centrally planned economies to capitalist regulated market economies.*

*In this chapter, Schroeder analyzes how this transition is hampered by the "legacies" of Soviet institutions, development strategies, and economic policies. Next she considers the specific measures necessary to accomplish a succcessful transformation, including stabilization, liberalization, privatization, creation of a new legal framework, and restructuring of production. Then she examines steps taken so far in different successor states. She concludes with an assessment of the economic and political factors affecting the future progress of economic reforms in these states.*

## INTRODUCTION

The Soviet Union, which played such a fateful role in world history for more than seven decades, is no more: in December 1991 it was replaced by 15 independent states, 11 of them loosely associated in a new entity called the Commonwealth of Independent States (CIS). The new states are in the throes of a societal transformation unprecedented in nature and scope. In essence, they are experiencing three, thus far largely peaceful, revolutions: (1) the transformation of governance from dictatorial rule to rule by participatory consensus, (2) the transformation of the economic system from socialist central plan-

* Reprinted from *The Former Soviet Union in Transition* (Study Papers Submitted to the Joint Economic Committee, U.S. Congress, 103d Cong., 1st Sess.) (Washington, D.C.: U.S. Government Printing Office, 1993), vol. 1, pp. 57–80, with the omission of references to unpublished papers and limited-circulation documents. Gertrude E. Schroeder is Professor of Economics at the University of Virginia.

ning to one based on private enterprise and markets, and (3) the transformation from units in a highly integrated and centrally managed empire to fully sovereign nation-states. Given the unique legacies of failed Communism, successful completion of any one of these revolutions would be daunting. Together, they pose challenges of such scope and complexity as almost to defy comprehension, let alone succinct description of the ongoing processes.

As these intertwined revolutionary processes unfold in the coming years, the need to assess the progress of the three transformations will be ever present. Evidence of progress (or regress) will take the form of innumerable actions at all level of society and in all arenas—political, economic, and social. The cacophony of daily happenings will constantly need to be put into a perspective framework, so as to avoid premature judgments based on the headline event of the moment. In assessing the pace of change, such perspective requires a clear picture of the state of affairs at the outset and of the legacies of the past. It requires an organized outline of what the transformations require in terms of institutions and physical and psychological reorientations based on understanding of the necessary underpinnings of the desired new order. And it requires that reasonable expectations be formed regarding the ease, speed, and smoothness of such fundamental changes in societal institutions and human behavior.

This study aims to develop such a perspective, focusing on the economic transformation. First we review the key physical and institutional legacies and the shared experiences which define the economic starting point for each of the new states that have emerged from former Soviet republics. These states are widely diverse in history, culture, ethnic composition, resource endowments, and level of development. Next we outline what must be done to accomplish a successful economic transformation from central planning to markets—the declared goal of all 15 states. Then we describe what has been accomplished thus far, for Russia in some detail, and for the other states more summarily. The study concludes with an evaluation of that brief record, putting it in perspective and speculating about the ability of the post-Soviet states to meet the many critical challenges that they face.

## THE LEGACIES OF SOCIALIST CENTRAL PLANNING: A COMMON INHERITANCE

The Soviet system of governance has left formidable legacies for its successor states. These legacies are to be found in the remnants of the institutions through which the economy was managed for many decades and in the habits and mindsets of the people whose behavior was molded by those institutions. Other legacies, perhaps even more terrible, stem from the development strategies that were pursued and are embodied in the physical capital stocks of each new state, in its land and its environment, and in the skills of its labor force. Related to those institutions and strategies are the legacies which are primarily the result of protectionist policies. Those policies insulated business firms not only from foreign competition, but from domestic competition as well. Nonetheless, the old system, despite its manifest flaws, did generate economic growth, secular gains in living standards, and an extraordinary degree of personal economic security. To maintain perspective on the emerging new economic orders in the successor states, one needs to keep in mind the totality of the old monolithic order and its legacies, both good and bad.

## Economic Institutions

Under the old regime, the economy functioned through a system that possessed its own internal logic and through institutions that were closely interconnected and mutually reinforcing.[1] Virtually all productive property was owned collectively, mainly by the state. Resources were formally allocated through centrally dictated plans for production and associated physical allocation of material inputs and capital to firms. Economic organization was hierarchical, with firms and farms functioning essentially as the lowest level units in a bureaucracy. Prices were set administratively, changed infrequently, and served mainly an accounting function (as was the case with money and bank credit). Thus, prices, money, and financial variables played only passive roles in the economy. Work incentives, while also job-related, were geared to meeting the centrally dictated production plans. Finally, the formal institutions were supplemented in practice by a variety of informal arrangements and behavioral norms (both semilegal and illegal, but marketlike in character) that on balance facilitated the functioning of the formal arrangements which proved to be so deeply flawed in practice. This so-called "second economy" functioned in the sphere of production as well as in consumption. Queuing and black markets were perennial features of everyday life.

The presence of these institutions meant that socialized property became nobody's property, with no one having a personal stake in maximizing its income stream and its value over time. It meant that firms throughout the production-distribution chain were oriented vertically toward satisfying their organizational superiors rather than horizontally toward pleasing their suppliers and customers. It meant that prices became accounting units which reflected neither relative costs nor relative scarcities even tolerably well. It meant that money was not real money in the sense of a universal carrier of options to buy goods and service of one's choice. It meant that there were no capital and financial markets and that banks acted essentially as accounting and money transfer agents for the government. Workers were educated and trained in the service of this institutional milieu. These institutions are the polar opposites of those characteristics of a well-functioning market economy.

---

[1] For discussion of this point see, in particular, Alastair McAuley, "Central Planning, Market Socialism, and Rapid Innovation," in *Technology Transfer and East-West Relations,* ed. Mark E. Schaffer (New York: St. Martin's Press, 1985), pp. 32–49; and Richard C. Ericson, "The Classical Soviet-Type Economy: Nature of the System and Implications for Reform," *Journal of Economic Perspectives* 5, no. 4 (Fall 1991), pp. 11–28.

## Development Strategies

A hallmark of Soviet development strategy was its long-continued addiction to unbalanced growth of the economy. To mobilize resources for economic growth, investment was pushed to a near-maximum at the expense of consumption. From the outset, investment was allocated disproportionately to the industrial sector, and within that sector to heavy industry and defense at the expense of consumer goods industries. Agriculture and the service sectors were relatively neglected, although in later years investment was directed disproportionately to agriculture as the perceived panacea for its perennial shortcomings. Moreover, Moscow-dictated regional development policies fostered specialization rather than diversification in each republic. The outcomes of this strategy are to be seen in the pattern of land use, in the nature and location of the physical capital stock, and in the deployment of the work force in each of the successor states. These are the physical facts of life with which they necessarily must begin their independent course. To one degree or another, their economies begin with overblown and distorted industrial sectors, unduly large amounts of resources tied up on farms, and grossly backward service sectors, where the accumulated backlog of neglect is awesome to behold.[2]

To speed up economic growth and to compensate for the manifest inability of Soviet-style institutions to economize resources, a mobilization strategy was pursued. Capital stocks were accumulated beyond the point of diminishing returns and at excessive costs in terms of consumption forgone by the population. Working-age adults were drawn into the labor force to such an extent that labor force participation rates are a near-maximum. Land was deployed and natural resources employed in the service of production, with scant attention paid to the environmental consequences. By the time of the Soviet Union's demise this growth strategy was no longer viable, and its legacies are visible and formidable. They are found in massive and largely obsolescent stocks of machinery, equipment, and buildings (often unsuitably located); in the fact that almost everyone has some job which is regarded as a right; and in the parlous state of the environment. These are other characteristics of the physical inheritance, in varying degrees and configurations, of each of the successor states.

## The Ultimate in Protectionism

The foreign trade institutions and policies in place in the USSR over many decades effectively shielded producers from all foreign competition. Within a general policy of trade aversion and, after World War II, a strong orientation toward trade with other socialist countries, Moscow planners decided what products were to be imported and in what quantities. The idea that imports should be used to spur efficiency in firms was completely alien. Rather, imports

---

[2] These and other severe economic distortions brought about by socialist central planning are described in Jan Winiecki, *The Distorted World of Soviet-Type Economies* (Pittsburgh, Pa.: University of Pittsburgh Press, 1988).

were obtained to fill gaps in domestic production essential to meeting overall plans. Procurement of imports through specialized government agencies and their allocation through supervising ministries also meant that business firms were insulated from contacts with their foreign suppliers. A bias toward import substitution figured importantly in planners' decisions about the expansion of domestic production capacities.

Similarly, firms were protected from having to try to sell their products on foreign markets. Planners decided what part of a firm's output was to be exported, and, if need be, accorded the firm special benefits to make its products salable abroad. In any case, the firm knew that whatever was not exported would be allocated to domestic customers. Exporters did not deal directly with their foreign customers, but instead, with state bureaucracies. In general, exports were viewed as a necessary evil, the price that had to be paid for unavoidable imports.

The protected environment for Soviet firms was enhanced by the fact that the bulk of trade throughout the postwar period was conducted within the framework of the Council for Mutual Economic Assistance (CMEA) trading system. Essentially, under that arrangement Soviet energy and raw materials were bartered for relatively inferior East European machinery and manufactures. It was a system of largely captive markets, in which sizable mutual economic interdependencies developed, but without the necessity to settle accounts in real money (hard currency). The accrued production interdependencies made all CMEA members and their firms highly vulnerable to any move to end the captive markets.

Extreme protectionism for business firms extended to the domestic arena as well. Firms did not have to compete with one another for customers or even to find them. Rather, a firm's products were "sold" or, more aptly put, "distributed" for it via its plan for "sales." To make matters worse, many firms were endowed with the ultimate in protection—monopoly or near-monopoly in the production of particular products. This ubiquitous situation arose from planners' misguided notions about the economic efficiencies to be had from concentrating output in giant agglomerations. The legacy of such policies is a world of monopolies. For example, according to Soviet data for the late 1980s, more than one third of all important machinery products (such as sewing machines, tram rails, and locomotive cranes) was made by only one producer, and another third was made by only two firms.[3]

This policy of "gigantomania" created large and critical interdependencies, which were reinforced in their geographical impact among republics by the central government's regional development and industrial location policies. These policies fostered specialization rather than diversification in each republic. Plants were designed and sited predominantly in the interest of the country

---

[3] These and a variety of other statistics showing the high degree of industrial concentration in the Soviet Union are cited in Heidi Kroll, "Monopoly and the Transition to the Market," *Soviet Economy* 7, no. 2 (April–June 1991), pp. 143–74.

as a whole. In a sense, this approach maximized inter-republic trade in an institutional setting that permitted firms to exchange their products in a highly protected market—another "captive market," in effect. As with foreign trade, these exchanges were arranged by state bureaucracies (mainly the industrial ministries and the State Committee for Supply) rather than by the firms themselves. Again, this situation made each republic and its producers highly vulnerable to dissolution of the internal Soviet market. To cite only one set of statistics characterizing the mutual vulnerabilities, in 1989, imports (domestic and foreign) provided from 15.7 percent (Russia) to 31.0 percent (Armenia) of republic consumption, and exports accounted for from 10.7 percent (Russia) to 27.1 percent (Azerbaidzhan) of republic production.[4] These mutual trade dependencies are deeply embedded in the production profiles, capital stocks, and labor skills in each new state and cannot be altered in any major way in the short run.

Finally, enterprises as well as republic governments themselves were insulated from bankruptcy or insolvency through a complex network of monetary transfers and by the highly centralized financial system. Firms did not have to seek out investors or banks to obtain new capital; instead, funds were supplied to them virtually without charge. If firms ran into financial difficulties, they could expect to be rescued by their parent ministry. Bankruptcy and closure because of insolvency were unknown. Republic governments did not have to concern themselves with raising revenue and balancing their budgets. Rather, their role was to administer budget revenues and expenditures largely determined for them by the central government. Whenever planned expenditures exceeded allocated revenues, the central government simply re-jiggered the flows or provided subsidies. If republic governments wanted to increase investment or social expenditures, they needed to lobby the fiscal authorities and central economic ministries in Moscow.

Individuals, too, were protected from economic vicissitudes. The state guaranteed jobs for everyone who wanted one. School-leavers could rely on the government to find them their first jobs. Reinforced by the fact that much housing and many welfare benefits were provided by employers, workers came to regard their particular jobs in particular firms as economic rights. Housing, health care, and education, although rationed in various ways, also came to be provided as social rights with only nominal charge, if any. To a large extent, a job entitled the employee to housing, recreational facilities, and social benefits financed by the employer. Social security systems provided income for the aged, the disabled, and families who lost a breadwinner. Finally, after World War II the rate of inflation was low, wages rose much more rapidly than prices, and social benefits were increased periodically. Such was the relatively secure

---

[4] These and other data on inter-republic dependencies are presented in my paper, "Economic Relations among the Soviet Republics," in *Investing in Reform: Doing Business in a Changing Soviet Union,* ed. Michael P. Claudon and Tamar L. Gutner (New York: New York University Press, 1991), pp. 19–37.

and predictable milieu that most people came to value and to associate with socialism.

## Economic Performance

Although nowadays almost universally discredited, the socialist production system proved able to generate fairly steady economic growth, albeit at markedly declining rates after 1975. According to the best measures available in either East or West (those of the U.S. Central Intelligence Agency), annual growth of GNP averaged 3.4 percent for the 40-year period 1951–90.[5] Growth was positive in every year but three—1963, 1979, and 1990. But while growth rates averaged about 5 percent in the 1950s and 1960s, the average rate fell to 2.5 percent in the 1970s and to 1.2 percent in the 1980s. Over the whole period, however, the Soviet growth rate was not able to keep up with Western Europe's, and it even ceased to gain on that of the United States after 1965. These relationships held true on a per capita basis as well. Thus, so-called "development gaps" were widening quantitatively and, as is now becoming ever more evident, qualitatively as well.

Moreover, in the postwar period, the Soviet people saw their lot improve dramatically, albeit from very low levels. With the higher priority accorded to consumption by post-Stalin leaderships, per capita consumption grew rapidly, registering an average annual growth of 2.8 percent during 1951–90. Again, however, the pace of gains in living standards slowed markedly—from a total gain of 35 percent in the 1950s to a mere 9 percent during the 1980s. Although "consumption gaps" with the West were widening, especially in qualitative terms, the Soviet people were able to perceive steady and palpable improvements in their living standards over the years in terms of more and better food; more clothing and footwear of more modern design; fast-growing stocks of consumer durables, including much-coveted automobiles; more spacious housing with more amenities; and additional services of many kinds. Antiquated though it was by Western standards, the USSR's cumbersome retail distribution system did manage to make most daily necessities available for purchase most of the time, at least until the end of the 1980s. While queuing was commonplace, people found a variety of ways to better their lot through informal channels. Judging from an extensive Western survey of Soviet emigrés, people were moderately well satisfied with their overall standard of living.[6] The significance of all this is that in the midst of today's turmoil, people can remember that socialism did work after a fashion.

Also part of the performance legacy of socialist central planning, however, is the fact that those gains in economic growth and living standards were

---

[5] *Measures of Soviet Gross National Product in 1982 Prices* (A Study Prepared for the Joint Economic Committee, U.S. Congress, 101st Cng., 2nd Sess.) (Washington, D.C.: U.S. Government Printing Office, 1990).

[6] *Politics, Work, and Daily Life in the USSR: A Survey of Former Soviet Citizens* (Cambridge, England: Cambridge University Press, 1987).

obtained at grossly excessive costs relative to the Western experience. Unlike in the West in general, Soviet growth was fueled by a massive buildup of capital stock, near-maximum mobilization of the population into the work force, profligate use of energy and raw materials, and an almost total disregard for the environmental consequences of what amounted to a policy of production at any cost. Whatever the disputes over the numerical calculations, it would be generally agreed that improvements in productivity beyond those embodied in the capital stock and a better-educated work force contributed little, if at all, to Soviet growth—a situation markedly different from Western growth experience.[7] Also, it is now generally agreed that the "technology gap"—as reflected in the quality and modernity of the physical technologies and processes used throughout the Soviet economy, and therefore embodied in present stocks of machinery and equipment—is large relative to the West and has been widening in recent years. There is no dispute either that the energy and raw materials intensity of Soviet production technologies exceeds those in the West by wide margins. This lamentable outcome is mainly the result of the fact that technological progress had to be "introduced" from above, because the system lacked incentives to generate it from below. Finally, observers agree that damage to the physical environment and to human beings has been inordinate; witness is given by the Chernobyl disaster and the title of a recent book, *Ecocide in the USSR: Health and Nature under Siege.*[8]

## A Treadmill of Attempts to Reform Socialism

Although the debilities of socialist central planning were visible from the start, they had become ever more evident by the mid-1960s, as economic performance indicators began to worsen and the sources of extensive growth began to dry up. Soviet leaderships from Khrushchev through Gorbachev believed that remedies could be found through within-system reforms. Their numerous actions were intended to make the system more efficient while leaving its essential features intact. Since it was those very features that influenced the behavior of economic agents and therefore economic outcomes, such efforts amounted to trying to square the circle and they came to naught.[9] Despite the

---

[7] For a masterful survey of Soviet growth experience, see Gur Ofer, "Soviet Economic Growth, 1928–1985," *Journal of Economic Literature* 25, no. 4 (December 1987), pp. 1767–1833.

[8] Murray Feshbach and Alfred Friendly, Jr., *Ecocide in the USSR: Health and Nature under Siege* (New York: Basic Books, 1992).

[9] This section relies on my papers on Soviet economic reforms, especially "Soviet Economy on a Treadmill of Reforms," in *Soviet Economy in a Time of Change* (A Compendium of Papers Submitted to the Joint Economic Committee, U.S. Congress, 96th Cong., 1st Sess.) (Washington, D.C.: U.S. Government Printing Office, 1979), vol. 1, pp. 312–40; "Soviet Economic Reform Decrees: More Steps on the Treadmill," in *Soviet Economy in the 1980s: Problems and Prospects* (Selected Papers Submitted to the Joint Economic Committee, U.S. Congress, 97th Cong., 2nd Sess.) (Washington, D.C.: U.S. Government Printing Office, 1982), pp. 68–88; and "Organizations and Hierarchies: The Perennial Search for Solutions," *Comparative Economic Studies* 29, no. 4 (Winter 1987), pp. 7–28.

perennial changes, and perhaps to some degree because of them, economic performance worsened. Until almost the very end of this process, there were three untouchables—the role of the Communist Party in the economy, the Communist system of property, and government determination of most production and prices. Within that framework, the numerous tinkerings reflected a ceaseless search for panaceas in three areas—economic organization, planning routines, and the degree of autonomy to be accorded to firms, along with incentive schemes for their managers.

Planners seemed to believe that discovery of the "ideal" arrangements for economic organizations would solve the economy's problems. The ensuing search and experimentation concerned (1) organizational relationships between the central government and republic and lower-level administrative units, (2) the structures of the economic bureaucracies, and (3) the organizational structures between these bureaucracies and the enterprises. The permutations and combinations that were tried out almost defy description. Some changes were major, such as Khrushchev's replacement of nearly all of the central economic ministries in 1957 with regional economic councils, and Brezhnev's subsequent restoration of the ministries in 1965. Also important were Brezhnev's drive in the 1970s to amalgamate enterprises into large associations and Gorbachev's establishment of seven supra-ministries (bureaus) during 1985–87 to coordinate the activities of several ministries with similar products or functions. Other innovations were of less consequence but were ubiquitous. For example, Gosplan underwent many reorganizations over the years; the responsibilities for central rationing and pricing were handed about; the number of ministries was increased and then decreased; ministries were divided and then reunited; ministries were shifted from all-union to union-republic status and back again. Through all this, the basic formal organizational structures endured, until Gorbachev's innovations brought about their destruction.

Another theme that prevaded the saga of reforms was the planners' seeming conviction that finding the "perfect" plan and planning routines would lead to similarly "perfect" performance by executants. In search of the optimal plan, postwar planners turned to modern computer technologies and mathematical models. Alterations were often made in planning procedures and routines. The number of plan targets set centrally for firms went through cycles of being decreased and then increased. Specific targets were redefined to make them more "scientific." Terminologies were changed—from mandatory "plan targets" to mandatory "state orders." Procedures were periodically altered in efforts to resolve the perennial tension between "branch" and "regional" planning. Planning through "program-goals" approaches and comprehensive planning for key industrial "complexes" and regions were added to Gosplan's burden and superimposed on the ordinary routines. The fecklessness of the persistent efforts to make central planning work better is shown by a growing divergence between plans and actual results. In the final Soviet 5-year plan (the twelfth) for example, the plan called for an average annual growth of 4 percent in GNP, but the rate achieved was less than 1 percent, as was also true for industrial production, for which average annual growth of 4.6 percent was targeted.

A third focus in the treadmill of within-system reforms was the degree of autonomy that should be given to enterprises and the design of incentive schemes for their managers. The situation was one of ebb and flow, in which the planners broadened the decision-making authority for firms in varying degrees and areas, and then retracted all or parts of the newly delegated authority. Although by no means removed from the dictates of their ministries and central plans, firms were given by far the most extensive delegation of authority when Gorbachev's 1987 package of reforms introduced a new Statute on the State Enterprise. In the growing macro-disarray of the late 1980s, firms in practice were able to exercise ever more independence. They found that they often could ignore the frantic efforts of their superiors to rein them in, and the behavior of firms contributed importantly to bringing down the system of centralized planning.

The frequent changes in the permitted autonomy for enterprises were accompanied by alterations in the criteria for assessing their success and rewarding their managers. While Stalin and Khrushchev focused almost single-mindedly on meeting plans for production in physical and value terms, their successors in their successive packages of reforms tried out a seemingly endless number of other combinations. In the 1965 package, meeting the plan targets for key products in physical units was still required, but bonuses were made dependent on targets for sales and profitability. When that complicated scheme did not bring the desired results, other criteria were added—notably meeting plans for labor productivity and improved product quality. Later, the emphasis shifted to contract fulfillment as the principal criterion for success. In effect, the planners sought to devise schemes that would induce socialist firms to increase production, improve efficiency across the board, improve the quality of products, and pay attention to customers. In a word, they were attempting to elicit capitalist behavior from socialist firms without placing them in a capitalist environment. This was one more failed attempt at squaring the circle.

## Ending the Treadmill of Soviet-Type Reforms

While Mikhail Gorbachev was fond of characterizing his reform initiatives taken before 1990 as both "radical" and "revolutionary," as formally laid out they were neither; in fact, they were a continuation of the decades-long treadmill.[10] But they did contain elements of radicalism, and they set in motion forces that unintentionally catapulted the Soviet economy off the venerable treadmill and into an era of reforms that in concept really are both radical and

---

[10] Details are given in my "Gorbachev: Radically Implementing Brezhnev's Reforms," *Soviet Economy* 2, no. 4 (October–December 1986), pp. 289–301, and "Anatomy of Gorbachev's Economic Reforms," *Soviet Economy* 3, no. 3 (July–September 1987), pp. 219–41.

revolutionary. The reforms adopted in Gorbachev's first few years of tenure contained two important innovations which were harbingers of things to come. First, he started a discussion about property ownership and launched an expansion of the private sector through legislation on private and cooperative economic activities. Second, he began the process of dismantling the state monopoly over foreign trade. But the real breakthrough occurred in 1990 in a series of developments that brought a sea change on the economic reform front. Since these events have been detailed elsewhere, a summary will suffice to make the point.[11]

In that momentous year, truly radical reform programs were promulgated and some of them were approved by more or less democratically elected legislative bodies. These programs were radical in the sense that if they had been implemented as intended, they would have dismantled the venerable institutions of socialist central planning and ultimately replaced them with those appropriate for a market economy with a sizable public sector. The harbinger of those historic developments was the so-called "Abalkin Blueprint"[12] set forth in the fall of 1989, which for the first time made property ownership the centerpiece of reform.[13] This theme also figured in a more subdued way in the more conservative programs set forth by the government of Prime Minister Ryzhkov in December 1989 and in May and September 1990. The most radical of the programs, however, appeared in August 1990 as the much-touted "500-day" (Shatalin) Plan.[14] This program was unprecedented both (1) for its stress on property ownership and (2) for its fast timetables for "destatizing" and privatizing state property and for decontrolling prices—steps that are essential to creating a market economy.

The basic features of the Shatalin Plan were incorporated in more general terms in the so-called Presidential Plan adopted by the federal legislature on October 19, 1990.[15] The language and character of this document stand in marked contrast to those in the 1987 package of reforms. Thus, the document states: "The choice of switching to a market has been made, a choice of historic importance for the country." Unlike its many predecessors, this official document outlined measures appropriate to that goal. Under its general authority, the government in early 1991 sharply increased both wholesale and retail prices, but also freed some 40 to 45 percent of them to be determined through contractual negotiations or to have ceilings, which proved largely un-

---

[11] Gertrude Schroeder, "A Critical Time for Perestroika," *Current History* 90, no. 558 (October 1991), pp. 323–27.

[12] Editor's note: Presented by then Deputy Prime Minister Leonid Abalkin.

[13] See Ed A. Hewett, "The New Soviet Plan," *Foreign Affairs* 69, no. 5 (Winter 1990/1991), pp. 146–67.

[14] Editor's note: Prepared by a group headed by Stanislav Shatalin.

[15] The formal title of the plan was "Basic Guidelines for Stabilization of the National Economy and Transition to a Market Economy."

enforceable. This unprecedented step by the central government made it easier for the successor republican governments to free most prices in January 1992.

In addition to comprehensive reform programs, the year 1990 also marked a watershed in the extent and kinds of reform legislation adopted by both the central and the republic governments. A mere list of their subjects shows their unprecedented nature. They concern property ownership in general; ownership and disposition of land; operating rules for enterprises regardless of ownership; promotion of small businesses; prevention of monopoly, and measures for demonopolization; establishment of a Western-style central bank and commercial banks; creation of a uniform system of taxation of profits; setting up joint-stock companies and securities markets; privatization of property; foreign investment; and entrepreneurship (private economic endeavors). Although legislative progress was uneven among republics and individual laws were flawed and sometimes conflicted with federal laws, this experience in 1990 and 1991 was a vital learning process for the new states-to-be; they did not have to start from scratch.

Other remarkable developments—and indeed essential ones—contributed to the breakthrough on the reform front in 1990 and its solidification in 1991. Above all, there was the meteoric ascendancy to power in republic governments. Even under the old order, this would have been required for effective economic reforms. In the new order, the republics gained experience for the first time in governing rather than merely administering their territories. Second, the central Communist Party's role in the economy and society was shattered—a sine qua non for market-oriented reforms. Third, the Marxist-Leninist ideology faded away, and there was a radical change in the language of economic discourse (although the ideology's mindset still seems to dominate much of the economics profession).[16] Fourth, the onrush of events dealt a fatal blow to the institutions of central planning, rendering them unable to enforce their will on economic agents. Fifth, the cumbersome and inefficient CMEA trading system was ended, along with the organization itself.

While these developments combined to bring about a fall in output, accelerating inflation, a sharp decline in inter-republican and foreign trade, and growing economic chaos, they effectively ended the treadmill of Soviet-type reforms. From then on, economic reform would take a totally different character. Moreover, amidst the mounting disarray in the macroeconomy, critically important things were happening that are essential to the future of the transition to the intended new economic order. At the microeconomic level, ordinary people began to take charge of their lives in myriad ways. Entrepreneurs ap-

---

[16] See Michael Alexeev, Clifford Gaddy, and Jim Leitzel, "Economics in the Former Soviet Union," *Journal of Economic Perspectives* 6, no. 2 (Spring 1992), pp. 137–48, and Pekka Sutela, *Economic Thought and Economic Reform in the Soviet Union* (Cambridge, England: Cambridge University Press, 1991).

peared in rapidly growing numbers. Enterprises acted ever more on their own in pursuit of self-interest. Local and regional governmental bodies started to run their own affairs. Foreign firms continued to invest in the region in increasing amounts and numbers (albeit still small in total). A multitude of individuals and organizations at all levels in society were interacting with their counterparts abroad in a wide range of endeavors. In its totality, the scale of all these developments is large and it is growing.

## FROM CENTRAL PLANNING TO A MARKET ECONOMY: WHAT IS TO BE DONE?

Before its demise in late 1991, the Soviet central government had committed itself to a choice of historical importance—to institute a market economy, with its radically different institutions, to replace the failed economic system of socialist central planning. This decision was a recognition at long last of the futility of further attempts to reform socialism. As of now, each of the 15 successor states has made a similar commitment. Their aim is to join the international community as well-functioning market economies that can generate economic growth and improve living standards for the people. The goal is often put as one of creating a "normal economy." Economic theory and world experience define clearly the basic characteristics of a successful market economy. They are: (1) The vast bulk (three quarters or more) of land and capital assets are in private hands, with property rights that are clearly defined and legally protected. (2) Production is guided by consumers through flexible prices. (3) The economic role of the state is limited to defining and enforcing property rights, ensuring macroeconomic stability, and providing public goods as chosen by the political process. For the new states bent on creating a market economy, this means, simply put, privatization of the vast bulk of now state-owned property, removal of controls on prices and economic activity, and institution of a new role for the state.

Whereas economics delineates the essential characteristics of a market economy, it has no agreed-upon theoretical model which prescribes an optimal strategy for transforming one economic system into another one. But when that possibility became real in the late 1980s (first in Eastern Europe), mapping the transition presented a new and exciting challenge for mainstream economists. Many of them quickly took it up. The result was a lively debate among Western economists, and a subdued one by Soviet economists, about what steps must be taken to achieve a market economy and about the sequence and speed with which the steps ought to be taken.[17] Early on, the issues came to be discussed

---

[17] There already is a large literature on the economics of transition, including the following: "Symposium on Economic Transition in the Soviet Union and Eastern Europe," *Journal of Economic Perspectives* 5, no. 4 (Fall 1991), pp. 3–162; "Symposium on the Economic Transition in Eastern Europe," *Comparative Economic Studies* 32, no. 2 (Summer 1991), pp. 9–177; *What Is to Be Done? Proposals for the Soviet Transition to the Market,* ed. Merton J. Peck and Thomas J.

in terms of "Big Bang" versus gradualism and in terms of whether macroeconomic stabilization should precede privatization or vice versa. Western economists were quick to provide their own "optimal" recipes for accomplishing both of these major tasks. In the process of proffering policy advice to the post-Communist governments and interacting with them, Western mainstream economists learned much about the entrenched economic and political legacies of socialism, and Soviet economists learned much about the desiderata for a market economy. In the meantime, the countries of Eastern Europe were providing models and experience in diverse transition paths and privatization schemes.

Out of these debates and experience has come a broad consensus about what must be done to transform a centrally planned economy into a market economy and to deal with the legacies of many decades of economic development under socialism. These tasks are the following, not necessarily in time sequence:

1. *Stabilization*. Inflation must be brought under control through drastic reduction in budget deficits and restricted credit.

2. *Liberalization*. Prices must be freed from controls. Profit-seeking business firms and farms must be allowed to decide for themselves what to produce and how to produce it. Firms must be able to engage freely in foreign trade. The currency should be made convertible as soon as feasible.

3. *Privatization*. Most land and capital assets must be put into private hands, and market arrangements must be set up for the exchange of such assets. Individuals and groups must be free to establish new private businesses with ease. Monopolies must be broken up.

4. *Regulation*. The state must assume the role of regulator of the macroeconomy and of business activity, using instruments that promote well-functioning markets through their influence on decisions of individuals and firms. The state itself should provide legal and social protection and supply public goods and services in amounts and kinds chosen by electorates.

5. *New institutions*. Legal, accounting, and statistical systems appropriate for a market economy must be established and new financial institu-

---

Richardson (New Haven, Conn.: Yale University Press, 1991); *The Emergence of Market Economies in Eastern Europe*, ed. Christopher Clague and Gordon C. Rausser (Cambridge, Mass.: Blackwell Publishers, 1992); *Transformation of Planned Economies: Property Rights Reform and Macroeconomic Stability*, ed. Hans Blommestein and Michael Marrese (Paris: Organization for Economic Cooperation and Development, 1991); Organization for Economic Cooperation and Development, *Reforming the Economies of Central and Eastern Europe* (Paris, 1992); entire special issue of *Economics of Planning* 25, no. 1, 1992; and János Kornai, *The Road to a Free Economy* (New York: W. W. Norton, 1990).

tions created, such as a central bank and a network of private commercial banks, insurance companies, and securities exchanges.

6. *Restructuring of production.* The mix of goods and services produced must change; land, capital, and labor resources must be redeployed in accord with the preferences of consumers at home and abroad. The state may play a role in such restructuring but ought not to dictate its directions, which should come from market signals.

Couched in summary form, these are the six major sets of tasks that must be carried out by each of the 15 successor states, if they are to create a reasonably well-functioning market economy starting from the physical, human, institutional, and economic legacies of central planning. Each of these major tasks encompasses a multitude of specific tasks and entails numerous and perhaps conflicting choices. What has to be done economically is gargantuan, and the tasks must be accomplished through political processes that are still in formation everywhere. While economists agree that stabilization—creating a credible currency—has to take precedence in the inflationary environment that was inherited from *perestroika*, the sheer magnitude of interconnectedness of the tasks would seem to require that a start be made on almost all fronts simultaneously. The new states will choose their own particular paths and paces of reform. Even though they have common legacies and large economic interdependencies, these choices will be influenced by the political, social, and economic particularities in each state.

## WHAT HAS BEEN ACCOMPLISHED?

During late 1990 and 1991, prior to the breakup of the USSR, all of the republics had adopted some of the kinds of legislation that represent steps toward a market economy. Several of them had promulgated their own comprehensive programs for economic reform. One republic—Estonia—had decontrolled most prices. Evidently convinced of the inability of the central government to spearhead reform, Russian President Boris Yeltsin in late October 1991 outlined a sweeping set of reforms that Russia intended to implement on its own within a short time. Following the center's demise, newly independent Russia began to carry out its program with vigor. Because of their interdependencies and the fact that the ruble is their common currency, the other new states have been forced to follow suit in some respects, notably in the decontrol of most prices. In other respects, the new states are going their own ways, most prominently in the methods and pace of privatization and in agricultural reform. With their independence now recognized by the international community, the former Soviet republics are being admitted to membership in the European Bank for Reconstruction and Development, the International Monetary Fund, and the World Bank with a speed that is unprecedented and astonishing. Delegations from these international organizations, along with many private advisers, are now working with the new states to further the process of reform.

Even at this very early stage, it is useful to review briefly what has been accomplished in the new states in less than a year of independence. In offering these brief surveys, we focus on major essentials and eschew a mass of detail. We also note the extraordinary difficulties in sorting out statements of intent, formal programs, laws passed, and implementation of legislated reforms in practice. Of course, each new state's progress deserves much fuller treatment than can be given in this study, and no doubt will get it as time passes. We reserve overall evaluation of the state of the reform process in the post-Soviet Union to a concluding section.

## Russia

In the course of its struggle for sovereignty in 1990 and 1991, Russia began to lay the foundations for radical economic reform. In those years, legislation was adopted on property ownership, land use, privatization of state property, joint stock companies, demonopolization, and freedom of enterprise. Subsequently, some of this legislation was amended and new reform-related laws and presidential decrees adopted. President Yeltsin's reform initiative in October 1991 outlined plans for bold action in the areas of price liberalization, currency stabilization, and privatization. This program was amended in February 1992, and in June 1992 a three–year program to implement specified reforms was announced.[18]

Progress has been made on a broad front. Prices have been freed for some 90 percent of consumer goods and 80 percent of producer goods. Some controlled prices, most notably for energy, are being raised manyfold. The initial price explosion in January 1992 eliminated the monetary overhang in the consumer sector and returned many goods to the shelves. The rate of inflation was brought down through sizable (albeit still insufficient) reductions in the budget deficit. It is proving difficult to reduce subsidies and restrict credit to large state enterprises. New value-added and generally uniform profits taxes were adopted. A start was made on banking reform, with interest rates raised sharply and a number of private commercial banks established. Many restrictions on freedom to found new businesses have been removed, most notably in the area of domestic trade. Moveover, all enterprises are now free to engage in foreign trade, with some products still subject to licensing and a requirement that half of all hard currency earnings be sold to the state at market rates of exchange. Foreign exchange rates have been unified and a nascent foreign exchange market is in being.

A program for extensive privatization taking a variety of forms is under way, with plans to adopt a voucher scheme later this year. A process of volun-

---

[18] For a full description and analysis of Russia's economic reform, see James H. Noren, "The Russian Economic Reform: Progress and Prospects," *Soviet Economy* 8, no. 1 (January–March 1992), pp. 3–41.

tary decollectivization of agriculture has been started, involving the transformation, by vote of the work force, of collective and state farms into cooperatives, joint-stock companies, or associations of individual peasant farms. As of July 1992, there were 130,000 such farms, and the number has been growing rapidly. New pension, unemployment compensation, and worker retraining programs are in place, with partial indexation of wages being sanctioned. Finally, an impressive start has been made on the restructuring of production, simply by virtue of a drastic reduction in military expenditures and a new program that allows defense enterprises to devise and execute their own strategies for conversion. It appears also that budgetary investment is being confined largely to financing economic and social infrastructure.

## Western Republics

Ukraine, Belarus, and Moldova have much in common. The governments in all three states have stated their intention to create a market economy and have taken significant steps to do so via legislation and programs, but implementation has been slow thus far. Most prices were freed in early January 1992, but more of them remain regulated than do in Russia. All three states have tentative plans to introduce their own currencies, Ukraine being the farthest along on this path. Each has its own national bank and has made a little progress toward commercializing its banking system. In 1992, each state reformed its tax system—replacing the old turnover and profits taxes with new value-added taxes, uniform profits taxes, and a variety of explicit excise taxes—but none has achieved adequate control over budgetary expenditures and bank credit. All three have social safety nets in place, with that of Ukraine being the most generous and containing provisions for nearly total indexation of wages to compensate for price increases.

By early 1992, the legislatures in the three states adopted laws on ownership of property and land, freedom of economic activity, demonopolization, and privatization of state property. A law on privatization of housing took effect in Belarus on July 1, 1992. Although the change in ownership of property has been miniscule thus far, the governments have recently announced plans to implement the process. All three have yet to do much in the area of agricultural reform, although Ukraine managed to create 10,000 private farms as of midyear 1992, despite much resistance.

Progress on reform in Moldova has been slowed not only by political conservatism, but also by the military conflict over the status of the Dniester region, and in Ukraine, by sparring with Russia about jurisdiction over the Crimea and over the military forces of the former USSR.

## Transcaucasia

Like the Western republics, Georgia, Azerbaidzhan, and Armenia have managed to adopt some of the key legislation needed to accomplish their stated objective of marketizing their economies, but (except for land reform in Armenia) little has been done to implement these laws and decrees. In their brief period of independence, these three states have been plagued with ethnic strife and (in Georgia and Azerbaidzhan) by struggles over control of the government. Following Russia's lead, the three states decontrolled most prices in early 1992. Azerbaidzhan and Armenia have plans to adopt their own currencies ultimately, and the new Georgian reform program raises that possibility. All three states now have their own national banks and a few private commercial banks, and all three have replaced the old turnover and profits tax arrangements with new value-added, profits, and excise taxes.

With respect to property ownership and privatization, the picture is one of diversity. Armenia has adopted such legislation, along with a program for land reform under which about 80 percent of all agricultural land formerly in the hands of state and collective farms has been privatized and some 165,000 individual farms established. Azerbaidzhan in early 1992 adopted two major pieces of reform legislation—a new law on land use and a decree on "Urgent Measures" for demonopolization, destatization, and privatization of property. It seems, however, that this decree has yet to be buttressed with specific legislation and a concrete plan for implementation. Although Georgia adopted major legislation on property (mainly in 1991), only in mid-May 1992 did it manage to formulate a comprehensive reform program, which calls for extensive privatization by a variety of methods over the next several years. Under the earlier legislation, however, the republic has put state housing into private hands through free transfers and has begun to give peasant families free plots of land of 1.25 hectares (about 3 acres). Under this land reform program the government plans to privatize roughly half of all agricultural land by mid-1992 and later on to begin disbanding the large state farms.

## Central Asia

Although there are important differences in the vigor of political support, the leaders of each of the Central Asian states (Kazakhstan, Kyrgyzstan, Tajikistan, Turkmenistan, and Uzbekistan) have stated that they are committed to achieving a market-oriented economy. Up to now, their approaches have been conservative, and on the whole not much has been accomplished yet. The vast bulk of prices have been freed in each republic, but each has rolled back some consumer prices in early 1992. Each has set up its own central bank, mainly based on laws adopted in 1991, but little has been done to commercialize the banking system. By early 1992, however, all five republics reformed their tax systems, with value-added, profits, and excise taxes replacing the old turnover tax and profits taxes. As of now, these states seem intent on remaining in the ruble zone, despite recent talk of establishing national currencies in some of them.

With regard to property ownership, destatization, and privatization, there is considerable diversity. By early 1992, all of these states adopted laws on land use, privatization, and freedom of economic activity. They (except apparently Tajikistan) have taken initial steps to destatize the farm sector. Uzbekistan, for example, has distributed free parcels of land to peasant families on the principle of extended leasing with inheritance rights; it plans to deal with loss-making collective farms in this way. Turkmenistan is taking a similar approach.

The region's frontrunners in the reform process—Kazakhstan and Kyrgyzstan—began agricultural reforms in 1991 with measures to create peasant farms; sell off or otherwise "privatize" loss-making farms; and transform collective farms and state farms into true producers' cooperatives. At the beginning of 1992, there were over 3,300 peasant farms in Kazakhstan and over 4,000 in Kyrgyzstan. A recent decree provides for rapid privatization of the food-processing industries. These two states are out in front also in their programs for privatization of the nonagricultural sectors. Both states are taking phased approaches that set ambitious targets for fairly speedy privatization of most state assets, including housing, in the next few years. Privatization is to be accomplished in a variety of ways, including distribution of free vouchers to employees. According to an official of the Kazakh State Property Committee, 2,426 small and medium-size establishments were sold by June 1, 1992. Although progress has been slow, both states have recently publicized measures to speed up the process.

## The Baltic States

During their three-year struggle for independence, Estonia, Latvia, and Lithuania led the rest of the former Soviet Union not only in setting the goal of establishing a market economy, but also in conceptualizing programs for accomplishing the transition and starting the process. All three republics freed most prices and abolished most consumer subsidies in 1991, earlier than elsewhere. Estonia dropped all subsidies on food and rents in May 1992—something not yet done even in Russia. All three states have central banks. In June 1992, Estonia adopted its own currency—the kroon, pegged to the German mark—and the other two Baltic states are moving to do so. All three have replaced their old Soviet-style tax systems with value-added, profits, and explicit excise taxes. The three states also have established their own social security systems and have taken measures to protect benefits from erosion by inflation.

With respect to the private sector, again the Baltics led the way. When individual labor activity and the formation of cooperatives were sanctioned by new Soviet laws in the 1980s, the share of new businesses formed in the Baltic republics significantly exceeded the share of these republics in the total Soviet population. Each state has adopted laws, and started implementing their declared intent, to dismantle the state and collective farms and encourage peasant farming. Their programs allow private ownership of land and involve restitution of property confiscated by Soviet authorities in the annexation of these states. A Lithuanian law also provides for the privatization of agricultural equipment. In Latvia, some 45,000 private farms were registered as of June 1992, compared with only 6,456 two years earlier. In the spring of 1992 there were 32,000 such farms in Lithuania and about 7,000 in Estonia. Latvia has nearly completed the transformation of state and collective farms, mainly into joint-stock companies eventually to be privatized, and a similar process is actively under way in Lithuania.

The three states also have adopted a variety of legislation concerning the privatization of nonagricultural property and housing. Their approaches differ, but all involve privatization by several means, including restitution of confiscated property and some kind of voucher scheme. Under the Lithuanian program, according to the Prime Minister, two thirds of the state's property was to be privatized by the end of 1992. Lithuania's legislation establishes investment accounts for citizens and indexes them partly for inflation. These funds can be used to purchase shares in firms or to buy housing. While sales of state firms have gotten off to a slow start, some 60 percent of eligible housing was sold by June 1992. Building on legislation passed in 1991, Latvia in Feburary–March 1992 adopted an array of legislation providing the legal basis for privatization and actively promoting the process, but implementation has been slowed by the unresolved question of who is a citizen of the republic eligible to participate in the process. Although Estonia has managed to privatize a small part of its services establishment and to convert a sizable number of firms to joint-stock companies, the process here, as in agriculture, has been slowed by the complexities of restoring property to former owners. Finally, all three states have rather liberal laws designed to attract foreign investment, and they (especially Estonia) appear to have been somewhat more successful than the other former Soviet republics in obtaining it, mainly from the Nordic countries.

While the reform agenda has by no means been neglected, the energies of Baltic governments have been severely taxed by the mechanics of establishing statehood, difficulties with the Russian government over trade and troop withdrawals, and efforts to cope with specific economic crises such as energy shortages.

## CONCLUSIONS

In its last year of existence, the USSR witnessed the culmination of the combined failures of courses of action it had long pursued in two critical realms— its attachment to within-system economic reforms and its vaunted "nationalities policies."

At long last the leadership was forced to recognize that Stalin's system of socialist central planning could not be reformed, and that escape from a progressive deterioration in economic performance across the board required replacement of that venerable system with the institutions of capitalism. As a consequence, this decades-long treadmill of attempts at within-system economic reform came to an end.

Moreover, the spectacular failure of nationalities policies to create a cohesive nation-state on a territory populated by many diverse ethnic groups was manifested in the dissolution of the Soviet Union itself. Indeed, by creating an administrative structure (the union republics) based on the traditional home-lands of major ethnic groups, the Soviet state had sown the seeds of its own destruction. Once the union government's reins were loosened under the poli-cies of *glasnost* and *perestroika,* the result was a bloodless revolt of the repub-lics that proceeded swiftly and ended in replacement on the world stage of the unitary Soviet state by 15 new sovereign states. Each is a nation-state in the sense that an indigenous ethnic group is dominant in its total population. The speed with which the Soviet state self-destructed gave its successor states (even giant Russia) scant time to assume the many tasks once performed by the center and to prepare for their new status in the international arena. The spear-heading of economic reform and the overall management of the macroeconomy were among the critical functions that had been assumed by the now defunct center.

To gain perspective on what the new states have accomplished thus far in economic reform, we must remind ourselves of what are the most urgent tasks of new statehood. The burden on their new inexperienced governments is immense.

In the area of foreign relations the new states must now formulate their own foreign policy, establish diplomatic relations with foreign states (among them the other former republics of the defunct USSR), and negotiate new international agreements on a wide range of matters. They also must establish a presence in a multitude of international organizations. The new states must decide on matters of national defense, including how to disentangle the for-merly unified Soviet defense establishment.

In the domestic political arena, the new states need new constitutions, laws, and administrative structures suited to independence. The political pro-cesses must be managed to ensure a reasonable degree of stability of govern-ment in order to formulate and execute policy over a broad spectrum. Among the most urgent issues for most of them is how to deal with their minority populations, including separatist demands in several states. In the social sphere, the new states must revamp their social systems and formulate policies to deal with urgent problems in public health, criminal justice, and the environ-ment.

In the economic realm, the tasks are even more daunting and also more pressing, since they concern the daily welfare of the entire population. Pursu-ing the complex tasks of systemic reform sketched above is only one of them, albeit an urgent one, if economic viability is to be sustained in the long run. While pushing the reform process forward, the beleaguered governments must cope with the daily crises stemming from the deep recession into which their economies have been plunged. The reasons for the recession include the col-lapse of the center with its ability to command, the steep decline in defense spending, the disarray in trade with the former CMEA and the former Soviet republics, worker strikes or strike threats, and ethnic strife. The new states must now manage their own public sectors and try to balance their own budgets. Moreover, they need to find ways to maintain social peace during the difficult period of transition and to build a political constituency for continuation of the reform process so as to maintain its credibility. In the international arena, the new states must forge new economic relationships with other countries, interact with them through international organizations, and seek economic aid and foreign investment.

Finally, the new states must deal with the cacophony of voices, both from their own economists and from those in the West, espousing one or another program for reform. Fascinated and challenged by the issues of systemic transformation, foreign and domestic economists have pelted the new governments with advice on how to do it. This advice is often conflicting and sometimes reflects inadequate understanding of the many legacies of the old ways and the political and societal constraints on the policymakers in these fledgling states.

Given the revolutionary nature of the many-faceted transformation from subservience to independence, the speed with which it occurred, and the excessive burden on the new governments, the progress on economic reform thus far is remarkable. In varying ways and degrees, the new states have been able to build on what has been accomplished while the old regime (although increasingly ineffectual) was still in place. That severe difficulties have been encountered in putting legislated changes into practice is only to be expected. Human attitudes and habitual ways of doing things change slowly in all societies. But there is much evidence that such changes are indeed taking place. That the details of specific facets of the reform agenda (e.g., privatization) are subjects of intense political controversy also is not surprising, since the new legislatures lack understanding of economics and are prone to populism. Despite all this, the reform process remains in motion everywhere as of now, even in those new states beset by ethnic conflict.

Meanwhile, market processes are arising from below, as individuals and firms alter their traditional behavior to cope with the new situations they face. That such behavior often may be suboptimal and may even seem unjust (so-called spontaneous privatization, for example) should be expected, especially in the present chaotic macroeconomic environment in all the new states, where governments are weak and legal systems unsettled.

Although systemic transformation is in process at long last in all of the successor states, large elements of the old system remain in place—a situation that could hardly be otherwise, given the short time since independence.

While formal central planning is absent, all of the states have retained the system of state orders ostensibly backed up with state-guaranteed supplies. The reason is their desperate efforts to implement inter-republic trade agreements and to meet what are considered essential state needs, such as assuring food supplies for the cities and securing key products for export for hard currency. State orders are no longer mandatory in Russia, however, and most other states plan to reduce their importance. Old-style bureaucratic structures still exist to administer such remnants of the old central rationing system. But the use of state orders to dictate, and allocate, even a decreasing share of production is becoming increasingly ineffective. Producers ignore state orders if they see fit, and regional units of the supply bureaucracies do likewise.

Governments are still trying to control the prices of some key products, notably energy, raw materials, and agricultural products, but such controls also are proving difficult to enforce. Moreover, the continuance of price controls is creating acute financial problems, as firms and farms struggle to survive in a milieu of prices, some free and some controlled. State ownership of property remains overwhelmingly dominant, and the process of privatization is proceeding slowly. A stable currency has yet to be achieved. Reform of financial institutions, in particular, is at an embryonic stage. Only spotty progress has been made toward revamping the old legal, accounting, and statistical systems.

In restructuring the mix of production, however, much change is occurring willy-nilly. Defense production falls and conversion to civilian products is attempted. Firms and farms, spontaneously or with government prodding, alter their product mixes. The private sector, oriented toward consumers, expands. Such investment as is taking place in the present chaotic conditions gravitates toward consumer-oriented sectors.

The tasks still ahead in establishing the conditions and institutions of a viable market economy are awesome. They would severely tax the political and social fabric of even the most seasoned, stable, and ethnically homogeneous democracy. But there is no *economic* reason why they cannot be accomplished in time. Under the best circumstances, the transformation will require many years. Given the physical and psychological legacies, the full recovery of the economies will be slow in coming. As is already clear, the transformation process will be characterized by much diversity. The Baltic states are already going their own ways, driven by their goal of becoming a part of Europe as soon as possible. Ukraine seems determined to take its own path to cementing statehood and achieving economic reform. For the other non-Russian states, what happens in Russia likely will be critical. If Russia continues to push ahead with economic reforms, the smaller states will be compelled to follow suit, at least as long as they remain in the ruble zone and heavily trade-dependent on their giant neighbor. They can learn from its experience.[19]

In the final analysis, the future of the transformation process in each of the 15 former Soviet republics will depend on factors that have little to do with economics. First and foremost is whether they will remain as states within their present borders. The demographic-ethnic inheritance contains much potential for conflict over territorial integrity, as is already evident. Second, the sustainability of economic reform is contingent upon whether the new entities can maintain reasonably stable and committed governments. Third, sustainability also depends on whether those governments and their populations can avoid

---

[19] For an elaboration of this argument, see my "On the Economic Viability of New Nation-States," *Journal of International Affairs* 45, no. 2 (Winter 1992), pp. 549–74.

consuming their energies and resources in ethnic conflict. Up to now, this factor has hampered the reform process and damaged the economies in several republics.

Although many observers are deeply pessimistic about the future course of economic transformation in the former Soviet republics, I am more sanguine. It is true that even with substantial Western aid, the chances of significant revival of their economies in the near term are slim. Given the likelihood of continued economic deprivation for much of the population and the consequent strains on the political process, economic transformation could stall. But progress by fits and starts is to be expected in any case and seems the most likely course of events. Patience is required both from participants in the transformation and from observers of it.

Nevertheless, the new states, whatever their configuration, have little choice but to make haste slowly toward a market economy, the only economic system that has proved its long-run viability. With so many of the impediments to systemic transformation removed by actions taken in the past two years, it would be a great tragedy if the people and the political leadership of any of the successor states failed to capitalize on those historic achievements and allowed the reform process to bog down in another treadmill of failed attempts to stay the course. Worse still would be attempts to restore the old socialist order. The new states need to hold fast long enough to cross the Rubicon. They must put a critical mass of market-oriented institutional reforms in motion, such that the behavior of most individuals and firms will change fundamentally so as to yield the fruits of the systemic transformation. But in contrast to the old treadmill of attempts to reform socialism, the goal of transition to a market economy is feasible and can have a high payoff, given time, patience, and appropriate international support.

## Chapter Twenty-five

# Privatization in Eastern Europe*

## *Morris Bornstein*[1]

*Privatization is a critical component of economic reform in a socialist centrally planned economy. This chapter provides a comprehensive view of the privatization process and its links with other elements of economic reform in Eastern Europe.*

*The chapter considers why privatization is necessary, which activities should be privatized (in what sequence and at what speed), how divestiture of state assets can be accomplished, and who the new owners might be. It analyzes how privatization can alter productive and allocative efficiency, output, employment, and the distribution of wealth and income. Also, it examines privatization's possible effects upon the government budget, the labor and capital markets, and the balance of payments.*

Economic reform in Eastern Europe has several main dimensions: macro-economic adjustment, marketization, restructuring, integration with the world economy, and privatization. All five dimensions have been involved, to some extent, in economic reforms in less developed countries.[2] However, privatization is more important in the transformation in Eastern Europe from a socialist centrally planned economy to a capitalist regulated market economy, than in

* Revised from Morris Bornstein, "Privatization in Eastern Europe," *Communist Economies and Economic Transformation* 4, no. 3, 1992, pp. 283–320, with the omission of references to foreign language sources, unpublished papers, and limited-circulation documents. Used with permission.

[1] Some of the research for this study was conducted while the author held a Senior Foreign Scientist Fellowship from the French Ministry of Research and Technology, under the auspices of a CNRS-ROSES project on economic reform in Eastern Europe directed by Professor Xavier Richet. Their support is gratefully acknowledged. The author also thanks Christina G. Farmer, Joseph K. O'Brien, and Kristi L. Thiese for their research assistance at the University of Michigan. Professor Ryszard Rapacki of the Warsaw School of Economics made many helpful comments.

[2] *Economic Liberalization in Developing Countries,* ed. Armeane M. Choksi and Demetris Papageorgiou (Oxford: Basil Blackwell, 1986); *Economic Reform and Stabilization in Latin America,* ed. Michael Connolly and Claudio González-Vega (New York: Praeger Publishers, 1987); Lance Taylor, *Varieties of Stabilization Experience* (Oxford: Clarendon Press, 1988); Bonnie K. Campbell and John Loxley, *Structural Adjustment in Africa* (New York: St. Martin's Press, 1989); *Economic Liberalization,* ed. Tariq Banuri (Oxford: Clarendon Press, 1990); and *Economic Crisis and Policy Choice,* ed. Joan M. Nelson (Princeton, N.J.: Princeton University Press, 1990).

economic reforms in countries in Africa, Latin America, and Asia that already have a large private sector. Hence, this study focuses on the role of privatization in East European economic reforms.

The first part is a theoretical and empirical analysis of principal elements of privatization. The next part examines relationships between privatization and four other dimensions of economic reform. The last part summarizes main findings and makes some comparisons with privatization in other regions.

In this study, "Eastern Europe" refers primarily to Hungary, Poland, Czechoslovakia (the Czech and Slovak Federal Republic, CSFR), Bulgaria, and Romania—five countries that have begun a transition toward a capitalist regulated market economy, although along different paths and at different speeds. However, each country's experience is not examined comprehensively or separately. Instead, some country experience is noted to illustrate features and problems of privatization.

The study does not address directly privatization in other areas sometimes included in "Eastern Europe." Privatization in eastern Germany, the territory of the former German Democratic Republic now part of a unified Germany, clearly is a special case. In the former Yugoslavia, privatization has been interrupted by war. Albania is only now starting political and economic reforms. Yet the analytical framework and findings of the study are relevant also to these areas, as well as to successor states of the former USSR.

## ELEMENTS OF PRIVATIZATION

The privatization process can be analyzed in regard to conception, objectives, scope and speed, and methods of divestiture of state assets.

### Concepts

In the broadest sense, "privatization" could embrace any increase in private activity, including the creation of brand-new (start-up) private enterprises, without any reduction in the activity of state enterprises.

Privatization could consist of the substitution of private for public activity by various means without a transfer of ownership of state assets.[3] One method is *franchising*, for example, the long-term grant to a private firm of the right to provide a particular service (such as telecommunications) in a specific geographical area. The firm uses its own plant, equipment, and personnel. Another approach is *contracting* with private firms, usually for shorter periods, for street repair, refuse collection, food service in hospitals, and so forth. In *management contracting*, a private firm manages a state enterprise, such as a hotel,

---

[3] Charles Vuylsteke, *Techniques of Privatization of State-Owned Enterprises, vol. I: Methods and Implementation* (Technical Paper no. 88; Washington, D.C.: World Bank, 1988), pp. 34–39; and *Privatization and State-Owned Enterprises: Lessons from the United States, Great Britain and Canada,* ed. Paul W. MacAvoy and others (Boston: Kluwer Academic Publishers, 1989), p. 46.

under some type of compensation arrangement. Under *leasing,* a private lessee of state assets makes rental payments for their use but assumes the full commercial risk of the operation and has the right to the residual net income.

A narrower, but probably most common, definition of privatization involves the transfer of ownership of state assets to private hands.

This study is concerned with the growth of the private sector through private start-ups and the transfer of ownership of state assets—the two main forms of privatization in Eastern Europe.

## Objectives

Privatization may have various economic, social, and political objectives.

**Economic Objectives.**   Privatization is expected to increase the efficiency of individual enterprises, branches composed of them, and thus the economy as a whole. Two types of efficiency may be distinguished: productive and allocative.

*Productive efficiency* can be improved if the same (or greater) output can be produced at lower cost. In state enterprises the incentives of managers and workers for productive efficiency are weak, for several reasons. Plan assignments stress output rather than cost reduction. Job security is a societal obligation of the enterprise. Losses are covered by budget grants or automatic bank credit. In contrast, under private ownership, without government support, enterprise managers are subject to contractual discipline by shareholders seeking profit maximization; to take-over discipline by potential private bidders; and to bankruptcy discipline by creditors.[4] Thus, privatization of a state enterprise can, for example, reduce overstaffing and cut excessive use of materials and energy.

*Allocative efficiency* entails the assignment of resources to their most productive uses by profit-seeking entrepreneurs when prices reflect relative scarcities—and production and trade controls and barriers to entry and exit are absent. Under public ownership, allocative efficiency may suffer because state enterprises, controlled by government directives and protected from competition by law and trade policies, have weak incentives to respond to prospective buyers' demands concerning quantity, quality, and assortment of goods and services.[5] Privatization can improve allocative, as well as productive, efficiency if competitive pressure is exerted by three forces: (1) the rivalry of many

---

[4] John Vickers and George Yarrow, *Privatization: An Economic Analysis* (Cambridge, Mass.: MIT Press, 1988), pp. 9–27.

[5] In a partial equilibrium framework, productive efficiency in making a given output could increase, even though that output was allocatively inefficient. In a general equilibrium framework, productive inefficiency would also imply allocative inefficiency, because inputs are allocated inefficiently if there exists a Pareto-superior structure of output and consumption. See Richard Hemming and Ali M. Mansoor, *Privatization and Public Enterprises* (Occasional Paper no. 56; Washington, D.C.: International Monetary Fund, 1988), p. 5.

domestic sellers and buyers of the same or substitute goods and services; (2) the lack of barriers to entry and exit; and (3) the absence of protection against imports.[6]

It is possible that a relatively small number of state enterprises could operate reasonably efficiently in an economic system where most economic activity is private. But a small private sector cannot operate successfully in a country dominated by the state sector. Such a country lacks the institutional framework of private ownership and the pressure of competition to stimulate efficiency.[7]

Other economic objectives of privatization include budget revenue from asset sales, absorption of some of the "monetary overhang" of household liquid assets, and an inflow of convertible currency from foreign direct investment. They are discussed further below.

**Social and Political Objectives.**  There are a number of social and political aims of privatization.

1.  Society can seek redress of past injustice when private property is expropriated by the state without proper compensation. In this case, restitution of the property (or, if that is not possible, financial compensation) is proposed.

2.  Another goal is to reduce inequality in the distribution of wealth and income by the repartition of some state property equally among all (resident adult) citizens, for instance, by free transfer of shares in operating companies or in holding companies that have shares in operating companies. Dividends from these shares would decrease inequality in the distribution of income. Also, it is hoped that such "popular capitalism" will create public (electoral) support for further privatization, for economic freedom, and for political pluralism and democratic institutions.[8]

3.  Finally, privatization can weaken the old power structure of Communist elites in state enterprises and the ministries and government agencies supervising ministries and enterprises. However, specific individuals from this *nomenklatura* may remain as managers, and perhaps become owners, of privatized enterprises, as discussed below.

---

[6] In developed capitalist market economies, comparisons of the efficiency of state-owned enterprises and private enterprises may be difficult for several reasons: (1) there are relatively few truly alike cases of public and private firms operating at the same time; (2) the length of time since privatization may be too short for before-and-after comparisons of the same firm; (3) and not all aspects of allocative efficiency are easily measured. See Vickers and Yarrow, *Privatization*, chap. 3. In contrast, the potential efficiency gains from privatization in East European economies are judged to be large by both national and outside analysts.

[7] Alan Gelb and Cheryl W. Gray, *The Transformation of Economies in Central and Eastern Europe: Issues, Progress, and Prospects* (Policy and Research Series, no. 17; Washington, D.C.: World Bank, 1991), pp. 31–32.

[8] Farid Dhanji and Branko Milanovic, "Privatization in East and Central Europe: Objectives, Constraints, and Models of Divestiture" (World Bank conference paper, June 1990), pp. 6–7.

There are some positive (mutually supporting) and negative (mutually conflicting) relationships among multiple objectives. For example, privatization can increase budget revenue, convertible currency receipts, and efficiency. On the other hand, demonopolization before asset sales should improve efficiency by increasing competition, but sale proceeds may be smaller because buyers are not paying to capitalize monopoly profits. Divestiture of state assets by free transfer, rather than sale, of company shares can accomplish widespread private ownership. But it sacrifices potential budget revenue in the short run and also efficiency in the long run if excessive dispersion of ownership weakens corporate governance.

## Scope and Speed

The potential scope for privatization is enormous in Eastern Europe, where 65–90 percent of gross domestic product (GDP) is generated by state enterprises—compared to average state shares of about 10 percent in developed market economies and 15 percent in less developed countries.

Some state assets are more likely to be privatized, to a greater extent and sooner, than others. The reasons include (1) the size of the unit and the amount a buyer must pay to acquire it; (2) the early efficiency gains expected; (3) the possibility of divestiture by a simple method such as auction sale, rather than a complex, yet-to-be-elaborated method such as voucher coupons for shares in holding companies; (4) the need for restructuring before privatization; and (5) political pressures for or against privatization.

Thus, for instance, privatization is likely to include, and may begin with, sale of apartments in state buildings to present tenants; restitution of some socialized agricultural land to previous owners; and sale of small restaurants, shops, and service facilities at auction. Privatization will also comprise small and medium-size manufacturing enterprises that are currently or potentially competitive without substantial restructuring.

In contrast, it will be more difficult to privatize many larger state enterprises in mining and manufacturing before considerable financial and organizational restructuring is accomplished and, in some countries (Poland, Czechoslovakia, and Romania), free transfer schemes are implemented.

Two categories less likely to be privatized are "natural" or technological monopolies and other branches deemed to be "strategic." The former include networks in power generation and distribution, oil and gas pipelines, telecommunications, and transportation, where only a single producer can exploit economies of scale. In such activities, it is possible that a regulated private monopoly might perform better than a public monopoly in regard to productive and allocative efficiency. The reasons are better managerial incentives for efficiency, discipline from the private capital market, and less political interference in enterprise decision making.[9] But in Eastern Europe the privatization of

---

[9] Hemming and Mansoor, pp. 12–13.

network monopolies does not appear probable. Domestic investors will not have sufficient capital. Foreign investors will not have enough interest in such highly regulated activities. The government may in any case consider these activities too "basic" or "strategic" for private ownership.

The state sector may also retain complete or majority ownership of weapons production, oil drilling and refining, mining, and shipping, on "strategic" grounds.

Privatization is likely to be much slower than initially envisioned, for several reasons.

1. In sequencing components of economic reform, governments will decide that privatization should be preceded by measures that establish a more favorable environment for the creation of new private start-ups, the divestiture of state enterprises, and the subsequent operation of private firms. For example, restrictive fiscal and monetary policies should reduce open and repressed inflation. Decontrol of prices should permit market forces to generate scarcity prices to guide resource allocation. In turn, competition in markets should be stimulated by demonopolization, import liberalization, and reduction of barriers to foreign direct investment. To assist workers who will be released when staffing is cut because of privatization, "social safety net" programs for unemployment compensation (and general welfare assistance) and retraining should be set up.

2. Speed may conflict with the attainment of some objectives of privatization. For instance, lower prices in asset sales may speed divestiture, but will reduce budget revenue. Free distribution of enterprise shares can be faster than their sale, but efficiency will suffer if mass share ownership impedes corporate governance. Speed may be achieved at the expense of efficiency if enterprises are privatized before demonopolization.

3. The pace of privatization will be constrained by the administrative capacity of government agencies responsible for it, on the one hand, and by the absorptive capacity of prospective private owners, on the other. In the first case, it will take time for new agencies to learn how to privatize sensibly a large number of varied enterprises. In the second case, it will take time for these agencies to find domestic and foreign buyers or to organize and carry out free transfers of state property. The issues involved are examined in the section below on methods of divestiture of state assets.

## Methods of Divestiture

Divestiture of state assets involves some preparatory steps, an evaluation of alternative approaches to sale and free transfer of property, and a choice of methods, or combinations of them, for divestiture of particular types of assets.

**Preparatory Steps.**   One important preliminary step is to establish clear ownership rights of the (national, regional, or local) government in an enterprise. Following that, privatization could involve either only the transfer of selected assets (to private hands through sale or leasing) or the sale of an entire enterprise as a unit. However, if private ownership is to be divisible, a joint-stock company must be created. Initially, the government will hold all the shares and appoint a board of directors to oversee the enterprise's activities.[10]

The government must decide who should have the responsibility for initiating the privatization of an enterprise or the disposal of some of its assets. One possibility is a state privatization (or "property" or "ownership transformation") agency for "privatization from above" in a centralized way. In contrast, in "privatization from below," the management and workers of an enterprise decide whether all or part of it should be sold, and if so, to whom, including themselves and other investors. Finally, in "external privatization," an outside (domestic or foreign) investor takes the initiative by approaching the state privatization agency or the enterprise.

The two more decentralized variants—privatization at the initiative of the enterprise or of an outside investor—may be faster than more centralized privatization led by a small and inevitably inexperienced agency (even with the help of domestic consultants and foreign advisers).

However, in such "spontaneous" privatizations there is a serious risk of insiders selling and acquiring state assets at unreasonably low prices by various techniques, as occurred in Poland and Hungary.[11] Hence, if decentralized modes of privatization are used, the state privatization agency still should exercise adequate supervision over them.

Finally, the initiator (and supervisor) of privatization must decide what kinds of organizational, financial, and physical restructuring of an enterprise are necessary before divestiture and how they should be accomplished. These issues are discussed below.

---

[10] This process is sometimes called *corporatization* or *commercialization*. The latter term is appropriate if the enterprise is to be run as a profit-maximizing business, but that stage may be achieved only after privatization.

[11] In Poland several techniques were used. (1) A private company was created to parallel a state enterprise. Both were run by the management of the state enterprise. It leased state assets free or at a nominal charge to the private company, which took on the most profitable orders. (2) Assets of a profitable unit of the state enterprise were sold to a private company that charged the state enterprise high prices for its services and also took over outside customers. (3) The state enterprise was "liquidated" through the sale of its assets to a new joint-stock company with diverse ownership but under the control of the managers of the former state enterprise. See Irena Grosfeld, "Prospects for Privatization in Poland," *European Economy* 43 (March 1990), pp. 147–48, and Jadwiga Staniszkis, " 'Political Capitalism' in Poland," *East European Politics and Societies* 5, no. 1 (Winter 1991), pp. 127–41.

Other techniques were employed in Hungary. (1) Managers sold some enterprises to outside investors at prices far too low in the light of assets or earnings. (2) In other cases, managers split state enterprises into new private companies and sold shares in the latter to individuals and other companies. The profitable operations went to the new private firms, and the original state enterprise became an "empty shell" with the less profitable or unprofitable activities, or sometimes only the enterprise's debts. See Organization for Economic Cooperation and Development (OECD), *Hungary* (Paris, 1991), pp. 113–14.

**Sale.**   From the experience of many other countries, there is a large body of knowledge about specific procedures for sale of state property through auctions of selected assets, management/employee buyouts, and public or private sales of shares by various techniques.[12]

However, all of these methods of sale require a valuation of assets or company shares. Ownership (or leases) of small shops, restaurants, or service facilities might be sold by auction, but the state would still want to specify a minimum (reservation) price based on its valuation. Similarly, valuation of assets is needed for employee buyouts, competitive tenders, and public share offerings. In Eastern Europe, accurate valuation of state enterprises is difficult for a number of reasons.

Therefore, the following discussion of sale as a method of divestiture begins with valuation problems. It then examines issues concerning sales of state property to different categories of possible buyers.

*Valuation.*   Proper valuation of state assets is important because sale will not be accomplished at an unduly high price. On the other hand, an unduly low price will reduce budget revenue. Also, asymmetry of information about the condition and prospects of an enterprise gives some potential buyers (e.g., managers, employees, and supervising government bureaucrats) an unfair advantage.[13]

In Eastern Europe, the value of enterprises is not well depicted in their financial statements. For example, balance sheets do not accurately represent assets, liabilities, and book values. In general, both assets and liabilities were recorded at nonscarcity prices. Land was not valued properly, if at all, because it was not traded. Plant and equipment may be shown at historical cost, or inadequately depreciated according to excessively conservative schedules. Assets include receivables not classified according to risk.

In enterprise income statements, revenues and expenditures have been entered at nonscarcity prices that are likely to be modified to different degrees as price decontrol proceeds. Revenues will change as output levels and mixes are adjusted (for example, because of the loss of sales to the former USSR and eastern Germany, and because of new competitive conditions from demonopolization and import liberalization). Costs will be altered by new prices for material inputs, reduction of restrictions on employment and wages, and government environmental protection regulations. Before-tax profits will be affected by the removal of subsidies, and after-tax profits by tax reforms.

International accounting firms can modify balance sheets and income statements to bring them closer to standards conventional in Western Europe. But their subsequent valuations based on revised book values, discounted average sustainable post-tax net earnings, or discounted future cash flow are likely still to be rather arbitrary.

---

[12] Vuylsteke, *Techniques,* pp. 8–40.

[13] Dhanji and Milanovic, "Privatization," pp. 15–16.

In developed capitalist market economies, with better accounting in enterprise financial statements than in Eastern Europe, one may seek guidance in pricing shares in state enterprises by examining the stock market's price-book value (P/B) or price-earnings (P/E) ratios for companies deemed similar in important respects. Yet stock market prices are often only loosely related to book values, even if the latter are revised by adjustments for inflation, treatment of depreciation of fixed assets, and unfunded liabilities. Furthermore, stock market prices reflect not only valuations of the worth of specific companies, but also business cycles, monetary policy actions affecting interest rates, battles for corporate control, and financial speculation.

However, Eastern Europe lacks broad stock exchanges to provide even such imperfect valuations of shares in private firms deemed comparable to state enterprises to be privatized. For example, in November 1991, the Warsaw stock exchange operated once a week to give a dozen traders the opportunity to deal in eight stocks. Hence, a privatization agency can reach only very rough, potentially rather inaccurate, valuations in order to set a fixed price for an initial public offering (IPO) or a reservation price for an auction, tenders, or a private sale.

Small investors will prefer a fixed price rather than an auction, which they are less likely to understand.[14] Yet there is a risk that the privatization agency will set too low a price, in an effort to get wider share ownership and to assure sale of the entire offering. This has occurred even in developed market economies, such as France and the United Kingdom, where shares were soon resold at 10–20 percent above the initial price.[15] Underpricing cuts budget revenue from privatization and, in effect, constitutes a transfer whereby the initial buyers at the low price gain at the expense of the taxpayers who make up the lost revenue.

In the case of sales to foreign investors before convertibility of the national currency has been achieved, there is the additional problem of determination of the exchange rate to be applied to valuations in domestic currency.

However imperfectly the valuation of state assets is handled, there are some specific issues that apply in sales of state property to (1) employees of a particular enterprise, (2) other domestic investors, and (3) foreign investors. In each case, there are advantages and disadvantages in regard to equity, efficiency, budget revenue, and speed.[16]

***Sale to Enterprise Employees.***    Employees can be offered the opportunity to buy all or some of the shares of their enterprise. In the former case, a leveraged buyout can occur as the employees acquire all the shares and control of the

---

[14] Vuylsteke, *Techniques*, p. 25.

[15] Tim Jenkinson and Colin Mayer, "The Privatization Process in France and the United Kingdom," *European Economic Review* 32, no. 2–3 (March 1988), pp. 482–90.

[16] Dhanji and Milanovic, "Privatization," pp. 23–26, and Branko Milanovic, "Privatization in Post-Communist Societies," *Communist Economies and Economic Transformation* 3, no. 1, 1991, pp. 26–30.

firm. For instance, in Poland, within a few months in 1991, in about 100 medium-size firms, employees paid for shares equal to 20 percent of the book value of the firm in cash up front and got the remaining 80 percent with government credit to be amortized over several years.[17] In the latter case, more relevant for larger enterprises, employees can be given the right to buy some (say 10–20 percent) of the shares at a concessional price—subject to limits for employees as a group and for individuals. For example, the 1990 Polish privatization law stipulated that workers could buy, at half price, up to 20 percent of the enterprise's shares, provided that their total purchases (at the discounted price) did not exceed one year's wage bill of the enterprise. If these purchases were proportionally distributed across the employees, each person's purchases would be restricted to a year's wages. However, the concessional price was interpreted to be a 50 percent discount from an actual sale price. If such an actual price is not determined from a general public offering, the method of concessional shares to employees cannot be used.

Sales of all or part of an enterprise's shares to its employees may have several *advantages*.

1. They are obvious potential buyers because they are acquainted with the enterprise, even though, like the population at large, they have no experience in the purchase and holding of shares.

2. Employees of successful enterprises are likely to respond to the chance to buy shares at a discount, especially if they can later resell them at a market price for a capital gain.

3. Employee share ownership may strengthen incentives for (at least productive, if not also allocative) efficiency.

4. Sale of shares at a concessional price compensates employees for a loss of property rights if workers' councils exercised some degree of control over production and investment decisions under state ownership of the enterprise. If workers get minority (10–20 percent) ownership under privatization, explicit property rights in the form of share ownership replace their previous implicit property rights in the form of (partial) control under state ownership.

5. Insofar as the value of existing assets resulted from employees' earlier decisions to forgo wages and benefits in order to reinvest enterprise revenues, it is fair to compensate them with the opportunity to buy shares at a discount.

Yet there are potential *disadvantages* to special provisions for employee share ownership.

---

[17] In Poland this process has the misleading name of "liquidation." This term does not mean that the enterprise actually stops operations and closes its doors. Instead, the firm is only juridically terminated as a state enterprise, through the transfer of its property to the new private company, but without any necessary implications that operations are interrupted.

1. Budget revenue will be lost if shares are sold at discount prices.

2. In regard to equity, concessional share prices for employees favor workers in some enterprises over the rest of the population. Employees in firms with greater capital intensity will have the opportunity for larger share purchases. For example, if, say, 20 percent of the shares in an enterprise are offered to its workers, the money value of shares available to its workers as a group and to each individual will be larger in more capital-intensive enterprises. Also, employees in more successful firms will be offered shares with greater potential dividends and appreciation. Finally, concessional arrangements for employees in enterprises subject to privatization treat them more favorably than people employed in activities not scheduled for privatization (e.g., health, education, network utilities) or people not employed (retirees, students).

3. With respect to efficiency, it is questionable how much employee share ownership improves efficiency in larger firms where harder work by an individual cannot make much difference in total profits. Moreover, if workers have control of the firm, there is a risk of excessive wages, avoidance of layoffs of surplus workers, and underinvestment in plant and equipment.

A comparison of the pros and cons suggests that on political and economic grounds concessional sales of shares to employees should be limited, say to a 25 or 50 percent discount on 10 or 20 percent of the shares.

*Sale to Other Domestic Investors.*    The assets of a smaller enterprise can be put up for sale at auction. The shares of larger enterprises, transformed into joint-stock companies, can be offered for sale at a fixed price or by auction to the highest bidder. Only part of the shares, say 30 or 50 percent, may be publicly offered, with some of the remainder allocated for concessional sales to employees and some retained by the government for subsequent sale. Also, shares in a number of enterprises might be offered at the same time.

Such public sales have several possible *advantages*. (1) They bring in more budget revenue than discounted sales to employees or free transfers of shares (discussed below). (2) With a given wealth distribution, sale by auction can achieve an optimal allocation of shares in the sense that they are purchased by the buyers willing to pay the most for them. (3) Compared with people acquiring shares by free transfers, buyers of shares are more likely to want, and may be more able, to exercise control over the enterprise.

The main *impediments* to public sale of shares are:

1. *Potential buyers' skimpy knowledge about equities.* In Eastern Europe, households (and institutions such as banks) lack experience in buying shares in IPOs or in a secondary market provided by a stock exchange. Prudent investment in shares requires understanding of the stock market as a whole, enough securities available at sufficiently low prices to diversify risk in a person's portfolio, a regulatory framework for disclosure of

relevant information about particular companies through prospectuses and financial reports, and independent advisory services furnishing evaluations of stocks and buy, hold, and sell recommendations.

Hence, for example, in 1990 Poland tried initially to privatize 20 enterprises through IPOs, but then reduced the number to 5. Of these five, only three were fully subscribed by the public, and a state development bank had to buy the shares necessary to complete the other two IPOs.

2. *Lack of capital to purchase many shares.* Even when there is interest in equity investments, domestic liquid assets of individuals are too small to purchase a significant portion of the thousands of state enterprises to be privatized. For instance, in Czechoslovakia domestic savings (not all of which would households want to devote to share purchases) were estimated to be equal to about 10 percent of the book value of state assets (which bore little relation to their market value).[18] In Poland the corresponding ratio between household savings and the book value of state property was 15 percent or less.[19]

3. *The likelihood of considerable inequality in purchases and ownership of shares.* The distribution of share ownership would likely be unequal, reflecting the existing distribution of wealth and the probability that the wealthier would be more inclined to invest in shares—partly because the wealthier include managers, bureaucrats, and others with better information about specific companies' status and prospects. Furthermore, among the wealthier will be former government or Communist Party officials or black marketeers who enriched themselves under the pre-reform regime.

Bank credit for more widespread household share purchases would increase the money supply and inflationary pressure. If, subsequently, the prices of their shares fell on the secondary market, borrowers might default on their loans, surrendering the collateral in shares. Another inflationary effect could occur from additional consumption spending if people believed that they had permanent additional wealth from the acquisition of shares.

Sometimes privatization through the sale of shares to institutional investors—such as banks, insurance companies, and pension funds—is recommended on the ground that they will be superior to individuals as buyers of shares because such institutions will have funds to buy large blocks of stock and will have greater interest and technical capacity to monitor and evaluate the performance of enterprise managements.

---

[18] Irena Grosfeld and Paul Hare, "Privatization in Hungary, Poland, and Czechoslovakia," *European Economy,* special edition no. 2, 1991, p. 41.

[19] Benjamin Slay, "The 'Mass Privatization' Program Unravels," *Report on Eastern Europe* (RFE/RL Research Institute) 2, no. 44 (November 1, 1991), p. 17.

However, in Eastern Europe there is no set of well-capitalized institutional investors able to buy large amounts of state property. Commercial banks are only now being developed, and it would be inflationary for them to create money to buy shares, although they might acquire some shares through debt-to-equity swaps for part of their outstanding (especially the bad) loans to enterprises. Only in the relatively distant future could shares be sold to institutions yet to be created and capitalized, such as insurance companies and pension funds.

***Sale to Foreign Investors.***   The *advantages* of sales to foreign investors, rather than to domestic buyers, include:

>    1. An inflow of capital into the economy, with payment in convertible currency.

>    2. Transfer of production technology and management and marketing skills.

>    3. Links with the world economy.

On the other hand, sale to foreign interests may be *opposed* on various grounds:

>    1. There may be reluctance to sell part of the national patrimony, created by decades of collective saving and investment, to outsiders.

>    2. Some specific branches or large enterprises may be deemed too "basic" or "strategic" to permit foreign control.

>    3. The consequences of underpricing may be considered more serious when foreigners gain at the expense of nationals.

**Free Transfer: Personal Entitlements.**   Divestiture of state property by free transfer, in addition to sale, has been advocated for various reasons, including equity, valuation problems, and the population's lack of funds to buy state assets.

Free transfer can involve personal entitlements (to former owners, employees, and the citizenry at large), endowments to institutions (such as banks and pension funds), or combinations of the two approaches, such as personal entitlements to shares in institutions such as mutual funds and holding companies.

***Restitution.***   In East European countries it is proposed to make restitution to people (or their heirs) whose property was taken by the state without adequate compensation.

Restitution can redress past injustice, repudiate policies of Communist rule, and privatize state assets.[20]

---

[20] Restitution is sometimes called "reprivatization," but the latter can also include divestiture of state assets, previously private and then nationalized, to private owners different from the original owners.

However, despite its appeal on moral and political grounds, restitution may prove difficult in practice and may even have some adverse consequences.

1. Will restitution address expropriation only of real property or also of financial assets? In the case of real property, will it include agricultural land; urban residential and commercial real estate; and manufacturing, trade, service, and transportation facilities? Will restitution of financial assets comprise bank accounts, stocks and bonds, and mortgages?

2. How will the restitution program allow for the deterioration, improvement, or transformation of physical assets since expropriation? How will it adjust the value of financial assets for inflation?

3. What will be the cutoff date for expropriation? For example, Jewish property was confiscated by Nazi or local fascist regimes during World War II before the advent of Communist regimes to power. Subsequently, Czechoslovakia, for example, nationalized larger businesses in manufacturing, construction, and commerce in 1948–50, and smaller businesses after 1955.

4. Must claimants be current citizens and residents of the country, or are emigrés eligible?

5. How soon must claims be filed, and how quickly will they be adjudicated?

Restitution through return of physical property can impede privatization by creating uncertainty about ownership title until claims are filed and resolved. Potential buyers of this property will be reluctant to do so until clear title is settled.

Hence, return of physical property is likely to be limited to selected categories of assets whose title may be established by the availability of good records, whose claimants can appear relatively soon, and whose physical character has not changed much since expropriation. Possible examples include agricultural land, housing, small shops, and Church schools.

Yet even for these assets financial compensation may be preferable. Then assets can be privatized sooner with a clear title for the new owner, before the state has completed resolution of claims to be settled with financial compensation. However, there are two issues concerning the amount and form of financial compensation:

1. Will the amount correspond to: (a) the original value 40 or more years ago, adjusted (how?) for inflation; (b) the present book value, perhaps revised for deficiencies in accounting; or (c) the estimated sale price in privatization?

2. Will payment be made in: (a) cash; (b) bonds (at what interest rate and with what restrictions on sale?); or (c) voucher coupons that can be used in auctions of state assets or purchases of shares in state enterprises to be privatized?

*Free Transfer to Enterprise Employees.*   In general, the discussion in an earlier section about sale of state property to enterprise employees applies also to free transfers to them. Indeed, the offer of shares to employees at a discount involves a personal entitlement. For example, the acquisition of 100 shares at a 50 percent discount is equivalent to the sum of a purchase of 50 shares at full price and a free transfer of 50 shares. The budget revenue lost is the same in both cases.

However, free transfer of shares to employees might be deemed more appropriate than concessional share prices for them if the aim is to compensate them for a loss of property rights exercised by workers' councils or for the value of assets resulting from employees' earlier decisions to forgo wages and benefits. Also, free transfers to employees of, say, 10 percent of the shares in an enterprise, instead of sale to them of 20 percent at a 50 percent discount, could make more shares available for a "core" (domestic or foreign) investor to control the enterprise.

*Free Transfer to Citizens.*   Under this approach, all resident adult citizens receive free shares in state enterprises transformed into joint-stock companies for full or partial privatization.[21] Some version of this approach is envisioned in Czechoslovakia, Poland, and Romania.

Several *advantages* are claimed for this approach: (1) It directly addresses the population's lack of enough liquid assets to buy much of the state property to be privatized. (2) It can therefore speed privatization significantly. (3) Also, it recognizes that the citizens already are supposed to own all state property collectively and seeks to split part of this property into divisible, personal, and eventually tradable shares. (4) Equal transfers to all citizens will reduce inequality in the distribution of wealth and of income from it. (5) Universal, or at least widespread, ownership of shares in firms (or investment trusts) promotes "popular capitalism." (6) Finally, free transfer of shares can avoid some of the valuation problems associated with sales of shares.

On the other hand, a number of *disadvantages* can be identified: (1) Insofar as the shares to be distributed free could instead be sold, budget revenue will be reduced. (2) Unlike sale of shares, free transfer of them does not absorb any of the monetary overhang. Furthermore, inflationary pressure could increase if people with a higher propensity to consume sell their free shares to others having a lower propensity to consume. (3) People who get shares free may have less interest, than those who buy them, in the operation of the respective enterprises. Also, the dispersion of share ownership, which impedes effective corporate governance, will be greater under free transfer than under sale of shares. (4) In contrast to sales to foreign investors, free transfers of shares to citizens will not infuse new capital, technology, and management skills into enterprises. (5) The state is likely to distribute free shares in enterprises which

---

[21] Dhanji and Milanovic, "Privatization," pp. 26–28, and Milanovic, "Privatization," pp. 30–31.

cannot be privatized by sales because of low profitability (or losses) and a need for restructuring.

There are three variants of free transfers of shares to citizens: (1) voucher coupons to bid for shares in operating companies; (2) actual shares in operating companies; and (3) shares in investment trusts such as mutual funds or holding companies that, in turn, possess shares in operating companies.

*Variant 1: Voucher Coupons for Share Auctions.* Each adult citizen is offered the right to buy, for a nominal sum intended to cover some of the administrative costs, a voucher book with a set of coupons that can be used to bid in auctions of some of the shares in some joint-stock companies. The coupons are denominated in points, not the national currency unit. Voucher books and their coupons are registered in the owner's name and are nontransferable. A person decides how many points to bid for a share of stock in a particular company. She or he can choose whether to bid points for shares in only one company, to spread them over several companies, or to pool them with other people to buy blocks of shares or even an entire small enterprise. The price of a share in terms of points is determined in the auction. A share price in money is established only when shares are later resold.[22]

The following *advantages* are asserted for this variant:

1. It is fair for these reasons: Everyone gets the same number of voucher points initially; the value of a voucher point in terms of company shares is established objectively in an auction; and the worth of a share in money (in dividends and resale price) is determined by the subsequent performance of the company.

2. Hence, no initial valuation of shares in money is required.

3. The citizen has the freedom to decide his or her own portfolio, with shares going to those willing to pay the most (points) for them.

Yet this variant has important *disadvantages*:

1. It is doubtful that citizens will have adequate knowledge to bid sensibly for company shares. People have no experience in such auctions. They will not be able to acquire enough reliable information about the past performance, present condition, and future prospects of individual companies. The average citizen might unwisely bid more heavily for shares in better-known firms, paying too much for them, while "insiders" (managers, workers, bureaucrats) with information about lesser-known companies might acquire shares in them at low prices (in points).

2. The unprecedented auction process will be extremely complex and confusing. Millions of people are to bid for shares in hundreds of enter-

---

[22] World Bank, *Czechoslovakia: Transition to a Market Economy* (Washington, D.C., 1991), pp. 89–90.

prises. An iterative process will be required until a price (in points) for each enterprise's shares is found such that all of the shares to be sold in all of the enterprises involved are placed among bidders, and all coupons offered are accepted. If the auction process leaves some unsold shares or some unabsorbed coupons, presumably the point valuations of the shares are not correct.[23]

3. Whenever resale, for money, of shares purchased with coupons is permitted, there will be great dissatisfaction on the part of "losers" whose shares command lower money prices and whose "investment" of voucher points proved disappointing in comparison with the outcomes of the bids of others. This dissatisfaction can weaken popular support for the privatization process, or at least for further use of this variant.

A version of this variant began in Czechoslovakia in 1992. Citizens could buy a voucher book with 14 sets of coupons, in denominations ranging from 100 to 1,000 "investment points," with a total of 11,000 points. To cover some of the administrative costs, there were fees of 35 korunas (a little more than US$1) for the book and 1,000 korunas (about US$33) for the right to use each set of coupons.

In May 1992, in the first "round" of the first "wave" of coupon privatization, shares in 1,491 companies, with a total book value of about 300 billion korunas, were offered. For every company, the opening price was 3 shares (each with a book value of 1,000 korunas) for 100 points. About 8.5 million people (out of the 11.5 million eligible) participated in the auction. Of the 8.5 million, 2.4 million chose to bid directly as individuals, and 6.1 million turned their coupons over to one of the more than 400 "privatization investment funds" (PIFs) formed as mutual funds to bid for company shares. In only 48 companies were all of the shares offered sold because demand equaled supply at the specified share price (in points). For shares of 469 firms, demand exceeded supply at the initial price, and all of the shares were offered again at a higher price in a second round starting in July 1992. In the case of firms for which demand was less than supply at the share price in the first round, the unsold shares were offered at a lower price in the second round. It is expected that about five rounds may be needed to place all the shares designated for the first wave of coupon privatization. A second wave, involving other firms' shares, is envisioned for 1993.

These auctions cover only a part of the shares in firms included in the coupon privatization program. For the first wave's 1,491 firms, the fraction of their equity to be placed through these auctions varies from 10 to 97 percent

---

[23] Eduardo Borensztein and Manmohan S. Kumar, "Proposals for Privatization in Eastern Europe," *International Monetary Fund Staff Papers* 38, no. 2 (June 1991), pp. 308–9.

(with 3 percent retained to meet possible restitution claims), and the average across all of these firms is only 50 percent. The remaining shares in these companies may be placed by other methods that involve sales for money. Also, many other firms will be privatized without the use of coupon privatization—for example, by public auctions, public tenders, and direct sales.

The first two rounds of the first wave of coupon privatization proceeded smoothly. However, important uncertainties remain about the number, size, branch distribution, and condition of the enterprises selected for this method of privatization; the fraction of their shares to be offered for coupon privatization; the ultimate outcome of the bidding process; and the operations of the as yet largely unregulated PIFs.

*Variant 2: Shares in Operating Companies.* In this variant, citizens receive free a portfolio of shares in a set of operating companies. Because the number of companies and shares will be small relative to the number of citizens, it is impractical to give the same portfolio to each citizen. Instead, there might be, say, 10 different portfolios, $I, II, \ldots, X$. Each portfolio could have approximately the same total book value, on the assumption that undervaluations and overvaluations, relative to unascertainable market values, would cancel out. A citizen would receive a portfolio determined by the last digit of the number of his or her national identity card. For example, Portfolio $I$ would go to a person whose card number ended in one, and Portfolio $X$ to someone whose card number ended in zero.

Compared to Variant 1, Variant 2 has some *advantages:* (1) The citizen is not asked to choose his or her portfolio in the absence of experience in investing and adequate information about individual enterprises. Nor will "insiders" with superior information be able to take advantage of it by choosing shares in particular companies. (2) Each citizen will get a diversified portfolio.

However, there are *disadvantages* as well: (1) Citizens have no choice about the shares in their portfolios. (2) Inevitably there will be protests that the portfolios were not truly constructed to be of equal value—as subsequently shown by the profit performance of companies and the market prices their shares command when trading is permitted.

*Variant 3: Shares in Investment Trusts.* This variant gives citizens free shares in an investment trust (IT) that, in turn, has been endowed with free shares in some operating companies. Each citizen receives the same portfolio of IT shares, say, one share in each of 5 or 10 ITs, although the ITs need not have the same portfolio of company shares. The IT shares will be nontradable until the value of ITs and their shares is established through trading in the shares of operating companies.

Compared to Variant 2, Variant 3 has some *advantages*: (1) It is fairer because every citizen gets the same portfolio of IT shares and thus of underlying operating company shares held by ITs. (2) A person's portfolio will be more diversified, because each of the 5 or 10 IT shares held corresponds to part of the IT's portfolio of shares in many companies. (3) Also, when company and IT shares become tradable, the prices of IT shares should be less volatile than the prices of shares of individual companies.

The success for Variant 3's approach will depend, however, on the nature and operation of the ITs that receive institutional endowments of company shares.

**Free Transfer: Institutional Endowments.**   Institutional endowments of company shares might be made to mutual funds, holding companies, banks, and pension funds.

*Mutual Funds.*   In this version of Variant 3, the IT is a mutual fund (MF) endowed with shares in various operating companies in different branches of the economy, and also with some money capital to enable it to trade in shares of operating companies when that is permitted.

MFs can provide diversification and, it is hoped, good portfolio management through trading in shares in operating companies. But as passive investors without controlling interests in operating companies, MFs can exercise discipline over company managements *only indirectly* by sales and purchases of company shares in a broad and active stock market—which may not exist in East European countries for a long time. MFs do not attempt to restructure companies or to select, motivate, and evaluate their managements. Because these roles are so important in privatization, it is proposed that ITs be holding companies instead of MFs.

*Holding Companies.*   In this version of Variant 3, the IT is a holding company (HC) endowed with a portfolio of operating company shares spread across branches, both to provide diversification and to avoid monopoly control in a particular branch. There might be 10–20 HCs, depending on the size of the country and the number of enterprises to be privatized in different branches. A "lead" HC will have a dominant position in each operating company, say at least 40 percent of the shares. Some of each operating company's shares will be held by other HCs, each of which has a small "passive investor" position. The lead HC is to exercise control of the operating company, even if the government retains a percentage of the shares greater than that given to the lead HC.

The lead HC's control of an operating company involves (1) restructuring it as necessary; (2) appointing, motivating, and evaluating the operating company's management; and (3) eventually disposing of shares in the operating company as part of a further stage of privatization. Shares might be sold on the stock market to citizens and other investors, or spun off to people with shares in the HC.

Because it promises effective corporate governance, the HC version is claimed to be superior to the MF version of Variant 3 and to Variants 1 and 2 of free transfer of shares as personal entitlements to the citizens.

There are uncertainties as to how well the HC version can operate on the scale envisioned for "mass" privatization in some East European countries:

1. How many HCs will be necessary for each operating company to be supervised effectively by a lead HC? For example, if an HC should have

no more than 5 operating companies with up to 10,000 employees, in the industrial sector of Czechoslovakia 300 HCs would be required. If there were only 10 HCs, each would have on the average 150 operating companies with a total of 300,000 employees.[24]

2. Will it be possible to find enough individuals or organizations qualified not merely to evaluate, purchase, and sell stocks (as in an MF), but rather to make strategic decisions about restructuring companies and to select and supervise their managements? Foreign advisers might be engaged, but the number of foreign organizations with successful HC experience is small relative to the number and range of privatizations to be accomplished in Eastern Europe.

3. How can adequate, but not too generous, incentives for HC managements be designed to attain the best performance in regard to maximization of the value of HC shares? For this purpose should HC managers have equity positions in the HC?

4. How can HC managements be insulated from political and economic pressures restraining them from painful restructuring of operating companies, including layoffs of personnel and even closure of facilities?

5. How can collusion among HCs be prevented?

6. How disposed will HC managements be to contracting their own activities by selling stock in operating companies and distributing the proceeds to HC shareholders, or by spinning off these stocks to HC shareholders?

Poland offers an illuminating example of an effort to implement the HC version of Variant 3.[25]

After considerable study and debate, a specific program was announced in June 1991. It covered 400 large state enterprises that accounted for about 25 percent of industrial output and 12 percent of the industrial labor force. After the transformation of the enterprises into joint-stock companies, 60 percent of the shares of each would be transferred to 10 HCs ("national wealth management funds") to be created. A lead HC would get 33 percent of an operating company's shares, and 27 percent would be divided equally among the other 9 HCs. Employees would get free 10 percent of an operating company's shares, and the government would retain 30 percent. Each adult citizen would get one share in each HC.

An ambitious timetable specified that by the end of October 1991 the 400 enterprises should be selected and transformed into joint-stock companies. The distribution of operating company shares among HCs was to be made between November 1991 and March 1992. By the end of 1992 lead HCs were to complete

---

[24] World Bank, *Czechoslovakia*, pp. 92–93.
[25] Grosfeld and Hare, "Privatization," pp. 141–46, and Slay, "The 'Mass Privatization' Program."

any necessary restructuring of their operating companies. Three more steps should be accomplished by early 1993: (1) Comparable performance data on the operating companies and the HCs should be published. (2) The HCs should start paying dividends to their shareholders. (3) Public trading, including by foreigners, should start in shares of the operating companies and the HCs.

Various *advantages* were claimed for this approach:

1. The lack of household capital to buy shares would be overcome by free endowment of HCs with operating company shares and free distribution of HC shares to the citizens.

2. The value of an operating company (and shares in it) need not be estimated initially.

3. Citizens would be treated equally because each would have an identical personal portfolio of HC shares, even though the various HCs had different portfolios of operating company shares.

4. The lead HCs would exercise corporate governance over operating companies they controlled by holding the largest block of shares (33 percent of the total).

This program was *criticized* on many grounds:

1. The idea of receiving shares in HCs not yet created to hold shares in operating companies not yet specified seemed nebulous to many.

2. Others believed that at least some of the operating company shares designated for free transfer should instead be sold to increase budget revenue and thereby reduce the budget deficit.

3. Some feared that as soon as trading in HC shares began, poorer citizens would sell them to richer buyers, including black marketeers, members of the former Communist *nomenklatura,* and foreigners.

4. It was unclear how responsibilities would be divided among HC managers, their foreign advisers, and operating company managers.

5. How could managers of operating companies and HCs be rewarded for increases in the values of companies and HC portfolios, if the initial values were not known?

6. It was argued that the relatively small number of relatively large HCs inevitably would have some monopoly power and would become powerful lobbies for "easy money" policies that would help increase the nominal value of the operating companies' shares in their portfolios.

7. The administrative burden of the program, whose overall cost was estimated in very round numbers at the equivalent of US$50 million, would be enormous. The Ministry of Ownership Transformation (MOT), with a staff of 200, was to create the HCs, distribute operating company shares among them, and monitor the HCs' subsequent activities—in addition to supervising all other kinds of privatization.

This unrealistic program could not be implemented. Of the approximately 400 enterprises envisioned for it, 170 were found to be too close to insolvency to be included, and 25 more enterprises were excluded for other reasons. In October 1991, the MOT announced that the program had been cut to 204 enterprises, accounting for only 7 percent of industrial output, and that distribution of free shares in HCs would be postponed to mid-1993. Some members of parliament have urged that the program to create HCs and distribute free shares in them be dropped altogether.

In Romania, 30 percent of the shares in each of an unspecified set of companies slated for privatization is to be given to five Private Ownership Funds (POFs). Each POF would have a varied portfolio of shares in companies in different branches. In turn, each citizen would receive free one share ("property certificate") in each POF. However, the full details of such a program have not yet between disclosed. Even if the entire 30 percent of the shares in an operating company were given to one POF, this would not appear likely to be sufficient for the POF to control the operating company. Hence, the POFs would resemble MFs rather than HCs.

*Other Institutions.*    Some shares in operating companies or investment trusts could be given free to banks and pension funds.

*Banks.* Free transfers of shares to banks can help recapitalize them, although the impact of these shares on banks' balance sheets will be unclear if the valuations of the shares are uncertain. Bank trading in shares can improve the efficiency of the (future) stock market. Representation of bank shareholders on the boards of directors of companies (or investment trusts) can be constructive, because banks have relevant financial expertise. However, banks should not be permitted to lend on preferential terms to companies in which they hold shares directly or through investment trusts.

Also, to avoid objections that state property has been given free to selected private interests (the private shareholders in the banks), the free transfers of shares should be made before banks are privatized.

*Pension Funds.* In Eastern Europe, state pensions have been provided as a form of social security for which payroll taxes were levied on enterprises. As part of the privatization of the economy, it is proposed that a number of non-state pension funds (PFs) be set up to handle pension programs of private firms.[26] To start these PFs, the government would give them free shares in operating companies, mutual funds, and/or holding companies. From these shares the PFs would receive dividends and, it is hoped, capital gains when trading in shares is permitted.

One argument for free transfers of shares to PFs is intergenerational equity. For example, free transfers of shares in today's assets to PFs will create future income flows for pensions to future workers who do not receive personal

---

[26] Gelb and Gray, *The Transformation,* pp. 43–44, and Dhanji and Milanovic, "Privatization," pp. 34–35.

entitlements to any of these assets, because they are now alive but too young to receive free shares as adult citizens, or because they are not yet born.

However, it is uncertain how fast such PFs can be created, how many workers they will cover, how pension contributions will be collected and what pension benefits will be offered, and how the PFs will be run in the absence of a stock market for portfolio changes. Therefore, rather than trying to allocate shares to PFs at the beginning of privatization, the government should reserve some shares for future distribution to PFs after they can be carefully established and an adequate stock market is in operation.

**Combinations of Methods.** Because each of the methods of divestiture of state assets has advantages and disadvantages, an East European country will employ more than one method, although not necessarily all of them. For example, all of the countries are likely to use sales to enterprise employees, other domestic investors, and foreign investors; personal entitlements in the form of restitution; and institutional endowments to banks. However, only Czechoslovakia, Poland, and Romania have (so far) chosen free transfers to the citizens; and only the latter two, institutional endowments to investment trusts.[27]

Moreover, several methods may be combined in the divestiture of a particular state enterprise. For instance, some of its shares may be sold to its employees, and some to other investors; or some shares may be sold by auction to domestic investors and others by sales negotiated with foreign investors. Finally, some enterprises may be only partly, rather than fully, privatized by the combination of methods chosen.

Certain methods, or combinations of them, are more likely for particular classes of assets, such as housing, agriculture land, small enterprises, and large enterprises.

*Housing.* In East European countries most housing is state-owned and rented, although there are some cooperative apartments and individually owned detached houses. Rents are low, usually below maintenance costs. Ten-

---

[27] Combinations envisioned in Poland are discussed in Stefan Kawalec, "Privatization of the Polish Economy," *Communist Economies* 1, no. 3, 1989, pp. 241–56; Janusz Lewandowski and Jan Szomburg, "Property Reform as a Basis for Social and Economic Reform," *Communist Economies* 1, no. 3, 1989, pp. 257–68; Piotr Jasinski, "Two Models of Privatization in Poland: A Critical Assessment," *Communist Economies* 2, no. 3, 1990, pp. 373–402; Grosfeld, "Prospects"; David Lipton and Jeffrey Sachs, "Privatization in Eastern Europe: The Case of Poland," *Brookings Papers on Economic Activity,* no. 2, 1990, pp. 293–339; Jan Mujzel, "Polish Economic Reforms and the Dilemma of Privatization," *Comparative Economic Studies* 33, no. 2 (Summer 1991), pp. 29–51; and Zbigniew M. Fallenbuchl, "Polish Privatization Policy," *Comparative Economic Studies* 33, no. 2 (Summer 1991), pp. 53–69. Proposals for Hungary are examined by János Kornai, *The Road to a Free Economy* (New York: Norton, 1990); Grosfeld and Hare, "Privatization," pp. 137–41; Keith Crane, "Property Rights Reform: Hungarian Country Study," in *Transformation of Planned Economies: Property Rights Reform and Macroeconomic Stability,* ed. Hans Blommestein and Michael Marrese (Paris: OECD, 1991), pp. 64–94; and OECD, *Hungary,* chap. V. On Czechoslovakia, see World Bank, *Czechoslovakia,* chap. 13, and Grosfeld and Hare, "Privatization," pp. 146–50.

ants' rights to apartments are strong, and occupancy rights usually pass to heirs within the family.

Restitution programs may cover a small part of state-owned housing. Financial compensation will be more common than physical restitution that could displace present tenants.

Widespread divestiture of state-owned apartments may be undertaken to privatize the housing stock and to reduce budget subsidies for its maintenance. Current tenants will receive personal entitlements in the form of free transfer of ownership to apartments or, more likely, the opportunity to buy them at nominal prices well below market values. The right to resell their apartments can create a housing market. For instance, such a program began in Hungary in the mid-1970s.[28]

However, the speed of this approach to privatization of housing will depend on (1) the extent to which rents are raised to market levels, to encourage tenants to buy apartments; (2) the size of households' liquid assets and their preferences about alternative uses of them; and (3) the availability of mortgages on favorable terms.

***Agricultural Land.***    Privatization involves the extent and manner of division of socialized (state and cooperative) farms' land and other assets (inventories, buildings, equipment, and livestock) among the families on the farms. Should families receive ownership of some or all of these assets free or by purchase at concessional prices? How much of the land should be covered by restitution programs that return it to previous owners (or their heirs), or provide them financial compensation?

Such issues have been addressed, but not fully resolved—in Hungary, for example.[29] Under June 1991 legislation, former owners (or their heirs) whose land was confiscated after June 8, 1949, are to receive restitution for part of the value of their property. Restitution is offered in one of three forms: (1) vouchers to buy state assets such as small businesses, apartments, or company shares; (2) annuities providing an annual income flow for life; or (3) land—not necessarily the original plot—under the condition that the claimant cultivate it for at least five years. The settlement for each claim will include a measure of land quality. The settlement will be regressive, in the sense that the larger the claim acknowledged, the smaller the proportion of it awarded in settlement.

However, it is too soon to appraise the implementation of this program. For instance, the worth of vouchers will depend on the prices in asset sales, and the purchasing power of annuities will be affected by the rate of inflation.

Hungary has made little progress in privatization of the agricultural cooperatives that control 70 percent of farm land and produce 73 percent of farm output. The government decided that the privatization process should not force

---

[28] OECD, *Hungary,* pp. 116–17.

[29] Michael Marrese, "Progress in Transforming Hungarian Agriculture," *Comparative Economic Studies* 33, no. 2 (Summer 1991), pp. 159–77.

all cooperatives to disband. On cooperatives considered for transformation, present land ownership is complex. On the average, the members already own 35 percent; the state, 5 percent, and the cooperatives themselves, 60 percent. The state, at least initially, wants half of the common land and other common assets, to compensate it for many years of subsidies to the farms. The remainder of the book value of the farms' common property may be distributed in shares ("wealth tickets") among present and retired members by an intricate formula. It apportions shares according to the weighted total (with decreasing weights) of up to the last 20 years of an individual's wages from the farm, divided by the summation of this weighted total over all present and retired members.

Wealth tickets may be sold, with a 20 percent tax due on the nominal value of the tickets. In many cases the nominal value is higher than the current market value because of great uncertainties facing Hungarian agriculture in regard, for instance, to demand, rising interest rates on farms' debts, and potential environmental liabilities.

Thus, privatization of agriculture by restitution with financial compensation and by the division of socialized farms' assets is complex, difficult, and slow. In contrast, it is fairly easy merely to transfer free the ownership of relatively small plots of land. For instance, in Romania, under a February 1991 law each farm family was initially allocated 10 hectares (25 acres). Although in principle land can be sold, those who previously owned no land (and thus were not entitled to any restitution) must wait 10 years to sell the land awarded them. Also, no family is to buy more then 100 hectares.

**Small Enterprises.**   Privatization of retail stores, restaurants, and service facilities is comparatively easy. Some establishments may be transferred to previous private owners (or their heirs) under a restitution program, although financial compensation is more likely than the return of physical property. More commonly, divestiture will occur through the lease or sale of facilities to private individuals or groups of them. An advantage of leasing is that the lessee does not need initial capital to buy fixed assets and only pays for their use, out of subsequent sales revenue. Sales of property can be through auctions or negotiated sales. The sale program can include, for example, preference for current enterprise employees as buyers, bank credit for purchases, and repayment of loans over 5 or 10 years, from enterprise income. Also, to assure provision of traditional services, it may be required that the private operator continue the same activity, rather than, for instance, transforming a shoe repair shop into a clothing and cosmetics boutique.

There are some potential problems in such sales. If the property is subject to physical restitution, it will be difficult to sell it, or even to lease it. Prospective buyers may not be able to obtain adequate information about the condition of the enterprise. At least in early rounds of sales, it will be difficult for the government to value enterprises accurately enough to set appropriate starting (reservation) prices for auctions or negotiated sales. Sufficient credit may not be available for private purchase and subsequent operation of the enterprise.

Yet, in Poland, privatization of small shops, restaurants, and service establishments by local governments proceeded rapidly. Privatization of small enterprises occurred as well in truck transportation, construction, and foreign trade. However, in all these fields, in addition to divestiture of state assets, new private start-ups were significant.

*Large Enterprises.*   Large state enterprises in mining and manufacturing—and thus most of industrial output—will be more difficult to privatize than housing, agricultural land, and small enterprises. Many large enterprises, grouped in vertical and/or horizontal trusts, have obsolete equipment, outdated product mixes, excess staffing, high costs, and low profitability or losses. They cannot be divested (by some combination of methods of sale and perhaps free transfer) without organizational and financial, if not also physical, restructuring.

The East European countries' privatization programs will differ for political and economic reasons. Political considerations include, for instance, the strength of the current government's concern for dislodging members of the old *nomenklatura* from economic power in state enterprises; its judgment about the need for preferential treatment of enterprise employees in the acquisition of state property; and its desire to gain popular support in return for free transfers of enterprise shares and of farm land. Economic factors considered are, for example, the need for budget revenue from divestiture of state assets; the desire for convertible currency from sales to foreign investors; and the importance attached to these investors' ability to improve technology, management skills, and export connections.

Yet in all the East European countries, because of its complexity and problems, divestiture of state assets will be smaller and slower than initially envisioned. Therefore the role of privatization through new start-ups will be important.

The scope, methods, and speed of privatization will affect, and be affected by, other dimensions of economic reform, as discussed next.

## PRIVATIZATION'S LINKS TO OTHER DIMENSIONS OF ECONOMIC REFORM

There are a number of links between privatization and other dimensions of economic reform in Eastern Europe—such as macroeconomic adjustment, marketization, restructuring, and integration with the world economy.

### Macroeconomic Adjustment

In Eastern Europe, macroeconomic adjustment involves a reduction in internal and external imbalances.[30] To shrink internal imbalances, the government must

---

[30] Michael Kaser, "The Technology of Decontrol: Some Macroeconomic Issues," *Economic Journal* 100, no. 401 (June 1990), pp. 596–615.

take three main steps. It must cut budget deficits by an increase in tax revenues and/or a decrease in expenditures. It must restrain the growth of the money supply. It must decontrol ("liberalize") prices to permit a comprehensive (not merely isolated or selective) movement of prices toward market-clearing levels that balance supply and demand.[31] In turn, to improve the balance of international payments, the government must act in two chief ways. One is to depreciate the exchange rate, in an effort to increase exports and decrease imports. The other is to negotiate agreements with creditors to reduce the burden of servicing prinicipal and interest on foreign debt. Privatization is linked to fiscal, monetary, and other aspects of macroeconomic adjustment.

**Fiscal Aspects.**    Privatization has short- and long-term implications for government revenues and expenditures.[32] There will be a one-time increase in budget *revenue* if assets or shares in state enterprises are divested by sale, rather than by free transfer, and if the proceeds go to the state treasury, rather than to the state enterprise.[33] The budget deficit will therefore decline, unless there is an offsetting increase in government expenditures. The proceeds of the sale may be used to retire government debt, and thus eliminate subsequent interest payments on it. However, insofar as the privatization sale aims to reduce the population's liquidity, the proceeds should not be spent at all.

On the other hand, government revenue from levies on profits of state enterprises will fall as these enterprises are privatized. Some of this revenue loss will be offset by taxes on profits of private firms that replace state enterprises. The magnitude of the offset will depend on the amount of profit under private operation and the tax rate applied to it. One might expect that efficiency and thus profitability will be greater under private ownership. However, the proportion of state enterprises' gross profits taken by the government has been high: for example, over 75 percent in Hungary, Czechoslovakia, and Romania. In contrast, profits tax rates on private firms are more likely to be 35–50 percent.[34] Hence, it is probable that privatization of state enterprises will reduce government revenue from profits taxes.[35] Therefore, to avoid an increase in the budget deficit, as a result of a loss of profits tax revenue, it will be necessary to curtail government expenditures and/or adopt new taxes.

---

[31] Because this movement entails a marked increase in the aggregate price level, as "repressed" inflation is transformed into "open" inflation, "stabilization" is a potentially misleading term for the macroeconomic adjustment process.

[32] Hemming and Mansoor, *Privatization,* pp. 16–18.

[33] As above, analyses of privatization commonly assume that the state treasury gets the proceeds. However, the enterprise might be permitted to retain some of the proceeds, for example, to finance restructuring measures.

[34] Borensztein and Kumar, "Proposals," p. 322.

[35] However, the government will get revenue from two other sources related to privatization. One is taxes on profits of private start-ups that were not previously state enterprises. The other is dividends on shares retained by the government in enterprises that were only partly, not fully, privatized.

Because of privatization, government *expenditures* may increase in the short term, for example, for the administration of privatization; restructuring of enterprises to be privatized; and unemployment compensation and retraining for displaced workers. However, budget outlays for subsidies should fall, because the government will be less willing to provide them to private firms than to state enterprises.

Government revenue and expenditure issues in connection with privatization are examined further in the discussion of fiscal reform in the section on "Marketization" below.

**Monetary Aspects.**   Privatization is one method to absorb some of the "monetary overhang" of excess liquidity of households (and enterprises) arising from past forced saving due to the unavailability of desired goods and services at controlled prices.[36]

Five approaches to reduction of the monetary overhang can be distinguished:

1. A *monetary reform* can directly confiscate some liquid assets by exchanging 1 unit of a new national currency for 10 (or 100 or 1,000) units of old currency. The exchange would affect both cash holdings and bank deposits. There is some historical experience, in various parts of the world, of successful monetary reforms of this kind as part of comprehensive programs to deal with hyperinflation. But such a monetary reform may lack popular support, because the incidence of the tax constituted by the monetary reform is not evenly distributed across the population. For instance, the rich may be more likely to keep a large share of their wealth in real assets, and the poor to hold chiefly monetary assets.

2. The *purchasing power* of liquid assets can be diminished by decontrol of prices. The resulting increase in the general price level can be deemed a tax on the real value of liquid assets. The incidence of the tax will vary across households according to their holdings of these assets. Yet it may be very difficult for the government to prevent what should be a one-time adjustment of prices, to market-clearing levels, from turning into a price-wage-price inflationary spiral.

3. Without a change in total liquidity, the excess or *involuntary part* of it can be decreased. For example, (real) interest rates on bank deposits can be increased to make it more attractive to people to hold liquid assets voluntarily (rather than try to spend them). However, there will be adverse effects on the government budget, in the form of (*a*) higher interest pay-

---

[36] Borensztein and Kumar, "Proposals," pp. 323–24, and Guillermo A. Calvo and Jacob Frenkel, "From Centrally Planned to Market Economy: The Road from CPE to PCPE," *International Monetary Fund Staff Papers* 38, no. 2 (June 1991), pp. 290–92.

ments on government borrowing from banks, and (*b*) larger subsidies to enterprises that the government assists in servicing their debt to the banks.

4. Liquidity may be reduced by an *exchange of money for goods*. For instance, insofar as currency convertibility and trade liberalization can be achieved, domestic currency can be spent for imports. But this approach weakens the trade balance.

5. Instead, people can *buy state assets*: for example, housing, a small state shop, or shares in a larger enterprise being privatized. Yet, as discussed above, people may not consider it advantageous to buy housing so long as rents are very low. They may not wish to become self-employed entrepreneurs. They will be unfamiliar with investments in shares. Also, they may be reluctant to put their funds in less liquid assets, preferring instead to keep money available to sustain purchases during the inflation they expect after the decontrol of prices.

Furthermore, macroeconomic adjustment calls for the early reduction of the monetary overhang. It can be cut much faster by monetary reform and/or decontrol of prices than by privatization, which will proceed slowly for reasons analyzed above.

Another monetary aspect is the potential impact of monetary policy on the financing of private businesses. This impact will affect the desire to acquire state assets or shares in firms being privatized, or to undertake private start-ups. Macroeconomic adjustment will include a restrictive monetary policy with constraints on the amount of bank credit and with higher real interest rates. There is a risk that bank lending will give preference to state enterprises over private enterprises, for several reasons. State enterprises will be considered traditional customers, unlike new private enterprises. The government may exert pressure on banks to finance state enterprises. This pressure may come through government ownership of shares in banks, or through suasion about "the national interest." In turn, banks may believe that loans to state enterprises are ultimately guaranteed by the government.

**Incomes Policies.**  Privatization can help achieve restraint on the growth of wages in connection with an incomes policy that is part of macroeconomic adjustment. As noted, decontrol of prices will lead to inflation. In order to moderate a resulting price-wage-price spiral, the government will want to control the growth of wages. In state enterprises, managers offer little resistance to workers' wage demands. Instead, managers side with workers in wage disputes with the government, seeking wage increases that are to be covered if necessary by (additional) budget subsidies. Therefore, in state enterprises it is difficult for the government to enforce an incomes policy—for instance through a tax on "excess wage growth"—that involves a fall in real wages.

In contrast, in private enterprises owners and their managers will restrain the growth of wages, because they want to keep prices competitive and to maximize profits. Hence, in the private sector there is less need for an "external" government-established and enforced incomes policy to curtail wage increases.

**Balance of Payments.**    Sales of state assets, or company shares, to foreign investors, can improve a country's balance-of-payments position. In the short run, the inflow of foreign currency strengthens the capital account. In the longer run, in the current account, foreign investment may generate additional exports (or reduce imports) by an amount greater than that devoted to the repatriation of profits.

Privatization through foreign investment is discussed further in a later section.

On balance, macroeconomic adjustment will help privatization more than privatization can assist macroeconomic adjustment.[37] Macroeconomic adjustment, however painful, should come early in the set of reform programs. It will establish a framework of aggregate demand, in balance with supply, and of relative prices, reflecting scarcities. In this framework, sensible privatization decisions can then be made.

Yet some kinds of privatization may be exceptions to the general principle that macroeconomic adjustment should be achieved first. For example, when housing is privatized, the stream of future services will usually be directly consumed by the owner. In the cases of small service enterprises and small plots of farm land, the future benefits of privatization will depend heavily on the owners' effort. In these cases, privatization can lead to an immediate increase in output that aids macroeconomic adjustment.

## Marketization

In Eastern Europe, economic reform entails the development of markets for goods, factors of production (labor, capital, and land), and foreign exchange. These markets will operate better if participating firms are independent, decentralized, and profit-seeking—namely, if they are private rather than state entities. Private firms are more likely than state enterprises to respond quickly and correctly to price signals in domestic and international markets.[38] This section analyzes links between privatization and marketization, in regard to the legal framework for private activity in the market, competition policy, fiscal reform, the capital market, and the labor market.

---

[37] Mario Nuti, "Privatization of Socialist Economies: General Issues and the Polish Case," in *Transformation,* ed. Blommestein and Marrese, pp. 59–60.

[38] Paul G. Hare, "From Central Planning to Market Economy: Some Microeconomic Issues," *Economic Journal* 100, no. 401 (June 1990), pp. 581–95.

**Legal Framework.**   Early in the privatization process the government must enact a set of measures to create a legal framework for a private enterprise economy. These measures include the following:[39]

1. Elimination of constitutional restrictions on private property and enterprise.
2. Company law covering the formation, registration, rights, responsibilities, and liabilities of firms.
3. Laws and regulations about a firm's relations with its shareholders, creditors, and the tax authorities—such as accounting regulations, disclosure requirements, and bankruptcy procedures.
4. Legislation about a firm's relations with its workers, including employment and dismissal, minimum wages, maximum normal hours and overtime compensation, safety and health conditions of work, and collective bargaining arrangements.
5. Legislation about a firm's relations with other firms; for example, contract law, procedures for resolution of disputes in court, and competition policy (discussed further below).
6. Foreign investment legislation, covering forbidden activities, procedures for registration and approval, percentage limits on shareholding, and repatriation of profits.
7. Legislation on business income taxes, value-added and excise taxes, property taxes, and personal income taxes (examined further below).
8. Legislation and procedures for divestiture of state property, including sale of state assets, and corporatization of state enterprises and sale or free transfer of shares in them.

It may take a year or more at the beginning of economic reform to draft, debate, and pass such a comprehensive set of legislation and regulations, and to establish a system of courts to interpret and enforce them.

**Competition Policy.**   The benefits from privatization will depend on the extent to which competition increases.[40]

Competition policy should address several ways in which competition may be curtailed: (1) Mergers and acquisitions decrease the number of rival sellers or buyers. (2) Patents, copyrights, and trademarks create market power by differentiating products. (3) Nominally separate firms may collude in pricing and market-sharing.

Competition policy also should consider how competition can be increased: (1) The number of rivals can be augmented by demonopolization as part of the restructuring of state enterprises before privatization (discussed further below). (2) Decontrol of prices will strengthen competition (and re-

---

[39] Dhanji and Milanovic, "Privatization," pp. 12–13.
[40] Vickers and Yarrow, *Privatization,* Chap. 3.

moval of subsidies will eliminate distortions of prices from costs). (3) Import liberalization is an alternative to competition among domestic firms. Import liberalization is the more important, the smaller the country and accordingly the fewer the domestic producers.

Finally, competition policy must take into account the extent and operation of the state sector, whose scope will be reduced through privatization more slowly than initially hoped. The markets in which private firms might operate will be less competitive, the greater the activity of state enterprises which are large, subsidized, and protected from foreign competition.

Without, or until, the privatization of state enterprises, the government should seek ways to get them to operate more nearly like commercial firms.[41] For instance, managers should be granted autonomy regarding inputs (including labor), pricing, and marketing. Managers should be assigned explicit objectives expressed in quantifiable performance criteria, such as growth of profits or a minimum return on capital. A performance information system should monitor actual results and analyze the reasons for them. An effective incentive structure should motivate managers and workers to achieve performance goals.[42] The state enterprise should be supervised by a government agency different from its old branch ministry accustomed to directing enterprises in a centrally planned economy. However, it will be unwise to assign the task of supervising state enterprises to the government privatization agency, unless the enterprises are being restructured for early privatization.[43]

**Fiscal Reform.**   In Eastern Europe, economic reform has important fiscal implications for the private sector. In the old system, the government tried to manage the dominant state sector by comprehensive central planning, detailed administrative orders, and direct controls. Under economic reform, the government seeks to exercise indirect macroeconomic control over a growing private sector through fiscal instruments of taxation and expenditure. Therefore, public spending is reoriented from outlays on the subsidization and development of state economic activity, toward the functions of the government in a capitalist regulated market economy: infrastructure, social services, and public goods. In turn, tax reform is imperative.[44]

In the traditional socialist centrally planned economy in Eastern Europe (from the late 1940s to the mid-1960s), tax revenue was collected from socialized enterprises in two main ways. (1) excise taxes (called "turnover taxes"),

---

[41] Barbara Lee and John Nellis, *Enterprise Reform and Privatization in Socialist Economies* (Discussion Paper no. 104; Washington, D.C.: World Bank, 1990), p. 24.

[42] Leroy P. Jones, *Performance Evaluation for Public Enterprises* (Discussion Paper no. 122; Washington, D.C.: World Bank, 1991).

[43] World Bank, *Czechoslovakia,* pp. 95–96.

[44] *Fiscal Policies in Economies in Transition,* ed. Vito Tanzi (Washington, D.C.: International Monetary Fund, 1992), and Cheryl W. Gray, "Tax Systems in Reforming Socialist Economies of Europe," *Communist Economies and Economic Transformation* 3, no. 1, 1991, pp. 63–79.

and (2) taxes on factors of production, such as social insurance charges on labor and profits taxes on capital. Other sources of revenue were taxes (in money or in kind) on agricultural land, taxes on urban property, and taxes on personal (chiefly nonwage) incomes.

Some changes in tax systems occurred under reform efforts in Eastern Europe from the mid-1960s through the late 1980s. For example, excise tax rates were differentiated further as their price-regulating role increased. Also, new taxes were introduced in some countries. A tax on fixed assets sought to obtain a specific return on capital regardless of actual profits. When the state ceased to set wages directly, it established a tax on excess wage increases by enterprises. A tax captured some of the excess profits on exports or imports arising from the combination of foreign prices, an overvalued official exchange rate, and nonscarcity domestic wholesale prices.

In the transition to a capitalist market economy beginning in 1990, tax reform is concerned with (1) adequacy of revenue to finance the government's activities; (2) efficiency in the use of factors of production; (3) reduction of inequality in the distribution of income and wealth; (4) ease of administration; and (5) interaction with foreign tax systems.

1. Because macroeconomic adjustment calls for a tight fiscal policy, the government does not want budget revenue to fall and therefore is reluctant to reduce old and reliable sources of revenue, such as excise taxes.

2. Privatization and the loosening of direct controls strengthen the influence of taxes on economic activity. Hence, there is a risk of disincentives from high marginal tax rates.

3. Taxation to reduce inequality in incomes becomes more important as differentiation of incomes—from labor, capital, and entrepreneurship—widens under economic reform.

4. Before reform, tax collection was relatively easy because taxes were collected from a comparatively small number of relatively large state enterprises, to whose records tax agencies had full access. In a private enterprise economy, there are many independent firms, as well as households, liable for taxes.

5. A reformed tax system similar to the tax systems of developed market economies can promote foreign direct investment from those economies (for instance, because it is easier to negotiate treaties against double taxation). Also, harmonization of an East European country's tax system with the system being adopted for the European Community can facilitate the country's future entry into the Community.

Hence, in an East European country a reformed tax system should include a company income tax with a maximum rate of 30–50 percent; a general personal income tax with a maximum rate under 50 percent; and a comprehensive retail value-added tax with a few, rather than many, rates.

Moreover, the new tax system should be constructed early in the reform process, in order to establish clear (and lasting) "rules of the game" for the activity of private enterprise.

**Capital Market.**   In a centrally planned economy, capital markets are virtually absent, because capital flows are determined by plan instructions. Some capital flows are budget grants, and others are bank loans at nominal interest rates that do not reflect the scarcity of capital.

In contrast, economic reform requires real capital markets with numerous independent units on both sides of the market, that is, private business firms demanding capital and private financial institutions supplying it. Banks will be the chief suppliers of capital, because the development of other sources such as insurance companies and pension funds will take many years.

Therefore, banking reform is critical for the success of privatization.[45] Banks should exercise independent credit judgments in their effort to make profits and to protect their capital position against losses from bad loans. Banks should allocate capital to firms that can use funds most effectively. Also, banks should exert financial discipline over firms, by requiring payment of loan interest and principal on time and by refusing additional credit to firms that fail to meet their obligations.

However, banks must be put on a sound footing before they can perform these functions. In East European countries commercial banks were created by the transfer of commercial banking activities formerly conducted by the State Bank ("monobank"). The commercial banks were set up to serve enterprises in particular sectors (industry, construction, agriculture) or, in some countries, on a regional basis. Competition among banks was restricted, because banks were not supposed to deal with enterprises other than those assigned to them.

The loan portfolios transferred by the State Bank to the commercial banks included many bad loans, often concentrated by enterprise and industrial branch. If these loans were marked down to realistic values, the banks' net worth would be negative. Moreover, these state-owned banks continue to make new loans, at negative real interest rates, to cover losses of state enterprises that are unable to pay interest and principal due on previous borrowing.

Hence, before banks can be privatized, they must be relieved of the obligation to make new bad loans, and their balance sheets must be cleaned up to eliminate the consequences of past bad loans. Bad loans must be removed from the banks' portfolios, for instance, by the transfer of bad loans to a separate "consolidation bank" in return for long-term government bonds with an adequate real interest rate. In addition, new capital must be injected. As discussed above, one method might be institutional endowments of shares in operating

---

[45] Lawrence J. Brainard, "Strategies for Economic Transformation in Central and Eastern Europe: The Role of Financial Markets Reform," in *Transformation,* ed. Blommestein and Marrese, pp. 95–108.

companies or investment trusts if free transfers are used in the divestiture of state assets.

Another issue in the privatization of banks is the "contestability" of the commercial bank market.[46] How many commercial banks should be authorized in a country or a region? Should there be separate banks for specific branches of the economy? Should commercial banking for business be separated from savings banking, personal loans, and mortgages for housing?

Finally, as in developed market economies, the central bank will need to use instruments such as reserve ratios and rediscount rates to regulate the amount of commercial (and other) bank lending. Also, it will need to monitor the creditworthiness of the banks' loan portfolios.

**Labor Market.**  Socialist centrally planned economies exercise tight control over the labor market, including wage-setting, employment ceilings for enterprises, and constraints on dismissals. Privatization of state enterprises will reduce overstaffing, transforming "disguised" unemployment into "open" unemployment. However, private start-ups will create new jobs. Also, compared with state enterprises, private firms will have greater wage differentiation that more accurately reflects labor market scarcities in training and skills, as well as productivity on the job.

To ease the transition from a controlled to a freer labor market, the government should adopt "social safety net" programs of unemployment compensation, retraining, early retirement, and anti-poverty income maintenance.

## Restructuring[47]

Economic reforms in East European countries change the conditions in which enterprises operate. Tight fiscal and monetary policies curtail subsidies and

---

[46] Gelb and Gray, *The Transformation,* annex 4.

[47] "Restructuring" in this study has a narrower, more specific content than "structural adjustment," which is often construed very broadly.

For example, the Organization for Economic Cooperation and Development considers structural adjustment to cover changes affecting all of the following (OECD, *Structural Adjustment and Economic Performance* [Paris, 1987]): (1) supply and allocation of factors of production—including the educational system, research and development, the labor market, and the financial system; (2) operation of product markets—including agriculture, "industrial policies," and international trade; and (3) organization and operation of the public sector—including regulation of the public sector, privatization, the tax system, and social policies for health, retirement pensions, and unemployment compensation.

The World Bank's Sectoral Adjustment Loan Program supports changes in all of the following (Samuel Paul, *Institutional Reforms in Sector Adjustment Operations: The World Bank's Experience* [Discussion Paper no. 92; Washington, D.C.: World Bank, 1990], pp. 4–5): (1) trade—including export promotion, import liberalization, tariff adjustment, and maintenance of flexible exchange rates; (2) finance—including reorganization of the financial system, interest rates, and control of budget expenditures; (3) the roles of the public and private sectors; and (4) production and investment—including decontrol of prices, tax and subsidy programs, and sector support services.

bank credit at negative real interest rates. Decontrol of prices alters the level and structure of prices. A new tax system modifies resource allocation and income distribution. New exchange rates and import liberalization expose enterprises to foreign competition. In addition, East European economies must adjust to the loss of markets in the former USSR and eastern Germany.

One set of enterprises can adapt reasonably well to these new circumstances and can be privatized without restructuring. A second set of enterprises is potentially competitive but requires restructuring before privatization. A third set of enterprises has poor prospects in a market economy and should be liquidated. Examples of each type can be identified in every branch of the economy. However, the first type is more likely to be found in parts of light industry and services; the second type in machine building and armaments; and the third type in mining and metallurgy.

This section analyzes financial, organizational, and physical restructuring of enterprises in connection with privatization.

**Financial Restructuring.**   There are several kinds of financial restructuring of enterprises:[48] (1) Assets recorded on balance sheets at book values well above estimated market values should be written down to market values. (2) Restructuring of liabilities may take various forms. For example, debt may be rescheduled by an extension of maturities. Debt may be converted into equity. The government may absorb some of an enterprise's debt, in order to give the enterprise adequate positive net worth. (3) An enterprise may be recapitalized by the injection of new capital. For instance, a state enterprise can be transformed into a new corporation whose equity consists of (*a*) the government's contribution in kind of assets of the former state enterprise, and (*b*) funds provided by private investors. (4) Bankruptcy acknowledges that liablities exceed assets, that the enterprise cannot be put on a sound footing, and that it should be terminated with some creditors' claims unsatisfied. Because creditors will commonly be other states enterprises or state banks, the government ultimately bears the losses of unsatisfied creditors.

Financial restructuring should be done by the state before, or in connection with, privatization—rather than be left to new private owners.

**Organizational Restructuring.**   Organizational restructuring usually involves the division of a larger entity into smaller parts:[49] (1) The enterprise (or a trust or combine composed of numerous enterprises) can be broken up into several legal entities. (2) The enterprise (or trust) can be transformed into a holding company with shares in subsidiary enterprises that acquire the assets and liabilities of the original enterprise. The aim is to privatize some, if not all, of the subsidiaries. (3) Some productive facilities may be sold. (4) Some nonbusiness

---

[48] Vuylsteke, *Techniques,* pp. 101–5.
[49] Vuylsteke, *Techniques,* pp. 23–24.

activities—such as housing, health care, and recreation for employees—can be taken over by local government agencies.

Demonopolization is an important aim of organizational restructuring in East European countries, where the average size of enterprises is much greater than in developed market economies. One reason for this concentration is the pursuit of economies of scale. Another is a high degree of vertical integration. As a response to supply shortages, enterprises often include units producing inputs and supplying services. In a market economy without such shortages, these component units would be independent firms. Further, parallel enterprises were grouped in trusts for ease of control by branch ministries and planning agencies. Also, in these networks of vertical and horizontal integration, there is extensive cross-subsidization of less profitable by more profitable units.

Organizational restructuring should be accomplished before privatization. All other things equal, it will be easier to sell smaller than larger units. The possibility of demonopolization actions after privatization would discourage buyers, or reduce the prices they would offer. The greater the number of firms in an industry, the more competitive it will be.

Yet it may be a serious technical problem to determine whether and, if so, how to break up large entities. The easy case is horizontal integration with multiple operations producing the same goods or services at different geographical locations, with few economies of scale. But in the other cases it often is difficult to measure economies of scale and to assess the efficiency of vertical integration.

Even when large units remain after organizational restructuring, they may still face competition from private start-ups (including by foreign investors) as well as from imports after trade liberalization.

**Physical Restructuring.**    Physical restructuring involves the upgrading or replacement of obsolete plant and equipment; the introduction of new technological processes; and investments for better energy efficiency and environmental protection.[50]

The government should avoid such rehabilitation of assets before divestiture. Particularly in a period of fiscal stringency under macroeconomic adjustment, the government should not incur additional costs for an enterprise that may not be recoverable at its sale. In any case, potential investors are likely to have different views than the government about how to rehabilitate the facility. Thus, physical restructuring should be left to the new private owners, who will carry it out in conjunction with changes in the level and composition of the firm's outputs and inputs.

---

[50] Ira Leiberman, *Industrial Restructuring: Policy and Practice* (Policy and Research Series, no. 9; Washington, D.C.: World Bank, 1990), pp. 17–18.

The difficulties of restructuring should not be underestimated. It inevitably will entail dismissals of workers, during a period when new jobs may be hard to find because aggregate demand is restrained by tight fiscal and monetary policies. Trade unions and local governments will oppose big layoffs and especially the closure of many or large enterprises.

Experience in the restructuring of enterprises in eastern Germany after reunification is enlightening and sobering. Despite the assistance of thousands of experts and the allocation of billions of marks from western Germany, restructuring in eastern Germany has been much slower and more costly than expected, for technical, economic, and social reasons.[51]

## Integration with the World Economy

Under socialist central planning, foreign trade was tightly controlled. For example, only certain enterprises were authorized to engage in foreign trade. There was comprehensive licensing of exports and imports. The currency was not convertible. A complex set of multiple exchange rates, established in the light of the relationship between domestic and foreign prices, sought to assure enterprises profitability in the fulfillment of plan assignments for the production of exports and the use of imports.

Also, the foreign trade of East European countries was excessively oriented toward other East European nations and the former USSR under arrangements in the Council for Mutual Economic Assistance (CMEA, the Soviet-led trade bloc dissolved at the beginning of 1991). In turn, the East European countries' trade with developed market economies and less developed countries was smaller than economically sensible in regard to comparative advantage and geographical proximity to Western Europe.

Economic reforms in Eastern Europe will strengthen its integration with the world economy. Trade liberalization, encouragement of foreign direct investment, and currency convertibility will have three effects. The ratio of foreign trade to gross national product will rise. A greater share of trade will be directed outside the former CMEA area. The commodity composition of foreign trade will be altered.[52] Privatization, in response to reform measures, will help generate these effects.

**Trade Liberalization.**   Trade liberalization includes removal of restrictions on firms' participation in foreign trade, elimination of comprehensive licensing of exports and imports, reduction of quantitative restrictions, decrease of unrea-

---

[51] Editor's note: See Chapter 10 in this book.

[52] Susan Collins and Dani Rodrik, *Eastern Europe and the Soviet Union in the World Economy* (Washington, D.C.: Institute for International Economics, 1991).

sonable customs fees, and abolition of practices such as import prefinancing requirements[53] that raise the cost of imports.[54]

These changes alter the market environment for domestic producers. Insofar as profit-maximizing private firms are more imaginative, aggressive, and flexible than state enterprises, privatization will enhance the economy's response to trade liberalization. For example, private firms will be more successful in cutting costs and improving goods to meet import competition, and in producing exportables and finding foreign markets for them.

Trade liberalization measures should also be taken by foreign countries to help East European nations expand exports. Foreign countries can increase access to their markets by cuts in tariffs (through Most-Favored-Nation treatment and Generalized-Special-Preference status) and by elimination or reduction of quantitative restrictions. The European Community (and European Free Trade Area) countries, for instance, have taken such measures to assist East European nations.[55]

**Foreign Direct Investment.**   Foreign direct investment (FDI)—which will be private—can provide (1) additional capital for the economy; (2) foreign currency receipts for the balance of payments; (3) know-how in technology, production, finance, and marketing; and (4) connections with export markets.

Privatization programs may impose some restrictions on FDI. For instance, some branches (transportation, energy, oil refining) may not be designated for privatization at all. FDI may be excluded from some branches (parts of retail trade and services) which are scheduled for privatization, but for which the government believes domestic sources have adequate capital, technology, and management ability.

Yet there will be many parts of light and heavy industry for which FDI will be sought. FDI may be promoted in various ways. (1) Foreign ownership may be authorized for most or all of a firm's equity. (2) Repatriation of profits and capital in convertible currencies may be promised. (3) Foreign investors can be

---

[53] Under the import prefinancing requirement in Hungary, for example, importers must deposit an amount equal to the value of intended imports in commercial banks when they seek a letter of credit. This is true even though payment of the corresponding foreign exchange occurs later, when the foreign exporter sends the bill. Importers typically wait several months before goods clear customs and are sold domestically. Meanwhile importers lose money, because they earn interest on these deposits at rates well below the market level, whereas they must borrow at much higher rates to obtain funds to establish deposits. At current high interest rates and with risk of depreciation of the forint [the Hungarian currency] because of high inflation, the prefinancing requirement significantly increases the cost of imported goods. This requirement thus is an implicit tax. Importers pass the additional costs, from the prefinancing requirement, on to consumers through higher prices, which reduce imports. See OECD, *Hungary,* p. 100.

[54] András Köves and Paul Marer, "Economic Liberalization in Eastern Europe and in Market Economies," in *Foreign Economic Liberalization: Transformation in Socialist and Market Economies,* ed. András Köves and Paul Marer (Boulder, Colo.: Westview Press, 1991), pp. 26–29.

[55] John Pinder, *The European Community and Eastern Europe* (London: Royal Institute of International Affairs, 1991).

given tax incentives such as reduction in profits taxes for 5 or 10 years. (4) Specific enterprises may be advertised abroad for privatization through FDI.[56]

However, FDI in connection with economic reforms in East European countries has been modest so far. Foreign investors are waiting to assess the political configuration and stability of individual countries, their progress in macroeconomic adjustment and marketization, and their implementation of privatization programs.

**Currency Convertibility.**   A currency is fully convertible only when any holder is free to convert it at the market exchange rate—fixed or flexible—into one of the major international reserve currencies. Convertibility may be restricted in various ways. There may be important differences in the degree of convertibility, for instance, between nonresidents and residents (and between different classes of residents, such as enterprises and households). The extent of convertibility also may vary by purpose, for example, for current account transactions such as enterprises' purchases of imports and payments for interest and repatriation of profits, *versus* capital account transactions.

There are four general preconditions for successful implementation of currency convertibility: (1) an appropriate exchange rate; (2) an adequate level of international liquidity; (3) sound monetary and fiscal policies; and (4) an environment in which economic agents respond well to market prices.[57]

In the last respect, domestic price reforms should lead to prices that reflect relative scarcities. Prices prevailing on world markets indicate relative scarcity values for tradable goods and services, which in turn affect appropriate prices for nontradables. Domestic producers and households must have both the incentives and the ability to increase supply and reduce demand in response to higher prices. Otherwise, the market–price mechanism will not function correctly, and the elimination of exchange and trade restrictions will not achieve efficiency in production and investment.

Compared to state enterprises not subject to the financial discipline of the market, profit-maximizing private firms will have stronger incentives to respond properly to domestic and foreign price signals.

Together with trade liberalization, currency convertibility stimulates import competition. In conjunction with favorable foreign investment legislation, currency convertibility encourages FDI by assuring repatriation of profits and capital. Yet convertibility need not be complete to achieve these aims.[58]

For example, enterprises, including foreign investors, should be free to buy foreign exchange at the official rate to make current account payments. In

---

[56] For instance, the Czech Republic has advertised internationally to offer for privatization through FDI 50 specific enterprises, ranging in size from 750 to 22,000 employees.

[57] Joshua E. Greene and Peter Isard, *Currency Convertibility and the Transformation of Centrally Planned Economies* (Occasional Paper no. 81; Washington, D.C.: International Monetary Fund, 1991), pp. 9–12.

[58] John Williamson, *The Economic Opening of Eastern Europe* (Washington, D.C.: Institute for International Economics, 1991), pp. 19–23.

turn, enterprises should be required to sell earnings of foreign exchange to the banking system at the official rate. Thus, in principle, foreign investors can pay for imports of goods and services and repatriate profits at the same exchange rate at which they earn foreign exchange through exports. Although export of capital would be subject to exchange control, a foreign investor should be able to repatriate whatever amount of capital was registered with the central bank when it entered the country.

On the other hand, the convertibility regime need not include a right for households to convert domestic currency into foreign currency, for instance, to make payments abroad or to maintain foreign currency accounts in the country (say as a hedge against inflation and depreciation of the exchange rate). Nor need convertibility involve a right for domestic enterprises or banks to make capital transfers to buy assets abroad.

## CONCLUSION

Through privatization East European governments wish to pursue economic objectives such as greater productive and allocative efficiency and budget revenue, as well as political and social goals such as weakening the old power structure and creating "popular capitalism" through widespread shareholding.

Each manner of divestiture of state property has numerous advantages and disadvantages. Hence, a country will use both centralized and decentralized approaches and a variety of methods. Despite serious valuation problems, some property will be sold to enterprise employees, other domestic investors, and/or foreign investors. Because domestic savings are small relative to the value of state property to be divested, free transfers may also be used, at least in some countries.

With respect to free transfers, personal entitlements may be given to enterprise employees and/or to the citizenry at large. There are three variants of free transfers to citizens: (1) voucher coupons to bid for shares in operating companies; (2) actual shares in these companies; and (3) shares in investment trusts (such as mutual funds and holding companies) that receive institutional endowments of shares in operating companies.

Certain divestiture methods, or combinations of them, are more likely for particular kinds of property, such as housing, agricultural land, small enterprises, and large enterprises.

Privatization is linked to other dimensions of economic reform. In the sphere of macroeconomic adjustment, privatization affects budget revenues and expenditures. Privatization can absorb some of the monetary overhang. Privatization will help achieve restraint on the growth of wages in connection with an incomes policy. Through sale of state assets or company shares to foreign investors, privatization can improve a country's balance-of-payments position in the short run and the long run.

Privatization will be affected by competition policy, tax reform, banking reform, and decontrol of the labor market.

Financial and organizational restructuring of state enterprises (and group-ings of them) should precede privatization, but physical restructuring should be left to new private owners.

Privatization is linked to an East European country's integration with the world economy. Foreign direct investment is itself a form of privatization. Private firms will respond better than state enterprises to changes occurring in the market environment from trade liberalization and currency convertibility.

A comparison of privatization in Eastern Europe and other regions reveals both similarities and differences.[59]

An important similarity is that privatization often was undertaken because of the ideology of newly empowered political forces. Through privatization they sought (a) to reduce the role of the state in economic decision making; (b) to gain budget revenue in the short run and cut budget subsidies in the longer run; (c) to increase productive and allocative efficiency; and (d) to achieve widespread ownership of company shares.

Also, in many countries, macroeconomic adjustment, decontrol of prices, and trade liberalization preceded or accompanied privatization, thereby helping to create a proper environment for it.

On the other hand, there are significant differences between privatization in Eastern Europe and in other regions.

1. The prospective scale of privatization is much greater in East Eu-ropean nations. For instance, in them, 70–90 percent of value added is produced by the state sector, in comparison with 5–10 percent in devel-oped market economies.[60] Network monopolies constitute much of the public enterprise sector in developed market economies, whereas in East-ern Europe the state sector includes all or most of mining, manufacturing, construction, trade, and services.

2. In other countries, only a few or scores of enterprises were privat-ized per year. For example, in Chile it took 15 years to privatize enter-prises producing 25 percent of gross domestic product (GDP), and in the United Kingdom 8 years to privatize enterprises accounting for 4.5 percent of GDP. At those rates, the privatization program contemplated in Poland,

---

[59] Vuylsteke, *Techniques*, synthesizes and compares privatization both in developed market economies and in less developed countries. Some detailed case studies appear in Helen Nankani, *Techniques of Privatization of State-Owned Enterprises, Vol. II: Selected Country Case Studies* (Technical Paper no. 89; Washington, D.C.: World Bank, 1988). For a comprehensive catalog of privatization experience in many countries, see Rebecca Candoy-Sekse, *Techniques of Privatiza-tion of State-Owned Enterprises, Vol. III: Inventory of Country Experience and Reference Mate-rials* (Technical Paper no. 90; Washington, D.C.: World Bank, 1988). See also *Privatization: The U.K. Experience and International Trends*, ed. Robert Fraser (Harlow, England: Longman, 1988); *Privatization in Developing Countries*, ed. V. V. Ramanadham (London: Routledge, 1987); and *Privatization in Less Developed Countries*, ed. Paul Cook and Colin Kirkpatrick (New York: St. Martin's Press, 1988).

[60] Dhanji and Milanovic, "Privatization," p. 5.

for instance (to cut the share of the state sector from 80 to 40 percent of GDP), would stretch far into the 21st century.[61]

3. To accomplish extensive privatization in a relatively short period, East European countries are using radical approaches not found elsewhere. In East European countries there is some "privatization from below," in which enterprise managers, with the acquiescence of workers, sell enterprises to their employees (including themselves), to other domestic enterprises, and/or to foreign investors. In contrast, in other countries state agencies exclusively decide which enterprises are to be privatized, and how. Also, to speed privatization, some East European countries expect to use free transfers (personal entitlements and institutional endowments) in divestiture of state assets. Countries in other regions used only various kinds of sales of state property.

4. In other regions, privatization occurred in nations with an appropriate legal system, a significant private sector, and markets for goods and factors of production. These features facilitated the transformation of state enterprises into private firms. In Eastern Europe, privatization is expected to help create a market economy.

Hence, in Eastern Europe privatization is an ambitious effort facing many obstacles. In all of the countries of the area, privatization will be slower and less extensive than initially envisioned. Its success will depend on progress in other dimensions of economic reform, such as macroeconomic adjustment, marketization, and integration with the world economy. The state sector will remain significant for a long time. Therefore the performance of the economy will be determined not only by the extent of privatization, but also by the speed and success of efforts to improve the operation of state enterprises.

Individual countries in the area will differ in the activities chosen for privatization, the combination of methods selected for divestiture, and the speed and results attained.

---

[61] Milanovic, "Privatization," pp. 20–21.

*Chapter Twenty-six*

# Structural Reform in Central and Eastern Europe*

*Richard Portes*[1]

*In this chapter Portes provides a concise, trenchant review of reasons why economic reform is proving more difficult than initially expected. The causes include external shocks such as the collapse of the Council for Mutual Economic Assistance (CMEA), the disruption caused by price liberalization, and poor coordination and sequencing of macroeconomic and microeconomic reform measures. Portes emphasizes problems in demonopolization and privatization of large state enterprises, banking, and industrial restructuring.*

## THE NEW EUROPESSIMISM: IS IT EXAGGERATED?

In little over a year, the prevailing mood among East Europeans themselves, as well as the Western analytical and policy community, has shifted from optimism and enthusiasm for the transformation to a most depressing pessimism.

Doubtless too much was expected, too quickly. Yet we might reasonably have expected that if the initial situation was anywhere near so bad as it appeared—if the distortions were so great and these economies so mismanaged—there must be some programs that would clearly make everyone better off.

* Reprinted by permission from the *European Economic Review* 36, no. 2–3 (April 1992), pp. 661–69, with the omission of references to foreign language sources and unpublished papers. Richard Portes is Professor of Economics at Birkbeck College, University of London, and Director of the Centre for Economic Policy Research (CEPR) in London.

[1] This paper has benefited by financial support from the Commission of the European Community (EC) within the framework of the PHARE program. It is part of a CEPR research program on Economic Transformation in Eastern Europe, supported by a grant from the Ford Foundation. [Editor's note: The PHARE program provides assistance for economic reform in Eastern Europe.]

But so far, even talk of a "J-curve" of economic transformation—in which the economy first goes downhill, then recovers to a higher level than the initial position—seems to be assuming too much. The picture from autumn 1989 to summer 1991 and the immediate prospects look rather more like an "L-curve."

Could the output collapses have been avoided? Will recovery be indefinitely postponed? Does the J-curve reflect a temporary dislocation, a necessary transition from the maximum achievable under socialist central planning to the higher levels possible in a capitalist market system? Or is it a sudden depreciation of organizational and human capital so great as to push these countries way down the league table of economic development? Perhaps the initial decline is a statistical illusion, reflecting the distortions and pervasive overestimation of performance in the old Soviet-type economies. Or if real, perhaps it is unnecessary, as some claim to be the major lesson of reform in China since 1978.[2]

To analyze what has gone wrong, we must distinguish the effects of exogenous demand and supply shocks; adjustment costs, broadly interpreted; misjudged sequencing; and other policy errors.

## Shocks

The external shocks are well known. The overall world economic slowdown with continued high real interest rates has presented an unfavorable environment. The collapse of CMEA trade, especially both Soviet markets and Soviet supplies, has been earlier and deeper than expected. It has forced acceleration of the transformation process and thereby harmed the coherence of reform programs. It has been followed at the beginning of 1991 by a price shock, as trade in the region shifted to "world market prices" and "convertible currency settlement."

For East Germany, there has also been the open border shock: not just monetary unification, but unhindered migration, radical shifts of preferences away from East German products to goods made in the West, and importing all West German institutions, including strong trade unions.[3]

## Adjustment Costs

The central feature of economic liberalization is a drastic change in relative prices, which is supposed to bring restructuring. But there will be adjustment costs. These will be lower, the greater is factor mobility. But deep-rooted problems in both capital and labor markets have substantially raised these costs of adjustment.

---

[2] See Athar Hussain and Nicholas Stern, "Effective Demand, Enterprise Reforms, and Public Finance in China," *Economic Policy* 12 (April 1991), pp. 141–78.

[3] Michael C. Burda, "Labor and Product Markets in Czechoslovakia and the ex-GDR: A Twin Study," *European Economy,* special edition no. 2, 1991, pp. 111–28.

**Capital Market Problems.**  Massive investment is necessary to replace the obsolescent existing capital stock. But domestic as well as foreign direct investment have been discouraged by pressures for restitution of property to previous owners (''reprivatization''), with attendant uncertainty of title; more generally, a legal framework ill-suited to private investment and evidently in transition; a totally inadequate financial infrastructure; regrettably justified uncertainties about access for exports to Western markets, in particular those of the European Community; and the debt overhang in Poland, Hungary, and Bulgaria. Delays in privatization and commercialization (*désétatisation*) of state-owned enterprises (SOEs) have also depressed investment.

Some of these factors have lowered the expected return from investment. All raised the *option value of waiting*: even if an investment is expected to be profitable, uncertainty makes it economically rational to wait and see how conditions may change (this is an explanation of hysteresis,[4] which supports the existing position). But the past year has lowered this barrier to action: a year later, potential investors observe that reforms are a durable process, that the economic regime does seem to have changed. So investment may pick up soon.

**Labor Market Errors.**  Labor market policies have been quite inadequate to encourage and channel the labor mobility necessary for economic restructuring. Both the magnitude of the required reallocation—not just from old or failing enterprises to new or flourishing ones, but also from industry and agriculture to services—and the institutional requirements are daunting: training, employment agencies, housing market reform.[5] In East Germany, the problems are compounded by a real wage too high for production and investment, though no higher than needed to limit migration. West German trade unions have contributed to wage-push in Eastern Germany, but it is not clear how policy could have resisted this, nor whether the greater influence of ''Austrian corporatism'' will moderate this pressure in the Czech and Slovak Federal Republic (CSFR).

## Sequencing Errors

It is much harder to change the expectations and behavior of firms than of households. Thus policy should initially have put less emphasis on the ''monetary overhang'' and household behavior, much more on the necessary changes in corporate control and the financial environment for state firms and on transforming the banking system.

---

[4] Editor's note: ''Hysteresis'' refers to a circumstance in which the path toward equilibrium depends on past history.

[5] Burda, ''Labor.''

## Macro and Micro

The main difference between Eastern Europe and Latin America was the initial absence of markets, hence huge distortions and supply-side failure. The Latin American experience and analogy, though instructive, have brought undue emphasis on macroeconomics for Eastern Europe. We are all supply-siders now, but since macro variables are more easily monitored and "controlled," they may still take undue attention. Nevertheless, macro remains important if it undermines micro (i.e., weakens the supply response).

Although macroeconomic stabilization takes absolute priority in pathological conditions such as incipient hyperinflation, we may have paid too much attention to macroeconomic instruments and performance as such. An important consequence was the failure of outside analysts, the international institutions, and domestic political leaders to press for wide-ranging importing of relevant European Community legal and regulatory frameworks. Similarly, we did not sufficiently stress the disastrous effects of restitution on investment.

*Ordnungspolitik*—creating the right institutional environment for markets but not intervening in them—is necessary. But it is not sufficient, nor would it have been even in Eastern Germany, absent the problems of restitution, migration, and trade unions. The authorities cannot just accept market outcomes because in Eastern Europe, much more so than in fully functioning market economies, economic policies will affect the market institutions themselves as well as the determinants of supply and demand.

## After the Shock

There is a somewhat technical explanation of the initial decline in output following major reforms.[6] This rests on how the consistency of expectations among households and firms underlies the coherence and sustainability of economic activity. The transformation process will require time to establish a credible new framework for economic decision making. It is essential to coordinate expectations around a relative price structure radically different from the old. Investment and trade rely heavily on the rules of a repeated game, in which participants learn over time about other participants' behavior, and the expectations that process creates. The transformation will change both. A repeated game can support multiple outcomes, of which the initial conditions are one, determined by history. That outcome underlies the initial expectations. Discontinuities in history—overriding hysteresis—however positive, may create a serious disequilibrium while a new set of consistent expectations evolves.

---

[6] David Newbery, "Reform in Hungary: Sequencing and Privatization," *European Economic Review* 35, no. 2–3 (April 1991), pp. 571–80.

# ENTERPRISES AND STRUCTURAL INERTIA

There is disagreement over the sequencing of demonopolization and associated restructuring of industry, domestic liberalization (free prices), trade liberalization (shifting from explicit or implicit quantity restrictions into tariffs), and privatization. Here we could contrast Newbery's[7] priority for deconcentration with the insistence of Sachs[8] on privatization as an urgent precondition of any progress. Grosfeld and Hare[9] emphasize the key role of privatization, but Charemza[10] as well as Hrnčíř and Klacek[11] stress the importance of demonopolization in the Czechoslovak context. It is much more difficult to change the behavior of firms than of households. Whatever the intended sequencing, in all countries there has been little progress with industrial restructuring from the center (i.e., deconcentration). Privatization will not cure that, so it will be necessary to improve conditions for entry and encourage new small and medium enterprises (not just one-person service establishments).

## The Delay of Institutional Change

Domestic firms have cut investment, and foreign direct investment has been much less than hoped, in good part because of uncertainty about the future rules of the game. Tax reform is difficult and takes considerable time, and here Hungary has the major advantage of the early starter.[12] It will still take a while to consolidate this advantage and eliminate the system uncertainty.

Other legislation has been delayed. It is common to attribute this not only to political conflicts, but also to the parliamentary bottleneck. The parliamentary time required could be much reduced, however, if parliaments could be convinced they need not—indeed, should not—try to adapt adequate general legislation, already operational elsewhere, to various supposed local special characteristics.

These countries should simply take over in their entirety applicable legislation from the EC, where appropriate, or a representative EC country. Austria would also do well, because it has made considerable efforts to adapt its own laws to those of the Community. There are qualifications—as experience in

---

[7] Newbery, "Reform."

[8] Jeffrey D. Sachs, "Accelerating Privatization in Eastern Europe" (paper for World Bank conference, April 1991).

[9] Irena Grosfeld and Paul Hare, "Privatization in Hungary, Poland, and Czechoslovakia," *European Economy,* special edition no. 2, 1991, pp. 129–56.

[10] Wojciech W. Charemza, "Alternative Paths to Macroeconomic Stability in Czechoslovakia," *European Economy,* special edition no. 2, 1991, pp. 41–56.

[11] Miroslav Hrnčíř and Jan Klacek, "Stabilization Policies and Currency Convertibility in Czechoslovakia," *European Economy,* special edition no. 2, 1991, pp. 17–39.

[12] Newbery, "Reform."

Eastern Germany suggests, not all West German laws, regulations, and economic institutions are market-friendly. And there are areas such as environmental standards where this approach would not be sensible. But in areas such as competition policy, this would be an appropriate condition for the EC to require for its aid.[13] At the same time, the Community should offer ample technical assistance in writing and implementing the laws.

### Enterprise Autonomy, Corporate Control, and Privatization

The transformation still has not established enterprise autonomy. "Tutelage" was a form of agents without principals, hence without responsibility or monitoring. But it is proving hard to substitute in large firms new mechanisms of corporate control that do permit initiative, reward risk-taking, and encourage investment.

Privatization of large firms has been delayed. It is technically difficult, but there has also been policy hesitation. Most of the obstacles were predictable and predicted,[14] and this is one area where it is not obvious that the optimal policy was full speed ahead regardless.[15] It is clear, however, that we did not recognize how much restitution would inhibit privatization and foreign direct investment. But the problems of legal framework, monopoly, and the difficulty of valuation under distortions have hindered conventional privatization and, absent alternatives, have led to give-away schemes.

It may be too late to influence significantly the outcome of the restitution debate in those countries where it has become a key issue. That and the other obstacles to privatization suggest we should give higher priority now to *désétatisation* (commercialization).

The principles underlying any approach to this problem of corporate control are clear.[16] Eliminate tutelage and the mechanisms and administrative hierarchies that supported it. Establish joint-stock status for firms, and initially let the government appoint independent boards. Commit to nonintervention—difficult without privatization, but essential. There will still be monitoring problems: regulatory capture (influence of the regulatees on the regulators), and the danger that if large state holding companies are used for control, they will

---

[13] Richard Portes, "The European Community and Eastern Europe after 1992," in *Europe after 1992: Three Essays,* ed. Tommaso Padoa-Schioppa (Essays in International Finance, no. 182; Princeton, N.J.: Princeton University Department of Economics, International Finance Section, May 1991), pp. 31–43.

[14] See Irena Grosfeld, "Prospects for Privatization in Poland," *European Economy* 43 (March 1990), pp. 139–50; and Richard Portes, "Introduction," *European Economy,* special edition no. 2, 1991, pp. 1–15.

[15] Grosfeld and Hare, "Privatization."

[16] See Grosfeld and Hare, "Privatization"; and David Begg, "Economic Reform in Czechoslovakia: Should We Believe in Santa Klaus?" *Economic Policy* 13 (October 1991), pp. 243–76.

become quangos,[17] or even new state ministries. But regulation is needed: especially if in the short run the authorities cannot change industrial structure (demonopolize), they must control conduct. This requires, however, a clear market test of efficiency, a level playing field (taxes and enterprise debts—see below), and transparency (regular monitoring of enterprise accounts, especially items such as supplier credit, tax arrears).

## FINANCIAL RESTRUCTURING

Stock markets are not the last thing these countries need, but they should not be high on the sequencing list. On the other hand, the banks have not proved able to take the roles that Corbett[18] suggested—partly because of the delay of financial restructuring. This lag is especially damaging because it vitiates external financial control, an important aspect of creating enterprise independence.

This problem of financial control is illustrated in the growth of inter-enterprise credit. This problem is not merely a phenomenon of the transition (firms going back to normal settlement terms rather than payment within seven days); rather, it dates back to the 1950s in Eastern Europe. Then as now, it was a response by the enterprises to avoid tougher state credit controls. Even then, they succeeded in evading strict rules against trade credit because the mono-bank was simply unable or unwilling to act. Why can the banking system not control this problem now? Some of the debts can be netted out within the enterprise sector, but some correspond to an increase in the enterprises' net debt to banks—and hence the monetary targets are bypassed by trade credit. If A does not pay B, then B does not pay bank interest on existing loans, so although the banks do not increase credit (they keep within monetary targets), nonperforming loans go up, although new loans do not.

But the authorities cannot close off this outlet if the banks themselves will not survive the squeeze. The banks do not have a capital base that could withstand significant bankruptcies. The authorities must clean out enterprise balance sheets to give transparency—to show which activities, as well as firms, are viable—so the banks are strong enough to force bankruptcy. Past debts are poor guides to future performance; hence tight money may give a bad restructuring.[19]

How should this be done? There are previous examples, such as Portugal,

---

[17] Editor's note: A "quango" is a quasi nongovernmental organization (i.e., a semipublic administrative body outside the civil service although financed by the government and with its top staff appointed by the government).

[18] Jenny Corbett, "Policy Issues in the Design of Banking and Financial Systems for Industrial Finance," *European Economy* 43 (March 1990), pp. 205–15.

[19] Begg, "Economic Reform."

from which the following suggestions draw.[20] In the Polish case, of course, inflation got rid of much of the enterprise debt, but I would still include Polish firms in a program of *immediately* forgiving all enterprise debt taken on before a certain date. Those bank assets would have to be replaced on the balance sheets of the banks by (low real) interest-bearing government debt. This is simply a transfer within (at this stage) the state sector. It should have no inflationary effect. It would raise the public debt—as recorded, but not really. It should be sufficiently clear that this is once-off for the danger of moral hazard[21] to be minimal; the whole point is to make firms and the banks forward- rather than backward-looking. The capital structure of enterprises will be rather odd for a while—all equity, no debt—but this will change.

This measure will not suffice. Bank staff are unable to implement selective bankruptcy or evaluate loan risk. Both need training and experience. Meanwhile, we have gone from subsidies provided by negative real interest rates to the taxes implicit in excessive intermediation margins.[22] There are dangers here of moral hazard and adverse selection: banks lending at high rates to risky firms and projects in the expectation of bailouts. Poorly qualified staff will be unable to cope. Moreover, the banking system in all these countries would benefit from much more competition, with appropriate regulation. All this suggests bringing in foreign banks on a large scale, with appropriate regulation (which should in any case be set up on the EC model).

Foreign banks wanting to enter could be required to absorb noncompetitive domestic banks. None of this resolves, however, the question of how the domestic commercial banks raise new capital. Privatization of those banks seems highly unpromising in the short run.

## DISTORTIONS AND INDUSTRIAL RESTRUCTURING

It is hard to stop throwing good money after bad if you cannot specify where the bad money is. Hare and Hughes[23] reveal for the first time in disaggregated detail the extent of distortions in industry in the CSFR, Hungary, and Poland. They calculate value added at world market prices for industrial branches. They find it poorly correlated with value added at domestic prices, and 20–25

---

[20] Jorge Braga de Macedo, "External Liberalization with Ambiguous Public Response: The Experience of Portugal," in *Unity with Diversity in the European Economy: The Community's Southern Frontier,* ed. Christopher Bliss and Jorge Braga de Macedo (Cambridge, England: Cambridge University Press, 1990), pp. 310–54.

[21] Editor's note: If it is clearly understood that the write-off of enterprise debt would occur only once to correct unique past problems, there would be less danger of "moral hazard" from borrowers undertaking new loans they expect to be written off.

[22] Editor's note: If lenders have larger margins (differences between interest rates they pay and those they charge), this raises costs and reduces profits for borrowing firms.

[23] Gordon Hughes and Paul Hare, "Competitiveness and Industrial Restructuring in Czechoslovakia, Hungary, and Poland," *European Economy,* special edition no. 2, 1991, pp. 83–110.

percent of manufacturing in each country operates at negative value added.[24] The protection of those industries could continue (though not through exchange rate depreciation), but this is simply wasteful. Yet there is also the question of what to do with the very low value-added activities.

A credit squeeze and forced bankruptcies will catch the wrong firms unless there is a financial cleanout beforehand. This is one aspect of the distinction between short- and long-run viability, in parallel with that between illiquidity and insolvency.[25] Exchange-rate undervaluation and maintaining a low real wage can give time for those that are not "value subtractors," but that time must be used.

Begg[26] suggests that this evaluation at world market prices shows (*a*) which loss-making SOEs to support; (*b*) which to privatize first (where divergence from domestic market value is least). In answer to the question whether there should be temporary assistance or protection to any negative value-added activities,[27] Newbery[28] responds that if firms are not viable with an undervalued exchange rate (low real wage) and low opportunity cost of capital, they should go.

But there must be some period of adjustment allowed. Automatic bankruptcy rules immediately after price reform will create unnecessary unemployment and be politically dangerous. Roland therefore suggests the authorities should "start with 'selective' bankruptcies . . . imposed from above in the case of enterprises where most indicators show and predict economic failure."[29] The Hare Hughes calculations could be extremely valuable in this regard, if extended to the enterprise level.

---

[24] Editor's note: However, these calculations used input-output data for industrial branches, rather than individual establishments, and included only goods traded on the world market.

[25] Portes, "Introduction."

[26] Begg, "Economic Reform."

[27] Ronald I. McKinnon, *The Order of Economic Liberalization: Financial Control in the Transition to a Market Economy* (Baltimore, Md: Johns Hopkins University Press, 1991).

[28] Newbery, "Reform."

[29] Gérard Roland, "Political Economy of Sequencing Tactics in the Transition Period," in *Systemic Change and Stabilization in Eastern Europe,* ed. László Csaba (Aldershot, England: Dartmouth Publishing Company, 1991), p. 60.

# Chapter Twenty-seven

# Transition to the Market:
# Theory and Evidence*

## László Csaba

*Csaba first notes the significance of political factors, rather than economic theory, in shaping economic reforms.*

*Then he draws a number of lessons from East European reform experience. For example, tight monetary-fiscal policies can restrain inflation, but they also curtail employment and output. Such macroeconomic stabilization is a necessary, but not sufficient, condition for marketization of the economy. Supply-side adjustments to economic reform measures are often slow. In this context, it is important for the government to promote investment for economic growth.*

*Csaba explains that, unlike stabilization, systemic change requires many years and thus will depend upon the sustainability of reform measures. He warns that economic reform programs cannot be implemented if they lack adequate popular and legislative support. In this respect, he mentions the widespread controversy in Eastern Europe over the need for an industrial policy to steer structural change. Also, he believes Eastern Europe should be cautious about adopting Western Europe's legal framework.*

*With regard to privatization, Csaba stresses that, although privatization is essential, it must be carefully designed in order to achieve the desired efficiency gains. Some experts argue that demonopolization is necessary for successful privatization and marketization of the economy, but in practice it often is difficult to identify the efficiency of individual components of a large entity. Also, changes in ownership structure may not improve enterprise management or owners' control over managers. Furthermore, governments may gain little net revenue from privatization.*

* Reprinted by permission from *On the Theory and Policy of Systemic Change*, ed. Hans-Jürgen Wagener (Heidelberg, Germany: Physica-Verlag, 1993), pp. 219–34, with the omission of references to foreign language sources, unpublished studies, and limited-circulation publications. László Csaba is a Department Head at Kopint-Datorg, Budapest, Hungary.

## INTRODUCTION

More than two years have elapsed since the Communist regimes of Central and Southeast Europe collapsed. In 1991 the Soviet Union also ceased to exist, and the artificial construct of Yugoslavia has also disintegrated. History is in the making.

Meanwhile, transformation of economic systems has become one of the favorite topics of general economic science. Any publishing house, any editorial office of some standing feels compelled to take part in this competition. Respected general economists, who never devoted any attention either to East European area studies or to comparative economics, make sweeping pronouncements, and even advise governments of ex-socialist states on how to transform the inherited bureaucratic systems.

Focusing attention on systemic transformation is quite justified, insofar as it is a unique historic opportunity to test available theoretical knowledge on a new empirical field. Whereas in developing countries, privatization, opening up to the world economy, and liberalization in general can mostly rely on prevailing structures of private property, in ex-socialist states the predominance of the public sector, lasting consequences of decades-long bureaucratic control, and the resultant distorted motivational and expectational structure of economic agents make the task truly unique. In other words, unlike in developing nations, transition to the market on the ruins of Communism has a value of its own, which is not subordinate to objectives of development economics.

With the Minsk agreements of December 1991, replacing the Soviet Union with a Commonwealth of Independent States, and the accession to power of Boris Yeltsin, new countries have given up tinkering with socialist reforms, and started to transform their systems into fully-fledged market economies. The stabilization program of the Gaidar team was clearly modeled on the Balcerowicz Plan.[1] Meanwhile, the Ukraine adopted a more phased, three-year plan of privatization. The mayor of Moscow, Gavril Popov, announced in November 1991 a scheme for overnight privatization of flats and the retail network in a town of Hungary's size. The Lithuanian Prime Minister Vagnorius forecasted that, by mid-1992, Lithuania will have become a fully-fledged market economy, having mastered the tasks of both privatization and stabilization by employing the voucher and employee stock ownership plan (ESOP) schemes.

It should be crystal-clear from the above that the same hopes, debates, and propositions are well under way in the one-time Soviet republics, as was the case in the Central European countries in the aftermath of the revolutions of November 1989. Still, unlike in the latter case, we possess at least some evidence of the use of given theoretical propositions in the East European postso-

---

[1] Editor's note: Former Deputy Prime Minister Yegor Gaidar's program for economic stabilization in Russia resembled in important respects the Polish economic stabilization program of former Deputy Prime Minister Leszek Balcerowicz.

cialist environment. In the following pages an attempt is made to sum these up. The proof of the pudding is eating, and the Central European countries, including the ex-GDR, have eaten some fruits of established economic science. Two years of experience must give some food for thought to policymakers and theorists alike.

The increased interest in transition is explained by the fact that in economics we rarely find an opportunity to test propositions so directly as in this case. True, the distance between the abstract theoretical models and the historically, politically, and culturally conditioned realities of any given country in transition remains considerable. Therefore the door is always open for the standard excuses, such as political ill-will, public ignorance, and the influence of vested interests having thwarted an otherwise perfect economic program. Established schools of thought will hardly disappear from the scene on the basis of East European experience, and various value judgments and priorities will justify widely divergent interpretations of the same facts also in the future.

Therefore the purpose of the present exercise should be made clear at the very outset. It is not about proving/disproving the futility/uses of neoclassical mainstream economics. It is not about elaborating a recipe about how to transform an imaginary or a given real country into one with a market economy. The present study is an attempt to survey *tentatively* what we have learned in the first two years of the transition when governments of several countries tried to implement the well or not-so-well-understood standard neoclassical propositions voiced by the experts of IMF and IBRD, Western theoretical economists, and their Eastern students. Since my purpose is not to play devil's advocate or to point my finger at any colleague and say "you were wrong," I shall discuss only propositions which are rather common in the exponentially growing literature on the subject, or are widely discussed among decision makers. Anybody who is not an absolute newcomer in the field will find more than enough examples on the given points.

## GENERAL REFLECTIONS

The first overwhelming experience of any observer of the East European scene is how little the conventional rationality, utility maximization assumption of economics influenced actors on the scene. If we put it in Marxist terms, it is very difficult to see how the economic base determines the political superstructure. Rather, on occasion, it is the tail wagging the dog. All in all, it is not very surprising that, at times of major historical changes, public choice might be mightier than elementary utility considerations. From the conversion rate of the Ostmark[2] to the Hungarian legislation prohibiting foreigners to buy agricultural arable land, the predominance of extra-economic considerations is rather obvious.

---

[2] Editor's note: The rate at which East German marks were converted into West German marks.

Theories about how to transform "a" socialist economy into "a" capitalist one proved to be of rather limited practical value. And, indeed, the crux of the problem is not the transition from a socialist bureaucratic economy to a capitalist free economy, but the collapse of a very specific historic construct, the Soviet empire.[3] This had at least three immediate consequences:

1. The problems facing the new regimes had little to do with abstract values and qualities postulated by the *ancien regime*. Instead they were confronted with such problems as the loss of a quarter or a third of their external markets due to the collapse of Comecon;[4] or the loss of value of a large share of fixed assets created specifically for the needs of an ideologically conditioned economic and defense community of countries.

2. What has been going on is hard to understand from the endogenous developments of any country or system, as it has been the changing geopolitical reality which superimposed its logic on the evolutionary tendencies in overripe socialist societies in the region.

3. The collapse of the Soviet empire implies also the collapse of the Russian state in its traditional form, created by sword and blood from the 16th century onward. Therefore the historic cataclysm, with its ideological, military, national, and power characteristics, renders economic considerations secondary. Any talk about the uses of a larger economic region or of a common currency simply misses the point, the given context of national secession. Whatever were the virtues of the Austro-Hungarian Monarchy, whatever were or were not the policies in 1917–18, the crux of the problem was that the story was over. Even if most or all participants lost in the *ex post* accounting, nobody thinks in these terms *ex ante*, and this loss seems inevitable.

Talk about interdependencies used to play a useful role in bringing about more accommodative approaches of certain political quarters during the 70s and 80s. However, the much too frequent invocation of this point proved to be rather misleading when the decisive role of national balance of power seems to have been overshadowed, at least for a while. The naive beliefs of external forces being able to keep together the Soviet Union or Yugoslavia were reflections of this twist of thought. Therefore much time and energy were spent on rather useless activities, whereas manageable ones, primarily the support for the Central European countries already making way in transforming their sys-

---

[3] It is not my intention to join the endless debate on what is/is not socialism, communism, and its many sorts. I use these terms in a purely descriptive, value-free sense. "Soviet socialism" is thus equivalent to "realexistierende Sozializmus" ["really existing socialism"], something which did exist in one half of the old continent [Europe].

[4] László Csaba, "The Rise and Fall of the Council for Mutual Economic Assistance," in *The Changing Soviet Union in the New Europe*, ed. Jyrki Iivonen (Aldershot, England: Edward Elgar, 1991), pp. 189–210.

tems, or helping the rather catastrophic situation in Albania and Bulgaria, received little or no attention. The belief that new immigration rules can keep these problems at arm's length is a further and no less dangerous illusion based on an opposite rationale. These "extra-economic" points relate directly to such narrow economic questions as the subject, object, and institutions of transition, economic opening, and convertibility. Newly introduced national currencies, as the Ukrainian grivna, are rather infrequently convertible, and there is more than one reason for its inconvertibility. Thus the limits of the instantaneous convertibility proposals are rather obvious in the given context.

As the socialist system was characterised by adverse selection according to loyalty, it is often believed[5] that competence in decision making is the single most important bottleneck in transforming the economic system. Still, experience of the last two years indicates that generally respected politicians, such as Balcerowicz or Klaus,[6] also have difficulty in getting their priorities implemented for a variety of reasons. As the new democratic systems emerged after the erosion of the old structures, no wonder that there is a limited capacity of implementing any central policies even in such small and ethnically homogenous countries like Hungary. The problems are obviously multiplied if national strife abounds. It is hard to restrict the money supply and credit creation over territories which do not accept the sovereignty of the central bank over themselves.

In retrospect, the international debate over gradualism versus cold turkey approach seems to have been overdimensioned and somewhat misplaced. Shock therapists, such as Klaus and Balcerowicz, have been heavily engaged in sequencing and gradual changes due to political exigencies, whereas the gradualist Hungarian government followed an absolute *laissez faire* policy against companies heavily hit by the collapse of Comecon markets. Moreover, experience has supported the thesis of Kolodko[7] that the entire question of "big bang" versus gradualism makes sense only in terms of stabilization, while it is entirely meaningless in terms of systemic change. The latter, as probably no one in the region would doubt, is a lengthy process, whereas stabilization can be mastered in a few months, as several historical examples indicate. Even in Vietnam, where Communist party rule excludes any talk of systemic transformation, it took only three months in 1989 to balance a previously very disequilibrated market.

---

[5] Pavel Pelikan, "The Dynamics of the Economic System," in *On the Theory and Policy of Systemic Change,* ed. Hans-Jürgen Wagener (Heidelberg, Germany: Physica-Verlag, 1993), pp. 67–94.

[6] Editor's note: Vaclav Klaus, Finance Minister and later Prime Minister, was the architect of the Czech economic reform program.

[7] Grzegorz Kolodko, "Stabilization Policy: Vision, Reality, Responsibility," in *Systemic Change and Stabilization in Eastern Europe,* ed. László Csaba (Aldershot, England: Dartmouth Publishing Company, 1991), pp. 79–90.

## THE PROOF OF THE PUDDING

In the following, I shall present some theses which attempt to sum up those lessons of postsocialist systemic transformations that are relevant for conventional economic approaches. I wish to stress the tentative nature of these findings, which are not meant to be "final" judgments on a process which is far from being completed at the time of writing.

1. Most economists tend to presuppose a *homo oeconomicus* [economic man], with utility maximizing ambitions expressed in monetary terms. This is a valid abstraction for a developed market economy, but, as development economics amply demonstrates, may be unfit for backward and traditional societies.

Under socialism, not only were labor markets missing, a capital market nonexistent, and savings limited, but also the societal environment was hostile to innovation, investment, and risk-taking, and it considered capital income as direct cheating rather than a risk premium. The problem is that, even if and when a reformed socialist system is monetized, people have various opportunities for putting their money to good use other than buying up the securities of bad public firms. In fact, unless old debts are completely forgiven, it makes little sense for most individuals to join in the privatization drive, as buying scarce hard currency and real estate, lending money at exorbitant interest rates, and many other activities may be more rewarding than buying up public firms. The lukewarm interest of foreign investors in East German firms is hardly a coincidence. On the other hand, forgiving all debts in a *reformed monetized* economy, such as Hungary or Slovenia, may be even embarrassing economically, as management did have responsibility for the debts, which reflected to some degree the market success of the firm. Taking over high debts, however, might cripple an otherwise sound restructuring plan of the new private owner.

Therefore the first thesis goes as follows: Conditions conducive to decisions of buying up the securities of public firms *are to be brought about by governmental activity*. Moreover, one of the main concerns of any government wanting to orchestrate a successful transition to the market has to be the priority of investment. Any money put into investment has to be preferentially treated over all other uses, especially over consumption even if, on distributional grounds, such an option may be politically controversial. Taxation principles of advanced welfare economies are hardly fit for fostering the process of capital accumulation in less developed and transition economies. Meanwhile, the differentiation between incomes invested and consumed may make disparities in wealth more acceptable than uniform taxation would.

2. In most economic models and, thus, in most suggestions on stabilization policies, there is an explicit or underlying thesis presuming the

*quasi-instantaneous adjustment of the supply side.* This is a rather common and convenient abstraction in economic theory. Still, in the East European reality it seems to be a far-fetched assumption. It is all the more important as politicians, and most recently Boris Yeltsin, make pronouncements asking for patience for about half a year or so. The promise/expectation of quick improvement is not alien to adherents of shock therapy in the economics profession either.[8]

One has to be rather clear about the time horizon of possible major improvements, since it has an immediate impact on the sociopolitical feasibility of any restructuring program. As the Polish election results of October 1991 and developments of the Russian winter of 1991–92 indicate, lavish promises may backfire. Unless it is made clear that free prices only redistribute availabilities in an economically more rational manner, the public would expect stabilization to improve living standards in general—which is fundamentally wrong. Thus, though the market will be equilibrated, the public will be disappointed and turn against those who have actually laid the foundations of longer-term improvement.

Experiences with standard IMF stabilization programs in Latin America are indicative of inevitably very high costs of adjustment in terms of growth.[9] It might take a decade before a new growth path is entered, if at all. Therefore, no matter how convenient the conventional assumption is, instantaneous adjustment of the supply side is a rather far-fetched assumption when applied to the East European reality. Moreover, in Latin America, the entire property rights issue cannot be invoked in explaining the sluggishness of adjustment. Hence the ritual reference to the need for quick privatization as the single most important precondition for improvement is inclusive at best.

The lesson might be summed up as follows: Rather than hoping for a quick and sizable adjustment on the supply side, the time horizon of the expectations has to be lengthened and the expectations of improvement simultaneously lowered. If one knows that systems, structures, and specialization patterns have to be changed in parallel, any forecast of a quick improvement sounds ill-conceived and incongruous with all the international experience. Free elections and a free press should increase the new governments' ability to tell this unpleasant truth to the public, as it might lower expectations and thus lengthen the tenure of the rulers.

---

[8] Jeffrey D. Sachs, "Poland and Eastern Europe: What Is to Be Done?" in *Foreign Economic Liberalization: Transformation in Socialist and Market Economies,* ed. András Köves and Paul Marer (Boulder, Colo.: Westview Press, 1991), pp. 235–46.

[9] László Halpern, "Hyperinflation, Credibility, and Expectations (Stabilization Theories and East European Stabilization Programs)," *Acta Oeconomica* [Budapest] 43, no. 1–2, 1991, pp. 89–109.

3. In abstract economic modeling it is relatively easy to demonstrate that *freeing prices will not lead to inflation* if monetary and fiscal policies are sufficiently tight. Correcting the general price level to where it clears the market is a once-for-all measure which can, and probably will, be followed by absolute price stability. This thesis, when translated into politics without qualifications, may give ground to mistaken expectations which might be turned against the reformist governments. Architects of the Polish stabilization program found it sufficient to rely on the figures of the first quarter of 1990 to conclude that *the phase of corrective inflation was over.*[10] As we all know, in 1990 Polish inflation was 250 percent, and in 1991 it was 60 percent. Thus hyperinflation caused by the Rakowski government has actually been broken. Moreover, knowing the size of recession and the collapse of the Soviet market, both figures sound respectable, though they are a far cry from the postulated price stability.

In Czechoslovakia, architects of the reform package of 1991 maintained, on the basis of the first two quarters, that the phase of corrective inflation was over, and a period of zero inflation lay ahead. Actually, annual inflation in Czechoslovakia in 1991 was 57.9 percent, and for 1992 a 15 percent figure was forecasted. These data are not measured against stagnant output, as in the models, but against heavily contracting output which itself should be anti-inflationary: a 25 percent drop in industrial production and 6.6 percent unemployment in Czechoslovakia. Again, the figures are reasonable but still a far cry from the statements of the politicians.

Elaborating the above-discussed theoretical standpoint, Cochrane and Ickes argue[11] that Latin American (bad) experience may not apply to Eastern Europe, as in the former case fiscal overspending, whereas in the latter price controls, are the primary culprits. The difference might well disappear in practice. Central European governments, widely condemned for an overdose of monetarism by their own public, have actually overspent fiscally in 1991 in Hungary, Czechoslovakia, and Poland alike. This did not happen because of incompetence or political laxity, but resulted from the deeper than expected recession in the respective economies. Due to the contraction of large-scale public activities which do pay taxes and the simultaneous expansion of private and unofficial activities which hardly pay any taxes, the maintenance of a deteriorating level of public services resulted in grave fiscal imbalances. In other words, a fair degree of precau-

---

[10] David Lipton and Jeffrey D. Sachs, "Poland's Economic Reform," *Foreign Affairs* 69, no. 3 (Summer 1990), pp. 47–66.

[11] John H. Cochrane and Barry W. Ickes, "Inflation Stabilization in Reforming Economies: The Myth of the Monetary Overhang," *Comparative Economic Studies* 33, no. 2 (Summer 1991), p. 117.

tion is needed if the governments want to avoid losing their credibility in fighting inflation. As inflation is known to be like fever (i.e., a sign, and only in part a cause, of illness) a successful fight against it is part and parcel of overall recovery. This is not to dispute away the prime importance of anti-inflationary policies, or the need to bring down inflation as much as possible for the well-known reasons. Still, a degree of realism is needed, as a period of protracted contraction might not be an ideal time for applying stringent monetary and fiscal policies as textbooks would prescribe.

4. It is widely accepted that *privatization* is not only a positive step, but an urgent one, which lays the *foundations for everything else*. Thus, it is argued, nothing will change irreversibly unless all or most of the assets will be in private hands. As a reflection of this approach, the *speed* of privatization has become a focal point of political debate in the three Central European countries. The number of firms outside the control of the government has become a kind of success indicator for the efficacy of the entire transformation process.

This approach seems to be a prime example of applying abstract theories without proper qualification directly to an untested empirical problem. In theory, and also in general international cross-country comparisons, private firms tend to outperform public ones for a number of reasons. Still, experience with actual privatization in both Britain and France[12] indicates that, if there is any correlation between efficiency and ownership change, it is *from* improved performance *to* privatization, not vice versa. Similarly, in most developing nations a maximum of 20 large companies were privatized, although the predominance of private property was already a given.

Similarly, Hungarian empirical studies[13] cast serious doubts over the omnipotence of abolishing public property. First, corporatized firms have indeed distanced themselves from the state administration, without however producing major efficiency gains. A very unhealthy phenomenon of cross-ownership emerged, with public firms owning each other, public banks owning companies, and companies owning banks. In this first phase of changes, in 1988–90, both the Treasury and the general public have been left out of the deal. When foreign direct investors appeared on the scene, they tended to buy up natural monopolies or, as in the sugar industry, created new ones. Wholesale and retail networks were bought up in a single package, producing a textbook case for transforming public monopolies into private ones. No wonder that no empirical evidence supports the

---

[12] Wladimir Andreff, "French Privatization Techniques and Experience: A Model for Central-Eastern Europe?" in *Privatization Process and the Role of the Public Sector: Recent Trends in Central-Eastern and Western Europe,* ed. Ferdinando Targetti (Aldershot, England: Dartmouth Publishing Company, 1992), pp. 135–54.

[13] M. Móra, "The (Pseudo) Privatization of State-Owned Enterprises (Changes in Organizational and Property Forms, 1987–1990)," *Acta Oeconomica* 43, no. 1–2, 1991, pp. 37–57.

efficiency argument for privatization in these cases. And, conversely, even public firms had to, and could indeed, adjust to market pressures when the collapse of the Soviet market forced them to export to the West or perish.

Therefore the empirical evidence in the Hungarian case indicates that too much attention has been devoted to privatization techniques as well as to the correct valuation of assets, whereas strategic issues tended to be neglected in sales deals. Sellers were often caught by surprise that buyers used the plant only for waste deposit or were interested just in getting rid of a competing firm. Though I do not belong to those who believe that a more vigorous governmental policy can do a lot against these practices, it is hard to escape the conclusion that *other elements than merely the property structure* also play a vital role in deciding the competitive nature and the quality of a market.

5. Many propositions have implied that the market is a relatively simple way of organizing economic activity, and thus it can be brought about by setting a few of its selected components correctly. Nobody in his right mind would doubt the need for setting priorities and quantitative targets in order to stabilize an economy. Still, the developing country analogy is misleading inasmuch as stabilizing any ex-socialist economy would not end up in its being transformed into a fully-fledged private market economy. On occasion, as in the case of the famous 1947 stabilization by Stalin,[14] considerations of systemic reforms and equilibrating the market might be positively contradictory. A single equilibrium rate of exchange, the introduction of market-clearing prices, or avoidance of budgetary deficits are all virtuous tasks of any reasonable economic policy but will fall short of creating such a comprehensive set of institutions as a modern market economy. The experiences of Bulgaria and Romania, and that of Poland in 1991, support the view that stabilization is a necessary but hardly a sufficient condition for attaining a functioning market order.

Whereas modern mainstream economics tends to abstract from institutional aspects that used to be part of classical political economy, this approach is hardly fruitful in the context where the heart of the job lies just in the change of the institutional setting and of the rules of the game. Thus reliance on disciplines studying the functioning and peculiarities of large bureaucratic organizations and of ascending economies needs to be an integral part of a successful transition strategy.

6. *Adoption of the legislation of other, well-functioning societies in their entirety* is often suggested[15] as a way to shortcut the laborious task of

---

[14] Editor's note: This Soviet stabilization program reduced the "monetary overhang" through a currency reform which exchanged 1 new ruble for 10 old rubles; kept money wages unchanged; and raised some retail prices. However, the socialist centrally planned economic system was not altered.

[15] Richard Portes, "Introduction," *European Economy*, special edition no. 2, 1991, pp. 1–15.

creating the framework of free enterprise. Also at the time of union, it was widely believed that taking over Federal German legislation was a great asset for the GDR.

Since then, the ambiguity of East German development has cast serious doubts over the advisability of heeding such propositions. Social responsiveness is normally seen as one of the strong points of the West German social market economy. However, legislating industrial, environmental, and social security relations tailored for a much more advanced economy has a fair share of direct responsibility for the unprecedented contraction of economic activity and employment in Eastern Germany. True, since the new provinces do not constitute a separate state any more, this might not be a major issue but, still, repercussions of adopting elsewhere-well-functioning rules should become obvious for any impartial observer.

It is important to bear in mind that learning a game and mastering it are two different things. For instance, the Hungarian legislation on unfair competition and antitrust policies, as embodied in Law No. 4/1984, were modeled on German juridical material. The law did not have a bite, as it would be hard to find anybody who has suffered seriously from this legislation. The case is anything but hand-picked. This is rather a rule for Hungarian legal practice. In other words, a more advanced legal framework might not compel the behavior in a more advanced manner.

Similarly, it is difficult to share the ambitions of the European Community Commission to unify everything possible and conceivable all across Europe. According to the basics of the theory of comparative advantage, a less developed country has very little to compete with if wages, pollution standards, opening hours, etc., are all the same as in more productive countries. Therefore the above-suggested shortcut is neither feasible nor advisable.

7. *Public reaction to a given policy-mix* is normally seen as *par excellence* cases of extra-economic issues. However, transition economics can hardly afford this luxury of economic science. For one, transforming the entire macrosystem makes sense only if it derives from a solid majority option of the public. In cases of balanced power relations between supporters and opponents of this course, as in Bulgaria, or with the *de facto* majority of those intending to preserve the underlying structure of inherited arrangements, as in Romania or the Central Asian Soviet republics, even setting the task makes no sense at all.

This thesis is well illustrated by the fate of the Markovic government in Yugoslavia or by the Yavlinsky Plan of September 1991 [in the USSR]. In both cases, professionally elaborate and congruous platforms were produced, while the respective power bases for implementing these policies silently disintegrated/eroded. It has nothing to do with the economic qualities of the Markovic Program that the Serbian leadership and its central bank adopted a course which was fundamentally inconsistent with the overall policy targets pursued by Markovic at the federal level. It has nothing to do with the economic merits of the Yavlinsky Plan that leaders of the major constituent republics decided to discontinue the 1922 treaty that had established the Soviet Union. One can discuss at length the costs and benefits of Ukrainian secession for that matter, but secession still remains an accomplished fact which renders the idea of a currency area irrelevant.

Adherents of people's capitalism of various brands normally assume that most people earnestly strive for property ownership. This underlying assumption is not supported by any sociological or historical evidence. Whereas restitution used to be the hottest issue in the Hungarian parliament, actually only a few thousand people have reclaimed their land. And this had a good economic reason. With 40 percent rates of interest, drastically decreased state subsidies, and a general overproduction of agricultural produce, it is not at all that easy to earn a living as a farming entrepreneur.

Meanwhile, the agricultural co-ops in Hungary have developed into diversified multipurpose ventures. Profits stem mostly from various nonagricultural activities. They do provide a certain level of social security and income for an oversized rural population. Therefore restitution would not imply getting land for nothing, but getting land in exchange for security in a very uncertain world with contracting economic activity.

In a similar macroeconomic environment, it is not a surprise that Czech citizens' interest is much more lukewarm concerning the voucher scheme than its fathers have envisaged. Whereas an enrollment of 4 million people was forecasted, in fact less than half have shown interest. Interest in the ESOP schemes is equally limited unless a *de facto* free distribution takes place under this slogan.

Thus the problem seems to be more conventional than postulated by the radical schemes (i.e., introducing a fair and broadly based tax system with enforceable collection rules, and applying an appropriate social safety net for those falling out of economic activity). The latter is particularly important as state socialism transformed East European societies into economies of wage earners, where a loss of job and the vulnerability to inflationary redistribution of saved incomes are particularly threatening for large social strata. In fact, the availability of those arrangements constituting postwar capitalism with a human face are the crucial factors for countries in the European cultural setting. Here, neither Japanese nor Wild-West types of options seem to enjoy much popularity. Compared to these options, the issue of how property is distributed macroeconomically seems to be a secondary issue for the populations concerned with transition to the market.

8. It is often suggested[16] that chopping up large public companies is a precondition for managing a successful transition to the market. In theory it is all very well. In practice, however, we face a lot of unsurmountable difficulties.

In Hungary, in the mid-80s, the government decided to deconcentrate industry in order to get rid of the much too strong pressure groups. Detailed case studies of this campaign[17] have demonstrated the difficulties in the economics of deconcentration. First and foremost, it is practically impossible to identify the efficiency of individual components of a conglomerate with a complicated set of internal transfer prices. Even theoretically viable parts may die if cut off artificially, or if the center manages to pass over a large share of old debts or sells new assets.

Moreover, parallel to economic transformation, the rule of law (*Rechtsstaatlichkeit*) must be established. Once public firms have been corporatized, it might be extremely troublesome for any state authority to interfere on general grounds of enhancing competition. Moreover, as seen above, foreign direct investors (FDI) are more often than not interested in creating monopoly positions of their own and buy up "natural monopolies." If the general policy is to encourage FDI, it is very difficult to legislate and even more to implement a policy of meticulous state controls and priorities. As the global competition among capital recipient countries is stiff, it seems to me illusory to put very strong beliefs in any governmental agency's ability to check and channel evolving market processes along macroeconomic considerations.

9. Considerations discussed above already foreshadow why we find a growing skepticism among authoritative economists in Hungary[18] against any form of producing *artificial proprietors* as well as against any attempt to *accelerate* the process of *evolutionary transformation artificially*. First, experiences with self-management in the 80s, and later with spontaneous privatization and the ESOP schemes were indicative of the crucial role of *control over management and managerial efficiency*. This has traditionally been an unresolved issue in agricultural and industrial co-ops alike.

What we have learned in recent years is that a change in the ownership structure might not lead to more efficient control over managerial activities or to more meritocratic selection of managers. There is a real

---

[16] David Newberry, "The Hungarian Economic Reform: Sequencing and Privatization," *European Economic Review* 35, no. 2–3 (April 1991), pp. 571–80.

[17] Eva Voszka, "Company Liquidation without a Legal Successor," *Acta Oeconomica* 37, no. 1–2, 1986, pp. 59–71; and Péter Vincze, "Transformation of Industrial Organization—without Genuine Changes," *Acta Oeconomica* 38, no. 1–2, 1987, pp. 117–31.

[18] András Köves, *Central and Eastern European Economies in Transition: The International Dimension* (Boulder, Colo.: Westview Press, 1991); and János Kornai, "The Principles of Privatization in Eastern Europe," *De Economist* [Amsterdam] 140, no. 2, 1992, pp. 153–76.

danger that social security directorates and municipalities will be endowed with sizable funds without creating competition and enhancing the presence of the private sector in the areas their services cover. There is no reason to expect that a further drop of efficiency would be avoided.

Restitution is basically excluded by the May 1991 ruling of the Constitutional Court in Hungary, whereas prerogatives of previous owners are severely restrained by the March 1991 regulations in Germany. Still, in other countries restitution is under way and it will be a controversial issue from both the economic and legal points of view. This is explained by the many-decades-long hiatus in the Baltic states and in Southeast Europe alike. From the economic point of view it is hard to see how a descendant with no prior experience can and will perform those proprietary functions conventionally postulated in textbooks.

Experiences in Poland, Romania, and probably also in Russia indicate that an overdose of radicalism might well backfire. It can accelerate the process for a while; yet later it produces a backlash. That side of the coin should also be added to the conventional story about the (actual) dangers of gradualism.

All in all, capitalism around the world has evolved basically in an evolutionary manner. As one does not see in Europe the cultural and historic background of Southeast Asia, the NICs[19] might become a model more for Vietnam than for any European ex-socialist country.

10. Hardly mentioned among theorists, it is all the more popular among decision makers to discuss: *What to do with* all the public *income* inflowing *from privatization*? Many people believe that establishment of new ventures should be fostered, others believe in reorganization programs, still others in amortizing public debt. In fact, international experience of privatization does not indicate its being a source of sizable governmental revenue. For one, the states normally want to get rid of bad firms, whose discounted future values are not particularly high. When good firms are being sold, more often than not the ideological concern of broadening the dispersion of ownership dominates. Therefore conscious underpricing of shares as a means of inducing common people to be involved was rather common in both Britain and France. In Germany, resulting costs are nearly always borne by the *Treuhand*,[20] which in 1991 (when good, and the best, companies were sold) ran a *deficit* of 20.8 billion DM. This sum might soar, according to some estimates, to 210–250 billion DM if present trends are extrapolated till 1995. If one thinks of costs of retraining, unemployment benefits, early retirement schemes, investment subsidies and bonuses, wage supports, etc., it is hard to believe that privatization would be a sizable source of current budgetary inflows. If there is good news for the

---

[19] Editor's note: Newly Industrializing Countries, such as South Korea, Taiwan, and Singapore.
[20] Editor's note: The agency responsible for privatizing East German state assets.

budget, it is that, in the future years, a private firm may not ask for the kind of automatic subsidization which is the rule for many public firms.

11. Besides the negative experiences there are some positive ones as well. Polish, Hungarian,[21] and East German experiences actually support the view of those who believed that *opening up to the world economy* is the core point of systemic transformation. If the import regime remains basically liberal, competition from abroad helps overcome most, if not all, difficulties stemming from the dominance of state ownership and from the preservation of much of the monopoly structure in transition economies. According to recent and yet unpublished studies of the Cartel Office in Hungary, out of the 25 cases of dominant market positions they examined in 1991, in 21 cases monopolists were simply not in the position to make use of their standing, as the collapse of the Soviet market coupled with competing imports from the West left simply no room for them to do so.

In all three cases of transition discussed above, there is a widespread controversy over the vices and virtues of "active structural policy" or "industrial policy" and in the Polish and Hungarian cases also over the "need to protect the domestic market," especially in agriculture. Many people, primarily from the unions and the chambers of trade and industry, are of the opinion that a more interventionist policy could make the transition smoother.

Against this view, there is the decade-long experience that state programs tend to conserve existing patterns, while in 1990–91 structural change did take place just because there was no governmental tutelage and empty budgets precluded governments from bailout actions and "active programs" alike.

12. Lessons of the first two years indicate that the *speed of process is not a good success indicator for transformation*. A modern market economy is a comprehensive set of structures, which will not come about overnight, no matter how competent our policies are. Once we have recognized the difference between stabilization and systemic change, we no longer believe this process could be over in weeks or months. If the nature of the change is such that, even after a shock treatment, it will take years to transform the system, *sustainability* becomes an independent variable and, moreover, an important success indicator. Liberalization of prices in the way the Gaidar team orchestrated [in Russia] might cause more harm than good, no matter how much we are committed to the idea of free pricing. Privatization programs along the lines of the Romanian govern-

---

[21] András Nagy, "Open We Must!" *Acta Oeconomica* 36, No. 3–4, 1986, pp. 219–39.

ment's proposals, with such a low degree of social approval as it had, could only have led to the intervention of miners.[22] In other words, between any two points the shortest way is a straight line. But if one of the points is at the top of a hill of 6,000 meters,[23] climbing directly might not be the safest or the fastest way of actually getting there.

Empirical evidence surveyed above supports the view that speed and quality might be contradictory considerations in orchestrating the transformation process. Cross-ownership between commercial banks and their clients was a right step in getting away from a property structure dominated by the rule of the state administration. Still, by now it has become a major obstacle in transforming corporations into truly private companies. Through the voucher and the ESOP schemes a wide dispersion of actual private ownership is being created for a while, but neither the problem of control over managerial efficiency nor the issue of *legitimacy* of property is being solved. Most people will rightly believe they were cheated, as they will hardly have a greater say in shaping their economic fortunes. Thus their support for the transition program might well be quite ephemeral.

This lends support to the view that thinking *ex ante* of the right sequence of measures to be taken not only makes sense but also is necessary if we are serious about getting to a more or less clearly defined terminus, say a social market economy.

## CONCLUDING REMARKS

It is hardly a coincidence that the present study did not touch upon many of the issues hotly debated in international literature. It is equally impossible to survey and reflect upon all important contributions. Still, as a kind of progress report, this reading of the events has, I hope, contributed to a better understanding of transformation economics.

The process of transition is far from being concluded. Empirical evidence in individual countries is manyfold and sometimes contradictory. At this point let me make two remarks, remembering that the present state of the art requires modesty in passing judgments of any sort.

First, no matter how depressing it may sound for a comparative economist, societies do not seem to possess the ability to learn from each other's mistakes. Thus even obvious policy and sequencing failures will probably be repeated when other countries join the process of transition to the market. Everybody seems to have the right to commit other people's/nations' mistakes,

---

[22] Editor's note: By strikes and demonstrations.
[23] Editor's note: 1,000 meters equal 0.62 mile.

and all of us stick to exercising this right. This might enable future analysts to show truly general regularities in this process, thus making national peculiarities more pronounced.

Second, even in sharing the agnostic view about the planability of systemic transformation, we should stick to the need of governmental management of the overall process, in which spontaneous evolution is bound to prevail. Most new institutions will never emerge without their being legislated. And, although governments can do fairly little in decreeing the market, they can always do a lot to sidetrack the transition process. Their responsibility for competent and efficient action, as well as for exercising the necessary restraint in most cases, remains, and rests with them alone.

# Chapter Twenty-eight

# Chinese Economic Reform Experience*

## The World Bank

*China has embarked on an extensive reform of its socialist centrally planned economy through privatization and marketization.*

*Most striking in the first respect are the abandonment of the commune and the return to individual household activity in agriculture, with a resultant sharp increase in incentives, output, and rural incomes. In addition, private and cooperative activity has significantly increased in services and light industry, creating employment and providing consumers larger quantities, greater variety, and better quality.*

*In the state sector, administrative planning of inputs and outputs has been reduced, freeing firms to negotiate some sales and purchases with each other. Partial relaxation of price control has led to a multiple system of administratively set state prices and flexible market prices. However, labor mobility is still limited, and wages remain closely controlled.*

*This chapter provides a comprehensive survey and appraisal of China's economic reform experience. First it explains key features of the Chinese economy before the reforms began in 1979. Next it discusses distinctive characteristics of the Chinese approach to economic reform, such as experimentation, gradualism, partial changes, and decentralization of decision making from the central government to local governments and to enterprises. Then it reviews the principal reform measures affecting agriculture and rural industry, foreign direct investment, trade, state enterprises, banking, and the labor force. It examines the effects of these measures on output, consumption, productivity, and foreign economic relations. It also analyzes the need for further reform steps in the operation of state enterprises, the financial sector, prices, and markets.*

*The chapter concludes by identifying five noteworthy elements of economic reform in China: (1) initial attention to agriculture, (2) emphasis on marketization*

* Reprinted by permission from World Bank, *China: Reform and the Role of the Plan in the 1990s* (Washington, D.C., 1992), pp. 34–69, with the omission of tables and charts, some footnotes, and references to foreign language sources, unpublished papers, and limited-circulation documents.

*rather than privatization in the state sector, (3) reorientation of the bureaucracy and the Communist Party, (4) export development, and (5) concern for social stability.*

*Chapter 29 subsequently draws major lessons from China's economic reform experience.*

## INTRODUCTION

It is now more than a decade since China launched its program of economic reform in late 1978. Much has been written and said about China's progress and experience since that time. This chapter is an attempt to examine the period of reform as a whole, to extract the essence of the Chinese reform experience and approach, and to assess the impact of the reform period on the Chinese economy. There are two main purposes for such an exercise. First, the length of the reform experience, and the availability of research results, now offer the scope to carry out such an assessment on a more rigorous basis. Second, now that the 1988–91 rectification program has been completed, China appears to have the opportunity and interest to enter a new reform era. In this regard, therefore, it seems appropriate to take stock of China's considerable reform achievements to date, and to assess not only how far China has already gone along the reform road, but also how much further it has to go to have in place the new economic system for which it is striving.

## INITIAL CONDITIONS

It is clear that the initial conditions under which China entered its reform era were very different from those of other reforming socialist economies, and were in general favorable to the rapid achievement of economic gains. It sometimes seems to be the opinion of commentators both inside and outside China that it is only in the reform period that China has achieved any economic or social success. However, there were many well-documented achievements of the first 30 years of China's socialist system since 1949,[1] most importantly in health and education. Moreover, China was not impelled to enter upon its reform path because of deep macroeconomic crisis—which removed the need for a strong dose of deflationary policy to accompany the launching of reforms.[2] Indeed, the fiscal and external accounts were in broad balance at this time, and savings mobilization was already high. Rather, the launching of reform stemmed from two main factors:

1. Dissatisfaction with the "extensive" growth model that had generated overall growth, but little if any improvement in productivity, and required in-

---

[1] See World Bank, *China: Socialist Economic Development* (Washington, D.C., 1983).

[2] For Central and East European countries, stabilization measures are estimated to account for about half of the output losses that have followed the launching of their reform programs [in the early 1990s].

creasing levels of investment to be maintained, thus preventing significant gains in personal consumption.

2. A political rejection of the extremes of "leftism" associated in particular with the period of the "Cultural Revolution."

It should be noted, however, that even at that time and despite the excesses of that period and the deaths of Mao Zedong and Zhou Enlai, there was no rejection of the socialist system *per se,* but rather a call for a radical reform away from the earlier approach to its implementation.

## Agriculture

The initial economic conditions laid the basis for a situation whereby the immediate benefits of the reforms selected outweighed the immediate costs. In agriculture, where reforms were launched, the commune system of socialized agriculture had achieved four of the five main goals for which it was established:

1. It had developed rural infrastructure, especially in terms of irrigation facilities and use of improved seeds and fertilizers.

2. It had created a rural management system, which not only served political and social needs, but also fostered economic support systems, such as input supply and marketing.

3. It had served to foster social aims, such as preventive medicine and attainment of universal education, through local (compulsory) mobilization of funds for such purposes.

4. It had diversified the rural sector from being a peasant agriculture on a self-sufficient basis.

What it had not done was improve agricultural productivity and thus output in quantity, quality, or variety. Grain output per capita was 283 kg. in 1952, but had risen to only 317 kg. in 1978. Moreover, agricultural productivity probably *fell* over this period, not least because of the absence of alternative, off-farm employment, as well as the two problems of the incentive system: there were virtually no incentives for individual efforts,[3] and agricultural prices were kept intentionally low to generate a surplus for industrial investment. Thus, prior to reform, the agricultural sector was endowed with reasonable physical, marketing, and human infrastructure, but without incentives. It was the sense of agricultural crisis that was perhaps as important as any other factor in creating the initial impetus for reform. Once individual incentives were introduced, and the role of the state was reformed, it was not surprising that the

---

[3] The commune system incorporated an arrangement for awarding "work points" to individuals in relation to individual effort. In practice, however, measurement of effort proved very difficult, not only because of intrinsic problems but also because of the general ethos of egalitarianism in that period.

output response was rapid. Improved output and productivity were the aims (and, indeed, the result) of agricultural reforms. As will be seen, increased savings available for investment and the release of surplus labor were unforeseen but perhaps even more significant side effects.

## Industrial Sector

In the industrial sector, there are three key factors with respect to the initial conditions.

1. China had changed from being an essentially rural, peasant economy in 1949 to one in which industry was very significant. The share of industry in national income had grown from 20 percent in 1952 to 49 percent in 1978. Of particular significance during this period was the first decade, and the 156 heavy industrial projects carried out with the assistance of the former Soviet Union.

2. Of critical importance was that by far the largest share of this industrial expansion was in heavy industry, and light industry was neglected, as would be expected in a Soviet-influenced approach. Heavy industry accounted for 57 percent of total output in 1978. The significance of this was twofold: (a) it meant that there was a significant industrial base from which to build; but (b) it meant that there were enormous opportunities for light industrial investment once investment decision making was decentralized.

3. Almost all this early industrial development took place through large- and medium-size state-owned enterprises (SOEs), with only a relatively small share in smaller, local enterprises. Indeed, these SOEs accounted for 78 percent of industrial output in 1978. This is of course to be expected, given the emphasis on heavy industry. But these large SOEs were burdened with excessive work forces and heavy social obligations and were managed in a largely administrative fashion, and this rendered them highly inflexible. Thus, when controls were released upon creation of small firms, the large SOEs were not able to squeeze out such firms or react rapidly to new opportunities. As with agriculture, the socialist system had laid a solid basis, but one which lacked incentives, and thus was ripe for reform.

## Provincial Autonomy

Another aspect relevant to the initial conditions is provincial autonomy. China after 1960 was never truly a centrally planned economy in the same sense as the former Soviet Union. There were only about 500 commodities under mandatory planning, compared with over 20,000 in the former USSR; and local governments always took the primary role in formulation and interpretation of plans. This had three particular consequences for the initial conditions. First, it meant that local implementation capacity was rather well-developed, with officials well able to respond to improved incentives. Second, with obvious exceptions, there was significantly less pressure for provincial autonomy in China than in other reforming socialist economies, such as those of the USSR or Yugoslavia, because of the relatively high ethnic homogeneity of the Chinese population. Third, while the emphasis on regional autonomy had generated good government capacity, it had also bred serious inefficiencies, especially in agriculture. It therefore offered enormous scope for gains from interprovincial trade.

Thus, China's initial domestic conditions in several key areas can be seen to have been ideal for reform. Unlike the case of many other socialist economies in transition, China's reform responded to socioeconomic pressures rather than to deep crisis, and the absence of the need for major stabilization meant that "shock therapy" was not needed. China also had the good fortune of its historic ties to Hong Kong and the overseas Chinese community, which have played a critical role. Above all, it had a set of conditions whereby the economy and its system of government were well-situated to respond rapidly to improved incentives by increasing output. Of course, not all results would be positive and not everyone would be a winner from reform, as the stop-go pattern of reform in China has amply demonstrated. Moreover, it is clear that several of these elements were distinct to the Chinese case, possibly reducing the applicability of the lessons from this experience. It is important to bear these initial conditions in mind in assessing the gains from reform. It can be cogently argued that part of the returns to reform in terms of efficiency gains and output growth are the delayed returns to the physical investment of the pre-reform era, which could not be reaped at that time because of inadequate incentives.

## CHINA'S REFORM STYLE

Because China began its reform program at the particular point in its economic history noted, it was able to develop its own distinctive approach to economic reform. This is most frequently described as "gradualist," although this only refers to the time taken rather than the depth of reforms. Indeed, the transformation of the Chinese economy that has occurred in these relatively few years since 1979 can hardly be regarded as a gradual change. China has not developed a well-defined reform strategy, nor has it drawn up a clear reform blueprint. Pre-announced reforms have often been withdrawn—such as the price and wage reform plan of 1989—and at other times, deep reforms have emerged suddenly, as with the grain price reform of May 1991.

It can be argued that China's reform philosophy or strategy is indeed *not* to plan reforms, but to push reforms forward in a coherent way when the economic, political, and social climate permits or demands it. This may itself be a response to the perceived failures of the planning system. It is generally agreed that a key reason why central planning fails—and *must* fail—is that it requires too much information. Not only can this information not be assembled and processed, but much of it is unobtainable by definition. It can be argued with equal coherence that to draw up a comprehensive reform blueprint would require a similar amount of information, much of it unobtainable. China did not and could not have foreseen the response of the rural sector to the agricultural reform, and the easing of restrictions on entry to the industrial sector. Therefore, it is argued, it is better to use the Chinese approach which moves and adapts as responses and results become evident.[4] But throughout the reform period, four features of the Chinese approach can be traced as consistent themes in implementation; gradualism, partial reforms, decentralization, and self-reinforcing reforms. It can perhaps be argued that these features, and especially the first three, were necessitated by the sheer size and diversity of China.

## Gradualism and Experimentation

In almost all areas of reform, implementation has been spread over time, often several years, and usually after experimentation.[5] Typically, such experiments take place in designated "reform areas," and after the results of trials are observed, they then spread to other parts of the country. Sometimes, this is the result of a well-publicized central government decision, and sometimes this happens "spontaneously," as other provinces copy the originating province. For example, the household contract responsibility system in agriculture began as an experiment in Sichuan province in 1980–81, and by the time it was formally endorsed by the central government in 1985, it had already spread throughout the whole country. Similarly, though less spontaneously, openness to foreign investment—and to foreign ownership of assets in general—started in a few areas and continues to be extended gradually over the whole country.

Sometimes, this gradualism is the result of the trial process. Other times it is opportunism frequently in response to rising fiscal pressures, and this is especially the case in price reform. In this area, there have been two attempts at formulating a comprehensive reform strategy, both of which have been abandoned. At other, sometimes unexpected, times, progress has been rapid. Perhaps the period from late 1989 to the end of 1991 (when reforms in general were receiving less attention) saw the most radical changes in relative prices in China in the whole reform period.

For some reforms, by their nature, gradualism is not possible, and an overnight change occurs. The central bank was established in 1984, and all its commercial transactions were rapidly transferred to the newly created Indus-

---

[4] See John McMillan and Barry Naughton, "How to Reform a Planned Economy: Lessons from China," *Oxford Review of Economic Policy* 8, no. 1 (Spring 1992), pp. 130–42, and Charles E. Lindblom, "The Science of 'Muddling Through,'" *Public Administration Review* 19, no. 2 (Spring 1959), pp. 79–88.

[5] What the Chinese call "feeling the stones to cross the river," in contrast to the maxim coined by President Vaclav Havel of the Czech and Slovak Federal Republic: "It is impossible to cross a chasm in two leaps."

trial and Commercial Bank, although, of course, it took longer for the People's Bank of China to take up its new functions fully. The foreign-exchange swap centers were all opened to domestic enterprises at the same time in 1988. But even in these areas, where arbitrage would suggest the impossibility of gradualism, the sheer size of the country and the inadequacy of the transport and telecommunications systems make gradualism possible.

The great advantages of this gradual approach, where it is possible, are clear:[6] severe shocks are avoided, trials permit mid-course corrections, institutional development can occur in line with the new systems, and economic agents can adjust slowly to the new conditions. China has thus been able to first bypass and later dismantle its administrative controls at the pace that market mechanisms capable of regulatory functions have emerged. This has meant not only that severe dislocations have in general been avoided, but also that China has been able to enjoy growth with reform. Of course, much of the reason that this has been possible has been the favorable initial conditions under which reform was launched.

But this approach has its drawbacks, and two in particular. The first is that some economic agents are unable to predict their future economic environment. In most areas of reform, the advantages of pragmatism override this,[7] but in other areas advance planning is important. This will be the case in the near future as China sets about reforming its import framework, for advance announcement of reduced protection will permit enterprises to adjust to the future set of arrangements. In such instances, there is a case for rapid implementation of the reform itself, but with adjustment to the new situation spread over time.

The second and potentially more serious charge is that gradual reforms can give time for those whose interests are threatened by reforms to regroup and either block progress along the gradual slope, or even reverse some reforms, and that failure to introduce reform rapidly will reduce the credibility of such reforms. This is clearly the fear of many policymakers in Central and Eastern Europe. There have indeed been such periods of reversal in China. The Communique of the Fifth Plenary Session of the 13th Central Committee in December 1989 clearly espoused a view that planning could solve the problems that had arisen during the course of reforms designed to address the shortcomings of planning. However, so far, each such reversal (or "one step back") has been temporary. It is clear that the new momentum of enterprise reform evident in 1992 is partly a conclusion of China's leaders that, during the "rectification program,"[8] the instruments of planning failed to come to grips with the fundamental problems of the state-owned enterprise sector. Thus, while periodic reversals occur, the overall direction continues. The reasons why planners have failed to regroup effectively in China are discussed below.

---

[6] World Bank, *World Development Report 1991* (Washington, D.C., 1991), p. 117.

[7] Indeed, in some areas pre-announcement is to be avoided. It was the *announcement* of future price reform in 1988, not the reform itself, which triggered inflation.

[8] Editor's note: The "rectification program" of 1989–90 slowed economic reforms.

## Partial Reforms

Closely related to the gradual/experimental approach to reform has been the use of partial reforms within sectors, and one of the more interesting results of the Chinese reform experience has been the apparent success of this approach. This has perhaps been most obvious in the two-tier pricing system, under which state enterprises have been permitted to sell above-plan output at market prices. It has been estimated that in 1989, on average, 38 percent of an SOE's outputs were sold on markets, and 56 percent of its inputs were procured on markets.[9] This dual price system has been of particular importance in the materials sector, for commodities such as coal, steel, timber, and cement, where differentials were sometimes very large indeed.

The two-tier price system, like the partial reform approach in general, has two particular advantages. First, it has been a powerful instrument of the gradualist approach, providing an underlying assurance of continuity of supply, while creating a situation where market skills can be learned. Second, and most important, it has created a situation where marginal resource allocation decisions have been made on the basis of market prices. In almost all sectors, enterprises' output targets are such that enterprise managers have sufficient capacity to make decisions based on the market as to how much above-plan output to produce. Only in the state coal, crude oil, and power sectors, as well as transport, does the command plan continue to leave little room for market-based resource allocation decisions.

This system has, however, had certain obvious drawbacks. The most important of these has been the incentive for leakage from the planned sector to the market sector, and the associated corruption this has engendered. One explanation of the difference between the percentage of outputs and inputs under the planning system is that output leaving enterprises under the plan then gets diverted to the market, or else undergoes price adjustment. It is estimated that of output under the plan, one third arrives at its intended destination at the plan price, one third arrives at the intended location but with the price adjusted to the market rate, and one third gets diverted entirely. Clearly, the incentives for corruption in this have been realized, and this not only has concerned policymakers in China, but was also one of the overt factors behind the May–June events of 1989.[10] What remains unclear is why these price differentials have persisted for so long, without arbitrage eliminating them. One factor is clearly the undeveloped transport and information system, but beyond this, provincial protectionism and import barriers explain how such differentials can continue. This partial reform approach is one whose benefits appear rapidly, but whose costs increase over time. Thus, if used as a transitional device, the

---

[9] Figures from a survey by the Chinese Academy of Social Sciences, cited in McMillan and Naughton, "How to Reform."

[10] Editor's note: Demonstrations in the center of Beijing, which the government suppressed by force.

approach has merits, but it has severe drawbacks as a long-term system. As discussed later, integration of the domestic market remains one of the major challenges.

## Decentralization

One of the features of China's initial conditions discussed above was the presence of a capable, in-place decentralized administration. This became a critical element in China's reform approach. As the central government released control, provincial, municipal, county, township, and even village administrations were ready to respond. This decentralization element of the reform approach is controversial in two ways. First, governments at local levels have frequently replaced reduced central planning with increased local planning. Second, at times the decentralization ran ahead of other reforms, and the local response was reacting to distorted relative prices—leading to inappropriate local investments, as in, for example, over 100 car assembly plants each with a capacity of less than 5,000 vehicles per year. But in general, and taken over the period, the unrelenting pursuit of economic development at the local level has clearly been a tremendous force for good and for progress as, for example, through the creation of so many new jobs in the township and village enterprises.

Moreover, decentralization has not just been to local governments, but to actors in all spheres of economic activity: to enterprises in making production and marketing decisions; to foreign trade corporations in selection of export products; to farmers in selecting crops; and, most important, to individuals, to a large extent with respect to purchases, though to a much lesser extent with respect to employment. Of course, this form of decentralization is how markets get created, for it is the absence of concentration of decision making that makes markets work, and thus the decentralization of decision making is at the heart of market creation. In China, the key to market creation without severe disruption has been twofold: as noted earlier, via gradual change which releases administrative controls only as markets develop; and via judicious balancing of markets and local governments. By decentralizing administrative power to lower levels of government, other forms of economic decentralization have been made more effective by local governments. For example, for most consumer goods, the government decentralized price controls to local governments in 1986, leaving it to them to decide when to release controls entirely, depending on the state of local market conditions. Decontrol moved rapidly in the dynamic South, with its many small firms, but more slowly in the Northeast, where state firms dominate. The direction of causality is open to debate, but the results seem to be positive in general.

Such decentralization has its dangers. Some conservative parts of China have moved slowly in some areas, such as for price decontrol in the Northeast and public ownership in Shanghai. It has also created a tendency toward overheating, as local development aspirations have forced a more rapid growth of credit than desired at the center. Thus, while the microeconomic effects appear to have been positive, it is less clear that the macroeconomic impact of decentralization has been wholly desirable.

Perhaps the greatest advantage of the decentralization approach has been to create interest groups in favor of further reforms, and to foster a climate for reform initiatives and "spontaneous" reform at the local level. This comes in two forms. First, many central reforms are "enabling," in the sense that they remove central prohibitions. Trade reform, for example, began in the mid-1980s with the removal of the prohibition on the creation of local foreign trade corporations. By 1990, 6,000 had been created where only 15 existed before. Second, as noted earlier, local reforms frequently spread, often from experiment in one area, and were later sanctioned nationally. It occurred in agriculture with the spread of the household contract responsibility system in 1981–82, and it appears to be repeated in social security systems at the present time. This spread is often the result of arbitrage pressures, when one province moves faster than a neighbor. It not only helps to build up increased confidence and interest in reforms, but also creates innovative approaches to reform.

## Self-Reinforcing Reforms

The fourth characteristic of China's approach to reform has been the self-reinforcing nature of reform: "Once a crack is opened in the monolith that is the centrally planned economy, natural forces take over and force the crack open ever more widely."[11] It can thus be seen with the benefit of hindsight how reforms in one area lead naturally to reforms in other areas, and can indeed *force* those reforms by creating pressures for change. This seems to refute the thesis that the gradualist approach permits the rise of countervailing forces. The initial agricultural reforms created surplus savings and labor, which created pressures for decentralization of authority to establish enterprises in rural areas, spawning the massive expansion of township and village enterprises. The creation of nonstate firms in turn created pressure of competition on the state-owned sector, forcing the state to relax control on the SOEs. This itself compelled the state to restructure its own sources and uses of revenue, and to reform the financial sector.

The key to the successful linking of one reform to another requires the appropriate response of policymakers. It would be possible, of course, for the pressure emerging from one area to be met with counterpressure rather than a complementary reform. For example, competition from township–village enterprises (TVEs) was met in 1989 by an initial attempt to restrict availability of credit for TVEs and to close some of them administratively. This attempt did occur to some extent for a time, but it was short-lived, and soon attention returned to how to solve the more serious problems affecting the SOEs. There is no clear way to ensure that the response of policymakers will be appropriate,

---

[11] McMillan and Naughton, "How to Reform."

but two factors seem paramount. First, the dynamics of the reform process create opportunities for the government to push forward with new reforms. Second, attempts to reverse reforms and reintroduce planning soon reveal its limitations again—just as attempts to solve the SOE problem in 1989–90 via planning have had little impact on restructuring and have instead fostered new interest in market-based solutions to these issues.

## CHINA'S MAJOR REFORM STEPS

This is not the occasion for a detailed review of individual reforms in China—a subject on which several books have already been written, and many more will come.[12] Nevertheless, it seems appropriate to consider briefly the main steps that were taken in each major reform area, and how they linked to others, not least so that the discussion of future reform priorities can be seen against the achievements of the past. The discussion that follows is divided into nine major sectoral areas, rather than chronologically. While it is useful to have this kind of periodic overview—and for the Chinese to put together the sort of document seen in the reform plan that accompanied the Eighth Five-Year Plan—the emphasis of China's reform approach will continue to be on individual interventions at the sectoral level, rather than the formulation of grand, cross-sectoral comprehensive blueprints. We have already discussed the strengths and weaknesses of this approach. It does seem likely that the approach will be more *balanced* than in the past, with an absence of emphasis on a leading reform sector, and with coordinated reforms in different areas, but this will remain well short of a blueprint approach.

### Major Reform Turning Points

There are different ways to define turning points in economic and political history. However, in this context, we are primarily concerned with key decisions taken by the Communist Party and the Government of China with regard to reforms. These decisions then became important reference works, and bear rereading for what they do and do not say about what is permitted after such decisions have been taken. The first of these is, of course, the decision of the 3rd Plenary Session of the 11th Central Committee of the Communist Party of China (CCP),[13] in December 1978. Its Communique officially launched the

---

[12] Among these, two are particularly recommended: Carl Riskin, *China's Political Economy: The Quest for Development since 1949* (Oxford, England: Oxford University Press, 1987), and *China: Modernization in the 1980s*, ed. Joseph Y. S. Cheng (Hong Kong: Chinese University Press, 1989). For an excellent shorter review, see Dwight Perkins, "Reforming China's Economic System," *Journal of Economic Literature* 26, no. 2 (June 1988), pp. 601–45.

[13] About every 5 years, the Communist Party holds a Congress at which it elects a Central Committee. The Central Committee meets in plenary session about 10 times between Congresses to make important decisions. The last (13th) Congress was in November 1987. Since then, 8 plenary sessions have been held. The next (14th) Congress is scheduled for the last quarter of 1992.

reform program and spawned the agricultural reforms and the beginning of the opening up to the outside world. Reforms in urban areas were only on a very limited experimental basis until the Third Plenary Session of the 12th CCP, which adopted the "Decision on Reform of the Economic Structures" October 20, 1984. It was this document that launched the acceleration of reforms in urban areas in 1985, and especially the two-tier price system and decentralization of enterprise management.

Despite these two milestones, the reform lacked a theoretical background and basis in socialist principles—it was based on Deng Xiaoping's principle of "seeking truth from facts," the basis for pragmatic decision making—but this came in October 1987 in the Report of Government to the 13th Party Congress, "Advance Along the Road of Socialism with Chinese Characteristics." This report adopted the theory of the "Primary Stage of Socialism," which provided the theoretical basis for Deng's approach, by showing the acceptability of multiple forms of ownership and economic systems during the early period of socialism that China would be likely to be in until well into the 21st century. This report also spawned the important guidelines, "the state regulates the market, and the market guides the enterprises," which remain the fundamental principle for China's "planned commodity economy." Finally, the adoption of the "Outline of the Eighth Five-Year Plan and the Ten-Year Development Program" is very significant, as it includes a clear description of China's reform approach for the coming period. It sets out reform intentions in a wide range of areas, marking the first occasion when the Plan was focused on policy issues as the key to development. However, it is likely in the future that this turning point will be seen to have been overtaken by the 14th Party Congress scheduled for the last quarter of 1992, which can be expected to take major decisions to guide the next phase of reforms.[14] Each of these four documents/decisions should be regarded as part of the enabling framework which has permitted the central and local governments to move on to define specific reform moves.

## Rural Reforms

These reforms are listed first, not only because reform started here, but also because they remain the most significant of all the reform efforts. As noted, China began the reform period with socialized agriculture operating on a reasonable technical basis, and at the heart of the reform was a return to individual, household agriculture with the breakup of the communes. With the return of the land to individuals on a long (15–25 year) lease basis, farmers had to agree to turn over a percentage of output to the state—in some areas the particular crops (especially rice in the south) were specified—hence the phrase *household contract responsibility system*. This measure was accompanied by

---

[14] Editor's note: The 14th Party Congress confirmed resumption of the main directions of economic reform discussed in this chapter.

a 25 percent (average) real increase in relative agricultural prices. Together, these improved incentives elicited a very rapid output response and generated large cash savings. Pressure for permission to utilize these savings for industrial use grew, resulting in the formal decision in 1984 for local authorities to create township and village enterprises.

Much has been written about the growth of rural industry,[15] and it remains the key to much of China's success in the 1980s. But *why* did this mushrooming of rural industry occur, apparently without *positive* policies, and as a result essentially of an enabling environment? We would offer three main reasons:

1. As suggested, the agricultural reforms created a surplus available for investment and released a pool of labor eager and available for new sources of employment.

2. The initial industrial conditions had—by neglecting the light industrial sector, and as a consequence of the socialist pricing system which favored light industry—created major opportunities for entry of small firms into this sector, where rapid, very high profits could be made.

3. Local governments were heavily committed to local economic development and played a key facilitating, and sometimes even entrepreneurial, role in fostering such industries.

In the South, the role of overseas Chinese is also relevant, while in provinces with large rural industrial sectors, such as Zhejiang and Jiangsu, domestic factors are paramount.

These are, in essence, the only two reforms of significance, and it was not until 1988 and 1991 that new reforms were launched, on the pricing/marketing side. In 1988, it was in the prices of nonstaples (sugar, eggs, vegetables, and pork) that price reform was successfully launched, and abandoned only after an attempted widening. But this approach—of converting product subsidies into wages—was the basis for the important grain and oilseeds price reform of 1991. It was accompanied by the introduction of wholesale and futures markets in grain, and China is slowly moving to a situation where markets will dominate agriculture.

## Foreign Direct Investment

It is sometimes forgotten that it was in the area of foreign direct investment (FDI) that the first industrial reforms were made, with the passing of the joint venture law in 1979 and the opening of the first four Special Economic Zones in 1980. Since that time, FDI has poured into China. The importance in Chinese terms was that it represented a major break with the autarkic principles of the pre-reform era, recognizing that China could not rely on its own resources

---

[15] See William Byrd and Lin Qingsong, *China's Rural Industry* (New York: Oxford University Press, 1990).

alone to catch up with the rest of the world in terms of technology. Thus, the importation of foreign technology and management techniques and their financing by overseas capital became a key strand of Deng's reform approach from the outset. Nevertheless, the early approach, focusing solely on export-oriented industries, severely limited the volume of FDI. Major modifications were introduced by the "22 Articles" in October 1986, which paved the way the following year for the opening up of the foreign exchange swap centers. They removed the most serious constraint, which had been China's attempt to force joint ventures to achieve self-sufficiency in foreign exchange. These "Articles" were further improved in 1990, when regulations were introduced to limit administrative interference with the operation of joint ventures.

It would have been surprising if the opening of China to FDI would not have been successful, given the size of its market and the cheapness and quality of Chinese labor. But the role of overseas Chinese communities, and of Hong Kong and Taiwan in particular, cannot be overemphasized. Fully three quarters of all foreign investment in China originated in Hong Kong—of course much of it by non-Hong Kong residents though channeled through Hong Kong—but this is of no matter. The turning point was the adoption of the "one country, two systems" policy, which led to the signing of the Sino-British accord in Hong Kong in 1986. It has in turn permitted a remarkable integration between the economies of China and Hong Kong.[16] While the regulations have been an important and appropriate enabling environment, it is the Hong Kong factor that explains, in our view, most of the great success of the open door policy.

## Commercial Reforms

One of the earlier reforms in China that appears to have been repeated in other reforming socialist economies has been the effective privatization of the commercial sector. This began in 1982, and by 1985 75 percent of all state-owned commercial and service companies had been sold or leased to private owners, and entry was permitted for any newcomers. The state sector remained important in three main areas: wholesaling of a wide range of products, especially agricultural; retailing of commodities under price controls and under the ration system; and operation of major commercial outlets employing large numbers of people, such as department stores. In addition to these formal retail channels, local governments have fostered the emergence throughout the country of "free markets" for food and consumer goods, especially clothing, frequently by providing basic facilities such as covered market stalls. Again, we have seen here the combination of the initial conditions of neglected consumption and facilitative local government.

---

[16] See Yun-Wing Sung, *The China–Hong Kong Connection: The Key to China's Open Door Policy* (Cambridge, England: Cambridge University Press, 1991).

It is no surprise that this proved a popular and successful reform, as it has in other countries, where improved commerce has been an early reform result. But two parallel results of this reform seem to merit mention. First, the private commercial system has provided a demand for backward linkage to the emerging new industrial sector, not least in alternative transport systems to deliver small quantities of goods to these outlets. This spawning of nonstate services seems set to continue in the 1990s, and indeed is now recognized by policymakers as a key source of future employment creation. Second, this area of reform has served as much as any to create a constituency in favor of the preservation and continuation of reforms, especially among the younger generation. It seems likely that this reform also had such instant results in China because the state commercial system had never been as all-encompassing in China as in other countries, and private commercial skills never completely disappeared, especially in rural areas.

## State-Owned Enterprise Reforms

There have been many detailed reforms related to the SOEs, but they really come down to two basic changes in the system. First, in 1983–84, the system of profit remittance to the central government was changed to one whereby enterprises paid income taxes and shared profits with their supervisory authority—with an increasing role for local industrial bureaus as supervisory authorities, compared with the earlier dominance of central ministries. The change was accompanied in 1984 by incentives to generate those now-retainable profits by the lowering of plan targets and permission to sell above-plan output on markets—together with the further decentralization of plan formulation and implementation. This led to "investment hunger" and very rapid industrial expansion in 1985. Second, the system became more structured from 1986 onward, as the agricultural contract responsibility system was applied to the SOEs under the *enterprise contract responsibility system*. It fixed profit remittance, retention rates, investment targets, etc., usually for a three-year period. By 1988 over 90 percent of all SOEs, accounting for over 50 percent of industrial output, were operating under this system, and by the end of 1991 most had signed a second contract.

Further innovations have been made—such as the Bankruptcy Law in 1987, the Enterprise Law in 1988, the use of enterprise groups and leasing of enterprises—but these are merely codification or variation of these two basic changes. Contrary to many general impressions, important efficiency gains have been achieved in the state sector as well as in the nonstate sector. They were obtained by gradually changing the focus of SOEs from concern with meeting output targets to one of meeting financial targets, by specifying the latter targets as the main performance criteria of the contracts, and by offering incentives for attaining and exceeding such targets. The key to ensuring that such gains have come by efficiency improvements has been the role of competition, not only from new nonstate enterprises, but also from other SOEs, given the size of the market in China. On the positive side, more gains have been made via this route than is frequently acknowledged. The key difficulty, as we discuss more below, is that the system is primarily one of positive inducements, without clear negative consequences of failure.

In short, China's enterprise reforms can be summed up in this way: it has been the "marketization" of such enterprises, as contrasted to the "privatization" approach of many other countries. Can state-owned enterprises operate fairly and effectively in the market? That is at the heart of the assessment of China's future.

## Financial Sector Reforms

Like most other socialist economies, China operated an essentially monolithic banking structure, and this has been one reform area where a classic sequencing of reforms over time has been planned and followed. The first step, in 1984, was to separate central banking from commercial banking, by creating the Industrial and Commercial Bank to take over the latter functions, leaving the People's Bank of China to focus mainly on central banking. This was extended in 1987 by the creation of two new universal banks to introduce slightly more nonprice competition into the banking sector. At the same time, financial innovations were encouraged, first by decentralizing authority to create nonbank financial institutions beginning in 1987, and second by forming new capital markets—essentially for secondary trading of government bonds in 1988–89 and more recently for trading in shares, beginning officially in 1991. This gradual deepening of the financial sector—at times ahead of the central institutional capacity to supervise and manage it—has been rapid and logical.

These financial innovations were necessary and "forced" by the change in the respective roles of the state and enterprises and individuals with respect to savings. The enterprise reforms meant that no longer would most surpluses be channeled via the government. Rather they would be retained by enterprises for investment, or passed along, in rising wages and bonuses, to workers, who then needed somewhere to lodge their financial savings. This rapid financial deepening of the economy also explains why China was able to sustain monetary expansion of close to 20 percent per annum throughout the decade of the 1980s without either revealed or repressed inflation.[17]

These financial innovations took place extremely rapidly in the mid-1980s, with little change since then. The commercial banking system remains 100 percent state-owned and operated—with a considerable share of total (especially working capital) lending influenced by the state through direct interven-

---

[17] Several studies have purported to estimate a high degree of repressed inflation in China, but they ignore the fact that rapid institutional development and financial deepening have reduced the velocity of money. See Andrew Feltenstein and Jming Ha, "Measurement of Repressed Inflation in China: The Lack of Coordination between Monetary Policy and Price Controls," *Journal of Development Economics* 36, no. 2 (October 1991), pp. 279–94.

tion to support its industrial policy, and seemingly only a relatively small proportion of total lending decided by banks on purely commercial grounds. Further reform in this area, then, also remains one of the major items on the unfinished agenda.

## Fiscal Reform

Many would argue that China has never had, and continues not to have, a *tax* system, but rather it has a *revenue* system. It should first of all be noted that China has always operated a decentralized taxation system, with the central government relying on provincial taxation bureaus to collect taxes. The main changes have been less concerned with a fundamental restructuring of sources of revenue than with changes in the way it has been collected and shared. In particular, the first big change has already been noted: profits began to be retained at the enterprise level, instead of being remitted almost in total to the state. This, of course, relieved the state of most of the burden of funding enterprise investment. The second big change came from the introduction of the *fiscal contract responsibility system,* the third of the four contract systems. This system was introduced over a few years beginning in 1985–86, when contracts were signed between the central and local governments. The contracts specify the taxes to be handed over to the center, those to be shared (and in what proportions), and those to be retained by the local government. Similar arrangements had always been in place, but the contract system formalized them.

Central tax revenues were squeezed because the fiscal contract responsibility system did not take account of inflation and because greater competition reduced the profitability of enterprises and hence profits taxes. However, after the initial rapid decline in revenues, the central government was able to introduce minor tax adjustments, especially for indirect taxes, to permit revenues to continue reasonably buoyant. China's tax or revenue system remains very unusual, however, with its reliance on contracted tax payments, layered indirect taxes, and near-total absence of personal taxes, as well as the absence of any centralized tax collection system. This is a second area where two major reforms occurred early (in 1986–88) with only minor adjustments since.

## Foreign Trade

In contrast to fiscal and financial reforms, the foreign trade area has seen evolutionary, gradual change, very much exemplifying the "Chinese model."[18] Not only has it progressed gradually as opportunity has arisen, but it has also involved partial reforms and has seen the "two steps forward, one step back"

---

[18] For a thorough review of foreign trade reforms, see Nicholas Lardy, *Foreign Trade and Economic Reform in China, 1978–1990* (New York: Cambridge University Press, 1992).

phenomenon. From its opening position of a system of about 15 foreign trade corporations (FTCs) operating under a nearly total mandatory trade plan, China rapidly moved to decentralize authority to create foreign trade corporations, while simultaneously reducing the scope of the trade plan, and permitting retention of foreign exchange at the local level. These measures rapidly spawned 1,500 new FTCs by the end of 1987, when the next two innovations were launched: (1) Certain sectors (garments, electronics, and agricultural sideline products) were essentially forced away from planning (and subsidy) and were given a high percentage for retention of foreign exchange. (2) A fourth *contract system* was instituted, *for sharing foreign exchange* between the center and local governments and for the level of "support" (provision of foreign exchange) from the center. Further power to create FTCs was delegated, and the number reached over 5,000 by 1990.

In January 1991 the third trade reform wave came when the second round of trade contracts was put in place. It eliminated central subsidies for exports and increased local retention of foreign exchange, which has increasingly been traded on the parallel market. Over the last five years, a series of devaluations has gradually corrected the overvalued exchange rate and eliminated all but 7 percent of the differential between the official and parallel rates. More than one third of all transactions now take place at the parallel rate. The results in terms of export performance are well-known. The emphasis of trade reform has always been on export promotion to finance "modernization" imports, and the import sector has never been seen as a source of competition. Now, however, with China once again seeking to resume its seat in the GATT, the fourth wave of trade reform can be expected to focus on liberalizing the import regime and making it more transparent.

It can thus be seen that the successful trade reforms have been driven by the desire to increase foreign exchange earnings to finance technology and materials imports. China has succeeded in this effort because of competition in the export sector, constant improvement in export incentives, and openness to foreign traders, especially from Hong Kong. In this regard, it has mirrored the Korean export experience a decade earlier. One final similarity should be noted: while import liberalization was left to the last, imports of raw materials and other inputs for exports have been open from the start, especially in the assembly industries of electronics, toys, and garments.

## Social Sector Reforms

China has left social sector reforms to the last. The reason seems to be twofold: First, by keeping the enterprise-based social safety net in place, it has postponed, or possibly avoided, many potential social problems. Second, because China continues to be very concerned about growth of large urban areas, it has resisted major labor reforms. In regard to labor, the main reform has been a preparatory one: the introduction of the labor contract system, whereby all new workers in SOEs since 1986 have been on contract, not permanent, status, and can theoretically be fired. This system covers about 20 percent of all state workers. The wage system has seen greater reliance on bonuses. On a national basis, the biggest change has been the growth of employment in nonstate enterprises, where rewards are usually on a piece-rate basis, and where nonwage benefits (housing, pension, health) generally do not exist, or are far less significant. Thus, the main change has not been to the basic state system, but in the development of a parallel system.

It is only very recently that the government has begun to move on a national basis with respect to areas such as housing, social security, and health financing, having largely focused on experiments so far. The difficulty is to move from a system of nonwage benefits tying the worker to his enterprise, to one where rewards are essentially monetary, with social facilities and services being made available to the worker through other mechanisms, both public and private. Given its potential for creating social instability, this is an area where the Chinese government is moving very cautiously indeed, as these reforms will also serve to loosen the state's control over labor mobility.

This brief overview of the main steps in China's reform illustrates many of the characteristics of Chinese reform discussed earlier: gradual (trade), decentralized (enterprise), partial (price), and self-reinforcing (financial). It also shows a clear trend throughout toward marketization of the economy, and the gradual evolution of arm's length, rules-based systems, although there remains a considerable way to go. Reforms have made the least progress the more they affect the state-owned enterprises in any adverse way, and the most progress where the opposite is the case. Thus, the challenges appear greatest in enterprise reform and in financial and fiscal reforms. However, before we address future reform priorities, it seems appropriate to review the impact of reforms to date, as an indicator of how far reforms have come.

## IMPACT OF REFORMS

Reform is not an end in itself. It is employed as a mechanism to foster development, and especially gains in efficiency, so that economies can enjoy growth and have a quality of growth that permits individuals to enjoy the benefits of growth. Fortunately, after more than 12 years of reform, and building on research results, we are now able to begin to assess quantitatively the impact of China's reform. We look here at measures in four areas that seem most pertinent: output and consumption; gains in productivity; the changing role of the state; and openness to the outside world. As we shall see, these results are impressive indeed, and a powerful source of justification for China's approach. They do not prove that China could not have done better with some alternative policies, perhaps avoiding some pitfalls. Such a counterfactual argument can also be raised and will be partially true. But the numbers show a strong response to reforms, in particular in terms of achieving the main goals: to generate rapid economic growth on the basis of efficiency gains and opening to the outside world, through a growing role for the market.

## Gains in Output and Welfare

China has had a strong growth performance for most of the period since 1949, and even during the Cultural Revolution.[19] This is not surprising, considering that the state has seen to it that over 30 percent of GNP has been invested every year. During the period 1965–80, real GNP grew by about 6.4 percent per year, with the gross value of industrial output rising by 10.3 percent and of agriculture by 3.1 percent. What we will see in the reform era is thus an *acceleration* of growth and welfare gains, rather than their introduction. It bears repeating that the purely economic gains of the pre-reform period were impressive, even if obtained at enormous cost—physical, political, and social. The reform era itself saw most rapid gains in 1982–88. With GNP growing at over 9 percent per year—and per capita GNP at 7.8 percent per year—there was a remarkably sustained increase in output over this period. Moreover, this growth in output was relatively balanced, especially during the early period, for agricultural performance also responded well to the reform. It is also not surprising, given the nature of reforms, that the tertiary sector saw the most rapid growth over this period. Indeed, the share of transport and commerce in national income fell from 13.6 percent in 1965 to 10.1 percent in 1980, but had risen to 14.8 percent by 1988.

But while output had grown during the pre-reform period, there had been relatively modest gains in private consumption per capita. Indeed, real wages saw little if any improvement over the period prior to 1979, with more of the increase in household income coming via growth in employment. From 1979 to 1988, availability of basic consumer goods and housing improved. Perhaps an even stronger indication of the real change in living standards is possession of major durable consumer goods. To take the three most startling examples: in 1981, there was less than 1 color television set per hundred urban households, but by 1990 the number had risen to 59; there were 0.2 refrigerators per hundred households in 1981, and 42.3 in 1990; and for washing machines, the figure rose from 6.3 to 78 per hundred households. Thus, the rapid growth in output translated into a very significant change in the standard of living in China over this period. The reason is that the reform era has seen intensive rather than extensive development, and thus rapid gains in total factor productivity.

These welfare gains are reflected in sharp reductions in the measured incidence of poverty during the reform era. The proportion of the population below the poverty line in China declined from 28 percent in 1978 to under 10 percent by the middle of the 1980s. However, no additional gains were made after 1984, as poverty in China is overwhelmingly a rural phenomenon, and the gains reflected the early gains from agricultural reforms. By 1990 some 11.5 percent of the rural population and 0.4 percent of the urban population re-

---

[19] Editor's note: The "Cultural Revolution" (1966–76) involved a struggle between conservative and reform forces that severely disrupted the Chinese economy.

mained in poverty. This meant, however, that over 160 million people had emerged from poverty during the reform era.

## Productivity Gains

Several studies, incorporating re-estimates of the value of China's capital stock, have begun to provide reliable estimates of gains in total factor productivity (TFP) during the reform period. These studies show very strong gains in TFP over the reform period in all sectors of the economy. We have already noted that the first half of the reform period focused on agriculture, with industrial reforms coming later, and the TFP gains reflect this, with TFP growth accelerating noticeably in industry after 1984. In agriculture, by contrast, productivity gains were rapid for a while, but then fell off, as most gains from increased effort were by then achieved. It is also of interest to note that TFP explains most growth in agriculture—land area fell, though use of fertilizers grew rapidly—but extensive growth (meaning greater use of inputs) continued to be the most important factor explaining industrial growth.

These gains in factor productivity are in stark contrast to the pre-reform era. Various estimates indicate that productivity was stagnant during the 1957–76 period. Indeed, one study showed a decline in combined agricultural and industrial TFP of −1.41 percent during 1957–65 and a gain of only 0.62 percent per year during 1965–76.[20]

These changes in TFP over time are supported by more conventional measures of efficiency gains. The accumulation–national income ratio (the Chinese equivalent of a capital–output ratio, given the absence of GNP data before 1978) rose from 3.79 in the first period (1953–59) to 4.30 in 1960–69, and to 5.39 in 1970–78. However, in 1978–88 it fell to 2.38, despite the surge in investment during the reform era. It is only during the slower growth performance of the rectification program of 1989–90 that the capital–output ratio has again risen.

Other results show that the reform in China is beginning to make the economy behave in ways similar to market economies. One of the distinctive features of the socialist system is that the inability of factors of production to move among alternative uses means that the government can fix the price system so that profits are a matter of administrative decision. Profits can vary widely among sectors, and the returns to factors of production in different uses can be very divergent. Evidence of equalizing profit rates and convergence of returns is a sign of effective marketization.

In 1980, profit rates in industry ranged from 7 to 98 percent. By 1989, the range fell to 8–23 percent, which is much more normal. In 1980, returns to labor

---

[20] See Perkins, "Reforming China's Economic System," and Kuan Chen, Gary H. Jefferson, Thomas G. Rawski, Hongchang Wang, and Yuxin Zheng, "New Estimates of Fixed Capital Stock for Chinese State Industry," *China Quarterly* 114 (June 1988), pp. 243–66.

in collective industry were only 48 percent of those in the state-owned sector, while this ratio rose to 55 percent by 1988. In contrast, returns to capital, which were 69 percent higher in the collective sector in 1980, were only 54 percent higher by 1988. Thus, not only are reforms serving to generate productivity gains, but they also appear to be improving resource allocation. This, it must be assumed, is the direct result of the rapid growth in competition, especially between state and nonstate industries.

## Role of the State

The primary purpose of reform in a centrally planned economy is to change the role of the state from one of planning and directing economic resources directly, to one where the state manages the policies which direct the resources. The impact of reform on the role of the state is shown in a variety of indicators which reveal how fundamental this change has been. The first and perhaps most dramatic change has been in the structure of output. In 1978, 78 percent of all industrial output came from the SOEs, operating entirely under the planning system. By 1989, the share of SOEs in total industrial output fell to 56 percent. This drop was *not* the result of privatization—for the effect of change in ownership of SOEs during this period was negligible, as it mostly occurred in the commercial sector—but rather was due to the growth of the nonstate sector. This outcome should thus be seen as one of the results of the gradual approach: that small incremental changes (in this case, via differential rates of growth) can over time add up to major structural reforms. In this regard, we may note the growth of output of township and village enterprises, individual enterprises, and joint ventures in particular.

Since the inception of urban reforms, the share of nonstate industry in the total has expanded enormously by virtue of very rapid growth rates. SOEs have been growing fast as well, but at only half the pace of nonstate enterprises. In fact, despite their low base, nonstate enterprises account for more than half of the total growth in industry over the 1985–90 period. Part of the explanation for the rapid growth of TFP is the relative growth of collective industry, where TFP gains have been particularly rapid.

This can be seen on a regional basis as well, from a comparison of gains in total factor productivity at the provincial level with the share of nonstate industry in total industrial output in different provinces. There is a generally close relationship between high-productivity provinces, such as Zhejiang, Jiangsu, and Guangdong, and the high share of nonstate industry, which in the extreme case of Zhejiang reached 68 percent in 1989. In contrast, provinces with very low shares of nonstate industry, especially those in the Northwest of China, had the lowest productivity. The only significant outlier is Shanghai, where the state sector appears to be most productive—perhaps as it is in Shanghai where much of the state's final goods production (automobiles, bicycles, electronics, cigarettes, processed food) is located.

The reform of the budget system and the decline in the role of budgetary financing show up very clearly in fiscal statistics. About one third of GNP passed through the budget in 1978, but this share fell to only 21 percent by 1989. The main effects concern the structure of government spending and the financing of investment.

Investment is now financed primarily from retained profits and bank loans. This is especially the case for the state-owned enterprises. In 1978, when they were remitting profits to the center, about 40 percent of their investment came from the budget. By 1989 this share fell to only 13 percent, with most of this change coming after 1984. While the state continues to *influence* investment very heavily through its approval system and via the banking system, it no longer has any significant direct financing role, especially in the productive sectors. Almost all budgetary investment is in infrastructure.

The corollary of the declining influence of the state in the financing of investment is the rising importance of the banking system in mobilizing savings. Not only has the use of bank loans for financing investment risen, but it has been made possible by the rapid growth of personal and enterprise deposits, although this does raise some of the key issues for the future. In 1978, savings deposits were only 8.6 percent of GDP. Since then they have more than tripled to 28 percent in 1989. Enterprise deposits have about doubled as a share of GDP, with the corollary being a decline in treasury and government department deposits. Indeed, overall marketization and financial deepening of the Chinese economy are among the more noticeable features of the reform period.

## External Sector

The fourth area of impact has been in the external sector, and in ways that distinguish China's reform effort from earlier socialist reform experiments. The key result is that China has become a much more significant participant in the world economy. This has been an area of reform where decentralization of decision making has been the primary factor behind the change. There are four aspects: trade, foreign exchange arrangements, technology, and foreign direct investment.

Perhaps trade is the most significant of these in many ways. Even in 1978 trade was relatively high in China, as by this time the program to import Western technology was already under way, but via the planning system. However, since 1978 trade has consistently grown at rates well above GDP growth rates. By 1990, trade had risen to the equivalent of 31.3 percent of GDP, making China, by this measure, the most open of all large countries—with a degree of openness more than twice that of India, Brazil, the United States, or Japan.[21] Note also that with the exception of the two retrenchment programs—

---

[21] Although it would not alter the conclusion, care should be taken in the use of these statistics. GDP may be somewhat underestimated, and trade statistics include the full value of exports based on processing of imported inputs, which tends to exaggerate the true role of trade in the economy.

in 1982–83 and 1990–91—a trade deficit has been recorded every year.[22] While no doubt some part of this growth in exports is the result of planning, more than half of all exports by the end of the 1980s fell outside any sort of planning. So these can be regarded as the result of the strong export incentives China has had in place.[23]

Of all such incentives—including foreign exchange retention, tax rebates, and direct subsidies on planned exports—the most important has been use of the exchange rate and foreign exchange markets. The exchange rate, which at the time was almost irrelevant for the determination of trade, was only Y[24] 1.72/$1 in 1978. It stands today at Y 5.38/$1, despite there having been only less than 30 percent more inflation in China than in the United States over the period. Thus we have witnessed a very strong real effective exchange rate depreciation in China. In fact, taking 1980 as 100, the real effective exchange rate index in June 1991 was only 34.6. With the reduction of trade planning and the aggressive use of the exchange rate, it seems reasonable to attribute a considerable share of the growth in trade to this depreciation. However, not all of this exchange rate change has been strictly "managed," since, as noted earlier, one of the reforms has been the introduction of the parallel foreign exchange market. In its first year, turnover on the parallel market was only $4 million, but it rose rapidly to an estimated $18 billion in 1991, accounting for about one third of all transactions. The growth of this market forced the realignment of the official rate since 1987, to the point where the differential between the official and parallel rates, which was close to 100 percent in 1988, is now less than 10 percent. Unification of the rates under a market-based system seems to be under active consideration.

Another aspect of the growth of China's trade is its impact on the level of technology in the country. About one third of all imports over the last 10 years have been of machinery and equipment. In other words, each year China has imported the equivalent of about 3 percent of GDP in capital goods, accounting for about 7.5 percent of all investment and about 15 percent of all investment in equipment. It can be assumed that this has had a marked impact upon the equipment manufacturing industry in China. Thus, while modernization and upgrading of equipment remain a priority, it can also be safely assumed that there is a wide range of Chinese industries where the vintage of capital equipment is not the primary issue in terms of competitiveness.

The fourth area of openness has been the impact of reform on foreign direct investment, which was the very first of the urban reforms. According to official statistics, contracts were signed over the period 1978–90 for over 29,000 joint ventures, with a contracted value of $45 billion. About half of these ventures are in operation, with an investment value of about $22 billion. This translates in the last few years to annual foreign direct investment of $2–3

---

[22] Trade surpluses have occurred in the two years *following* the main stabilization efforts of 1981 and 1989.

[23] See Lardy, *Foreign Trade,* Chap. 3.

[24] Editor's note: Y is the symbol for the yuan, China's currency.

billion, which is of the same order as inflows of either official borrowing (World Bank, Asian Development Bank, Japan, etc.) or commercial borrowing. More important, as many of these investments have been export-oriented, especially in the southern provinces of Guangdong and Fujian, this has been the other major explanatory factor behind China's export growth, since the economies of China, Hong Kong, and Taiwan have been more closely linked. Indeed, some 70 percent of all foreign investment in China, and over one third of its trade, originates in Hong Kong. To put this in a global perspective, China is the destination for about 10–15 percent of all foreign direct investment in low- and middle-income countries.[25]

Thus, reforms have led to a situation in which China has become a major player in world markets, through its own trade links and the integration of its manufacturing sector through foreign direct investment, and this distinguishes China's reform efforts. However, as discussed below, this effort in the export sector has proceeded faster than—and has not been the result of—import liberalization, which remains high on the unfinished agenda.

## REFORM PRIORITIES

We have seen from the preceding parts of this chapter that China has come a long way in its economic reform and that the economic impact has been measurably strong. However, many problems remain, and while progress has been great and the overall economic performance of the last decade is remarkable, it seems clear that much indeed remains to be done. Indeed, this conclusion follows from the Chinese approach to reform, which expects the reform process to last a long time. This section therefore is concerned with the main items on the unfinished agenda. In terms of the major priority areas, it seems to us that there are six of particular importance. These are: the state-owned enterprises, the financial sector, public finance, the external sector, prices and markets, and the role of the state. While actions in each area are distinct, reform of the SOEs is the key constraint and the main obstacle to be overcome.

### State-Owned Enterprises

Many incentives have changed for the state-owned enterprises, and their focus has shifted considerably away from achieving output targets and providing social services toward making profits and improving efficiency. Nevertheless, while the role of the nonstate enterprise sector has changed dramatically, the fundamental relationships between the state and the SOEs, and between the SOEs and their workers, remain unchanged. Enterprises remain subject to administrative interference in day-to-day operations, the negative consequences of failure remain unclear (in contrast to the positive rewards for success), and workers continue to be assigned to enterprises administratively and

---

[25] See Sung, *The China-Hong Kong Connection.*

to be bound to those enterprises through the housing, health, education, and social security systems. China's state-owned enterprises therefore continue to display many characteristics of public enterprises throughout the world—not least in making losses funded both via the budget and in a less open way through the banking system.

However, China requires that the publicly owned enterprises remain dominant in China's society. Therefore, the reform priority in the state enterprise sector relates not so much to the issue of privatization, as to the regulatory and competition framework. Three shortcomings seem to be paramount in this regard:

1. In terms of *ownership,* property rights remain vague, and there continues to be the need for new institutional mechanisms to separate the roles of government as regulator, owner, and manager of enterprises.

2. The *regulatory and legal framework* remains largely underdeveloped. For example, the absence of company law makes the development of an arm's length trading system difficult.

3. The SOEs continue to be protected from the full impact of domestic and foreign *market forces*. Nonstate enterprises have less than equal access to credit, they are restricted from entry to sectors where they would threaten SOEs, foreign investment is not permitted to compete with existing SOEs, and trade is restricted. Finally, bankruptcy remains extremely limited, and while the use of mergers is gaining, it is being carried out in a largely administrative fashion.

The challenge is therefore to create a framework in which public enterprises operate within a clear system of regulation and are subject to the full force and consequences of competition, so that they behave much as private enterprises would in the same situation. Progress in this aspect will be both key to, and closely linked to, progress in the financial sector. While there are several reform experiments under way or planned for this problem, it is not at all clear what Chinese policymakers are trying to achieve, or what concept of the future Chinese SOE they have in mind. Although in such areas as price reform and the tax system the final goal seems clear, it is in SOE reform that new thinking seems most needed.

## Financial Sector Issues

Dramatic change was introduced in the financial sector in China during the first years of urban reforms, but, aside from some encouraging developments in capital markets, reform in this sector seems to have stalled since 1988. At the heart of the problem is the excessive use of the banking system by the state to meet its own economic aims, via directed lending and "policy" lending. This practice effectively prevents the banking system from performing its key role of allocating savings to their priority uses. Furthermore, if the state is directing resources toward, for example, the covering of SOE losses, it could be storing up enormous portfolio problems for the banking system.

Associated with this problem is the continued relative weakness of China's central bank in its ability to regulate and supervise the financial sector and to formulate monetary policy and implement it via indirect instruments. Instead, monetary policy appears still to be heavily influenced by (among others) provincial leaders, and it is implemented largely by use of direct credit controls. This situation suggests three key areas for priority development in the financial sector:

1. Development of alternative methods of financing for government policy objectives, including the budget itself and capital market development.

2. Continued strengthening—in terms of both technical capability and status— of the central bank in formulating and implementing monetary policy and in carrying out its regulatory/supervisory functions.

3. Further efforts to increase the use of indirect instruments of financial control, such as the interest rate structure and use of open market operations via new instruments such as short-term treasury bonds.

Although the financial sector has yet to face a serious crisis, portfolios of banks deteriorated during 1989–91 through a combination of heavy lending (made possible by very high savings) and the weak economy. While the recovery should bring some relief, financial sector problems still pose a threat to the long-term success of the Chinese approach to economic reform. Short-term action in these three areas is most urgent.

## Public Finance

The second of the three strands of macroeconomic management in China relates to public finance. As with the financial sector, public finance underwent one massive reform—the shift from profit remittance to corporate income tax—but only minor change since. China continues to have a revenue system rather than a tax system, and it is one bound by contracts. As such, it is tied inextricably to the old economic system that links the state, enterprises, and workers. It thus perpetuates the old economic system and will need dramatic overhaul if it is to *promote* a new economic system. There are three aspects in particular:

1. Taxes are *contracted* (both at the enterprise and at the provincial level), and taxes will have to be clearly separated from such contracts.

2. The tax system is heavily based on the state production enterprise system— the primary tax collection point—and will have to be diversified with greater reliance on the personal income tax and final-sales-point taxes, in line with progress in converting nonwage into wage income.

3. The indirect tax system cascades[26] and makes incentives very unclear. It should be replaced by more transparent rules-based systems such as value-added taxes.

---

[26] Editor's note: Indirect taxes are levied at different stages in the production of one good.

Finally, it must be noted that one third of all public expenditures are for price and enterprise subsidies, at the expense of infrastructure investment and social expenditures. The solution to this problem lies primarily in the areas of price and enterprise reform. The growing pressure on the budget seems to be lending some urgency to the attention given to fiscal issues because it takes time to implement reforms once they are formulated.

## External Sector

It was observed earlier that great progress has been achieved not only in expanding trade but also in making exports responsive to economic signals. Yet two factors in the trade regime continue to be of particular importance. First, external trade is still dominated by foreign trade corporations of various kinds, and participation of production enterprises directly in trade is limited. Second, the import regime continues to offer a high degree of protection to domestic industry, and thus imports are regarded primarily as a source of embodied technology. This protection is provided by an opaque and unpredictable system of import licensing and by an uneven tariff structure, albeit with apparent frequent exemptions to reduce the anti-export bias. There are two primary areas of focus for future trade reform:

1. Reform of the *import regime* by moving to a system of management by indirect control, with a lower level of protection effected by tariffs rather than licenses and administrative barriers, and with transparent control mechanisms.
2. Continued efforts at institutional reform of *FTCs,* through further reduction of their effective monopsony and greater entry to export markets for production enterprises.

It is logical that the existing import regime has been accompanied by a foreign direct investment system that, while offering good incentives, restricted the competitive impact of foreign enterprises and therefore developed a complex and lengthy approval process. Similarly, efforts in this area should be directed toward further opening of the domestic market, and improved efficiency and transparency in the approval process. With a very strong trade balance, and about nine months of imports in foreign exchange reserves, now would seem a most opportune time to launch such reforms.

## Prices and Markets

In terms of reform progress, we stressed that more than half (perhaps two thirds) of all transactions are now carried out at market prices. Moreover, a key factor is that most marginal resource allocation decisions are made at market prices. However, at least one third of all transactions are at controlled prices and many remain subject to the materials allocation system. In theory, these conditions need not matter, as the state should be able to adjust for them in other ways. For example, low coal prices reduce the attractiveness of investment in coal for local governments, and reduce available financial surpluses at coal mines for reinvestment. Theoretically, and in practice in the pre-reform situation, the planning system could compensate with fiscal transfers, but the state no longer has the fiscal resource control to do so. The result is unbalanced investment, and unfair interprovincial income distribution, in addition to obvious microeconomic consequences such as waste of energy.

Price reform in the sense of new price formulation systems, especially for raw materials and grain, will require not only lifting of controls or adjustment of fixed prices, but also development of market infrastructure, such as transport and storage facilities, and information systems. It will also require price-sensitive consumers, and a major accompanying reform must be the conversion of price subsidies into wages. Thus, reforms in these areas would need to focus on the following:

1. Removal of remaining price controls for most commodities, usually preceded by price adjustments and accompanied by market infrastructure investments. Priorities seem to be in prices of energy, transport, certain raw materials, and grain. Such measures should be accompanied by the development of regulatory mechanisms and institutions to guard against abuse of monopoly powers.
2. Conversion of remaining consumer price subsidies—especially for grain—into wages, so that state procurement and distribution can be gradually eliminated.

It appears that with recent price adjustments there are no longer any "sacred cows" in pricing. Given the continued favorable demand–supply balance in most markets, there is plenty of scope for rapid movement in this area at the present time.

## Role of the State

Much has already changed with respect to the role of the state, as it has fostered the growth of nonstate enterprises and yielded control over prices, revenues, and materials. Much of what has already been covered in this section is concerned with continued progress in this direction. Other elements that have been mentioned imply things that the state will have to do *more*, such as indirect macroeconomic management and development of a legal framework. In short, the role of the state and of planning must continue to evolve.

There are two other key areas where the role of the state will have to change dramatically and where little concrete progress has been made so far. First, social services of one kind or another—especially housing, health insurance, and pensions—are still provided primarily by the enterprise sector. Also, by virtue of the gradual reform process and emphasis on development of new enterprises rather than radical reform of existing enterprises, the state enterprise system has continued to offer protection against unemployment. Here there is a new role for the state either in direct provision of such services or by creating a framework for nonstate, nonenterprise-based systems, such as private pensions and health insurance. It is only by removing this burden from enterprises that true enterprise reform can begin, and the state must directly promote appropriate solutions.

Finally, virtually no significant progress has been made in the labor market. Most workers continue to be assigned jobs, and movement between geographical areas remains highly restricted. Even movement between enterprises within one geographical area is difficult, because of nontransferability of accumulated nonwage benefits and housing. These factors are compounded by a set of antiemployment-creation policies such as low interest rates and low energy prices, coupled with a bias against labor-intensive sectors such as service industries and private enterprises. These conditions suggest three aspects of primary focus:

1. Conversion of nonwage benefits into wages, and separation of the provision of social services from enterprises.

2. Gradual relaxation of labor allocation systems, both vocational and geographical.

3. Continued attention to removal of antiemployment policies, especially those that encourage high capital–labor ratios, such as low input prices and interest rates, and policies that discriminate against township–village enterprises.

## SOME TENTATIVE CONCLUSIONS

This chapter has been concerned with the way China has gone about its reform program and the impact on the economy of these reforms. It is clear that the Chinese approach has worked well in the initial conditions under which it was launched. This is not to say that the outcome was *optimal*, and other measures could have made the results even better. For example, it is now generally accepted in China that stronger monetary management in 1988 and more rapid price reform in 1990 would have improved matters. It must also be stressed that one of the key features of China's initial conditions was the absence of a need for harsh stabilization measures, and there were no simultaneous external shocks, such as the collapse of the CMEA which has so strongly affected the countries of Central and Eastern Europe. Five key features of the Chinese reform experience seem to be key elements of success which may have some more general applicability, irrespective of issues related to the gradual approach and to special conditions unique to both China and its approach to reform.

### Five Key Features

At the start of the reform program, China had a large and relatively well-developed industrial system but was nevertheless fundamentally a rural economy. Moreover, as the discussion of initial conditions suggested, the agricultural sector was highly repressed and was thus ripe to respond to reforms. These factors supported the appropriateness of the decision to use *agriculture as the entry point*. Not only did agriculture respond rapidly—as it has in other countries such as Vietnam—but this response generated the rural savings and surplus labor necessary to launch the next phase of reform and created a constituency for reform.

The second element of particular significance in China was the emphasis on *marketization instead of privatization* and on the role of growth of the nonstate sector in diversifying ownership patterns. The spectacular growth of nonstate enterprise has served two key functions. (1) It created economic growth and generated employment opportunities, thus bringing out significant gains from reform. (2) It generated competitive pressure on state-owned enterprises, forcing change in their behavior, even though this process remains far from complete.

This process can be regarded as "privatization from below" in that within just a few years 45 percent of industrial output is now from nonstate industries. More generally, emphasis on creation of new nonstate industries suggests the possibility of creating a competitive framework in which state enterprises can be made more efficient without recourse to direct privatization programs.

The gradual approach to reform runs the risk that the losers from reform can regroup either to oppose further change or even to attempt reversal. Of course, this same factor can also work in the opposite direction, as reform skeptics can be won over when the pace of reform is gradual and benefits start to emerge. The particular problem in a socialist system is how to *change the interest of the bureaucracy and the Communist Party*. Bureaucrats, especially at the national level, are among the major losers from reform, with loss of power, prestige, and, in particular, nonwage income. Nevertheless, China had some success in reorienting the bureaucracy. The reforms created pressure on the planners because they reduced central revenues and the profitability of state enterprises. Although to some extent this pressure caused part of the bureaucracy to seek to protect their profits and interests, it also redirected the interest of the bureaucracy toward ensuring that their enterprises were oriented toward profit-making. This trend has seen setbacks at times, but the periods of resurgence of planning theology (as in 1989–90) have proved short-lived, as even planners have found it hard to preserve their interests through such methods in the face of past reforms. We can observe in 1992 a recognition of the failure of planning solutions to achieve significant restructuring of state-owned enterprises during the previous three years. Thus, the use of decentralization and promotion of nonstate industry generated a reorientation of the interest of the bureaucracy away from planning goals toward economic performance. This coincided with the interests of the Party, which saw its political interests geared increasingly to the achievement of economic success.

The fourth distinctive element of the Chinese approach is its emphasis on *export development* and more generally its entry into world markets. The big difference between this approach and that of other countries has been the postponement of import liberalization to late in the reform process, although it has had the result of a relatively high level of importation of advanced technology. This outcome has been possible for two reasons: First, the size of the domestic economy has made it possible to generate competitive forces, especially among smaller enterprises vying for export business. Second, while China had been closed to import competition, it has been very open to influence from outside in its export industry—especially from Hong Kong entrepreneurs who have been permitted to impose rigorous export design and quality control standards. The unique relationship between China and Hong Kong may reduce the replicability of this element of the strategy.

The fifth key factor in the Chinese approach has been the *role of the state in maintaining social stability*. By using the gradual approach and by not subjecting the state sector to major shocks, China has succeeded in avoiding severe social costs during its transition. The Chinese effort has focused much less on changing old enterprises and more on generating new opportunities. Moreover, postponing social reforms to the end of the reform process has given China the opportunity to develop over time the institutional framework for a new social security system. What remains to be tested is whether China can now move to address the more fundamental issues of the state enterprise sector and the dismantling of this social system—and indeed the issue of whether the state wishes to carry out this aspect of reform. Nevertheless, it is clear that this approach has avoided some of the serious social consequences that could have undermined the case for further reform.

## Sustainability

A key question in considering the Chinese approach to economic reform is whether this approach is sustainable over the medium to long term, or whether it is simply postponing problems that will later "come home to roost." Three potential issues for the future need to be addressed:

1. The danger of future insolvency of some large banks with limited capital bases and small loan loss provisions, as they acquire an increasingly weak loan portfolio by funding losses of SOEs. It is further argued by some that this problem will *worsen* as the influence of nonstate industry rises and SOEs lose some access to resources.

2. The argument that so long as SOEs remain dominant, they will never be able to achieve efficiency at internationally competitive levels. So long as this position is maintained, China will always be a highly protected economy, and the benefits of present reforms will fade away to stagnation until this issue is addressed.

3. That social tensions will mount in two directions. First, greater provincial autonomy and self-sufficiency will increase further the growing regional disparities in China, leading to increasing conflicts. Second, the fight against poverty in China is showing fragile gains, with many persons only just above

the poverty line. With reforms and further difficulties for the central government, the present social safety net could collapse, pulling millions back into poverty.

In other words, these arguments suggest that the gradual approach has limitations, and that China will eventually approach these limits. This view is based primarily on the recent experiences of the formerly socialist countries of Eastern and Central Europe. These are serious issues, and the possibility of such a collapse—forcing China into its own "big bang"—should not be dismissed out of hand. Moreover, it must be recognized explicitly that China's reform is indeed one which does not have successful historical precedent. But two important factors must be stressed as sources of reassurance:

1. Over the reform period, China has generally responded to problems of reform by introducing *new* reforms and by deepening existing reforms. Thus, we can see an incremental reform movement over the entire period of the reform era, albeit at varying speeds. This gives reassurance that as new problems emerge they, too, will be met by incremental movement, so that, as in the past 10 years, deep crisis simply will not occur. For example, there could be incremental reforms which restructure existing SOEs, and these reforms in turn could correct, on an incremental basis, the genuine portfolio problems of banks.

2. The gains of the reform era have been "intensive" rather than "extensive," as measured by the strong productivity gains registered, and China has succeeded in maintaining the momentum of GDP growth even during periods of adjustment. These productivity gains are not restricted to new industries, but have been recorded also in existing SOEs. This outcome suggests that the economic results of the Chinese approach to reform may be qualitatively different from the experiences of some other countries. We would suggest that this difference could lend credence to sustainability and to the possibility that China will grow out of its problems. The secret of this success has been China's use of "marketization" and the vigorous development of the nonstate sector, which has been unique to the Chinese approach.

The key to sustainability thus rests, in our view, not on any theoretical or philosophical issues about the ultimate level of efficiency that publicly owned enterprises can achieve, but rather on the solutions that China will develop toward the unfinished agenda. In particular, this position relates to solutions to the problems of the financial sector and the state-owned enterprise sector and its environment. If appropriate incremental reforms are instituted, stressing growing "marketization" and a continued associated increase of competitive forces via growth of the nonstate sector and trade reform, the remarkable experience of the past decade lends hope that the Chinese approach can indeed lead to a sustainable pattern of growth with reform. The question is how well future policy will address the unfinished agenda.

## Chapter Twenty-nine

# Lessons from China's Economic Reform*

*Kang Chen,*
*Gary H. Jefferson,*
*and*
*Inderjit Singh*[1]

*This chapter discusses six principal lessons—four positive and two negative—from China's economic reform experience.*

1. *In China there was a leading sector (agriculture) whose reform could in turn strongly stimulate reform in other sectors of the economy.*

2. *In China, the urban industrial reform effort was piecemeal and gradual, rather than comprehensive and fast. Nevertheless it significantly increased factor productivity and allocative efficiency.*

3. *As trading partner, financier, and intermediary and facilitator, Hong Kong exerted a powerful influence on the reform of China's economy.*

4. *In China, there are strong pressures for reform from local governments and enterprises.*

5. *The Chinese economic reform process has been hampered by weak indirect macroeconomic management and poor monetary and fiscal policies. Also, government policies have discriminated against labor-intensive activities which can help absorb unemployment resulting from urban labor market reforms.*

* Reprinted by permission from the *Journal of Comparative Economics* 16, no. 2 (June 1992), pp. 201–25, with the omission of Chinese terms, tables, and references to foreign language sources, unpublished papers, and limited-circulation documents. Copyright © by Academic Press, Inc. Kang Chen is Professor of Economics at the National University of Singapore. Gary H. Jefferson is Professor of Economics at Brandeis University. Inderjit Singh is an economist in the Socialist Economies Reform Unit in the Country Economics Department at the World Bank.

[1] The authors deeply appreciate the insightful and detailed comments given by Tom Rawski and Shahid Yusuf and the helpful suggestions of two anonymous referees. All errors, including those of interpretation, remain those of the authors.

6. *The greater authority which economic reform promised enterprises has been limited by administrative interference, manipulation of prices, and corruption.*

*The authors conclude that, in comparison with China, it is less appropriate for Eastern Europe and the successor states of the former Soviet Union to focus on agriculture first, or to pursue piecemeal rather than more extensive and more rapid reforms. Nor do these countries have a counterpart of Hong Kong to aid their reforms. On the other hand, as in China, poor macroeconomic policies and excessive administrative interference can imperil economic reforms in other nations.*

## INTRODUCTION

Prior to the breathtaking acceleration of economic restructuring in Eastern Europe and the Soviet Union in the late 1980s, three socialist countries, Yugoslavia, Hungary, and China, had each accumulated a decade or more of reform experience. The purpose of this study is to summarize key lessons of China's economic reforms—both the important successes and the failures of the experiment—that may bear upon choices facing reformers in Eastern Europe, the former Soviet republics, and China in the 1990s.[2]

By a number of statistical measures, China's economic reform program has achieved notable success. Key statistical indicators of this success are summarized below:[3]

*1. Rapid growth.* During 1965–80, China's real GDP grew by 6.4 percent per year; during 1980–88, real GDP growth accelerated to 10.4 percent.[4] Total GNP increased 2.5-fold from 1978 to 1988.

*2. Accelerated employment growth.* During 1978–88, total employment grew at an average rate of 3 percent, exceeding the rate of 2 percent achieved during 1958–78. As labor productivity in agriculture rose rapidly, releasing workers from farm production, during 1978–88, nonagricultural employment growth accelerated to an average rate of 6.5 percent. More impressively, even as the baby-boom generation born in the 1960s was moving into the labor force, the urban unemployment rate, which stood at 5.3 percent in 1978, fell to 2 percent during 1986–88.

---

[2] The perspectives and analysis developed in this study are drawn from many sources. In addition to first-hand observation and personal research, our views are informed by the extensive literature of other scholars who study China's economy, numerous World Bank reports on various facets of the reform program, and several sets of enterprise survey data that are being collected or analyzed with the participation of one or more of us.

[3] Unless otherwise specified, statistics reported in this section are drawn or derived from various volumes of the *Statistical Yearbook of China* (State Statistical Bureau, Chinese editions).

[4] These estimates are likely to be biased upward. Sources of upward bias in official statistics of industrial output that are associated with formation of new establishments, new product innovation, and changes in value-added ratios are investigated in Gary H. Jefferson, "Growth and Productivity Change in Chinese Industry: Problems of Measurement," in *Adaptive Innovation in Asian Economies,* ed. M. Dutta and Z. L. Zhang (Greenwich, Conn.: JAI Press, 1992), pp. 30–47.

3. *Rapidly expanding external sector.* Under the open door policy, foreign trade expanded fivefold, from 20.6 billion current U.S. dollars in 1978 to 102.8 billion in 1988. Exports which accounted for 4.8 percent of Chinese GDP in 1978 expanded to 13 percent in 1988.[5] Equally impressive have been qualitative changes associated with the growth of trade, as product quality, production technologies, managerial efficiency, and marketing strategies have all been substantially upgraded.

4. *Rising living standards.* During 1978–88, per capita GNP doubled in real terms. During 1978–88, the per capita real income of rural residents grew at 9.6 percent per year; the comparable rate for urban residents was 6.3 percent. During the 1980s, the average living space per urban resident doubled to 8.5 square meters, and the average rural living area per capita also doubled from 8.1 to 16.0 square meters.

In a comparison of the consumption of basic needs and consumer durables in 1952, 1978, and 1988, the data show a sharp contrast between the two time periods 1952–78 and 1978–88. Even if per capita ownership of consumer durables in 1952 were zero, the gains reported during the 10 years of reform are multiples of the gains recorded during the previous 26 years.

These achievements have not been obtained without substantial costs: growing economic inequality, rising economic insecurity, greater price instability, rising corruption, and greater political and social instability.[6] In weighing the role of economic reform in creating these conditions, however, it is necessary to acknowledge several factors.

First, we distinguish between conditions arising from the transition and those that promise to persist, and perhaps grow in magnitude, under the new order. The dual pricing system, intended to be a transitional device, has invited pervasive corruption that should diminish as prices become increasingly uniform and competitively determined. On the other hand, economic insecurity, intrinsic to the market system, may become more, not less, pronounced, as labor market reform proceeds. In a risk-averse society, for which we find evidence in the case of China, incomes must be higher to compensate individuals for the increased disutility of risk.[7] Some portion of the spectacular rise in

---

[5] Due to an underestimate of China's GNP measured in dollars (the measure used for imports and exports), these ratios are overstated. See Nicholas Lardy, *Foreign Trade and Economic Reform in China, 1978–1990* (New York: Cambridge University Press, 1992). Nonetheless, they are probably representative of the rate of increase in the openness of China's economy.

[6] The extent to which economic inequality has risen or fallen in the sense of changes in the Gini coefficient is debatable. During 1978–84 rapid growth of output and incomes within the rural sector relative to the urban sector is likely to have reduced overall inequality. Within each of these sectors, however, it is likely that emergence of wealthy households has increased inequality. Also income differences between coastal regions and interior provinces have almost certainly increased.

[7] Note that in a survey of workers, only 11.7 percent of respondents expressed willingness to "accept the risk of being out of a job" in exchange for their incomes quadrupling. See *Reform in China: Challenges and Choices (A Summary and Analysis of the Chinese Economic System Reform Research Institute Survey)*, ed. Bruce L. Reynolds (Armonk, N.Y.: M. E. Sharpe, 1987), p. 156.

incomes cited above is therefore needed just to make Chinese citizens feel no worse off as they begin to cope with the rigors of life in a market economy.

Second, some of the problems encountered during the transition might have been avoided, or substantially mitigated, through the choice of an alternative or revised reform strategy; they were not inevitable consequences of reform. Among these problems are accelerating inflation during 1988 and 1989 and the socially corrosive corruption made more extensive and visible as inflation increased the spread between certain plan and market prices, thus raising the potential gains from corruption.

Third, economic system reform inevitably raises major issues that challenge the core of Communist ideology and the apparatus of control. Certain problems, however—such as the democracy movement and its subsequent suppression during the spring of 1989 and the decline of political stability—may not so much be symptoms of economic reform as they are manifestations of China's recurring problem of leadership succession within a highly personalized authoritarian regime.

## KEY LESSONS OF REFORM

China's reform experience yields many lessons. Here we have chosen to stress the six that we consider to be most salient. These are (1) importance of a leading sector, an important element of the sequencing problem; (2) the efficacy of gradual and partial reform, relating to the issue of the speed and comprehensiveness of reform; (3) importance of proximate, kindred economies as reform models and sources of resource transfer; (4) importance of the distinction between centrally managed reform and bottom-up reform; (5) the tendency for flawed institutions and bad policy to obstruct reform; and (6) the need for checks and balances and the uncertain ability of a government with a monopoly of political power to establish such measures.

### The Importance of a Leading Sector

Few of the achievements or failures of China's reform program can be viewed in isolation. Dynamic change in one sector has invariably spilled over into change in other sectors. To understand the successful features of China's reforms, it is vital to understand the synergy that caused the cumulative impact of reform to be far greater than the sum of its parts.

China's economic reform started with rural agriculture. The initial success of the agricultural reforms is beyond dispute. With the restoration of family-based farming, agricultural production grew rapidly. Crop production grew at 6.8 percent for 1979–84, well above the 2.5 percent growth rate for the 1953–78 period. Agricultural productivity and farm incomes rose, and the quality and quantity of food available to consumers improved vastly.

Rather than the success of the agricultural reforms, the focus of this section concerns the impact of China's successful agricultural transformation on other sectors, that is, the role of a leading reform sector played by agriculture.

While the agricultural reforms greatly increased agricultural productivity, their impact on other parts of the system is the important lesson to be drawn from their success. Specifically, the agricultural reforms must be credited with the impetus they gave to rural industry.

In recent years, rural industry, also called township–village enterprises or TVEs, has become the most dynamic sector of China's economy.[8] In the 1980–88 period, over 30 percent of the growth of China's total material production was contributed by rural TVEs. The share of the value of rural TVEs' output in GNP increased from 13 percent in 1980 to 21 percent in 1988. The growth of rural TVEs is even more significant, considering that TVEs receive no budgetary investment allocation and subsidies from the state.

This remarkable growth would have been unachievable without two conditions: first, liberalization of the state material allocation system, which allowed industrial goods produced by the state sector to be purchased by the emerging TVE sector, and, second, the agricultural reforms. Through their impetus to agricultural labor productivity, which rose at an annual rate of 4.7 percent during 1978–84, the agricultural reforms motivated higher incomes and savings and a pool of surplus labor—thereby generating abundant sources of capital and labor that, in turn, fueled the dynamic growth of rural enterprise.[9]

**Capital.**    In 1978, the assets owned by Chinese peasants were estimated at 80 billion yuan.[10] Each rural resident owned, on average, just 100 yuan, equivalent to 60 U.S. dollars, of assets. Almost all rural assets were collectively owned (i.e., owned by the people's communes).

After the reforms, 800 million Chinese peasants regained the right to accumulate private assets and the right to engage in nonagricultural activities. By 1985, rural private assets exceeded 700 billion yuan, growing in excess of 27 percent per year. In that same year, gross fixed assets of the TVE sector amounted to approximately 120 billion yuan, just a fraction of the enormous pool of assets that had been accumulated during the first 7 years of rural reform.

**Labor.**    Prior to the reforms, China's food allocation system, work point system, and resident registration system limited peasants to working in agricultural activity at the places where they were born. In 1978, about 10 percent of

---

[8] Rural TVEs, called commune and brigade enterprises prior to the reform, are established at the township and village level and at below-village levels. In general, TVEs face harder budget constraints, have clearer ownership status, and are more independent compared with state-owned enterprises. For a more in-depth discussion of rural industry, see *China's Rural Industry: Structure, Development, and Reform,* ed. William Byrd and Lin Qingsong (New York: Oxford University Press, 1990).

[9] This estimate is certain to be low, since many workers who were registered as agricultural workers increasingly allocated a part of their labor to nonagricultural activities or left agriculture altogether.

[10] Editor's note: The yuan is the Chinese currency.

the rural labor force engaged in nonagricultural activities. As agricultural labor productivity rapidly rose, enabling the country's food requirements to be satisfied by a shrinking number of workers, and as restrictions on off-farm work were relaxed, off-farm employment rose sharply. By 1988, 21 percent of the rural work force was engaged in nonagricultural activities as a *de facto* rural labor market emerged. During the 1980s, more than 67 million rural workers were absorbed by TVE enterprises. Yet, the rapid increase of employment in rural TVEs did not curtail labor productivity growth in that sector. Over 1980–88, labor productivity in rural industry rose by an average of 12 percent per year, high by any standard.[11]

Through its dynamic growth, the TVE sector has itself become a leading sector, now generating intersectoral and systemic benefits. Specifically, the development of TVEs has (1) mitigated the problem of rural surplus labor and the flight of workers to cities; (2) expanded the scope of market activity, bringing competitive pressure to bear on state-owned enterprises; (3) diffused the potential under the reforms for a growing division between urban and rural areas; and (4) contributed to the economy's export performance.

This latter consequence is further demonstration of China's virtuous circle of economic reform. Initially, great distances and many sectors separated what are probably China's two most successful reforms, its rural reforms and its open-door policy. The former transformed agricultural production, whereas the latter has given rise to a growing export sector which, in turn, finances the purchase of a wide range of new industrial technologies and equipment. But the success of these reform initiatives is not unrelated. The rise in agricultural labor productivity that generated the surplus labor and abundant savings critical to the expansion of TVEs also served indirectly to finance the growth of industrial exports. In 1989, rural TVE exports grew by 30 percent, reaching $10.5 billion, approaching one quarter of China's total export volume.

While we have stressed the positive role of a lead sector and the potential for intersectoral linkages in generating synergy in the reform process, the intersectoral impacts of individual reforms can also have negative consequences. One such case, also relating to the linkage between agriculture and TVEs, concerns the abrupt slowdown in agricultural growth in 1985.[12] The slowdown followed the 1984 decision to sanction officially the development of private rural enterprise and to allow rural credit cooperatives to lend more freely to rural industry and services.[13] Together with various other nonagricultural mea-

---

[11] This figure is somewhat inflated due to upward bias in constant price measures of the growth of TVEs' output. China's State Statistical Bureau openly acknowledges that it does not have a reliable output deflator for the TVE sector. Nonetheless, even a generous downward adjustment from 12 to 8 percent would still attest to extraordinary productivity growth in TVE industry.

[12] The annual growth rate of crop production fell from 6.8 percent during 1978–84 to 1.0 percent during 1984–88.

[13] Other reasons suggested for the slowdown include the full implementation of the household responsibility system in 1984 and a decline in the availability of chemical fertilizers.

sures and in combination with agricultural price controls, these actions depressed the relative competitiveness of agriculture and accelerated the flow of labor and capital to nonagricultural activities. Hence, controls in one sector may require second-best measures in which controls become appropriate for sectors capturing disproportionate shares of resources. Viewed dynamically over the last decade, however, the reforms that led to rapid TVE growth have, in turn, created a positive-sum outcome. That is, these reforms created greater efficiency and more resources throughout the economy than would have existed in their absence. In this sense, the sequence of China's first decade of reforms was fortuitous.

## The Efficacy of Gradual and Partial Reform

China's urban industrial reforms did not begin formally until 1984. Various reforms that were enacted piecemeal during 1978–84 were considerably expanded in 1984, but the 1984 reform package was not characteristic of the "big bang" programs being tested or advocated in Eastern Europe and the former Soviet republics. In particular, China's urban industrial reform program emphasized an expansion of enterprise autonomy and incentives and the reduction, but not elimination, of plan allocations.[14] Among the more important of the urban industrial reforms are:

1. Multi-year management responsibility contracts that set various management targets, the most important of which are those for profits, profit remittance, and taxes.[15]

2. Profit retention and the authority to invest and distribute bonuses out of retained profits.

3. At the margin, considerably expanded authority to choose the level and mix of production, to sell output and acquire material inputs on the market, and to set, or at least to negotiate, prices.

These reforms have had the effect of providing a discretionary source of funds that, within regulated bounds, can be used to reward profit-seeking behavior and to finance new investment. The result has been a widespread reorientation of enterprise managers and workers toward competitive, profit-seeking behavior and a greater tendency for the more profitable enterprises to capture a larger share of investment resources.

Establishment of the dual price system was widely regarded as (*a*) representing a compromise that preserves planned allocation while drawing incre-

---

[14] For a more complete account of the status of China's industrial reforms as of the mid-1980s, see *China's Industrial Reform,* ed. Gene Tidrick and Jiyuan Chen (New York: Oxford University Press, 1987).

[15] Regarding several earlier applications of the enterprise contract responsibility system, see Anthony Y. C. Koo, "The Contract Responsibility System: Transition from a Planned to a Market Economy," *Economic Development and Cultural Change* 38, no. 4 (July 1990), pp. 796–820.

mental output into a market system, and (*b*) softening the risk of economic reform by "changing a big earthquake into several small tremors."[16] The incremental aspect of the two-track system also allowed for implementing price reform and enterprise reform in tandem.

Although enterprise autonomy and initiative are substantially greater than they were at the outset of the reforms, analysts frequently emphasize the incomplete and unsatisfactory extent of China's industrial reforms. Chief among the shortcomings of the existing reform regime are: (1) the persistence of weak labor markets, which complicates the problem of worker discipline and incentives; (2) excessive intervention of local officials in the affairs of enterprises, which erodes the authority and effectiveness of enterprise managers; (3) the persistence of soft budget constraints; and (4) the tendency of local government to inhibit competition and interregional trade for the purpose of accumulating resources and revenues.[17] Moreover, as Dwight Perkins observes, "The whole approach was *ad hoc* and highly experimental, with many forward movements and reversals in one area or another." Evidence of these and other problems leads analysts to ask whether the enterprise reform program has really created the conditions required to improve enterprise performance fundamentally, or if it has simply empowered local governments with the authority previously held at the center and complicated the task of management so much that gains will be negligible.

Because, from an institutional perspective, persuasive arguments can be made on either side concerning the effectiveness of China's urban industrial reform program, here we focus on the impact of the reforms in promoting productivity growth and economic efficiency—key objectives of the urban industrial reforms. Specifically, we present evidence concerning: (1) industrial productivity growth, including evidence concerning the impact of specific reforms on factor productivity growth, and (2) changes in productive efficiency resulting from a tendency for returns to factor inputs to become more equal, as we would expect if profit-seeking behavior were becoming more pronounced and factor and product markets were becoming more complete and competitive.

**Productivity Growth.**   Evidence that the industrial reforms have raised factor efficiency is reported by Jefferson, Rawski, and Zheng, who find that during 1980–88, total factor productivity (TFP) in state industry rose at an average

---

[16] These objectives of the dual pricing system are discussed by Wu Jianling and Zhao Renwei, "The Dual Pricing System in China's Industry," *Journal of Comparative Economics* 11, no. 3 (September 1987), pp. 309–18.

[17] Kang Chen, "The Failure of Recentralization in China: Interplays among Enterprises, Local Governments, and the Center," in *Markets and Politicians*, ed. Arye L. Hillman (Boston: Kluwer Academic Publishers, 1991), pp. 209–29. On the issue of managerial authority, see Andrew Walder, "Factory and Manager in an Era of Reform," *China Quarterly* 118 (June 1989), pp. 242–64.

annual rate of 2.4 percent.[18] The comparable rate for the collective sector (including TVEs) was 4.6 percent.[19] This finding of robust TFP growth compares favorably with an earlier finding reported by these authors and their colleagues,[20] that during 1957–78, productivity growth in state industry was virtually stagnant.

While several research programs are under way to identify the contribution of individual reforms to this vastly improved productivity performance, some preliminary evidence is available. Using a small sample of 20 state- and collective-owned industrial enterprises, Jefferson and Xu[21] find that increased enterprise autonomy, profit retention, and market exposure have each motivated higher rates of factor productivity growth. Specifically, their findings show the following: (1) By empowering factory managers to rationalize the allocation of workers within the enterprise, the "optimal labor combination program" has accelerated labor-productivity growth in factories adopting the program relative to those that have not. (2) Among enterprises relying most heavily on self-financed investment, capital productivity has risen most rapidly. (3) Enterprises purchasing the largest share of material inputs on the market reveal comparatively high rates of material input productivity growth.[22]

**Convergence of Factor Returns.**   In an economy consisting of profit-maximizing enterprises operating within competitive product and factor markets, we expect uniform prices of comparable goods and factor inputs and a tendency for the equalization of returns to capital, labor, and intermediate inputs among sectors and enterprises. Recently, evidence compiled by Jefferson and Xu shows a tendency within Chinese industry for factor returns to have converged during the 1980s. The coefficients of variation measure the dispersion of returns to labor, capital, and materials across 226 large and medium-size state indus-

---

[18] Gary H. Jefferson, Thomas G. Rawski, and Yuxin Zheng, "Growth, Efficiency, and Convergence in China's State and Collective Industry," *Economic Development and Cultural Change* 40, no. 2 (January 1992), pp. 239–66. Unlike previous studies of Chinese industrial productivity growth, this study (*a*) includes intermediate inputs and (*b*) develops price deflators for investment goods and intermediate inputs, so that these, as well as output and labor, can be treated as constant price valuations or physical quantities.

[19] Coverage of the collective sector excludes village-level TVEs.

[20] Kuan Chen, Gary H. Jefferson, Thomas G. Rawski, Hongchang Wang, and Yuxin Zheng, "Productivity Change in Chinese Industry: 1953–85," *Journal of Comparative Economics* 12, no. 4 (December 1988), pp. 570–91.

[21] Gary H. Jefferson and Wenyi Xu, "The Impact of Reform on Socialist Enterprises in Transition: Structure, Conduct, and Performance in Chinese Industry," *Journal of Comparative Economics* 15, no. 1 (March 1991), pp. 45–64.

[22] The finding regarding capital productivity may alternatively be interpreted as showing that the higher the rate of growth of capital productivity, the greater the share of self-financed investment. In either case, the finding points to a benefit of higher profit retention rates.

trial enterprises and within specific industrial branches.[23] Declining values reveal a pattern in which factor returns are becoming more nearly equal over time. Since the convergence of factor returns implies the growth of allocative efficiency, some part of the growth in industrial total factor productivity, reported above, appears to reflect improving resource allocation at the core of China's industrial sector. Consistent with these findings, Naughton reports that from 1980 to 1989 across 38 industrial branches of state industry the coefficient of variation of profit rates fell from 0.78 to 0.44.[24]

During the 1980s, China's strategy for a dual-track economy with the state sector's share gradually declining in favor of alternative ownership forms, including private and cooperatively owned enterprises, has yielded striking success.[25] Arguing for rapid marketization and privatization, some analysts and participants in the economic transformation of Eastern Europe and the Soviet Union contend that a chasm cannot be leaped in two jumps. China's industrial reforms offer a vivid example of halfway reform, the first of the two or more jumps required to attain the level of industrial efficiency envisaged by China's reformers. Nonetheless, while partial and gradual reform has succeeded within state industry, it is unlikely that these gains would have materialized if the state had not sanctioned rapid reform in the rural sector and relaxed the state's monopoly on industrial production that existed at the outset of the reforms. The rapid entry and growth of nonstate enterprises, particularly TVEs, has created a competitive industrial environment which has eroded profits in the state sector and required state factory managers to upgrade their operations.[26]

## The Important Role of a Kindred Model

Since the introduction of the open-door policy in 1979, China has moved with remarkable speed from near complete autarky during the 1960s and early 1970s to a position in 1988 in which China's reported trade ratio exceeded those of India, the United States, and Japan, the three largest market-oriented coun-

---

[23] This study for the World Bank uses average revenue products as a proxy for marginal measures. In order to relax the underlying assumption of identical production technologies (output elasticities) across industrial branches, the authors investigate the tendency of factor returns to converge within individual branches and find further confirmation of significant patterns of convergence.

[24] Measured as the ratio of the sum of profits and taxes to capital. See Barry Naughton, "Implications of the State Monopoly on Industry and its Relaxation," *Modern China* 18, no. 1 (January 1992), pp. 14–41.

[25] In 1978 the state sector represented 90 percent of the gross value of China's industrial output. Currently this share barely exceeds 60 percent.

[26] This argument is developed in John McMillan and Barry Naughton, "How to Reform a Planned Economy: Lessons from China," *Oxford Review of Economic Policy* 8, no. 1 (Spring 1992), pp. 130–42.

tries.[27] In addition to direct trade promotion, the opening of China has been greatly facilitated by the expansion of foreign direct investment and the designation of special economic zones.

One conspicuous and significant feature concerning the internationalization of the Chinese economy, particularly the outward-oriented provinces of the southeast, is the dominant role of Hong Kong and growing influence of Taiwan. As trading partner, financier, and intermediary and facilitator, Hong Kong has had a profound and pervasive effect on the development path of a country with 200 times the population of this small but dynamic entrepot.

**Trading Partner.**    Because Chinese trade statistics do not distinguish between direct and indirect, or entrepot, trade, we use Hong Kong statistical sources.[28] These statistics show that in 1988 exports to Hong Kong represented 40.8 percent of China's total exports. Hong Kong was the final destination for only a quarter of this share, while three quarters were reexported, a substantial share having been processed in Hong Kong before being shipped out.[29] On the import side, 30.8 percent of total Chinese imports came from Hong Kong, of which more than two thirds were processed in China and reexported through Hong Kong.

**Financier.**    The dominance of Hong Kong in China's external relations is also reflected in Hong Kong's role as a source of foreign direct investment. Of the $3.2 billion in foreign direct investment in China in 1988, $2.1 billion (two thirds of the total) originated in Hong Kong and Macao. The fact that Guangdong province accounts for 43 percent of China's total foreign direct investment further underscores the importance of proximity to Hong Kong—not only for Hong Kong investors, but also for other foreign investors for whom access to Hong Kong's services, skills, market, and infrastructure, unobstructed by language or cultural barriers, are critical assets. The rapid growth of trade between China and Hong Kong partly reflects patterns of investment, particularly Hong Kong investment in low-wage processing and assembling operations in China. Hong Kong firms supply such operations with the required raw materials and components, part of which are made in Hong Kong.

---

[27] This comparison of trade ratios should be treated with some skepticism, since imports and exports are measured in U.S. dollars, China's GNP is understated due to omitted items and underreporting, and there is the usual problem of using different relative prices to value traded and nontraded goods. See Lardy, *Foreign Trade,* Appendix. 2.

[28] Time lags and differences between f.o.b. and c.i.f. are ignored.

[29] Reexported trade does not include transshipments, since these pass through the port without clearing customs.

**Intermediary and Facilitator.**  A further measure of the important role of the kindred economy is the spectacularly large number of foreign visits of kindred Chinese living in Hong Kong, Macao, and Taiwan (i.e., those Chinese referred to by Beijing as *tongbao,* literally, same womb). In 1988, of 31.7 million visits to China, 29.8 million, over 90 percent, were Chinese from Hong Kong, Macao, and Taiwan, the balance consisting of foreigners and overseas Chinese. The predominance of *tongbao* visitors reflects the frequency with which Chinese investors, managers, traders, technicians, and other economic agents, including discriminating consumers, cross into China. The vision of nearly 100,000 trips per day underscores the tremendous volume of resources, skills, and attitudes being transplanted from Hong Kong into China.

These statistics do not fully capture the important impact of Hong Kong on China. The tens of thousands of transactions per day between Hong Kong and nearby areas in China, particularly Guangdong province, serve to challenge the institutions and attitudes of central planning. In particular, the presence of Hong Kong trade, capital, and middlemen:

1. Challenges trade and investment monopolies and substantially reduces transaction costs associated with both trade and investment.

2. Abets China's thriving black market in foreign trade, forcing planners to maintain a more realistic exchange rate for the Chinese yuan.

3. Provides a laboratory, so that reform initiatives with respect to pricing, investment incentives, and trade measures are able to generate rapid feedback to allow planners to gauge the effectiveness of reform policy.

In the long run, the biggest role Hong Kong can play in the Chinese economy is that of a model demonstrating the efficacy of the market. In the following section, we discuss the critical distinction between centrally managed and bottom-up reform. During the past decade of reform, it is unlikely that any one area or collection of persons has provided more inspiration and guidance in the ways of spontaneous reform than Hong Kong.

In recent years, with the relaxation of restraints on travel and investment in China, Taiwan has emerged as a second source of kindred resources and know-how. Since its foreign exchange reserves are the world's largest, the potential for Taiwan to reinforce and expand the impact that kindred Chinese have made to China's first decade of reform is considerable.

In the case of east and west Germany, the western dog is clearly wagging the eastern tail. In the case of China, however, it is arguable that, in a more subtle and protracted way, Hong Kong, Macao, and Taiwan—specifically the accumulated capital, technologies, and skills of their combined population of less than 30 million persons—may, more than any other single factor, be responsible for the ongoing economic transformation of the lives of over 1 billion people. If so, this will be the case of the tail wagging the dog, initially through the transformation of Guangdong province and then fanning out to Fujian and Hainan provinces and beyond.

## The Critical Distinction between Centrally Managed Reform and Bottom-Up (or Spontaneous) Reform

Reform has a proactive connotation. Indeed, China's economic reform program was deliberately initiated; these initiatives constitute an impressive list of reform measures. Notable among these initiatives are the establishment of special economic zones (SEZs), provisions for the retention of profits and the distribution of bonuses, and the enterprise contract responsibility system. The direct impact of these initiatives from the center has been substantial. However, three points require emphasis.

First, it is critical to realize that many of these reforms are enabling reforms. That is, they authorize local initiatives but do not guarantee achievement of their intended effect. In order for reform initiatives from the central government to be effective, microlevel actors—households, enterprises, and localities—must respond favorably to these initiatives.

Second, many reforms have followed *de facto* change. The government consented or sanctioned important reforms only after they had become widespread. The most dramatic example is China's rural reforms. Contrary to popular belief, these reforms were not planned by the central government. In fact, leasing land for household farming and setting quotas on a household basis, the two most important ingredients of the household production responsibility system, were in 1979 explicitly banned by China's leadership. Initially opposing land tenure and the household contract system, the central government gradually recognized that these innovations from below were widely supported and constituted a viable mode of agricultural production. Although these measures were initially authorized for remote regions in 1980, it was not until 1985 that the government sanctioned the key administrative measures that led to China's successful agricultural reforms. Yet, by the end of 1984, over 93 percent of China's cultivated land had been contracted to households, and nearly 100 percent of China's rural villages were fixing quotas on a household basis. More recent examples of bottom-up initiatives that only later became accepted by authorities at the center include stock exchanges in Shanghai and Shenzhen and Shanghai's Pudong development zone.

Third, many reforms remain unsanctioned. Unsanctioned reform has been widespread during the past decade, but as the government became increasingly reticent to back reforms during the 1988–90 austerity program and particularly during the period following the crackdown in Tianamen Square,[30] the phenomenon of unsanctioned reform has become more important. While some of these unsanctioned reforms, such as the growth of private banking, are well publicized, most are surreptitious. Among these are the establishment of subsidiaries in rural areas of Guangdong province for the purpose of processing or

---

[30] Editor's note: Pro-democracy demonstrations in 1989 were forcibly suppressed by the government.

distributing goods that would otherwise be subject to state allocations and price regulation. More generally, many enterprises consciously develop counterpolicies that are formulated to counter or thwart government policy or regulations that inhibit local initiative or profit.

Spontaneous reform has, at a minimum, been a necessary complement to managed reform, and sometimes it has been a necessary prerequisite to managed reform. Among the conditions that have caused spontaneous reform to be so important and effective are the following:

1. The tradition of a relatively weak central government, aided by China's geographic size and diversity.

2. The pent-up dissatisfaction and widespread desire for reform and greater local and individual initiative.

3. A population that has not lost the recipe for commerce and entrepreneurship, in part because classical socialism had been in force for just two decades (approximately 1957–77).

4. The open-door policy and the proximity of kindred models and resources.

The capacity for spontaneous economic reform is an important resource that the government should not stifle. It generates signals where the greatest returns are to be gained from incremental reform.

The challenge to the Chinese government is twofold. First, it should establish the macroeconomic controls and appropriate regulatory environment within which spontaneous, unbalanced reform can evolve. Second, it should establish a system that can monitor feedback from the reform process and formulate relevant policy initiatives to resolve bottlenecks and distortions as they appear within China's piecemeal reform program. More emphasis should be placed on creating institutions with these capabilities and maintaining flexibility in the formulation of policy, particularly the use of indirect instruments, rather than relying upon traditional capabilities and methods of state planning. The final two lessons address this latter point.

## Flawed Institutions and Bad Policy Impede Reform

Economic reform is impeded not just by the lack of a feasible and coherent strategy, the lack of political will, or the fear of economic dislocation. At certain junctures of China's reform process, flawed institutions or policy instruments and bad policy have also made key reforms difficult to initiate or to sustain. During the past decade, significant examples of obstacles to reform include: (1) flawed instruments of indirect macroeconomic management that have necessitated reliance on direct, administered measures, and (2) various policies that retard the generation of employment and thus increase the prospect of vast unemployment associated with expanded labor mobility and labor markets.

**Macroeconomic Management.**     Among the key instruments of macroeconomic stability in a market economy are an independent central bank, flexible interest rates, and an efficient revenue system. The absence or compromise of these instruments requires the use of direct controls. In the case of China, the implementation of a macroeconomic stabilization program during 1988–90 required the excessive use of direct administrative means—such as price controls, credit and materials allocations, and forced open market operations (e.g., substituting bonds for workers' cash wages). The effect was to contravene prior reforms and create a more serious hiatus in the reform program than required had the instruments of indirect macroeconomic stabilization been in place.

Specifically, the following shortcomings in China's system of macroeconomic management have necessitated direct administrative intervention:

*(a) Lack of Independence.*     The independence of China's central banking system is weakened in several ways. First, under the existing structure, the financial system, government plans, and the state budget are still interdependent. Most loans by the specialized banks (the People's Construction Bank and the Industrial and Commercial Bank in the industrial sphere) are covered by the mandatory plan. This means, in effect, that the State Planning Commission and local planning commissions assign to banks the responsibility of financing investment projects that have been approved by the planning system. The Planning Commission approves projects, the Ministry of Finance pays the bills, and the banks lend money accordingly. When the government does not have enough money in the bank, printing money has been the usual solution for overdraft. In this sense, the money supply is endogenous; there is no consciously independent monetary policy.

Independence of China's banking establishment is also compromised by its system of governance. Because banks operate under the close supervision of local governments, which wield influence over the careers of bank directors and their families, banks are careful to listen to local government priorities. Acting in the interest of the region is more important than profits or policies of the banking system. Local governments do not like to see local banks remit excess reserves to the next level in the hierarchy, or to see banks lend excess reserves to banks in other localities, even to branches of the same bank. The rule of the game has been to keep deposits within the local boundary, and to annex resources through attempts to force the hand of the central bank. The effect is to swell the volume of local reserves and credit so as to require the use of direct credit controls.

*(b) Inflexible Interest Rates.*     A prominent feature of China's financial system is the considerable appetite of enterprises for investment resources. This condition is motivated by low, often negative, real rates of interest. During the 1980s, nominal interest charges were gradually adjusted upward, but not as rapidly as the rise of inflation. The effect was declining real costs of capital that spurred more investment demand and greater macroeconomic instability at precisely the time when interest rates should have been used to moderate the demand for

credit.[31] Arresting this growing imbalance of supply and demand for investment funds required more credit rationing and greater intervention in the banking system.

*(c) Inelastic Revenue System.*   China differs from most other countries in that the central government collects very few of its own taxes. Apart from customs duties and selected excises, the center relies on local government for the collection of revenues, most of which originate with state industry. Some portion of revenues collected locally is remitted to the center as specified by a system of financial responsibility contracts. Under this scheme, local governments remit revenue to the center in accord with a fixed target. In some cases, a fraction of revenues in excess of the target is also remitted.

The problem with this revenue scheme is that it has been found to be highly inefficient, that is, inelastic with respect to the growth of nominal income. In particular, as inflation accelerates (as it did during 1987–88), the tax base of the center, fixed in nominal terms, declines in real terms. Furthermore, once they have satisfied their contracted revenue targets with the center, localities tend to hide revenues of which a portion is supposed to be remitted to Beijing.[32] During the latter half of the 1980s, the inflationary growth of central government expenditures led to a growing gap between expenditures and revenues that, in turn, required deficit financing and the printing of money.

China's breakdown in macroeconomic stability during the late 1980s arose from many sources, but clearly the problem was made worse by an insufficiently independent banking system, inflexible interest rates, and an inefficient revenue system. The acceleration of inflation during the last half of the 1980s and the use of clumsy administrative means to combat it took a considerable toll on the reform program, beyond the use of various counterreform measures. Inflation undermined the enthusiasm of the public for the reform process, particularly price reform, and damaged the confidence and credibility of reformers in their ability to superintend an orderly transition to a market economy. Although inflation has been curtailed, its underlying structural causes remain fundamentally unaltered.

**Anti-Employment Policies.**   A second major area in which flawed institutions or bad policies, in this case the latter, have inhibited critical reform initiatives is labor market reform. Urban labor market reform is needed both (1) to enforce

---

[31] For enterprises selling in the market during 1985–88, the user cost of capital (the real rate of interest plus the depreciation rate) was virtually zero. See Gary H. Jefferson and Thomas G. Rawski, "Urban Unemployment, Underemployment, and Employment Policy in Chinese Industry," *Modern China* 18, no. 1 (January 1992), pp. 42–71.

[32] There are innumerable ways in which local governments can divert revenues or arrange payments from enterprises in lieu of taxes. For example, an enterprise makes a deal to accelerate repayment of its loan in lieu of taxes to a locality which has already met its minimum revenue obligation.

greater discipline and efficiency within China's industrial enterprises and (2) to create the flexibility required to support structural adjustment entailing the reallocation of workers across sectors, industrial branches, and individual enterprises.

China has adopted a wide range of policies and pricing conventions that have the unintended consequence of discriminating against labor-intensive activities. By suppressing employment-creating economic activity and increasing the likelihood of a large increase in urban unemployment if enterprises are given more freedom to lay off redundant workers, these policies make it all the more difficult to implement meaningful urban labor market reforms. In particular, there are five areas of anti-employment policy: (1) anti-agricultural bias motivating labor to leave labor-intensive farming; (2) anti-service sector bias, which retards the development of this labor-intensive sector; (3) bias against labor-intensive forms of enterprise ownership, particularly small-scale private enterprise; (4) export policies and practices that mitigate against the development of labor-intensive sectors that accord with China's international comparative advantage; and (5) distorted factor prices that motivate enterprises to substitute capital, energy, and materials for labor.[33]

The persistence of this formidable set of anti-employment policies creates a legitimate fear among China's reformers and political leadership that further relaxation of controls on labor allocation and mobility will lead to unacceptable levels of unemployment in urban areas. The government has taken initial steps toward effective labor market reform. Among these are curtailment of the labor allocation system; the optimal labor combination program to rationalize the allocation of workers within enterprises; and the creation of pension and unemployment programs that pool the expense of retirement and unemployment benefits among enterprises. The creation of a fluid and competitive labor market, however, will require a more aggressive set of reforms—which will become tenable only as the constraints on market-based generation of employment (described above) are eliminated.

## The Importance of Checks and Balances and the Difficulty of Achieving These under a Communist Regime

The intent of China's enterprise reform program was to establish enterprises on an administratively and financially independent footing. Yet, the devolution of administrative control to local government, already begun in the early 1970s, has intensified local administrative interference in enterprise management, price manipulation, and corruption. The question is whether a Communist government, accustomed to political monopoly and unfettered control over economic resources, can create a legal and regulatory framework within which enterprises can further broaden their autonomy.

---

[33] See Jefferson and Rawski, "Urban Unemployment."

**Administrative Interference.**  Almost every Chinese enterprise reports to numerous supervisory agencies, often at different levels of government. These agencies exercise authority over production, sales, material supply, investment, working capital, labor allocations, and Communist Party organizations. Resistant to efforts to curtail the system of perpetual negotiations about taxes, subsidies, allocations, and favors, local officials have been extremely inventive in capturing power and expanding control over enterprises through a variety of informal mechanisms, as well as through their control over geographically immobile factors and resources.

This complex, meddlesome administrative environment seriously undermines the autonomy and operations of factory directors.[34] Not atypical of the directors, one, already a seasoned engineer and manager at the time he assumed the directorship of a state enterprise, reported that it took 4 years and most of his time and energy just to establish effective working relations with various supervisory agencies. Others complained bitterly that they wanted their *popo*,[35] or supervisory agencies, "off their backs."

**Price Manipulation.**  Originally, when the two-track system was established, it was anticipated that enterprises would grow out of subordination to the plan. This has occurred somewhat, but not as rapidly or uniformly as expected. First, some government organizations continually increase enterprise quotas and planning targets. For example, in many of Shanghai's industrial branches (especially in metallurgy, textiles, and some machine-building enterprises), production was almost 100 percent planned in 1988. Output produced above the state quota is also often subject to compulsory local plans.

Even though the scope of markets continues to expand—so that capital goods subject to the state mandatory plan have been reduced from more than 80 percent of the total to only 20–30 percent—multiple prices have not shown a tendency to merge. Sometimes, the difference between list prices and market prices may not be so big on paper, but numerous trading units tack on additional margins and demand handling fees in cash. Prices of raw materials may rise several times during the distribution process.

**Corruption.**  Multiple prices, while an improvement over fixed state prices, provide extensive opportunities for corruption. Officials with the power to approve distribution targets under state plans often fall to the temptation of bribes. For enterprises, whether material inputs can be obtained at list prices or must be acquired at market prices can make the difference between profit- or loss-making operations. The authority of local officials to set and enforce government allocations thus serves as a direct link between power and money.

---

[34] Walder, "Factory," and World Bank, *China's Finance and Investment* (Washington, D.C. 1988).
[35] Literally translated as "mother-in-law."

Government organizations have been using their authority to force enterprises to sell their above-quota products to government-run companies at low prices. Some local governments have gone so far as to close down markets and deliberately create multiple prices for certain products. Thus, profits from high market prices have fallen into the hands of the profiteering officials.

Administrative interference, price manipulation, and corruption, as well as attempts to monopolize production and trade at the local level, underscore the need for checks and balances in an effective market economy. Among these checks and balances are competitive markets; an autonomous banking system; a comprehensive system of enterprise, commercial, and criminal law; an independent legal system to enforce and interpret the law; and an independent watchdog press to bring to public attention abusive officials and economic crimes.

In addition, a key to limiting the *ad hoc* interventions of the Chinese bureaucracy in enterprise operations is private ownership and a code of property rights. The Chinese government has effectively stalled on the issue of privatizing state and collective enterprises. We have emphasized the effectiveness of gradual and partial reform within state industry. However, in large part this success reflects the enormous inefficiency within the industrial sector at the beginning of the reform program—which allowed various halfway measures (including the enterprise contract responsibility system and dual pricing) to motivate significant improvements in productivity. Under these halfway measures, however, serious distortions persist. Eventually, probably sooner rather than later, extensive privatization and more complete marketization will be required for China to join the club of newly industrialized economies—those developing economies that have acquired the capacity to spawn new products and technologies and to export them at competitive prices.

This list of needed institutional innovations raises a key question which for now remains unresolved, that is, the extent to which political reform is a prerequisite for a full transition to an effective market-oriented economy. Since multiparty systems have eliminated the Communist party's monopoly on power in Eastern Europe and the former Soviet republics, it may be that this issue will have to be resolved with reference to the experience of a single country, China. During the first decade, China's Communist party demonstrated sufficient flexibility to achieve reforms in the economic system that could not have been contemplated in 1978. Whether a new generation of leaders can manage the transition toward more complete markets and private ownership should become evident during the next decade.

## CONCLUSIONS

During the 1950s, development economists debated the relative merits of balanced and unbalanced development strategies in which advocates of the former argued that the interconnectedness of development required a big push on all fronts.[36] Citing limited resources, both financial and administrative, advocates of unbalanced development emphasized that as bottlenecks become manifest, resources can and will be allocated to alleviate them. The schizophrenia among specialists in transition economics regarding the "big bang" or sweeping reform versus those advocating a piecemeal, evolutionary approach mirrors this earlier debate.

To a significant degree, China's reform demonstrates that gradual and partial reform can be successful. The viability of a reform strategy depends in part on the extent to which there are substitutes and complements in the reform process.[37] China's reform experience shows that privatizing state enterprises has not been essential for the near- to medium-term success of its industrial reform program. Expanding managerial autonomy and incentives and ending the state's monopoly over industry have, to a substantial degree, substituted for the privatization of state enterprises. On the other hand, China's experience also suggests that there are complements, or fixed proportions, in the production of successful reform outcomes. A set of indirect instruments of macroeconomic policy, more complete than those currently in place in China, are necessary to sustain enterprise autonomy during periods of retrenchment. The alternative to indirect instruments is to infringe on enterprise autonomy through the direct control of inputs, outputs, and credit to enterprises.

Still, the extent to which piecemeal, evolutionary reform can succeed may well depend upon particular characteristics of the reforming economy. The proportionately smaller rural economies in Eastern Europe and their greater capital intensity and inflexibility may limit the potential for a single leading sector to drive reform in other sectors. In these countries, it is less likely that a phenomenon comparable to China's rural industry could emerge with competitive spillover impacts on the state sector. Since competition is more likely to come directly from established, world-class firms in Western Europe, there is a stronger argument for rapid, comprehensive reform with privatization as its centerpiece. In this case, management reform may not be an effective substitute for privatization.

In varying degrees, the countries of Eastern Europe, through their proximity to Western Europe and expatriate communities, have access to significant resources that can transcend distance, language, and cultural barriers. This is less true for the former Soviet republics. The Baltic republics maintain stronger

---

[36] See the debate among Ragnar Nurkse, *Problems of Capital Formation in Underdeveloped Countries* (Oxford: Basil Blackwell, 1953); Albert Hirschman, *The Strategy of Economic Development* (New Haven, Conn.: Yale University Press, 1958); and P. N. Rosenstein-Rodan, "Notes on the Theory of the 'Big Push,'" in *Economic Development for Latin America,* ed. Howard S. Ellis (London: Macmillan, 1961), pp. 57–67.

[37] Jefferson and Rawski, "Urban Unemployment," show how the government's formulation of reform strategy is analogous to the firm's investment decision. Their model develops the distinction between complements and substitutes in the technique of reform.

links with the West than the Russian heartland does, but distance, language, and culture, as well as nearly 75 years of Communist rule, have attenuated the access of other former Soviet republics to resources, skills, and attitudes of the market economies.

The relative merit of rapid versus gradual reform also depends upon the degree of certainty regarding the desired set of post-reform arrangements and the effectiveness of various reform instruments. While the East Europeans are moving with alacrity to replicate the West European model, the Chinese are groping toward a solution with Chinese characteristics that will include some as-yet-unclear mix of East Asian and Western-style capitalist arrangements. Attitudes of governments and residents toward risk also condition the pace of reform. By growing out of the plan rather than scrapping it, the Chinese government has chosen to limit the downside risk of a substantial increase in urban unemployment and political instability—in contrast with the East Europeans, who seem intent on eliminating the old order at virtually any cost.

With the possible exception of the annexation of East Germany by West Germany, it is now clear that no transition unfolds in a precise, predictable way. Through the protracted interplay of politics and economic reform, China's transition experience promises to be as messy and unpredictable as any. Four of the conditions identified above—China's leading dynamic rural sector, the ability of piecemeal reform to generate real gains, the inspiration of kindred models, and the bottom-up dynamic of Chinese reform—together guarantee that China's reforms will continue to move forward. The other two conditions—the tendency for bad policy and flawed institutions to obstruct reform and the absence of checks on political power—will cause the path of reform to be halting and unpredictable.

# Suggestions for Further Reading
# for Part IV

*Socialist Central Planning*

Frateschi, Carlo, ed. *Fluctuations and Cycles in Socialist Economies*. Brookfield, Vt.: Avebury, 1989.

Hare, Paul G. *Central Planning*. Chur, Switzerland: Harwood Academic Publishers, 1991.

Kornai, János. *The Socialist System: The Political Economy of Communism*. Princeton, N.J.: Princeton University Press, 1991.

Peebles, Gavin. *A Short History of Socialist Money*. Sydney, Australia: Allen & Unwin, 1991.

Wolf, Thomas A. *Foreign Trade in the Centrally Planned Economy*. Chur, Switzerland: Harwood Academic Publishers, 1988.

*Economic Transformation*

Brabant, Jozef M. van. *Privatizing Eastern Europe: The Role of Markets and Ownership in the Transition*. Dordrecht, the Netherlands: Kluwer Academic Publishers, 1992.

Commander, Simon, ed. *Managing Inflation in Socialist Economies in Transition*. Washington, D.C.: World Bank, 1991.

Corbo, Vittorio; Fabrizio Coricelli; and Jan Bossak, eds. *Reforming Central and East European Economies: Initial Results and Challenges*. Washington, D.C.: World Bank, 1991.

Islam, Shafiqul, and Michael Mandelbaum, eds. *Making Markets: Economic Transformation in Eastern Europe and the Post-Soviet States*. New York: Council on Foreign Relations Press, 1993.

Marer, Paul, and Salvatore Zecchini, eds. *The Transition to a Market Economy*. 2 vols. Paris: Organization for Economic Cooperation and Development, 1991.

Organization for Economic Cooperation and Development. *Reforming the Economies of Central and Eastern Europe*. Paris, 1992.

Siebert, Horst, ed. *Privatization*. Tübingen, Germany: Mohr, Siebeck, 1992.

———, ed. *The Transformation of Socialist Economies*. Tübingen, Germany: Mohr, Siebeck, 1992.

Tanzi, Vito, ed. *Fiscal Policies in Transition*. Washington, D.C.: International Monetary Fund, 1992.

Targetti, Ferdinando, ed. *Privatization in Europe: West and East Experience*. Aldershot, England: Dartmouth Publishing Company, 1992.

Wagener, Hans-Jürgen, ed. *On the Theory and Policy of Systemic Change*. Heidelberg, Germany: Physica-Verlag, 1993.

### Agriculture

Boyd, Michael L. *Organization, Performance, and System Choice: East European Agricultural Development*. Boulder, Colo.: Westview Press, 1991.

Gray, Kenneth R., ed. *Soviet Agriculture: Comparative Perspectives*. Ames, Iowa: Iowa University Press, 1990.

Pryor, Frederic L. *The Rise and Fall of Collectivized Agriculture in Marxist Regimes*. Princeton, N.J.: Princeton University Press, 1992.

Wädekin, Karl-Eugen, ed. *Communist Agriculture: Farming in the Far East and Cuba*. London: Routledge, 1990.

————, ed. *Communist Agriculture: Farming in the Soviet Union and Eastern Europe*. London: Routledge, 1990.

### Soviet Union

Aslund, Anders. *Gorbachev's Struggle for Economic Reform*. 2nd ed. Ithaca, N.Y.: Cornell University Press, 1991.

Cooper, Julian. *The Soviet Defence Industry: Conversion and Economic Reform*. London: Royal Institute of International Affairs, 1991.

Flakierski, Henryk. *Income Inequalities in the Former Soviet Union and Its Republics*. Armonk, N.Y.: M. E. Sharpe, 1993.

Goldman, Marshall I. *What Went Wrong with Perestroika*. New York: Norton, 1991.

Hewett, Ed A. *Reforming the Soviet Economy: Equality versus Efficiency*. Washington, D.C.: Brookings Institution, 1988.

International Monetary Fund, World Bank, Organization for Economic Cooperation and Development, and European Bank for Reconstruction and Development. *A Study of the Soviet Economy*. 3 vols. Paris, 1991.

Kushnirsky, Fyodor I. *Growth and Inflation in the Soviet Economy*. Boulder, Colo.: Westview Press, 1989.

Malle, Silvana. *Employment Planning in the Soviet Union*. New York: St. Martin's Press, 1990.

Porket, J. L. *Work, Employment, and Unemployment in the Soviet Union*. London: Macmillan Press, 1989.

Standing, Guy, ed. *In Search of Flexibility: The New Soviet Labor Market*. Geneva: International Labor Office, 1991.

World Bank. *Food and Agricultural Policy Reforms in the Former USSR: An Agenda for the Transition*. Washington, D.C., 1992.

————. *Russian Economic Reform: Crossing the Threshold of Structural Change*. Washington, D.C., 1992.

*Eastern Europe*

Berend, Ivan. *The Hungarian Economic Reforms, 1953–1988*. Cambridge, England: Cambridge University Press, 1990.

Clarke, Roger, ed. *Hungary: The Second Decade of Economic Reform*. London: Longman, 1989.

Köves, András. *Central and East European Economies in Transition*. Boulder, Colo.: Westview Press, 1992.

Székely, István P., and David M. G. Newbery, eds. *Hungary in Transition*. Cambridge, England: Cambridge University Press, 1993.

World Bank. *Czechoslovakia: Transition to a Market Economy*. Washington, D.C., 1991.

———. *Poland: Economic Management for a New Era*. Washington, D.C., 1990.

*China*

Byrd, William A. *The Market Mechanism and Economic Reforms in China*. Armonk. N.Y.: M. E. Sharpe, 1991.

———, ed. *Chinese Industrial Firms under Reform*. Oxford: Oxford University Press, 1992.

Dorn, James A., and Wang Xi, eds. *Economic Reform in China: Problems and Prospects*. Chicago: University of Chicago Press, 1990.

Lee, Peter N. S. *Industrial Management and Economic Reform in China, 1949–1984*. Hong Kong: Oxford University Press, 1987.

Shenkar, Oded, ed. *Organization and Management in China, 1979–1990*. Armonk, N.Y.: M. E. Sharpe, 1991.

White, Gordon, ed. *The Chinese State in the Era of Economic Reform: The Road to Crisis*. Armonk, N.Y.: M. E. Sharpe, 1991.

World Bank. *China: Reform and the Role of the Plan in the 1990s*. Washington, D.C., 1992.

# Part V

# Selected Aspects of Economic Systems

The next two chapters compare economic systems in two related aspects. Chapter 30 analyzes the types and forms of unemployment, and the corresponding antiunemployment measures, in capitalist regulated market economies (CRMEs) and socialist centrally planned economies (SCPEs). Chapter 31 discusses similarities and differences in illegal economic activity, including the use of labor, in CRMEs and SCPEs.

The Suggestions for Further Reading following Chapter 31 contain references on cross-system comparisons of not only these but also other aspects of economic systems.

## Chapter Thirty

# Unemployment in Capitalist Regulated Market Economies and Socialist Centrally Planned Economies*

## *Morris Bornstein*

*For systemic reasons, the nature of unemployment and of antiunemployment measures differs in capitalist regulated market economies (CRMEs) and socialist centrally planned economies (SCPEs).*

*Although seasonal, frictional, and structural types of unemployment occur in SCPEs, they do not have cyclical unemployment problems comparable to those in CRMEs. "Open" unemployment of people seeking jobs is smaller in SCPEs than in CRMEs. But "disguised" unemployment—the underutilization of employed workers—is larger in SCPEs than in CRMEs.*

*In turn, in regard to antiunemployment measures, CRMEs stress job creation and matching the unemployed with vacant jobs. The SCPEs strive to "mobilize hidden reserves" of effort and productivity of labor already employed but underutilized.*

*Economic reforms in SCPEs are likely to reduce "disguised" unemployment and increase "open" unemployment. In response, governments will pursue job creation, job matching, and unemployment compensation programs. Thus, labor markets in such reforming countries will become more like those in CRMEs.*

The comparative economic systems literature commonly distinguishes two major types of economic systems—capitalist regulated market economies (CRMEs) and socialist centrally planned economies (SCPEs).

CRMEs have several key characteristics: (1) Most of the means of production are privately owned. (2) Market forces chiefly determine the level of eco-

---

* Revised from Morris Bornstein, "Unemployment in Capitalist Regulated Market Economies and in Socialist Centrally Planned Economies," *American Economic Review* 68, no. 2 (May 1978), pp. 38–43. Material from the original version is reprinted by permission. New material copyright © 1993 by Morris Bornstein.

nomic activity, the rate of growth, the composition of output, and the distribution of income. But (3) the government intervenes in the economy in various ways to deal with problems of growth, monopoly, inflation, unemployment, income distribution, and so forth. The CRMEs include, for example, the United States, Canada, Western Europe, Japan, and Australia.

In SCPEs, on the other hand: (1) Most means of production are collectively owned. (2) A large administrative bureaucracy attempts to direct resource allocation and income distribution through comprehensive and detailed planning. (3) A combination of administrative allocation and a controlled labor market distributes workers among jobs. (4) A combination of a controlled market and official and unofficial rationing distributes consumer goods and services among households. The SCPEs have included the USSR, most East European countries, and China.

This study compares the two systems in regard to types of unemployment and antiunemployment measures. The experience of particular countries, such as the United States or the USSR, is mentioned by way of illustration, but it is not suggested that they are prototypical or ideal examples of their respective economic systems. There are interesting differences in regard to unemployment among the CRMEs and among the SCPEs, arising from differences in the level of economic development, the structure of the economy, the demographic composition of the labor force, and social and institutional arrangements. But space limitations preclude discussion of such intragroup differences. Also, lack of relevant data for the SCPEs prevents reliable statistical comparisons of unemployment rates in the two systems.[1] Finally, the study does not consider unemployment in a third type of economic system—a socialist regulated market economy—because the sample of countries (Yugoslavia) is too small to permit sound generalizations about systemic characteristics transcending particular national circumstances.


## TYPES OF UNEMPLOYMENT

Unemployment may be analyzed in terms of its origin or its form. The first approach is more common, but the second is perhaps more illuminating in comparing economic systems.

---

[1] For an effort to compare Soviet and U.S. unemployment rates, see Paul R. Gregory and Irwin L. Collier, Jr., "Unemployment in the Soviet Union: Evidence from the Soviet Interview Project," *American Economic Review* 78, no. 4 (September 1988), pp. 613–32. See also I. Adirim, "A Note on the Current Level, Pattern, and Trends of Unemployment in the USSR," *Soviet Studies* 41, no. 3 (July 1989), pp. 449–61, and J. L. Porket, *Employment and Unemployment in the Soviet Union* (London: Macmillan, 1989).

## Origin

In CRMEs four kinds of unemployment are commonly identified.[2] *Seasonal* unemployment arises from regular seasonal fluctuations in the demand for and supply of labor. On the demand side, seasonal variations in labor requirements are common, for instance, in agriculture, construction, and vacation resort activities. On the supply side, the school calendar affects the labor force participation of young people. *Frictional* unemployment involves those seeking their first jobs and those between jobs after quitting or being dismissed. *Structural* unemployment occurs when people are unable over a long period to find work, because of a lack of appropriate skills or a shortage of jobs in their particular labor market areas, although national aggregate demand may be high. Finally, *cyclical* unemployment results from a general decline in business activity, with a subsequent recovery leading to reemployment.

In CRMEs, seasonal and frictional unemployment are considered part of the normal process by which the market mechanism adjusts production to demand. Thus a seasonally adjusted frictional unemployment rate of, say, 3 to 4 percent of the labor force could be considered compatible with "full employment." On the other hand, cyclical and structural unemployment have more serious economic and social consequences and more urgently require corrective government action.

SCPEs may have seasonal unemployment due to natural factors, such as agricultural production cycles, and institutional arrangements, such as the academic calendar. In turn, some frictional unemployment is expected so long as new entrants into the labor force can choose their first jobs, workers are free to quit, or enterprise managers are permitted to dismiss unsatisfactory or surplus workers. But authorities in SCPEs may complain about job changes on the initiative of workers—stressing the costs to the economy in lost production during periods of unemployment, in low productivity when workers begin new jobs, and in retraining programs.

In SCPEs, structural unemployment is regarded as evidence of deficiencies in planning, which is supposed to balance the supply of and demand for labor though accurate estimates of the labor force and correct decisions on training programs, technological progress, location of new capacity, and relative wages. This is an extremely difficult task, and in the USSR, for instance, structural unemployment has persisted in certain regions and among women in smaller cities and rural areas.[3]

---

[2] On unemployment in CRMEs, see, for example, K. G. Knight, *Unemployment: An Economic Analysis* (London: Croom Helm, 1987); Stephen J. Nickell, "Unemployment: A Survey," *Economic Journal* 100, no. 401 (June 1990), pp. 391–439; and Lawrence H. Summers, *Understanding Unemployment* (Cambridge, Mass.: MIT Press, 1990).

[3] See Silvana Malle, *Employment Planning in the Soviet Union* (New York: St. Martin's Press, 1990), and David Lane, *Soviet Labor and the Ethic of Communism: Full Employment and the Labor Process in the USSR* (Boulder, Colo.: Westview Press, 1987), chap. 4.

In contrast, SCPEs do not show the recurrent pattern of cyclical unemployment common in CRMEs. The reason include the SCPEs' "taut" planning
for ambitious growth targets and their measures to insulate the domestic economy from external shocks. Aside from harvest variations, fluctuations in economic activity in SCPEs result primarily from changes in growth rates of investment and output, without periodic recessions in which workers are laid
off.[4]

## Form

The distinction between "open" and "disguised" unemployment in some ways
parallels the more familiar contrast between "open" and "repressed" inflation.
The openly unemployed are seeking jobs but cannot find them. Disguised unemployment—or underemployment—occurs when workers have jobs but are
underutilized (1) because they wish full-time jobs but can get only part-time
work; (2) because their full-time jobs do not use all their skills and training; or
(3) because, though employed full-time in jobs matching their qualifications,
their productivity is low.

The first kind of disguised unemployment—part-time work when full-time
jobs are sought—is more common in CRMEs than in SCPEs. In the latter, part-
time work is more often a way to draw into the labor force pensioners, home-
makers, and others not available for full-time jobs.

The second category—work below skill level—occurs in both systems
because training opportunities and choices are not correctly matched with
(future) employment possibilities, information on vacancies is imperfect, or
mobility is limited.

The causes of low productivity may include late delivery of materials,
equipment breakdowns, poor organization of production, low output norms,
weak incentives due to the level and structure of compensation, and hoarding
of labor by enterprise management. All of these may be found in both CRMEs
and SCPEs, but only labor hoarding will be considered here.

In SCPEs such hoarding is explained by the combination of the "ratchet"
principle in planning, tight labor market conditions, and restrictions on the
dismissal of redundant workers. The first makes management expect that already ambitious production assignments will be "jacked up" continually in
future periods. The second makes management believe that it may be difficult
to replace workers who quit or to hire additional workers authorized for the
extra output. Therefore, management wants a pool of "reserve" workers on
the payroll, not because they are needed now but because they are likely to be
required, but perhaps unavailable, in the future. Finally, there may be restric-

---

[4] See Barry W. Ickes, "Cyclical Fluctuations in Centrally Planned Economies: A Critique of the
Literature," *Soviet Studies* 38, no. 1 (January 1986), pp. 36–52, and *Fluctuations and Cycles in
Socialist Economies,* ed. Carlo Frateschi (Brookfield, Vt.: Avebury, 1989).

tions of law or custom on management's ability to discharge unneeded workers.[5]

Labor hoarding also exists in CRMEs when labor input is not adjusted fully to changes in output. Inaccurate sales forecasts can cause "unplanned" hoarding. Conscious "planned" hoarding occurs because of legal commitments, indivisibilities in production, morale considerations, transaction costs in firing and hiring, and expectations of future changes in demand. The Japanese version is sometimes called "permanent" or "lifetime" employment.

Thus, a comparison of unemployment in CRMEs and SCPEs must consider both the open and the disguised forms. One may hypothesize that central planning's effort to mobilize resources for rapid growth and socialism's ideological commitment to the "right to work" tend to hold open unemployment in SCPEs below the rates observed in CRMEs. At the same time, these two factors may lead to more disguised unemployment in SCPEs than in CRMEs.

Unfortunately, the statistical data to test such hypotheses are lacking. However, the relative importance of the two forms of unemployment may be inferred from the focus of policy discussions and antiunemployment measures in the two systems. In CRMEs, the chief concern is with open unemployment, while SCPEs pay much more attention to underemployment. Thus, SCPEs stress that "full employment" means not only (1) that there is a job for everyone who wants one, but also (2) that labor should be allocated rationally across the economy and (3) that it should be used efficiently inside the enterprise. Similarly, whereas the concept of "labor reserve" has been applied in the United States to refer to potential workers currently outside the labor force, in the USSR it encompasses as well "hidden" or "internal" reserves in the labor input of the employed but underutilized.

## ANTIUNEMPLOYMENT MEASURES

In turn, the two systems differ in their approach to reducing unemployment.

### CRMEs

In CRMEs there are two types of constraints on antiunemployment measures. At the micro level, society is loath to impose restrictions on the freedom of workers to choose and quit jobs and on the freedom of firms to determine the amount and kind of labor input. At the macro level, it is widely believed that a reduction in unemployment will be accompanied by an increase in inflation. Thus, policymakers try to determine a "tolerable" rate and composition of unemployment. Efforts to reduce unemployment include (1) job creation, (2)

---

[5] See, for instance, Nick Lampert, "Job Security and the Law in the USSR," in *Labor and Employment in the USSR*, ed. David Lane (New York: New York University Press, 1986), chap. 15, and David Granick, *Job Rights in the Soviet Union: Their Consequences* (New York: Cambridge University Press, 1987).

matching the unemployed with job vacancies, and (3) reducing the size of the "labor force" desiring employment.[6]

In CRMEs the conventional approach has been to create jobs in the private sector by stimulating aggregate demand through expansionary monetary policies, tax cuts, and increases in government purchases of goods and services. Some CRME governments have subsidized part of private firms' wage costs to induce them (1) to maintain the employment of workers who would otherwise be laid off or (2) to hire additional workers from the unemployed. Finally, additional (temporary or permanent) public sector jobs can be established at the national, regional, or local levels.

The matching of unemployed workers with existing or newly created job vacancies is attempted through placement services, retraining, relocation assistance, and area development schemes.

The unemployment rate can also be decreased by reducing the size of the "labor force" wishing paid employment. Labor force participation of the "old" can be cut by lowering the retirement age and by raising pensions so fewer "retirees" seek work. In turn, the entry of the "young" into the labor force can be delayed by extending compulsory secondary education and by increasing tuition and maintenance subsidies for postsecondary training.

In addition, the effects of unemployment on household income may be at least partially offset by unemployment insurance schemes and welfare programs.

## SCPEs

In SCPEs the attainment of the political leaders' goal of full mobilization of labor resources is constrained by the extent of workers' freedom to quit—which was much greater in Eastern Europe than in China—as well as by the inability of planning agencies to control enterprise operations and regulate labor markets exactly as they wish. But in SCPEs the inflation–unemployment trade-off is regarded with much less concern than in CRMEs. The SCPEs are more confident about their ability to curtail inflationary pressure by tax and credit measures or to repress it by comprehensive price controls.

In SCPEs jobs are created by ambitious development plans implemented by detailed administrative orders, government expenditure programs, and an accommodating monetary policy. The socialist character of the economy resolves the issue of public versus private sector employment overwhelmingly in favor of the former—with the private sector usually limited to subsidiary agriculture, handicrafts, and selected personal services. Explicit wage subsidies to public enterprises are the exception rather than the rule. But firms attempt to

---

[6] See, for example, Richard Jackman, Christopher Pissarides, and Savvas Savouri, "Labor Market Policies and Unemployment in the OECD," *Economic Policy* 11 (October 1990), pp. 450–90.

cover the cost of surplus labor by negotiating larger wage bills in their annual plans and by securing higher prices from central agencies, which usually set prices to cover planned branch-average cost plus a profit markup on it.

For matching workers with job vacancies, SCPEs emphasize training programs, and organized mass recruitment for new towns. Although employment bureaus are useful for the latter, the official attitude toward them in SCPEs is ambivalent. The authorities fear that such bureaus may not only help in centrally planned labor placement, but may also facilitate (1) enterprises' efforts to build up "reserve" labor pools and (2) "unplanned" labor turnover at the initiative of workers. Thus, in the USSR for instance, these bureaus were supposed to screen all requests for workers and reject those inconsistent with an enterprise's labor plan, and one indicator of the bureaus' performance was how long workers stayed in the jobs in which they were placed.

In SCPEs the relocation of workers to new areas is difficult. One factor is social and cultural obstacles to mobility similar to those in CRMEs. Also, housing shortages are widespread and persistent because of investment plans' neglect of infrastructure. Furthermore, the high participation rate of married women in the labor force requires suitable jobs for both spouses in the new city. Thus, except where location decisions are determined by natural factors such as mineral deposits, it has usually proved more feasible to place new capacity in labor surplus areas than to relocate workers.

The governments of SCPEs have traditionally regarded unemployment insurance as unnecessary and indeed harmful. A high level of aggregate demand is supposed to assure enough jobs for all. Furthermore, when a worker is no longer needed by a firm, because of changes in output assignments or production methods (for example, mechanization or automation), the management is expected or even legally obligated (1) if possible to reassign the worker, with retraining if necessary, inside the enterprise; or (2) to arrange for placement in another firm in the same area. Therefore, the authorities have considered that unemployment is voluntary, rather than involuntary, and that compensation for it not only is unjustified but could extend the unemployment period by financing a longer job search. A similar view may be found in the discussion in the United States about the disincentive effects of unemployment compensation.

## CONCLUSION

Contrary to some official claims, unemployment does occur in SCPEs—because of nature, workers' freedom of job choice, and imperfect planning. Although seasonal, frictional, and structural unemployment exist in SCPEs, they do not have cyclical unemployment problems comparable to those in CRMEs. However, the distinction between open and disguised unemployment—alternative forms of inefficiency—is important. In SCPEs a high level of aggregate demand due to ambitious national plans can create a labor shortage at the macro level, while there are labor surpluses at the micro level as a result of the firm's reaction to taut plans and tight labor markets.

These differences are in turn reflected in the emphasis of antiunemployment measures in the two systems. CRMEs stress job creation, with controversy over the shares for the private and public sectors. The CRMEs maintain income and support the job search of the unemployed through unemployment compensation. In the unreformed SCPE the authorities consider unemployment compensation unnecessary and detrimental, and they try through demanding plans to mobilize "internal" reserves of the employed but underutilized.

Economic reforms in SCPEs reduce "concealed" unemployment (underemployment) and increase "open" unemployment.[7]

In pursuit of profit (rather than output or sales) as the chief performance indicator, enterprise managements seek to economize on labor inputs by not hiring unneeded workers and by releasing excess personnel, as well as to increase the productivity of those on the payroll. Pressure to make such changes is exerted also by the hardening of "soft budget constraints," as government subsidies and automatic bank credit are curtailed.

The distribution of jobs is altered by economic reforms. In the shift toward a market economy, the composition of output becomes more responsive to consumers' sovereignty, and it moves from intermediate and producers' goods toward consumers' goods, and from material products to services. Also, the share of small and medium-size firms in total employment rises. One reason is the change in the composition of output. The maximum efficient size (at the minimum point on the average cost curve) is lower in light industry and most services than in heavy industry. Another reason is privatization, under which small private firms are started and large state enterprises are broken up.

In a reforming economy, the government responds to these changes in employment opportunities by developing new programs for (1) job creation, (2) job matching, and (3) income maintenance.

1. The ability of the government to bolster aggregate demand to sustain employment during a significant restructuring of production is constrained by the pursuit of restrictive monetary-fiscal policies to curb inflation after prices are decontrolled. Still, the government may try to create jobs by loans to start new enterprises (especially in areas with high unemployment), and it may undertake public works programs, for instance, improvement of the infrastructure of roads and health and education facilities.

2. The government is likely to establish, or strengthen, employment services which provide job information, counseling, and placement. Also,

---

[7] See, for instance, Alastair McAuley, "The Economic Transition in Eastern Europe: Employment, Income Distribution, and the Social Security Net," *Oxford Review of Economic Policy* 7, no. 4 (Winter 1991), pp. 93–105, and Alberto Chilosi, "On the Social and Economic Consequences of Institutional Transformation in Eastern Europe," in *On the Theory and Policy of Systemic Change,* ed. Hans-Jürgen Wagener (Heidelberg, Germany: Physica-Verlag, 1993), chap. 9.

it will expand training and retraining programs. Further, the government can increase labor mobility by aiding the construction of dwellings to reduce housing shortages which impede the relocation of workers.

3. To maintain the incomes of unemployed workers, in a reforming economy the government provides unemployment compensation, which was deemed unnecessary in an SCPE. This assistance may be linked to participation in a training or retraining program. However, the challenge is to design an unemployment compensation program with benefits whose amount and duration are generous enough to sustain incomes and ease the adaptation to structural change, but not so liberal as to undermine people's incentives for early reemployment.[8]

In these ways, as economic reform programs are implemented, and job security is reduced and labor mobility is increased, the labor market in a reforming former SCPE will become in important respects more like that of a CRME.

---

[8] On this and other elements of the "social safety net" under economic reforms, see, for example, Robert Holzmann, "Social Policy in Transition from Plan to Market," *Journal of Public Policy* 12, no. 1 (January–March 1992), pp. 1–35, and Kalman Rupp, "Democracy, Market, and Social Safety Nets: Implications for Postcommunist Eastern Europe," *Public Policy* 12, no. 1 (January–March 1992), pp. 37–59.

## Chapter Thirty-one

# The Underground Economy in the West and the East: A Comparative Approach*

*Bruno Dallago*[1]

*In addition to the legal "regular" economy, an illegal "irregular" or "underground" economy exists in both capitalist regulated market economies (CRMEs) and socialist centrally planned economies (SCPEs). This chapter compares underground economic activity in the two systems (which the author refers to as the "capitalist-type economy" and the "Soviet-type economy").*

*In certain respects underground activity in CRMEs and SCPEs is similar. For example, in both systems underground enterprises tend to specialize in labor-intensive activities without significant economies of scale. Also, underground enterprises may get inputs from, or supply outputs to, firms in the "regular" economy. In both systems, by omitting underground activity, official statistics understate employment, production, and consumption.*

*But in other important ways the underground economy in CRMEs and SCPEs differs. The main reason for underground activity in CRMEs is evasion of taxes and government regulations. In SCPEs, the chief reason is to produce goods and*

* Reprinted by permission from *The Unofficial Economy: Consequences and Perspectives in Different Economic Systems*, ed. Sergio Alessandrini and Bruno Dallago (Aldershot, England: Gower Publishing Company Limited, 1987), pp. 147–63, with the omission of references to foreign language sources. Bruno Dallago is Professor of Economics at the Università degli Studi di Trento, Italy.

[1] Parts of this research have been supported by a grant from the Consiglio Nazionale delle Ricerche (CNR 85.01150.10) and by a grant from the Ministero della Pubblica Istruzione for a research project on "Formal and Real Decentralization in Soviet-Type Economies." The author would like to thank, in particular, Professor Gregory Grossman of the University of California at Berkeley for the valuable help and hospitality received while the author was a guest of the Department of Economics at Berkeley, and the Russian and East European Center of the University of Illinois at Urbana-Champaign. The author, of course, bears all responsibility for the final product and its content.

*services in shortage at official prices set below market-clearing levels. Thus, in CRMEs customers usually pay lower prices for underground goods and services than for the output of regular firms, whereas in SCPEs they pay higher prices for underground products than for regular output. Also, with open unemployment common in CRMEs but not in SCPEs (as explained in Chapter 30), underground work in CRMEs often is a person's primary job, while in SCPEs it usually is supplementary to regular employment.*

## INTRODUCTION

An irregular (unofficial) increase in the supply of goods and services (here termed the underground economy) is present in Soviet and in capitalist-type economies. Similar characteristics manifest themselves in both economic systems. In general, underground production is present in labor-intensive and less standardized activities, where economies of scale are irrelevant and technology permits the splitting up of the production process into smaller units. Some goods and services produced underground are legal and are also produced in the regular economy. They belong to the irregular economy because of the way they are obtained. Generally, the producing enterprise or part of its production is underground (i.e., does not officially exist). Often this happens when operation of a certain type of enterprise is prohibited by law. The underground economy is strictly interwoven with other irregular activities. In many instances, they are different components of the same economic process (e.g., underground production and corruption or tax evasion). The aspect of production will be the focus of this study.

## BASIC FEATURES OF THE UNDERGROUND ECONOMY

*In the Soviet-type economic system* there are two major components which together form the so-called underground entrepreneurial sector: underground private enterprises and underground private activities.[2]

Underground private enterprises are real enterprises run by private owners and entrepreneurs; these enterprises hire workers in order to gain a profit. They are—and will remain—underground because this type of enterprise is prohibited by law or because an underground existence is more profitable. Underground private enterprises generally supply consumption goods and personal services because of their simpler and less risky marketability. Less frequent is the case of the supply of production goods and services, including to socialist enterprises. The vast range of production items includes garments, footwear, household articles, houses, home-brew alcohol, and various services

---

[2] Gregory Grossman, "The 'Second Economy' of the USSR," *Problems of Communism* 26, no. 5 (September–October 1977), pp. 25–40; A. Katsenelinboigen, "Colored Markets in the Soviet Union," *Soviet Studies* 29, no. 1 (January 1977), pp. 62–85; and Konstantin M. Simis, *USSR: The Corrupt Society: The Secret World of Soviet Capitalism* (New York: Simon & Schuster, 1982).

(car and home repair, sewing and tailoring of garments, transportation of persons and goods, and the like).

Underground private activities, on the other hand, reach large dimensions and are not independent, but are in symbiosis with a socialist enterprise. The latter unofficially produces goods and services, using inputs paid for by private persons, owners of the products and services supplied.

Another example of this symbiosis between regular and irregular activities is typified by socialist enterprises managed and run as virtually private enterprises. Here, production takes place according to plan but yields a higher quantity. The surplus remains underground and is sold on the irregular market; and the revenue is taken by organizers of the underground activity. It is evident that without widespread corruption, this type of mechanism could not function.

*In the capitalist-type economic system*, private activity has few limits and the underground economy is confined to relatively few sectors. Among the most typical are (1) such acts of illegality as illegal construction, production of alcohol, transportation of goods and persons, and the illegal or irregular supply of professional services (e.g., dental technicians working as dentists); (2) acts of forgery, such as forgery of documents, banknotes, records, and paintings; and (3) underground production induced by other underground activities (such as the production of speedboats for smugglers).[3] There are also many examples of underground production of goods and components in manufacturing, such as in the garment, footwear, and car industries. In the capitalist-type economic system, there exist independent underground activities as well as activities vertically integrated with regular enterprises.

## CAUSES OF UNDERGROUND ACTIVITY

Activities are said to be underground because they break the law, escape regulation, or transgress social agreements. They either are prohibited (such as private enterprises in certain sectors of Soviet-type economies) or are performed underground to circumvent prohibitions, limitations, and controls. The existence of these activities is explained by the institutional structure of the economic system.

### Producers

*In the Soviet-type economic system,* underground activities are all-pervasive. They seem to prosper mainly because there is a wide demand for goods and services not satisfied by the regular economy, and because underground activi-

---

[3] Edgar L. Feige, "How Big Is the Irregular Economy?" *Challenge* 22, no. 5 (November–December 1979), pp. 5–13; Peter M. Gutmann, "The Subterranean Economy," *Financial Analysis Journal* 33, no. 6 (November–December 1977), pp. 26–28; and Carl P. Simon and Ann D. Witte, *Beating the System: The Underground Economy* (Boston: Auburn House Publishing Company, 1982).

ties grant the organizers considerable rewards. The institutional organization of the economy causes shortage in the regular economy, thereby fostering demand for goods and services supplied by underground activities.[4]

There exist three major groups of goods. The first group consists of goods and services utilized by enterprises. When enterprises have no inner constraints against input increases (as in the Soviet-type economic system), only an administrative policy is effective.[5] In such circumstances, input shortage is unavoidable, creating ample room for irregular activity. However, owing to technological factors, and control and repression activity, the underground economy is confined mostly to irregular exchange of production goods and services among socialist enterprises and much less to underground production.

A second group is made up of consumption goods and services utilized by consumers (families) and the private sector of the economy. Both consumers and the private sector have hard inner constraints against demand increases. Here shortage can be regulated and controlled also by monetary policy. Underground activity permits an increase in both income and consumption. This group of goods constitutes the main area of underground production; controls are difficult, and production technology is often simple.

Goods and services utilized by enterprises, on the one hand, and families and the private sector, on the other, make up the third group. This is a very wide category and the most difficult to control through economic policy. In fact, there is an imbalance between socialist enterprises and families, since only the latter have an inner constraint against demand increases. For this reason, economic policy produces a displacement effect to the disadvantage of families. Utilization of policy instruments to limit demand will be effective on the consumers' side but will have little effect on discouraging enterprise demand. The consequence for aggregate demand may be negligible.

In fact, a relative strengthening of the enterprise's position may develop, inducing enterprises to increase their demand even further. In doing so, they may be indirectly aided by a central policy aimed at increasing production in order to increase consumption. As a result, economic policy may be a good means of controlling consumer demand; but only administrative measures can effectively control enterprise demand. This displacement effect, which forms the basis for the incapability of the traditional Soviet-type economy to increase consumption rapidly, further stimulates the demand for underground production by families.

The pervasiveness of shortage creates ample space for the underground economy. On the one hand, shortage means that demand is higher than supply and that people and enterprises have purchasing power (both monetary and

---

[4] János Kornai, *Economics of Shortage,* 2 vols. (Amsterdam: North Holland Publishing Co., 1980).

[5] Editor's note: Enterprises may not have "inner" constraints against input increases if they want to maximize output without regard to cost and profit. However, administrative allocation of scarce inputs imposes "external" constraints against input increases.

nonmonetary) higher than that necessary to buy or obtain all the available (regular) goods and services. Goods and services in shortage, or goods and services of better quality, can be procured from the underground economy. On the other hand, the underground economy provides the possibility of increasing individual incomes.

*In a capitalist-type economy*, the causes of the unofficial economy differ radically from those described above. An enterprise (with an inner constraint to gain a profit) will try to control its input demand and diminish costs, (1) to increase its profit rate or (2) to decrease prices to gain a higher market share, to keep the previous share, or simply to survive. The underground economy may provide a powerful means of reaching one or more of these targets without decreasing input utilization. This, however, depends on four major factors: technology, the structure of costs, the role of regulation, and flexibility.

The underground economy may be utilized in industries where production consists of many stages, which can be decentralized or performed with different technology.[6] Underground production has no role in industries characterized by a continuous production process (such as the chemical and metallurgical industries).

One of the major motivations for utilizing the underground economy is the possibility of diminishing costs. In particular, underground activities evade taxes, social contributions, and sometimes monopoly prices (e.g., on state monopoly products, such as cigarettes and alcohol). For this reason, the underground economy is found particularly in labor-intensive production and is most useful for those industries in which at least one stage of production is labor-intensive or may be replaced by a cheaper, labor-intensive technology. In an oligopolistic market, when costs decrease there is a tendency to keep the previous price level, thus raising the profit rate.[7] Underground activities, when vertically integrated with regular activities, may give rise to a higher rate of profit for regular enterprises.

Regulation is introduced to protect society or individual groups from the harmful consequences of firms pursuing microeconomic gain (e.g., pollution and other forms of environmental destruction, product adulteration, and the like). However, for individual market producers, regulation may increase costs and decrease flexibility and adaptability to changing market conditions. Regulation may also create a shortage of certain goods (e.g., regulation of building land). The underground economy allows producers to avoid regulation and may result in an increased supply of goods (e.g., illegal construction on protected land).

Finally, the underground economy may increase the flexibility of input utilization (mainly labor), preserving managerial control over the enterprise's

---

[6] B. Contini, "The Anatomy of the Irregular Economy" (Mimeo, January 1981).

[7] Piero Sraffa, "The Laws of Return under Competitive Conditions," *Economic Journal* 36 (December 1926), pp. 535–50.

inner life (e.g., avoiding trade-union controls). An enterprise operating in a growing industry can decide not to expand its regular productive capacity and can instead decentralize a part of its production [to the underground economy]. This prevents its production structure from growing rigid and prevents social and internal control problems in the enterprise from growing stronger (for example, because of a stronger trade-union organization).[8]

## Consumers

The situation of consumers in the two economic systems is more alike than that of enterprises. In both economic systems, consumers have inner constraints against demand increases.

However, the macroeconomic situation of consumption differs in the two systems. In a capitalist-type economy, where demand is often low relative to potential supply and there is no relevant displacement effect from consumer to enterprise demand, consumers demand underground production mainly because of a lower price level. In a Soviet-type economy, owing to shortage, consumers demand underground products mainly because of their better quality or simply because they are the only available products, even if their price is higher.

## Workers

The situation in the labor market *in a capitalist-type economy* is often characterized by unemployment of primary workers and by a supply of labor by marginal workers (women, students, retired people, immigrants). Marginal workers are willing to supply labor in the underground economy because of flexibility of working time, lack of alternatives in the regular economy, and the fact that the net wage is often higher than in the regular economy (due to evasion of taxes and social contributions). The underground economy also offers primary workers the opportunity to increase income through moonlighting. The demand for underground labor is fostered by a low gross wage level (caused by evasion of taxes and social contributions) and by greater flexibility [for managers in the use of labor].

*In a Soviet-type economy*, full employment prevails. People supply labor in the underground market to increase their income (net wage rates being generally much higher than in the regular economy) and to obtain personal satisfaction. The latter is true mainly for underground entrepreneurs and craftsmen. Underground labor demand is generally high because it is the only type that underground enterprises can utilize. Underground labor demand is determined, therefore, by institutional and structural factors.

---

[8] G. Gaetani-D'Aragona, "The Hidden Economy: Concealed Labor Markets in Italy," *Rivista Internazionale di Scienze Economiche e Commerciali* 28, no. 3 (March 1981), pp. 270–89.

# THE UNDERGROUND MARKET FOR CONSUMPTION GOODS AND PRODUCTION INPUTS

## Consumption Goods

Depending on the intensity of shortage in the regular market and differences in quality and price level between the two markets, consumers *in a Soviet-type economy* take advantage of the underground market for consumption goods and services. This is determined by their income and ability to pay with acceptable payment means; the situation in the market for substitutes and alternative goods; and the willingness of people to substitute for the goods in shortage. . . .

Supply depends on four main factors:

- The possibility of the underground producer to find production inputs.
- The efficiency of repression or, alternatively, of corruption.
- The possibility of buyers to offer acceptable payment means (in a situation of high inflation or excess purchasing power, the country's official currency may be replaced by convertible currencies or goods such as alcohol, cigarettes, or imported goods).
- The possibility of the producer to spend the revenue obtained or to gain particular satisfaction from underground performance.

*In a capitalist-type economy*, underground producers have to compete with regular producers to create demand. Given certain disadvantages of an underground market (such as lower confidence of consumers, difficulties of location, and smaller dimensions), underground producers can be successful only if they are more competitive than regular ones—in price, quality, time necessary to obtain goods or services, or regulation. Where shortage is the cause of going underground, the situation may be similar to that of a Soviet-type economy (as in the case of building land or the underground market for personal papers and certificates).

## Labor

In the labor market of *a Soviet-type economy*, there is no unemployment. As a consequence, working time in the underground economy is supplementary to, and not substitutive for, regular working time. Therefore, labor supply is entirely made up of the moonlighting of primary workers and of labor by marginal workers who do not accept a regular job. Labor supply in the underground economy by workers absent from their regular jobs is also widespread.

Underground labor demand in both economic systems depends on the level of underground activity; that is, on the level of demand for goods and services produced underground (given the efficiency of repression and corruption). However, in a Soviet-type economy, costs are secondary to enterprises—in contrast to capitalist-type economies, where the difference between wages in the regular and underground economies is an important one.

*In a capitalist-type economy*, a large part of the underground labor supply depends on the existence of unemployment. In many instances (unemployed people, illegal aliens, marginal workers), underground employment may be the only way to get a job.

In any case, the underground economy offers flexible jobs and permits tax evasion, paying a net wage sometimes higher than the regular one. In fact, net and gross wages coincide or are very close to each other.

The underground labor market has a dual structure composed of strong and weak workers. The underground economy offers strong workers the opportunity to increase personal income. They supply labor, depending on the net wage level. This group is made of primary workers with a job in the regular economy, often with qualifications for which there is an overall shortage. On the other hand, there exists a group of weak workers, for whom the underground economy offers the only possibility of getting a job and for whom the net wage rate is not the only determinant. The weakest group is clearly that of illegal aliens.[9]

Between these two groups of workers, there are many others whose families already have an income, however modest, and for whom the underground economy offers the only or most favorable opportunity to increase personal or family income (unemployed people receiving unemployment benefits, retired people with a pension, housewives and students who enjoy security thanks to their family position).

As a consequence, in a capitalist-type economy, the underground labor supply supplements as well as substitutes for the regular labor supply. . . .

## Capital

*In a Soviet-type economy*, the demand for and supply of capital are basically seen in physical terms, because of the inexistence of a regular financial market. On the one side, it is very hard for an underground entrepreneur to find investment goods in the regular market. Even if this were possible, a private individual buying investment goods would raise suspicions. For these reasons, an underground entrepreneur is able to obtain investment goods mainly through a regular enterprise, either with its cooperation or by stealing from it.[10]

---

[9] Sasha G. Lewis, *Slave Trade Today: American Exploitation of Illegal Aliens* (Boston: Beacon Press, 1979); David S. North and Marion F. Houstoun, *The Characteristics and Role of Illegal Aliens in the U.S. Labor Market: An Exploratory Study* (Washington, D.C.: Linton and Co., 1976); Edwin P. Reubens, "Aliens, Jobs, and Immigration Policy," *The Public Interest*, no. 51 (Spring 1978), pp. 113–34; Sidney Weintraub and Stanley R. Ross, *The Illegal Alien from Mexico. Policy Choices for an Intractable Issue* (Austin, Texas: The University of Texas Press, 1980); and Sidney Weintraub and Stanley R. Ross, *"Temporary" Alien Workers in the United States: Designing Policy from Fact and Opinion* (Boulder, Colo.: Westview Press, 1982).

[10] Grossman, "The 'Second Economy,'" and Simis, *USSR: The Corrupt Society*.

On the other side, the underground supply of financial capital is limited. Underground entrepreneurs often initiate their activity utilizing personal savings or the savings of relatives and friends. However, a large share of this money is spent on corruption.

The underground market for investment goods is rather active and relatively widespread. Goods and services exchanged include:

- Stolen goods and services. Investment goods needed by an underground entrepreneur are stolen from a regular enterprise, often by its employees. The same refers to services: regularly employed workers perform a service (e.g., transportation) for an underground enterprise during regular working time and with the use of regular enterprise assets.

- Goods and services irregularly obtained from a regular enterprise, through an illegal agreement with its managers. This form involves widespread corruption of control and repression bodies.

- Use of goods and services of, and within, a regular enterprise during or after regular working time. This form is widespread when the underground activity is in symbiosis with the regular activity.

- Goods and services bought on the regular market. This possibility is limited.

- Goods and services exchanged on the underground market.

- Goods built or transformed by the promoter of the underground activity. This category basically comprises tools and small machines for underground craftsmen.

Given the efficiency of repression or, alternatively, of corruption, shortage determines the level of production, and therefore the underground demand for investment goods and services. The effect of repression varies according to the type enforced. Successful repression may cause a decrease in demand and in underground activity in general only if it is continuous and seen as permanent. In this case, corruption loses its effectiveness. However, even successful repression, seen as temporary and discontinuous, is likely to foster demand (in order to replace confiscated goods) and increase corruption. Due to shortages in Soviet-type economies, monetary factors (the price of investment goods and services, the interest rate on borrowed capital) are not very effective.

As to supply, two main causes can be isolated. Supply and investment decisions are explained by the drive to gain a higher personal income (through profit and rent). Psychological and social factors (personal satisfaction and prestige) are also important. However, the supply of investment goods, services, and monetary capital may have passive motivations. Reinvestment in underground activities is dictated by a lack of alternatives, in particular when underground entrepreneurs and capitalists are unable to consume their underground income, mainly because of the fear of exposure.

At this point, a question is legitimate: Why should people try to increase their personal income in a shortage economy? Shortage should eliminate every incentive to gain a higher income, because spending is limited. However, shortage at both macro- and microeconomic levels does not mean that individual consumers are unable to spend additional income.

There are four possible adjustments to a shortage situation in which the underground economy plays a role. One widespread form of adjustment is "queuing up": The buyer is unable to find in the regular market the good or service he is looking for and waits for his turn in a queue. If he has additional income from underground activity, he is able to "shorten" or "jump over" the queue and immediately obtain the good or service by offering a reward (tip, bribe, present) to the allocator (worker, seller, bureaucrat).

Another adjustment is forced substitution: The buyer is unable to find the needed good or service in the regular market and is forced to buy a substitute of lower quality or at a higher price. Additional income from underground activity permits him to buy a substitute of higher quality (and higher price) or allows him to offer the allocator a reward, thereby persuading the allocator to find the needed good or service.

A third possible adjustment is forced saving. Although forced saving (in the traditional sense of unspendable money due to absolute shortage) does not play a role, saving in order later to buy an expensive good or service (a house or a long pleasure journey) certainly exists. In this case, additional underground income is helpful.

Finally, the buyer can turn directly to the underground market for goods and services in shortage in the regular market or for those of a higher quality (although generally at a higher price).

*In a capitalist economy*, the underground capital market is similar to the regular one. Because private capital flow and utilization are almost unconstrained, there is no such thing as lack of investment alternatives. On the contrary, a private capitalist will balance various alternatives open to him, including the possibility of investment in the underground economy, when this becomes more profitable. To make a decision, he has to base his calculation on three important elements.

One element is determined by direct costs, that is, those costs to be paid directly by the capitalist. In the irregular economy, these costs are lower due to lower gross wage rates and tax evasion. However, taxes and social contributions which burden regular enterprises may be momentarily reduced or paid for by the government, decreasing the comparative advantage of going underground. Also, underground enterprises have higher costs than regular ones: costs of hiding their activity; difficulties of access to the regular market; and the danger of growing beyond a certain dimension. Therefore, economies of scale cannot play a relevant role, and technical progress may be slower due to organizational difficulties. Sometimes underground enterprises have to pay bribes. The risk of being caught may make it more difficult to find financial capital and inputs. In short, the cost of avoiding regulation and control may be high in time, bribes, risk, and uncertainty.

A second element consists of labor productivity and flexibility. Due to the absence of trade unions and to flexibility in hiring and dismissing workers, labor productivity (including labor intensity) and flexibility in the productive structure of underground enterprises may be higher than in regular enterprises. However, labor mobility may be too high and out of enterpreneurial control. Moreover, the underground economy often cannot survive alone and has to enter into a symbiotic relationship with a regular enterprise (usually larger), losing its independence.

Lastly, final market prices of underground products play a role in underground entrepreneurial calculation. As already seen, underground market prices are generally lower than in the regular economy, and may be a disincentive to investment.

Taking these elements into account, entrepreneurs can get an idea of the underground profit rate, probably higher in many fields than the regular one. However, they must also consider the efficiency of repression, which adds risk and additional cost to underground economic activity. When an entrepreneur has decided to invest in an underground activity and financial capital is available, there are no particular problems in finding investment goods, apart from the possibility of control by authorities.

The case of capital coming from irregular activities (drug production and trade, illegal gambling, and the like), is different. In this case, the underground economy offers a good opportunity to "launder" illegal money by investing it in the production of regular goods. From here, it is easier to invest this money in the regular economy. This is important for the Mafia, for instance. Given the overall demand for goods and services, the technology, and the situation in the labor market, capital in a capitalist-type economy flows from the underground to the regular economy and vice versa with few obstacles, according to differences between regular and underground profit rates and the risk coming from repression.

## ADVANTAGES AND DISADVANTAGES OF UNDERGROUND ACTIVITIES

Underground enterprises *in Soviet-type economies* have both advantages and disadvantages in comparison to regular enterprises. Diffusion of the underground economy depends on their balance.

One major field of analysis is input procurement. Because of the nonexistence of a regular free market of capital and investment goods and services, underground enterprises are clearly at a disadvantage. Input procurement is a permanent worry for them and may expose them to detection. Shortage worsens the situation. (The same applies to regular enterprises.) In the labor market, there are no particular disadvantages to underground enterprises. They are generally able to obtain the labor they need because they can pay higher [net] wages than regular enterprises.

From the point of view of costs, the situation of underground enterprises seems unproblematic. Material inputs are often obtained for a low price or free, with only a bribe or reward to the supplier. However, an underground enterprise has additional costs of hiding and protecting the underground activity. These range from material and human costs of performing the activity in hidden places or by night, to costs for bribes and those costs incurred by the impossibility of utilizing the regular trade system. Finally to be taken into account are the monetary, material, and human costs in case of detection. As to wages, underground enterprises have no particular advantages. On the contrary, they generally pay higher wages, and evasion of taxes and social contributions lends only a modest advantage.

The comparison of advantages and disadvantages on a cost basis has little significance in a Soviet-type economy, where regular enterprises remain insensitive to costs and pervasive shortage exists. Therefore, it can be supposed that underground enterprises would exist and flourish even with much higher costs and prices than regular enterprises. Due to shortage, both underground and regular enterprises have no serious problems selling products. However, underground enterprises must care about quality in order to sell goods and services supplied by regular enterprises. On the other hand, shortage makes demand relatively price-inelastic and this allows for higher selling prices.

The main advantage of underground enterprises lies in the flexibility, participation, and interest of the collective. Due to institutional and organizational factors, there is a close connection between the economic outcome of the enterprise and personal income of its participants. Psychological and social motivations of workers, entrepreneurs, and capitalists promote higher efficiency and productivity. However, these same motivations in difficult times may cause abandonment of the enterprise. The threat of difficulties of economic origin may provide a powerful incentive towards entrepreneurial performance, better organization, and productive flexibility.

In Soviet-type economies, underground enterprises have very soft constraints on the production side. Shortage assures an almost endless market for their supply and excludes any room for competition with regular enterprises. However, they have multiple social and political constraints. There is a considerable difference between underground and regular enterprises, and for this reason underground enterprises are easily detectable. They spend more energy and resources on hiding their activity and on bribery. The main advantage they have compared to regular enterprises lies in the participation and interest of the employee collective, which gives rise to a higher quality of production, with final (consumer) prices generally higher.

*In a capitalist-type economy* the advantages and disadvantages are quite different [from those in a Soviet-type economy], due to the different situation in both regular and underground enterprises. A fundamental difference lies in the fact that both regular and underground enterprises are cost-sensitive. There are no particular differences between the two enterprise types as far as input procurement is concerned. Both procurement difficulties and prices are approximately the same. However, underground enterprises can easily evade taxes, on both inputs and outputs, as well as social and other contributions (e.g., costs for being granted a license or a permit to produce and sell). Very often, underground production is decentralized, taking place in workers' homes. In this case, a part of the fixed costs is saved by the underground enterprise.

Evasion increases the risk of detection and compels underground enterprises to defend themselves by hiding the activity (both physically and economically) and by bribing public officials in charge of the repression of underground activities. This increases costs and decreases the possibility of spending profits and rents gained from underground activity. Moreover, their relative advantage over regular enterprises in the field of taxes and contributions may be diminished by governmental policy which decreases these burdens in certain economic sectors.

As to flexibility, the advantage to underground enterprises is clear. Flexibility is increased by avoidance of regulation and by easier management of labor. Trade unions do not exist in underground enterprises, and it is generally easy to hire and dismiss workers. However, due to their irregular existence, underground enterprises face other previously mentioned costs.

Concerning final demand, underground enterprises have no particular advantages or disadvantages over regular ones. They must compete with each other in the same market for a generally limited demand or vertically integrate with regular enterprises.

Overall, in a capitalist-type economy, underground enterprises have very soft social and political constraints, since they are relatively similar to regular enterprises. Their survival and growth depend strictly on economic factors. They require a higher profit rate and a looser organization than do regular enterprises in order to compensate for the disadvantages of an underground existence. For this reason, they develop only in labor-intensive industries where economies of scale are irrelevant and technology permits subdivision of the production process.

## THE RELATIONSHIP BETWEEN REGULAR AND UNDERGROUND ENTERPRISES

Relationships between regular and underground enterprises are manifold, depending on such factors as the dimension of enterprises, the sector of activity, and the overall situation of the economy. However, common features may be found in the two economic systems.

*In a Soviet-type economy* the situation is asymmetric on the two sides of the economic process—production and input procurement. Due to shortage, regular and underground enterprises do not compete in sales with each other, because the market can absorb their production. At most, if the quality of underground production is higher, consumers may become discontented with regular enterprises; but this may be compensated for by price differentials.

Shortage also exists on the input side. Government authorities directly allocate regular inputs to regular enterprises, and only irregularly produced inputs are available to underground enterprises, though in modest quantity since underground enterprises almost exclusively produce consumption goods and services. For this reason, hard competition develops in the input market between regular and underground enterprises. Due to lack of a true market for investment goods and services, underground economies try to obtain part of the inputs allocated to regular enterprises, or to utilize both [regular and irregular inputs] when possible. Underground enterprises are parasitic on regular enterprises, increasing input shortage. However, regular enterprises can ask the central allocator for a greater quantity of inputs, and generally obtain them. This is less true for labor, where [the additional] supply comes from moonlighters and marginal workers, who, supposedly, are not willing to offer labor to regular enterprises. However, absenteeism is a widespread phenomenon that [augments] underground labor supply.

*In a capitalist-type economy*, regular and underground enterprises compete in a similar way for inputs—the only major difference in their position being in the regular financial market, where underground enterprises have difficulties of access. In the output market, it is necessary to take into account the role of underground enterprises.

If underground enterprises produce goods and services equal to those of regular enterprises, hard competition may develop where there is limited demand. In this case, the result depends on the difference in costs and on economic policy. As already surmised, underground enterprises enjoy lower unit costs. Regular enterprises may react, accelerating technical progress. But, where underground enterprises can, they may [through competition] expel regular enterprises from the market, when government does not help regular enterprises by diminishing taxes and social contributions.

When underground enterprises produce goods and services that enter the regular production process as inputs, the situation is quite different. Here mutually advantageous vertical integration may develop. A widespread phenomenon is that of a regular enterprise decentralizing a stage of its production process to an underground enterprise, sometimes created by itself. In this case, the regular economy can take advantage of the lower costs that characterize underground enterprises, since the regular economy can control the underground economy by controlling its output market. A regular enterprise vertically integrated with an underground enterprise presumably has lower unit production costs or enjoys a higher profit rate, and may expand its market share without having to invest in new technology. Here, underground enterprises may help competition with completely regular enterprises.

In an oligopolistic market, vertical integration may substitute a higher price in order to increase profit; or, in the case of a price decrease, may permit the survival of less efficient enterprises without the reorganization of the production process. This form of vertical integration may also serve as a substitute for capital export to countries where labor cost is lower. . . .

## SOME MACROECONOMIC CONSEQUENCES

The underground economy can have quantitative and qualitative macroeconomic consequences. Considering the former, because underground enterprises produce goods and services, the overall (regular and underground) national income is higher than regular income alone. At the same time, the existence of underground enterprises modifies the working and structure of the overall economic system. Particularly relevant are distributive effects.

Consequences of quantity and quality represent two different sides of the same phenomenon, which conveniently bear separate analysis. Once again, the situation is quite different in the two economic systems.

*In the Soviet-type economic system*, underground enterprises distort economic information and calculation. Through irregular appropriation of regular inputs, underground enterprises are able to charge a great part of their costs to regular enterprises. This gives regular enterprises the opportunity to demand more inputs from the central allocator. Consequently, governmental bodies possess distorted information about the characteristics and working of the economy.

Wrong information leads to wrong decisions. Planning and economic policies are less efficient. The government has to increase allocation of state budget resources to enterprises and, therefore, will also increase centralized enterprise revenue. Administrative intervention is fostered, and economic reforms are impeded.

The situation in the labor market is also distorted, as a consequence of the fact that underground enterprises operate in a shortage economy with full employment of workers willing to offer labor to the regular economy. On the one hand, there is an intensification of labor shortage in the economy, due to demand coming from underground enterprises. Increased shortage is experienced by regular enterprises through increased absenteeism of primary workers. Moreover, moonlighters are probably tired and their productivity is decreased. All this may have negative social (e.g., in family relations) and health consequences. On the other hand, underground enterprises help diminish labor slack existing in regular enterprises ("unemployment behind the doors") when workers are utilized in underground sections of regular enterprises (underground enterprises in symbiosis with regular enterprises). As a consequence, there is an increase in working time actually supplied to the overall economy (regular and underground). The increase in jobs is much lower and is limited to marginal workers willing to work only in the underground market.

Assuming that underground enterprises exclusively produce consumption goods and services (a supposition close to reality), the demand for investment goods and services as well as the supply of consumption goods and services are increased. Because of the way in which material inputs are obtained, net income is generated (equal to the aggregate price of goods and services produced, minus the aggregate price of material inputs) that approximates gross income. Income is distributed to underground workers, entrepreneurs, and capitalists, but not to the state, which contributes a large part of the inputs. Income is spent almost exclusively in the market for consumption goods and services (both regular and underground). Shortage in this market is attenuated, therefore, only as far as a portion of underground income is saved: for example, because no luxury goods are available or because underground entrepreneurs fear detection is made easier by luxury consumption. The same result is reached if underground income is partially utilized to buy imported goods, which may be accomplished through the underground market (e.g., in the black market for convertible currency).

It is seen, therefore, that underground activities increase shortage in the market for investment goods and services, and only slightly attentuate shortage in the market for consumption goods and services. . . . This means that actual consumption of goods and services is higher than the official [figure. But the] underground economy is not, in itself, a solution to the problem of shortage, which can be eliminated only by a comprehensive reform of the economic system.

Suppose that *in a capitalist-type economy*, underground enterprises exclusively produce consumption goods and services. . . . If regular and underground enterprises supply the same goods and services (or close substitutes) and if underground enterprises sell for lower prices (due to lower costs), regular enterprises can be displaced from the market, since the overall increase of consumption demand is lower than the increase in overall supply of consumption goods and services. In fact, a part of the underground income is spent in the (regular) market for investment goods and services, and another part saved. An overall positive effect will result only if cheaper underground products are exported. As a consequence, regular enterprises tend to concentrate more on the production of investment goods and services and less on the production of consumption goods and services than [they would] in the absence of underground enterprises. Therefore, underground activities have an expansive effect on the regular production of investment goods and services and a recessive effect on the regular production of consumption goods and services.

When underground enterprises are vertically integrated with regular enterprises, there is a displacement effect against regular enterprises not integrated with underground enterprises; and integrated regular enterprises can decrease prices and/or increase profits. This impedes the introduction of new technology, because competition is based on cost evasion (of taxes and the like) and not on productivity increase.

Overall, if the existence of the underground economy is accounted for, production, national income, and the standard of living are higher. Moreover, a dual price level may develop, in particular where the role of autonomous workers is relevant: a higher level for regular activities (generally for the public sector and large private enterprises) and a lower level for goods and services supplied to individual consumers and small enterprises (if an underground agreement is accepted that leads to tax evasion for the supplier). Finally, technical progress may be slowed down, because a simpler and less expensive solution, such as going underground, is available.

Quite different is the situation of the government. By definition, underground activities evade taxes and social contributions, but utilize goods and services offered by the government. As a consequence, the underground economy increases the state budget deficit and is a direct cause of the increase in taxation and social contributions burdening regular activities. As far as taxation has a depressive effect on economic activity, the underground economy is a cause, not just the consequence.

In the labor market, on the one side, the underground economy increases labor market flexibility, because irregular activities are utilized to weaken the workers' position. On the other side, as a consequence of an underground demand for labor, workers (as a group and as individuals) are in a stronger position. The danger of true unemployment is less pressing. . . . Given this stronger position, workers, as a group and as individuals, are less ready to accept a wage decrease in order to keep their regular jobs in a time of crisis. Regular wages then become more rigid.

Policy consequences are also relevant. Mistaken and insufficient information leads to wrong decisions; and policies (in particular, demand control policies) lose effectiveness.[11] The existence of an underground economy has a relevant role in causing present economic problems, and it impairs the ability of economic policy to solve them.

---

[11] Feige, "How Big Is the Irregular Economy?"

# Suggestions for Further Reading
## for Part V

*Unemployment*

Deacon, Bob, ed. *The New Eastern Europe: Social Policy Past, Present, and Future.* London: Sage Publications, 1992.

Evers, Adalbert, and Helmut Wintersberger, eds. *Shifts in the Welfare Mix: Their Impact on Work, Social Services, and Welfare Policies.* Boulder, Colo.: Westview Press, 1990.

Jackman, Richard; Christopher Pissarides; and Savvas Savouri. "Labor Market Policies and Unemployment in the OECD." *Economic Policy* 11 (October 1990), pp. 450–90.

Knight, K. G. *Unemployment: An Economic Analysis.* London: Croom Helm, 1987.

Malle, Silvana. *Employment Planning in the Soviet Union.* New York: St. Martin's Press, 1990.

Nickell, Stephen J. "Unemployment: A Survey," *Economic Journal* 100, no. 401 (June 1990), pp. 391–439.

Porket, J. L. *Employment and Unemployment in the Soviet Union.* London: Macmillan, 1989.

Summers, Lawrence H. *Understanding Unemployment.* Cambridge, Mass.: MIT Press, 1990.

*Underground Economy*

Brzezinski, Horst. *The Shadow Economy: An Assessment of Its Operation in Free Market, Socialist, and Developing Countries.* Boulder, Colo.: Westview Press, 1990.

Cowell, Frank A. *Cheating the Government: The Economics of Evasion.* Cambridge, Mass.: MIT Press, 1990.

Dallago, Bruno. *The Irregular Economy: The "Underground" Economy and the "Black" Labor Market.* Aldershot, England: Dartmouth Publishing Company, 1990.

Feige, Edgar L., ed. *The Underground Economies: Tax Evasion and Information Distortion.* Cambridge, England: Cambridge University Press, 1989.

Łoś, Maria, ed. *The Second Economy in Marxist States.* New York: St. Martin's Press, 1990.

Portes, Alejandro; Manuel Castells; and Lauren A. Benton. *The Informal Economy: Studies in Advanced and Less Developed Countries.* Baltimore, Md.: Johns Hopkins University Press, 1989.

*Other Aspects of Economic Systems*

Atkinson, Anthony B., and John Micklewright. *Economic Transformation in Eastern Europe and the Distribution of Income*. Cambridge, England: Cambridge University Press, 1992.

Bergson, Abram. "Comparative Productivity: The USSR, Eastern Europe, and the West." *American Economic Review* 77, no. 3 (June 1987), pp. 342–57.

Birman, Igor. *Personal Consumption in the USSR and the USA*. New York: St. Martin's Press, 1989.

Buck, Trevor. *Comparative Industrial Systems*. New York: St. Martin's Press, 1982.

Hanson, Philip. "The Economics of Research and Development: Some East–West Comparisons." *European Economic Review* 32, no. 2–3 (March 1988), pp. 604–10.

Melvin, Michael, and Su Zhou. "Do Centrally Planned Exchange Rates Behave Differently from Capitalist Rates?" *Journal of Comparative Economics* 13, no. 2 (June 1989), pp. 325–34.

Moroney, John R. "Energy Consumption, Capital, and Real Output: A Comparison of Market and Planned Economies." *Journal of Comparative Economics* 14, no. 2 (June 1990), pp. 199–220.

Murrell, Peter, *The Nature of Socialist Economies: Lessons from Eastern European Foreign Trade*. Princeton, N.J.: Princeton University Press, 1990.

Stollar, Andrew J., and G. Rodney Thompson. "Sectoral Employment Shares: A Comparative Systems Context." *Journal of Comparative Economics* 11, no. 1 (March 1987), pp. 62–80.

# Index